# Issues in Financial Regulation

*edited by*

# FRANKLIN R. EDWARDS

*Professor, Graduate School of Business, Columbia University*

*Columbia University Center for Law and Economic Studies*

McGRAW-HILL BOOK COMPANY

*New York  St. Louis  San Francisco  Auckland  Bogotá  Düsseldorf*
*Johannesburg  London  Madrid  Mexico  Montreal  New Delhi*
*Panama  Paris  São Paulo  Singapore  Sydney  Tokyo  Toronto*

**Library of Congress Cataloging in Publication Data**

Main entry under title:

Issues in financial regulation.

(Regulation of American Business and industry series)
"These papers . . . are the outgrowth of a series of
faculty seminars held during the 1976–1977 academic year
by Columbia University's Center for Law and Economic
Studies."

Includes index.

l. Banking law--United States--Addresses, essays,
lectures.      2. Finance--United States--Law--Addresses,
essays, lectures.      I. Edwards, Franklin R., 1937-
II. Columbia University. Center for Law and Economic
Studies.      III. Series.

KF974.A2I84      346'.73'082      78-12028
ISBN 0-07-019049-6

1234567890   DODO   7865432109

The editors for this book were Ellen M. Poler and Virginia
Fechtmann Blair, the designer was Elliot Epstein, and the
production supervisor was Sally Fleiss. It was set in
Palatino by University Graphics, Incorporated

It was printed and bound by R. R. Donnelly.

# Issues in
# Financial Regulation

## REGULATION OF AMERICAN BUSINESS AND INDUSTRY SERIES

# Contents

# Acknowledgments

This volume and the seminar series from which it stemmed were made possible through funding provided by eight founders of the Center for Law and Economic Studies, Columbia University. Corporations to whom a debt of gratitude is owed are: Amoco Foundation, Inc., the Bell System, Exxon Corporation, Citibank, General Electric Foundation, IBM Corporation, Kraftco Corporation, and Xerox Corporation.

# Preface

The purpose of this book is to explore the legal and economic dimensions of financial regulation. It contains nine chapters that analyze major issues in financial regulation. The papers, together with the related comments and discussion, are the outgrowth of a series of faculty seminars held during the 1976–1977 academic year by Columbia University's Center for Law and Economic Studies. The papers are analytical rather than policy oriented, and they seek both to delineate the conceptual foundations for government intervention in financial markets and to determine the likely effects of this intervention.

This volume differs from past studies of financial regulation in that it is not constrained by the necessity of reaching harmonious recommendations. Nor is it subject to political exigency. And, rather than focusing on differences in conclusions, it emphasizes differences in reasoning.

A major strength of the book is that it contains the views of both legal and economic scholars. These scholars are also asked to defend their views in the debate which follows each paper. Both economists and lawyers play a key role in the regulatory process, and mutual understanding is essential to the formulation of wise and effective regulation. Too often, lawyers cope with the consequence without understanding the cause; too often, economists ignore the consequence while searching for the cause. By employing an interdisciplinary approach, we have attempted to fuse these disparate views and to provide new insights into old controversies and fresh analyses of new problems, all the while consciously and gingerly crossing the minefield of interdisciplinary research.

The book opens (Chapter 1) with a paper on the dual banking system by Kenneth Scott. This is an ideal topic with which to begin, since discussion of it requires a complete description of the administrative structure covering the regulation of banking and related financial institutions. Scott focuses on two aspects of our dual system of federal and state regulation. The first is the legislative and legal underpinnings of this system. After thorough analysis of its legal history, he concludes that there is little support for the notion that Congress expressly wished to maintain a system of dual regulation by federal and state authorities. On the contrary, there are sound reasons to believe that it wished to achieve the opposite: a monolithic system of federal regulation. This is a particularly important finding in view of the recent flurry of court decisions premised on the legislative sanctity of the dual banking system.

The second aspect Scott addresses is of far-reaching importance: the implications of divided regulatory authority, of competition between regulators. Bank regulation has a notorious history of competition between federal and state regulators, with national banks switching to state charters, and vice versa. The issues emerging from this kind of regulatory structure are similar to those surrounding the current debate over the chartering of corporations by states. Some states have few or no chartering requirements, while others have substantial requirements, and a company is free to choose the state in which it wishes to incorporate. Scott's analysis of the consequences of competition among regulators, as well as the related comments by Walter Gellhorn, William Niskanen, and Bernard Shull, are cogent not only to the problems of bank regulation but to many other regulated industries as well. A central issue is whether competition among regulators erodes regulation to the point where it fails to achieve its public interest goals.

In Chapter 2, Franklin Edwards and James Scott examine the question of solvency regulation. Maintaining the solvency or soundness of the financial system is the fundamental public purpose for government's long-standing regulatory presence in financial markets. Edwards and Scott begin with a description of the current structure of solvency regulation applicable to depository institutions. Next, they examine the purported public policy rationales that underlie this structure. Finally, they ask the critical question: What kind of regulatory structure is needed to meet the legitimate public interest goals?

Edwards and Scott conclude that some form of deposit insurance is needed, but that there is at present too much solvency regulation and that eliminating much of it would enhance the social welfare. They contend that regulators should rely primarily on balance sheet regulations to guarantee bank soundness: By varying equity capital and liquidity requirements, regulators can adequately control the probability of a bank's failure, and these controls do not impose significant costs on society. Regulatory control over entry, branching, pricing (such as Regulation Q), and the activities banks engage in can be eliminated without jeopardizing bank soundness, and this elimination will increase competition and, therefore, enhance public welfare.

Edwards and Scott also analyze the feasibility of substituting a variable-premium deposit insurance scheme for the present uniform-premium system, and they conclude that a variable-premium system is probably both feasible and desirable. The discussants, Paul Horvitz and William Young, concentrate on the question of whether a variable-premium deposit insurance system would be desirable, and they provide many useful insights into the workings of such a system.

In Chapter 3, Roy Schotland and Sam Peltzman discuss the appropriate regulatory approach to controlling conflict-of-interest abuses by the managers of financial institutions. This is a slippery issue which has not received much scholarly attention in the past. Schotland describes the innumerable kinds of conflicts of interest that can and do arise in financial institutions and attempts to distinguish abusive from innocuous conflicts. He argues that abusive conflicts are so pervasive as to require greater regulatory control, and that past controls have been inadequate.

Peltzman's view is markedly different. He maintains that abusive conflicts of interest arise largely because of imperfectly competitive markets, so that the appropriate solution to such conflicts is to eliminate restrictions on competition. Further, even in the imperfectly competitive world of banking, Peltzman argues that many of the conflicts we observe may be socially beneficial, not harmful. Blanket prohibitions of certain kinds of suspected behavior, therefore, may eliminate more good than evil.

This debate provides one of the very few substantive discussions of the conflict-of-interest question—an issue historically veiled by shibboleth and misunderstanding. While the outcome of the debate may not be to everyone's liking, it clearly helps to delineate the grounds upon which the debate should focus. One of these is the extent to which information is readily available to consumers of financial services; another is the extent to which consumers can make use of such information.

In Chapter 4, these issues are analyzed. As an economic commodity, *information* is surrounded by misunderstanding and confusion. Why, and under what circumstances, will management choose not to disclose relevant and timely information? Instances of blatant abuse of inside information by managers are easy to find and, perhaps, have diminished our desire to understand why they occur. However, effective regulation in this area, just as in others, requires an understanding of the market shortcomings with respect to information.

Stephen Ross's paper on disclosure regulation is an important step toward elucidating the market process by which information is or is not made available. Ross begins by summarizing the traditional economic theories of information, arguing that these theories are incomplete because they do not take into consideration all the forces operating on managers to encourage them to make information available. Further, without an understanding of these forces, it is impossible to recognize the circumstances under which informational failures may occur, or, alternatively, to determine the kinds of regulatory responses that can be effective in eliminating such deficiencies. Ross's approach is to use signaling theory to explain what motivates managers to make available relevant and truthful information. He shows that under conditions of perfect competition, particularly with respect to managerial services, the private market should work well to make information available to the public in a timely way.

A major contribution of this paper is to bring the debate over disclosure laws back to the fundamental issue of why and how the market system fails us. As is so often the case, competition is seen to play a critical role. If there are information abuses, they exist because of competitive failures; and Ross would have us concentrate on eliminating the competitive imperfections, and not on controlling information per se. Of particular interest is his analysis of the kinds of contracts that would have to exist between stockholders and managers in order to assure the timely flow of relevant and accurate information.

The commentary by Homer Kripke on Ross's paper, together with the debate which follows, reveals clearly the chasm that separates lawyers and economists. Kripke finds little of value in a signaling theory approach, arguing that it completely fails to describe the world as we know it. He is particularly impatient with a theory whose applicability is based on a type of managerial compensation contract that never has existed and never will. Kripke points with force to the fact that informational abuses are common, and that regulation has helped considerably.

While no clear policy prescriptions emerge from this debate, Ross's attempt to develop a more complete theory of information is provocative and will undoubtedly elicit controversy. Potential implications go far beyond the issues that surround the debate over the proposed disclosure requirements for financial institutions.

In Chapter 5 Robert Shay examines the burgeoning area of consumer protection law applicable to financial institutions. While usury laws have existed in most states for decades, new efforts are under way to protect small borrowers in a host of other ways. In particular, truth-in-lending laws have recently been adopted, and major efforts have been made to bolster debtors' rights and remedies. Discrimination in lending is also coming under close scrutiny.

To assess the need for government regulation and its impact in this area, Shay concentrates on the laws that prohibit creditors from garnisheeing the wages of borrowers in default. These laws, like many other debtor protections, circumscribe the freedom of contract between borrowers and lenders, limiting the rights of creditors. Shay examines the purported legal and economic rationales for this kind of regulation, and he advances a procedure for evaluating it—essentially by assessing the costs and benefits which result from regulation. His analysis demonstrates the difficulty of establishing the net social value of these laws.

Three commentaries on Shay's paper, by Leonard Lapidus, Kellis

Parker, and Robert Pitofsky, as well as the discussion which follows,
vividly exhibit the different predilections of lawyers and economists. The standard assumptions made by economists that lenders and borrowers possess adequate information and behave in a rational way (or in a way that furthers their own interests) come under fire. Although all participants agree that some sort of cost-benefit test is appropriate, it is clear that individual preconceptions and prejudices influence one's assessment of these costs and benefits. Those who contemplate further expansion of debtor protections will wish to resolve many of the issues debated here before proceeding.

Chapter 6 explores the regulatory implications of the new payments technology. Widespread bank adoption of electronic funds transfer systems (EFTs) threatens to make drastic changes in our financial structure—from the elimination of "money" as we now know it to the formation of nationwide banking cartels. These implications are explored in three papers: Almarin Phillips analyzes the implications for conducting monetary policy; Elinor Solomon examines the implications for future competition and the structure of financial markets; and Alan Westin explores the possible impacts on our privacy. While both Solomon and Westin see potentially serious problems associated with EFT systems and urge a cautious approach, Phillips is forthright in his call for immediate change. Unless the payment of interest is allowed on both demand deposits and banks' reserve balances, Phillips foresees great problems in the future management of monetary policy. Discussion from the floor following these papers is particularly insightful in elucidating the potential monetary policy pitfalls.

In Chapter 7, the wisdom of social programs to allocate credit is debated. A considerable amount of financial regulation, either directly or indirectly, is aimed at allocating credit among the various sectors of the economy. Housing stands out clearly as a favored recipient. In the major paper, Stanley Diller argues that the fungibility of credit largely dooms credit allocation schemes to failure: They will not affect real spending in any way. Further, such schemes are likely to have perverse distributive (or income) effects. Diller singles out housing for intensive study and concludes that neither secular trends nor cyclical fluctuations in real housing expenditures can be attributed to either the cost or the availability of credit. These general conclusions are reinforced by Burton Zwick's and Michael Hamburger's examination of attempts to control consumer credit in the early 1950s. They find that efforts to allocate consumer credit had no effect on consumers' real expenditures.

In contrast, Lester Thurow argues forcefully that credit allocation schemes can work and are desirable. He argues that credit markets are already quite imperfect, so that the availability of credit is already distorted, and in ways that have regressive income distribution consequences. A credit allocation program can hardly hurt, and it may help. In particular, Thurow favors the use of differential reserve requirements on banks' assets, which he contends will alter relative credit costs, thereby changing the composition of real expenditures. In addition, they can be used to alter the distribution of income in a progressive direction. Dwight Jaffee and George Cooper, the last two discussants, attempt to assess all the arguments and to present a balanced view.

In Chapter 8, the regulatory consequences of the interplay between domestic and international financial markets are examined. With banks and other financial institutions increasingly operating in more than one country, national differences in regulation are assuming greater importance, and disputes over alleged competitive disadvantages and unequal reciprocal treatment are occurring with increasing frequency. There is also growing concern that transnational differences in regulation may dilute bank regulation to the point where the soundness of the financial system will be jeopardized.

James W. Dean and Herbert Grubel try to assess the seriousness of these concerns, and to determine what, if any, regulatory responses are appropriate. An important contribution of their paper is their formulation of an explicit theory of multinational banking to explain the proliferation of multicountry operations. In this framework, transaction costs and information costs occupy a central role, along with regulatory differences among countries. Dean and Grubel conclude that there are sound economic reasons for the spread of multinational banking, and that its development has resulted in some clear social benefits, but that it has also created some thorny regulatory issues. They are especially concerned about maintaining the solvency of large banks and preserving the orderliness of world financial markets. To this end, they propose the establishment of an international deposit insurance scheme—an international equivalent to the United States' Federal Deposit Insurance Corporation.

Discussants Raymond Vernon and Henry Bloch both challenge Dean's and Grubel's theory of multinational banking, arguing that it is too narrow to capture the economic and business essence of international banking. They provide counterexamples, which, they believe, better illustrate the fundamental reasons for the spread of multinational banking. They are also less sanguine than Dean and Grubel about its ultimate public policy implications: Future developments may require more regulatory controls and greater international cooperation than Dean and Grubel contemplate. Finally, in the debate that follows, Dean's and Grubel's proposal of an international deposit insurance scheme comes under attack: Both its economic and political feasibility are questioned.

In the last chapter, Arnold Heggestad surveys empirical studies of the relationship between market structure and bank performance. Regulatory control of entry, branching, and merging alters the structure of local banking markets and thereby indirectly affects the competitive behavior of banks—or their willingness to engage in price competition, nonprice rivalry, etc. The formulation of regulatory policies toward competition depends critically upon knowledge of the nexus between the various dimensions of market structure and bank performance.

During the last few years, there has been a remarkable number of new empirical studies on this issue, using different data and methodologies, which have examined heretofore unexplored dimensions of market structure and performance. Heggestad's review of some 45 of these studies should be of great aid to practicing lawyers, regulators, and bankers, as well as to academics. In particular, he provides us with a single summary table of these studies in which the following aspects are compared: Type of bank performance examined (price, profits, etc.); dimension of market structure analyzed (concentration, entry conditions, etc.); other variables employed; statistical methodology and data used; and their findings. He also gives his own opinion of each study, indicating its strengths and weaknesses. While these assessments are unlikely to go unchallenged, Heggestad's organization and summary of these studies fills an obvious and important need.

In summary, in this book, considerable scholarly talent is brought to bear on a wide range of key topics in financial regulation, and the result is a lively intellectual exchange. While the book does not offer a blueprint for regulatory reform—such an end was not envisioned—certain of its themes should not go unnoticed. In particular, although the need for some regulation in financial markets is widely acknowledged, the tenor of the discourse is clearly toward the opinion that financial institutions are currently overregulated, that a considerable amount of financial regulation could be relaxed or eliminated without jeopardizing the public policy goals which underlie such regulation. Another theme is the healthy skepticism toward regulation exhibited by many participants. Even when regulation is conceptually desirable, there is doubt about the ability of government to implement policies that can effectively achieve the stated social goals. Last, as between lawyers and economists, lawyers show a clear proclivity to rely on regulation to check abusive markets. Economists are more confident in the ultimate power of impersonal market forces to eradicate abusive behavior, and they are more skeptical about the wisdom and abilities of government regulators. Lawyers are more confident that the case-by-case wisdom of regulators, however imperfect, is still superior to the frailties of the market. Thus, while not a guide to regulatory change, this book is, nevertheless, an intellectual lighthouse by which would-be reformers can chart their ways. In these waters, the shoals to be avoided are not always as clear as the shores to be reached.

FRANKLIN R. EDWARDS

*Professor of Business,*
*Graduate School of Business,*
*Columbia University*

# Issues in
# Financial Regulation

CHAPTER ONE

# Bureaucratic Competition and the Structure of Bank Regulation

## THE DUAL BANKING SYSTEM: A MODEL OF COMPETITION IN REGULATION

Kenneth E. Scott, *Professor of Law, Stanford University*

In banking circles, the dual system of both state and national banks and banking agencies is an object of almost universal veneration. When hearings are held on legislative proposals affecting banking operations and regulation, witnesses from the banking industry or even from the banking regulatory agencies, as well as the members of Congress themselves, customarily include in their remarks some statement of their fidelity to the principle of dual banking. Typical is the comment of a representative of the National Association of Supervisors of State Banks: "The dual banking system . . . is a vital national goal with roots deep in our constitutional history, and one of the very reasons why this country has achieved an economic growth unparalleled among the nations of the world."[1] Discordant voices have not been completely lacking; for example, Senator Carter Glass's flat statement in 1932: "I think the curse of the banking business of this country is the dual system."[2] But, on the whole, the critics have made little headway.

The issue of the structure of bank regulation was reopened by the entry into the debate of former Chairman of the Board of Governors of

---

1. *Hearings on Consolidation of Bank Examining and Supervisory Functions (H.R. 107 and H.R. 6885) Before the Subcomm. on Bank Supervision and Insurance of the House Comm. on Banking and Currency and Before the House Comm. on Banking and Currency,* 89th Cong., 1st Sess. 120 (1965) (statement of F. Shelby Cullom) [hereinafter cited as *1965 Consolidation Hearings*]. See also *Hearings on the Financial Institutions Supervisory Act of 1966 (S. 3158) Before the Subcomm. on Financial Institutions of the Senate Comm. on Banking and Currency,* 89th Cong., 2d Sess. 34–37 (1966).

2. *Hearings on the Operation of the National and Federal Reserve Banking System Before the Senate Comm. on Banking and Currency,* 72d Cong., 1st Sess., Pt. II, 395 (1932). For a more contemporary dissent, see Robertson, "Federal Regulation of Banking: A Plea for Unification," 31 *Law and Contemporary Problems* 673 (1966).

the Federal Reserve System, Dr. Arthur F. Burns. Chairman Burns took the occasion of his address to the annual convention of the American Bankers Association in 1974 to criticize "the diffusion of authority and accountability that characterizes the present regulatory system" and to state that "the danger of continuing as we have in the past should be apparent to all objective observers."[3] Subsequently, he was joined by Governor Sheehan, who excoriated the "hodgepodge of bank regulation as it has evolved in this country,"[4] and by Governor Bucher, who concluded that "the existing system of bank regulation is not only overlapping and confusing—but, in many respects, fails sufficiently to serve the public interest."[5]

With that, the controversy moved into the legislative area. In 1975, Senator Proxmire, the Chairman of the Senate Banking Committee, introduced a bill to consolidate all federal bank regulatory activities into a single Federal Bank Commission.[6] On the House side, Banking Committee Chairman Reuss and Subcommittee (on Financial Institutions Supervision, Regulation and Insurance) Chairman St. Germain released "Discussion Principles" in connection with their Financial Institutions and the Nation's Economy (FINE) study project. Their recommendations called for a Federal Depository Institutions Commission that would combine into one agency the supervisory and regulatory functions of not only the three federal banking agencies but also the Federal Home Loan Bank Board and the National Credit Union Administration.[7] Hearings were held, substantial controversy and opposition developed, and no bills were enacted in 1976.

In part, of course, these differences in viewpoint derive from differences in objectives and values. But on closer examination, there also proves to be considerable disagreement about what the essential features of the dual banking system are and how it actually operates. It is the purpose of this study to undertake an examination of the present structure of the dual banking system and its consequences for banking regulation.

We will begin by describing the component parts of this dual system, in terms of the agencies and institutions involved. Then, we will examine it in operation to understand precisely what is at stake. Efforts

---

**3.** Address by Chairman Arthur Burns, *Maintaining the Soundness of our Banking System* 19, American Bankers Ass'n Convention Honolulu, Oct. 21, 1974.

**4.** Address by Federal Reserve Governor Sheehan, *1975—The Year for Federal Banking Regulation Reform* 2, Institutional Investors Institute, New York City, Dec. 10, 1974.

**5.** Address by Federal Reserve Governor Bucher, *Federal Bank Regulatory Reform* 5, Western Independent Bankers Ass'n Convention, San Francisco, March 11, 1975.

**6.** S. 2298, 94th Cong., 1st Sess. (1975). This action had long been urged by Governor Robertson. See Robertson, N. 2 *supra* at 674–675.

**7.** House Comm. on Banking, Currency and Housing, *FINE Discussion Principles* 11–13 94th Cong., 1st Sess. (Comm. Print 1975).

at countering the dual system or preventing its operation will be considered, and finally, we will undertake a preliminary application of this analysis to some current issues.

## A DESCRIPTION OF THE DUAL SYSTEM

In references to the dual banking system, banking is sometimes thought of solely in terms of commercial banks and sometimes, more broadly, as comprising savings and loan associations (S&Ls) and mutual savings banks (MSBs) as well. We will use the broader sense; though most of our attention will be centered on commercial banking, some of the data and illustrations will be drawn from the S&Ls and MSBs.

The structure of regulation of these institutions is complex. The duality of the system involves state and federal chartering, but there is actually more to it than that. Beginning with commercial banking, there are four possible patterns of regulation, which are set forth below with figures indicating the magnitude of each one at year-end 1975. (1) National banks are chartered by the Comptroller of the Currency (a quasi-independent officer in the Department of Treasury) and are automatically members of the Federal Reserve System and insured by the Federal Deposit Insurance Corporation (FDIC). Currently, most of the very large banks are national banks; in the aggregate at year-end 1975, 4,741 national banks held 58 percent of total commercial banking assets. (2) State banks may be members of the Federal Reserve System (in which case they are also automatically insured by FDIC), and most of the larger ones are. A total of 1,046 state banks were members, holding 19 percent of commercial banking assets, at year-end 1975. (3) State banks may be insured by FDIC without joining the Federal Reserve System, and that is the position of most of the numerous small state banks. There were 8,585 insured nonmember banks, holding 22 percent of commercial banking assets. (4) Finally, in a number of states, a state bank may operate without federal deposit insurance. This is viewed as competitively very disadvantageous, and there were only 253 banks in this category, holding 1 percent of commercial banking assets.[8]

For savings and loan associations, there is a similar pattern. (1) Federal S&Ls are chartered by the Federal Home Loan Bank Board (FHLBB), and they are automatically members of the Federal Home Loan Bank (FHLB) system and insured by the Federal Savings and Loan Insurance Corporation (FSLIC). The latter two agencies are legally separate entities with differing memberships, but they are administered by the same three-member FHLBB. There were 2,048 federal associations, holding 58 percent of industry assets. (2) State associations may obtain FSLIC insurance of accounts, in which event they are now also required

---

8. 62 Fed. Res. Bull. A14, Dec. 1976.

as a matter of informal policy to become members of the FHLB system. In this category were 2,030 state S&Ls with 40 percent of industry assets.[9] (3) Some state associations belong to the FHLB system but do not have federal insurance of accounts. A mere 124 associations, with 0.6 percent of industry assets, compose this group. (4) A somewhat larger number of generally quite small state associations has neither FSLIC insurance nor FHLB membership. There were 762 associations, with 1.8 percent of industry assets, in this category.[10]

Mutual savings banks do not have a dual system in the traditional sense; they are located in only 17 states, and have no federal counterpart. Nonetheless, several different regulatory configurations do exist. (1) About two-thirds (or 329) of the MSBs, with 89 percent of the industry's assets, have FDIC insurance of deposits. Mutual savings banks are eligible to be members of the Federal Reserve System, but none is; 74 were members of the FHLB system.[11] (2) The remaining one-third were virtually all Massachusetts savings banks insured by a state fund corporation.[12]

The foregoing data and regulatory patterns are set forth in Table 1-1. This constitutes the skeleton of the dual system, and a few salient differences should be emphasized. Mutual savings banks have no choice at the chartering level and have, in fact, obtained federal deposit insurance only from FDIC directly. S&Ls have a choice between state and federal chartering, but confront the same federal authority when it comes to account insurance and borrowing from a central bank. Commercial banks have not only state and federal chartering but separate federal routes to deposit insurance as well. In effect, the different banking institutions represent different degrees or varying extents of a dual system.

The content of regulation is what adds flesh to this jurisdictional skeleton. Banking regulation is exceedingly detailed and comprehensive, and it defies generalizations that are both simple and accurate, even on the federal level.[13] When all 50 states are brought into the picture, an attempt to be comprehensive almost inevitably bogs down in detail.

---

9. United States League of Savings Ass'ns, *1976 Savings and Loan Fact Book* 50, 96 (1976). Maintenance of membership in the FHLB system is made a condition of the approval of the application for account insurance. See Form FHLBB - 140, *Application for Insurance of Accounts*, Instruction 2; FSLIC, *Outline of Information*, Exhibit G #6.

10. About half of the non-FSLIC-insured associations belong to state insurance fund organizations in four states: Maryland, Massachusetts, North Carolina, and Ohio. U. S. League of Savings Ass'ns, N. 9 *supra* at 50, 96.

11. Statistical Series, Table S.3.3, Federal Home Loan Bank Bd. J. 84 (April 1975).

12. National Ass'n of Mutual Savings Banks, *1976 Fact Book* 5.

13. For an excellent but lengthy survey, see the two-part article by the former general counsel of the Federal Reserve Board, H. Hackley, "Our Baffling Banking System," 52 Va. L. Rev. 565, 771 (1966).

**TABLE 1-1  Number and Total Assets of Banks and Savings and Loan Associations**
December 31, 1975 (in billions of dollars)

**Banks**

| Item | All banks | Commercial Banks | | | | | | | Mutual Savings Banks (State) | | |
| | | Total | FDIC insured | | | | | | Total | FDIC insured | Noninsured |
| | | | Total | FRS Member Banks | | | Nonmember Banks (State) | | | | |
| | Total | | | Total | National | State | FDIC insured | Noninsured | | | |
|------|------|------|------|------|------|------|------|------|------|------|------|
| Number | 15,109 | 14,633 | 14,372 | 5,788 | 4,741 | 1,046 | 8,585 | 261 | 476 | 329 | 147 |
| Percent of total | 100 | 96.8 | 95.1 | 38.3 | 31.4 | 6.9 | 56.8 | 1.7 | 3.2 | 2.2 | 1.0 |
| Total assets | $1086.0 | 964.9 | 944.7 | 733.6 | 553.3 | 180.5 | 210.9 | 20.5 | 121.1 | 107.3 | 13.8 |
| Percent of total | 100 | 88.8 | 87.0 | 67.6 | 50.9 | 16.6 | 19.4 | 1.9 | 11.2 | 9.9 | 1.3 |

**Savings and Loan Associations**

| Item | All associations | FHLB Member Associations | | | | | | | Nonmember noninsured associations (state) |
| | | Total | FSLIC Insured | | | | | Noninsured (state) | |
| | | | Total | Mutual | | | Stock (state) | | |
| | Total | | | Total | Federal | State | | | |
|------|------|------|------|------|------|------|------|------|------|
| Number | 4,964 | 4,202 | 4,078 | 3,462 | 2,048 | 1,414 | 616 | 124 | 762 |
| Percent of total | 100 | 84.6 | 82.2 | 69.8 | 41.3 | 28.5 | 12.4 | 2.5 | 15.4 |
| Total assets | $338.4 | 332.2 | 330.3 | 262.1 | 195.4 | 66.7 | 68.1 | 1.9 | 6.2 |
| Percent of total | 100 | 98.2 | 97.6 | 77.4 | 57.7 | 19.7 | 20.1 | .6 | 1.8 |

*Sources:* 62 *Federal Reserve Bulletin,* July 1976, table A 14.    U.S. League of Savings Associations, *1976 Fact Book,* tables 40, 41, 79, 91.
1975 FDIC *Annual Report,* table 108.    FSLIC data.

It is not the purpose of this study to set forth and examine the content of banking regulation as such. That would be a distinctly different, and more arduous, task. Nonetheless, it is not possible to understand the working of the dual system without a general knowledge of how the distribution of regulatory functions corresponds to the structure of agency jurisdiction. We will, therefore, present a very condensed account of the substance of banking regulation, with the caveat that it does not include all the pertinent qualifications and detail.

The initial distinction to be borne in mind is that between the primary level and the secondary level of supervision. The primary level is that of the chartering authority, historically, for a long period, the only level.[14] The most basic and pervasive functions of regulation and supervision are performed at the primary level by state law and state banking boards or superintendents or commissioners for state banks or S&Ls, and by federal law and the Comptroller of the Currency or the FHLBB for national banks or federal S&Ls. This primary law, which varies significantly among different jurisdictions, defines the powers of the institutions established under it and limits the activities in which they can engage and the investments they can make. The primary supervisory agency customarily has discretionary control over entry (through approval of charter applications), exit (through power to close a bank and put it into receivership), and market structure in general (through approval of branches and mergers). The primary supervisor also examines all the institutions under its jurisdiction, a process combining a review of the bank's records and operations with criticism and comments on management's performance and judgments, and usually exercises a variety of specific approval powers. On this level, for banks and S&Ls (but not mutual savings banks), the system is one of duality; an institution may operate in a particular locale under either the state or federal supervisor and law.

Overlaid on this primary level is a secondary system of regulation and supervision, exclusively federal in origin and much more scattered and specialized in content. It is least intrusive for national banks. Being a member of the Federal Reserve means being subject to its determinations as to asset reserve requirements on demand and time deposits, interest ceilings, and foreign branches, and being insured by FDIC means mainly paying its annual insurance premium. But, for a state bank, being a Fed member means being subject, in addition, to its examination powers, cease-and-desist authority, and approval powers over domestic and foreign branches and merger acquisitions. State member banks likewise incur an additional set of statutory prohibitions and restrictions, some of them imported into the Federal Reserve Act

---

14. State banks date back to the beginning of the republic, and the system of national banks to 1863; the Federal Reserve Board did not appear on the scene until 1913, and FDIC until 1933. Similarly, state S&Ls trace their origins to the first part of the nineteenth century, while the FHLB system was not created until 1932 and the FSLIC until 1934.

from the National Bank Act, on such matters as capital requirements and dividend payments, purchases of corporate stock, underwriting, dealing in investment securities, and interlocking directorates. If a state bank is FDIC insured but does not join the Fed, the layer of federal control is considerably thinner. All the statutory restrictions mentioned disappear, as do the Fed's reserve requirements. The bank is still subject, however, to federal examination, interest rate ceilings on time and savings deposits, cease-and-desist authority and approval power over domestic branches and merger acquisitions.

The resulting pattern of regulation of banks is depicted, if not clarified, in Figure 1-1.

For an S&L, the secondary level of federal control is less comprehen-

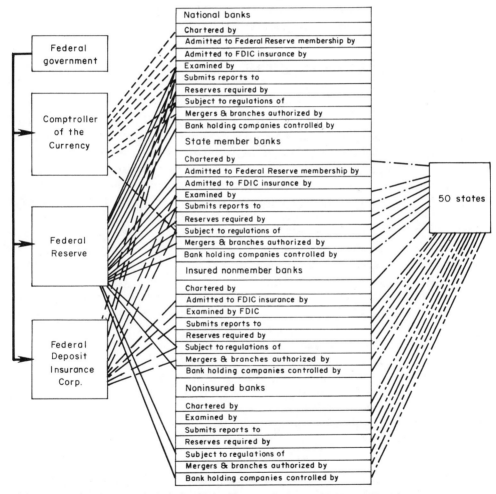

**FIGURE 1-1 The tangled web of bank regulations. (*Source:* Hearings on Financial Structure and Regulation before the Subcommittee on Financial Institutions of the Senate Committee on Banking, Housing and Urban Affairs, *93d Cong., 1st Sess., 1973, p. 619.*)**

sive. FSLIC insurance means a member institution is subject to federal examination and cease-and-desist authority, approval of its forms of accounts and their advertising, geographical restrictions on its lending activities, minimum net worth reserve requirements, and interest rate ceilings on savings accounts. Membership in the FHLB system subjects an institution to limited federal examination authority, interest rate control, and certain liquid asset requirements; it is the least pervasive of any of these regulatory structures.

This account, summary though it is, may be sufficient to give a sense of how the content of regulatory restriction and control relates to where the institution is positioned in the jurisdictional structure outlined in Table 1-1.[15] We will have occasion later to consider some facets of regulation in more detail, by way of illustration and example. For the moment, it is enough to be aware of the extent and importance of diversity in banking regulation.

## THE OPERATION OF THE DUAL SYSTEM

### The Principle of Choice

Given such regulatory diversity, what are its implications? In effect, bankers at all times have a choice as to which set of laws and administrators they wish to operate under. This is most evident in terms of entry; a group wishing to go into the banking business may apply to the Comptroller for a national bank charter or to the state for a state bank charter, and along with the latter, it might seek Fed membership or simply FDIC insurance, or conceivably neither.

Perhaps less evident, but in practice much more important, is the fact that an existing bank also at all times has the same choice. A state bank can choose to withdraw from the Fed, or even from FDIC (so far as legal right is concerned), whenever it wishes. Furthermore, under "reciprocity" statutes, national banks can at any time convert to state banks, and vice versa, with the approval of the system they are seeking to enter but without any power on the part of the system they are leaving to block the move.

This right to switch charters in either direction, whether the regulatory authority whose ship is being abandoned likes it or not, is a key element in the dual system's operation. It is not a product of any original intent or design; in fact, the exact opposite is true. When the national banking system was created during the Civil War, it was

---

15. A number of laws of more general applicability have been omitted from this analysis—for example, the Civil Rights Acts of 1964 and 1968, dealing with nondiscrimination in employment and housing, and the Consumer Credit Protection Act of 1968, as amended, dealing with truth-in-lending disclosures, credit billing, and consumer credit reporting. Such laws are not primarily concerned with banking regulation, and for the most part, they would apply to a bank no matter where it is located in the jurisdictional structure.

expected to replace state banks,[16] a process that the passage in 1865 of a prohibitive 10 percent per annum tax on state bank notes[17] was intended to assure. To facilitate the transition from state to national banks, Congress provided that any state bank "may, by authority of *this act,* become a national association"[18]; no authority from or consent by the state was deemed necessary, a proposition whose "validity cannot be doubted," according to the Supreme Court in *Casey* v. *Galli.*[19] The law remained in that posture until 1913, when the Federal Reserve Act added a proviso "[t]hat said conversion shall not be in contravention of the State law"[20] and thereby allowed the state to interpose a veto.

In 1934, when Congress again wanted to promote the development of a new system of federal institutions (this time, savings and loan associations) it used the same device: Section 5(i) of the Home Owners' Act of 1933[21] was amended to authorize any state S&L that was an FHLB member to convert into a federal S&L by a majority vote of its shareholders, whether or not state law permitted such a transformation.[22] But then the Supreme Court in *Hopkins Federal Savings and Loan Association v. Cleary*[23] held such a conversion provision to be an unconstitutional encroachment upon the reserved powers of the states under the Tenth Amendment: "The state, which brings [S&Ls] into being, has an interest in preserving their existence, for only thus can they attain the ends of their creation."[24]

Thus, by 1935, the power of the chartering jurisdiction—whether state or national—to block a conversion was enthroned in both statutory and constitutional law. A state bank could not convert to national charter unless state law allowed it; there was no provision whatever permitting a national bank to convert to state charter. In practice,

---

16. Act of Feb. 25, 1863, Ch. 58, 12 Stat. 665 (repealed 1864, current version at 12 U.S.C. § 21-221 (1970; Supp. V, 1975)). Neither this act nor the 1864 act, see N. 18 *infra,* was officially titled a National Bank Act at the time of enactment; the 1864 act was subsequently so titled by the Act of June 30, 1874, Ch. 343, 18 Stat. 123.

17. Act of March 3, 1865, Ch. 78, § 6, 13 Stat. 484. This was reenacted by the Act of July 13, 1866, Ch. 184, § 9, 14 Stat. 146 (superseded by the Internal Revenue Code of 1939). See Hackley (Pt. 1), N. 13 *supra* at 570–573.

18. Act of June 3, 1864, Ch. 106, § 44, 13 Stat. 112 (superseded by Revised Statutes of 1873, Title 65) (Emphasis added.) Needless to say, there was no provision for conversion the other way.

19. Casey v. Galli, 94 U.S. 673, 678 (1876).

20. Federal Reserve Act of 1913, Ch. 6, § 8, 38 Stat. 258 (codified at 12 U.S.C. § 35 (1970)).

21. Home Owners' Loan Act of 1933, Ch. 64, § 5(i), 48 Stat. 134 (current version at 12 U.S.C. § 1464(i) (1970)).

22. Act of April 27, 1934, Ch. 168, § 5, 48 Stat. 645 (codified in 12 U.S.C. § 1464(i) (1970)).

23. 296 U.S. 315 (1935).

24. *Id.* at 337. It is unlikely that the view taken in the opinion of the limitations of national power would prevail today.

however, movement from one system to the other was not particularly difficult. Many states had enacted provisions authorizing conversion to national charter, usually without a requirement of approval by the state banking department.[25] And national banks had found a substitute for direct conversion through adoption of voluntary liquidation, in which all assets and liabilities would be transferred to an existing or newly organized state bank and the business carried on much as before.[26] Though somewhat cumbersome and burdened with an undesirable flavor of insolvency, voluntary dissolution was free from any requirement of the Comptroller's consent.

When it appeared that the liquidation device might be treated as the occasion for realization of a capital gain and result in substantial tax costs, the banking industry obtained the enactment in 1950 of a federal conversion statute[27] permitting direct conversions to or mergers with state banks without the Comptroller's consent. The argument for the "two-way street" bill was that "a tax obstacle should not stand in the way of complete duality."[28] In addition, the new statute contained a reciprocity clause barring such transfers "unless under the law of the State in which such national banking association is located State banks may *without approval by any State authority* convert into and merge or consolidate with national banking associations under limitations or conditions no more restrictive" than those for national banks.[29] Although both the automatic consent feature and the reciprocity clause were important changes in the National Bank Act, they occasioned no discussion in the hearings and drew no opposition from the federal banking agencies.[30] Once the dual system was invoked, nothing more was necessary.

---

25. E.g., Act of July 31, 1927, Ch. 857, § 6, 1927 Cal. Stats. 1796 (current version at Cal. Fin. Code §§ 2090, 2092 (West 1968)); Act of April 16, 1914, Ch. 369 § 137, 1914 N.Y. Laws 1314 (current version at N.Y. Banking Law § 137 (McKinney 1971)).

26. See Act of June 3, 1864, Ch. 106, § 42, 13 Stat. 112 (current version at 12 U.S.C. §§ 181–186 (1970)).

27. Act of Aug. 17, 1950, Ch. 729, 64 Stat. 455 (codified at 12 U.S.C. § 214 (1970)).

28. S. Rep. No. 1104, 81st Cong., 1st Sess. 2 (1949).

29. 12 U.S.C. § 214c (1970). (Emphasis added.) It will be noted that the section refers to three transfer routes: conversion, merger and consolidation. It has been held that there must be state reciprocity as to the particular route chosen (and perhaps as to all three?) for transfer to be permissible. Ellis v. State Nat'l Bank of Alabama, 434 F. 2d 1182 (5th Cir. 1970), *cert. denied* 402 U.S. 973 (1971).

30. See *Miscellaneous Hearings: Hearings on H.R.J. Res. 196, H.R.J. 197, and H.R. 5745, 5120, 5792, 6102, 6909, 7726, and S. 2128 and S. 2252 Before the House Comm. on Banking and Currency,* 82d Cong., 1st & 2d Sess. 105–106 (1951–1952); *Miscellaneous Hearings: Hearings on H.R. 1161, 1060, 1732, 2730, 5044, 5533, 6305, and H.R.J. Res. 188 Before the House Committee on Banking and Currency,* 81st Cong., 1st Sess., 66–76 (Vol. 1, 1950); *Conversion of National Banks into State Banks: Hearings on H.R. 1161 Before the Subcomm. on Federal Reserve Matters of the Senate Comm. on Banking and Currency,* 81st Cong., 1st Sess. 10–13 (1949).

The impact of the federal reciprocity clause was substantial; in the next two decades, some 36 states enacted or broadened statutory provisions permitting banks to switch from state charters.[31] The typical state banking statute today merely states that no approval is required to convert or merge out of its system,[32] while a few contain a counterpart to the federal reciprocity condition.[33] The end result is a legal structure in which financial institutions are able at any time to leave a regulatory jurisdiction.[34]

Thus, the effect of this series of federal and state conversion statutes has been to negate the premise of *Hopkins Federal* that the state has an interest in preserving the existence of its creatures and preventing them from becoming "creatures of the nation."[35] Instead, state institutions may become national, and vice versa, at their own discretion and without any form of administrative approval by agencies of the jurisdiction they are leaving. It is this ability of the firm to change from one set of regulatory laws and agencies to another that is the unique feature of banking's dual system.[36]

But what is the value of that ability, and when is it exercised? Proponents and critics of the dual system offer quite divergent answers. A study written for the American Bankers Association concludes that "the historic value of dual banking lies in its ability to provide an escape valve from arbitrary or discriminatory chartering and regulatory policies at either the state or Federal level. . . . One of the historic objectives of dual banking has been to provide alternative supervisory frameworks under which commercial banks may choose to operate, thereby safeguarding against the extension of harsh, oppressive, and discriminatory supervision to institutions without recourse to alternative arrangements."[37] Arguments against proposals for a federal bank-

---

31. Ellis v. State National Bank of Alabama, 434 F.2d 1182, 1189 n. 9 (5th Cir. 1970), *cert. denied* 402 U.S. 973 (1971).

32. See, e.g., N.Y. Banking Law § 137 (McKinney 1971); Cal. Fin. Code §§ 2090, 2092 (West 1968); Ill. Rev. Stat. Ch. 16½, § 120 (1973); Ohio Rev. Code Ann. §§ 1121.02–1121.04 (Page 1968); Fla. Stat. §§ 661.02(2), 661.08(1) (1973).

33. See, e.g., N.J. Stat. Ann. §§ 17:9A–148(D) (2), 17:9A–154.1 (West 1963, Supp. 1977); Pa. Stat. Ann., Tit. 7, §§ 1602(b), 1709 (Purdon 1967).

34. See, e.g., Federal Home Loan Bank Bd. v. Greater Delaware Valley Fed. Savings & Loan Ass'n, 277 F.2d 437 (3d Cir. 1960). (Board can control only manner of obtaining membership approval of conversion.) A reciprocal conversion statute for federal S&Ls was enacted in 1948 as an amendment to Section 5(i) of the Home Owner's Loan Act of 1933. See Act of July 3, 1948, Ch. 825, § 1, 62 Stat. 1239 (codified at 12 U.S.C. § 1464(i) (1970)).

35. 296 U.S. 315, 337 (1935).

36. The closest, though limited, analogy is probably the ability of a business to change the state of its incorporation. For a disenchanted appraisal of the consequences, see Cary, "Federalism and Corporate Law: Reflections Upon Delaware," 83 Yale L. J. 663 (1974).

37. Brown, *The Dual Banking System in the United States* 59, 64–65 (New York: American Bankers Ass'n Dep't of Economics and Research, 1968).

ing commission in 1965 sounded the same note: The essential attribute of the dual system was that it provided "an opportunity to escape arbitrary supervision"[38] and "a vital check against the development of oppressive or capricious supervisory practices."[39]

When seen through the eyes of the supervisor, a markedly different picture sometimes emerges. To former Federal Reserve Governor J. L. Robertson, the existing structure creates "a dangerous tendency toward a 'race of laxity' in bank supervision that will lead, at an accelerating rate, to deterioration of the standards of sound banking which it is a function of bank supervision to maintain."[40] Chairman Burns, in his 1974 address, agreed: "The present regulatory system fosters what has sometimes been called 'competition in laxity.' . . . I need not explain to bankers the well-understood fact that regulatory agencies are sometimes played off against one another."[41]

When a bank switches regulators or charters, is it fleeing from oppressive supervision or opting for lax supervision? It is not necessary to choose up sides according to these terms. A more neutral, and useful, way of considering the question is in economic terms, derived from the theory of the firm.[42] A bank, like any other enterprise, may be thought of as engaged in trying to maximize the value of the firm—i.e., to maximize the present value of the stream of anticipated future earnings. One of the factors affecting those estimates of future earnings is the legal environment: the combination of statutory constraints and regulatory policies that define the investment opportunities open to the firm and affect its costs of operation. If the differences in regulatory options open to a bank give rise to significant differences in estimations of future earnings, one would expect the bank to prefer the more profitable option. If conversion were required to obtain it, the costs of conversion would have to be less than the increase in present value generated by it for an actual switch to take place.

In the economic view, then, establishment of a regulatory equilibrium between the different dual system options might be expected. The advantages and disadvantages of each option would be evaluated by each bank in terms of its own location, type of business, set of competitors, and so on; banks would distribute themselves across the available options in accordance with their profitability estimates. But as laws or

---

38. *1965 Consolidation Hearings,* N. 1 *supra* at 178 (statement of Ralph Zaun).

39. *Id.* at 187.

40. *Proposed Federal Banking Commission and Federal Deposit and Savings Insurance Board: Hearings on H.R. 729 and H.R. 5874 Before the Subcomm. on Bank Supervision and Insurance of the House Comm. on Banking and Currency,* 88th Cong., 1st Sess. 177 (1963) [hereinafter cited as *1963 Commission Hearings*].

41. Address by Chairman Arthur Burns, N. 3 *supra* at 18–19.

42. See generally Cohen and Cyert, *Theory of the Firm: Resource Allocation in a Market Economy* (Englewood Cliffs, N.J.: 2d ed., Prentice-Hall, 1975); Niskanen, *Bureaucracy and Representative Government* 36–42 (Chicago: Aldine, Atherton, 1971).

regulators change, or as the economic environment of the bank changes, profitability estimates may change also, and switching among regulatory options will take place until a new equilibrium is established. We will now examine this process more closely.

## The Sources of Relative Advantage

Unless there are differences among the regulatory options, choice among them is without importance. Differences in the substance of banking regulation are what make the dual system function, and it is richly endowed with opportunities for them to arise. They are built into the regulatory structure at many different levels, with corresponding degrees of permanence or ephemerality.

### CONSTITUTIONAL—THE FEDERAL INSTRUMENTALITY DOCTRINE

A few inequalities are seen as having a constitutional foundation.[43] Since national banks are chartered by the federal government and governed by the terms of federal law, they are also the potential beneficiaries of federal supremacy. Under the Supremacy Clause of Article VI of the Constitution, Congress can override conflicting provisions of state law in the course of exercising its delegated powers. Though the creation of national banks is not listed among the powers delegated to Congress, the Supreme Court in 1819, in the historic case of *McCulloch v. Maryland*,[44] upheld the power of Congress to incorporate a bank as a necessary and proper incident of its power to lay and collect taxes and borrow money, the bank in question being the Second Bank of the United States. The Court went on to consider the point directly at issue in the case—the power of the state to impose a tax on the bank's operations (note issuance):

> [I]f the States may tax one instrument, employed by the government in the execution of its powers, they may tax any and every other instrument. They may tax the mail; they may tax the mint; they may tax patent rights; they may tax the papers of the custom-house; they may tax judicial process; they may tax all the means employed by the government, to an excess which would defeat all the ends of government. . . . The question is, in truth, a question of supremacy; and if the right of the States to tax the means employed by the general government be conceded, the declaration that the constitution, and the laws made in pursuance thereof, shall be the supreme law of the land, is empty and unmeaning declamation. . . .

> The Court has bestowed on this subject its most deliberate consideration. The result is a conviction that the States have no power, by taxation or

---

**43.** See, e.g., Hackley, "Our Discriminatory Banking Structure," 55 Va. L. Rev. 1421, 1429–1435 (1969); Hackley, N. 13, *supra* at 585–586; Wille, "State Banking: A Study in Dual Regulation," 31 *Law & Contemporary Problems* 733, 742–743 (1966).

**44.** 17 U.S. (4 Wheat.) 316 (1819).

otherwise, to retard, impede, burden, or in any manner control the operations of the constitutional laws enacted by Congress to carry into execution the powers vested in the general government.[45]

Thus the Court by constitutional implication found the Second Bank of the United States immune from such taxation by the State of Maryland.

Although the Second Bank of the United States was not a governmental central bank in the modern sense, there was a major public element in its operations. The federal government owned 20 percent of its stock and appointed 20 percent of its board of directors; the Bank acted as fiscal agent for the United States and as the depository for public monies, and its circulating notes were legal tender for all debts to the federal government.[46] The Bank also was assured that no other would be chartered by Congress during its 20-year life.[47]

By contrast, the National Bank Acts of 1863[48] and 1864[49] contemplated, and achieved, a system of thousands of banks completely privately owned. In the Court's view, that made no difference; national banks were still "instruments designed to be used to aid the government in the administration of an important branch of the public service," and therefore "the States can exercise no control over them, nor in anywise affect their operation, except in so far as Congress may see proper to permit."[50]

In certain areas, Congress was specific about what it intended to permit or not permit. For example, in the field of taxation, whose importance McCulloch had so underscored, Congress, in the 1864 act, allowed states to impose nondiscriminatory taxes on stock in national banks and on real estate owned by national banks.[51] And that, said the Supreme Court, was the full "measure of the power of a state to tax national banks, their property, or their franchises."[52] After the decision in *First Agricultural Nat'l Bank v. State Tax Commission*[53] that a national

---

45. *Id.* at 432–433, 436.

46. Act of April 10, 1816, Ch. 44, 3 Stat. 266.

47. *Id.*, § 21, at 276.

48. Act of Feb. 25, 1863, Ch. 58, 12 Stat. 665 (repealed 1864, current version in scattered sections of 12 U.S.C., including 12 U.S.C. §§ 21–221 (1970, Supp. V, 1975)).

49. Act of June 3, 1864, Ch. 106, 13 Stat. 99 (superseded by Revised Statutes of 1873, Title 65) (current version in scattered sections of 12 U.S.C., including 12 U.S.C. §§ 21–221 (1970, Supp. V, 1975)).

50. Farmers' and Mechanics' Nat'l Bank v. Dearing, 91 U.S. 29, 33–34 (1875).

51. Act of June 3, 1864, Ch. 106, § 41, 13 Stat. 112 (codified at 12 U.S.C. § 548 (1970)).

52. Owensboro Nat'l Bank v. Owensboro, 173 U.S. 664, 669 (1899). The doctrine of intergovernmental tax immunities, which had provided much of the intellectual foundation of this position, was sharply contracted in Graves v. State Tax Comm'n *ex. rel.* O'Keefe, 306 U.S. 466 (1939). Nonetheless, this provision, as somewhat broadened by later amendments, still was construed as setting a limit on state powers of taxation. First Agricultural Nat'l Bank v. State Tax Comm'n, 392 U.S. 339 (1968).

53. 392 U.S. 339 (1968).

bank did not have to pay state sales and use taxes on its purchases, Congress changed the law to provide that "a national bank shall be treated as a bank organized and existing under the laws of the State or other jurisdiction within which its principal office is located" for purposes of state taxation.[54] Congress has also allowed the states to impose their usury ceilings upon national banks, at least in part.[55]

On the other hand, Congress has from time to time enacted special rules for national banks that consciously carve out a privileged position in comparison to their state counterparts. Although national banks may be sued in state as well as federal courts, they may be sued only in the county or district in which they are "located" or "established"[56]—that is, only at the location of the bank's principal office, even though it may have branches or offices or activities elsewhere which would clearly support local jurisdiction and venue under the usual rules.[57] And, even when properly sued in state court, a national bank has a limited immunity from preliminary injunction or attachment.[58]

In most areas, however, Congress has said nothing explicit, and thereby has left matters to the courts. In theory, the courts might create an entire system of federal law to govern all aspects of the operations of

---

**54.** Act of Dec. 24, 1969, Pub. L. No. 91-156 § 2(a), 83 Stat. 434 (codified at 12 U.S.C. § 548 (1970)), as amended by State Taxation of Depositories Act, Pub. L. No. 94-222 § 1, 90 Stat. 197 (1976). The provision did not become fully effective until Sept. 12, 1976, with the expiration of a moratorium on state "doing business" taxes on out-of-state banks. *Id.*

**55.** Act of June 3, 1864, Ch. 106, § 30, 13 Stat. 108 (as amended, this section is codified in 12 U.S.C. §§ 85–86 (1970, Supp. V, 1975)).

**56.** Act of Feb. 18, 1875, Ch. 80, § 1, 18 Stat. 320 (codified in 12 U.S.C. § 94 (1970)). It derives from Act of June 3, 1864, Ch. 106, § 57, 13 Stat. 116.

**57.** See National Bank of North America v. Associates of Obstetrics and Female Surgery, Inc., 425 U.S. 460 (1976); Northside Iron & Metal Co. v. Dobson & Johnson, Inc., 480 F.2d 798 (5th Cir. 1973); United States Nat'l Bank v. Hill, 434 F.2d 1019 (9th Cir. 1970).

Some inroads, however, have been made on the venue privilege. It does not apply to "local"or *in rem* actions in which the suit is one to determine interests in property at its situs. Casey v. Adams, 102 U.S. 66 (1880); Chateau Lafayette Apartments v. Meadow Brook Nat'l Bank, 416 F.2d 301 (5th Cir. 1969); Central Bank v. Superior Court, 30 Cal. App. 3d 962, 106 Cal. Rptr. 912 (3d Dist. 1973) (dictum). It is subject to doctrines, of uncertain scope, of "implied waiver" or consent by the bank. Charlotte Nat'l Bank v. Morgan, 132 U.S. 141 (1889); Reaves v. Bank of America, 352 F. supp. 745 (S.D. Cal. 1973); Michigan Nat'l Bank v. Superior Court, 23 Cal. App. 3d 1, 99 Cal. Rptr. 823 (1st Dist. 1972), *cert. denied* 409 U.S. 1125 (1973). See generally Steinberg, "Waiver of Venue Under the National Bank Act: Preferential Treatment for National Banks," 62 Iowa L. Rev. 129 (1976). On the other hand, it is not overridden by the broad venue provisions of the federal securities laws. Radzanower v. Touche Ross & Co., 426 U.S. 148 (1976).

A more radical contention—that federal court venue may lie only where the bank's principal office is "established," but state court venue is proper wherever the branch of the bank is "located"—is tested in Citizens & Southern Nat'l Bank v. Bougas, 138 Ga. App. 706, 227 S.E.2d 434 (1976), *cert. granted* 429 U.S. 1071 (1977).

**58.** Act of March 3, 1973, Ch. 269, § 2, 17 Stat. 603 (codified in 12 U.S.C. § 91 (1970)). The Supreme Court has given a narrow reading to Section 91, confining the bar to actions brought by creditors of a national bank seeking to reach its assets, not by debtors of a national bank seeking to protect their property from mortgage foreclosure and sale; Third Nat'l Bank in Nashville v. Impac, Ltd., 97 S. Ct. 2307 (1977).

national banks.[59] But in practice, the courts have settled for a much more limited effort at creating governing federal rules, leaving most relationships to be dealt with by the state law. The result, as summarized by the Supreme Court in 1944, is that "national banks are subject to state laws, unless those laws infringe the national banking laws or impose an undue burden on the performance of the banks' functions."[60] Of course, that leaves the crucial question as to what aspects of state law may so interfere with the attainment of the objectives of the national banking system that they must be rendered inapplicable or replaced by a uniform federal rule. The answer is far from easy to divine, but there is a scattering of holdings. For example, a state criminal statute making it an offense to accept deposits with knowledge that the bank is insolvent was held invalid as applied to officers of national banks.[61] State unclaimed property or escheat laws, on the other hand, may be applied to deposits in national banks.[62] And a recent decision upheld a state law requiring federal, as well as state, mortgage lenders to pay interest on escrow accounts.[63]

Possibly the most important area in which the courts have seen fit to create federal rules to the advantage of national banks has to do with interstate operations. States typically require out-of-state corporations to "qualify" to do local business and to pay local taxes based upon that business, with one sanction being that they are barred from the use of local courts to enforce their rights if they do not so qualify and pay. If the out-of-state corporation is a national bank, however, these "doing business" statutes have been construed not to apply or have been held invalid.[64] For major banks seeking to operate in national markets, this may be a significant advantage.[65]

---

59. See, e.g., Clearfield Trust Co. v. United States, 318 U.S. 363, 366-367 (1943).

60. Anderson Nat'l Bank v. Luckett, 321 U.S. 233, 248 (1944). The earliest formulation was that "the agencies of the Federal Government are only exempted from State legislation, so far as that legislation may interfere with, or impair their efficiency in performing the functions by which they are designed to serve that government." First Nat'l Bank v. Kentucky, 76 U.S. 353, 362 (1869). See also Davis v. Elmira Savings Bank, 161 U.S. 275 (1896).

61. Easton v. Iowa, 188 U.S. 220 (1903). But cf. Stathes v. Maryland, 29 Md. App. 474, 349 A.2d 254 (1975), *appeal dism'd*, 428 U.S. 803 (1976). (The embezzlement statute was concerned only with the criminal behavior of national bank employees and not the affairs of the national bank.) See also Franklin Nat'l Bank v. New York, 347 U.S. 373 (1954).

62. Anderson Nat'l Bank v. Luckett, 321 U.S. 233 (1944); Roth v. Delano, 338 U.S. 226 (1949); Standard Oil Co. v. New Jersey, 341 U.S. 428 (1951).

63. Federal Nat'l Mortgage Ass'n v. Lefkowitz, 390 F. Supp. 1364 (S.D.N.Y. 1975).

64. See, e.g., Steward v. Atlantic Nat'l Bank, 27 F.2d 224, 228 (9th Cir. 1928); Bank of America v. Lima, 103 F. Supp. 916 (D. Mass. 1952); State Nat'l Bank v. Laura, 45 Misc. 2d 430, 431–432, 256 N.Y.S.2d 1004, 1006 (Westchester County Ct. 1965).

65. See Hackley, N. 43, *supra* at 1432-1435. Furthermore, if the business being done locally fell within the ambit of the banking business, state statutes would frequently purport to limit or exclude the right of out-of-state banks to engage in it at all.

The federal instrumentality doctrine continues to be, then, a source of somewhat uncertain dimensions for differences between the state and national banking systems. Although it has some constitutional and statutory foundations, much of it rests in the hands of the courts, dependent primarily upon inferences about what is necessary to achieve legislative objectives; it is, therefore, subject to alteration by congressional action in any particular respect. But so long as national banks are regarded as arms of the federal government,[66] the availability of the federal judiciary to protect them, on occasion, from otherwise governing state law, even in the absence of any congressional enactment to that effect, constitutes one category of divergencies within the dual system.

STATUTORY—THE VARIATIONS IN RELEVANT LEGISLATION

A more obvious source of differences, and one not automatically favoring national institutions, consists of the fact that the state and federal laws authorizing the limiting banking operations are far from identical.[67] In the words of one long-time participant in banking regulation: "Volumes could be written about the lack of uniformity among the laws of the fifty states and the District of Columbia relating to the operations of commercial banks."[68] It will suffice here to mention a few of the more salient examples.

One characteristic of banking laws is the imposition of reserve requirements—that is, a requirement that a bank hold presumably safe and liquid assets in a minimum amount equal to a specified percentage of its deposit liabilities. While the Federal Reserve System and every state but Illinois have a reserve requirement, set either by statute or by the supervisory authority within a permitted range, the percentages vary widely. Even more important is the statutory definition of assets that satisfy the requirement. The Federal Reserve System requirement, applicable to all national banks and state member banks, counts only the bank's holding of coin and currency ("vault cash") and its balance with the local Federal Reserve Bank, which are nonearning assets, while most state requirements count certain types of government securities, which are earning assets, in addition to vault cash and balances with other banks. To the extent that reserve requirements force a bank to hold more nonearning or low-earning assets than it would otherwise

---

66. Cf. First Agricultural Nat'l Bank v. State Tax Comm'n, 392 U.S. 339, 348–359 (1968) (Marshall, J., dissenting). (Changing circumstances have erased relevant differences between federal and state chartered banks.)

67. A useful summary comparison, as of 1963, is contained in *Comparative Regulations of Financial Institutions, Subcomm. on Domestic Finance of the House Comm. on Banking and Currency*, 88th Cong., lst Sess. 1–133 (Subcomm. Print 1963), [hereinafter cited as *Comparative Regulations*].

68. Hackley, N. 13 *supra* at 580.

choose to hold in the normal conduct of its business, they amount to a kind of tax on banking operations—and one which varies a great deal among jurisdictions.[69] The variations make comparison complicated, but, at least in the Fed's view, the present structure of reserve requirements, on the whole, puts its members at a significant competitive disadvantage.[70]

For a second illustration, all the state and national banking laws contain limitations on loans by a bank to a single borrower, but the definition and the amount of those limitations are far from uniform. The limitation formula is usually a percentage of the bank's equity capital or net worth, with the percentage ranging from 10 to 35 percent and the base sometimes restricted to the capital and surplus accounts and sometimes extended to include undivided profits and capital debentures.[71] There are also numerous exceptions, or categories of loans and investments to which the limitations do not apply,[72] and these, too, vary widely from one jurisdiction to another. In many instances, the result is to define differently the size of the line of credit a bank can extend to its largest customers, depending on whether the bank holds national or state charter.

The third example, to change the setting, is from the savings and loan field. State branch laws for S&Ls, like banks, cover a spectrum from prohibiting branches through an array of forms of limited branching to full statewide branching.[73] The statute for federal S&Ls made no reference to the subject of branching[74] and, hence, imposed no limitations; the FHLBB, as a matter of policy, has said it would permit federal S&Ls to branch in a particular state if the state law or practice permitted "savings and loan associations, savings banks or similar institutions or commercial banks . . .to establish branches in such State or to conduct chain, group, or affiliate operations."[75] The result of this "most-favored-institution" policy was that in a state like Illinois, the FHLBB in

---

69. For a current survey, see American Bankers Ass'n *State Banking Law Service*, 19–24, 34–44 (1976).

70. See, e.g., Burns, "The Structure of Reserve Requirements," 59 Fed. Res. Bull., 339, 341 (May 1973). A study that supports this conclusion is Gray, "Bank Regulation, Bank Profitability, and Federal Reserve Membership," 1 Nat'l Banking Rev. 207 (1963).

71. *Comparative Regulations*, N. 67 *supra* at 29-36.

72. See. e.g., the long list of exceptions contained in 12 U.S.C. § 84 (1970, Supp. V, 1975).

73. *Comparative Regulations*, N. 67 *supra* at 133.

74. It has been held, nonetheless, to confer upon the FHLBB by implication the power to authorize branches. North Arlington Nat'l Bank v. Kearny Fed. Savings & Loan Ass'n, 187 F.2d 564 (3d Cir.), *cert. denied* 342 U.S. 816 (1951); First Nat'l Bank of McKeesport v. First Fed. Savings & Loan Ass'n of Homestead, 225 F.2d 33 (D.C. Cir. 1955).

75. 12 C.F.R. § 556.5(b) (1) (1977). For an earlier announcement of this position, see *Financial Institutions Act of 1957: Hearings on S. 1451 and H.R. 7026 Before the House Comm. on Banking and Currency*, 85th Cong., 2d Sess., Pt. 2, p. 880 (1958).

1973 announced it would allow federal S&Ls to branch, although state S&Ls could not.[76] Discrepancies between alternative jurisdictions in a matter as important for an institution's growth as branching are of obvious significance.

Examples could be multiplied, but it seems unnecessary. The point is simply that banking regulation is a field in which the powers conferred on banks and the restrictions to which they are subject are diverse in a multitude of ways, some minor and some major, as among the various state and federal laws. It is not a field in which much standardization has occurred, along the lines of the Uniform Commercial Code or other uniform state acts.

POLICY—THE EXERCISE OF ADMINISTRATIVE DISCRETION

Even where the statutory language for different jurisdictions is identical, its application by different agencies will give rise to different interpretations. This is accentuated when the statute explicitly confers a broad approval power on the agency over some species of transactions (e.g., mergers), but it will occur even on the level of merely defining the agency view of the meaning of a statutory provision.

Numerous examples of the latter were provided by the controversies in the early 1960s between Comptroller of the Currency James Saxon and the Federal Reserve Board. One well-publicized dispute involved the bond underwriting authority of national and state member banks.[77] The Banking Act of 1933,[78] in undertaking to divorce commercial banking from investment banking, prohibited national banks from underwriting—that is, purchasing from the issuer to distribute to the public— any securities, but with an exception for "general obligations of any State or any political subdivision thereof."[79] At the same time, the Federal Reserve Act was amended so that "State member banks shall be subject to the same limitations and conditions with respect to . . . underwriting . . . as are applicable in the case of national banks."[80] From the outset, the Fed took the position that the exception for general obligation bonds did not cover revenue bonds or any other bonds not

---

76. 38 Fed. Reg. 4361 (1973); "Illinois Federals May File De Novo Branch Applications," Fed. Home Loan Bank Bd. J., 30 (Feb. 1973).

77. See *To Permit National Banks to Underwrite and Deal in "Revenue Bonds": Hearings on H.R. 7539 Before the House Comm. on Banking and Currency*, 89th Cong., 1st Sess. 10–13 (1965), (statement of James J. Saxon); *Increased Flexibility for Financial Institutions: Hearings on H.R. 5845, 7878, 8230, 8245, 8247, 8459, and 8541 Before the House Committee on Banking and Currency*, 88th Cong., 1st Sess. 6 (1964); See also Robertson, N. 2 *supra* at 680-683.

78. Act of June 16, 1933, Ch. 89, 48 Stat. 162 (codified in scattered sections of 12 U.S.C.).

79. 12 U.S.C. § 24 (Seventh) (Supp. V, 1975).

80. 12 U.S.C. § 335 (1970).

backed by general powers of taxation. In 1963, however, the Comptroller began a series of rulings that state revenue bonds and bonds issued by political subdivisions and authorities not having any general tax powers were within the exception, so that national banks could underwrite and deal in them.[81] The Fed was unmoved and promptly advised state member banks that, in its view, the Comptroller's rulings were invalid.[82]

Thus, statutes aimed at identical treatment produced, in the hands of two different agencies, diametrically opposing outcomes. The same thing happened with respect to the power of a bank to establish and invest in a subsidiary corporation, as a means of carrying on part of its banking operations. A national bank is prohibited from purchasing for its own account "any shares of stock of any corporation," except as "otherwise permitted by law";[83] state member banks are subject to "the same limitations and conditions."[84] Comptroller Saxon found the necessary legal permission to invest in an operations subsidiary by a broad interpretation, as was his wont, of the clause authorizing a national bank to exercise "all such incidental powers as shall be necessary to carry on the business of banking."[85] The Federal Reserve Board, however, reaffirmed its long-standing position that the incidental-powers clause was not sufficient to open up an area of exceptions from the stock-purchase prohibition.[86]

Where the statutory language explicitly confers on several administering agencies a range of approval discretion, there is obviously a still greater likelihood of divergencies in policy and application, even though a list of factors or standards to be "considered" is written into the law. The standards may, of course, be so general as to be devoid of almost all limiting content, such as requirements that approval be based on the "public interest" or "convenience and needs of the community," in which case it is evident that the course of decision may vary greatly from one administrator or agency to another. In the banking field, decisions on new charters and branches are made under statutes that

---

81. See, e.g., 12 C.F.R. § 1.127 (state revenue bonds), § 1.167 (nontaxing authority) (1977).

82. See, e.g., 12 C.F.R. § 250.121 (b) (5) (1977) (originally published in 28 Fed. Reg. 12,611 (1963)). The conflict was ultimately taken to court and resolved in favor of the Fed's position. Port of New York Authority v. Baker, Watts & Co., 392 F.2d 497 (D.C. Cir. 1968).

83. 12 U.S.C. § 24 (Seventh) (Supp. V, 1975).

84. 12 U.S.C. § 335 (1970).

85. 12 U.S.C. § 24 (Seventh) (Supp. V, 1975); 2 Nat'l Banking Rev. 430, 576 (1965); 12 C.F.R. § 7.7376 (1977).

86. See 31 Fed. Reg. 10,021 (1966); "Member Bank Purchase of Stocks of Operations Subsidiaries," 52 Fed. Res. Bull. 1151 (1966). This time the Fed ultimately yielded and adopted the Comptroller's view; see 12 C.F.R. § 250.141 (1977); Ns. 100–103 *infra* and accompanying text.

customarily contain such vaporous standards, or none at all.[87] An administrator is therefore free to be as restrictive or liberal with approvals as he pleases, regardless of the policy being followed by other regulators. Comptroller Saxon, for example, was noted for embarking on a policy of ready approval of new banks and branches,[88] to the consternation of many state supervisors and bankers.[89]

A somewhat more detailed, or at least longer, list of statutory approval standards does very little to change the picture. The Bank Merger Act of 1960[90] prescribed no less than seven identical "factors"[91] that were to be considered by the Comptroller, the Fed, and FDIC in determining whether to approve "in the public interest" a merger acquisition by a bank under its jurisdiction. "In the interests of uniform standards," the law required each agency to request a report on the competitive factors from both the other two banking agencies and the Attorney General.[92] Somehow, Congress declared, this would mean that the three agencies "must review applications with the same attitude, and must give the same weight to the various banking and competitive factors."[93] In fact, of course, that did not happen; each agency went its own way, and three different patterns emerged. To oversimplify, the Comptroller saw mergers as increasing competition in the size category of the resulting bank and, therefore, almost never disapproved a merger on competitive grounds, while the Fed displayed considerable concern with the degree of concentration being produced in local banking markets and followed a notably tighter course on merger applications. FDIC occupied an intermediate position, closer to that of the Comptroller in the early period and moving markedly toward the stricter attitude of the Fed after 1970 (when Frank Wille became

---

87. See Scott, "In Quest of Reason: The Licensing Decisions of the Federal Banking Agencies," 42 U. Chi. L. Rev. 235 (1975).

88. See, e.g., Hackley, N. 13 *supra* at 772–773.

89. See, e.g., *Conflict of Federal and State Banking Laws: Hearings Before the House Comm. on Banking and Currency,* 88th Cong., 1st Sess. (passim 1963) [hereinafter cited as *1963 Hearings on Banking Law Conflicts*].

90. Act of May 13, 1960, Pub. L. No. 86-463, 74 Stat. 129 (current version at 12 U.S.C. § 1828 (c) (5) (1970)).

91. There were six "banking" factors—"the financial history and condition of each of the banks involved, the adequacy of its capital structure, its future earnings prospects, the general character of its management, the convenience and needs of the community to be served, and whether or not its corporate powers are consistent with the purposes" of the Federal Deposit Insurance Act—and one "competitive" factor—the effect of the transaction on competition, "including any tendency toward monopoly"—to be taken into consideration. *Id.*

92. *Id.* at § 1828 (c) (4).

93. S. Rep. 196, 86th Cong., 1st Sess. 23 (1959). Cf. H.R. Rep. 1416, 86th Cong., 2d Sess. 12 (1960).

Chairman).[94] The result, despite the statute, was a clear lack of uniformity among the agencies in their treatment of bank mergers,[95] as interested banks quickly came to perceive.[96]

SUMMARY

Thus, the opportunities are legion for discrepancies to arise between the different regulatory options available to an institution under the dual system. Predicting when and where those opportunities will materialize is another and more difficult matter. Any favorable or unfavorable shift in law or policy in one regulatory configuration that is not matched in the others creates such a divergence. If most economic regulation is viewed as the outcome of a continuing struggle for advantage among various interest groups, then what is required is a different balance of political forces bearing on the components of each dual system option.[97] That seems intuitively very likely in such a structure, but its detailed exploration lies outside the scope of this study.

## Initial Responses

When regulatory divergencies do arise and are significant in terms of estimates of future profitability for a bank, there should be observable behavioral consequences for both banking entry and banking operations. This is the area we shall examine next, for the period from 1950 to 1974.

In the preceding discussion of regulatory divergencies, it will have been noted that many of the examples were from the period in which James Saxon was Comptroller of the Currency (November 15, 1961 to November 15, 1966). Comptroller Saxon was widely regarded as an aggressive proponent of the national banking system; his interpretative and policy innovations were generally in the direction of expansion of the operations and activities of national banks. He was also viewed as much more liberal in his chartering policies than his predecessors or most state supervisors. One measure of the correctness of those views

---

94. An extensive analysis of the 1960–1962 decisions may be found in Hall and Phillips, *Bank Mergers and The Regulatory Agencies* (Fed. Reserve Bd., Washington, D.C., 1964). An interesting statistical appraisal of the 1,916 merger applications acted upon by the three agencies between 1960 and 1972, in terms of the competitive factor reports submitted by the Attorney General and other agencies, is contained in R. Eisenbeis, "Differences in Federal Regulatory Agencies' Bank Merger Policies," 7 J. of Money, Credit and Banking 93 (1975).

95. See Eisenbeis *id.* at 104.

96. Examples are cited in Hackley, N. 13 *supra* at 627–628 and Hackley, N. 43 *supra* at 1456–1457.

97. For a discussion of such a view of regulation and some of its theoretical shortcomings, see Posner, "Theories of Economic Regulation," 5 Bell J. of Economics & Management Science, 335 (1974).

and the significance of his actions is to examine the extent of response

by banks themselves.

ENTRY FLOWS

The organizers of a new bank in any locale would obviously prefer the regulatory configuration that they believed would prove the most profitable, but they would also have to take into account the supervisor's attitude toward the entry of a new competitor and, hence, their prospects of success in the application. The entry figures in Table 1-2 necessarily reflect both elements.

The bulk of bank entry, as can be seen, occurred in the form of

**TABLE 1-2   New Banks**
(1950–1974)

| Year | National banks | State banks | | |
| | | FRS member | Nonmember FDIC insured | Non-FDIC-insured |
|---|---|---|---|---|
| 1950 | 6 | 8 | 44 | 9 |
| 1951 | 9 | 2 | 40 | 7 |
| 1952 | 15 | 4 | 42 | 5 |
| 1953 | 12 | 10 | 37 | 5 |
| 1954 | 18 | 6 | 42 | 6 |
| 1955 | 28 | 4 | 71 | 12 |
| 1956 | 29 | 6 | 72 | 10 |
| 1957 | 20 | 3 | 50 | 11 |
| 1958 | 18 | 2 | 63 | 9 |
| 1959 | 23 | 4 | 75 | 12 |
| 1960 | 32 | 4 | 75 | 14 |
| 1961 | 26 | 2 | 70 | 10 |
| 1962 | 63 | 4 | 100 | 12 |
| 1963 | 163 | 3 | 115 | 19 |
| 1964 | 200 | 3 | 120 | 12 |
| 1965 | 88 | 4 | 90 | 13 |
| 1966 | 25 | 4 | 70 | 22 |
| 1967 | 18 | 3 | 73 | 13 |
| 1968 | 15 | 1 | 65 | 4 |
| 1969 | 16 | 7 | 92 | 15 |
| 1970 | 40 | 8 | 130 | 5 |
| 1971 | 37 | 9 | 150 | 5 |
| 1972 | 55 | 13 | 167 | 6 |
| 1973 | 90 | 26 | 216 | 5 |
| 1974 | 97 | 35 | 232 | 25 |
| Total | 1143 | 175 | 2301 | 266 |
| Percent | 29.4 | 4.5 | 59:2 | 6.8 |

*Source:* FDIC Annual Reports, Tables 101 (1950–1959, 1964–1974), 102 (1960–1963).

national banks and nonmember insured state banks; very few state banks chose to commence business as Federal Reserve System members. In percentage terms, national banks accounted for 29 percent of new bank entry, and nonmember insured state banks for 59 percent.

If the period is divided between the five Saxon years (1962–1966) and the balance, some sharp contrasts appear. In the Saxon years, 48 percent of new entry came from national banks and only 44 percent from nonmember insureds, while for the rest of the period, national banks produced only 19 percent and a dominant 68 percent came from nonmember insureds. The data of Table 1-2 are summarized in Table 1-3. Interestingly enough, the tables suggest that the Saxon edge was rather quickly lost, a phenomenon to which we shall return.

CONVERSION FLOWS

Far more important, in terms of their immediate impact on the banking system, are the shifts made by existing banks within the dual-system options. The numbers of converting commercial banks moving in different directions is set forth in Table 1-4. (Movement from insured to uninsured status is so infrequent that it is omitted from the tabulation.) As used here, any switch from one regulatory configuration to another is referred to as a conversion whether or not it also involves a change between state and national charter. As the totals indicate, there have been significant tendencies for uninsured banks to change to FDIC insured status, for state member banks to leave the Fed and remain solely under FDIC, and recently, for national banks to switch to state insureds. In Table 1-5, the data are summarized in terms simply of movement into and out of the national banking system.

During the Saxon years, the number of banks entering the national banking system by conversion was almost three times the number leaving it, while the ratio in the earlier period was 2 to 1 and in the later

**TABLE 1-3   New Banks**
(1950–1974)

| Years | Total new banks | National banks | State banks | | |
|---|---|---|---|---|---|
| | | | FRS Member | Nonmember FDIC insured | Non-FDIC-insured |
| 1960–1961 | 1084 | 236 | 55 | 683 | 110 |
| Percentage | | 21.8 | 5.1 | 63 | 10.1 |
| 1962–1966 | 1130 | 539 | 18 | 495 | 78 |
| Percentage | | 47.7 | 1.6 | 43.8 | 6.9 |
| 1967–1974 | 1571 | 268 | 102 | 1123 | 78 |
| Percentage | | 17.1 | 6.5 | 71.5 | 5 |

*Source:* Table 1-2 data.

FDIC Annual Reports, Tables 101 (1950–1959, 1964–1974), 102 (1960–1963).

**TABLE 1-4   Bank Conversions: Number**
(1950–1974)

| | From: | Uninsured | | | FDIC | | FRS | | National bank | |
|---|---|---|---|---|---|---|---|---|---|---|
| | | (1) | (2) | (3) | (4) | (5) | (6) | (7) | (8) | (9) |
| Year | To: | FDIC | FRS | N.B. | N.B. | FRS | FDIC | N.B. | FDIC | FRS |
| 1950 | | 38 | 3 | 2 | 1 | 6 | 4 | 3 | 1 | 0 |
| 1951 | | 24 | 2 | 0 | 2 | 6 | 11 | 0 | 1 | 0 |
| 1952 | | 20 | 0 | 0 | 0 | 12 | 9 | 0 | 6 | 1 |
| 1953 | | 37 | 3 | 0 | 1 | 7 | 4 | 1 | 4 | 0 |
| 1954 | | 24 | 1 | 1 | 7 | 11 | 4 | 4 | 4 | 0 |
| 1955 | | 35 | 1 | 1 | 5 | 15 | 2 | 2 | 4 | 1 |
| 1956 | | 60 | 2 | 1 | 6 | 8 | 14 | 2 | 3 | 0 |
| 1957 | | 21 | 0 | 0 | 2 | 7 | 13 | 3 | 4 | 0 |
| 1958 | | 26 | 1 | 0 | 4 | 6 | 15 | 3 | 1 | 0 |
| 1959 | | 50 | 2 | 0 | 1 | 3 | 15 | 6 | 2 | 0 |
| 1960 | | 24 | 0 | 0 | 6 | 7 | 26 | 9 | 9 | 1 |
| 1961 | | 29 | 1 | 1 | 5 | 4 | 16 | 4 | 1 | 0 |
| 1962 | | 17 | 0 | 2 | 8 | 5 | 26 | 3 | 6 | 0 |
| 1963 | | 37 | 1 | 0 | 18 | 3 | 22 | 8 | 13 | 0 |
| 1964 | | 20 | 0 | 0 | 19 | 4 | 19 | 13 | 5 | 1 |
| 1965 | | 16 | 0 | 0 | 13 | 1 | 23 | 10 | 7 | 0 |
| 1966 | | 24 | 0 | 0 | 10 | 4 | 32 | 13 | 7 | 2 |
| 1967 | | 21 | 0 | 0 | 7 | 1 | 21 | 4 | 5 | 0 |
| 1968 | | 18 | 0 | 0 | 6 | 3 | 40 | 7 | 12 | 0 |
| 1969 | | 16 | 2 | 0 | 9 | 1 | 41 | 8 | 28 | 3 |
| 1970 | | 12 | 0 | 1 | 5 | 0 | 38 | 6 | 39 | 0 |
| 1971 | | 6 | 0 | 0 | 7 | 4 | 20 | 3 | 21 | 0 |
| 1972 | | 5 | 0 | 0 | 12 | 6 | 36 | 7 | 22 | 1 |
| 1973 | | 9 | 1 | 1 | 8 | 4 | 28 | 8 | 21 | 0 |
| 1974 | | 5 | 1 | 0 | 8 | 9 | 28 | 7 | 20 | 0 |
| Total | | 593 | 21 | 10 | 170 | 137 | 507 | 134 | 246 | 10 |
| Percentage | | 32.4 | 1.1 | 0.5 | 9.3 | 7.5 | 27.7 | 7.3 | 13.5 | 0.5 |

*Sources:* FRB, Annual Reports of Bank Changes (G.4.5), 1950–1974.

   FDIC, List of Yearly Changes Among Banks, 1950–1974.

**TABLE 1-5   Bank Conversions: Number**
(1950–1974)

| Years | To national bank | From national bank |
|---|---|---|
| 1950–1961 | 83 | 43 |
| 1962–1966 | 117 | 41 |
| 1967–1974 | 114 | 172 |

*Source:* Table 1-4 data

   FRB, Annual Reports of Bank Changes (G.4,5), 1950–1974.

   FDIC, List of Yearly Changes Among Banks, 1950–1974.

period, 2 to 3. Again, it will be noted that the apparent advantage of the national banking system during the Saxon period did not long endure and was, in fact, soon reversed, at least in numbers.

But numbers alone do not tell the whole story, or even the most interesting part. The size of the converting commercial banks is a more useful dimension in understanding how the dual system operates. Table 1-6 presents the same conversion picture as Table 1-5, but in terms of the aggregate assets of the converting institutions. When depicted in asset terms, it is evident that the Fed has been the heavy loser as a regulator, while the numerically largest category of institu-

**TABLE 1-6   Bank Conversions: Assets**
(millions of dollars)
(1950–1974)

| | From: | Uninsured | | | FDIC | | FRS | | Nat. Bank | |
|---|---|---|---|---|---|---|---|---|---|---|
| | | (1) | (2) | (3) | (4) | (5) | (6) | (7) | (8) | (9) |
| Year | To: | FDIC | FRS | N.B. | N.B. | FRS | FDIC | N.B. | FDIC | FRS |
| 1950 | | 181.8 | 35.6 | 2.8 | 2.9 | 19.1 | 12.3 | 55.8 | 3.2 | 0 |
| 1951 | | 42.3 | 94.6 | 0 | 9.6 | 21.4 | 72.5 | 0 | 1.1 | 0 |
| 1952 | | 40.3 | 0 | 0 | 0 | 42 | 440.3 | 0 | 35.3 | 58 |
| 1953 | | 86.2 | 8.9 | 0 | 2.6 | 137.3 | 50.5 | 8 | 25.5 | 0 |
| 1954 | | 179.1 | 2.7 | 1.8 | 99.5 | 228.6 | 15.4 | 69.1 | 28.7 | 0 |
| 1955 | | 42.8 | 9 | 1.9 | 36.2 | 123.8 | 7.1 | 14.3 | 12 | 11.4 |
| 1956 | | 154.6 | 4.9 | 2.8 | 78 | 69.5 | 90.2 | 46.8 | 3.8 | 0 |
| 1957 | | 71.5 | 0 | 0 | 21.4 | 57 | 86.3 | 21.6 | 13.6 | 0 |
| 1958 | | 48.9 | 2.4 | 0 | 51.8 | 171.5 | 94.8 | 59 | 10.2 | 0 |
| 1959 | | 371.9 | 4 | 0 | 6.3 | 20.8 | 126.5 | 156.1 | 2.9 | 0 |
| 1960 | | 41.6 | 0 | 0 | 53.1 | 69.5 | 343.3 | 294.2 | 32.6 | 54.4 |
| 1961 | | 66.4 | 4.3 | .8 | 62.6 | 12.7 | 107.4 | 243.9 | 1.9 | 0 |
| 1962 | | 55.6 | 0 | 7.3 | 187.3 | 54.4 | 397.3 | 38.4 | 33.9 | 0 |
| 1963 | | 53.4 | .2 | 0 | 112.7 | 21.8 | 157.7 | 319.8 | 162.3 | 0 |
| 1964 | | 28.9 | 0 | 0 | 188.4 | 98.2 | 263.3 | 1908.3 | 38.8 | 1.9 |
| 1965 | | 25 | 0 | 0 | 74.2 | 39.5 | 492.7 | 13553.5 | 71.1 | 0 |
| 1966 | | 174.8 | 0 | 0 | 251.1 | 62.5 | 479.3 | 633.4 | 74 | 66.6 |
| 1967 | | 65.9 | 0 | 0 | 82.3 | 18.2 | 424.5 | 154 | 18.6 | 0 |
| 1968 | | 30.1 | 0 | 0 | 92.6 | 73 | 456.2 | 5050.5 | 72.8 | 0 |
| 1969 | | 58.2 | 3.8 | 0 | 54.8 | 1.9 | 684.4 | 2997.2 | 1173 | 102.3 |
| 1970 | | 92.2 | 0 | 12.4 | 116.5 | 0 | 389.4 | 176 | 552 | 0 |
| 1971 | | 364.1 | 0 | 0 | 58.3 | 156.5 | 275.4 | 85.7 | 411 | 0 |
| 1972 | | 99.4 | 0 | 0 | 147.5 | 463.2 | 1360.1 | 1158.5 | 592.3 | 198.6 |
| 1973 | | 54.9 | 1.2 | 47.2 | 135.4 | 121.1 | 1401.3 | 403 | 499.4 | 0 |
| 1974 | | 38.4 | 4.7 | 0 | 143 | 608.2 | 1388.1 | 3980.7 | 1736.7 | 0 |

*Sources:*  FRB, Annual Reports of Bank Changes (G.4.5), 1950–1974.

FDIC, List of Yearly Changes Among Banks, 1950–1974.

Rand McNally International Bankers Directory.

tional conversions (from uninsured to FDIC) shrinks greatly in importance.

If comparisons are to be made over a period as long as 25 years, however, these asset figures must be related to the size of the commercial banking system at the time; while the banking system has remained relatively static in number of firms, its assets have grown during this period from $156 billion at the start of 1950 to $835 billion by the beginning of 1974. Table 1-7 expresses the asset figures of Table 1-6 in terms of hundredths of a percent of the total assets of the commercial banking system at the beginning of the year (i.e., as of December 31 of the preceding year).

**TABLE 1-7  Bank Conversions: Asset Percentages**
(1/100 percent of total commercial bank assets)
(1950–1974)

| Year | Total commercial bank assets (billion $) | From: To: Uninsured (1) FDIC | (2) FRS | (3) N.B. | FDIC (4) N.B. | (5) FRS | FRS (6) FDIC | (7) N.B. | Nat. Bank (8) FDIC | (9) FRS |
|------|------|------|------|------|------|------|------|------|------|------|
| 1950 | 156.0 | 11.7 | 2.3 | 0.2 | 0.2 | 1.2 | 0.8 | 3.6 | 0.2 | 0 |
| 1951 | 167.0 | 2.5 | 5.7 | 0 | 0.6 | 1.3 | 4.3 | 0 | 0.1 | 0 |
| 1952 | 178.6 | 2.3 | 0 | 0 | 0 | 2.4 | 24.7 | 0 | 2.0 | 3.2 |
| 1953 | 188.6 | 4.6 | 0.5 | 0 | 0.1 | 7.3 | 2.7 | 0.4 | 1.4 | 0 |
| 1954 | 193.1 | 9.3 | 0.1 | 0.1 | 5.2 | 11.8 | 0.8 | 3.6 | 1.5 | 0 |
| 1955 | 202.4 | 2.1 | 0.4 | 0.1 | 1.8 | 6.1 | 0.4 | 0.7 | 0.6 | 0.6 |
| 1956 | 210.7 | 7.3 | 0.2 | 0.1 | 3.7 | 3.3 | 4.3 | 2.2 | 0.2 | 0 |
| 1957 | 217.4 | 3.3 | 0 | 0 | 1.0 | 2.6 | 4.0 | 1.0 | 0.6 | 0 |
| 1958 | 222.8 | 2.2 | 0.1 | 0 | 2.3 | 7.7 | 4.3 | 2.6 | 0.5 | 0 |
| 1959 | 238.6 | 15.6 | 0.2 | 0 | 0.3 | 0.9 | 5.3 | 6.5 | 0.1 | 0 |
| 1960 | 244.7 | 1.7 | 0 | 0 | 2.2 | 2.8 | 14 | 12 | 1.3 | 2.2 |
| 1961 | 257.6 | 2.6 | 0.2 | 0 | 2.4 | 0.5 | 4.2 | 9.5 | 0.1 | 0 |
| 1962 | 278.6 | 2.0 | 0 | 0.3 | 6.7 | 2.0 | 14.3 | 1.4 | 1.2 | 0 |
| 1963 | 297.1 | 1.8 | 0 | 0 | 3.8 | 0.7 | 5.3 | 10.8 | 5.5 | 0 |
| 1964 | 312.7 | 0.9 | 0 | 0 | 6.0 | 3.1 | 8.4 | 61 | 1.2 | 0.1 |
| 1965 | 346.8 | 0.7 | 0 | 0 | 2.1 | 1.1 | 14.2 | 390.8 | 2.1 | 0 |
| 1966 | 377.2 | 4.6 | 0 | 0 | 6.7 | 1.7 | 12.7 | 16.8 | 2.0 | 1.8 |
| 1967 | 404.6 | 1.6 | 0 | 0 | 2.0 | 0.4 | 10.5 | 3.8 | 0.5 | 0 |
| 1968 | 452.3 | 0.7 | 0 | 0 | 2.0 | 1.6 | 10.1 | 111.7 | 1.6 | 0 |
| 1969 | 501.9 | 1.1 | 0.1 | 0 | 1.1 | 0 | 13.6 | 59.7 | 23.4 | 2.0 |
| 1970 | 531.7 | 1.7 | 0 | 0.2 | 2.2 | 0 | 7.3 | 3.3 | 10.4 | 0 |
| 1971 | 577.2 | 6.3 | 0 | 0 | 1.0 | 2.7 | 4.8 | 1.5 | 7.1 | 0 |
| 1972 | 640.9 | 1.6 | 0 | 0 | 2.3 | 7.2 | 21.2 | 18.1 | 9.2 | 3.1 |
| 1973 | 739.6 | 0.7 | 0 | 0.6 | 1.8 | 1.6 | 18.9 | 5.4 | 6.8 | 0 |
| 1974 | 835.1 | 0.5 | 0 | 0 | 1.7 | 7.3 | 16.6 | 47.7 | 20.8 | 0 |

*Sources:* Table 1-6 data.

FRB, *Federal Reserve Bulletin*, Table A14 (Commercial banks, by classes) (December 1976 and prior years).

The annual conversion rate figures of Table 1-7 can be viewed from a number of perspectives. If the data are grouped from the standpoint of the national banking system during the Saxon and non-Saxon years, as before, the pattern that results is shown in Table 1-8.

When compared to Table 1-5, a much more impressive picture appears of banks in the Saxon period shifting to the national bank regulatory option. The average annual rate of conversion to national banks goes up 20 times over the prior decade, and becomes 36 times as large as the rate of conversion out of the national banking system.

DISCUSSION

In some sense, the numbers at which we have been looking are not very large, in terms of the entire banking system; at its height, in the Saxon period, the net rate of accretion to the national banking system through conversion amounted to only about 1 percent per year. On the other hand, these numbers cumulate; if a trend is sustained over 5 or 10 years, even at levels well below 1 percent, it can become quite appreciable.

The rate of conversion to national banks in the 1960s was certainly regarded at the time as dramatic, even alarming. James Saxon and his successor as Comptroller, William Camp, were denounced as destroyers of the dual banking system; bankers fulminated, and so did their congressional allies. But, in fact, the tides running so strongly in favor of the national banking system in the Saxon years, as shown in Tables 1-5 and 1-8, thereafter slackened or reversed, and for several reasons, that is what one would expect. As the attractiveness of one regulatory option increases, due to policy shifts by a new incumbent or for any other cause, those institutions that are at the margin will be induced to shift. Once they have done so, however, a new regulatory equilibrium will be established, and the tide will not continue to run except as other factors continue to change and work in its favor; it is a simple fallacy to project such trends automatically, especially to a terminal point where one of the regulatory systems is extinct. Furthermore, and perhaps even

**TABLE 1-8  Bank Conversions: Average Annual Asset Percentages**
(1/100 percent of total commercial bank assets)
(1950–1974)

| Years | To national bank | From national bank |
|-------|------------------|--------------------|
| 1950–1961 | 5.2 | 1.2 |
| 1962–1966 | 101.3 | 2.8 |
| 1967–1974 | 33.3 | 10.6 |

*Source:* Table 1-7 data.

FRB, *Federal Reserve Bulletin,* Table A14 (Commercial banks, by classes) (December 1976 and prior years).

but dynamic. A strong conversion trend in favor of one regulatory
system seems to induce changes in response by the alternative regulatory systems, and it is to that aspect of the dual banking system that we
turn next.

## Secondary Responses

AGENCY REACTION

Any marked conversion flow implies a significant diminution in the
size and importance of the regulatory agencies losing members, and
that is a matter not taken lightly. This becomes most evident in a
dramatic case such as the shift of a single, very large bank. For example,
in 1968, the $5 billion Wells Fargo Bank, the largest state-chartered bank
in California, converted to a national bank. The California Superintendent of Banks, James Hall, promptly issued a press statement in which
he forecast "radical change" in the fundamental structure of banking in
the United States and the "elimination of a significant dual banking
system," and not-so-incidentally noted that the conversion would
reduce the revenue (from assessments levied on state banks) of the state
banking department by 30 percent.[98]

Similar impacts were felt by the banking departments of New York,
when the $13 billion Chase Manhattan Bank converted to national
charter in 1965, and of North Carolina, when the $1.6 billion Wachovia
Bank decided in 1968 to become a national bank. The state bank
supervisors attributed these and other conversions not only to the
inducements created by the policies and interpretations of the Comptroller, but also to the constraints imposed by the Fed upon its member
state banks. A contemporary account of a conference attended by
bankers and bank regulators in May 1968 reported that "smoldering
dissatisfaction" with the Fed's policies "boiled up" at a panel
discussion.[99]

That dissatisfaction intensified with the Wells Fargo and Wachovia
conversion decisions, and led to a meeting in August 1968 between a
delegation of state bank supervisors and the Board of Governors of the
Fed.[100] The next day, the Fed abruptly made a complete reversal of
position on two of the issues on which it had differed with the Comptroller: the authority of banks to invest in an operations subsidiary[101]
and the necessity for approval of "loan production offices" as
branches.[102] In both cases, the Fed abandoned its prior legal interpreta-

98. Statement by James Hall, California Superintendent of Banks, June 14, 1968.

99. "FR Administration Hit at ABA Conference," *American Banker* 1 (May 23, 1968).

100. Hackley, N. 43 *supra* at 1447.

101. See Ns. 83–86 and accompanying text.

102. Hackley, N. 43 *supra* at 1449–1450.

tion and adopted the more permissive view of the Comptroller, to the applause of its member banks (and the pain of its legal staff).[103]

In more general terms, of course, the problem for the losing regulatory system can be expressed as one of enhancing its profitability for member banks, and that can be achieved in a number of different ways, corresponding to the sources of relative advantage or disadvantage previously discussed.[104] Within the agency's own control are matters of regulatory policy, such as the exercise of discretionary approval powers over mergers or branches, and questions of interpretation of existing statutes, within the bounds allowed by language and legal conscience. Thus, the Fed could in a day's time drop two restrictions that were contributing to the decision of large state member banks to switch to national charters.

If a restriction or cost rests upon express statutory provisions, then its alteration requires action by the legislature. That is a forum in which rival economic interests can more effectively come to bear, and in which the agency cannot control outcomes. For the last two decades, the Fed has been more concerned with the continuing outflow of small member banks to state insured status,[105] which puts them entirely beyond its jurisdiction, than it was with the shift in the 1960s of some large state banks to national charter, which meant that they were still FRS members. The common view is that the loss of small member banks is attributable primarily to the cost of reserve requirements.[106] This cost can be eliminated only by amending the statute, and the Fed proposed precisely that step: an amendment of the Federal Reserve Act to provide for the payment of interest on reserve balances.[107] There can be no doubt that payment of interest on reserves could markedly change profitability calculations and assist the Fed in retaining or obtaining members, but it will also affect the present competitive interaction between banks and other financial institutions; the latter may be expected to automatically oppose the measure before Congress, and the outcome becomes problematical.

GENERAL TENDENCIES

Under the dual banking system, the regulatory agencies can be seen as firms producing different brands of regulation and engaged in a species

---

103. See *Federal Rulings Regarding Loan Production Offices and Purchases of Operating Subsidiaries: Hearings Before the House Comm. on Banking and Currency*, 90th Cong., 2d Sess. (1968).

104. See earlier section on The Sources of Relative Advantage, pp. 13–22.

105. See Tables 1-4 and 1-7, cols. 6 and 8, pp. 25 and 27.

106. See both Burns and Gray, N. 70 *supra*.

107. S. 1664, 95th Cong., 1st Sess. § 202(b) (1977); See Fed. Reserve Bd., *The Impact of the Payment of Interest on Demand Deposits* 90–98 (Jan. 31, 1977); B.N.A. *Washington Financial Rep.*, No. 10, p. A-10 (March 14, 1977).

of competition for market shares. At the same time, the analogy with
the behavior of private firms in private markets should not be pushed
too far; our theories of government regulation and bureaucracy do not
permit us to posit with confidence well-specified models of bank supervisory agencies.[108] Profit maximizers they are not, nor do simple models
of empire building or power aggrandizement seem to fit too well. For
the most part, the banking agencies seem to respond more vigorously to
the loss of existing members than to the prospects for obtaining new
members. Behavior is more defensive than aggressive; a Saxon stands
out as atypical.

Nonetheless, a few tentative propositions on the tendencies of such a
system of agency competition may be worth offering for consideration
and testing and refinement, rather than as demonstrated conclusions.
First, limitations on bank competition with nonbank enterprises will
tend to be eroded, insofar as they rest on agency discretion and interpretation. It is true that the supervisory agency is subject to some
conflicting considerations and pressures: It sees new activities and lines
of business as "risky" (as if old lines were not) or, at least, as unfamiliar
(which makes more difficult its examining and supervising duties), and
it is conscious of being held responsible by the legislature and press
every time a bank gets into trouble or fails. But if a breakthrough occurs
within one of the regulatory options so that the "business of banking"
becomes defined in a new and broader way and banks start shifting to
that option because it is significantly more profitable, the pressures on
the other regulatory agencies to conform, insofar as it is within their
power, seem well-nigh irresistible.[109]

Second, an agency will find it difficult to unilaterally raise or impose
regulations on bank operations designed to protect depositors by preventing bank failures—regulations relating to matters such as liquidity,
capital adequacy, and portfolio loans and investments. Such requirements impose costs on the subject banks, and are obviously vulnerable

---

**108.** There is a small body of interesting literature developing in this field. See, e.g., W.
Niskanen, N. 42 *supra;* Noll, "The Behavior of Regulatory Agencies," 29 *Review of Social
Economy* 15 (1971).

**109.** Indeed, under such circumstances, even the legislature is likely to feel that it has little
choice but to adopt a matching amendment to the statute, if that is what is needed; it is,
after all, only "equitable" that state banks have the same powers as their federal counterparts or vice versa. Nonbank competitors will find it hard to stem the tide before a
legislature asked to take matching action, particularly if it is a state legislature; their main
hope is to repeal the breakthrough by court decision or legislative enactment where it
occurred.

In short, there is competition at the legislative level as well as at the agency level. The
mutual savings bank industry has been keenly aware of its disadvantage in not being able
to subject state legislatures to this form of competitive pressure and has been campaigning for 15 years to get a "federal charter" bill through Congress. See *Federal Charter
Legislation for Mutual Savings Banks: Hearings on H.R. 258 Before the Subcomm. on Bank
Supervision and Insurance of the House Comm. on Banking and Currency,* 88th Cong., 1st
Sess. (1963).

to dual system avoidance unless matched by the other jurisdictions. At the same time, it seems likely that the banking agencies are less inclined to unilaterally reduce such requirements in the competition for market shares, since they would see the reduction as increasing the probability of bank failures and of the concomitant political investigation into why the agency ever allowed such an undesirable event to occur.

Third, restrictions on interbank competition will tend to be eroded, and here, the contrast with regulatory agencies in the traditional or monopoly mold is a sharp one. The traditional regulatory agency—the ICC or CAB or state licensing board—has been only too effective as a device for cartel administration: limiting entry, dividing markets, raising price, and restricting output.[110] No one would contend that the bank regulators have not significantly reduced the entry of new banks,[111] but they cannot hold a candle to the spotless record of the CAB, which in almost four decades of existence has never authorized a single new trunkline air carrier.[112] At least one of the reasons that new entry in banking has not been so effectively stifled is the fact that it is not administered by a single agency.[113] There are, for any business location, two chartering authorities (state and Comptroller) and three routes to deposit insurance (Comptroller, FRB and FDIC). While the banking industry could presumably always find general agreement on the proposition that new entry is risky and unnecessary and should not be permitted, the regulatory agency has the countervailing consideration of protecting its market share.

The same forces bear on other aspects of cartel management. Banks would prefer not to pay interest on demand deposits, and they disapprove of the invasion of their market territories by branches of other

---

110. The literature is becoming overwhelming. See, e.g., MacAvoy, *The Economic Effects of Regulation* (Cambridge: M.I.T. Press, 1965); A. Friedlaender, *The Dilemma of Freight Transport Regulation* (Washington, D.C.: Brookings Institution, 1969); Jordan, *Airline Regulation in America* (Baltimore: Johns Hopkins Press, 1970); Douglas and Miller, *Economic Regulation of Domestic Air Transport* (Washington, D.C.: Brookings Institution, 1974); Moore, "The Purpose of Licensing," 4 J. Law & Economics 93 (1961); Gellhorn, "The Abuse of Occupational Licensing," 44 U. Chi. L. Rev. 6 (1976).

111. Peltzman, "Entry in Commercial Banking," 8 J. Law & Economics 11 (1965). Peltzman estimated that the 2,272 banks formed during the 1936–1962 period represented about a 58 percent reduction in rate of entry. Cf. F. Edwards & L. Edwards, "Measuring the Effectiveness of Regulation: The Case of Bank Entry Regulation," 17 J. of Law & Economics 445 (1974). Authors would lower the reduction effect substantially, but still leave it at the quite appreciable level of almost 1,500 bank formations that were prevented.

112. Civil Aeronautics Bd. Practices & Procedures, *Report of the Subcommittee on Administrative Practice and Procedure of the Senate Committee on the Judiciary*, 94th Cong., 1st Sess. 6 (Comm. Print 1975).

113. This point is recognized, though presented in somewhat different terms, in Golembe, "Our Remarkable Banking System," 53 Va. L. Rev. 1091, 1107–1108 (1967); American Bankers Ass'n, *The Bank Chartering History and Policies of the United States* 12 (1935).

banks or financial institutions. If one supervisor sees his way clear to transform interest-bearing savings accounts into a species of checking account[114] or to adopt a much more liberal attitude toward branch approvals, it may be predicted that his actions will be met with criticism and condemnation from other segments of the banking community. But if neither the criticisms nor political pressures are successful in putting an end to such a move, the pressure will soon shift to the other regulators to bring their own positions into conformity.

In short, the dual system prevents the formation in banking of a single industry cartel, enforced through the rules and powers of a single government agency. The closest approximation that can be obtained involves several competing cartels, or a situation akin to oligopoly. As banking history suggests, under such circumstances, coordination of policies keeps breaking down in light of the gains to be reaped from breaking through competitive restrictions, and effective punishment of the "violators" is rendered very difficult.

Whatever the accuracy or completeness of the foregoing assay at some generalized tendencies, the underlying point seems indisputable: The dual banking system is a dynamic and interactive regulatory structure, so that a change in the content or effect of regulation in one sector sets in motion a whole series of forces. Banks reassess their profitability estimations; those at the margin may convert; and the agencies respond with further changes in regulatory content or policy. This is certainly perceived, if not necessarily clearly articulated, by those involved with banks and their regulation, and, in a number of ways, it finds reflection in banking legislation. Further understanding of the dual banking structure may be gained from examining some of the special features of bank regulatory laws attributable to efforts to counteract it.

## Limiting the Dual System

If your objectives are served by giving a free rein to the tendencies of the dual banking system, then, of course, there is no need to do anything special to bring that about. The competition among agencies will automatically take over, pressing the agencies in their policy choices in the direction (if our prior generalizations are correct) of broader operating authority and lowered constraints on profitability.

The same pressures will bear on the legislature, but as we have noted, the outcome there will be affected more by counterpressure from other economic interest groups.[115] To remove that contingency, the banking industry in 29 states has obtained the passage of "wild card"

---

114. In the case of "negotiable order of withdrawal" or NOW accounts, the initial shift in statutory interpretation was effected by a court rather than by a favorably disposed agency: Consumers Savings Bank. v. Commissioner of Banks, 361 Mass. 717, 282 N.E. 2d 416 (1972).

115. See text accompanying Ns. 105–107 *supra*.

provisions, which, with some variations, authorize state supervisors to allow state banks to engage in any "activity" permitted national banks.[116] This makes matching extensions of statutory authority automatic, without subjection to the vicissitudes and costs of the legislative process.

On the other hand, if your objectives are to impose and maintain some form of effective constraint, a need may be perceived to protect it from the operation of dual system forces. An inspection of banking legislation discloses numerous efforts in this vein. They are of varying degrees of comprehensiveness, but all are directed toward preventing or removing the sources of discrepancy between regulatory options on which the dual system works and thus reducing the scope of agency competition.

STATUTORY HARMONIZATION

Earlier we noted the extent to which statutory variation gave rise to areas of relative advantage for one dual system option as compared to another. Here, we will consider some of the ways in which elimination of such areas has been proposed or attempted.

The problem grows out of the potential discrepancies inherent in the combination of the laws of 50 states with three different federal jurisdictions. One approach that has been urged is that a uniform banking code be prepared and pressed on the states for adoption, following the precedent of the Uniform Commercial Code and other uniform acts drafted over the years by the National Conference of Commissioners on Uniform State Laws.[117] In fact, a Model State Banking Code was published by the American Bankers Association in 1950;[118] it has had an effect on revisions of the banking laws in various states, but was nowhere adopted intact in the mode of a uniform law. This route to harmonization has remained at the stage of a suggestion.

On the national level, there have also been efforts to make uniform the statutory provisions and standards applied by the three federal banking agencies, in certain areas. The most prominent recent examples are the Bank Merger Act of 1960[119] and the Financial Institutions Supervisory Act of 1966.[120] The effectiveness of identical statutes in achieving identical results is, of course, dependent upon the amount of interpretative leeway or approval discretion conferred by the statute

---

116. American Bankers Ass'n, *State Banking Law Service* 119–145 (1976).

117. Address by Federal Reserve Governor Mitchell, Coordination and Substance of Bank Regulation 2-3, New Jersey Bankers Ass'n Annual Convention, Bermuda, April 23, 1975.

118. American Bankers Ass'n, *State Banking Law Service*, Pt. IV (1965).

119. Act of May 13, 1960, Pub. L. No. 86-463, 74 Stat. 129 (codified at 12 U.S.C. § 1828(c) (1970, Supp. V, 1975)).

120. Act of Oct. 16, 1966, Pub. L. No. 89-695, Tit. II, 80 Stat 1046 (codified at 12 U.S.C. § 1818 (1970, Supp. V, 1975)).

upon the administering agency; the widely different outcomes that were produced in the area of bank mergers have already been commented upon.[121] However, so long as every insured bank is subject to the same statutory constraint through one of the three federal agencies, a degree of uniformity is obtained and the dual system has a narrower scope within which to work.

An alternative approach to uniformity is effected by having the federal law governing national banks simply adopt by reference the content of whatever the state law provides on a particular subject. The leading example is the branching authority of national banks, first granted by the McFadden Act of 1927.[122] In its present form,[123] the federal law permits national banks to establish "inside" branches (located in the same community as the bank's main office) and "outside" branches (located elsewhere in the same state) only if a state statute expressly authorizes branches in such locations for a state bank similarly headquartered. This produces somewhat uniform bounds on branching by state and national banks on a state-by-state basis, though, of course, there is no uniformity at all across states; furthermore, in any given state, there can still be marked differences in the extent to which, within those statutory bounds, the supervisory authorities are inclined to issue branch approvals. It is, nonetheless, clear that this device has enabled branching to be limited (and markets to be protected) over a long period, in a way that would never have been possible if state and federal laws had followed independent branching policies. Outside the branching example, the technique of adoption of state law restrictions has not found wide employment;[124] it does, after all, demand an abdication of any national policy in favor of the vagaries of state legislation.

## POLICY COORDINATION

Identical statutes reduce, but do not eliminate, the opportunity for differences between the regulatory options; there is still the potential, as we have observed, for varying interpretations and policies. Banking legislation displays several approaches to coping with that source of divergence.

A mild step is to require formal consultation among the agencies administering the statute, in the hope that differences will be resolved and a line established that will then be held. When interest rate ceilings on time and savings accounts were extended in 1966 to include savings

---

121. See text accompanying Ns. 77–95 *supra*.

122. Act of Feb. 25, 1927, Ch. 191, § 7, 44 Stat. 1224 (codified in scattered sections of 12 U.S.C. (1970 & Supp. V 1975)).

123. 12 U.S.C. § 36(c) (1970).

124. For other instances of state law incorporation, see 12 U.S.C. § 24 (eighth) (1970) (charitable contributions), § 85 (1970, Supp. V, 1975) (usury ceilings), § 90 (1970) (pledging to secure public deposits), and § 92(a) (trust powers).

and loan associations as well as banks, Congress required that the limits be set after consultation among the Fed (with jurisdiction over member banks), FDIC (with jurisdiction over nonmember insured commercial banks and mutual savings banks) and the FHLBB (with jurisdiction over insured and member S&Ls).[125] Under this authority, the Fed and FDIC have established a ceiling rate of 5 percent for savings deposits in banks,[126] while the ceiling for regular savings accounts in S&Ls and mutual savings banks is 5¼ percent.[127] The ceilings for deposits with specified minimum maturities and amounts are scaled higher, but the same ¼ percent differential in favor of thrift institutions is maintained, up to deposits of $100,000 or more (which have no ceiling). This statutory advantage is obviously a matter of heated controversy between the banking and S&L businesses, and maintaining it puts the regulatory agencies under a great deal of pressure from their members. In 1975, Congress decided to place less trust in consultation among the agencies and required that any elimination or reduction of the interest rate differential receive congressional approval by concurrent resolution before becoming effective.[128] In essence, veto power over increases in the bank ceiling rates has been vested in the FHLBB.

Formal centralization in one agency of all power to issue regulations and interpretations under a statute administered and enforced by all the agencies is the next step in this progression, and one being taken more often of late. The most prominent example is the Truth-in-Lending Act,[129] which gave to the Federal Reserve Board the power to prescribe the extensive regulations needed for determination of the "annual percentage rate" and other disclosures,[130] while dividing administrative enforcement among the four banking agencies and others as well.[131] The same pattern—regulation and interpretation committed to the Fed alone, with shared enforcement responsibilities—has been followed in the Equal Credit Opportunity Act of 1974[132] and the Home Mortgage Disclosure Act of 1975.[133] There can be no doubt that this technique greatly narrows the opportunity for divergencies among the

---

125. Act of Sept. 21, 1966, Pub. L. No. 89-597, §§ 2–4, 80 Stat. 824 (codified at 12 U.S.C. §§ 371b, 461, 1425b, 1828(g) (1970, Supp. V. 1975)).

126. 12 C.F.R. §§ 217.7(c), 329.6(c) (1977).

127. *Id.* at §§ 526.3, 329.7(b).

128. Act of Dec. 31, 1975, Pub. L. No. 94-200, § 102.89 Stat. 1124 (codified at 12 U.S.C. § 461 (Supp. V, 1975)). The Fed subsequently found a limited way around the statute by establishing a new form of account for use in retirement savings plans at a ceiling equal to that for S&Ls. See 42 Fed. Reg. 20,284, 32,764 (1977).

129. 15 U.S.C. §§ 1601-1665 (1970, Supp. V, 1975).

130. 15 U.S.C. § 1604 (1970).

131. 15 U.S.C. § 1607 (1970, Supp. V, 1975).

132. 15 U.S.C. §§ 1691–1691e (Supp. V, 1975), as amended by Act of March 23, 1976, Pub. L. No. 94-239, § 2, 90 Stat. 251.

133. 12 U.S.C. §§ 2801-2809 (Supp. V, 1975).

regulatory options, almost to the vanishing point—almost, but not quite. There is still room for the play of agency discretion as to enforcement effort and appropriate enforcement sanctions. Differences between the banking agencies in this regard have not yet become a source of visible controversy, but it may be predicted with some confidence that they will.

CENTRALIZED ENFORCEMENT

The only way to rule out all sources of difference and relative advantage is to vest both interpretation and enforcement in a single agency. That is what Congress did in the Bank Holding Company Act,[134] which, as amended in 1970, now applies to and limits a company owning only one bank and, thereby, indirectly constitutes an important new definition of the banking business. It does not matter whether the subsidiary bank is a national bank, a state member bank, or a state nonmember insured bank; jurisdiction over the activities of the holding company lies exclusively with the Federal Reserve Board. The Act even applies to a holding company for a bank that is not FDIC-insured at all, and thus largely free of federal regulation.[135]

As to the matters covered by the Bank Holding Company Act, the dual system no longer has any way to operate; for better or worse, competition among regulatory options is ended, except insofar as one option is not to do a banking business in the holding company form. It is noteworthy, however, how infrequently there has been recourse to this final answer to dual system pressures.[136] Most banking legislation that displays awareness of the way in which restrictions are undermined by regulatory divergence attempts to limit it in one of the less effectual ways previously discussed.

## CONCLUSION

By this point, it should at least be clear that the unique administrative structure of banking regulation in the United States has had a pervasive

---

**134.** Act of May 9, 1956, Ch. 240, § 2, 70 Stat. 133 (current version at 12 U.S.C. § § 1841–1850 (1970)).

**135.** Curiously, the holding company control triggers a provision that requires the subsidiary bank to "become and remain" an insured bank. 12 U.S.C. § 1842(e) (1970). On the other hand, the FDIC does not have to grant insurance if it feels the bank does not qualify, which raises interesting possibilities. See S. Rep. No. 91-1084, 91st Cong., 2d Sess. 25 (1970).

**136.** The Federal Reserve Board has been campaigning for several decades to have its reserve requirements made mandatory for all banks, nonmembers as well as members, to staunch its membership drain; see Burns, N. 70 *supra* at 339, 341–42. The Board's failure to make any progress in getting Congress to take this step has undoubtedly contributed to its recent proposal for the payment of interest on reserve balances. See N. 107 *supra* and accompanying text.

influence on the design and operation of banking legislation. It has also given rise to reams of argumentative nonsense.

One species of nonsense is perpetrated by the more fervid proponents of the dual system, who characterize it solely in terms of unrestricted choice among differing regulatory alternatives and attribute the existence of that choice to some sort of grand design on the part of the founding fathers or, at least, the Civil War Congress. As we have seen, it cannot be characterized so simply; there are elements of both freedom of choice and limitations on choice. And the intent of the Civil War Congress was not to create a complex structure of choice at all but to supplant the state banks with a national banking system that could more effectively assist in financing the war.[137] Out of the quite undesired failure of that intent has come our present structure, by inadvertence and not original design.

Another species of nonsense is currently taking hold in the judicial system, with the aid of some inept over-generalizations, and that is the proposition that the dual banking system reflects a congressional desire to promote "competitive equality" between state and national banks. Recently, for example, in the case of *Independent Bankers Association of America v. Smith*, the United States Court of Appeals for the District of Columbia Circuit founded an important decision on the following premise: "When Congress established our dual banking system, it wisely placed at one cornerstone the principle of competitive equality between state and national banks."[138]

That "cornerstone" principle is no less than a tour de force in standing reality on its head. The very core of the dual banking system is the simultaneous existence of different regulatory options which are *not* alike in terms of statutory provisions, regulatory implementation, and administrative policy; there is no "principle" whatever of initial identity. Indeed, the only real way to obtain legal equality among all competing banks, as we have seen, would be to put an end to the dual banking system entirely and replace it with a single federal regulatory agency in the traditional centralized mode, which is precisely what Congress has not done.

A more modest reading of the *Independent Bankers* dictum would confine it to the issues in the particular case, which involved the question of whether bank electronic-funds-transfer (EFT) terminals were branches. Branching is one of the few areas in which the federal law incorporates by reference state law restrictions,[139] and the Supreme Court cases from which the *Independent Bankers* court drew its "compet-

---

137. See text accompanying Ns. 16–18 *supra*.

138. Independent Bankers Ass'n of America v. Smith, 534 F.2d 921, 932 (D.C. Cir.), *cert. denied* 429 U.S. 862 (1976); Nebraskans for Independent Banking, Inc. v. Omaha Nat'l Bank, 530 F.2d 755, 759, 762 (8th Cir.), *vacated and remanded* 426 U.S. 310 (1976).

139. See Ns. 122–124 *supra* and accompanying text. For a general discussion, see Baxter, Cootner, and Scott, *Retail Banking in the Electronic Age: The Law and Economics of Electronic Funds Transfer* (Montclair, N.J.: Allanheld, Osmund 1977) 121–127.

itive equality" principle were also branching cases.[140] But even so confined, the competitive-equality touchstone is inaccurate and no substitute for a more careful and thoughtful probing for legislative purpose and its limits. For example, a national bank may establish a branch in a particular location only if under state law such a branch would be authorized for state banks "expressly" or "affirmatively and not merely by implication."[141] If state banks were in fact branching, but on the basis of liberal state administrative or judicial interpretation of statutes that were ambiguous or silent on the subject, national banks would not be able to do the same.[142] The draftsmen neither sought nor achieved competitive equality as such, and the equality principle is a misleading guide to construction of the National Bank Act.

That brings us to yet another brand of nonsense: outcries about the "destruction of the dual banking system" that arise whenever newly adopted legislative or administrative policy confers a significant advantage on one of the regulatory options, and especially whenever actual conversion flows are occurring in substantial amount. In particular, the notion that a rough "balance" or size equality between the various regulatory segments of the dual banking system is somehow mandated by statute, or required in theory, is totally specious.[143] Such outcries are not to be taken literally or seriously; they are merely part of the tactics of political pressure whereby other regulatory options are led to adopt matching positions. Those maneuverings show the dual system in operation in its customary mode, not its destruction.

The effective destruction of the dual banking system could, on the other hand, be brought about very simply, without an alarming centralization of authority in a single federal agency, by a measure never pressed or even considered—abolition of the right of banks to convert out of their existing regulatory jurisdiction without approval, or at all.[144] This, the real cornerstone of the dual banking system, was not

---

140. See First Nat'l Bank in Plant City v. Dickinson, 396 U.S. 122, 131–33 (1969); First National Bank of Logan v. Walker Bank, 385 U.S. 252, 261–262 (1966).

141. 12 U.S.C. § 36(c) (1970).

142. The *Independent Bankers* court overcame this difficulty for its supposed principle by an act of force majeure—in order not "to frustrate legislative intent," it simply proceeded to "reject" the quite unequivocal language of 12 U.S.C. § 36(c). 534 F. 2d at 948 N. 104.

143. For example, the fourth banking option—that of a state chartered non-FDIC-insured bank—though chosen by only 2 percent of banks, nonetheless exerts force by its mere existence. A recent illustration would be the need Congress has felt to exert rate control authority over uninsured institutions. See 12 U.S.C. § 1832 (Supp. V, 1975) (barring the extension of NOW accounts as interest-paying checking accounts); 12 U.S.C. § 1425b(a) (1970) (extending FHLBB rate control authority over nonmember associations not under state rate controls).

144. Consideration of the Franklin National Bank failure led the House Government Operations Committee so far as to recommend that the receiving federal agency require a certification from the former regulator that "the bank is in sound condition and in compliance with all existing supervisory requirements." H.R. Rep. No. 94-1669, 94th Cong., 2d Sess. 9 (1976).

cemented into place until remarkably recently,[145] and has always drawn very little attention. Even if conversions were blocked, it is true that new bank entry and differential growth rates would continue to affect the market share possessed by different regulatory agencies, but the process would operate far more slowly and the pressures toward conformity would be much reduced.

One of the major objectives of this study, therefore, is to provide a more sound and useful basis for the consideration of dual system issues by those who find themselves concerned with them from time to time— and that includes the courts and the Congress, as well as the regulatory agencies. Too much discussion on the structure of bank regulation has consisted of a battle of slogans and straw men. Proposed changes are debated in terms of a choice between tyranny and laxity, and the debate never progresses very far. Such straw men may, in fact, represent crudely one or another aspect of the dual banking system, but they are not helpful in framing the issues in a way that leads to deeper analysis and understanding.

"Competitive equality," for example, is an appealing slogan but a woeful guide for the courts in resolving interpretative issues under the National Bank Act, because there is no such central purpose underlying the statute. The mischief wrought by this false lodestar has spread to other sections where there is some reference to state law. For instance, in *St. Louis County National Bank v. Mercantile Trust Co.*[146] the court held that a national bank's ability to establish trust offices under 12 U.S.C. § 92a also is subject to the branching limitations of 12 U.S.C. § 36. "The policy of competitive equality was incorporated into section 92a,"[147] the court declared, and therefore "to allow Mercantile to accomplish what a state bank could not would frustrate the purpose of section 92a."[148] But, however seductively simple the slogan may be, it does not describe accurately the dual banking system, in either its whole or its parts, and by giving it their allegiance, the courts will merely be led astray.

The propositions we have examined likewise find application to the choices of policy and procedure that confront the banking agencies in endeavoring to discharge their functions. The Board of Governors of the Federal Reserve System, as we have noted, has become increasingly sensitive to the loss of members created by the costs of its reserve requirements and has responded in several ways. For a long time, the Fed tried to get Congress to extend its reserve requirements across all

---

**145.** See text accompanying Ns. 16–36 *supra.*

**146.** 548 F.2d 716 (8th Cir. 1976), *cert. denied* 97 S. Ct. 2975 (1977).

**147.** Since the provisions of Section 92a derive from Section 11 (k) of the Federal Reserve Act of 1913, 38 Stat. 262, as amended by the Act of Sept. 26, 1918, 40 Stat. 967, it will be noted that the policy in question cannot rest on the McFadden Act of 1927, Ch. 191, 44 Stat. 1224 (codified in scattered sections of 12 U.S.C.).

**148.** 548 F.2d at 720.

banks, members or not, so that the requirements would be beyond the

reach of dual system switching, but it met with no success. Quite recently, the Fed has changed tactics and advocated the payment of interest on reserve balances, thereby reducing their cost to member banks, but that also requires legislation by Congress, which may not be forthcoming.[149]

If the problem is seen, not in terms of the reserve requirement by itself or the "inequity" of its application to only one (self-chosen) category of banks, but in terms of a general balance of bank profitability across different options, a broader range of response opens up. Obviously, the banks that are leaving Fed membership are those at the margin, for whom the costs of membership, net of the advantages of membership, are greater than under one of the other regulatory options.[150] Not all banks are leaving, and those that are likely to leave probably have some common characteristics which can be identified with fair accuracy. All that need be done to stem the "membership drain" is to improve somewhat the profitability picture for that marginal group of banks, and that can be done in any of a number of ways.

Quite a few recent actions by the Federal Reserve Board can be interpreted in this light as moves to enlarge the benefits and reduce the costs of System membership. In 1968, the Fed completed and published a comprehensive "Reappraisal of the Federal Reserve Discount Mechanism," which proposed extending member bank borrowing privileges from emergency or very short-term loans to more of a regular line of credit, available at what generally amounts to a subsidized interest rate.[151] The recommendations have been partially implemented, including a more liberal "seasonal" borrowing privilege.[152] Likewise, in contemplating the adoption of a schedule of charges for services provided by Reserve Banks to automated clearing houses to which both member and nonmember banks and institutions belong, the Board noted that the price schedule would reflect consideration of "the burden of required reserves maintained by member banks";[153] that amounts to saying that member banks would receive the services at a subsidized rate. A more selective tailoring of System benefits and burdens to the position of the marginal banks can be found in the reserve require-

---

149. See text accompanying Ns. 104–107 *supra*. The bill reported out by the Senate Banking Committee on August 3, 1977, S. 1873, 95th Cong., 1st Sess. (1977), does provide for interest payment on reserve balances, but at a much lower rate than the Fed proposed.

150. Cf. Knight, "Comparative Burdens of Federal Reserve Member and Nonmember Banks," *Monthly Review*, FRB of Kansas City, March 1977, p. 13, with L. Kreider, "Optional Affiliation with the Federal Reserve System is Consistent with Equitable Treatment Between Banks," Conference of State Bank Supervisors, 1976.

151. See "Reappraisal of the Federal Reserve Discount Mechanism," 54 Fed. Res. Bull. 545–551 (1968).

152. See 62 Fed. Res. Bull. 787 (1976); 12 C.F.R. § 201.2(d) (1977).

153. Proposed Reg. J, 41 Fed. Reg. 3097, 3098 (1976).

ments themselves, which are lower for banks that are smaller in deposit size.[154]

But none of these actions constitutes an attempt that is especially designed, or perhaps even consciously designed, to change the profitability calculations of precisely that group of marginal banks whose departure from System membership continues to bother the Board so much.[155] If the Board deliberately embarked on such a course, it would amount to an effort to price discriminate among customers, and that can present practical difficulties that are by no means insignificant. In addition, there is the underlying substantive question of just how important it is to bring the Fed's membership attrition to an end, for monetary policy or other reasons.[156] However, the point here is a narrower one: The agency has a wide range of choice in affecting the profitability calculations that are the driving force in dual system switching. The Board need not define its problem, properly understood, in terms of the reserve requirement in isolation.

For either a regulatory agency or a court, the dual banking system must be taken as a "given"; they cannot change its essential workings, but their actions will be more effective and better reasoned if they understand it clearly. Congress is less confined, and from its standpoint, this study has broader implications.

To begin with, Congress, too, might benefit, in evaluating the arguments and contentions presented to it, from more insight into the nature of the dual system. As one example, whenever Congress has under consideration the possibility of extending the branching authority of national banks or of expanding their geographical scope of operation through devices as varied as holding companies and EFT terminals, it is sure to hear at length about how such measures would spell the end of the dual banking system. It is true that such measures would mean, if not the end, at least a partial impairment of geographically protected market areas. But the existence of a competing set of regulatory alternatives would continue as before. It is not even likely that their relative market shares would be much affected. The states that are highly restrictive in their approach to territorial competition among banks would quickly match an expansion in the scope of national bank

---

154. See 12 C.F.R. § § 204.2(a), 204.5 (1977), S. 1873, 95th Cong., 1st Sess. (1977), would carry still further the reduction for small banks.

155. See statement by Arthur F. Burns, Chairman, Board of Governors of the FRS, before the Senate Comm. on Banking, Housing and Urban Affairs, March 10, 1977, in 63 Fed. Res. Bull. 238, 243–244 (1977).

156. Outside the Fed, at least, many economists do not think that the effective implementation of monetary policy is much affected by the extent of System membership. See, e.g., Friedman, *A Program for Monetary Stability*, (New York: Fordham University Press, 1959); Warburton, "Non-Member Banks and the Effectiveness of Monetary Policy," in *Monetary Management* 339 (Comm'n on Money and Credit, 1963); Robertson and Phillips, "Are Uniform Reserve Requirements Really Necessary?" 91 Banking Law J. 403 (1974).

operations, in a manner that merely exemplifies how the dual system works in practice, rather than auguring its demise.

More fundamentally, however, the dual banking system is not something to which Congress can only react and adapt; it is the product, intentional or not, of Congress's own actions and may be shaped as Congress sees fit. Recently, the subject of "reform" of the structure of bank regulation again has come to the forefront of attention in Congress and elsewhere.[157] Reform proposals can take many forms;[158] one of the most sweeping and significant (and persistent) would create a Federal Bank Commission, and it is this proposal that we will examine in terms of the analysis of this study.

As introduced by Senate Banking Committee Chairman Proxmire, the Federal Bank Commission Act of 1977[159] would vest in a new five-member commission all the functions of the Comptroller of the Currency and FDIC, and all the bank supervisory functions of the Board of Governors of the Federal Reserve System, leaving the latter to continue to exercise monetary policy functions, including the operation of the discount window and the establishment of reserve requirements. What would be the effects of such a measure? Opponents see "reason to be concerned that undue concentration of regulatory authority will destroy the dual banking system which historically has been very innovative and responsive to the public interest."[160] Supporters expect "the elimination of what you have frequently heard described as the 'competition of laxity' between the agencies."[161] Were the bill enacted, both might find their expectations unfulfilled, at least in substantial part.

The Federal Bank Commission bill would centralize the administration of the federal banking statutes in one agency, but it would not eliminate the differences in their coverage. There would still be four

---

157. See, e.g., *Federal Bank Commission Act—1976: Hearings on S. 2298 Before the Senate Committee on Banking, Housing and Urban Affairs,* 94th Cong., 2d Sess. (1976) [hereinafter cited as *1976 Hearings*]; *Federal Bank Commission Act: Hearings on S. 2298 Before the Senate Comm. on Banking, Housing and Urban Affairs,* 94th Cong., 1st Sess. (1976) [hereinafter cited as *1975 Hearings*]; *Financial Institutions and the Nation's Economy, Discussion Principles: Hearings Before the Subcomm. on Financial Institutions Supervision, Regulation and Insurance of the House Comm. on Banking, Currency and Housing,* 94th Cong., 1st & 2d Sess., Pts. 1–3 (1975–1976); *Hearings on H.R. 8024 Before the Subcomm. on Financial Institutions Supervision, Regulation and Insurance of the House Committee on Banking, Currency and Housing,* 94th Cong., 1st Sess. 876–880, 1189–1199 (1975); *Report of the President's Commission on Financial Structure and Regulation, Senate Committee on Banking, Housing and Urban Affairs,* 93d Cong., 1st Sess. 87–95 (Comm. Print 1973).

158. See U.S. General Accounting Office, *The Debate on the Structure of Federal Regulation of Banks* 5–11 (April 14, 1977).

159. S. 684, 95th Cong., 1st Sess. (1977).

160. *1976 Hearings,* N. 157 *supra* at 188 (statement of John Chisholm for the American Bankers Association).

161. *Id.* at 206 (statement of Michael Harper of the Center for Law and Social Policy for the National Consumer Congress and Americans for Democratic Action).

distinct regulatory options, and banks would still be free to move between them. The structure of the dual system would remain; what would be eliminated would be competition in the exercise of agency discretion, as one of the sources of divergencies and comparative advantage, and that would be the extent of the change wrought by the legislation.

How important a change would that be? It would put banks in essentially the same position as the S&Ls occupy vis-à-vis the FHLBB. The dual system still operates, but with diminished scope. It ought to be possible to judge how much outcomes would differ under the two regimes by an empirical comparison of the S&L regulatory history under the FHLBB with that of the banks under their present structure, but that examination remains unattempted. In its absence, one can venture only a few suggestions. The first is that entry can be much more tightly controlled; the S&L structure affords only one route to deposit insurance, since the same board that makes the chartering decision for federal associations also makes the insurance decision for state associations.[162] That substantially simplifies the problems of cartel enforcement and, hence, one would expect to see it employed to a greater degree. A second possibility is that the outward expansion of activity limitations would proceed more slowly. To the extent that the contours of permitted business are vaguely defined in the statute,[163] or that the scope of restrictive provisions is subject to a measure of interpretation, competition among jurisdictions has been an important factor in wearing away the protective bulwarks that rival industries and trade groups have obtained from the legislature.

The latter point may be made clearer by considering another reform proposal. Former FDIC Chairman Wille has recommended the retention of the Comptroller and the establishment of a Federal Supervisor of State Banks (who would exercise over state banks the supervisory powers of the Fed and FDIC) and a Federal Banking Board (which would operate the insurance fund and exercise rulemaking authority in those areas applicable to all banks.[164] As part of his proposal, Wille would vest in the Comptroller and the new Federal Supervisor the power to approve or deny nonbank acquisitions by bank holding companies owning a single bank that falls within his jurisdiction. This would divide between two jurisdictions part of the approval power

---

162. Historically, the FHLBB always has viewed itself as exercising the same broad discretion in the two situations, but this position was recently rejected by the court in West Helena Savings & Loan Ass'n v. Fed. Home Loan Bank Bd., 553 F.2d 1175 (8th Cir. 1977). If it prevails, the decision will open up entry to much more agency competition.

163. This is true of the banking business to a greater degree than the savings and loan business. Compare 12 U.S.C. § 24 (Seventh) (1970, Supp. V, 1975) (national banks) with 12 U.S.C. § 1464(c) (1970, Supp. V, 1975) (federal S&Ls), as amended by Act of Aug. 3, 1976, Pub. L. No. 94-375, § 22, 90 Stat. 1078.

164. *1975 Hearings*, N. 157 *supra* at 275–280.

now held exclusively by the Federal Reserve Board and open up a new

area to dual system competition. It should be a safe prediction that
expansion through acquisition of nonbank businesses would proceed
at a somewhat faster pace.[165]

In conclusion, this study has attempted to take a macroview of the
functioning of administrative agencies—looking not at how arrangements within a single agency affect its performance but at how arrangements between a number of agencies on both the state and federal level
affect their combined performance of the substantive functions
assigned them. It is hoped that a better understanding of what the dual
banking system means, and how it operates in practice, has been
achieved. Some general propositions about the workings of the relatively unusual phenomenon of agency competition have been offered,
but in tentative form and with recognition of the need for more rigorous
formulation and testing. But, even if there were full acceptance of the
propositions here advanced, there would not be full agreement on the
appropriate responses, in terms of agency procedure and jurisdiction,
for that inevitably depends on each person's own evaluation of the
merits of the various kinds of bank regulation presently employed.
Banking is quite possibly the most extensively regulated of all industries, and there is a growing body of opinion that much of the regulation is ineffectual, costly to the public, and, in view of the existence of
federal deposit insurance since 1933, redundant.[166] If those views are
correct, there is a good deal to be said on behalf of the dual banking
system, but not exactly in the terms either its friends or its critics
customarily employ.

---

**165.** Likewise, entry competition could be deliberately enhanced if the FDIC and the FSLIC
were made rivals, by broadening the insuring jurisdiction of each to include the other's
clientele and allowing each to adopt and adjust a premium classification schedule.

**166.** See Scott and Mayer, "Risk and Regulation in Banking: Some Proposals for Federal
Deposit Insurance Reform," 23 Stan. L. Rev. 857 (1975); Clark, "The Soundness of
Financial Intermediaries," 86 Yale L. J. 1 (1976); Meltzer, "Major Issues in the Regulation
of Financial Institutions," 76 J. of Political Economy 482 (1967); and Edwards and Scott,
"Regulating the Solvency of Depository Institutions: A Perspective for Deregulation," in
this volume.

# COMMENTARY

William Niskanen, *Director-Economics, Ford Motor Company*

Competitive regulation seems to be a contradiction in terms. How can one regulate the behavior of persons or businesses if they can select the body of regulations to which they are to be subject? My reflections on this subject, however, lead me to believe that competitive regulation is neither as unusual nor as undesirable as it is often believed.

Let me begin by discussing a theory of regulatory behavior. There is no apparent consensus within the economic community on a theory of behavior of regulatory commissions—on what they maximize, on what their objectives are. Stigler, Posner, and others have recently postulated a variety of objectives, but there has not been any testing of which objective function best explains regulatory behavior.

Let me give you my view. We should start with the members of Congress and interpret their objective function (as they write regulatory legislation) as trying to maximize their "brokerage" fees. They can do this in one of two ways: if a company asks a member of Congress for a special favor, that company should expect the legislator to extract a good bit of the net benefits in terms of contributions to the legislator and/or services to constituents. That hypothesis is quite consistent with the declining rate of return in almost all regulated industries as a function of the period of time that they have been regulated. Typically, when regulations are first put in place, the "capture theory" makes sense—the regulations serve the interests of the regulated parties. Over time, however, the evidence is quite clear that the rate of return in the regulated industry declines gradually as net benefits to the regulated parties are eroded by various types of costs, such as for litigation.

What happens in an industry that has not asked for any favors from the government? In that case, Congress passes specific punitive legislation which it is prepared to relieve in exchange for special favors. So, if

you never ask for special favors, you still cannot expect to be off the
hook.

The best way to explain why Congress, as well as most state legislatures, have uniformly rejected the advice of the economic profession dealing with environmental matters—to use some sort of effluent tax approach rather than a regulatory approach—is that the regulatory approach serves the interests of Congress or legislators better than the tax approach. This rather cynical theory of regulatory behavior is consistent with my reading of the long history of regulation. One has the feeling that the major long-term beneficiaries of regulation are the legislators, the people to whom they distribute special favors, and the regulators themselves.

Professor Scott has valuably described the dual system in banking regulation and some of its effects. Both commercial banks and savings banks may choose either a national or a state charter. All the documented effects of this system, from my point of view, seem to be desirable, at least to new entrants or potential new entrants to the industry, and to bank customers.

A national charter is often the way around restrictions on entry and other restrictive characteristics of state banking legislation. Alternatively, the opportunity to operate under state charter, outside the Federal Reserve System, has reduced the power of the FRS and of other federal regulatory agencies.

Moreover, banking regulation is even more competitive than the dual system Scott describes. A group of bank investors also has the choice of whether it wants to operate as a commercial bank or as a savings bank. There is competition between commercial and savings bank charters within a state, as well as between national and state charters for each type of bank. As a result of this competition between the regulators, there is increasing competition between commercial and savings banks. Several states permit NOW accounts, and in some areas, drafts on credit union shares are accepted by local merchants as equivalent to checks. Commercial banks have responded to this behavior by savings and loan associations and credit unions by developing overdraft accounts, and they may soon be forced to compete by paying interest on checking accounts.

The only identifiable losers from all this competition, I believe, are some regulators and those investors in some less aggressive existing banks. Competition among regulators has substantially reduced the power of this rather cozy cartel.

Given this competition among regulators, what changes in the banking system itself and bank regulations should we expect in the future—say, within the next decade or two?

I expect to see the following sequence of actions: I think state chartered banks will probably continue to leave the Federal Reserve System, primarily to reduce their reserve requirements. The FRS most likely will respond, possibly rather quickly, by either paying interest on reserve accounts in the Federal Reserve banks or by permitting banks to include government bonds in their required reserves. This will make both FRS membership and a national charter much more attractive than either one is at the moment.

I believe you should also expect the following effects: NOW accounts will be available on a national basis within a decade; commercial banks will probably pay interest on checking accounts with some threshold balance; somewhat less pretentious bank buildings will be built to service retail accounts; and the banking system will become more competitive with nonbanking institutions, such as consumer credit companies. A major reform in the American banking system, I think, will be accomplished in an evolutionary manner, without the dubious benefit of a presidential commission and the blessings of Congress.

What are likely to be the equilibrium characteristics of banking regulation, given this competition both between national and state regulation and between different types of banking and financial institutions? More specifically, is there a Gresham's law for banking regulations — will bad regulation drive out good regulation? Will any effective regulation remain, in time, if such competition is effective?

My tentative answer to the last two questions is no. The public purpose of much bank regulation has been to prevent a run on banks that could deteriorate into a general bank panic. This is a legacy of pre-1930 conditions. The creation of federal deposit insurance for both commercial and savings banks in the 1930s, I believe, has largely eliminated the need for this type of regulation. The private purpose of much banking regulation has been to restrict entry and maintain cartel prices. Charter mongering by banking commissions is most likely to eliminate just those regulations that no longer serve a public purpose by undermining the various restrictions on entry that only serve the purposes of existing cartels.

Now, what type of regulations are likely to remain after all this sorting out? Some type of regulation will surely continue to be enforced, either directly or indirectly, by suppliers of deposit insurance. The moral hazard problems—of distinguishing between bank failures attributable to actions by insured banks themselves as opposed to actions originating outside the banks—are so great that some restrictions on bank behavior will almost surely remain a condition for deposit insurance. On the other side of the market, given the strong competitive advantage of deposit insurance, banks will continue to be willing to accept these conditions unless they become so onerous that some sort of private deposit insurance becomes preferable. The ultimate limit, of course, on the restrictions that banks will accept (to be eligible for the federal deposit insurance) will be the comparative advantage of federal versus some form of private deposit insurance.

Some form of regulation will also continue to be demanded by banks—particularly new small banks—as a certificate of their worthiness. A great deal of current regulation ought to be regarded as a

certification process. (Further, the closer regulation approaches the
certification process, the less harm it is likely to do.) For major banks, their names and reputations serve this purpose. For others, however, some type of regulation, if nothing more than bank examination and some minimum constraints on their behavior, serves this purpose. The mere use of the word "national" in names such as the First National Bank of Ypsilanti, or whatever, conveys a certain set of restrictions on behavior as well as structural characteristics of the balance sheet that banks are willing to accept.

In a competitive equilibrium, I would expect banking commissions to serve two primary roles: to screen and monitor eligibility for deposit insurance, and to certificate new banks. Competition among regulators is necessary to limit them to these rules. In the absence of such competition, they would be induced to use their monopoly power to serve some wholly inappropriate public purpose, such as credit allocation, or to serve some wholly inappropriate private purpose, such as maintaining a cartel of existing banks. One should not expect, in short, monopoly power to go unexploited—monopoly power will be used for some purpose. Its use will be determined by whoever most strongly affects the behavior of the person exercising that monopoly.

One example of competitive regulation that is close to long-term equilibrium is the chartering of general corporations. Most corporations (outside banking and transportation) are allowed to obtain a corporate charter in any state, regardless of where they operate. This competition—in this case, not just between one state and the federal government, but among all 50 state corporation commissions—has greatly reduced but has not eliminated the restrictions on corporate charters. Many corporations that are now large were incorporated in Delaware, the least restrictive state, but most corporations are incorporated elsewhere.

A number of legal scholars have attributed many of the evils of the modern world to the lenient Delaware law, and have proposed that all large corporations be chartered by the federal government. As far as I know, there is no evidence whatsoever to support their case. The body of literature which supports federal chartering seems to conjecture that since the Delaware law clearly serves the interests of corporate management, it must therefore not serve the interests of minority stockholders. A recent empirical study, however, concludes that the interests of minority stockholders are also significantly improved by corporations moving to Delaware, and that there is no transfer of benefits between the minority and the majority stockholders.[1]

Competition for corporate charters reduces the restrictions imposed by these charters. No one's interests are served by such restrictions, except those who would use corporations for their own purpose with-

---

1. Hyman, *Economics of State Corporations Law: The Delaware Controversy* (Law & Economics Center, Univ. of Miami, Working Paper, March 2, 1977).

out the burden of buying any stock. All restrictions on corporate charters have not disappeared, however, because they still serve the value of certification, conveying to interested parties how certain legal issues affecting the corporation are likely to be handled by the courts and regulatory commissions in that state.

An example of competitive regulation that is not an equilibrium is the state licensing of doctors and lawyers. This licensing is competitive only to the extent that the entry requirements are different among states, and there exist reciprocity agreements that permit these professionals to practice in another state. We should recognize the AMA and the ABA for what they are—national professional cartels that survive only because they can maintain near uniformity in state licensing procedures and/or restrict reciprocity.

Now that taxpayers are paying a large part of medical and legal bills, legislators might give more attention to these cartels. The easiest way to reduce their power would be to require reciprocity among states. In time, this would have the effect of reducing both the medical and the legal license to a certificate. In other words, an Alabama or a California doctor could practice anywhere in the United States. All of us, at least as consumers, would benefit.

My position, in summary, is that competitive regulation is good because most regulation is bad. Our system of dual banking regulation, rather by inadvertance, is evolving in a direction from which we can only benefit.

Beware of those who would create a monopoly of the right to do mischief.

# COMMENTARY

**Bernard Shull,** *Professor of Economics, Hunter College of the City University of New York*

Professor Scott has provided us with an illuminating description of the dual banking system. I am particularly struck by his showing that its seemingly key element, which he calls the "principle of choice"— permitting shifts, or threats of shifts, from state to national regulatory systems and vice versa—has only recently become firmly established in law. Of course, the Federal Reserve and the FDIC options do not predate those institutions.

Somehow, the dual banking system in its modern form has managed to generate instant tradition and profound reverence. Dual banking produced dual irony in 1963 when state banking associations throughout the country celebrated the centennial of the system—the one hundredth anniversary of a law designed to eliminate state banks, the celebration of a system whose "principle of choice" was no more than a few decades old.

I have few comments on Professor Scott's description of the system. I agree with him that the "principle of choice" is an important element but note that competition between the Comptroller and state supervisory agencies would exist (and has existed) in its absence, in the granting of new charters and branches in desirable locations.

I think, also, that too sharp a line is drawn between bankers, who favor, and regulators, who oppose, the system. No doubt, the bankers are for it. But with the exception of a few regulators from the Federal Reserve—Robertson, in particular—the regulators seem to be for it, too.

Professor Scott's model of the system is of particular interest. He assumes commercial banks to be profit maximizing firms within a legal-regulatory environment that affects their costs of operation and, perhaps, the demand curves for their products. He further assumes that bank regulatory agencies are in competition for "regulatees," that is, for "market shares," but that the agencies respond more vigorously to the loss of existing members than to the prospect of obtaining new members. Divergencies of material significance in the regulatory options available to commercial banks then arise—presumably out of the constitutional and statutory differences affecting different regulatory categories and through the exercise of administrative discretion. Such differences lead to the shifting of banks to more advantageous regulatory options until a "regulatory equilibrium" is established. The shifting is limited by the fact that not all banks find it profitable to shift and, also, by defensive modifications of regulatory options which have become disfavored.

This model is plausible, and it is possible to classify a good many developments of the recent past, particularly during the Saxon years in the Office of the Comptroller, within its framework. But I have some questions about its ability to explain events in other years.

The major implication of the model is that competition among the agencies will, from time to time, erode regulation. For example, there will be an erosion of restrictions permitting more intense competition between banks and nonbank financial institutions. In the Saxon years, and thereafter, this certainly seems to have been the case.

There is room for caution, however, in attributing this erosion of regulation to agency competition alone. Before 1966, commercial banks repeatedly prevailed upon the Federal Reserve (with FDIC cooperation, not competition) to raise Regulation Q maximums to permit more effective price competition with savings institutions. Substantial erosion in activity restrictions occurred in the late 1960s, when large banks discovered the one-bank holding company mechanism, a development which did not require any agency to relax its regulations. The initial pressure banks felt to escape the traditional bounds of commercial banking, and which overrode regulatory restrictions regardless of cooperation or competition among the agencies, is also reflected in the permissive interpretations of the National Banking Act by Comptroller of the Currency Saxon. The changes he introduced were vigorously advocated by bankers whose views he had solicited.[1]

The model's prediction that regulations separating commercial banks from other financial institutions will erode seems accurate beyond the Saxon years. But it is not clear that competition among the agencies was decisive in this result. One might speculate that had James Saxon not reinterpreted the incidental powers of the national banks, large banks would simply have found the one-bank holding company mechanism earlier.

---

1. U.S. Comptroller of the Currency, *National Banks and The Future* (Washington, D.C., 1963).

The model also predicts that the regulatory agencies will compete

away chartering restrictions. Again, evidence of the Saxon years serves as a basis for this view.

The 1940s and 1950s, however, were decades in which the harshest chartering restrictions ever to exist in banking were established and maintained—as dual banking with the "principle of choice" emerged in its modern form. Moreover, the tradition of "free banking"— amounting to free entry by new charter—predates dual banking in the United States, and emerged under single state regulatory agencies before there was a federal chartering option.

There are, I believe, at least two factors insufficiently elaborated in Professor Scott's model that help explain the weakening of restraints on commercial banks engaging in nontraditional activities in the post-Saxon years and restraints on chartering in the United States in the pre-Saxon years. First, there is the existence of a lightly regulated financial sector with which commercial banks must compete. In effect, there is a broader dualism in our financial system than that represented by dual banking. Competition from the nonregulated sector has placed pressure on commercial banks to innovate and to escape regulation. The pressure is transferred to the bank supervisor, whether one or more, cooperative or competitive.

Second, the conception of agency motivation in the model is probably too narrow. I am not sure that an oligopoly theory throws much light on the matter. The agencies cannot really "cheat" by giving "secret" concessions. (This was certainly not Saxon's approach.) Unfortunately, the factors determining when and to what extent the agencies will cooperate or compete are not specified. As a result, the model tells us that sometimes banks will be able to play one regulator off against another, and sometimes not.

It should be remembered that each supervisory system was superimposed on the previous one to enforce new and presumably more effective regulation. The historical mission of these agencies was to shore up regulation in the face of what was generally considered to be previous regulatory failure leading to serious financial distress. The agencies' legitimacy in Congress, with the public, and even with commercial banks, depends, at least in part, on their effectiveness in this regard. As a result, they probably cooperate more tenaciously than is suggested by a defensive "market share" strategy alone.

The contribution of the dual banking system to the erosion of particular kinds of regulation, then, is not clear. I see no way to accurately determine what it has been. However, it does seem reasonable to identify some erosion of regulation with the intensification of regulatory competition. There is evidence, for example, that it is difficult to establish and maintain procompetitive restrictions on mergers and acquisitions under dual banking. In the absence of antitrust restrictions in the 1950s, the agencies permitted enormous horizontal combina-

tions.[2] Had options been available to holding companies, there probably would have been many enormous market-extension acquisitions.[3]
The corrosive effect of agency competition on merger regulation, with
at least potential anticompetitive results, is still evident.[4]

In conclusion, I would suggest that while the model is plausible, the
importance, if not the validity, of its implications may be questioned.
Puzzling observations as to the workings of the dual banking system
remain. For this and other reasons, it is difficult to accept the conclusion
that "dual banking" makes an important contribution to the intensification of competition. Finally, while the benefits of "dual banking" are
moot, it is also necessary to consider its costs. Some concern over the
difficulties regulatory agencies have had in imposing capital requirements would seem warranted.

---

2. In 1955, for example, Chase National, with close to $6 billion in assets at the time, was
permitted to merge with Manhattan Bank, with close to $2 billion in assets; National City
Bank, also with over $6 billion, was permitted to merge with First National, with close to
$1 billion. In 1963, the Supreme Court superseded "dual banking" by clearly establishing
the applicability of the antitrust laws. The agency approvals were not accorded even
presumptive validity. United States v. Philadelphia Nat'l Bank, 374 U.S. 321 (1963).

3. In 1962, for example, Morgan Guaranty tried to form a holding company that would
affiliate Morgan and six of the largest upstate New York banks, each with a leading
position in Buffalo, Rochester, Albany, Binghamton, Syracuse, and Utica. The New York
State Banking Department approved the acquisition. The Federal Reserve Board, with the
final say, turned it down. "Morgan New York State Corporation to become a Bank
Holding Company," 48 Fed. Res. Bull. no. 5, 567–582 (May 1962). Under New York State
law at the time, there was no further recourse, because state law did not permit branching
throughout the state. There is evidence to support the procompetitive impact of the
denial. See Shull, "Multiple Office Banking and the Structure of Banking Markets: The
New York and Virginia Experience," *Proceedings of a Conference on Bank Structures and
Competition* (Fed. Res. Bank of Chicago, 1972).

4. There was a remarkably explicit example two years ago. In December 1974, the FDIC
turned down a merger between two small Texas banks (Bank of South Texas and First
National Bank of Alice) by a 2 to 1 vote—with the Comptroller of the Currency, a member
of the FDIC Board, dissenting. The bank requested a reconsideration by the FDIC,
reminding it that the merger could be restructured so that the resulting bank was a
national bank. The FDIC reconsidered in August of 1975 and this time approved the
merger by a 2 to 1 vote, with Chairman Wille dissenting.

# COMMENTARY

Walter Gellhorn, *University Professor Emeritus, Columbia University*

Thirty-eight years ago, I wrote a monograph on the Federal Reserve System and yet another on the Federal Deposit Insurance Corporation and the Comptroller of the Currency.[1] When I then considered the matter, I persuaded myself that harmonizing regulation among the various agencies was badly needed. Of course, it was a much simpler thing in those days, since the nation then had only 48 states and not 50. Even so, efforts to achieve harmonization in those distant days could produce only a makeshift voluntary cooperation that would not suffice. What we needed, I said then, was "thoroughgoing coordination and unification of the several banking authorities, a possibility which is now being considered by the appropriate congressional committees." That possibility has apparently been considered fairly continuously for almost four decades, and I daresay it will continue to be considered for another four decades.

Professor Scott's paper and the discussion of it thus far have, I think, given us a reasonably persuasive demonstration of the soundness of Justice Holmes's aphorism, "Sometimes a page of history is worth more than a volume of logic."

Nobody starting from scratch today would dream of creating the regulatory design we actually have; but once a structure exists, no matter how ill-designed it may be, reasons will be found to maintain it. Reorganizing an administrative structure, an extremely difficult task at any time, becomes especially difficult when the structure creeps across the jurisdictional boundaries of different governmental entities.

The Scott paper, though giving support to the Holmes aphorism,

---

1. Printed, respectively, in S. Doc. No. 186, 76th Cong., 3d Sess. (1940), and S. Doc. No. 10, 77th Cong., 1st Sess. (1941).

rather tends to undermine another aphorism that appeals to people who, like Professor Edwards and Dr. Niskanen, think that government regulation is a terrible thing. The aphorism to which I refer is, of course, the one proclaiming that that government is best which governs least. Professor Scott's paper seems to suggest that that government which governs the most—or, at least, has the largest number of administrative agencies with a finger in the pot—is likely to produce enough chaos to cause virtually a state of nonregulation or deregulation.

Demands to get rid of or modify the dual banking system seem to me to be related to demands in different contexts, constantly heard nowadays, for greater centralization of authority in order to eliminate inefficiency. The pressure to centralize is felt in almost all areas of life—noneconomic as well as economic.

Yet, currents run contradictorily and intermittently in diverse directions. New York City, for example, has a passion at the moment for decentralization of school administration. Does anyone think that that is going to make for efficiency of educational administration? This is very unlikely, I would suppose. Those who advocate decentralization are reflecting dissatisfaction with the rigidities that efficiency sometimes produces.

We have evidence at the moment of mounting federal interest in hospital administration. Until now, hospitals have been local concerns. They have been subject not merely to dual administration, but to God knows how many administrations, if you think of all the local and state agencies that deal with health care facilities. The same has been true of welfare administration. Now, the question is being asked whether the broth might not be better if only one master chef, that is, the federal government, determined what are to be its ingredients.

This sort of battle about multiple agencies concerned with one or another phase of a problem, where all the phases interweave to create master problems, will be an element of American life for a long time to come. It is not a peculiarity of banking regulation.

For whatever it is worth, my guess is that centralization will prevail in a very spotty manner indeed. Much can be said for maintaining the diversity which in a sense makes for less forcefulness of administration than would a truly centralist system.

*Myers v. United States,*[2] dealt with a different matter, namely, the separation of powers among the three great branches of government. Congress had sought to restrict the power of the president to remove postmasters. The majority of the Supreme Court said that that was an unconstitutional interference with the Executive. Justice Brandeis, dissenting, thought that this was a mistaken view of the Constitution.[3] "The doctrine of the separation of powers," he wrote, "was adopted by the Convention of 1787, not to promote efficiency but to preclude the

---

2. Myers v. United States, 272 U.S. 52 (1926).

3. *Id.* at 293.

exercise of arbitrary power. The purpose was, not to avoid friction, but, by means of the inevitable friction incident to the distribution of the governmental powers among three departments to save the people from autocracy."

The Brandeis dissent is pertinent to our discussion. Something in the same general vein and changing very few words indeed might be said, and probably will be said, about such things as the dual banking system by those who cherish it. They will not seek to defend it on the ground that it is the best possible system, but they will defend it by arguing that the inevitable frictions of diverse regulatory demands may prevent the worst possible system. Persons who focus only upon the effectiveness of the structural form of regulation, according to the proponents of pluralism, are likely to produce despotic regulation.

I predict that opinion will flow in the direction of pluralism, though I myself am unpersuaded by the kind of argument I have just sketched. All in all, I favor the centralization of authority. Though it does open the door to the danger of arbitrariness in administration, it also focuses attention and responsibility. My own belief, based on observations of governmental functions for some time, is that when one can identify an area that should be of concern to right-minded people, attention can successfully be drawn (sometimes after too long an elapse of time, to be sure) to autocratic or unwise administrative policies. Recognizing the perils of concentrated power, nevertheless I deem them less than the perils of confused and conflicting administration.

I should like to comment briefly on the conclusion Professor Scott stated at the very end of his paper. He says that "banking is overregulated . . . and (in view of the existence of federal deposit insurance since 1933) redundant." That is also Dr. Niskanen's apparent view, although not Professor Shull's.

I identify myself as a Shullite rather than a Scottite.

In discussions of deregulation, I have felt, at times, that we have been inadequately attentive to the conditions that called regulation into being in the first place. Having perceived an inadequacy or an ineptitude in regulatory practice, we have quickly assumed that the solution of difficulties is to end regulation altogether. Is this, in fact, the correct approach?

Banking regulations, for example, have some function other than safeguarding depositors against loss of their funds if their bank collapses. A major Swiss bank failure, so widely reported in the press, apparently did not destroy the depositors. Nevertheless, even though the depositors were paid off to the last centime, the whole financial community in Switzerland apparently felt the repercussions of the disaster that struck that one bank. Similarly, in our own country, repercussions would be felt despite the existence of insurance against loss for depositors. Deposit insurance is a highly desirable protection for small people like me, but it is not an impregnable safeguard of society.

When I reread my 1939 monograph on the Federal Reserve System and reminded myself about the conditions that brought the system into being, I wondered whether, in point of fact, deregulating or significantly diminishing regulation of banking would meet the various elements of public need that had evoked the Federal Reserve System in 1913. If, suddenly, deregulators had their way and the forces of competition were given free rein, would the problems and deficiencies of the past not reappear in their old guise or in new form? I put aside current events such as the Truth-in-Lending Act and similar developments that might, in themselves, suggest new areas for regulation rather than deregulation.

The circumstances that have enlarged public regulation of banks were not imagined evils, puffed into life by a bureaucrat who sought to fool the public in order to swell the area of regulation and thus add to his staff and strengthen the hold of his tentacles upon the body politic. They reflected, rather, felt needs. Dealing with those needs by governmental activity was thought to be more desirable than ignoring them or leaving them to the uncertainties of self help.

When I hear discussions about the optimal organization of banking regulations and realize that for some, the optimal organization is no organization at all, I want to be certain that I know exactly what areas of public concern will no longer be matters of public concern if the federal or the state agencies are eliminated from the scene.

# DISCUSSION

FRANKLIN R. EDWARDS: (MODERATOR)

Today's session deals with the administrative structure of bank supervision in the United States, and, in particular, with implications of the dual banking system.

Thank you all for your excellent presentations. Professor Goldschmid would like to ask the first question.

HARVEY J. GOLDSCHMID:

The problem we are talking about today is not so much centralization of federal supervision, but the ability of the regulated to choose the regulator. It is the same problem as the race to the bottom (or to Delaware) that has occurred in the chartering of corporations.

If you assume some public purpose rationale for regulation, then doesn't multiple regulation, where the regulated have a choice, invariably undermine that purpose?

WILLIAM NISKANEN:

But you must compare what monopoly regulators do with what in fact happens under this kind of dual (or competitive) regulation. You should not compare such regulation with what you would do if you were king and had full authority and perfect knowledge. What you actually get from monopoly regulation is the kind of regulation you have at the CAB and the FCC, and that is not desirable.

GOLDSCHMID: You do not need to have monopoly regulation. For instance, with respect to federal chartering of corporations, you could adopt a minimum standards act but still allow dual regulation on the state and federal level. This would still avoid the problem of having those regulated being able to evade regulation.

NISKANEN: The effects are the same. Kenneth Scott pointed that out very well. If you prohibit corporations from changing to another set of regulations, you are really instituting monopoly regulation. The key feature of monopoly is that you cannot make such change.

EDWARDS: Would it be correct to summarize your position by saying that although there may be a public interest reason for regulation, the kind of regulations that actually emerge from the congressional activity you describe, and from the regulatory process, are not in fact those which advance the public interest. The question is whether the regulation that actually emerges is better than no regulation at all or little regulation. The virtue of the dual banking system is that competition among regulators erodes what might otherwise be bad regulation.

NISKANEN: The equilibrium regulation is not necessarily zero, of course. Delaware has some restrictions. I do not think that you are going to find a zero equilibrium in bank regulation either, for two reasons: One is that banks will have to accept some kind of restriction to be eligible for deposit insurance, and the other is that regulation serves a useful certification function—it serves much the same function as do the brand names of major consumer products. Certification identifies certain quality characteristics of banks. To be able to convey that set of quality characteristics by identifying who your certificator is can serve a valuable social purpose. It ought to be provided somehow, although not necessarily by the government. Conceivably, it could be provided by a private certificating agency.

JOHN D. HAWKE: In the last couple of years, there have been a number of regulatory developments worth noting.

First, the existence of the NHC coordinating agency has served to even out a lot of the disparity in regulations among the agencies. It has provided a mechanism for avoiding such disparities which has worked quite well, at least among the banking agencies.

Second, there is an increasing tendency to assign regulations to the Federal Reserve System rather than to divide them among the various regulatory agencies. All consumer regulations, for example, have been assigned to the rule-writing division of the Federal Reserve. Again, there is some competition, perhaps, in the enforcement of those regulations, but the basic rule-writing is done by the Federal Reserve.

In another area, the promulgation of security regulations, Congress substantially removed regulatory disparity in 1974 by saying that the banking agencies have to follow the SEC. Here again is congressional pressure toward the homogenization of regulation.

Finally, the Justice Department has come to assume an important role in deciding mergers, as a result of the 1966 amendments to the Bank Merger Act and recent Supreme Court decisions.

There is clearly a drift towards more centralization of authority.

PHILLIP CAGAN: If we look at the regulations that we have had, I would say that they have pretty well satisfied the function that was intended: to guarantee a stable money supply. Regulations have controlled the instability which I think would occur if the banking system were left on its own. Of course, people who engage in regulation do not always understand its purpose, so we may also have regulation of all kinds of other things. There is clearly a tendency toward overregulation. From that point of view, I agree with Niskanen that the dual banking system has not been a bad thing. It has enabled us to achieve our fundamental public purpose, but at the same time, it has eroded this tendency toward overregulation. It would be better if there did not exist a tendency toward overregulation, of course, but we cannot have everything.

EDWARDS: You have hit upon a point that was not discussed. If I understand you correctly, you are arguing that under competitive regulation, regulators will still supply at least enough regulation to achieve the public interest goals which underlie that regulation. This occurs in banking, in my opinion, because regulators are motivated by a desire to avoid bank failures, and the concomitant adverse publicity.

Once you say that, it seems like a stroke of genius to have invented the dual banking system: It prevents regulators from choosing the monopoly supply of regulation. Nevertheless, I am somewhat uncomfortable defending a regulatory structure because it erodes regulation.

One final remark. By now, most of us have given up hope for any major reform legislation in banking. This discussion leads me to believe that instead of working for deregulation, we should propose the creation of additional, competing, regulatory agencies to achieve the same purpose.

KENNETH SCOTT: That has already been proposed. That was, for example, one of the more interesting features of Chairman Frank Wille's (FDIC) proposal to reorganize banking regulation in 1975. His scheme was to take bank holding company regulation and chop it up into three parts: Take it away from the Federal Reserve and give some of it to the FDIC and the Comptroller, depending on whether the subsidiary bank was a national or state insured bank, or a state member bank.

One can predict very easily what the results of that would be. The heart of this area of regulation concerns definition of the proper scope of the banking business that can be conducted through the holding company mechanism, and this depends upon the way regulatory agencies see activities. Are they closely related to banking, or a proper incident thereto? This is not language of high intrinsic content. The agency can do a lot with it, and it does.

If regulatory authority were split between three agencies, it is clear that you would start to accelerate the tendency toward more expansive definitions of banking activities. This is exactly the kind of proposition that I am trying to highlight in my study.

CHAPTER TWO
# Solvency Regulation and Bank Soundness

## REGULATING THE SOLVENCY OF DEPOSITORY INSTITUTIONS: A PERSPECTIVE FOR DEREGULATION

**Franklin R. Edwards,** *Professor, Graduate School of Business,*
*Columbia University*
**James Scott,** *Associate Professor, Graduate School of Business,*
*Columbia University*

*Another economic area that raises particularly difficult problems is the monetary system. Government responsibility for the monetary system has long been recognized. It is explicitly provided for in the constitutional provision which gives Congress the power "to coin money, regulate the value thereof, and of foreign coin." There is probably no other area of economic activity with respect to which government action has been so uniformly accepted. This habitual and by now almost unthinking acceptance of governmental responsibility makes thorough understanding of the grounds for such responsibility all the more necessary, since it enhances the danger that the scope of government will spread from activities that are, to those that are not, appropriate to a free society, from providing a monetary framework to determining the allocation of resources among individuals.*

MILTON FRIEDMAN

## INTRODUCTION

The regulation of financial institutions, and of depository institutions in particular, is considered to be a sine qua non for a prosperous economy, and proposals to relax this regulation are almost always greeted with images of wholesale economic instability. The recurring financial panics experienced during the late years of the nineteenth century are taken as proof that unregulated financial markets are inherently destructive. This seemingly irrefutable view of history has to a large extent circumscribed efforts to appraise the fundamental wisdom and effectiveness of financial regulation. Although during the last fifteen years, two presidentially appointed committees conducted extensive reviews of financial regulation, their analyses and ultimate recommendations were largely limited to making marginal changes to a regulatory structure basically accepted as sound. Whether because of

We are indebted to members of this seminar series for helpful comments. Philip Cagan, Linda Edwards, and Walter Gellhorn, in particular, provided many insightful comments.

political exigency or fundamental belief, the reform proposals of these committees represent little more than backwaters in the historical current toward greater and greater regulation. That regulation spawns more regulation in response to evils perceived by regulators is a principle as old as regulation itself.

Fundamental to financial regulation is the desire to protect the solvency of financial institutions. Any serious effort to evaluate such regulation, therefore, must center on solvency regulation, regulations designed to maintain the solvency of commercial banks and other depository institutions. The lack of a clear understanding of the objectives and functions of regulations may be the single most important roadblock to reform. The primary objective of this paper, therefore, is to provide a comprehensive review and analysis of the regulatory structure currently used to maintain the soundness of depository institutions.

While the focus of this paper is on regulations that promote the soundness of our financial system, it is not always easy to determine the major or primary social goal of a particular regulation. Indeed, a regulation may sometimes have more than one purpose. Thus, our procedure in this paper is to analyze all regulations which have an important bearing on solvency and to appraise the contribution these make to soundness. We believe that a necessary first step to an overall assessment of our regulatory system is agreement about what controls are required to guarantee financial soundness.

It is perhaps noteworthy in passing to point out that not all students of financial markets agree on what kinds of solvency regulations are required. For example, in his classic work, *The Wealth of Nations,* Adam Smith argued that the only necessary restrictions on banking are the prohibition of small bank notes and the requirement that all notes shall be repaid on demand. Otherwise, Smith says, banking "may, with safety to the public, be rendered in all respects perfectly free."[1] More recently, Milton Friedman has pointed to the plethora of banking regulations as an example of a government activity that cannot be justified.[2] Neither author, however, makes clear the bases for his conclusion. Is all regulation unnecessary, or just some of it? And if we are to retain any regulation, which should it be?

Recent events also suggest a need to rethink our system of solvency regulation. During the last few years, a number of uncommonly large banks have failed. Since 1970, we have witnessed the failure of the U. S. National Bank of San Diego, California (deposits of $922 million), the American Bank and Trust Company of Orangeburg, South Carolina (deposits of $112 million), the Franklin National Bank in New York

---

1. Smith, *The Wealth of Nations* 313 (New York: Modern Library, Random House, Inc., 1937).

2. Friedman, *Capitalism and Freedom* 35. (Univ. of Chicago Press, Chicago, 1962).

(deposits of $1.4 billion),[3] the Hamilton National Bank in Chattanooga, Tennessee (deposits of $400 million), the American Bank and Trust Company in New Orleans (deposits of $162 million), and the Northern Ohio Bank (deposits of $96 million). In addition, in 1972, the Bank of the Commonwealth of Detroit (deposits of $992 million) survived only with the assistance of the Federal Deposit Insurance Corporation (FDIC), and in 1975, the Security National Bank in New York (deposits of $1.3 billion) was merged into another institution on an emergency basis. Finally, in February 1977, the FDIC arranged an emergency takeover of the Banco Economico in Puerto Rico (deposits of $183 million), narrowly averting what would have been the fifth largest bank failure ever handled by the agency.[4] Table 2-1 and Figure 2-1 show the trend of bank failures since 1945.

At least part of the reason for this surge in bank insolvencies is the rapidly changing nature of the banking business. During the last two decades, banks have expanded their operations into more risky areas, such as direct lease financing, the underwriting of revenue bonds, and various foreign activities not permissible at home. In addition, banks

---

3. Six months before its demise, Franklin National had deposits of $3.5 billion.

4. See Horvitz, "Failures of Large Banks: Implications for Banking Supervision and Deposit Insurance," 10 J. Financial and Quantitative Analysis, No. 4, 589–601 (Nov. 1975); "New Orleans Bank is Ordered Closed," New York Times, Dec. 4, 1976, p. 31, col. 6; and "Spaniards in Emergency Takeover of the 4th Largest Puerto Rican Bank," New York Times, Feb. 21, 1977, p. 33, col. 5.

**TABLE 2-1    Bank Failures 1946–1975**

| Year | Number of banks closed per year | Total deposits of closed banks per year (millions) | Largest bank failure during period (millions) |
|------|--------------------------------|----------------------------------------------------|-----------------------------------------------|
| 1946–1950 | 5.0 | $     7 | $     7.9 |
| 1951–1955 | 4.6 | 14 | 17.0 |
| 1956–1960 | 4.0 | 9 | 7.0 |
| 1961–1965 | 6.6 | 24.4 | 40.2 |
| 1966–1970 | 6.4 | 46.6 | 93.0 |
| 1971–1975 | 6.8 | 1,021.2 | 1,440.5 |
| 1971 | 6 | 132.0 | 66.8 |
| 1972* | 4 | 1,092.0 | 992.0 |
| 1973 | 6 | 971.0 | 932.0 |
| 1974 | 4 | 1,571.0 | 1,440.5 |
| 1975† | 14 | 1,340.0 | 1,300.0 |

*Includes Bank of the Commonwealth, which did not close but which received financial assistance from the FDIC.

†Includes Security National Bank of New York, which was merged on an emergency basis.

*Source: FDIC, Annual Report, 1945–1975.*

now engage in extensive liability management, aggressively buying all
kinds of short-term funds (such as Certificates of Deposits, commercial
paper, and Eurodollars) for both liquidity and growth reasons. Thus, an
obvious question is whether the current regulatory system has been
responsive enough to these changes to maintain the soundness of the
banking system.

The following analysis of solvency regulation is set out in three

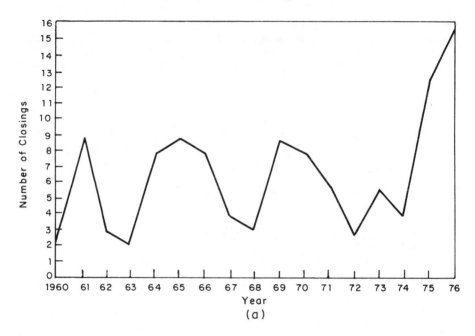

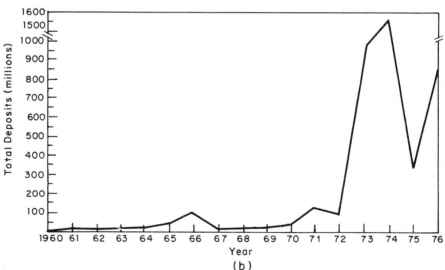

FIGURE 2-1  (a) Number of banks closed, 1960–1976; (b) Total deposits of
closed banks, 1960–1976. (*Source: U.S. Comptroller General,* Federal Supervision of State and National Banks, *Jan. 1977, p. 9-2.*)

sections. The first section describes the existing regulatory structure for

maintaining bank soundness and examines the roles of a lender-of-last-resort, of deposit insurance, and of the various detailed solvency regulations in maintaining bank soundness. As part of the latter, we discuss entry restrictions, activity restrictions, pricing constraints, balance sheet constraints, and regulations to curb self-dealing and conflicts of interest. In the next section, the various rationales for government regulation of financial markets are examined with a view toward determining what kinds of regulation are necessary to achieve these goals. We discuss both "efficiency" and "equity" rationales for regulation and conclude that all of these ends can be attained by the adoption of a sound deposit-insurance system: Relying solely on a lender-of-last-resort is unwise and is likely to be less efficient. Further, if detailed solvency regulation has a role to play, it is as a necessary concomitant to deposit insurance. In the third section, alternative deposit insurance plans are analyzed. We discuss the problems associated with the present uniform-premium system, and assess the wisdom and feasibility of instituting a variable-premium insurance system. Also, the function of detailed solvency regulation under each type of insurance scheme is examined.

Our major conclusion is that, for purposes of soundness, most detailed solvency regulations are unnecessary under either type of insurance system: All such regulation should be eliminated except for balance sheet controls (or equity capital and liquidity requirements). Finally, after reviewing the various "nonsolvency" ramifications of eliminating these regulations, we conclude that deregulation along these lines would result in a net social benefit.

## EXISTING REGULATORY STRUCTURE

The current regulatory structure for maintaining the soundness of the banking system is three-dimensional. The first two regulatory supports are the Federal Reserve's lender-of-last-resort capability and federal deposit insurance, both of which are directed at insuring the solvency and stability of the entire financial system. The third is a set of detailed regulations which seeks to reduce the likelihood that any single bank will fail. These three regulatory supports are not independent of one another, but their economic functions are sufficiently distinct to warrant separate discussion.

Before launching into a discussion of them, however, one thing should be made clear: By designating a regulation as a solvency regulation, we do not mean to suggest that the political reason for the existence of the regulation is to insure bank soundness. The political and economic forces that converge to make law and regulation are more often than not so complex as to be unfathomable. Our objective is not to examine the political history of banking regulation, but to describe, classify, and analyze the laws and regulations having an impact on bank soundness, whether or not this effect is intended.

## Lender-of-Last-Resort

A major reason for the creation of the Federal Reserve in 1913 was to establish a lender-of-last-resort capable of preventing the collapse of the financial system in times of acute crisis. In such times, the outstanding need is for an increase in bank reserves and an expansion of loans. A bank panic is characterized by two phenomena, either of which can cause a substantial contraction of the money supply: In response to a threatened deposit run, banks attempt to increase their reserve ratios; and individuals attempt to acquire currency in exchange for their deposits. As individuals exchange deposits for currency, bank reserves fall, requiring a contraction of the money supply; and as banks increase their reserve holdings, the expansionary effect of each dollar of reserves (or the size of the money supply multiplier) is diminished. Both together can result in a severe contraction of money and credit at just that time when liquidity is most needed. Individual banks are incapable of offsetting this phenomenon through unilateral action—their prudence may only hasten the crisis. The Federal Reserve, on the other hand, can increase bank reserves by purchasing securities and lending to banks, thereby preventing a contraction of bank deposits and bank credit.

Indirectly, therefore, through its function as a lender-of-last-resort, the Federal Reserve, at times, may be in a position to prevent the insolvency of banks that would otherwise succumb to the onslaught of panic-stricken depositors. While its chief mission is to stabilize and control the supply of money, it accomplishes this, in times of bank panics, by keeping banks from failing. Even so, some banks will fail, and some depositors will suffer losses. The function of the lender-of-last-resort is not to protect all banks and depositors, but only to protect aggregate bank deposits. In the process of achieving this goal, it may also protect depositors, but not all depositors.

## Deposit Insurance

The current scheme of deposit insurance insures all deposit accounts up to a maximum of $40,000 and is funded by the imposition of a fixed-level premium on banks' deposits. While deposit insurance may seem, at first glance, to be directed at safeguarding depositors' assets when a failure does occur, its major purpose is actually to reduce the number of bank insolvencies by reducing or eliminating the threat of a "bank run." Before the age of deposit insurance, it was not uncommon for one bankruptcy in a community to precipitate others by raising doubts in the minds of depositors about the solvency of all banks in the community. An attempt by a large group of depositors to withdraw their money from even sound banks may threaten the solvency of these banks. In the face of a bank run, potential investors who might otherwise be willing to extend credit to such banks may lose confidence in these banks and refuse to buy their securities. Banks will then have to

sell large amounts of assets under unfavorable circumstances, greatly depressing the value of these assets and threatening the solvency of the banks.[5] Deposit insurance greatly reduces the probability of this occurring, and by guaranteeing the funds of depositors, it eliminates most incentives for the wholesale withdrawal of these funds. The primary benefit of deposit insurance, therefore, flows from its external effect of discouraging bank runs: It reduces the likelihood that one failure (or the failure of one badly managed bank) will result in other failures. As such, deposit insurance simultaneously reduces the frequency of bank failure while protecting (and reimbursing) the depositors of those banks that do fail.

The current federal deposit-insurance system levies a premium on all bank deposits of one-twelfth of 1 percent of total assessable deposits. This premium has not been high enough for the FDIC to accumulate a large reserve fund: It now holds about $6 billion in reserves. It also has authority to draw an additional $3 billion from the United States Treasury, if necessary. Thus, total funds available to meet potential claims of depositors constitute about 1.5 percent of total insured bank deposits (estimated to be about $600 billion). This reserve fund does not seem excessive when it is remembered that during the 1971–1975 period, banks with deposits of more than $5 billion failed. (See Table 2-1.)

## Detailed Solvency Regulations

The most complex and misunderstood dimension of solvency regulation is the plethora of detailed regulations imposed on banks by either federal or state regulatory authorities, which either directly or indirectly affect bank solvency. These regulations can be classified into the following general categories of constraints: entry restrictions, activity (or diversification) restrictions, pricing constraints, balance sheet (structure) constraints, and restrictions on insider conduct (intended to curb self-dealing and conflicts of interest).

### ENTRY RESTRICTIONS

Existing banks are protected from new competition by various regulations that limit entry into the banking industry, or that limit entry into specific banking markets by restricting branching. The alleged reason for these restrictions is to prevent "excessive" competition from bringing about an unstable banking system, or one characterized by frequent

---

**5.** To the extent that the central bank is willing to lend to banks subject to deposit runs, deposit insurance would be unnecessary. See discussion concerning the deficiencies of relying solely on a lender-of-last-resort capability.

bankruptcies. For example, in analyzing the effect of entry restrictions on entry in banking, Sam Peltzman states:

> The prime justification for bank entry restriction becomes clear by noting the date of its adoption—1935; it was designed to prevent a repetition of the collapse of the banking system such as had taken place in the early 1930's. . . . Bank entry restriction was designed to . . . [insure] against a high rate of failure. Entry restriction is supposed to accomplish this in two ways. First, it weeds out those applicants who value their own chances more highly than do the regulators. . . . Second, it reduces interbank competition generally. In this way, . . . the whole distribution of profit rates in banking will be greater than it would be under free entry, and fewer banks will incur losses that cause them to fail.[6]

The major obstacle to entry into the banking industry is the chartering authority exercised by both federal and state banking regulatory authorities. Economic barriers to entry, such as capital needs and economies of scale, are of minimal importance. In exercising their chartering authority, regulators customarily use the "convenience and needs of the community" test to restrict entry to a level where existing banks, whether efficient or not, can continue to prosper. The possibility that an existing bank will be driven into bankruptcy by aggressive entrants is nearly eliminated.

Existing banks are protected from entry by two kinds of regulation: restrictions on the formation of new banks, and restrictions on branching. The effect of the first of these is to limit the number of new banks allowed to enter all banking markets.[7] The major impact of this constraint is probably felt in small, rural banking markets (or towns), where new, small banks can become significant competitors in a short period of time. In cities, where large banks are dominant, entry by small banks is less likely to have a significant competitive effect. In these markets, potential entry through new branch formation by nonlo-

---

6. Peltzman, "Bank Entry Regulation: Its Impact and Purpose," 3 Nat'l Banking Rev., No. 2, 172 (Dec. 1965). For similar views, see Alhadeff, "A Reconsideration of Restrictions on Bank Entry," 76 Q. J. Econ., No. 2, 246–263 (May 1962); and Tussing, "The Case for Bank Failure," 10 J. Law & Econ. 129–147, (Oct. 1967). Other reasons sometimes cited for controlling entry are to prevent entry by the clearly incompetent or by members of organized crime. However, even if regulators can discriminate among potential entrants in a way that permits them to achieve these goals (which is debatable), the major impact of entry control on bank soundness still derives from its effect on limiting overall competition. Even if all "incompetents" and "criminals" were kept out, entry would still pose a significant competitive threat to existing banks. Thus, from solely a solvency perspective, we do not believe that these subsidiary reasons for entry regulation are of critical importance. They may serve other public policy ends, however.

7. See Edwards and Edwards, "Measuring the Effectiveness of Regulation: The Case of Bank Entry Regulation," 17 J. Law & Econ., No. 2, 445–460 (Oct. 1974).

cal, large banks is far more important. Limitations on inter- and intra-state branching, therefore, are the significant factor in these markets.

ACTIVITY RESTRICTIONS

Although increasing liberalization of our banking laws has broadened the scope of permissible banking activities, banks are still quite restricted with respect to the assets they can hold and the activities they can pursue. While they now engage in many nontraditional financial activities, such as equipment leasing and acting as insurance agents, banks are prohibited from pursuing nonfinancial activities, such as owning a manufacturing subsidiary, and they are prohibited from providing certain financial services, like underwriting insurance, operating as brokers or dealers in stock, and underwriting corporate stocks and bonds. In addition, there are limitations on the amounts that banks can lend to a single customer. The primary reason for these restrictions is to assure that banks will remain solvent:

> The restrictions on the types of business to be conducted by national banks were intended, first, to prevent them from undue speculation, and, second, to prevent them from tying up their funds, in assets which, although safe, might be unsalable so that they would not be readily available to meet the demands of the depositors.[8]

Historically, the business of commercial banking has been viewed as one of "discount and deposit," or as the business of accepting deposits and making short-term, self-liquidating loans to finance goods in the process of production and exchange.[9] This narrow view of banking emphasized the safety and liquidity of depositors' funds and the fiduciary relationship between banks and depositors. Indeed, many banking scholars have expressed complete disapproval of all investments other than commercial loans, maintaining that if the latter were not available in sufficient volume, the proper remedy was "a diminution of the amount of capital invested in the banking business rather than a change in the form of its investment."[10]

Although this view prevailed in the United States for more than a half century, the nature of commercial banking began to change in the early 1900s. In particular, banks began to increase their participation in the long-term capital market. During the last sixty years, banks (especially large banks) have steadily expanded their activities to the point where the term "department store" banking seems considerably more

---

8. See Peach, *The Security Affiliates of National Banks* 52. (John Hopkins Press, Baltimore, Md., 1941).

9. See Scott, *Money and Banking* (2d ed. rev., H. Holt & Co., New York 1903).

10. *Id.* at 129–130.

accurate than does "commercial" banking. Today, large banks are unquestionably the most generalized financial institutions in existence, bearing little resemblance to their ancestors. Thus, as old barriers fall and new functions are assumed, some critical questions are: How much of a threat to bank solvency are these new activities? Have we already gone too far in liberalizing the scope of bank activities?[11]

PRICING CONSTRAINTS

The major pricing constraints in banking are the restrictions imposed on the interest rates that banks can pay on deposits, both demand and savings deposits (Regulation Q). No interest at all can be paid on demand deposits, and only a specified maximum can be paid on various types of savings deposits. Although negotiable certificates of deposit in denominations of more than $100,000 are now exempt from this ceiling rate, as are Eurodollar deposits, these pricing limitations are still effective constraints for all but the very largest banks.

Again, the alleged reason for these restrictions is to insure solvency. Experience prior to the Banking Act of 1933, when banks could pay unlimited interest on their deposits, led many observers to conclude that unrestricted competition for deposits only resulted in higher costs to banks, which forced them to reach for higher yielding, higher risk assets, making them more susceptible to bankruptcy.[12]

The earliest attack on the practice of paying interest on deposits in the United States came on the heels of the banking panic of 1857. Symbolic of these attacks was the following statement by a committee of the New York Clearing House Association:

> A bank, having committed this first error of paying interest on its deposits, is therefore compelled by the necessities of its position to take the second false step and expand its operations beyond all prudent bounds.

> Banks are properly lenders of capital, and not borrowers, and it is not one of their legitimate functions to disturb the national current of trade by borrowing at one price to lend at a higher one. Such transactions constitute speculation in money, which is dangerous to all, and which ultimately reacts on the banks themselves with destructive power. From the nature of their organization, they should be conservative.[13]

---

11. Another, somewhat different, kind of activity constraint is the prohibition by some states of bank branching. This is an old issue, but one that is still hotly debated, although for reasons other than its implications for bank solvency. An obvious question, however, is: Are banks with many offices more vulnerable to insolvency or less? The analysis required to answer this question is similar to that which may be used to assess the broader question of the impact of activity restrictions on bank solvency.

12. See Benston, "Interest Payments of Demand Deposits and Bank Investment Behavior," 72 J. Political Economy, No. 5, 431–449 (Oct. 1964).

13. *Proceedings of the New York Clearing House Association* (March 5, 1858).

More recently, the Commission on Money and Credit recommended continuation of interest constraints on the rationale that "this legislation was adopted to reduce competition for deposits among commercial banks and thereby to relieve pressure for increased earnings which led to imprudent loans and investments."[14]

Regardless of the validity of these arguments, one historical consequence of pricing constraints is clear: They have reduced competition among banks, and between banks and other nonbank depository institutions. In addition, the elimination of price competition for deposits curtails competition on the loan side as well. Without the flexibility to alter deposit flows through variations in interest rates, banks are essentially left without the raw materials they need to alter the volume of their loans. As such, there is little incentive for them to increase loan volume by undercutting the loan rates of rivals. Further, there are good reasons to think that nonprice rivalry has not been an effective substitute for price competition. In particular, since most banking markets are tight oligopolies to begin with, restrictions on price rivalry have undoubtedly facilitated tacit agreements among banks to curtail all forms of competition.[15] Thus, it seems reasonably safe to conclude that pricing constraints have reduced competition and, consequently, raised bank profitability above what it would otherwise be.

### BALANCE SHEET CONSTRAINTS

Perhaps the best known solvency regulations are those imposed on the structure of a bank's balance sheet, such as requirements that banks maintain specified levels of capital and liquidity.[16] The ostensible rationale underlying these constraints is twofold: to make banks less vulnerable to insolvency by requiring that they hold a diversified portfolio and to insulate them from bankruptcy in the event of an earnings (or asset) problem by requiring that they maintain a sizable capital buffer.

The rationale for this kind of regulation can perhaps be best understood by examining capital regulation in more detail. To begin with, capital regulation is made operational by the process of bank examination by supervisory agencies. The major task of bank examiners is to make a determination of the riskiness of a bank's assets on the one hand and the adequacy of its capital on the other. Examiners attempt to gauge the probability of a decline in bank asset values and the ability of a

---

14. *Report of the Commission on Financial Institutions to the President of the United States* 20 (Washington, D.C., 1967).

15. For a similar argument, see Phillips, "Competition, Confusion, and Commercial Banking," 19 J. Finance, No. 1, pp. 32–45 (March 1964).

16. Requirements that member banks keep non-interest-bearing reserves with the Federal Reserve System are, in our opinion, associated more with monetary policy than with bank solvency.

bank's capital to absorb such declines without depositors incurring losses. If a bank's assets are deemed to be too risky, or its capital inadequate, the relevant supervisory agency will compel the bank to alter its balance sheet: increase its capital, or decrease its risk assets. More capital and less risky assets are seen by regulators as being substitutes in the bank's portfolio, and an important goal of the examination process is to achieve an appropriate mix of the two. In practice, however, the emphasis is on regulating capital rather than on the details of the asset portfolio, since it is considered difficult for a bank examiner to judge accurately the riskiness of the many different kinds of bank assets.[17]

Thus, the arguments are that capital regulation makes banks less vulnerable to unexpected losses by providing them with a capital buffer, while liquidity regulations make them less prone to bankruptcy by requiring that they hold a more liquid asset portfolio.

A brief review of the discussion of entry restrictions, activity restrictions, pricing constraints, and balance sheet constraints suggests that these regulations can be divided into two types of regulatory constraints: those that enhance solvency by increasing bank profits through the restriction of competition; and those that bolster solvency by restricting the freedom of banks to engage in risky activities or to hold high-risk portfolios. The first category clearly includes entry restrictions and pricing constraints, and the latter, activity and balance sheet constraints. While activity restrictions also diminish competition, they do so in "nonbanking" markets rather than banking markets.

### SELF-DEALING AND CONFLICTS OF INTEREST

The last set of solvency regulations is directed at insider misconduct: self-dealing and conflicts of interest. Of those banks that do fail, many fail because of self-serving loans made to directors and affiliates, or as a result of outright fraud and embezzlement.[18] Thus, a host of regulations have been imposed on managers to restrict the potential scope of such misconduct.

---

17. For supporting views, see *The Impact of Examination Practices on Bank Lending Policies,* Subcomm. on Domestic Finance of the House Comm. on Banking and Currency, 88th Cong., 2d Sess. 21–22, 37 ff (1964); and Peltzman, "Capital Investment in Commercial Banking and its Relationship to Portfolio Regulation," 78 J. Political Economy, No. 1, p. 3 (Jan. Feb. 1970).

18. In a recent study of thirty banks that failed between 1971 and 1976, the General Accounting Office reports that fourteen of the banks failed because the management made "improper or self-serving loans," eight because of "general loan management weaknesses," and eight because of "embezzlement or other crimes." See Comptroller General of the United States, *Federal Supervision of State and National Banks,* Ch. 9 (Washington, D.C., 1977). In the absence of solvency regulations, of course, "improper or self-serving loans" would probably account for a small proportion of failures because so many more banks would fail for "economic" reasons.

These regulations are essentially an administrative substitute for

common-law remedies through private litigation. While the previously discussed solvency regulations seek to enhance bank soundness by imposing additional restrictions on banks (compared to what the common law would impose), insider misconduct regulation arguably increases soundness by using a more efficient scheme for policing managerial behavior than that available under the common-law system of privately enforced rights. By reducing the expected net benefits of misconduct, it, in effect, raises the level of honesty among bank managers.

Because the nature of insider misconduct regulation is fundamentally quite different from the anticompetitive and portfolio-constraining regulations discussed earlier, we do not attempt to evaluate its usefulness in maintaining bank soundness. Such an assessment would entail an examination of the inadequacies of common-law remedies and of the effectiveness and costs of administratively policing managerial behavior.[19]

Before concluding this discussion of detailed solvency regulations, it may be useful to indicate the role that periodic bank examination by regulatory authorities plays in the overall scheme of solvency regulation. All banks are now subject to examination by one or more regulatory agencies, either by the relevant state authority, or by one or more of the federal regulatory agencies—the Comptroller of the Currency, the Federal Reserve, or the FDIC. The purpose of such examination is, first, to enforce the body of laws and regulations that pertain to banks, of which solvency regulations are only a part; and second, to act as a kind of "shadow" management to reduce the incidence of mismanagement. Thus, with respect to solvency regulation, examination is more of an enforcement device than a supplement.

There is, of course, some question whether examination is an effective or efficient enforcement device, or whether it should be used to second-guess management, but these issues are not central to this paper.[20]

## OBJECTIVES OF SOLVENCY REGULATION:
## HOW MUCH REGULATION IS ENOUGH?

Two reasons commonly advanced to support the regulation of any industry are: to enhance economic efficiency and to protect certain

---

19. See Clark, "The Soundness of Financial Intermediaries," 86 Yale L. J., No. 1, 79–86 (Nov. 1976).

20. Recent and pending changes suggest that in the future bank examination will focus more on a bank's internal control system in an effort to protect against fraud or defalcation and potential conflicts of interest. For a useful discussion of bank examinations, see Benston, *Bank Examination*, Reprint Series, No. C-16 (Center for Research in Gov't Policy & Business, Univ. of Rochester, May 1973). See also the recent report to the Congress by the Comptroller General of the United States, N. 18 *supra* at Ch. 7.

classes of consumers. From the point of view of economic theory, the efficiency rationale stems from the existence of certain widely recognized market failings. Specifically, traditional theory focuses on the maximization of allocative efficiency and acknowledges the existence of four kinds of market failure: increasing returns to scale (or natural monopoly), public goods, goods with external effects, and informational deficiencies.[21] In the presence of any of these market failures, regulation can, in principle, enhance allocative efficiency—it can improve at least someone's economic lot without making anybody worse off. One issue, therefore, is whether any of these market failures occurs in banking and financial markets, and if so, why?

The desire to protect a certain class of consumers is a fundamentally different reason for regulation. It presumes the existence of maximum economic efficiency, but it still seeks to improve the well-being of certain consumer groups. By definition, therefore, this can be accomplished only be reducing the well-being of other consumer groups. Such reasoning is commonly referred to as the "equity" or "distributional" rationale for regulation. Thus, to evaluate a regulation from this perspective, it is necessary to identify the protected class of consumers and to determine which groups are made better off and which worse off by the regulation.

## Efficiency Reasons for Regulation

Banks provide three major economic services or products. First, they are a ready source of liquidity for all sectors of the economy. Their ability to extend credit and to create money in response to economic conditions is a critical lubricant for economic activity. Second, they provide a payments mechanism (checking accounts), which facilitates economic exchange. And, third, they provide a low-risk, highly-divisible, investment asset (savings deposits), which arguably enhances the ability of consumers to maximize intertemporal utility.

Will banks operating in a free-market environment fail to provide these products? Or will they provide them in ways that are not socially optimal? Or, alternatively, is one or more of these products subject to the deficiencies associated with natural monopoly, public goods, externalities, or informational inadequacies? Conclusions about which solvency regulations are necessary and which are not must rest on a clear understanding of why such market failure occurs.

THE LIQUIDITY RATIONALE

The liquidity rationale for regulation is essentially one of protecting the nation's money supply from widespread bank runs. This rationale is

---

**21.** See Edwards, *Regulation Under Attack: New and Old Perspectives on the Economics of Regulation,* Working Paper No. 151 (New York: Graduate School of Business, Columbia Univ., 1977). This paper discusses other theories of regulation as well.

probably the most frequently cited reason (either explicitly or implicitly) for regulating banks.

The successive financial crises of 1873, 1884, 1890, 1893, and 1907 brought widespread demand for increased regulation of banking, culminating in the enactment of the Federal Reserve Act of 1913. Similarly, the wholesale collapse of the financial system in the 1930–1933 period quickly spawned the Federal Deposit Insurance Act of 1933 and the Banking Act of 1935. These crises, understandably, led to the view that government regulation is necessary to insure against a wholesale refusal by banks to convert deposits into currency on demand during periods of acute stress (and to prevent the concomitant disruptions in the flow of credit).

Runs on banks are characterized by uninformed (or misinformed) depositors attempting to convert deposits into currency. Runs can be precipitated by either the withdrawals of depositors with "legitimate" concerns or the withdrawals of frightened and uninformed depositors (who have an erroneous view of a bank's financial position). In either case, the "external" effect of such a run is to force banks to sell assets simultaneously, which depresses bank asset values below equilibrium values, and which, if depositor demands are to be met, may cause insolvency. Further, any wholesale failure of banks causes a sharp fall in the money supply and in overall liquidity, which almost always causes a general curtailment of economic activity. Thus, since control of the money supply is central to maintaining economic stability, and since such control cannot be assured if the banking system is vulnerable to financial panic, government regulation of banking is presumed necessary. This rationale is essentially a public-good argument, where economic stability (and the implied stability of the money supply) is the public good.

Although this argument implies some form of government intervention, the required scope of regulation is not clear. One view is that only a lender-of-last-resort facility for controlling the money supply is necessary. In the event of a bank run, the Federal Reserve could prevent a bank crisis by lending directly to besieged banks or by purchasing their assets on favorable terms (perhaps under repurchase agreements). The Federal Reserve clearly has both the legal and the economic power to do this. Further, once the panic subsides, the potentially undesirable expansionary effects of such actions can be reversed if the Federal Reserve sells assets and raises reserve requirements. The success of such an operation will depend on the swiftness and decisiveness with which the Federal Reserve diagnoses and responds to the problem, as well as its skill in taking subsequent offsetting actions. Given an inclination to do so, however, it does not seem overly optimistic (at least in principle) to think that the Federal Reserve could respond quickly enough, and effectively enough, to prevent serious bank runs.

The argument that still more government safeguards are needed rests on two grounds: history and transaction costs. First, the history of bank failures in the United States provides striking evidence that the mere existence of the Federal Reserve may not be a sufficient guarantee of financial soundness. In the 50-year period prior to the creation of the Federal Reserve System in early 1914, from 1864 to 1913, the average annual number of *national* bank failures was 11. In contrast, during the nine-year period from July 1, 1920, to June 30, 1929, 4,925 banks closed their doors, more than 20 percent of all banks—an average of 547 banks each year. Of these banks, 697 were national banks, an average of 77 national bank failures each year.

> In view of the safeguards instituted by the Federal Reserve it seemed little short of incredible that we should suffer in the decade of the twenties a veritable holocaust of bank suspensions—the number of failures finding no parallel since the collapse of "wild cat" banking schemes in the thirties and forties of the past century.[22]

What happened in the 1929 to 1933 period is well known. The Great Depression began in the winter of 1929 and culminated in 1933 in as severe a banking crisis as the United States had ever known, with all banks in the country finally suspending operations. Although most banks subsequently reopened, in the four-year period from June 30, 1929, to June 30, 1933, there were 8,493 bank insolvencies. Indeed, the number of banks definitely labeled as insolvent in the three days March 14–March 16, 1933, exceeded the total number of suspensions in the 48 years from 1864–1912.[23] Further, the money supply ($M_1$) fell from $26.4 billion in 1929 to a low of $19.4 billion in 1933 (a 27 percent decrease).[24]

Confronted with these facts, it is indeed difficult to place confidence in the willingness and ability of the Federal Reserve to contain a potential bank crisis. In theory, a lender-of-last-resort facility is sufficient; in practice, it does not seem to be.

The second argument for additional government intervention stems from the belief that, even if a lender-of-last-resort facility were sufficient to prevent a banking debacle, the social costs of relying only on this facility would be substantial. Other regulatory schemes, such as deposit insurance, which impose a lower cost on society, can be used to maintain soundness.

Even assuming the existence of a lender-of-last-resort that can and does stabilize the money supply, individual depositors will still always have some uncertainty about the safety of their own deposits, and the soundness of their own banks. There will continue to exist some chance that "your" bank may fail, and that you may suffer losses. Consequently, any individual depositor will have an incentive to withdraw

---

22. See Harold G. Moulton, *Financial Organization and the Economic System*, Ch. XXII (McGraw-Hill, New York 1938, reprinted by Arno Press, New York 1975).

23. *Id.* at 354–357.

24. See Temin, *Did Monetary Forces Cause the Great Depression?* 4–5 (W. W. Norton & Co., Inc., New York 1976).

his funds in times of uncertainty, thereby setting in action the forces of which banking crises are made. If central banks spot the problem quickly and act decisively, they may be able to avert a major banking crisis. But stopping bank runs after they begin may be considerably more costly to society than not having them at all. The costs associated with bank runs and bank crises are clearly substantial, ranging from the costs associated with the transportation of large amounts of currency to the enormous opportunity costs incurred by depositors, borrowers, and banks in attempting to secure their positions (not to mention the possible costs associated with a serious error of judgment or timing by the Federal Reserve).[25] A regulatory scheme that could reduce or eliminate these "transaction" costs would be socially preferable to relying on only a lender-of-last-resort facility.

Deposit insurance is such an alternative regulatory scheme. The United States adopted it in 1933 as a supplement to its lender-of-last-resort facility. Deposit insurance largely eliminates depositors' incentives to demand cash in times of uncertainty, and therefore virtually eliminates the possibility of a bank run. Even if banks fail, depositors are assured of quick reimbursement. Thus, while a lender-of-last-resort facility may not provide sufficient protection, a deposit-insurance system which enjoys the public's confidence certainly does.

THE PAYMENTS-SYSTEM RATIONALE

A second argument for the regulation of banking is that, by providing checking account service, banks provide a superior payments system which, in the absence of regulation, would be underutilized. This argument rests on the notion that a bank-supplied payments system lowers the transaction costs of economic exchange, increases the volume of exchange, and thereby enhances general economic welfare. In essence, it is an externality argument: One person's decision to use (and accept) checks in payment for goods confers benefit on many others (as well as himself) because it makes it easier for them to use the payments system. In other words, the value of a checking account to a person partially depends upon how many other people use and accept checks (just as the value of a telephone depends upon how many people

---

25. These potential costs may be glimpsed by examining the repercussions in the Eurodollar market following the bankruptcy of Bankhaus I. D. Herstatt in 1974. Its collapse set off a run on the deposits of smaller Eurobanks so that many sound banks found it difficult to renew deposits at any price for several weeks thereafter, thereby pushing them to the brink of insolvency. The largest Japanese and Italian banks also had to pay substantial interest-rate premiums to renew their short-term deposits. Finally, there was a major disruption in the market as bankers refused to deal with all but the strongest banks. A major crisis was averted only by the intervention of central banks. That this happened in a market where all the participants were large and financially sophisticated suggests that the costs of bankruptcy would be considerable in markets where there are thousands of small banks and millions of small depositors and borrowers.

have a telephone). Solvency regulation lowers the risk (and, therefore, cost) of holding demand deposit balances, which are an essential component of the widespread use of checks as a payments vehicle. Consequently, it should increase the use of this payments system.

It is probably safe to conclude that regulation has succeeded in increasing the use of demand deposits (or checking accounts), although it is by no means a necessary result of the current regulatory system. Present regulation does two things: Undoubtedly, it makes demand deposits less risky, thereby tending to increase the public's use of these deposits, but it also results in lower interest rates being paid on demand deposits, which tends to reduce public demand for these deposits. Thus, while regulation increases the "quality" (or safety) of demand deposits, it does so at the cost of reducing the pecuniary yield on these deposits. The net effect of these competing forces is unclear. Conceivably, regulation may raise quality by too much, causing the public to use demand deposits excessively (in a Pareto optimal sense). Too many resources devoted to providing a service or product are just as (allocatively) inefficient as are too few devoted to the task. Nevertheless, given the positive externalities associated with the use of demand deposits, one's judgment may still be that regulation, on balance, does yield a social benefit.

However, if the sole objective of regulation is to encourage the use of demand deposits, deposit insurance again seems to be sufficient to accomplish this goal.

### THE SAVINGS ASSET RATIONALE

The third efficiency rationale for regulating banks is to make available at low social cost an attractive, riskless, investment vehicle for savings. Savings deposits under the present regulatory framework are virtually risk-free. They can be held in very small increments of $1 or less, and, frequently, they yield an attractive pecuniary return. The existence of such an asset arguably permits households to better allocate their consumption over time, enabling them to achieve greater utility than would otherwise be possible. This argument is applicable not only to commercial banks; it applies to all financial institutions that, because of regulation, are able to provide a low-risk savings asset—mutual savings banks, savings and loan associations, consumer credit unions, etc.

This argument rests on the proposition that an unregulated market will be unable to provide an equally attractive savings asset. Although we can only speculate about this, our guess is that the market would do a reasonably good job at generating good (although not perfect) substitutes for government-insured savings deposits. To begin with, in the absence of regulation, banks and other savings institutions would still provide savings deposits, although these deposits would not be entirely riskless. However, banks at the same time would almost surely pay higher yields on these deposits, so that many savers might very

well be indifferent between low-paying regulated and high-paying,
higher-risk, unregulated savings deposits. Private deposit insurance
schemes are also a possibility, although even these do not guarantee
totally riskless deposits—insurance companies may also be subject to
failure. In addition, mutual funds that hold only risk-free government
securities and sell shares in small denominations (much like the money
market funds of recent years) are a possibility, although these, too,
would not be totally riskless because of the risk of fraud and embezzlement. Thus, left to its own devices, the free market would probably
develop some close substitutes for government-insured savings deposits. Perfect substitutes, however, may not be forthcoming. As such,
there may be a case for the government's providing risk-free savings
deposits by insuring bank deposits.

INFORMATION COSTS

A final efficiency argument for solvency regulation is that such regulation can substantially reduce the information costs of depositors. If each
depositor has to rely solely on his own wit and resources to evaluate the
soundness of banks when deciding where to place his deposits, each
will incur sizable informational costs. In some cases, these costs will
even exceed the potential benefits of the information, so that depositors
will either forgo search entirely or not use bank deposits. In other
cases (such as large depositors), depositors will engage in extensive
search and will incur substantial informational costs. Arguably, government can intervene to reduce these costs and produce a *net* savings.
The argument rests upon the notion that there are significant economies
of scale in acquiring information, and that information cannot be
bought and sold successfully in private markets because of its public-
good characteristics. Consequently, it will be more efficient for the
government (rather than for all depositors acting individually) to
assemble information pertinent to bank soundness and use it to protect
depositors.

In principle, however, solvency regulation is still unnecessary. If it is
assumed that depositors are capable of digesting and intelligently utilizing information, the government can simply collect the requisite
information and make it available to depositors, possibly at a zero
price. In theory, the public's informational needs can be efficiently met
by the government if it simply acts as a collector and a dispenser of
information. Regulation to protect those who possess the information
and the wit to protect themselves is not supportable on grounds of
economic efficiency (although it may be on other grounds).

In sum, the most compelling efficiency rationale for governmental
solvency regulation is probably what we have called the "liquidity
rationale": the need to prevent "bank runs" in order to maintain control
of the money supply. The "payments mechanism," the "savings asset,"
and the "informational deficiency" arguments offer considerably less

convincing rationales for direct regulation, although informational deficiencies do call for some form of government involvement. Further,
none of these rationales calls for more than the adoption of a viable
system of deposit insurance that enjoys the confidence of the public.
Detailed solvency regulations only seem necessary to the extent that
they constitute an indispensable part of such a deposit insurance system. Also, a lender-of-last-resort facility is superfluous unless public
confidence in the insurance system is somehow undermined. (In any
case, such a facility will, of course, exist for purposes of monetary
policy.)

## Fairness and the Protection of the Financially Illiterate

There may be other reasons for regulating banks and financial institutions than to enhance economic (or allocative) efficiency. "Equity" or
"fairness" is often cited by both regulators and the courts as a reason for
regulation. The notion that banks stand in a fiduciary position vis-à-vis
depositors is a common historical theme: "Short-term, self-liquidating
loans to finance goods in the process of production and exchange were
best adapted to meet the requirements of commercial banks because of
their fiduciary relationship to depositors."[26]

This "fiduciary" view sees banks as custodians of peoples' monies,
and therefore subject to a higher standard of care. Of course, all businesses that borrow in capital markets are, to some extent, custodians of
money. The distinction between banks (as well as other financial institutions) and other debtor-firms is perhaps not that they borrow more,
but that their creditors are often small and unsophisticated depositors,
who, arguably, are incapable of making judgments about the soundness of banks, even if the requisite information were available. Thus,
they must be protected from excessively speculative banking practices
and unscrupulous and dishonest bankers. This rationale is fundamentally paternalistic, and it is much the same as that used to justify the
licensing of doctors, lawyers, accountants, barbers, beauticians, automobile repair shops, etc.[27]

As a rationale for regulation, it is also a mixture of equity and
efficiency considerations. If consumers (or depositors) are not able to
use information wisely, so that they sometimes make choices different
from those that they would make if they processed information efficiently (or different from those that a financially sophisticated person
would make in possession of the same information and having the
same utility function), the result will be economic inefficiency and

---

26. Peach, N. 8 *supra* at 9. Also see Dewey, *State Banking Before the Civil War* (Gov't Print
1910); and First Nat'l Bank v. Converse, 200 U.S. 425 (1906); First Nat'l Bank v. Stokes, 203
S.W. 1026 (Ark. 1918).

27. But see Gellhorn, "The Abuse of Occupational Licensing," 44 U. Chic. L. Rev., No. 1, 6
(Fall 1976).

welfare loss, just as in the case where consumers act rationally but are imperfectly informed. In addition, these customers will suffer private losses (or costs) as well. However, in these cases, the primary motive for regulation is usually to protect the small and unsophisticated rather than to enhance economic efficiency. The vision of "little people" losing their life savings is a powerful restraint on those who would advocate "freer" banking.

Faced with this kind of "irrational" behavior, there is, in general, only one regulatory response: direct control of the products offered for sale. Regulation must restrict the range of products or options available to the consumer by prohibiting the sale of low-quality or high-risk products. This control is usually effected by the imposition of either licensing requirements (as for doctors) or certification standards (as for drugs and foods). In banking, solvency regulation seeks to eliminate high-risk banks through a combination of licensing and certification standards.

Such a policy normally has both benefits and costs. Its benefits derive from the fact that it removes alternatives that some people "should not" have chosen; its costs, from the fact that it eliminates choices that some people "should" have made.[28] In banking, some depositors may conceivably prefer to take more risk and earn a higher rate of return, and in the absence of regulation, they could, if they desired, deal with a riskier bank that paid a higher interest rate. This would be a viable option for large savers, for example, who have extensive diversification possibilities; and it might also be a reasonable alternative for many small savers, such as those without important financial responsibilities (those who are young, without families, and with enough human capital to make reasonably certain an adequate future income). There is simply no a priori way to know whether regulations of this type will improve or worsen economic welfare. Moreover, evaluation of such regulation requires information on consumer tastes (or risk preferences), which is difficult to obtain, in principle as well as in practice.[29]

Viewed in this light, banking does not stand out as a case where financial illiteracy will result in especially severe injury to the small and unsophisticated. The risks clearly do not approximate those associated with undergoing a surgical operation or riding on an unsafe airplane. The financially unsophisticated will, of course, make mistakes and suffer losses, but the consequences of these poor choices are unlikely to be catastrophic. Even small savers have alternatives: They can avoid risk entirely by not using any bank—they can use cash instead of

---

**28.** See Colantoni, Davis, and Swaminuthan, "Imperfect Consumers and Welfare Comparisons of Policies Concerning Information and Regulation," Bell J. Econ. 602–618 (Autumn 1976).

**29.** Information is needed on transformation functions between products and their characteristics and, of course, on the costs of implementing and policing the regulations. See *id.* at 613.

demand deposits and hold the bulk of their savings in, say, government savings bonds. Such behavior will entail greater transaction costs, of course, but the reduction of these costs is an efficiency reason for regulation, not an equity reason. In contrast, there is little alternative to undergoing emergency medical treatment when the circumstances require it. Finally, even small savers may have diversification possibilities: houses, automobiles, other financial assets, education, etc. It is noteworthy that regulation does not do much to protect against the possibility of buying an unsafe used automobile, or a structurally unsound house, or even a poor education (although there are common-law remedies in some circumstances). With respect to these items, poor choices may expose savers to potentially greater losses than poor choice of a bank.

There is obviously no way to resolve this argument to everyone's satisfaction. We do not now, and never will, have enough information about consumers' tastes (and transformation functions) to make scientific judgments about the impact of such regulation on economic efficiency. Further, beliefs about the need and the wisdom of protecting the unsophisticated consumer of financial services depend more on subjective judgments than on scientific assessments, and, of course, on one's feeling about the effectiveness and costs of government regulation. At one extreme are those who would protect every small saver from loss, no matter what the economic cost; at the other, perhaps, are the "efficiency" advocates, who favor regulation only if the economic benefits exceed its costs, no matter what the distributive consequences may be. In between, there is large scope for misunderstanding and debate. Whatever one's belief, however, it is clear that a viable deposit insurance system will provide all the protection necessary to satisfy the social goal of fairness.

## DETAILED SOLVENCY REGULATION AND ALTERNATIVE DEPOSIT INSURANCE SCHEMES: SUGGESTED REFORMS

Thus far, our analysis suggests that all the social goals of solvency regulation can be attained by adopting a sound deposit-insurance scheme—one that the public believes will guarantee prompt repayment in the event of insolvency. In this view, the role of detailed solvency regulation, if any, is to support or maintain the soundness of the deposit-insurance system. If a sound and efficient insurance system can exist in the absence of such solvency regulations, these controls are, a fortiori, unnecessary. This section examines the role of detailed solvency regulation under the assumption that some form of deposit insurance is in existence. Given deposit insurance, are all the solvency controls discussed in the second section necessary? The answer to this question, as we shall see, partially depends upon precisely what kind of deposit-insurance system is adopted. Consequently, we also discuss the strengths and weaknesses of alternative insurance systems—specif-

ically, a uniform- versus a variable-premium system.

The discussion is divided into four subsections. In the first, we
analyze the contribution that each type of solvency regulation makes to
bank soundness *under the assumption that the present system of deposit
insurance (uniform-level-premium)* is in force. We conclude that most of
the detailed solvency regulations are superfluous and could be discarded without jeopardizing the soundness of the banking system.
Further, after assessing the potential benefits and costs of eliminating
these regulations, we conclude that their elimination would be in the
public interest. In the second subsection, the feasibility and potential
benefits of substituting a variable-premium deposit-insurance system
for the present uniform-premium system is examined. In the third
subsection, the issue of whether all deposits should be insured is
discussed; and in the last subsection, the practicality and the potential
gains from using private insurers to supply some or all of the required
deposit-insurance coverage is explored.

Our strongest conclusion is that, no matter what kind of deposit-
insurance system is adopted, all detailed solvency regulations, except
for balance sheet controls, should be eliminated. Entry restrictions
(both on new bank formations and on branching), price controls, and
activity constraints are not necessary to maintain soundness, and at
least the first two impose significant net costs on society. (Our discussion of the social [nonsolvency] implications of discarding activity
restraints shows these to be far-reaching and deserving of careful
consideration.) We also conclude that some form of variable-premium
deposit insurance would be an improvement.

## Detailed Solvency Regulation Under
## A Uniform-Premium Insurance System

Under the present insurance system, the government guarantees the
safety of deposits up to $40,000 per account and charges banks a
premium per dollar of deposits that is independent of the insured
institution's risk exposure. In the absence of other solvency regulations,
this insurance system would create socially dangerous incentives for
financial institutions. In particular, since the holding of risky assets by
banks would neither increase their insurance premiums nor result in
deposit withdrawals, many institutions would find it optimal to substantially increase the riskiness of their asset portfolios.[30] Also, because
the cost of insured deposits will not be affected by changes in an

---

30. A fuller analysis of the nature of the dangers inherent in the existing deposit-insurance
system as well as a more rigorous justification for the statements contained in the text
appears in Scott, *Moral Hazard in the U.S. System of Deposit Insurance,* Working Paper
(Graduate School of Business, Columbia Univ., Sept. 1977).

institution's ratio of debt and equity capital to deposits, institutions have an incentive to replace high-cost debt and equity capital with low-cost, government guaranteed, deposits.[31]

Both an increase in asset risk and a decrease in capital reduce institutional soundness and therefore increase the risk exposure of the government insurer. More precisely, both increase the probability of bank insolvency. Further, the increase in asset risk reduces the liquidity of a bank's assets and impairs the amount the government insurer could recover in the event of insolvency. This incentive problem is common to insurance and is known as the problem of "moral hazard." Moral hazard arises when the nature of the insurance contract induces the insured party to act in ways harmful to the insurer.[32]

The problem of moral hazard is increased by de facto regulatory guarantees of uninsured deposits and debt. Rather than allow unsound institutions to fail, regulators often arrange for a merger with another sound institution, especially in the case of large institutions. Such a merger results in higher payments to uninsured creditors and stockholders than would otherwise occur.[33] This type of de facto insurance also encourages banks to substitute uninsured debt and deposits for equity capital.

The purpose of detailed solvency regulations should be clear: They are to check the managerial tendencies which are the obvious result of an insurance system that provides for riskless deposits while at the same time charging a uniform premium not reflective of individual banks' risk exposures.

ARE ALL THE PRESENT DETAILED SOLVENCY REGULATIONS NECESSARY?

In our discussion of existing regulatory structure, it was shown that detailed solvency regulations essentially work through two routes: Either they increase solvency by restricting competition, or they limit the opportunities open to banks to engage in risky activities (or to hold risky portfolios). Entry restrictions (including branching restrictions),

---

31. The incentive for banks to alter their portfolios in response to deposit insurance is supported by an empirical study by Sam Peltzman. He finds that "virtually all of the decline in the capital-deposits ratio since the 1920's can be accounted for by substitution of deposit insurance for capital." See Peltzman, N. 17 *supra* at 17.

32. On the issue of moral hazard, see Arrow, "Insurance, Risk, and Resource Allocation," *Aspects of the Theory of Risk-Bearing* (Helsinki 1965); Pauly, "The Economics of Moral Hazard: Comment," 43 American Economic Rev., No. 3, 531–537 (June 1968); and Grubel, "Risk, Uncertainty, and Moral Hazard," 38 J. Risk & Insurance, No. 1, 99–106 (March 1971).

33. E.g., Barnett, Horvitz, and Silverberg, "Deposit Insurance: The Present System and Some Alternatives," 94 Banking L. J. 304–332 (April 1977). For a discussion of the dangers of allowing a large bank to fail but which, nevertheless, argues that some large banks should be allowed to fail, see Mayer, "Should Large Banks Be Allowed to Fail," 10 J. Financial & Quantitative Analysis 603–610 (Nov. 1975).

pricing controls, and activity restrictions (as currently administered) fall into the first category, while balance sheet controls (e.g., liquidity and capital requirements) are in the second.[34] In a separate paper, we analyzed the likely effects of these regulations on bank soundness and concluded that only balance sheet controls are necessary to give regulators effective control over bank soundness.[35]

The impact of these regulations on bank solvency has been debated for some time, but there has been little rigorous analysis of exactly how they affect the likelihood of bank insolvency. Shibboleth, more than reason, has pervaded the debate. Empirical testing in this area has also been deficient because of the lack of a satisfactory theoretical structure on which to base statistical tests. Recent advances in the theory of finance generally, and in the theory of bankruptcy in particular, provide, however, a more satisfactory structure for analysis. Further, when these solvency regulations are appraised within the context of such a structure, the complexity of their effects becomes clearer: Most have ambiguous effects on bank soundness. To be specific, anticompetitive regulations are of dubious value, while a combination of liquidity and equity capital regulations appears to be sufficient to maintain bank soundness.

More specifically, in our recent study of the effects of various detailed solvency regulations, we arrived at the following conclusions:

> While entry restrictions probably reduce the probability of failure for "full access" banks (banks with complete access to capital markets), they have ambiguous effects on "partial access" banks (banks which can raise funds in an emergency only by selling their own assets);

> Activity restrictions may either increase or decrease the likelihood of failure depending on the relationship between the prohibited activity (or asset) and the bank's portfolio of other assets;

> Although ceilings on the payment of interest on deposits should reduce the probability of failure for all banks in the short-run, the long-run effects of such regulation are uncertain for both partial and full access banks;

> Liquidity requirements are likely to reduce the probability of failure for the partial access bank but may increase it for the full access bank;

> The effectiveness of capital requirements depends on the nature of the regulation (debt or equity) and on how the bank uses the additional funds. Additional debt financing is likely to increase the probability of failure for all banks, while additional equity funding is likely to reduce it.[36]

---

**34.** Activity restrictions that were not absolute prohibitions against certain activities but were in the form of diversification limits would fall into the second category along with balance sheet controls. These are not the kind of activity constraints we have in the United States, although such constraints are in use in some foreign countries like Germany.

**35.** Scott and Edwards, *Bank Solvency Regulation in the United States: A Theoretical Analysis,* Research Paper, No. 190 (Columbia Univ. School of Business 1977).

**36.** *Id.* at 41–42.

Thus, the major thrust of our analysis was to show that through a combination of equity capital and liquidity controls, regulators can successfully control bank solvency; and that bank soundness need not diminish if entry restrictions, activity constraints, and interest rate ceilings are relaxed or eliminated. Unless there are strong nonsolvency reasons for maintaining these regulations, they should be discarded. The social benefit of discarding (or at least relaxing) them is clear: increased competition.[37]

RAMIFICATIONS OF POLICY RECOMMENDATIONS

*Relaxing Restrictions on New Bank Formation.* Historically, entry restrictions have been a major impediment to competition in banking. Studies of entry controls show that such restrictions have reduced the number of new bank formations by as much as 40 to 60 percent since 1935.[38] When it is remembered that most banking markets in the United States have only a few banks, restrictions on entry take on special importance.[39] Even in markets with many banks, the threat of entry can be a significant competitive element, and the erection of entry barriers can greatly diminish competition. Indeed, empirical studies confirm that this is not an academic matter: Restrictions on new bank formation clearly worsen bank performance.[40]

The most significant regulatory impediment to new entry is imposed

---

37. For a thorough review of the adverse competitive effects of entry controls, see Heggestad, "Market Structure, Competition, and Performance in Financial Industries: A Survey of Banking Studies," in this volume. For an analysis of the effects of interest rate ceilings, see Robbins, "The Effects of State Usury Ceilings on Single Family Homebuilding," J. Finance 227–236 (March 1974); Greer, "Rate Ceilings, Market Structure, and the Supply of Finance Company Personal Loans," J. Finance 1363–1382 (Dec. 1974); and Pyle, "The Losses in Savings Deposits from Interest Rate Regulation," 5 Bell J. Economics & Management Science, No. 2, 614–622 (Autumn 1974). For an analysis of activity restrictions, see Black, Miller, and Posner, "An Approach to the Regulation of Bank Holding Companies," forthcoming.

38. See Peltzman, "Entry into Commercial Banking," 8 J. Law & Econ. 11–50 (Oct. 1965); and Edwards and Edwards, "Measuring the Effectiveness of Regulation: The Case of Bank Entry Regulation," J. Law & Econ. 445–460 (Oct. 1974).

39. Using a common measure of concentration, the Herfindahl Index and its corresponding "number-equivalent" index, it can be shown that the average rural county in the United States has a numbers-equivalent of less than 2.2 banks, and that the average Standard Metropolitan Statistical Area (SMSA) has a numbers-equivalent of about 4.5 banks. Only 10 percent of SMSAs have a numbers-equivalent of more than 9.3 banks, and only 20 percent of rural counties have a numbers-equivalent that exceeds 3.9 banks. Clearly, these figures do not suggest the existence of highly competitive markets. See Heggestad, N. 37 *supra* at 8–9.

40. See, for example, Fraser and Rose, "Bank Entry and Bank Performance," J. Finance 65–78 (March 1972); McCall and Peterson, *The Impact of DeNovo Commercial Bank Entry*, Working Paper, No. 76–77 (Fed. Deposit Ins. Corp., Div. of Research 1976); and Edwards and Edwards, No. 38 *supra*.

under the guise of the "convenience and needs" requirement. This stipulates that regulators should not permit entry unless another bank would serve the "convenience and needs" of the community. In practice, regulators have interpreted this to mean that they should not permit entry into markets that already have enough banks. Of course, what constitutes "adequately banked" is far from clear, at least in practice. In general, however, if regulators believe that new entry is likely to result in the exit of some other (already existing) bank(s), they would consider the community to be adequately banked and refuse to permit the new entry. It goes without saying that the prediction of such a market result is often well beyond the limits of human wisdom; and regulators tend to err on the side of permitting too little rather than too much entry, since they do not relish the prospect of bank failures (even given a sound deposit insurance system).[41] Thus, entry restrictions can be expected to diminish competition and the social benefits which derive from it; and the elimination of entry restrictions, at least those based on the convenience and needs requirement, can be expected to increase competition and the concomitant social benefits. Further, if the absence of such restrictions were seriously to threaten bank soundness (which is doubtful), regulators could always rely more extensively on the use of capital and liquidity regulations to maintain bank solvency.

There are other, lesser, regulatory impediments to new entry. Of particular concern may be the requirement that those seeking a charter show "good character." Elimination of these may arguably permit the wholesale infiltration of banking by organized crime. In addition, applicants are required to demonstrate a certain managerial expertise, and to have adequate capital backing. None of these, we believe, presently constitutes a substantial barrier to entry, so that their retention will not significantly reduce the benefits of an otherwise easy-entry policy.

In conclusion, all regulatory impediments to entry based on the "convenience and needs" requirement should be abolished.[42] In addition to the benefits of greater competition that will flow from the adoption of such a policy, an important saving will result from a reduction in the substantial legal and administrative costs now associated with obtaining a bank charter. These, too, are social benefits.[43]

*Relaxing Branching Restrictions.*   Just as restrictions on new bank formation diminish the threat of entry, so, too, do restrictions on branch-

---

41. For a discussion of entry policy, see Scott, "In Quest of Reason: The Licensing Decisions of the Federal Banking Agencies," 42 U. Chi. L. Rev. 235 (1975).

42. A recent study argues that, historically, free entry into banking did not lead to a chaotic banking system with large losses for bank customers. See Rockoff, "The Free Banking ERA: A Reexamination," J. Money, Credit, & Banking 141–168 (May 1974).

43. See Posner, "The Social Costs of Monopoly and Regulation," 83 J. Political Economy, No. 4, 807–829 (Aug. 1975).

ing. These are another regulatory obstacle to entry, and their adverse effects on bank performance are well-documented. Eliminating them would increase competition and clearly enhance social welfare.[44]

There will also be efficiency benefits from more extensive branching. First, and most important, freer branching will result in more convenient banking service: the cost of operating a branch office is considerably lower than operating a completely separate banking entity, so that the result should be more offices per capita, everything else equal.[45] This will reduce customers' transaction costs. Second, where branching is prohibited, multibank holding companies are often used as a substitute, and holding companies are more expensive to operate than an analogous branching network. Third, freer branching will result in larger banks, which will be able to take advantage of any scale economies that exist. Although most studies of economies of scale in banking do not show substantial benefits to scale, these studies do not examine all banking products or services. They also do not fully account for possible capital (or financial) economies.[46]

Against these benefits, there are two potential negatives associated with more extensive branching. First, branching will eliminate the *local* bank-customer nexus. It has been argued that the result will be poorer bank service, or at least service that is less responsive to local needs. Evaluating the validity and importance of this argument is obviously difficult. However, there is no evidence to suggest that people are at present being better served in unit-banking states than in branching states. Further, if people prefer to deal with a local bank rather than a large branch bank, presumably they will be willing to pay for it: They will either use existing local banks at higher cost, or they will create a market environment conducive to the formation of a local bank.

Second, freer branching may ultimately result in the reduction of competition. If there are economies associated with size, at least up to some rather large size, it is conceivable that with extensive branching, the number of banks in the United States may diminish sharply. That such a reduction will occur is indisputable. What is in doubt is the exact number of banks that will remain. Will it be 5,000, 500, 50, or 5? Our knowledge of economies of scale in banking suggests that a large number of banks will remain, say, 500.[47] But, there is no way to predict

---

44. See Jacobs, *Business Loan Costs and Bank Market Structure: An Empirical Estimate of Their Relations*, Occasional Paper, No. 115 (Nat'l Bureau of Econ. Research 1971); Horvitz and Shull, "The Impact of Branch Banking on Bank Performance," Nat'l Banking Rev. 113–179 (Dec. 1964); and Heggestad and Mingo, "The Competitive Condition of U.S. Banking Markets and the Impact of Structure Reform," 32 J. Finance, No. 3, 649–662 (June 1977).

45. See Bell and Murphy, *Economies of Scale in Commercial Banking* (Fed. Res. Bank of Boston 1967).

46. See, for example, *id.*

47. *Id.*

the outcome with certainty. However, two points seem worth noting:

First, to the extent that greater efficiency is the cause of the reduction in
the number of banks, this gain must be weighed against the loss
resulting from a curtailment of competition; and, second, the preserva-
tion of competitive banking markets seems more properly in the regulatory sphere of competition (or antitrust) policy than branching law.
Severe restraints on branching succeed in limiting the potential economic power of banks at the cost of forgoing the fruits of greater
competition and more efficiency.

In sum, the case for permitting branching is a strong one, and there
is no reason to retain branching restrictions out of considerations for
bank soundness. Indeed, the diversification advantages of branch
banks probably make them less vulnerable to bankruptcy. However, it
would be prudent to accompany more permissive branching with strict
antitrust laws.[48]

*Relaxing Activity Restrictions.* Activity restrictions are still another
form of entry barrier: They prevent full competition between commercial banks and other financial institutions. As such, they also diminish
competition in financial markets, and for this reason, their elimination
would be in the public interest.[49] Further, as indicated previously, the
argument that these restrictions increase bank soundness is quite weak;
there is actually good reason to think that, as a diversification constraint, they make banks more vulnerable to insolvency. To the extent
that banks imprudently engage in certain high-risk activities, regulators can respond by varying capital and liquidity requirements to
maintain bank solvency.

Is there any reason to keep activity restrictions? There are three
arguments against eliminating them. First, the end of these restrictions
may also spell the end of specialized financial institutions. If regulations treat all institutions equally, and if there are significant economies
associated with scale or with greater diversification, single-product
financial institutions may not remain competitive, and may disappear
through absorption and acquisition. The present financial landscape of
consumer finance companies, factors, savings and loan associations,
investment bankers, etc., may change to one of large, multiproduct, all-
purpose, financial institutions, all competing against one another. This

---

**48.** In particular, the issue of the "linkage theory of oligopoly" remains unresolved. See E.
Solomon, "Bank Merger Policy and Problems: A Linkage Theory of Oligopoly," 11 J.
Money, Credit, & Banking, No. 3, 323–336 (Aug. 1970); and Heggestad and Rhoades,
"The Influence of Multi-Market Links on Local Market Competition," Rev. of Econ. &
Statistics, forthcoming.

**49.** Studies of inter-institutional competition are Stolz, "Local Banking Markets, Structure,
and Conduct in Rural Areas," *Bank Structure and Competition* 134–148 (Fed. Res. Bank of
Chicago 1976); White, "Price Regulation and Quality Rivalry in a Profit-Maximizing
Model: The Case of Branch Banking," J. Money, Credit, & Banking 107–118 (Feb. 1976);
and Heggestad and Mingo, N. 44 *supra*.

vision is reinforced by the prospect of nationwide branching and extensive electronic fund transfer systems.[50]

The issue, therefore, is whether specialized financial institutions should be preserved by regulatory constraint. A common argument is that multiproduct financial institutions would not adequately serve all segments of financial consumers. But, in this event, what is to prevent specialized institutions from entering and serving this group? With free entry, an unfilled market demand will attract attention: Profit opportunities will be seized, if not by multiproduct firms, then by specialized institutions.

Perhaps the crux of the argument for regulatory restrictions that protect specialized financial institutions lies in the belief that the free market will not serve certain segments of the populace to a degree consistent with the social welfare—or in the belief that there are externalities present. For example, a major role of specialized financial institutions has been to make certain that there is ample financing to support housing expenditures. In other words, specialized institutions are necessary to allocate credit and resources into certain sectors of the economy, like housing. Presumably, the market, left to its own workings, will not serve these sectors adequately.

Present knowledge of how such credit allocation schemes have worked, however, suggests that they have been a failure. Credit is a fungible commodity, and it is highly doubtful that the credit flows generated by specialized financial institutions have had an appreciable effect on the volume of real expenditures in the designated sectors.[51] Further, regulatory provisions directed at preserving specialized financial institutions, such as ceilings on savings rates, clearly have had regressive distributive consequences: High-income groups have benefited at the expense of low-income groups.[52] If subsidization of certain sectors of the economy is desirable, there are probably more obvious, more efficient, and more effective devices available (such as tax concessions). Thus, the desire to allocate credit is not a reason to retain specialized financial institutions, and is, therefore, not a reason to retain activity restrictions.

The second reason for activity constraints is the conflicts-of-interest problem. For example, a traditional argument against permitting commercial banks to act as investment bankers (and to underwrite corpo-

---

50. See, for example, Phillips, "Implications of the New Payments Technology for Monetary Policy," in this volume; and Baxter, Cootner, and Scott, *Retail Banking in the Electronic Funds Transfer* (Allanheld, Osum Co. Publishers, Inc., Montclair, N.J., 1977).

51. See Diller, "Credit Allocation and Housing," and Hamburger and Zwick, "Credit Allocation and Consumer Expenditures: The Case of Installment Credit Controls," and related comments in this volume. See also Kane, "Good Intentions and Unintended Evil: The Case Against Selective Credit Allocation," J. Money, Credit & Banking 55–69 (Feb. 1977).

52. See Pyle, "The Losses on Savings Deposits from Interest Rate Regulation," Bell J. Econ. & Management Science 614–622 (Autumn 1974).

rate securities) is that bank managers will be subject to more self-dealing and conflicts-of-interest temptations than at present. This argument is complex, and its analysis is beyond the scope of this paper.[53].

Nevertheless, three observations seem pertinent. First, to the extent that competition is enhanced by the relaxation of regulation, the conflicts-of-interest problem may diminish, not increase. The greater the competitive pressure, the more bank managers will be measured by the competitive yardstick, and the less will be the opportunity to indulge in self-dealing and other conflict-of-interest practices.[54] Second, at present, regulatory restrictions on banks' activities are not consistent with the goal of eliminating conflicts of interest. In particular, the massive trust operations of commercial banks already pose conflict-of-interest issues as troublesome as any likely to be encountered. If the reason for retaining activity restrictions is to minimize conflicts of interest, a complete revision and rearrangement of these restrictions is called for. Third, control of self-dealing and conflicts of interest might be better effected by the development of clear administrative provisions and remedies directed at specific practices, rather than the wholesale prohibition of certain activities. A strengthening of common-law remedies would also be useful. At present, banking regulations and bank regulators are quite unclear about the limits of permissible managerial conduct in this area.

The third argument for keeping activity restrictions is to prevent banks from acquiring "undue" political and economic power. If banks could engage in all kinds of activities and own all kinds of businesses, they might well become huge enterprises with tentacles reaching into all areas (even without violating any current antitrust laws). The present banking structure in Germany may be a reasonably accurate representation of what might happen here. The pros and cons of such a development are beyond the purview of this paper, as are possible alternative regulatory approaches, such as limiting the *absolute* size of banks irrespective of the activities they engage in. That this is an issue of considerable social importance is clear enough.[55]

In sum, activity restrictions should not be retained on the grounds

---

53. See, for example, Schotland, "Conflicts of Interest Within the Financial Firm: Regulatory Implications," and a critique of this paper by Peltzman in this volume.

54. For development of this argument, see Peltzman, *ibid.*

55. For a discussion of the issues involved in breaking up large firms, see Posner, *Antitrust Law: An Economic Perspective*, Ch. 5 (Univ. of Chicago Press 1976). For a discussion of the public policy issues associated with large conglomerate firms, see Williamson, *Markets and Hierarchies: Analysis and Antitrust Implications*, Ch. 9 (Free Press, London, 1975). For a discussion of the possible role of banks in large conglomerate organizations, see Bronfenbrenner, "Japan's Galbraithian Economy," Public Interest 149–157 (Fall 1970). For a discussion of the reciprocal business practices that might emerge with banks as part of a conglomerate organization, see Edwards, "The Economics of 'Tying' Arrangements: Some Proposed Guidelines for Bank Holding-Company Regulation," 6 Antitrust L. & Economics Rev. 87 (1973).

that they are necessary to maintain bank soundness. There are better ways of maintaining soundness. These restrictions also are not useful in allocating credit to meet social priorities; and they do not contribute much to the resolution of the conflict-of-interest problem. Whether they are necessary or efficient devices with which to curb the development of concentrations of economic and political power is an open issue which needs careful consideration.

*Eliminating Price Controls.* The major price controls imposed on financial institutions are the prohibition against paying interest on demand deposits and the interest ceilings on the savings deposits of banks and thrift institutions. As indicated earlier, both of these prohibitions have uncertain effects on long-run bank solvency. They are also clear restrictions on competition, both as between banks themselves and between banks and other financial institutions; and their harmful effects are well known.[56]

If solvency considerations are ruled out, there is no obvious reason to prohibit the payment of interest on demand deposits. Indeed, in many cases, such interest is already being paid, either indirectly through the provision of services, or directly through such devices as NOW accounts and Eurodollar accounts. Much the same thing can be said about interest ceilings on savings accounts, although here the arguments are complicated by the introduction of competition between commercial banks and nonbank savings institutions.

The major nonsolvency reason for maintaining interest ceilings on savings deposits is obviously the thrift institution problem—the fear that outright competition between banks and thrift institutions will drive thrift institutions out of business and/or divert savings flows away from housing. The use of specialized institutions to allocate credit has already been discussed, and its effectiveness has been questioned. Further, if activity restrictions are eliminated or eased, specialized financial institutions will probably disappear in any case, so that the thrift institution problem will no longer exist. However, if the decision is made to retain specialized institutions, interest ceilings can still be eliminated. There are alternative ways to keep specialized institutions viable. For example, thrifts (as well as banks) could be permitted to use variable-rate mortgages. The pros and cons of this solution have been discussed extensively in the literature, and there is no need to rehash them here.[57] Our conclusion is that there is neither a sound solvency nor an important nonsolvency reason to retain interest ceilings.

---

56. See Pyle, N. 37 *supra*; White, N. 49 *supra*.

57. See D. Jaffee, "What to do About Savings and Loan Associations," J. Money, Credit & Banking, 537–550 (Nov. 1974); Cambs, "Variable Rate Mortgages—Their Potential in the U.S.," J. Money, Credit & Banking, 245–251 (May 1975). Interest ceilings also almost certainly have been the major reason for the "credit crunches" of 1966 and 1969–1970.

The elimination of interest ceilings, besides increasing competition,

will have another very important social benefit: It will prevent the
erosion of the effectiveness of monetary policy in a world with electronic fund transfer systems (a world that may not be too distant).
Without the freedom to pay competitive interest rates on demand and
savings deposits, the definition of "money" will become less certain
and the ability of the Federal Reserve to control it even less certain.[58]

*Reliance on Balance Sheet Controls.* A central tenet of our policy recommendations thus far is that regulators should rely more on a combination of liquidity and equity capital requirements to maintain bank
solvency at the desired level. We have argued that these controls are
effective and that other solvency regulations are unlikely to be as
effective. A remaining question is whether greater reliance on these
controls (or higher equity capital and liquidity requirements, if necessary) will impose significant costs on society. If so, the gains from
eliminating the other regulations must be weighed against these additional costs.

Recent developments in the theory of finance suggest that balance
sheet controls are likely to impose small costs on society. In particular,
in a world of perfect capital markets, without taxes and without bankruptcy costs, the allocation of resources will be independent of the
balance sheets adopted by firms (or mandated by regulation). "Higher"
equity capital requirements, for example, will reduce both stockholder
returns and risk in a way that will leave total stockholder wealth and
total investment unchanged—the allocation of resources will be
unaffected.[59]

In a world with taxes and bankruptcy costs, the issue is less clear. To
begin with, the allocation of resources will then be partially determined
by the tax structure, even in the absence of regulation. Second, the
imposition of "higher" capital requirements on banks will clearly
reduce the after-tax return in banking relative to risk, so that less
resources will flow to banking. The problem of determining the social
costs associated with this reallocation, however, is that we must compare two "second-best" allocations, and as usual, we have little to say
about this kind of trade-off. Nevertheless, in a world of taxes, it does
seem appropriate to point out that any misallocation of resources will,
in all likelihood, be partly due to the existence of taxes, so that any
undesirable allocative consequences of balance sheet controls can, in
principle, be "undone" by appropriate changes in the tax system. It is,

---

**58.** Probably, it also will be necessary for the Federal Reserve to pay interest on the reserve
balances kept with it by financial institutions in order to keep them from leaving the
system (or not joining it). For a fuller discussion of this issue, see Phillips, N. 50 *supra.*

**59.** See Modigliani and Miller, "The Cost of Capital, Corporation Finance, and the Theory of
Investment," 48 Am. Econ. Rev., No. 3, 261–297 (June 1958).

after all, not the balance sheet controls per se that cause the misalloca-tion but the combining of these controls with a tax structure that encourages the adoption of certain balance sheet positions that would not otherwise be attractive. In sum, the case that balance sheet controls impose important costs on society seems weak.

This is not to say that such controls will not impose significant *private* costs on financial institutions. For example, at present, interest payments are deductible from taxable corporate income, so that if a financial institution increases its ratio of debt plus deposits to equity, its taxes will fall. This tax saving is a major private benefit to extensive use of debt.[60] Hence, if financial institutions are required to hold more equity, the major private cost will be higher taxes.

Similarly, the imposition of liquidity requirements on financial insti-tutions may result in private costs, but not in social costs. If financial institutions are required to hold more liquidity than they would other-wise, there will be private costs in the form of lower earnings, but we would not expect a significant reallocation of resources to occur. Greater commercial bank purchases of, say, treasury bills will only result in the withdrawal of other buyers from this market; and the fungibility of credit assures that credit allocation will not significantly affect real spending.[61]

In sum, present knowledge suggests that the social costs associated with anticompetitive solvency regulations are likely to be much greater than those associated with balance sheet controls, and that significant social benefits can be derived from either abolishing or relaxing sol-vency regulations that restrict competition.

## Use of Variable Instead of Uniform Insurance Premiums

PROBLEMS WITH THE PRESENT INSURANCE SYSTEM

The present uniform-premium insurance system has two intrinsic problems. First, as discussed above, it creates a socially detrimental set of incentives for bank managers: It induces them to reduce their capital and increase the riskiness of their assets. Thus, in the absence of solvency regulations to maintain adequate levels of liquidity and capi-tal, particularly equity capital, the entire banking system could become

---

60. Modigliani and Miller, "Corporate Income Taxes and the Cost of Capital: A Correction," Am. Econ. Rev. 433–443 (June 1963); and Scott, "A Theory of Optimal Capital Structure," 7 Bell J. Econ., No. 1, 33–54 (Spring 1976). In the personal tax structure, capital gains are taxed at a lower rate than ordinary income. Many argue that this reduces the tax benefits a corporation ultimately reaps from the issuance of debt, e.g., Merton Miller, "Debt and Taxes," 32 J. Finance, No. 2, 261–276 (May 1977). The issue is empirical. To the extent that this is true, it reduces the private costs that a financial institution, forced to hold equity capital, might bear.

61. See N. 51 *supra* and related discussion.

unsound; and this can happen even though depositors are confident

about the safety of their deposits.

The second problem is that under the present system, regulators have difficulty controlling banks. Although present capital and liquidity controls may, in theory, be adequate to maintain bank soundness, the historical evidence suggests that banks (and particularly large banks) have, nevertheless, continually decreased their capital and liquidity positions, despite the wishes of regulators. [62] The reasons for this trend are complex, but at least part of the answer lies with the inadequacy of the traditional regulatory tools: sanctions to enforce balance sheet constraints, such as denial of insurance, are so severe that regulators are reluctant to use them until it is too late.[63] Thus, although adequate controls may exist, regulators are often reluctant to use them to enforce existing regulations.

BENEFITS OF A VARIABLE-PREMIUM SYSTEM

The use of a variable- rather than a uniform-premium insurance system can reduce the severity of both these problems.[64] First, it alters managerial incentives in a favorable way. Premiums that are lower for conservative banks and higher for risky banks encourage managerial decisions that maintain soundness. Indeed, if variable insurance premiums could be set often enough and accurately enough (so that the premium-risk structure were exactly correct), the use of variable premiums would completely eliminate the moral-hazard problem.

Second, a variable premium provides regulators with a "pricing" tool that may have several advantages. To begin with, the activity of continually setting (and changing) insurance premiums will force regulators to focus much more sharply on the determinants of the soundness of individual financial institutions. In addition, changing a bank's insurance premium, especially if it is a common occurrence, will not be nearly as severe as would denying it insurance entirely, so that regulators may be less reluctant to respond to poor management practices.

---

62. Total bank capital dropped from 9.1 percent of total assets in 1960 to 8.1 percent in 1975; and the ratio of total capital to loans dropped from nearly 20 percent to 14.3 percent over the same period. Also, for the largest 15 holding companies, debt capital increased to almost 30 percent of total capital. See also Peltzman, "Capital Investment," N. 17 *supra*; and Horvitz, "Failures of Large Banks," N. 4 *supra*, especially Table 2-2.

63. For a similar view, see Mayer, "Should Large Banks Be Allowed to Fail?" J. Financial & Quantitative Analysis 603–610 (Nov. 1975).

64. Variable-premium deposit insurance has been proposed by others. See, for example, Mayer, "A Graduated Deposit Insurance Plan," 47 Rev. of Econ. & Statistics 114–116 (Feb. 1965); Shapiro and White, "A Graduated Deposit Insurance Plan: Some Comments," 47 Rev. of Econ. & Statistics 116 (Feb. 1965); Meltzer, "Major Issues in the Regulation of Financial Institutions," 75 J. Political Economy 482–501 (Aug. 1967); Tussing, "Meaningful Bank Failures: A Proposal," 18 J. Industrial Econ., No. 3, 242–254 (July 1970).

The most common criticism of a variable-premium system is that it would be difficult or impossible to set the premiums.[65] It is true that, historically, there have not been enough bank failures to establish an actuarial system. More important, the relevant failure data one would need is the loss experience in a market *without* detailed solvency regulation but *with* a viable deposit insurance scheme. Such data, obviously, do not exist. Nevertheless, there are other plausible ways to set premium levels. Government examiners already assess the riskiness of individual financial institutions in order to determine the appropriate regulatory actions. Indeed, regulatory authorities already use objective risk-classification schemes.[66] Further, regulatory agencies, as well as others, are currently developing procedures for assessing risk in financial institutions that are increasingly sophisticated, accurate, and objective.[67] While there may be initial design costs in developing a risk classification system and in relating the insurance premium structure to it, these costs are likely to be relatively small.[68] Thus, the technical, economic, and regulatory difficulties involved in establishing a variable-premium insurance system appear surmountable.

ADMINISTRATION OF A VARIABLE-PREMIUM SYSTEM

Setting variable insurance premiums on a regular basis requires the frequent collection and interpretation of data from each insured institution. Since most of, if not all, the required data already are being collected and interpreted by regulators, the administration of a variable-premium system could rely primarily on the regulatory apparatus in place.

Two administrative issues may, however, arise. First, banks in high premium classifications, or banks whose premiums are increased, may protest that they have been treated unfairly. Such charges may make

---

65. See Scott and Mayer, "Risk and Regulation in Banking: Some Proposals for Federal Deposit Insurance Reform," 23 Stan. L. Rev., 857–902 (May 1971). Also Tussing, N. 64 *supra.*

66. For a description of the capital adequacy formula used by the Federal Reserve System, see Bank Examination Dep't, Fed. Res. Bank of New York, *A Measure of Minimum Capital Adequacy* (Mimeographed 1952).

67. For example, Sinkey, "A Multivariate Statistical Analysis of the Characteristics of Problem Banks," J. Finance, 853–868 (Sept. 1970); Altman, Haldeman, and Narayanan, "ZETA Analysis: A New Model to Identify Bankruptcy Risk of Corporations," 1 J. Banking & Finance, 29–54 (June 1977); and Merton, "An Analytic Derivation of the Cost of Deposit Insurance and Loan Guarantees: An Application of Modern Option Pricing Theory," 1 J. Banking & Finance, 1–11 (June 1977).

68. Using only one percent of the net annual premium income for the FDIC and FSLIC would provide more than $2 million, more than enough to develop the system. See Scott and Mayer, N. 65, *supra* at 893.

regulators reluctant to change premiums. Larger banks and banks with more political clout also may be able to obtain favorable treatment.[69] A completely accurate risk classification of all banks, however, is not necessary to insure the viability of either the insurance fund or the financial system. It is sufficient if premiums are accurate on average; the system will remain viable as long as there are no systematic errors in the setting of premiums. But, to reduce administrative problems (and possible unfairness), the risk-classification scheme should be as objective as possible, even if somewhat arbitrary. This will help to divert the charges of discriminatory treatment toward the premium structure itself, which would actually be a positive development.

Second, there is the question of whether the premium rates levied on individual banks should be publicly disclosed. We believe that there are strong reasons why they should be. There will obviously be opposition to public disclosure from high-risk banks, and from banks that may be threatened with being placed in a high-risk classification. Regulators, too, may wish to avoid the public attention that will accompany such disclosure. Nevertheless, public disclosure will provide more information to the private capital markets, which are important under both the existing and the proposed regulatory system, because they reinforce the discipline imposed by regulators. If private capital markets are sufficiently informed, riskier institutions will find it more costly to raise external debt and equity capital relative to sounder institutions. If these markets do not receive sufficient information to perform this function, the burden of maintaining bank soundness will fall solely on government regulators. Different insurance ratings, while not perfect, clearly contain information useful to suppliers of capital and should be discussed openly. (In general, nondisclosure is inappropriate for a regulatory system which relies on *partial* deposit insurance, since the effectiveness of such a system depends importantly on the existence of a well-informed private capital market.)

Public disclosure will have additional benefits. If regulators disclose their rating scheme, and if it is consistent and objective, charges by individual banks that they are being treated unfairly are less likely to arise. There will also be more pressure to develop a defensible and—it is to be hoped—a better premium-classification scheme. In addition, disclosure will encourage public discussion of institutional practices affecting soundness, which should result in more sophistication about these practices. Last, disclosure of how regulators respond to a bank's activities—or change in the bank's insurance premium—will act as a restraint on discriminatory and arbitrary regulatory action.

Would disclosure reduce public confidence in the financial system? We think not. The confidence of both insured and uninsured depositors returned quickly after recent large bank failures, and recent public

---

69. Scott and Mayer believe this to be the main drawback of a variable premium system, *id.*

disclosures of substantial bank losses around the world have disrupted, but not incapacitated, financial markets. (Indeed, given the efficiency with which regulators have handled these problems, depositor confidence may have increased.) In any case, it seems likely that the reaction of insured depositors to disclosure of bank premiums will not be one of panic but of indifference, while uninsured depositors, creditors, and stockholders will just as clearly not be indifferent. But that is the whole point. The confidence of these suppliers of capital in some banks will be greater than in others. Further, a highly informed capital market should be more efficient than a poorly informed market, so that the result may be more confidence in the system as a whole, not less. Finally, in the event of an irrational bank run by uninsured depositors, there is always the lender-of-last-resort.

The significance of the disclosure of insurance premium classifications may also be easily overstated. Such disclosure may not add much information to that already available to sophisticated (uninsured) creditors. Further, even if it is viewed as highly significant information, it will still not be the only determinant of an institution's cost of capital. Additional information will still be required to value uninsured debt and equity.

SOLVENCY REGULATION UNDER A VARIABLE-PREMIUM SYSTEM

Although a variable-premium system appears to be both viable and feasible, there may still be some role for balance sheet controls under such a system. In practice, a variable-premium system may be insufficient to offset completely the moral-hazard risks introduced by the provision of deposit insurance, for two reasons: Perfectly accurate assessments of risk may not be possible, and it may not be feasible or "efficient" to adjust premiums frequently. Until regulators have had sufficient experience to evaluate the problems associated with these operational difficulties, it would seem prudent to continue to use balance sheet controls to limit managerial options. Ultimately, it is possible that even these will be unnecessary.

## 100-Percent Insurance

Should the government require banks to insure all their deposits, or just some of them, such as under the present $40,000 account limit? There are, at least, three arguments in favor of 100-percent insurance.[70] First, because various state regulations affect the proportion of uninsured deposits that are effectively guaranteed at present, 100-percent coverage would be more equitable. Second, broader insurance coverage

---

**70.** A useful discussion of the pros and cons of 100 percent insurance, along with several possible proposals, appears in Barnett, Horvitz, and Silverberg, "Deposit Insurance: The Present System and Some Alternatives," 94 Banking L. J., 304–332 (April 1977).

would further reduce the likelihood of bank runs. In particular, the

possibility of a run by large depositors would be eliminated. Third, 100-percent insurance would facilitate the disclosure of financial information relating to specific institutions. That is, with 100-percent insurance, regulators will not have to be as concerned about precipitating a bank run by the disclosure of unfavorable information. (Of course, such information would also be less interesting to depositors.)

There is, however, an important drawback to 100-percent insurance: It will increase the moral-hazard risks implicit in a deposit insurance system. If large depositors are also indifferent to bank soundness, all market discipline will disappear. In such a world, balance sheet controls will be even more necessary and variable premiums even more desirable.[71] Our judgment is that it would be unwise to substitute completely the judgment of regulators for the proven discipline of the marketplace.

## Private Insurance

The analysis in this paper does not contain an a priori reason to conclude that the private provision of deposit insurance could not work. Conceivably, some or all of the insurance provided by federal agencies could be provided instead by private insurance companies.[72] Although the cost of insurance for individual institutions is already low, the substitution of profit-maximizing insurers for nonprofit insurers may increase efficiency and reduce costs still further, unless there are substantial economies of scale associated with the provision of such insurance. More important, competition induced by having a number of private insurance companies engaged in the determination of premium levels may result in a more accurate assessment of bank soundness and risk.

Insurance companies can also protect themselves from moral-hazard risks by requiring various agreements with respect to a bank's capital and liquidity (as well as other aspects of its balance sheet), similar to the nonprice covenants customarily imposed on borrowers by creditors in loan agreements (and similar to the present balance sheet regulations). Deft use of these tools seemingly could provide private insurers with as much protection as they would a government insurer. However, the intangible effect on depositor confidence of having a government insurer rather than a private insurer, no matter how sound, is difficult to assess and could, in practice, be quite significant.

Even in a private deposit-insurance system, government would still have two important functions: to act as lender-of-last-resort, and to

---

71. Even without 100-percent coverage, uninsured creditors may still be insured de facto, which also increases hazard risk.

72. See, for example, Meltzer, N. 64 *supra* and Scott and Mayer, N. 65 *supra*.

require that all banks obtain deposit insurance from some private insurer. It is necessary to make deposit insurance compulsory because of the "free-rider" problem. Deposit insurance has the character of a public good: It bestows benefits upon all banks because of its effect in eliminating bank runs, whether or not they themselves are insured. Consequently, all banks must be made to share the cost of these benefits. Finally, although it is not clear that a lender-of-last-resort is even needed, the presence of such a government facility obviously will inspire public confidence in the insurance system. (As we mentioned earlier, however, such a facility will exist, in any case, as part of the governmental mechanism necessary to implement monetary policy.)

## CONCLUSION

Analysis of the present structure of solvency regulation strongly suggests that it is more elaborate than required to guarantee the soundness of the banking system. Many of the existing regulations are ineffective and of little value, and some may even be detrimental to soundness. Further, these regulations impose a significant cost on society, mainly because of the inhibiting effect they have on competition. Our general conclusion is that selected deregulation of the banking industry would enhance social welfare.

Our main conclusions with respect to the erection of a better regulatory structure are, at minimum:

1. Retain some type of federal deposit insurance system.

2. Retain and place greater reliance upon balance sheet controls, especially liquidity and equity capital requirements, which we believe are adequate to maintain bank soundness.

3. Eliminate all restrictions on branching.

4. Eliminate most, and possibly all, restrictions on *de novo* entry.

5. Eliminate price controls, such as those imposed on the payment of interest on demand and savings deposits.

6. Relax activity restrictions to an extent consistent with other (nonsolvency) social goals.

7. Apply a vigorous antitrust policy to financial institutions.

These changes need not alter the soundness of the banking system in one direction or the other. Their main thrust is to increase the social efficiency of the regulatory system, primarily by increasing the degree of competition among banks and between banks and other financial institutions. Under the proposed system, bank soundness can still be set at any level that is desired by altering liquidity and capital requirements.

Our analysis also suggests that efficiency may be further enhanced if a variable-premium deposit insurance system is used instead of the present uniform-premium system. Such a system can be made operational with little change in the present regulatory structure, and its use may permit more effective control of the moral-hazard risks implicit in a deposit-insurance system. Finally, whatever the type of deposit-insurance system used, we do not believe that 100-percent insurance coverage is wise.

# COMMENTARY

Paul M. Horvitz, *Assistant to the Chairman,*
*Federal Deposit Insurance Corporation, Washington, D.C.*

Literature on the regulation of financial institutions is probably the weakest in the field of finance, consisting in large part of unverified assertions and untested hypotheses concerning the appropriate approach to achieving unspecified objectives. This has continued to the present time, even though there have been vast strides in finance theory in recent years. The attempts by Edwards and Scott to analyze the regulations pertaining to the solvency of financial institutions in a rigorous manner is an admirable objective.[1]

The authors begin by setting forth a classification of solvency regulations into restrictions on entry, on activity, on pricing, on balance sheet relationships, and on self-dealing. This is a useful and appropriate classification, though as the authors note, the reasons for the continuation of some of these regulations lie in other considerations than safety and soundness. Restrictions on entry and pricing are favored by most bankers because restrictions limit competition and improve bank earnings. By so doing, they reduce bank failures, which makes a nice rationale for keeping these restrictions. Even so, it is difficult for those favoring such restrictions to argue with the Edwards-Scott conclusion that the most important regulations on banks, from the point of view of safety and soundness, are the balance sheet constraints.

The desirability of bank regulation is generally taken for granted. It is widely believed that bank failures are more calamitous than failures

---

1. Although this paper comments only on the Edwards-Scott paper included in this volume, in the original seminar their paper also incorporated much of the material now contained in their paper, *Bank Solvency Regulation in the U.S.: A Theoretical Analysis*, Research Paper, No. 190, (Columbia Univ. School of Business 1977).

of other businesses for reasons that are rarely spelled out.[2] Edwards and Scott examine carefully the reasons for social concern with minimizing the risks of bank failure. Their conclusions are sound, though I would give more weight to their "savings asset" argument. The availability of a risk-free asset is important in modern portfolio theory. Edwards and Scott underestimate the loss to bank depositors if such assets are not available from banks. Their suggestion that bank customers may be indifferent between a riskless asset and one with risk but paying a higher rate (reflecting, in part, the saving in insurance premiums) must recognize that the current cost of federal deposit insurance is only about one-thirtieth of 1 percent.

The discussion of the "payments system" rationale also does not make clear the extent of the resource misallocation due to our present regulatory system. Banks cannot pay interest on demand deposits, so they compete by providing checking services at below-cost prices. Bank customers devote resources to minimizing the size of their demand deposits (a socially wasteful activity, since such deposits can be created at low cost) and write an excessive number of checks (since they are not bearing the cost of handling those checks).[3]

Edwards and Scott note that an important part of the existing regulatory structure is the existence of a lender-of-last-resort, the Federal Reserve. Their initial definition of this function stresses that it is directed at stability of the financial *system,* a definition in accord with the traditional central bank lender-of-last-resort responsibility described by Thornton and Bagehot. In recent years, however, the Federal Reserve has shifted its concern to *individual banks.* This raises the question of whether lending $1.5 billion to Franklin National Bank is an appropriate exercise of lender-of-last-resort responsibilities at a time in which there was no general banking panic or liquidity pressure (i.e., at the time of the Franklin loan, no solvent banks were having difficulty obtaining funds).

The Edwards-Scott analysis leads to a conclusion that I can easily endorse: "All of the social goals of solvency regulation can be attained by simply adopting a sound deposit-insurance scheme." It is unfortunate that the paper did not conclude at this point. Having reached a sound conclusion on the role of deposit insurance, the authors go on to

---

2. Though, on one occasion, I argued that "the closing of the only bank in town is less serious than the closing of the mill in a one-mill town." *Monetary Policy and the Financial System,* 106 (Prentice-Hall, Inc., New York, 1974).

3. This paper focuses on the minimum regulation needed and does not analyze the social waste of regulations in excess of the necessary minimum. Perhaps some amplification of why elimination of redundant regulation is important would be useful. Let me cite one example. Given the demand deposit competitive situation noted above, it is difficult to introduce an improved technology for handling payments. Since the bank customer is not bearing the cost of the present payments system, he is not likely to be interested in electronic funds transfer systems whose major social advantage is lower cost.

draw some questionable conclusions as to the workings of alternative deposit-insurance schemes.

The discussion of the "moral hazard" in deposit insurance is not convincing. Edwards and Scott argue that bank management will respond to level-premium (such as we now have) insurance by increasing their risk-taking, and even if premiums are increased, "banks will behave in a way that will result in an *upward spiral* of risk-taking" [italics added]. I do not see the logic of this. If I insure my house against burglary, I may become less careful about locking doors. But if the insurance company raises my premium, I have no incentive to become more careless. I may drive less carefully if my car is insured, but that is not a function of the level of the premium. Likewise, the insured bank does not have to fear that a risky investment policy will result in withdrawals of deposits by nervous depositors, so the level of risk-taking will increase. But this does not impair the soundness of the deposit-insurance system (though if that level of risk-taking is considered excessive, it will require solvency regulations).

Edwards and Scott conclude from their analysis that a variable-rate premium insurance scheme is preferable. This is a topic that has long been argued in the literature.[4] It cannot easily be disposed of here, but a few comments may be relevant. Such a system would involve a higher average premium than the present system. Since the present system involves premiums of only about one-thirtieth of 1 percent, there is not much room to reduce premiums for banks opting for a conservative investment policy. It is hard to see the advantage of that, though Edwards and Scott claim that the present premium level "has not been high enough for the FDIC to accumulate a large reserve fund." In my view, the FDIC reserve fund is very large (and probably excessive). Edwards and Scott make the irrelevant comparison between the size of the fund and the total deposits of banks that failed in recent years. The relevant comparison is between the fund and the ultimate *losses* involved in these failures.[5]

The usual objection to a variable insurance premium is the difficulty of setting the rate structure. It is impossible to set an actuarially accurate premium structure that would lead to an efficient allocation of resources, but I would not necessarily rule out the idea of variable-rate insurance. It might be feasible to establish a simple, seemingly arbitrary system that has the effect of putting banks into, say, three, four, or five risk categories. These might be based on a few simple ratios relating such variables as capital ratios, asset mix, income ratios, etc., without attempting to defend the premiums in actuarial terms. Rather, the premiums would be related to factors the supervisors consider relevant, and their level would be set so as to bring about some desired

---

4. Cf. Barnett, Horvitz, and Silverberg, "Deposit Insurance: The Present System and Some Alternatives," Banking L. J. (April 1977), and the references cited therein.

5. Thus, FDIC net income in each year exceeds the total losses in all failures since 1934.

result in terms of bank portfolios. Insofar as a bank placed into a high-risk class was unhappy, it could adjust its policies to change its risk category. In that sense, there would be an element of choice in such a system.

The premiums set under such a system, and the levels of particular financial ratios, would be essentially arbitrary. But that is not far removed from our present system. The authors make the valid point that the problem of setting variable rates is no more difficult, conceptually, than evaluating the capital adequacy of individual banks—something bank examiners presumably do every day. In fact, examiners do not do this very well. When they make mistakes and demand higher capital than the banker thinks necessary, the banker has several options: He can argue, stall, compromise, or refuse to raise capital. These options would not be available if the bank received a bill for higher insurance premiums. My point is simply that if a government agency does not know what it is doing, it is better not to give it a lot of power to enforce its rules. The "mushiness" of the present system, whereby the examiner must nag and harass to get the bank to meet his view of capital adequacy is better than one that would give greater enforcement powers to the FDIC.

Edwards and Scott also argue that private insurance may be feasible. While I have no objection to private deposit insurance, I fail to see the advantage. We have already noted the low cost of the present insurance system. It is hard to imagine private insurance as offering great cost savings. More important, how would such a system get started? In the view of Edwards and Scott, a deposit insurance system needs a very large reserve fund. Where would that come from?

In any case, Edwards and Scott note the possible need for some government regulation of private insurance companies. If all we do is add another layer of regulation to the structure, it is hard to see a net gain.

My criticisms of the Edwards-Scott conclusions on deposit insurance are aimed at what is essentially a specific implementation of the results of their analysis. Their principal conclusions as to the importance of deposit insurance and the redundancy of most of the types of banking regulation we now have are sound. Those who espouse entry controls and pricing and actuarial constraints should be required to defend them on grounds other than their essentiality to preserving bank soundness.

# COMMENTARY

William F. Young, *James L. Dohr*
*Professor of Law, Columbia University*

We have been informed of the objectives of "detailed solvency regulations" for banks: They include liquidity, support for the payments system, and accessibility of savings. Other arrangements serving more or less the same objectives are a lender-of-last-resort facility and deposit insurance. My assignment is to comment on deposit insurance.

In the paper presented to us by Professors Edwards and Scott, the question is persistently raised whether or not a viable deposit insurance system is workable *without* detailed insolvency controls. I counted some half-dozen allusions to it, somewhat plaintive in tone. Doubtless, it is a serious question, seriously intended.

Unfortunately, I do not have the answer. Much would depend, of course, upon the character of the insuring system. Is it to be compulsory or not? Is it to be a "social" insuring system? Would private insurers have an entree into the field—with or without competition from a government-sponsored enterprise? To what extent would the supposed insurance be provided on the mutual plan? May we suppose that experience rating plays a part? About these and other questions, we are left free to speculate; for the only clear specification given in the paper is that, unlike deposit insurance provided by the system in place, the insurance envisaged would be written on a variable-rating plan. That is to say, factors of risk other than amounts on deposit would be taken into account in pricing the insurance. The key submission, then, is that *underwriting* in relation to deposit insurance largely may serve the objectives mentioned above, in lieu of detailed solvency regulations.

(The paper itself does not disclose that the authors envisage a private market in deposit insurance. It does not allude to possibilities of coinsurance, reinsurance, or the like. Professor Edwards indicated, in an oral presentation, that private, and compulsory, insurance is contemplated.)

Underwriting has won great kudos among us as an efficient way to distribute the burden of risk assessment. It is generally praised for encouraging enterprise. Ventures are undertaken the more readily because some of the risks may be laid off through insurance—notably those that appear imponderable to the adventurers. One supposes instinctively that professional underwriting, in a market context, conserves the exertions devoted by a community to risk-assessment. Professors Edwards and Scott have pointed out forcefully that deposit insurance, as we have it now, is *not* conducted in a market context. For that reason, it may fail to realize the whole potential that it has for economizing on risk-assessment. Obviously, savers and others who utilize bank deposits do not (in that role) fit the model of adventurers who might be encouraged to accept risks by having access to underwriting services; yet it is safe to suppose that the fact and the degree of deposit insurance affects materially the behavior of depositors and prospective depositors in relation to the risk of bank failure. Considerations of efficiency in risk-assessment have certainly contributed to insuring plans, voluntarily and privately instituted, which cater to very much the same classes comprised by savings-account depositors. (At present we are asked to attend only to bank deposit insurance; but it will be appropriate to notice in a moment that arguments germane to bank operations may apply also to those of other financial institutions.) It comes easy to suppose that through reliance on underwriting, we can increase efficiency in the necessary work of assessing risks of bank failure.

But efficiency is not the only consideration affecting views about underwriting. The view that Brandeis took toward fidelity insurance is an excellent illustration of this fact. He thought it an abomination. Among the first duties of a manager, he thought, was that of knowing the character of his employees; to have them bonded is to flout that duty.[1] Brandeis was moved by moral considerations. His concern is not comprehended in the expression "moral hazard," as the expression is commonly used in insurance circles. However, the fact of moral hazard and the Brandeisian conception of fiduciary responsibility are both aspects of the important public question: Where in a society should particular functions of risk assessment be assigned? As everyone knows, bargaining processes do not always make assignments that suit

---

1. "[T]o him it was the very negation of managerial responsibility to divest itself of the duty and the risk of knowing the character of trusted employees." Freund, *On Understanding the Supreme Court* 54 (Little, Brown, Boston, 1949).

"For Brandeis, the insurance principle had taken over too large a sector of modern life, accentuating the drift, already too strong, toward the anonymity and the obscuring of responsibility that accompanies giant corporate or public enterprises." Freund, *On Law and Justice* 134 (Belknap Press of Harvard Univ. Press, Cambridge, 1968).

us; and when they do not, a legislative assignment is likely to occur. A rather recent example is the institution of FAIR plans, whereby fire coverage and some others are made available in blighted urban areas. In this instance, the decision was made to break out the catastrophe risk. Underwriters for the plans have a standing order to suppress consideration of environmental risks, with a view to moderating the costs of insuring through the plans. Here, again, a moral principle is at work—one that might have appealed to Brandeis. It is that a property owner ought not to have an undue burden cast on him by the neglect of neighboring properties, but he should be held to account only for risks that are in some measure his to control.

A salient point about deposit insurance as we have it is that the risk of catastrophe figures largely in its design. In this context, "catastrophe" signifies the contagion of a bank run. Edwards and Scott acknowledge most explicitly that underwriting, in relation to deposit insurance, must contemplate widespread bank runs, as a risk to be evaluated. This is precisely the rub, of course, in a proposal for variable-rate deposit insurance. From the standpoint of a single bank's management, such a prospect has the character of an environmental risk. If we disregard differences of size among banks, provisionally, then we may say that the *only* risk actually underwritten at present by deposit insurance is the environmental risk. In underwriting terms, the effect of introducing variable rating would be to "package" this risk with others, the most notable one being that of a bank's bad investment strategy.

As the foregoing paragraph suggests, one way of approaching the Edwards-Scott proposal is to ask whether or not underwriting of the bank-run risk should be encouraged separately from other risks (bad management) that deposit insurance presently encompasses. This question assumes that the managerial risk and what I have termed the environmental, or "catastrophe," risk are so far distinctive that underwriters could assign separate values to them. Given this assumption—a problematical one—then, in principle, I suppose that the underwriters should be encouraged to do so. Otherwise, we should not gain the full benefits of a private insurance market in allocating the function of risk-assessments. However, it is not clear to me that Edwards and Scott would have us seize those benefits to the full extent that is possible. They seem to assume that underwriters would have no techniques at hand for dealing with the bank-run risk, other than a catastrophe loading of premiums. They contemplate compulsory insuring of deposits, presumably under standardized terms. They are evidently preoccupied with the problem mentioned above: whether or not elements of the failure risk are divisible for rating purposes. The issue would look very different to them if it were assumed that a deposit insurer had no access to such sources for recouping a loss as, for example, the bank's capital accounts and insurance against employees' infidelity. To characterize their work this way does nothing to discredit it, naturally, but does make the comment that Edwards and Scott have set constraints on

the design of deposit insurance for the special purpose of making it do duty in lieu of solvency regulation. Or perhaps it is fairer to say that they would adapt the existing design for that purpose. In either case, they do not profess to explore at large the merits of underwriting in relation to bank failure.

Over the last quarter of a century, private insurers have attended carefully to the packaging of risks, as a means of reducing transaction costs in the marketing of insurance. Much might be said about the merits of packaging the bank-run risk with other risks of banking, and we have reason to hope that Edwards and Scott will pursue the subject. Given only the usual objects in designing insurance, the idea would not attract much enthusiasm, I daresay. Some time ago, when brokerage houses sought to insure their customers' accounts in the private market, the complaint was raised that the carriers would deal only with the largest houses. Since this insurance is roughly comparable to bank deposit insurance, the experience does not augur well for deposit underwriting in the private sector.

The discussion so far exhibits chiefly what the appeal of underwriting is, in relation to bank failure: It is precisely as a surrogate for "detailed insolvency regulation" that one would espouse variable-rating for deposit insurance. So, evidently, it is regarded by Edwards and Scott. Their question, be it remembered, is not whether such a system is meritorious, but whether it is "viable." In the question itself, there is an assumption that the current assignments of risk-evaluation in relation to bank failure are not satisfactory. That is the proposition, indeed, of the paper before us. As the authors come to examine a reassignment of the function, away from the legions of bank examiners and toward underwriters, they will doubtless draw lessons from the history of the insurance business. One of the certain lessons is that insurers readily succumb to the temptation to *control* the risks they assume, adding that control to the function of *assessing* risks, which is underwriting in the proper sense. The phenomenon was noted in a classic dissertation at Columbia 75 years ago:

> Insurers of boilers have their inspectors, fire insurance companies have their patrols, burglary insurance companies their private watchmen, and so on through the list. The part of the premium which is used in carrying out these protective measures ought not to be considered as part of the cost of insurance.[2]

I believe there is a lesson for us in the proclivity of insurance managers to exercise risk control, when thinking of deposit insurance. Though we may mean to exploit the insurance mechanism for the purpose of

---

2. Willett, *The Economic Theory of Risk and Insurance* (Ph.D. thesis, Columbia Univ., New York 1901).

displacing solvency regulation, we must contemplate the possibility that the expectation is self-defeating. And this prospect does not depend on whether the insurance managers are public officials; for, as we also know from experience, many of the legal safeguards of our lives and fortunes are the handiwork of private insurers.

Deposit insurance is singularly exempt from the various objections that may be leveled against many other forms of insurance. Losses occasioned by bank runs are a prominent (though largely indeterminate) part of the risk transferred, as we have noticed; and since runs feed on the subjective insecurities of depositors, it may be supposed that deposit insurance strongly tends to suppress the risks it covers. That is a grand virtue. It is especially pronounced in the form that deposit insurance presently takes, wherein underwriting is confined to the catastrophe risk. In whatever form, the insurance doubtless induces, among its beneficiaries, a cavalier attitude toward the risks it covers. This was the basis for the complaint that Brandeis made against fidelity insurance, as we have seen. But this complaint hardly applies to deposit insurance, at least so long as modest dollar limits continue to apply; for no one would ask small depositors to embrace the risks that fiduciaries do (or should). Unlike some forms of catastrophe insurance (e.g., dread disease insurance), deposit insurance does not entail heavy transaction costs. In this respect, it has the usual virtue of group insurance. The administration of claims is intrinsically efficient, because the event insured against is a matter of easy and high definition: the suspension of bank payments. In this respect, deposit insurance compares favorably even with life insurance, as to which the fact and the cause of death are not infrequently controversial matters. A comparison with credit life insurance suggests itself. And, here again, deposit insurance fares well, for it does not arouse the creditors' incentive—known as reverse competition—to load the premium. (But note that Professors Edwards and Scott may be read to suggest that uniform-rate deposit insurance distorts the incentives of debtor banks; in that form, deposit insurance may well "reverse" competition.)

Taking all these characteristics of deposit insurance together, one may fairly wonder that the scheme is considered to be insurance at all. The institutions subscribing to the federal brand are compelled by the sponsor, in form of law, to advertise their membership. The advertising is supposed to, and presumably does, reduce the incidence of loss. The accessibility of the "insurance" does not induce any enterprise much more hazardous than taking money out of a mattress. (Or, if this be overdrawn, it may become more literally true as the age of electronic fund transfers advances.) These and other curious incidents of deposit insurance may justify us in thinking of the scheme as one of *pseudo-insurance*. But that is not to depreciate it. It is an important and valuable institution.

Much of the importance and peculiarity of deposit insurance depends upon the fact that its patrons are a special breed. (It is banks that Edwards and Scott have brought into the focus; but even if some

kindred institutions such as credit unions were included, the set of
subscribers would still be sharply defined.) The rationale for singling
out these patrons is partly the existence of the solvency regulations that
we are taught to suspect. If the regulations be subtracted, is there still a
sufficient rationale for *bank* deposit insurance? Or for some other
chosen set of target customers? The principle of variable-rate insurance,
if accepted, naturally raises the question, Variable as among whom? If
underwriters can successfully discriminate among banks, with respect
to the risk of failure, can they not also discriminate among a good many
other firms more or less involved in the country's payments system? I
set these questions, not so much for answers, as to put a point upon a
simple observation. It is this: The choice between "uniform" and
"variable" rating of deposit insurance ought to rest on some reflection
about the range of entitlements that we wish to reinforce by the
insuring arrangement. In the absence of detailed solvency regulation—
which has helped to define that range, though it creates its own
expectations—we might choose to place a rather different set of interests under insurance protection. The problem is, in any case, not one to
be solved by efficiency considerations alone. Just as in relation to
fidelity and fire insurance we are entitled to make legislative choices on
other grounds, so are we in relation to deposit insurance. That is
peculiarly so if the device is wanted to assure liquidity of credits and
other great social needs.

Because deposit insurance is an important and valuable arrangement, it is important to allocate its costs, and specify its beneficiaries,
with care and discrimination. One object of the paper before us is to
renew our concern about that. Professor Edwards and Professor Scott
have succeeded in that, with me; and I am certain, at the least, that their
questioning and further deliberations, as promised, are quite justified.

# DISCUSSION

FRANKLIN R. EDWARDS: Thank you, gentlemen. Who would like to ask the first question?

BERNARD SHULL: I was in the Comptroller's Office in the early 1960s when Don Silverman of the San Francisco National Bank was evaluated as a highly competent bank manager. Since George Vojta is here, and he has advocated that the evaluation of management by regulators might be a better way of protecting solvency than specific regulations (such as capital and liquidity requirements), I would like to ask him what he believes to be the competencies needed by bank regulators to evaluate bank management?

GEORGE VOJTA: Current trends within the Comptroller's Office are already moving in this direction. The Comptroller's examination processes are being changed to ones more akin to CPA-type procedures: Instead of going into a direct examination of the loan portfolio—loan by loan—the focus is on the processes by which a bank is managed, with particular emphasis on its control functions. These evaluations will be made on the basis of interaction with bank

---

The discussion here pertains to both the paper in this volume and to a companion paper, Scott and Edwards, *Bank Solvency Regulation in the United States: A Theoretical Analysis*, Research Paper, No. 190 (Columbia Univ. School of Business 1977).

management and will be verified by a direct
sampling procedure, where appropriate.

This is a very constructive development. Scrutinizing a bank's process for asset acquisition, its financial control system, its internal audit system, etc., and determining how all this compares with financial results, is, to my mind, a more relevant supervisory perspective. It boils down to an emphasis on the quality and integrity of management, which will ultimately show up in the bank's profitability.

ROBERT SHAY: In your theoretical model of bank solvency, you distinguish between full access banks and partial access banks. Is it not possible that a full-access bank can, overnight, become a partial-access bank?

JAMES SCOTT: I would argue that under normal conditions— no bank panic, etc.—people lose confidence in a bank only when it reaches the point where its current losses and people's expectations of its future profitability are such that the bank is effectively judged to be insolvent. Insolvency does not occur in a 10-minute period, of course. There may be a six-month or a one-year interval before the corpse of the bank actually falls onto the street, but it is all over when the earnings (losses) fall below the bankruptcy point as we have represented it.

PETER J. KOLESAR: In your analysis, in crisis, certain institutions sell assets while others sell equity, and this dichotomy is often critical to your assessment of the effect of a regulation. Are there data that you can look at to determine whether banks do one or the other, in fact? And what kinds of banks do which?

EDWARDS: Perhaps Paul Horvitz can answer this question.

HORVITZ: I would say that it is more frequent for small banks to resolve their problems by the sale of equity than it is for a large bank. A small bank can raise sufficient money by the sale of equity, to insiders, without making public disclosures. A large bank in difficulty cannot raise equity capital without complying with securities laws, which require disclosure, and disclosure of its conditions might produce a "run," as well as other problems. So, in terms of access to the equity market for a bank in difficulty, small banks may more easily have access than large banks.

SCOTT: Just one caveat. A large bank may still be able to sell debt more easily; and when it sells debt, it is still selling a claim to its future cash flows. Ideally, it might like to sell equity; however, it can raise almost as much money by selling debt and then later replacing the debt with equity.

ALVIN MARTY: I would like to point out that there is no insurance in terms of the real value of the dollar. All proposed insurance schemes cover only nominal values. In that sense, there is an argument for paying interest on demand deposits as a way of insuring the real or commodity value. In your analysis, you say that if you pay interest on demand deposits, you may increase the possibility of loss in nominal values. I would say that paying interest on demand deposits is a way of insulating the opportunity costs of holding the real value of money. And this becomes increasingly important during a period of inflation and variability in rates of inflation.

EDWARDS: Our analysis is focused on the probability of bank failure, and not on the extent of depositor losses. In addition, we think banks should be allowed to pay interest on deposits.

JANUSZ ORDOVER: I have a couple of minor technical points.

As I was listening to the comments made before, it occurred to me that one problem with respect to your theoretical model is that it is static and not dynamic. It might be preferable, perhaps, to model the bankruptcy process as some sort of a statistical model in which the next period earnings are a result of this period's decisions, plus a random element, and then look at how regulatory policies affect this income stream, rather than focus on the next period's income realization.

I am also puzzled by the fact that even though you talk so lovingly about insurance, you do not seem to be too concerned about the moral-hazard problem. Banks can purchase insurance and then undertake various investments, which may or may not increase the probability of their becoming insolvent in the next period and having to be bailed out. So when you talk about insurance, via the depository scheme, you may want to consider the fact that one will need to have a very sophisticated scheme of observing what, in fact, the banks do.

EDWARDS: We are concerned with it but believe that it is not a problem, if you can accurately set risk premiums. If you can set premiums commensurate with the portfolio risk of the bank, and the bank knows that the regulators will walk back into the bank at a future time and reset it, it will not make sense for the bank to increase its portfolio risk. In the long run, the bank will have to go continually to higher and higher risk levels, and the premium will follow. Finally, the bank will reach a point where it will find itself at too high a risk level. By revising its risk and its insurance premium, it will be able to increase its value. In sum, we believe that the moral-hazard problem only occurs if you believe that banks operate in a myopic way.

ORDOVER: I believe it may also occur because of improper monitoring of bank activities. What you are saying is that, over the long run, all thieves are caught.

EDWARDS: That is essentially our argument.

SCOTT: As far as the question of statics versus dynamics is concerned, we really have a dynamic model in the case of the "full access" bank. The mathematics in our theoretical model shows how changes in different kinds of regulations affect future earnings, and how these changes in future earnings impact on the probability of bankruptcy in the coming period, and in every period thereafter. However, with respect to the "partial access" bank, the analysis encompasses only the probability of insolvency for one period ahead.

ROBERT POZEN: I have some problem with your definition of insolvency. You have a formula for it, but as you talk about it, you seem to be referring often to some event that does not have a one-to-one relationship with the formula. You seem to have two insolvency points: one as defined by your formula, and the other defined in almost a psychological way, based on investors' expectations. It seems to me that it is very difficult to capture in any formula the point of insolvency: The critical point is the investors' expectations. Perhaps you could ask the institutional placers of CDs, what are the real factors that determine expectations and the point of insolvency? I do not think your formula for insolvency really captures that critical point.

SCOTT: Our bankruptcy formula for the bank with full access to the capital market, in fact, depends crucially on investor expectations. If losses exceed what investors believe the present value of the bank's future earnings to be, the bank goes bankrupt. Your comments seem to imply that you want the losses to have a second effect. That is, you want to have such losses reduce investors' expectations of future earnings. That is not currently in the model, but I doubt that its incorporation would change any of the model's results.

VOJTA: The phenomenon of expectations is basic. The agent which triggers the ultimate problem can be an investor, a CD placer, or a regulator who makes an assessment and, on the basis of that assessment, derives an expectational conclusion about the bank. The agent could also be a correspondent bank presented with a request for borrowing *in extremis* by its failing bank correspondent.

I think your model does not fully capture this phenomenon.

WILLIAM VICKREY: I am a bit puzzled by the characterization of deposit insurance as such a beautiful form of insurance. If it were so beautiful, without any of the usual problems of insurance, why did we not have it before 1933? And, why do we not have it now with respect to certificates of deposit, in particular? The idea of having a premium that will be adjusted *ex post* by an appraisal of the riskiness of the bank's assets or the riskiness of the bank's overall position, seems to me a little bit like asking the insurers to second-guess all the bank's portfolio decisions. This, in effect, is a modification of the moral-hazard problem. Instead of the bank's having an incentive to engage in more risky investments, which you may have if the premium is fixed, you have an attempt to second-guess what the person who assesses the premium will think about your investment. You will try to invest in assets that are riskier, in fact, than the auditor will think they are. Thus, I do not think you have gotten away from the moral-hazard problem. Accordingly, I am not really convinced that you have dealt with what I think is the essential reason why we did not have private insurance of deposits, which is the difficulty of dealing with the moral-hazard problem, and the lack of a positive countervailing incentive for those who would effectively decide to insure.

HORVITZ: I would like to say something about why we did not have insurance before, and why we do not have 100-percent deposit insurance now.

There has always been, and is now, a lot of opposition to insurance from people who have interests at stake. One hundred percent deposit insurance, for example, changes the relative attractiveness of large banks versus small banks. With 100-percent insurance, those firms or depositors who now prefer to have their $1 million deposits in Citibank would be indifferent as to where they put their deposit—a small bank in Iowa would be just as good. So, it is probably in Citibank's interest not to have 100-percent deposit insurance.

WILLIAM K. JONES: On the question of moral hazard, I think I am correct in saying that insurance would relate to deposits and not to the equity interests of the stockholders of the bank. Nor would it relate to the positions held by the managers in the bank, so that, even in institutions in which there is no equity position, presumably there is an interest in retention of managerial positions on the part of those in control.

These factors clearly affect the inclinations of management to seek riskier investments. After all, their jobs are at stake, and, to the extent that there is an equity interest in the institution, the interest of the equity holders is at stake. Granted, we want some kind of regulatory supervision to prevent self-dealing and fraud. If we have that, we really do not have to worry so much about the problems of differential risk premiums and of managements taking excessive risk, assuming that we have a comprehensive insurance program that is related to deposits.

YOUNG:  I think you are absolutely right. One of the distinctive features of deposit insurance is that it is bought by entities subject to subrogation. That is to say, upon a payout to depositors, the insurance enterprise expects to recover, as far as it can, from the managers— those who chose to place the insurance where they did.

If I may just add to that: It seems to me one problem with deposit insurance is that it segregates one part of the risk facing depositors. I think that management and the owners (stock interests) in banks will insist on fidelity insurance, and on other kinds of insurance, "passing on" the premiums, so to speak. That breaks out a significant part of the total risk that depositors face. And it tends to throw on deposit insurance only what I would call the catastrophe risk or the "environmental" risk—of bank runs and the like.

## CHAPTER THREE

# Alternative Views on Regulating Conflicts of Interest in the Financial Firm

## CONFLICTS OF INTEREST WITHIN THE FINANCIAL FIRM: REGULATORY IMPLICATIONS

Roy A. Schotland, *Professor of Law, Georgetown University*

### INTRODUCTION

*Item:* The sixth largest bank in Washington, D.C., Madison National, had $84 million in deposits and $46.2 million in loans at the end of 1974. It made virtually no home mortgage loans, though 13 other District of Columbia commercial banks, both larger and smaller, did. Less than 10 percent of its loans went to consumers, a much lower proportion than at 15 other commercial banks in the District, including all the larger banks. But, 24 percent of its loans—$11.1 million—went to directors, stockholders, their partners, or former bank employees. (In contrast, at the two largest District of Columbia banks, 7 percent and 9 percent of loans were so made.) All but one of its large (more than $100,000) real estate loans went to members of that group. All the bank's four offices were rented or purchased from directors, major stockholders, or their partners. One of the purchases was at a price approximately $10.75 per square foot higher than paid by the sellers—two directors and the family of a third—when they bought three years earlier, *after* the bank had secured approval for a branch there, and although property prices during that period in that immediate area had declined. Lest there be

---

Since 1972, I have worked under Twentieth Century Fund auspices, with William Cary, Benjamin Cohen, Roger Murray, William Stott, and the Fund's Director, Murray Rossant, on a project to explore conflicts of interest in securities markets. Thus far, we have published monographs by different authors on Broker-Dealers, Investment Bankers, Commercial Bank Trust Departments, Corporate Pension Funds, State and Local Pension Funds, Union Pension Funds, and Nonprofit Institutions. We will publish a book reproducing all of those studies and one more, on Real Estate Investment Trusts, as well as conclusions and recommendations. Those monographs are the sources for factual material in this paper, unless otherwise indicated. While I have benefited immeasurably from work with Cary, *et al.* and the authors of the monographs, the views expressed here are merely my own.

doubt: The bank and persons in question have "distinguished" reputations in the community, with no presence of persons, or ties to persons, of questionable reputation.

*Item:* County Federal Savings & Loan of Maryland, near Washington, kept substantial non-interest-bearing deposits at the two largest banks in Washington. Ten directors of County Federal owned 23 percent of a real estate company which borrowed from those banks. The bank extending one such loan, of $1.5 million, wrote that it was on the understanding "we will have on deposit from County Federal a minimum balance of $300,000." The three principal directors involved included a former county judge and a former state bar association president.

*Preliminary Answers:* As to Item 1, as the FDIC's director of bank supervision has put it, when a bank in a city with more than one or two banks gives more than 5 percent of its loan money to directors and major stockholders, "you get a suggestion that the bank, which is a public resource, is not serving the public as it should." No information is available about any later developments in the Madison situation. Regarding Item 2: Here, there have been later developments. The Federal Home Loan Bank Board confidentially recommended that the three principal directors leave County Federal's board, which they did with no public explanation by anyone. Further, the key director, and prime beneficiary of the transactions, has been indicted for misappropriating $355,000 of County Federal's funds. Also worth noting is an earlier event: In 1970, the Justice Department, finding the kind of conduct in Item 2 "fairly widespread" among bankers, sent a warning to banks that such practices might result in prosecutions for misappropriation.

*Full Answer:* That takes the rest of this paper, to which we turn after two caveats. Lest the caveats turn the reader away instead of serving merely to caution, let me here summarize the themes of this paper:

1. Conflicts of interest are frequent, nearly ubiquitous. Few result in abuses, but abuses are not so rare or inconsequential as to allow us to ignore the area. Conflicts are frequent because they are inevitable: Whenever one person (or firm) performs a variety of functions or performs one function for a number of people, conflicts may arise. Since many combinations of functions also produce valuable efficiencies, the question becomes how to live with the conflicts.

2. The question, in the context of any specific conflict, is *several-fold:* (a) Is this conflict easily removable, or would valuable efficiencies be lost if the existing arrangement were broken up? (b) How likely is abuse; how severe the injuries if abuse occurs? (c) If steps are warranted to reduce the likelihood or severity of abuse, can their cost be kept lower than the costs of the injuries?

3. These questions need consideration because conflicts matter: (a) When abuses do occur, there are always losses in fairness, and there may be losses in economic efficiency. (b) Since conflicts are so frequent and abuses so troublesome, many steps have been taken to reduce the likelihood of abuse. Since these steps in themselves involve costs, we should make sure that the steps are meaningful and the costs worthwhile. (c) "The importance of appearances" is perhaps overemphasized currently, but conflicts of interests in financial institutions are a matter in which appearances can count tangibly. If conflicts exist but corrective steps have not been taken and a problem does arise (e.g., the Penn Central bankruptcy), it will be hard to persuade juries and legislators that conflicts between, say, a bank's commercial and trust departments, were not abused. Thus, unless appearances are considered, unwarranted liabilities or regulatory intrusion are more likely. Moreover, if abuses occur and as a result confidence in the integrity of financial institutions declines, willingness to deal with such institutions will decline, entailing higher transaction costs for society. (d) While conflicts of interest are ubiquitous, those in financial institutions have unusual significance because of the size, role, and pervasive impact of such institutions.

4. Competition can eliminate or reduce some conflicts, but most conflicts occur where competition cannot be effective. Competition is a limited or inapplicable answer for many of these problems.

5. For some conflicts, disclosure should be sufficient safeguard; for others, changes in firm or market structure or regulatory requirements may be warranted. Solutions to these problems must be particularized rather than procrustean. The same kind of conflict may need different responses for, say, banks as distinguished from broker-dealers, and for big firms as distinguished from smaller ones.

6. The aim of efforts to eliminate abusive conflicts is not merely to reduce specific injuries, but to reduce undisclosed, unmeasured pricing and non-neutral allocation.

*Caveat:* The episodes noted above[1] are typical conflicts-of-interest episodes. Some people believe that episodes are best reserved for use by storytellers and cracker-barrel philosophers. Other people, including me, believe that while some episodes say nothing of general interest, others are illuminating about general practices, and sometimes even a single episode may warrant taking steps to promote the episode's repetition or nonrepetition. I refer not to the use of "horror stories" to build popular support, e.g., for legislative action, but rather to the use of episodic information to provide, in the words of Learned Hand, "the kind of evidence on which responsible persons are accustomed to rely in serious affairs."[2] That is, the conclusions about reality which this paper proffers rest on less firm evidence than might be needed to win a lawsuit, or than some people—though not I—might deem sufficient to justify legislative or regulatory action.

Some lawyers may, by force of their episode- or case-oriented training and practice, be too prepared to act on the basis of one "story" of a wounded widow, and too unthinking about the frequency of such wounds or whether the proposed "cure" may be more hurtful to widows generally or to society generally than it would be to let the wounds lie. On the other hand, some economists may, by force of their training and practice, tend to be too reluctant to act without information about the severity and frequency of the wounds, and too unthinking about whether, in the interim, grave harm may be suffered as wounds recur, deepen, or spread.

Each perspective has value and major roots, lawyers' concern for justice, and economists' concern for the finitude of resources. From either perspective, at what point is enough known to warrant governmental intervention in theretofore private—or, at least, not specifically regulated—conduct? That involves three questions: two obvious, and one warranting a little spelling out. First, what is the nature and severity of the injuries suffered in the two episodes above? For example, who are the stockholders who are hurt—sophisticated, rich investors, or poor widows, or both? Who in the community is hurt by being refused loans because of undue preference for insiders? How much are they hurt, how much is the community as a whole hurt—is that even answerable? Second, what specific intervention is proposed? Less of a showing is needed to support governmentally mandated disclosure of specific conduct than to support governmentally mandated prescriptions or proscriptions shaping that conduct.

Third, what is the feasibility and likelihood of getting either fuller information (or nonepisodic information) before acting? For example, if the press unearthed and legislators pointed with alarm at an episode of flagrant abuse by a bank in the course of conducting its own real estate investment activities at the same time as managing a real estate investment trust for public stockholders (in this hypothetical case, managing that trust in an improperly self-serving manner), what information could be secured to make a reasonably informed judgment about whether to change the law "chartering" real estate investment trusts so as to require their management by firms without any conflicting real estate activity? Could any but episodic information be secured?

## DEFINITION, TERMS, AND TYPES

The very phrase *conflict of interest* is like Pandora's box, connoting trouble. To point to a conflict of interest is to open a burdensome tangle of explanation. Some people will say that to be active at all is to have conflicts. But one may no more shrug off a particular conflict of interest or set of conflicts by noting that they exist in some degree almost everywhere than one would shrug off starvation or disease by noting that in the long run, we die.

*interest,*[3] and to distinguish that from ordinary marketplace conflict and
from such sure and blatant abuses as fraud, embezzlement, and
bribery.

*Alternative
Views on
Regulating
Conflicts of
Interest in the
Financial Firm*

## Definition of Conflicts, Abuse, and "The Issue"

The crux of a conflict of interest lies in the label itself: Two or more
interests are legitimately present and competing or conflicting; the
person (or firm) making the decision which will affect those interests
usually has a larger stake in one of the interests than the other(s),
although he is expected, indeed obligated, to serve each interest
affected regardless of his own stake.

1. There is self-interest (itself not always unconflicted, as in the conflict
   between desire for self and desire for reputation or self-image).

2. There is the interest created by the special obligations of certain kinds of
   careers. A lawyer or investment adviser, by merely opening his door to
   "do business," is under "fiduciary" obligations to do business in a
   certain way, whereas the used car salesman is not. The fiduciary's
   obligation, as a guardian's to a ward, is to give an unusual primacy to
   promoting and protecting the interests of the client, to such an extent
   that the client may repose trust that his interests are the only ones being
   considered (in matters affecting him) unless and until he is told otherwise. Even when the client is told otherwise, as in the setting of fees, the
   fiduciary is not free to seek what the traffic will bear but is supposed to
   use not only honest but "disinterested" judgment in determining what
   is reasonable compensation.

3. There is the interest created by the special obligations of certain kinds of
   roles, taken on in addition to regular jobs or tasks, such as the bank
   official who becomes a director of a borrower corporation. Before
   becoming a director, his only obligations are as agent, with most dealings at arm's length, but with the directorship also come fiduciary
   obligations to the borrowing corporation's stockholders.

4. There is the interest created by general legal obligations. For example, in
   recent years (although not without precedent at least as far back as 60 to
   70 years ago, and not without analogies going further back), the law has
   imposed obligations to faceless third parties, or "the marketplace," such

---

**3.** One of the few studies of conflict of interest, focusing as have most others on the conflict
between a public official's governmental responsibilities and his private economic interests, opened with the statement that for 175 years, officials, scholars and others have
attempted to define a . . .

> vague, nebulous thing called "conflict of interest." Interestingly, The Dictionary of
> American Politics, Black's Law Dictionary, and The Encyclopedia of Social Sciences
> fail to list the phrase among their many thousands of entries.

Frier, *Conflict of Interest in the Eisenhower Administration* 3 (Iowa St. Univ. Press, Ames
1969), reprinted by Pelican Books, New York 1970.

as to refrain from trading in securities if possessed of material information not known publicly.

It is imperative to emphasize that the self-serving opportunities present in conflict situations are usually not exploited. If this were not so, fiduciary relationships would seldom have survived, reputations would rarely be intact, and the law would have had to intervene far more than it has.

Thus, to say a conflict is present is only to say that there is a *potential* for self-serving abuse. To say a conflict has been *abused* is quite different. Our corporate law long ago abandoned the notion that mere presence of a conflict voided a transaction. Today, many questions come down to whether, having admitted the frequency of conflicts, we have adequate safeguards to prevent or redress their abuse.

Conflicts are frequent, indeed nearly ubiquitous, because valuable efficiencies can be enjoyed by having one person (or firm) perform a variety of functions. To bar conflicts would be to lose those efficiencies. The challenge is not to bar all or suffer all but to evaluate in each kind of situation how likely is abuse, how severe the loss if abuse occurs, and how valuable the efficiencies which keep one from simply barring the conflict. Then, if some safeguard against abuse is found desirable, the answer lies in tailoring remedies which give enough protection without undue costs. It is in such particularistic evaluation that we find the true issue(s) of conflict of interest.

## Conflicts' Distant Cousins: Embezzlement, Bribery, Fraud

One reason conflicts stir even more concern than they deserve is that they are confused, or lumped together, with conduct that is simply criminal. Though some conflict situations may invoke criminal sanctions, they are almost entirely left to civil sanctions. I believe this is so, first, because of the very nature of a conflict—two interests *legitimately* present—and, second, because of the difficulty of knowing (let alone knowing beyond a reasonable doubt) whether the conflict was abused or, alternatively, whether the same transaction would have occurred and on the same terms, even if no conflict had been present. Sometimes, the facts will be blatant, as in the County Federal situation noted above. But not usually. A corporate officer who embezzles, appropriating to his or her own use funds or property which he or she controlled but did not own, could not claim any legitimate interest in personal use of that property. In contrast, a corporate officer responsible for purchasing supplies and whose brother is one of the main sellers of an item the officer must purchase, has a conflict because it is legitimate for the officer, indeed incumbent upon him or her, to consider whether to purchase from a brother or, in light of the conflict, to have superior officers make the decision on that one item. But if the brother is chosen to supply the item—even if chosen by the superior officers—it would not be clear whether the conflict hurt the purchasing corporation unless the price and terms can be readily compared with alternative suppliers. Indeed, even if the price were somewhat high, whether that was unfair

**129**

*Alternative
Views on
Regulating
Conflicts of
Interest in the
Financial Firm*

turns on whether this was an item which is scarce at times, or needs much servicing, and so forth. In contrast, if the purchasing officer received "gifts" (above, roughly, Paul Douglas's $2 value—inflation-adjusted?)[4] from the seller, there was no legitimate interest in such receipt, and there need be little hesitancy in treating it as a criminal kickback or bribe.

A minor confusion in my distinction between crimes and conflicts is the conflict problem associated with use of inside information about issuers. The law on that problem, and on some conflicts within operating corporations, has grown under Rule 10b-5, where "fraud," an old *malum in se* concept, is much spoken of and where criminal sanctions are available. Suffice it here to note that "securities fraud" is far broader than common-law fraud, and that although criminal prosecutions are possible as a matter of law, it is rare—indeed, not a single instance comes to mind[5]—that the statutory criminal armory is brought to bear in the lively, interesting area of 10b-5. Thus, the actual treatment of "securities law fraud," rather than its mere legal wording, further supports the above distinction between crimes and conflicts.

## Marketplace Conflicts

Conflicts in the marketplace, or what the law calls arm's-length bargains between buyers and sellers, are not conflicts of interest in the sense of this paper and related literature. Of course, all sellers are obligated not to be untruthful, and in some situations sellers may have special duties, e.g., when a buyer relies upon a seller to select an article for a particular use. But we do not think of such obligations as fiduciary, nor of such situations as conflicts of interest, and despite the similarities between such situations and fiduciary ones, the differences lead to important distinctions. For all the difficulty purchasers may have in selecting a bottle of wine or repairing a television set, the commercial marketplace generally does an efficient and effective job of resolving the conflicts of interest between buyer and seller; at worst, the buyers lose a few dollars and switch to another seller. In situations in which the consequences of bad selection or advice may be more severe, as with drugs, elaborate licensing and related regulation exist.

In the marketplace for professional services, such as medical treatment, legal advice, and investment management, the situation is different. First, the need or wish for confidentiality makes marketplace-type

---

4. A routine of repeated "little" gifts can create acute difficulty, even injustice, in defining *"de minimis."* See, e.g., Schuck, "The Curious Case of the Indicted Meat Inspectors," 245 Harper's Magazine, No. 1466, 81–88 (Sept. 1972): "The old-timers always say, 'It isn't a good inspector who pays for his Sunday dinner.' I figure the job is hard enough without having the other inspectors [and the meat-packers] suspicious of you."

5. Possibly excepting United States v. Simon, 425 F.2d 796 (2d Cir. 1969), *cert. denied* 397 U.S. 1006 (1970).

shopping unfeasible. Second, the importance of the service rendered makes the cost of a mistake too high to justify reliance on the trial-and-error approach that a consumer may use in the commercial marketplace. Finally, the buyer is simply unable to evaluate not only the worth of the services but even what services are required. Even after the transaction has been completed, it is hard for the buyer to determine whether the service was appropriate and the fee reasonable. The combination of these conditions has led the law to invite buyers of professional services to put aside caveat emptor and to repose trust in the seller.

This "trust" is not merely a cosy, gemeinschaft feeling: It involves giving the trusted person or firm decisional power over one's property (or health, or legal affairs), with an inseparable power to exploit that trust toward the trustee's own ends instead of merely the beneficiary's. In the financial field, this trust is expressed in the fiduciary obligations of the brokers, dealers, lawyers, accountants, pension fund officials, trustees, underwriters, and other professionals.

## Why Do Conflicts Matter?

"To some extent the concern over conflicts of interest reveals a step forward in the morality of the marketplace, for it means that open fraud has become far less common."[6] We have here both a problem of morality, in the sense of fairness, and one of the marketplace, in the sense of efficient operations and resource allocation.

INJURIES SUFFERED

When abuses do occur in conflict situations, the injuries caused come down to one thing: Someone helps himself to an economic advantage to which he is not entitled. "Entitlement" here refers to the price the market would put on the goods or services (or the allocation the market would effect), or, if there is no market, then the value that a disinterested judgment would deem appropriate.

There are two kinds of objections to such injuries: The first is equity or fairness, in that the self-server takes what belongs to others. The second is economic, in that the self-dealing lowers operating efficiency or leads to an inefficient allocation of resources. Some injuries invite cries of "unfair" more clearly than attacks as "unsound economically," but rarely would an abuse not draw both kinds of objections.

For example, if trustees (or a corporate management group) help themselves to excessive compensation, the beneficiaries of the trust (or the corporation's stockholders) are *pro tanto* deprived of dollars that would have been theirs. The unfairness is clear. As for the economic

---

**6.** Mayer, *Conflicts of Interest in Broker-Dealer Firms* 69 (Twentieth Century Fund, New York 1975).

impact, at least at first blush, the money simply has been transferred inefficiently: The trustees or management would have performed the same services for lesser compensation, since if they could not have taken advantage of a conflicted situation, they would have had no choice but to work for "market-determined" compensation. The excessive compensation, used otherwise, might have made the trust or corporation more efficient if spent on such things as research or quality control, or retained for future needs, or might have permitted the firm to lower the cost of its products or services and so enable it to gain a larger or more secure share of its market. However, if, in fact, there were neither current nor future "efficient uses" for those dollars (unlikely as that is), then while the management or trustee acted unfairly, it is possible that no overall inefficiency resulted.

Excessive compensation is merely the simplest example of unfairness and probable operating inefficiency. If a manager of Our Corp. also owns a private firm, His Corp., and he causes Our to enter transactions with His at prices unduly favorable to His, again he improperly siphons dollars away from the company he is obligated to manage disinterestedly. However, in addition to the clear unfairness to Our stockholders and probable harm to Our's operating efficiency, this example includes the possibility of harm to His's competitors. Even if His is less efficient than its competitors, its ability to get business it could not win in market competition protects it from the consequences of its inefficiency. Thus, resources are inefficiently allocated to a weak enterprise. If the inefficient firm secures enough business on such preferential, noneconomic bases, it may drive out more efficient competitors, hurting the competitors' customers by a decline in overall operating efficiency. Such declines are not only economic losses; they are unfair to other participants in those markets—and their employees and stockholders—who are entitled to operate on the expectation that their success or failure will turn on their ability, effort, and related performance, and not on the bases of improper preferences which, if discovered, would be barred by law.

In short, to the extent that transactions are affected by exploitation of a conflict of interest rather than market factors and disinterested judgments, we are likely to suffer less efficient operations, less efficient allocation of resources, and unfairness. Depending on how many people are treated unfairly, how substantial that unfairness is, and how substantial the inefficiencies caused are, the conflict may be a matter of real social concern.

THE IMPORTANCE OF APPEARANCES

An additional reason why conflicts matter, even if not abused, relates to the effect of image or appearance on public confidence in financial institutions. In the post-Watergate era, perhaps too much is made of appearances and perhaps too little of the costs of living in sterilized glass houses.[7] On the other hand, in this specific sphere, appearances have tangible significance. If something goes wrong and a conflict of interest was involved, then it will be easy to persuade outsiders that the conflict was abused. That difficulty of persuasion can have measurable importance if a lawsuit arises over whatever went wrong. To take a leading example, if the Penn Central goes into bankruptcy and a bank was a large creditor also having large stock holdings in its trust department, then if substantial sales were being made shortly before the bankruptcy, there is bound to be a claim that inside information was used illegally. Unless the bank has well-established, strong procedures to prevent such an abuse, the bank's credibility and integrity are highly vulnerable. Indeed, without such preventive systems, the mere existence of the conflict leaves the bank vulnerable to attack whatever it does in a situation like Penn Central: Where there was little or no selling of the trust holdings, it has been claimed (in a suit against Continental Illinois, the Penn Central's lead bank) that the trust beneficiaries were being victimized to protect the bank's creditor interests.

Conflicts have a "bad name," and their mere presence creates the difficulty of persuading outsiders that no abuse occurs, precisely because conflicts are brought to full visibility only when something has gone wrong. If Penn Central had flourished, how loud would have been the complaints over the Continental Illinois's dual role? However, this is not like some suits claiming "unsuitable" investments, in which one may reasonably conclude that the moaning, injured widow was a greedy old woman who wanted to swing and guessed wrong. The victims of conflict situations, more often than not, were likely unaware of the duality or multiplicity of roles before a loss occurred and caused them to explore more fully. Thus, a fiduciary operating with a conflict is at risk: If losses occur which arguably involved the conflict, that fiduciary has a considerable problem, even if the loss was caused externally and not at all as a result of abuse of the conflict.

The concern for credibility is not merely a matter of individual firms' vulnerability to suit. At least as important is the industry's vulnerability to regulatory intervention aimed at correcting what appear to be failures of the marketplace or of integrity, or both. Such failures may occur only at less competent or less reputable firms, but it is rare indeed that the regulatory intervention will be limited to such firms. Moreover, as noted earlier, the regulatory requirements will impose at least some costs, possibly substantial ones.

Clearly, then, if an industry is to function well, and be so understood to function well, so that there will be little or no tendency for govern-

---

7. A caricaturist might argue, in light of some governmental moves in recent years, that since government is an art and since "in art, appearance is the only reality" (Bernard Berenson), it is foolish to be concerned about whether appearances affect substance.

mental intrusion to correct experienced wrongs, it will need to take **133**
reasonable steps to protect against abuse of conflicts.

*Alternative
Views on
Regulating
Conflicts of
Interest in the
Financial Firm*

mental intrusion to correct experienced wrongs, it will need to take
reasonable steps to protect against abuse of conflicts.

Probably more important is the impact on confidence. Confidence in
financial intermediaries encourages and lowers transaction costs,[8] indirectly if not directly, in finance and the securities markets.

THE SPECIAL IMPORTANCE OF CONFLICTS IN FINANCIAL INSTITUTIONS

The sums directly involved in financial institutions are huge. Bank trust
departments, the largest institutional investors, now manage over $400
billion of assets. The largest category of institutional accounts, pension
fund portfolios, now total about $370 billion (over $165 billion of which
is managed by bank trust departments, and $88 billion by life insurance
companies).[9]

Such institutions constitute the bulk of our primary capital markets,
providing new external long-term funds to the private sector of our
economy, and play a critical role in our secondary capital markets,
trading and pricing corporate securities that have been issued. Therefore, the efficiency and fairness of these institutions' performance have
an important impact on virtually the entire private sector.

Such institutions also usually perform a variety of functions. For
example, almost every trust department is part of a commercial bank.
Broker-dealers perform many different functions for the same customers. Therefore, conflict situations in these firms are unusually frequent and unusually complex.

Finally, financial institutions are subjected to the strongest legal
obligations for the benefit of their ultimate customers. These obligations increase the importance of conflicts. The most famous statement
of the level of those obligations is, of course, that of Cardozo in
*Meinhard* v. *Salmon*.[10]

## EXPERIENCED PROBLEMS

It is one thing to abstract typologies of kinds of conflicts and kinds of
injuries; it is quite another to slot actual situations into the constructed

---

8. Since abuses of conflicts are at least a major cause of bank failures (see Subsection on
Banks, *infra*) and since other banks and larger corporations take substantial steps to avoid
losses due to failure of a debtor, higher transaction costs are assumed.

9. For private noninsured pension funds as of end-1976, SEC quarterly report, B.N.A.
Pension Rep., No. 141, p. A-1 (June 13, 1977); for private insured funds as of end-1976,
Institute of Life Insurance; for state and local funds as of 1975–1976, U.S. Dep't of
Commerce, *Pensions & Investments* 11 (June 6, 1977); and for banks' share as of end-1975,
FDIC, *Trusts Assets of Commercial Banks—1975*.

10. 249 N.Y. 458, 464, 164 N.E. 545, 546 (1928): "A trustee is held to something stricter than
the morals of the market place. Not honesty alone, but the punctilio of an honor the most
sensitive, is then the standard of behavior."

pigeonholes. For one thing, some situations belong in more than one pigeonhole; life does not obediently line up according to abstract constructs. For another, the situations are more easily understood if presented not by intellectual-construct categories but, rather, as they arise in particular lines of activity, such as broker-dealing, pension fund managing, etc. Also, I prefer to risk erring on the side of fuller presentation of episodes that seem significant rather than selection of only enough to validate each feature of my construct.

The episodes presented in this section are intended to provide a sense of the types of themes and variations sounded by conflicts in financial firms, and to support the recommendations which follow. In most instances, the episode "speaks for itself."

## Broker-Dealers

GOLDMAN, SACHS (GS) AND PENN CENTRAL COMMERCIAL PAPER

GS is the leading dealer in America in commercial paper (at least, paper of nonfinancial corporations). As a multifunction firm and one of our largest investment bankers, it often has other relationships with companies in whose commercial paper it makes a market. For example, during the two years GS made a market in Penn Central's commercial paper, GS—according to an SEC Report—had with Penn Central about six other relations, either functioning or discussed.

> As late as March 1970, despite a string of unfavorable reports from the company, Goldman, Sachs still awarded Penn Central its "prime" rating and was active in persuading the National Credit Office (NCO, a Dun & Bradstreet subsidiary) to give Penn Central an apparently independent "prime rating" that carried more credibility. An internal memo from Robert Wilson of Goldman, Sachs informed the senior partners of the firm that the director of NCO had said "that as long as Goldman, Sachs was going to continue to handle the company's c/p (commercial paper) he would keep the prime rating." Goldman, Sachs salesmen, however, continued to stress the NCO rating as an outside appraisal in their discussions with customers.

> Until late April 1970, Goldman, Sachs salesmen kept recommending Penn Central paper to the firm's customers, scoffing at stories that the company's cash flow would not sustain its debt structure. But the firm's own inventory, which had been as high as $15 million in February, went down to zero. Ten million dollars of that total was bought back ahead of schedule by the struggling railroad itself at Goldman, Sachs' insistence; the remaining five million was taken back when the paper expired. When the ship went down, Goldman, Sachs as captain was safely aboard another ship; its customers were dunked to the extent of $82 million.

> Some of the customers to whom Goldman, Sachs sold Penn Central paper were highly sophisticated investors: the last large sale, on May 1, 1970, was $5 million to American Express. The interest rate required to move Penn

**135**

*Alternative
Views on
Regulating
Conflicts of
Interest in the
Financial Firm*

Central paper after February 1970 was significantly higher than that being paid by other "prime" borrowers in this market—partly because Penn Central was trying to sell longer-term paper—and this difference should have alerted even less experienced customers to the possibility of risk. But the customers were not told that Goldman, Sachs was no longer carrying an inventory of Penn Central paper—or that the firm was using its management of Penn Central's commercial paper offerings as an entree to what appeared to be very profitable business ("could amount to as much as a billion-dollar underwriting") from the railroad.

The SEC report on this situation concluded that "most of the institutions and corporations" that purchased the paper "were not sophisticated in terms of their ability to gather and analyze the necessary information. . . . And . . . almost all of the customers were relying on Goldman, Sachs' recommendation." Two examples were cited in the report. One was a textile manufacturer in Clinton, South Carolina, for whom Goldman, Sachs had arranged mergers in 1964 and 1968, who had $1 million to invest pending the closing of another merger; the textile man instructed his treasurer to put the money in commercial paper, "relying on the recommendation of Goldman, Sachs and no one else." The other was Muhlenberg College in Pennsylvania, which added $300,000 to an existing inventory of $400,000 of Penn Central paper on March 30, 1970, relying on a representation by a Goldman, Sachs salesman that "there was no need for concern since total assets exceeded 6½ billion."

In defense Goldman, Sachs argued that the Dun & Bradstreet credit raters were not so dependent on its advice as the SEC staff contended; that its reduction of its Penn Central inventory was consonant with its action as dealer in the commercial paper of other, wholly solvent companies during the tight-money period of early 1970; that the salesman did not specifically push Penn Central paper but marketed a full range of commercial paper; and that the SEC staff went into print with comments from Goldman, Sachs' customers without seeking Goldman, Sachs' side of the story. But the firm has entered into one of those SEC consent decrees that permit it to say that it did nothing wrong but won't do it again. Virtually all the holders of defaulted Penn Central paper sued Goldman, Sachs. The firm settled cases involving more than half of the money its customers lost, paying off at rates varying from twelve to twenty-six cents. More patient customers may collect more; in the first cases to come to trial, in September 1974, a jury awarded the holders of the commercial paper the full face value, to be paid by Goldman, Sachs.[11]

BLOCK TRANSACTIONS—"WHOLESALE" STOCK MARKET MEETS "RETAIL"

In earlier days when a 10,000,000-share daily volume seemed as remote as heaven (and as desirable), specialists stood at the heart of exchange market activity, acting both as broker and dealer, dealing for their own accounts but under an obligation—well met by almost all of them almost always—to serve as a "balance wheel" meeting or melding

---

**11.** Mayer, N. 6 *supra* at 20–21 (footnotes omitted).

public orders so as to assure an orderly, reasonably liquid market. Because of many conflicts in their activity, since at least the SEC's 1936 study on whether to segregate the broker and dealer functions, there has been a constant effort—whether serious or merely for show depends on the viewer's perspective—to monitor specialist performance and, via a panoply of rules, assure against abuse of the conflicts.

With the expansion of institutional investors and their activity, the specialist system proved inadequate (for a number of reasons having little, if anything, to do with conflicts) and a similar function came to be performed off the exchange floor by major brokerage houses, almost all of which also performed numerous other functions—e.g., as research sources or investment managers themselves, or as investment bankers, or as retail "wire houses." However, unlike the highly regulated specialists, the "block houses" have virtually no regulatory burdens or safeguards, despite some seemingly highly troublesome new conflicts. Examples of possible abuses are:

a) A potential conflict of interest exists when a block trade assembler places its discretionary accounts on the passive side of block trades. Insofar as the participation of such accounts eliminates or reduces the need for block positioning, it allows the block trade assembler to avoid a very risky and often unprofitable activity, while at the same time increasing its commissions earned to the extent of that participation. The block trade assembler may well be tempted to put its accounts into such transactions at unfavorable prices to earn the brokerage commissions on both those shares and the other shares in the block trade.

[The study then gave this case:] [T]he block trade assembler had made a bid for its own account, which the seller had rejected. Thereupon the broker bought the bundle for a discretionary account at a slightly higher price, earning $29,000 in brokerage commissions—a maneuver not unlike that of a Swiss bank that sells securities it has underwritten directly to its managed accounts; the activity would be illegal for underwriters in the United States without elaborate disclosure precautions, but is not illegal for block positioners.[12]

b) Before 1971 the price of the block as printed on the tape had a known meaning. If 50,000 shares changed hands at $50 and the commission at that price worked out to 1 percent, the world knew that the buyer had paid $50.50, the seller had received $49.50, and the block broker had taken $1; and if he had positioned 10,000 shares, he had done so at an effective price to him of $49.50 (and if he sold out at $48.50, he was still going to make money on the total deal, because he had $40,000 of gross commission income on the cross to set against his $10,000 loss on positioning).

Today, when a cross (a transaction where the same broker represents both buyer and seller) prints at $50, nobody can tell if that was really the price. With commissions negotiable, the broker and his customers can allocate differing proportions of the money to commis-

---

12. *Id.* at 30–31.

**137**

*Alternative
Views on
Regulating
Conflicts of
Interest in the
Financial Firm*

sion and to price. It may make a considerable difference to the positioner's profitability on his acquired inventory whether the price of a 50,000-share deal prints at $49.75 or at $50.25; under the new rate structure, he and his customers can decide which of these numbers they would like to see on the tape.

"Even the printed price doesn't mean anything," a senior partner at one of the oldest Wall Street investment banking houses insists, "because you never know what the side deal is." Institutions and the block brokers are constantly doing business with each other; the institution that sells to the broker today will be buying from him tomorrow. Thus a party that gains an advantage on one deal can make amends on the next. [For example, one of the biggest "block" dealers,] Salomon Brothers, while handling blocks of Equity Funding common stock, was dealing with Equity Funding as a customer for the debt instruments of others. . . . A specialist, contrasting his work with that of a block trade, says insinuatingly: "Of course, I'm not influenced by what happened yesterday in the corporate bond department, or by the chance for a trade in the municipal bond department. . . ."[13]

c) When a wire house does a block business and distributes securities to its retail customers, the legal, ethical, and practical elements of decision are difficult to assess. The customer does benefit from the broker-dealer's wholesale purchase price and from elimination of the commission charge. On the other hand, securities are made available at retail in connection with a block transaction only when wholesale customers cannot be found, and presumably the wholesale customers know what they are doing. Merrill Lynch has an absolute rule that such distributions will be made only when the research department independently recommends the stock, and several others say they are "comfortable" with such operations only when they have a research recommendation.[14]

Almost certainly one of the best routes to reducing abuses of conflicts by specialists is to promote—surely not *bar*, as has been the situation—competition among specialists, so that the better market-maker will drive out the self-server. We already have vigorous competition among "block houses."

INSIDE INFORMATION

If a broker-dealer manages accounts or even merely furnishes investment advice and is also on an issuer's board, which obligation (as director or as broker-dealer) prevails? The answer has always seemed to me so clear, and by now there is so much written and even understood that only the most summary treatment seems warranted here. Suffice it to note that (1) this is a conflict problem; (2) it arises in a number

---

13. *Id.* at 31–32.

14. *Id.* at 32.

of settings—broker-dealer/director, broker-dealer/investment banker, broker-dealer in both public markets and in private placements, etc.; and, (3) in some of those settings (e.g., directorships), the answer may be to eliminate the conflict by eliminating the "conflicted" directorships, but in others (e.g., the multi-function firm), the answer gets into the intricacies of whether sufficient protection can be secured by such procedural devices as "Chinese walls," a problem treated below.

Note also that misuse of inside information on behalf of one's own clients (1) *helps* them—unless other firms do likewise; (2) may secure an unfair competitive advantage for the investment manager so acting; and (3) certainly injures other participants in the market, and thus, likely weakens the market as a whole.

### Broker-Dealing Combined with Investment Banking

Bernstein-Macaulay, as a Hayden, Stone subsidiary (as a result of a merger the firm is now Shearson Hayden Stone) . . . at first refused to recommend to its advisory clients any securities underwritten by Hayden, Stone. This policy, however, was eventually relaxed under pressure from advisory clients who wanted to have the advantage of Hayden Stone's specific knowledge about companies for which it served as investment banker. "We did it, in several cases, and it worked out perfectly," Bernstein says. "My hand didn't tremble for a minute." . . . [But later:] In September 1971, Hayden, Stone (at that time known as CBWL-Hayden, Stone) served as investment banker in a private sale of $5,250,000 of Topper [Corp.] debentures, receiving an underwriting fee of $157,500 for its role in the transaction. Hayden, Stone's affiliate, Bernstein-Macaulay, recommended the securities to three pension funds it advised—two of them New York City union funds, the third a union fund in Massachusetts—as a result of which all three funds took positions in Topper. Topper at that time was considered a red-hot go-go security; during 1971 its common stock price had more than doubled, and at one time it had been on the American Stock Exchange's most actively traded list for six consecutive days. Bernstein-Macaulay insists that, in recommending the debentures to its fund clients, it complied with the Investment Advisers Act of 1940 by fully disclosing all pertinent data including the fact that Hayden, Stone represented the seller in the transaction. Indeed, Peter Bernstein, far from acting defensive about recommending the Topper securities, made a virtue of his firm's close association with the company; he wrote at the time to one of his clients, Teamster Local 816, that "our close knowledge of this company gives me confidence that the deal is a sound one" and went on to describe in glowing terms an ingenious new Topper toy intended to teach a child to spell. The funds bought the securities and paid Bernstein's fee with commission dollars.

Unfortunately, though, Topper did not flourish as predicted. In February 1973, hit with heavy returns that forced it to liquidate much of its inventory at discount prices, the firm filed under Chapter 11 of the Bankruptcy Act.[15]

---

15. Brooks, *Conflicts of Interest: Corporate Pension Fund Management*, 39 (Twentieth Century Fund, New York 1975).

*Alternative
Views on
Regulating
Conflicts of
Interest in the
Financial Firm*

The investment banker is in at least a three-way conflict: obligations to the buying public, to corporate issuers, plus self-interest. Consider the difficulty of accommodating obligations which, at first blush, pull in three potentially different directions:

PRICING THE ISSUE

> The investment banker must ensure that the price is low enough to constitute a reasonable buy for his customers. Too low an offering price, however, starves the corporation of needed working capital and harms members of the buying public attracted by long-term-investment prospects.

> An artificially low offering price may inflate demand and release a runaway hot issue in which the price of the stock climbs rapidly in aftermarket trading. Soon the stock price may descend rapidly, burning the unlucky members of the public who bought the stock at a premium from its initial purchasers. These unfortunates were not smart enough or well connected enough to buy the new issue at the lower offering price.

> The price must be "fair" to the company going public. The price must provide adequate proceeds so that the corporation can do those things that caused it to go public in the first place.

> Investors who already hold shares in the corporation and who want to continue to hold them will benefit from the highest possible initial offering price. The more others pay in, the greater the worth of their initial investment.

> Investors who control the corporation will profit from a high offering price because the value of their equity holdings increases as the price rises. On the other hand, a low price may create a wild hot issue after-market in which they can unload at great profit.[16]

SELF-UNDERWRITING

A peculiar, but telling, example of how conflicts arise, and how challenging their resolution is, lies in the problem of broker-dealer firms going public.

> At the time, the NASD rules prohibited a broker-dealer firm from underwriting its own securities. Although the policy reasons were sound, the idea seemed absurd. Imagine the competitive turmoil that would be caused if Bache & Co. were underwritten by Merrill Lynch, or *vice versa*. A broker-dealer is a fiduciary, and Bache, if the facts warranted, would have the legal obligation of recommending the securities of Merrill Lynch over its own.

---

**16.** Wolfson, *Conflicts of Interest in Investment Banking*, 30 (Twentieth Century Fund, New York 1976).

Moreover, if the deal soured, Bache, the investment banker, would end up holding Merrill Lynch stock.

A final NASD compromise in 1971 eliminated some of the black humor in this scenario, but not all. To begin with, the rules do permit self-underwriting, but there remain certain standards that the member-firm must uphold. It must have been in the investment banking and securities business for at least five years, three of the five years must have been profitable, and a majority of the board of directors on the filing date and the effective date of the prospectus must have been active in the investment banking and securities field for that five-year period. These requirements may serve as anticompetitive barriers to the entry or growth of new firms. . . .[17]

## Banks[18]

### ENDING UP WRONG: SELF-DEALING AND FAILURES

According to a recent FDIC study of 92 banks that failed between 1960–1977, 58.6 percent failed because of improper loans to insiders or out-of-bank's territory borrowers (who, presumably, have some special relationship with the insiders); 25.3 percent because of fraud; and 16.1 percent because of general weakness of management of lending.[19]

### STARTING OUT WRONG: SELF-DEALING AND PURCHASE OF CONTROL

Often, when a group of investors or bankers seek to buy control of a bank—call it Bank *A*—they borrow the purchase price from another bank, *B*, putting up as collateral the very stock they buy with the loan. Unsurprisingly, Bank *A* almost always is in a correspondent banking relationship with *B*, which necessarily and properly means regularly leaving compensating balances at Bank *B* in return for such services as check clearing. The FDIC studied whether banks whose control groups had such "stock loans" maintained at the correspondent lending banks larger compensating balances than did banks without such loans.[20] (The study used 1971 data on 98 Texas banks with stock loans, compared with a group of 246 Texas banks without such loans.)

---

17. *Id.*, at 57–58.

18. For consideration of conflicts in bank holding companies, see Schotland, *Bank Holding Companies and Public Policy Today*, Pt. I, pp. 233, 269–277, on BHCs and REITs. House Banking Comm., "FINE" Study Papers Compendium, 94th Cong., 2d Sess. (1976).

19. FDIC, *Why 67 Insured Banks Failed, 1960–74* (FDIC Liquidation Div., update to May 31, 1977).

20. Paterson and McLaughlin, *Conflict of Interest and the Financing of Commercial Bank Stock Ownership* (FDIC 1973).

First, they found that some of the stock loans were at 3 percent and 4 percent interest rates; the mean interest rate on these loans was below 4.5 percent, or about three-quarters of the prime rate at that time. The study further found that, as you would expect (unless you think those lending banks are eleemosynary institutions or fools), the stock-loan banks did maintain significantly higher balances at the lending correspondent banks. In some cases, correspondent relations were established with the lending bank just after the stock loan was made, and balances thereafter held were substantially larger than reserve requirements or operating needs would dictate. However, there was no difference in average profitability between the banks which had stock loans and unduly high correspondent balances and other banks. That is, though the new managements financed so much of their personal loans by having their banks maintain unnecessarily large, unproductive correspondent balances, this did not result in any demonstrable loss, on average, to stockholders. For one thing, unsurprisingly, the stock-loan banks maintained much lower amounts of vault cash (and similar holdings) than the other banks. For a second thing, the stock-loan banks maintained significantly larger proportions of their assets as loans rather than as investments, compared with the non-stock-loan banks. The authors did not explain this difference in readiness to lend. My own speculation is that the people who have the imagination to arrange such stock loans—not a secret stunt by any means, but not the world's most conservative practice either—also would be likely to run their banks less conservatively. Of course, the method of financing their loans is still an undisclosed siphoning to themselves of earning power which belongs to their bank and its stockholders. (That their greater willingness to lend may constitute a greater service to the bank's community does not justify the siphoning.)*

### CONFLICTS BETWEEN CUSTOMERS—THE UNFRIENDLY TAKEOVER

Conflicts of interest are a minor part of the corporate warfare that breaks out when Company *A* seeks to take over an unwilling Company *B*. But, if one financial institution is a fiduciary for both *A* and *B*, a difficult conflicts problem is inescapable. This has come to be known as "the Microdot situation" because, in 1975, that company was the target of a takeover attempt by General Cable.

Irving Trust had been General Cable's lead bank for many years. Four of General Cable's 11 directors were also directors of Irving or its parent holding company; and General Cable had an outstanding line of credit from the Irving for more than the sum they sought from that bank to finance the tender offer. According to Microdot, Irving Trust also had been Microdot's lead bank for many years, and in that capacity, the bank received quarterly statements of Microdot's operations on a nonpublic divisional basis, as well as daily nonpublic statements of Micro-

---

* This was written before the Bert Lance matter became notorious.

dot's cash position.[21] Whether or not these facts establish any abuse by Irving Trust, it seems clear that this kind of problem will recur, and ground rules for this situation are needed. Certainly, the problem cannot be dismissed out-of-hand, as it recently was with unlawyer-like rashness by bank counsel from a leading firm: "sheer nonsense . . . I personally would never advise anyone not to finance a transaction they would ordinarily finance, even though the target company may be one of their customers."[22] There may be times that a bank must stand back. Just when that is necessary, when specific steps might permit participation by a bank, and what steps would be appropriate for an investment banker, go into detail beyond the scope of this paper.

## Bank Trust Departments

PRIVATE PLACEMENTS

According to a study for the Pennsylvania Public School Employees' Retirement Fund, the Mellon Bank, the fund's main investment adviser, placed from 1960 to 1966 an unusually large proportion of the Fund's assets in private placements, yet earned an inexplicably low return on those investments, lower than was earned on similar investments by a group of life insurance companies.[23] While the Mellon's performance improved after 1967, relations with that major fund have deteriorated severely (which, according to the Bank, is mere politics). A frequent anti-bank claim by nonbankers is that banks compete for private placements by offering rates which are hard to explain unless they are abusing captive trust accounts.

---

**21.** There is substantial question whether Irving Trust was still Microdot's lead bank at the time of the takeover. By 1975, another large bank had a director interlocked with Microdot as well as acting as its transfer agent and registrar; five other banks had banking relationships with it; the line of credit at the Irving was only 20 percent of Microdot's total bank lines and had been barely used during 1975; and the relationship had been declining. Moreover, it appears that General Cable had arranged and decided upon the tender offer before telling Irving Trust that it was going to draw upon the line of credit. Further, there was no showing (indeed, there was a flat denial) that Irving Trust furnished any advice or confidential information or did anything but comply with the drawdown on General Cable's existing line of credit. See *Hearings on Corporate Takeover, Senate Banking Comm.*, 94th Cong., 2d Sess. 2–11, 33–41, and 44–45 (Feb. 16, 1976), (testimony of Rudolph Eberstadt, president of Microdot, and Gordon T. Wallis, chairman of Irving Trust).

**22.** Statement of Richard S. Simmons in panel on "Financing and other Aspects of Cash Tender Offers," 32 Bus. Law., No. 4, pp. 1415, 1419, 1421 (1977)

See also comments by Raymond S. Troubh, *id.*, at 1301, 1303: "Try not to go after companies where you suspect that a kind of defense is going to be thrown up such as in the General Cable tender offer for Microdot. Ultimately, Microdot was sold to another company in a higher offer, but it's an extremely serious, difficult and expensive trauma to fight that kind of defense."

**23.** Guttentag and Stoll, *Performance, Policy & Management of PPSERF,* 50 (Univ. of Pennsylvania Fels Center of Gov't, Feb. 1973).

One of the most ancient precepts of trust law is that the trustee shall not deal with or profit from the corpus, except for his agreed fees. One of the most long-standing, widespread practices among trust departments has been to place uninvested cash—either awaiting (or between) investments or distribution—in own-bank *demand* deposits. (Indeed, the Federal Reserve and Comptroller have promoted for trust accounts an astonishing vehicle, the *non*-interest-bearing *time* deposit, which enables the bank not only to reap the interest but also to reduce its reserve requirements.)

For most accounts, of course, the potential interest lost is not large. For most trust departments, the aggregate has always been large and, at most banks, is the difference between profit or loss on trust operations.

This time-honored dishonoring of the trustees' obligation has changed considerably in the last two or three years. Three forces have forced the improvement: First, as interest rates soared in the last two tight-credit periods, the amounts involved doubled, and people became more conscious of cash management (as is most evident in the rise and success of "money market" funds). Second, the biggest clients of the major banks, the pension accounts, run mostly by corporate officers who are particularly sophisticated about cash management, clamored for—and got—the full benefit of interest on uninvested cash. Third, the spread of computer systems enabled banks to lower the cost of moving money between checking accounts and interest-bearing vehicles. (Probably unrelated, but a possible fourth force ending this abuse, was the antitrust-motivated ending of another widespread abuse of trust accounts: the banks' use of brokerage generated by those accounts to win demand deposits from the brokers.) Long before the pressures heightened to end this abuse, one bank, the Hartford National, maintained several thousand savings accounts in thrift institutions for its trust accounts' uninvested cash.

Such practices by trust departments enabled them to offer investment management services for what misleadingly appeared to be unusually low fees, and doubtless were low ones for sophisticated clients.

TYING

Is it conflict of interest for a bank to use commercial-side relationships to win investment management business? What if a trust account, comprised of assets which are not the borrower's own, is given to a bank to assure the flow of loans? If a corporation manages its employees' pension fund, as most do, and the corporation itself does not (as many corporations do not) stand behind that fund when the fund assets do not meet its liabilities, then the corporate management is serving the stockholders' interests, at the expense of the pension beneficiaries' interest, if they pick an investment manager on any basis other than investment competence. This may involve abuse of a conflict of interest by the *borrower*.

### "CONFLICTED" HOLDINGS

In a variety of settings, particular holdings in the trust department raise a range of conflicts, from inside information problems, to common directorships, to concern over whether investment judgments are affected—or displaced—by a concern to further or protect commercial banking relationships, to use of assets in some accounts to further the interests of other accounts' holdings, etc. In short, the fact that a bank is likely to lend to a number of companies represented in its trust department portfolio creates conflicts. At what point may abuse arise?

1. Continental Illinois was lead bank for Penn Central. Should it have avoided holding any PC stock in the trust department? If so, (a) because it was lead bank? Or (b) because any large credit relationship should bar an equity position in the trust department? If the latter (and possibly even the former), one is effectively compelling all large banks to separate themselves, wholly or nearly so, from their trust departments.

2. Connecticut Bank & Trust held so much stock in W. T. Grant, via family and family-related foundation trust accounts that, whether or not the trustee was in a "control" position, it had unusual access to information. Rightly or wrongly, whether out of a concern to abide by law against misuse of such information or other concerns, substantial stock sales were made but brought to a halt when stock remaining in those CBT accounts totaled about $300 million market value—at that moment. Not too long after the halt on the sales, of course, Grant went broke. Is CBT liable to the accounts now holding wallpaper? If so, for precisely what abuse(s)?

3. What of the conflicts in smaller cities or towns, where substantial blocks of shares in many local businesses are virtually bound to be placed by settlors into trust accounts at the one or few local trust departments? In addition to the spider web of interrelationships between a bank and those firms, many of those banks will have few, or *no*, full-time trust personnel.

4. Trust departments, large and small, have long found themselves holding substantial amounts of stock in their own banks. Should they sell, unless there are substantial reasons for the particular account to continue to hold? Should the bank itself be able to vote any such shares?

The Federal Comptroller of the Currency bars trust departments in national banks from voting such shares, but only in electing directors. California law "sterilized" the votes of such shares. Is either course sound?

Ohio law bars trust departments from voting any shares in their own banks. Since most of the larger banks and their trust departments are in bank holding companies, only the holding company owns shares in the bank, everyone else owning shares in the holding company. Ohio practice is to have the trust department vote shares in its own bank holding company.

## Pension Funds

The notorious problems with corporate and union pension funds have not been in the conflicts areas. The major corporate problems were deprivation of allegedly "vested" retirement benefits, either by the closing of the employer, most dramatically at Studebaker, or by inadequacies of disclosure or unfair firing. The major union problems were embezzlement, most dramatically at one or two of the several Teamsters' funds. Still, serious conflicts problems certainly were here before ERISA (Congress's "Pension Reform Act of 1974," or Employment Retirement Income Security Act), and almost certainly have not been banished by that complex, ill-administered law.

Also, one of the most serious conflicts problems in state and local pension funds (not under ERISA, although the subject of a pending bill to impose similar regulation) has always been their large holdings of their own communities' tax-exempt securities—ridiculous from an investment point of view for any tax-exempt portfolio. That practice receded greatly over the last decade, but roared back in one spectacular situation: the New York City problem.

The most interesting commentary on these three classes of funds—corporate, union, and state and local—is the basic similarity of conflicts and abuses. In each class, the fund is to be managed in the interest of pension beneficiaries, but there are incentives to use the assets in the managers' interests.

1. Corporate pension funds are run by corporate officers, with *no* employee representation (at least, I know of no such instances). Thus, the fund is a large pot of other people's liquid assets under corporate officers' control. In cases in which the corporation stands liable to meet any liabilities the fund cannot meet, what happens to the fund does not matter to fund beneficiaries—unless the corporation folds. Not a problem with United States Steel; but once we have seen such ancient honorables as Penn Central and W. T. Grant fall, we know that assuring the soundness of pension funds is truly important at most corporations. (ERISA includes a pension benefit insurance scheme.) The managers of the fund, though fiduciaries for present and potential pension beneficiaries, have an obvious incentive to utilize such a large pot for *corporate* purposes. For example, 26 percent of Woolworth's pension fund assets in 1971 were in Woolworth real estate—under ERISA, this is illegal. Or, a few years earlier—though clearly violative of securities laws—both Georgia-Pacific and Genesco used their pension fund assets to buy their own stock in a manipulative fashion so as to reduce the amounts the

corporations owed for recently-acquired smaller corporations. Many corporate pension funds held large proportions of their assets in the corporations' own stock, with the dual effect of (1) increasing pension beneficiaries' dependence on the employers' solvency, and (2) increasing management's power to insulate itself from potential shareholder-vote accountability. (ERISA limits the holding of employer stock or other property; profit-sharing funds are different.)

2. Almost all union pension funds are run, pursuant to the Taft-Hartley Act, by "joint boards," composed of equal representation from labor and management. Almost all such funds are found in industries with a relatively large number of relatively small employers, e.g., hotels and restaurants, textiles, trucking. In fact, the "multi-employer" representatives have been most notable for their passivity, leaving fund management almost wholly to the labor representatives. Union officers in a few funds have had virtual carte blanche in putting funds heavily into real estate and similar ventures in which the officials or their associates were also investing; or in using their funds to buy from themselves and their associates; or lend to, etc.

3. State and local pension funds are usually run by a board consisting of a mix of state officials—sometimes ex officio (perhaps from elective offices) and sometimes appointed; and "public representatives," who usually (sometimes by statutory requirement) are "knowledgeable in investments and finance." Some boards have beneficiary representation, but very few are entirely or dominantly so composed.

Almost all state statutes bar any member of the fund board from benefiting, directly or indirectly, from any business with the fund. Yet, one of the most pervasive conflicts facing such funds is the pressure to do business with local broker-dealers, banks, etc. "Home Sweet Home" does not hurt the fund in New York or California, et al., where there are numerous highly competent firms. It is another matter in smaller states and cities; the funds often appear to be captive vehicles for covert subsidies to local firms. Since the board members' firms usually are the more significant and perhaps more competent firms, it would probably be a hardship for the fund to do without those firms' services, or the relatively scarce expertise of those board members. I know of only one state where a significant effort is made to reduce this conflict, Connecticut: Each year a different major insurance company has a representative on the state's pension fund board, and during that year that company can do no business with the fund.

In addition to these direct conflicts, public officials on the board—or even if off—feel considerable pressure to use the fund to buy locally issued securities, particularly tax-exempts, but also smaller local firms' securities.

The most extreme instance of this problem occurs in New York, where about $7 billion in state pension fund assets are managed by a single individual, Comptroller Arthur Levitt, who is also responsible for the issuance of New York State securities. Without Levitt's reputation, that structure would be intolerable.

**147**

*Alternative
Views on
Regulating
Conflicts of
Interest in the
Financial Firm*

The list of similar pension fund conflicts in each sphere does not exhaust the conflicts. But there are two more items. First, there is the problem of corporate pension fund managers, who are also officers of the funding corporation, "juggling the actuarial assumptions" which determine how much in new funds must be contributed to the fund to meet its liabilities. For example, United States Steel reported earnings of $147.5 million in 1970 and $154.5 million in 1971. In 1971, United States Steel said: "Pension costs were lower in 1971 than in 1970. . . . The interest rate assumption for funding pension costs was revised, as it has been from time to time, in light of the actual experience of the pension fund." Data later in the report showed that the revision added $42.7 million to net earnings. Similarly, in 1972, Sohio's revisions turned a marginal gain into a solid one.[24] Today, ERISA requires that actuaries "certify" their pension plan assumptions, and changes in actuaries or assumptions must be reported to the Department of Labor.

Last is the most acute current problem confronting union funds and ERISA administrators. As noted, employers contributing to such funds tend to be small firms. Many of them, especially in such industries as the construction trades, tend to operate on little working capital. Frequently, they have difficulty meeting payments when due—payments for everyone and everything, not merely pension contributions. Their creditors tend to know well whom to trust for how much and how long, and so do the union representatives on the pension fund board. But at what point is "necessary tolerance" of delinquent pension payments an abusive pattern in which the fund is really extending continuous credit to the employer, and at what point is it essential to survival of marginal firms? The fuzziness of that line may be one reason why multiemployer representatives on the boards of these funds tend to go along so much with the union representatives. Otherwise, the union representatives might take a hard line toward "tolerance." (The Labor Department has been asserting that these are unsecured loans to parties in interest, and all illegal.)

## Investment Companies

Mutual funds, or open-end investment companies, have a management structure which is hard to believe. The fund holders do not vote for their management but for a board of directors, which, in the main, merely contracts the fund's management out to an outside or "external" management company. Those directors, however, consist of persons from the management company—plus, by requirement of the Investment Company Act of 1940, several "independent," or "unaffiliated," or "disinterested" directors. Thus, the management contract is not entered into after a search of the market for such services but, instead, in a rather cosy setting. Indeed, the basis for requiring the independent

---

24. Brooks, N. 15 *supra* at 32–33.

directors is precisely a concern to keep the "negotiation" of the contract from being too cosy, the terms too sweet. In fact, a very strong showing could be made, and many informed persons are convinced, that the industry pattern has been one of management terms far too sweet. Are "independent" directors—even if exclusively responsible for the negotiation, and even if they were a majority—a sufficient safeguard? A highly interested skeptic, plaintiffs' attorney Abe Pomerantz, stated:

> In real life I have found that the independent directors are not really independent. I don't mean that they are bad men or that they are ogres. I simply mean that, since it is the affiliated directors who habitually and historically appoint the unaffiliated directors or designate them for directorial office, it won't surprise any sophisticated person to learn that the affiliated people don't pick toughies. They pick fellows who are friends of theirs and who are likely to be kind of—again I don't want to use harsh adjectives like "submissive" or "dominated," but let's say friendly. Let's say they are friendly. They are not watchdogs.
>
> Because if you really want to have a watchdog watch a man, you don't have the man select the watchdog.[25]

Can outside representation be made a meaningful safeguard? Perhaps the basic "external management" structure makes no sense.

A second statutory safeguard arises from that same lack of arm's-length bargaining or accountability between the managements of such a fund and the fund. No sale or purchase of property may occur between fund and "affiliated persons" except after specific application to the SEC, public notice and opportunity to present views, and, finally, SEC approval. It is clear that this greatly inhibits transactions and that it is acceptable only if one assumes that many of the transactions would be abusive. All transactions by all managements, however impeccable their records, must run a gauntlet of expense, delay, and substantive review by government. The SEC also has here a considerable burden.

Third, when bank holding companies applied to the Federal Reserve Board for permission to manage closed-end investment companies, there was opposition from existing investment companies, and vehement claims that the conflicts of interest would be too troublesome. The Board granted permission, but with a number of conditions aimed at safeguarding against conflict problems—e.g., barring the use of the banks' names on the investment companies, lest the latter be sold (overtly or not) on the basis of the bank's reputation for soundness and even, perhaps, with some confusion as to just how far from insured deposits any such investment would be. Perhaps the FRB required the safeguards because of the opposition from the competitors, or perhaps because of sensitivity (in light of the Glass-Steagall Act) about preserv-

---

25. *Mutual Fund Legislation of 1967, Senate Banking Comm.*, 90th Cong., 1st Sess., 691 (Aug. 4, 1967) (testimony of Abe Pomerantz).

ing a line between banking and securities activity, or perhaps because the FRB saw the conflict problems unusually clearly as a result of the long federal experience in regulating investment companies.

In any event, when only a few months earlier the FRB allowed bank holding companies to manage similar vehicles—real estate investment trusts (REIT)—there was no similar concern for safeguards against conflicts. The conflicts in managing REITs seem even *more* acute because of the pricing of investments there and the BHC sponsor of the REIT conducting competing real estate activity for its own account.[26]

## WHAT TO DO? EXPERIENCED AND SUGGESTED LINES FOR REGULATION

### Premises

In the nineteenth century, courts spoke as if it were possible to keep dualities of interest, and thus conflict situations, from even arising. For example, in 1846, the Supreme Court said:

> The general rule stands upon our great moral obligation to refrain from placing ourselves in relations which ordinarily excite a conflict between self-interest and integrity. . . . In this conflict of interest the law wisely interposes. It acts not on the possibility that, in some case, the sense of that duty may prevail over the motives of self-interest, but it provides against the probability in many cases, and the danger in all cases, that the dictates of self-interest will exercise a predominant influence, and supersede that of duty.[27]

As the Court said in 1880, "Constituted as humanity is, in the majority of cases duty would be over-borne in the struggle."[28]

Condemnation of efforts to serve two masters goes back as far as the Sermon on the Mount,[29] and even earlier. Plato sought to avoid conflicts by recommending that his philosopher kings be stripped of all personal assets.[30] But as a noted scholar stressed, "Plato was, after all, talking of the Kingdom of Heaven, and the same anthology in which Matthew appears speaks also of rendering unto two different masters that service which is the due of each."[31]

In the past century, with no weakening of moral fiber but rather

---

26. See further Schotland, N. 18 *supra* at 274–83.

27. Michoud v. Girod, 4 How. 503, 554, 11 L. Ed. 1076, 1099 (1846).

28. Wardell v. Union Pacific R.R., 103 U.S. 651, 658 (1880).

29. Matthew, 6:24.

30. Plato, *The Republic,* Book VII, p. 543.

31. Manning, "The Purity Potlatch: An Essay on Conflicts of Interest, American Government and Moral Escalation," 24 Fed. B.J., No. 3, p. 239 (Summer 1964), citing also Mark, 12:17.

rising recognition of the great and growing scope of the variety and complexity of doing business in corporate forms, we came to understand that to bar all dualities of interest was impossible outside the Kingdom of Heaven, or at least was an incalculable impediment to earthly efficiency. It was also recognized that the legal, ethical, and other concerns over the potential for self-serving abuses, inherent whenever duality of interest became conflict of interest, could be protected against by using more subtle, detailed devices.

Allowing the market to take care of problems is highly desirable. But there are many problems the market does not reach or reach well, from the lawyers' setting of fees, to South Dakota's needing its only broker-dealers to bring their expertise onto the State's pension fund board, to the problem of delinquent payments to union pension funds. By definition, conflicted transactions occur wholly or partly outside the play of market forces.

Of course, the best answer is the integrity of the persons involved. But that cannot be the only answer, for at least two reasons:

1. While most people strongly want to perform with full integrity, many of the conflict situations are fairly complex, and guidelines and practices are far better than requiring each individual, in each situation, to go through de novo thinking about what is the right course of conduct.

2. Integrity is not merely a matter of purity of heart but, at least in finance, with its frequent complexities, is also a matter of judgment that usually comes with experience. Our financial institutions are so large and in such flux, and our society enjoys such personal career mobility and constant emergence of new firms, that many people have substantial fiduciary responsibilities and obligations without having had the prior experience that prepares them to anticipate conflict situations. Established policies and practices might be dispensable in a scene where few new firms emerge and where personnel turnover is limited enough that word-of-mouth training and shared experience could do the job. That is not our scene.

## Answers

The *first* implication for regulators—whether at the legislative, the administrative, or the judicial stage of a problem—is to recognize that in complex financial instruments or institutions, conflicts are virtually bound to be present. They must be canvassed, and their avoidability must be assessed: Can the structure be redesigned to eliminate or reduce them, or at least reduce their likelihood of abuse and the severity if abused?

The *second* implication is that precisely because conflicts are so widespread, varied, and intricate, direct regulation cannot be the sole solution. Rather, the regulatory framework must embrace direct efforts to stimulate market and self-regulatory corrections. This means three kinds of regulation.

*Alternative
Views on
Regulating
Conflicts of
Interest in the
Financial Firm*

This is an indispensable part of the scheme of safeguards needed for many conflicts, and may be the sole step for some. Disclosure can serve several purposes, in addition to its best-known use: "sunlight as disinfectant." For example, if a firm is not required to have any specific procedures on X but must disclose what procedures it does have on X, then it will probably establish at least minimal procedures; and, if clients care about how X is handled, then there will be some healthy competition among firms to offer more satisfactory procedures on X. There, as in many other settings, disclosure is helping market choices operate better. Examples are:

1. In situations such as the control of use of inside information in such multifunction firms as major broker-dealers or banks with trust departments, there should be not only disclosure of what practices or procedures the firm does employ, but also specific answers to specific questions. For example, which commercial-side personnel have what, if any, trust-side functions? If there are any common personnel, what steps are taken to avoid abuse of conflicts—does the commercial-side person stay away when "conflicted" stocks are up for investment decisions? What, if any, common use is made of research facilities? What procedures are followed if material inside information does come into the hands of investment personnel? Are clients apprised, loud and clear, that they should not expect to benefit from any inside information the firm may secure?

2. In situations in which a firm acts sometimes as broker and sometimes as dealer, data might be required to be available upon request by any client considering a dealer transaction, as to the dealer's current inventory in that security and recent inventory trend.

3. In situations in which a firm acts as trustee, investment manager, or adviser, explicit disclosure of any conflicts should be made if a "conflicted investment" is recommended or selected. Did the firm underwrite? Is the private placement coming from a customer of another arm of the firm? Etc.

   Also, in such situations, an important overall safeguard would be to require disclosure of the median risk-adjusted investment performance of each category of accounts under the firm's management, and comparable data on each account willing to pay for compiling the data. Then, each personal trust account beneficiary, or pension account principal, would be able to see how his account had fared, compared with similar accounts. Of course, there are many differences among accounts, but making the firm accountable for explaining will go far—with little cost— to assuring that no accounts are simply abused, or that if they are, investors will see it and move elsewhere. The market in investment management services would improve greatly.

4. Beneficiaries of collective accounts such as pension funds must have full, periodic data on risk-adjusted investment performance, measured against other comparable funds; compensation to each provider of services, and the process of its selection; and the process of valuation of

any nonpublic market investments, such as real estate or private placements; etc.

In short, mandated disclosure of key systems and key data serves as a powerful protector but is not intrusive into business judgments.

MANDATED SELF-REGULATORY MECHANISMS

Disclosure, even if done with sophisticated diversity of methods of dissemination, cannot communicate the whole message. Moreover, disclosure has invaluable, but not unlimited, impacts on the process of making decisions. There must also be appropriate representativeness. This does not mean "consumer" members on a bank's board. It does mean some directors who are not only "outside" but also (1) are not "affiliated," as a borrower would be "affiliated" with a bank; (2) meet criteria, established by statute or regulation, of relevant background; and (3) are assured, in proportion to the firm's resources, both direct compensation and also an adequate budget for such support (as counsel, accountant, or whatever) as they may need, on occasion, if they are to be more than rubber stamps. Indeed, steps by former SEC Chairman Hills, and the New York Stock Exchange (NYSE), have moved impressively (on at least some of these lines) to require outside directors and board audit committee members for listed corporations.

Appropriate representativeness in pension fund management would go far indeed to reducing conflict abuses. I believe it sheer anachronism that corporate, and so many state and local, funds are managed entirely by "management." Collective bargaining tends not to correct this because improving the system gets a lower priority than improving the pay, or level of benefits, or working conditions.

It seems amusingly obvious that one of the surest correctives of conflicts of interest is to make certain that each interest is represented (as near as may be practicable).

MANDATED PRIVATE ENFORCEMENT MECHANISMS

Disclosure and representativeness need their "stick behind the door." This means, at least, consideration of the availability of class action suits for beneficiaries of collective accounts, or for clients (or beneficiaries) of accounts managed by one firm, for injurious conduct allegedly in abuse of a conflict of interest.

In any such suits or administrative proceedings (e.g., before a bank regulator or the SEC), where there are time-tested procedural safeguards against frivolous litigation, the tribunals might be authorized to award reasonable attorneys' fees and costs to a private party who substantially prevails, or who, in the discretion of the tribunal, has rendered a service to the administration of the account or accounts in question. This would be merely an adaptation of what ERISA already provides pension beneficiaries.

The *third* implication is that existing regulators, particularly of depository institutions and insurance companies, must raise the priority they assign to assuring against abuses of conflicts. These agencies' long-standing primary concern with financial soundness and their emerging concern with consumer protection both require systematic review of the regulated firms' systems for handling conflicts of interest. The Comptroller of the Currency has changed its examinations of trust departments in that direction.

Such review, or "systems worthiness assessment," as the Federal Aviation Administration (FAA) calls an analogous program reviewing airline safety, entails extremely limited additional burden on regulators already performing close and intricate reviews of all regulated firms. Moreover, assuring that each firm has a system tailored to its own situation and also covering the kinds of problems broad experience has shown need coverage is the strongest means of avoiding abuses and procrustean legal requirements.

The *fourth* implication is the acute need to avoid procrustean requirements, since the problems are so varied and the firms' resources so diverse. All problems can be met with integrity if appropriate guidance and support are furnished. Also, we must not, in the name of "conflict-proofing," unduly burden smaller firms. As one small trust department's chief officer said after hearing the full range of steps Citibank took to build its "Chinese Wall," "We can't afford two dining rooms."

The Chinese Wall excellently exemplifies the need for flexibility. It might be that the Wall is not really worth full consideration, if one believes it cannot work when it is really needed. In that case, one would have to consider separating trust from commercial functions, which raises so many additional questions as to need another paper.[32] Here, on the assumption that we will not force separation and so avoid these conflicts, suffice it to note that a giant bank can do far more than a smaller bank; that there are acute conflicts at every size level; and that even the smallest banks can take special steps to reduce conflicts in the more acute situations, as by not acquiring shares in "conflicted" local firms and trying to liquidate "inherited" positions in such stocks.

---

32. For some years, there has been considerable discussion of splitting bank trust departments away from bank commercial departments. Some people favor this as an answer to what they perceive as undue concentration of economic power in banks; others favor it, or favor it also, as a step to prevent abuses of conflict of interest.

Whether bank trust departments should be wholly separated from their banks (or bank holding companies) raises many issues which go beyond conflicts of interest, such as how the newly independent trust operations would be capitalized; whether insurance or bonding might suffice instead of, or in addition to, capital; more important, what impact such a change would have on cost of services and conditions of competition in the investment advisory market; and, perhaps most important and least predictable, how the change would affect the quality and type of personnel coming into the trust industry. Moreover, while total separation might be feasible for large banks—leaving aside its cost or worth—in most communities, a forced splitting of the bank from its trust operations would result too often in the community's losing local trust services.

The *fifth* and last implication is that there must continue to be, just as there have been, a variety of intrusive prescriptive or proscriptive requirements, lest we run undue risks of abuse. I refer to existing requirements such as (1) limiting the amount of employer's stock (or other property) a pension fund may hold; (2) limits on an investment banker's trading activity in the period just after a new issuance; (3) limits on banks' loans to insiders; etc. Some of the new limits should be plain from the text examples above: (1) requiring that REIT sponsors engaged in concurrent, competitive activity, invest *pari pacsu* with their REIT and give the REIT an effective right of first refusal; (2) certainly requiring trust departments not only to refrain from buying their own bank or bank holding company stock (already taken care of), but also to "pass through" to trust account principals all the votes on any such shares "inherited" by the trust department and retained because of the wishes of account principals; (3) taking steps to limit the likelihood of conflicts or impact of abuse by limiting the size of equity positions any single investment manager may hold (size measured as a proportion of each company's stock outstanding, with flexibility, so that institutional investors would not be barred from investing in smaller companies); and (4) limiting routine purchases and sales by "conflicted" investment managers—e.g., an issuer's investment banker or substantial creditor—to certain periods such as the two weeks following each quarterly report.

With disclosure, we have a clear principle and the challenge of tailoring its implementation so as to be effective in particular situations. With prescriptive and proscriptive requirements, little generalization seems possible, but there is some. Such requirements too often involve more than anticipated burdens on regulators and costs for regulated firms, with *undesired* negative impacts on smaller firms. We have long recognized, in regulatory schemes, the need to reduce burdens on smaller firms, but we have made far too few distinctions and have been begrudging with those few (as in the SEC's incredibly late upward revision of its $300,000 level for lesser reporting requirements on new issues). We have, so far as I know, not even begun to recognize that (1) firms which have presented problems relatively frequently might well be subjected to closer monitoring or stricter requirements than other firms; and/or (2) firms with unblemished records might be freed of requirements such as *advance* approval of certain transactions. Such differentiation puts burdens more where they belong, thus creating additional incentives to meet public policy needs for protection against abuse of conflicts of interest.

# COMMENTARY

Sam Peltzman, *Professor, Graduate School of Business, University of Chicago*

I came to this conference in the hope that I would find out about a problem called "conflict of interest." After reading Schotland's paper, my ignorance about this problem remains unvanquished. My search for a workable definition, or even a tractable delineation of its boundaries, proved fruitless. What I got instead from Schotland's paper was a vague sense of unease with a variety of conduct that, I would argue, more easily fits within more familiar categories: monopoly pricing, exploitation of ignorance, or even the age-old desire to get something for nothing.

As we all know, conflict is an inherent companion of many social relationships. I would like my mechanic to turn my car into a Rolls Royce for free; he would like to charge me the price of a Rolls Royce for a knowing gaze under the hood. We also know that our social system relies mainly on competition within a set of defined and enforced property rules to mobilize these conflicts of interest for mutual advantage. Schotland is well aware of all this, and his emphasis on the role of competition in turning inherent conflict into a creative force is commendable. But I believe that, because his view of the role of competition is too limited, Schotland has either exaggerated or misunderstood the problems that remain.

Since I despair of finding a meaningful definition of the problem, let me illustrate this point by treating conflict of interest the way Schotland does—by heuristic illustration. Consider his example of the "two-hat problem." We academics are quite familiar with this problem: We are hired to teach children, and we are hired by publishers to write textbooks. There is often a remarkable coincidence between the name of the teacher and the author of the textbook his students purchase. Is there something wrong with this that we ought to guard against procedurally? Let me say immediately that sometimes there is something wrong, in the sense that the student would, at times, have gained from a different combination of teacher and textbook. But, here, I presume we have to deal with the more difficult issue of whether the harm is likely to be so great and pervasive as to commend a costly remedy. I submit to you consumers of our services that, on some reflection, you are unlikely to want us debarred or restricted from using our own textbooks. That cozy arrangement will usually profit the student as it does us, because part of what we communicate to the student is unique: our mode of analyzing problems, our sense of what is important and what is trivial, etc. This can frequently be put across better if the student reads us as well as hears us. You would risk your son's or daughter's loss of more that is valuable in this arrangement than you would be likely to gain by restriction of it.

Why should I be so confident in this essentially empirical judgment? You would, after all, have justification for suspecting that my judgment is nothing more than self-interested apologia. The reason for my confidence, however, goes back to the broader view of competition that I find missing in Schotland's paper. Despite our best efforts, we academics have not been terribly successful in isolating ourselves from this competition. It is a competition that goes far beyond attracting *your* son or daughter to our classroom. We are constrained to seek their goodwill after they graduate, to maintain our reputation, to contribute to that of our institution and profession—all this, not necessarily because it flatters our vanity but because to do otherwise would be bad for business. You are not constrained by our temporary monopoly over the tender judgments of this year's class, nor ought you to rely on some unselfish sense of professional obligation for us to do right by our students. Look, instead, to the potential impairment of our comforts that would ultimately attend our regularly falling behind our competitors.

Of course, I mean all this to be a much more general comment on Schotland's mode of analysis. He places heavy weight on the specific exploitation of short-run advantage—the bank that dumps bad loans onto its REIT, the mutual fund manager who votes himself a handsome management fee, etc. These can commend themselves to us as intractably serious problems when we are attracted by the apparent weakness of competition in the specific instance. But I must insist that this is not what competition is all about. It is not simply that this REIT will be impaired in competing for capital or that the mutual fund will risk redemptions, important as these considerations may be. It is that the bank and the mutual fund manager risk loss of reputation and, consequently, of future business, perhaps in fields far beyond real estate lending and investment management. Indeed, let me argue that market competition, broadly understood, will make this risk increase in proportion to the danger of short-run exploitation.

To understand my argument, I want you to notice how many of the instances of potential exploitation Schotland cites occur in service markets. Indeed, Schotland makes explicit what he regards as the weaknesses of ordinary competitive forces (narrowly conceived) in these

markets—the usual consumer informational requirements are unlikely
to be met, shopping for something you cannot see, feel, or smell is
expensive, etc. But, now, notice something else about these markets—
the prevalence of client relationships. We are frequently prone to speak
of "my doctor" or "my lawyer" or even "my mechanic" as we are not
prone to speak of "my department store" or "my restaurant." This
connection between services and client relationships is neither accidental nor unrelated to the problem at hand. It is, first, a method by which
the customer brings to bear on a specific transaction a competition for
future business. The seller will be less eager to exploit a short-run
informational advantage if he thereby risks losing a lifetime of my
business. Second, it invites a competition among sellers for reputation.
The seller who expects to have me as client can also expect me to
communicate the broad range of my experience to others seeking a
similar service. The force of this competition for future business and for
reputation can sometimes be strengthened by some of the very practices that appear ominously pregnant with conflicts of interest. If the
seller wears two hats instead of one, the future value of my business in
either line can be held hostage to his current performance in the other.
So, too, is his wider reputation in either line put at greater jeopardy by
improper performance in one. The ability to wear two hats successfully
is, of course, greatly constrained by the advantages of specialization. I
would be leery of having my doctor defend me in court. But when
knowledge and technique are sufficiently similar, I may eagerly seek
conflicts of interest. The possibility, for example, that my banker might
lose both my brokerage business and my deposit and lending business
if he *either* churned my portfolio *or* overcharged for a loan may well
make him a better broker and a better banker.

Is there, then, a conflict-of-interest problem worth talking about?
Since this conference must presume such a problem, my responsibilities to it seem to demand more than the Panglossian view that conflict
of interest is really a good thing. So, let me state that there may be a
problem, but I am not sure it has much to do with conflict of interest,
however vaguely that is defined. It is a corollary to my argument, so far,
that the absence or weakness of competition in all its relevant dimensions is a necessary precondition for what may be called "abuse" of
conflict of interest. Let me make it clear at the outset that I mean to talk
about activity that is important and pervasive enough to merit consideration of important and permanent remedies. And, if my corollary is
apt, this requires us to focus on cases where the forces of competition
are significantly and permanently weak. What I would like to argue is
that, in these cases, we will often be misled if we search for conflict-of-
interest abuse when we ought to be looking for more general manifesta-
tions of monopoly power. That is, the relevant theory is the more
familiar and more precise theory of monopoly pricing.

Consider the example of the bank which grants loans on preferential
terms to insiders. What might ordinarily constrain this? At one level, a

precise definition of the property rights of depositors and investors might do this—as Schotland points out, some such activities may more usefully be treated as a breach of criminal law. (Before I lay such cases aside, I should mention one reason why property rights may be ill-defined for banks. This is the government monopoly of deposit insurance, with its associated, subsidized insurance rate structure. This makes it unclear whether the depositor is lending his funds to the care of the bank or, ultimately, to the care of the FDIC, and so weakens the depositors' interest in guarding against fraud or robbery.) When the property law is inapplicable, what defense has the depositor or investor against what he would regard as an imprudent management decision? My lawyer friends will hastily consult the law of trusts. I am convinced that they vastly exaggerate the importance of such concepts as fiduciary responsibility generally, and especially when applied to ongoing management decisions. I see no important distinction between the trust I repose in my banker to treat my investment funds wisely and the trust I repose in Macy's to treat my shopping funds wisely. Nor should I expect the motives of either in soliciting my funds to differ greatly, so the special obligations imposed by the law on my banker ought not be relied on too heavily (or may even foreclose some mutually advantageous investments). It all ultimately comes down to competition. When my banker is shielded from competition, by entry control or maximum deposit rates, I have to expect that my deposit will earn less than otherwise. If I am one of a multitude of potential investors, and the bank organizers have a scarce talent in securing a bank charter, I ought to expect that they, rather than I, will receive the benefits of noncompetitive returns in banking. It is fundamentally this noncompetitive margin that makes for the possibility of a regular, pervasive "exploitation" of conflict-of-interest situations.

But ought we to expect this particular form of exploitation to be a major component of monopolistic exploitation? While I am prepared to be persuaded by evidence, the logic of economics argues against this— or it suggests that the practice may mitigate the effects of monopoly. Return to our bank officer who is able to extract monopoly rents from depositors. Assume, in the first instance, that he must act competitively for loan business, because of the wide range of nonbank alternatives available to his borrowers. Then, if he lends to himself at low rates, and he is not an efficient user of these funds, all he has done is to shuffle money from one pocket to the other, while bearing the cost of his inefficiency. Assume, for example, that his inefficient business earns 8 percent on its funds, while a comparable efficient business is willing to pay 10 percent. There is simply no way our banker can avoid losing this 2 percent differential by lending to himself at less than 8 percent. Of course, if he earns more than 10 percent, he ought to be encouraged to exploit his conflict of interest. The point, here, is quite general: We ought to expect a monopolist, no more or less than a competitor, to exploit his position efficiently. If it is indeed the case that a conflicted activity promotes inefficiency, we ought not to worry over its impor- **159** tance or we ought to be concerned about any barrier to substitution of the more efficient activity.

Now consider the alternative circumstance: The loan market, or some segment of it, like small business loans, is not competitive, because alternatives to banks are scarce. Loan rates, then, exceed the cost of funds. This monopoly loan rate induces the borrower to substitute labor for capital. From the social viewpoint, this substitution, induced by the monopoly loan rate, is inefficient; it raises the real cost of the borrower's output. A borrower adept enough to do so will now have an incentive to organize a bank and use his bank's funds in his business. By charging himself a competitive loan rate, the combined profits and efficiency of his bank and other business will have increased. To the suspicious outsider, this bargain loan rate looks like abuse of a conflict of interest, but it is the sort of abuse we would do well to encourage, for it mitigates the inefficiency brought about by monopoly.

If you think this story is fanciful, I would ask you to consider the sorts of markets where this kind of self-dealing ("vertical integration" is a more neutral term) may have aroused your suspicion. How frequently are these characterized by some legal restraint on competition, as is the case with many parts of our capital markets? If you want to see the generality of my point, ponder the structural changes that have accompanied deregulation. Look, for example, at the gradual unbundling that has taken place in the brokerage business since May Day. The fact that institutions and, to a lesser extent, individuals are now increasingly buying brokerage, research, investment management, etc. from different sources ought to lead you to reevaluate the practices that grew up under noncompetitive fixed rates. That structure could not suppress all forms of competition, but it constrained brokers to compete by offering services below cost rather than lower rates. Seen in this light, "touting" stocks in a firm's inventory may be a sinister name for holding a large inventory and shaving the bid-asked spread to attract brokerage customers. Channeling managed funds through a captive broker provides opportunities for cutting rates by servicing the funds below cost, etc. Analogues in banking will not be hard to find—low trust management fees will be a way to avoid legal deposit rate ceilings, for example.

Such evasion of constraints on competition is not, to be sure, an unmixed blessing. It does help to overcome monopolistic inefficiency, but it does this unevenly. Some customers will have better alternatives than others, and this means that some customers will pay the full monopoly price while others do not. Not every bank borrower can organize a bank, nor does every trust customer have a fat deposit account to trade for superior trust services. The price discrimination that effectively results from this can create its own inefficiencies and— perhaps more important from the perspective of Schotland's paper— inequities. But let us be clear on the source of these inequities. They have far less to do with abuse of conflict of interest than with the working of noncompetitive markets. The widow whose trust account is managed less attentively than a large depositor's may well be obtaining the management on competitive terms. The seeming inequity stems from the bank's incentive to undercharge the large depositor. The widow can expect no better overall terms if the bank is required to stop doing better by the large account. About all that could be expected from such a rule is a weakening of competition for large deposits. In general, if we focus on eliminating abuses of conflict of interest, we run the risk of gaining their elimination at the cost of strengthening monopoly. We would, I think, be better off to eliminate the monopoly and let competition attack the abuses.

I should emphasize something that has been lurking in my remarks and that my professional colleagues will already have seen. Abuses of conflict of interest will be with us always, no matter how few the restraints on competition. So, too, will most other forms of evil. All of us, I think, realize this and, if we pursue the logic rigorously enough, understand the modesty this imposes on our goals. Put in our jargon, there is a socially efficient amount of evil. Schotland surely understands this, but his exposition, and, I fear, that of many policy-oriented lawyers, inevitably ends up obscuring this fundamental truth. He takes seriously the ability of well-selected episodes to tell us whether there is too much abuse of conflict of interest. In the end, though, we find out only that these abuses exist. This, I am afraid, tells me no more about the utility of our legal system than would a similar taxonomic description of this week's murders.

I do not mean by this to imply that the status quo is appropriate in either case. My purpose is, rather, to suggest how I think we ought to go about analyzing such problems. We ought to begin by asking what forces nurture a phenomenon and what forces constrain its growth, which goals the phenomenon is consistent with and which inconsistent. In short, we should start from a theory which predicts the extent and incidence of the phenomenon, and then see whether that theory is consistent with the facts. Unless we have some basis for knowing why and when conflicts of interest arise, I find it difficult to understand how we could conclude that there is too much of it or how we could design an appropriate remedy. I have tried to adapt some essential elements of economics to shed light on the why and when of conflict of interest. This led me to conclude that we ought to find it more prevalent in service markets than goods markets, more prevalent in noncompetitive than competitive markets. These implications can be checked against evidence, and if they are found wanting, I will have to reexamine my conclusion about the social utility of this form of behavior, and the dangers of regulating it directly. I say reexamine rather than abandon because I still would want to understand the why and when before I can sensibly jump to policy conclusions.

Schotland has been sensible enough to ask and answer the right questions often enough to be restrained in his own policy conclusions. I do not believe these will effectively deal with whatever problem is at hand because I see the relevant phenomenon in a different light. I could quarrel with his recommendations on other grounds, but that would take us too far afield into the economics of disclosure. I see enough work to be done in the analysis of financial institution practices to keep us busy for a long time.

# DISCUSSION

SCHOTLAND: Let me make three points. First, I agree that I have a more limited view of competition than Professor Peltzman. I do not agree that it means I underestimate competition. That means merely that I do not think competition solves all problems or solves them soon enough. Nor do I believe it means that competition is problem-free. That is, competition does create its own problems.

Second, Peltzman makes several flat errors. He commits the cardinal error of many economists: overaggregation. He aggregates what has to be kept separate, and so he misses the points where the action lies.

For instance, he speaks of bank loans to insiders, and says that if a banker lends to himself at low rates and is not an efficient user of these funds, all he has done is shuffle money from one pocket to another.

Now, we have about 15,000 banks. I doubt that there are 50 of them that are in the 100 percent possession of a single person. They are owned by large numbers of stockholders. Preferential insider loans will occur at the expense of the marginal outside borrower, who is knocked out when the money goes to the insider.

In addition, he says the bank which manages an REIT will not abuse the conflict because of the potential loss of reputation, overlooking the fact that the bank has more at stake in its reputation as a bank than as an REIT.

He also overlooks that many abuses will not come to light and, therefore, will not affect reputation. Even if they do come to light, they may be too small to matter as compared with other aspects that make up reputation. They also may be too small to be redressed: There may be too little incentive—or legal barriers—to private or public suits.

Peltzman says the multiservice firm will be less likely to abuse conflicts because it fears losing confidence in each line. However, I may need to stay with the bank and, therefore, will be more willing to tolerate lesser performance in the investment management end. I have no doubt that occurs.

Last, all of Peltzman's treatment is either general or hypothetical. I would like him, if we have the time, to deal concretely with the few episodes of abuse in the paper and tell us whether (1) he would simply tolerate them, and (2) if not, how competition would operate to reduce the problems—for example, would allowing more firms to have fiduciary powers be a good thing; and (3) if the problem is not to be tolerated and competition will not reduce it, just exactly what he would do, other than having us all invest only in gold and use only electronic fund transfers.

PELTZMAN: First, let me clarify a point. By discussing the possibility of conflict of interest abuses in service markets and noncompetitive markets, I did not mean thereby to limit the domain of the discussion. My point—I hope I can get this across—is that we are calling abuses, in many instances, what is simply called price cutting in these markets. So, it is not that I want to dismiss the importance of the practice by focusing on only a few cases where it occurs. I am making quite a different point: Something that might look harmful to us can actually improve efficiency.

I will not discuss in detail all the specific examples cited by Professor Schotland; that would take all day, and I do not think would be very useful methodologically. Let me deal with just a couple of his points.

He talks about the denial of the benefits of a loan to somebody else if it is made to an insider. Of course, that denial is going to happen. The insider uses the loan and forecloses some alternative. My point is that we ought not to expect the choice to promote inefficiency. We ought not to expect the banker to make a loan to himself if he could avoid the inefficiency by lending the money to somebody more efficient than himself.

With respect to stockholders, again let me reemphasize that banks are competing for capital. Entry into the business is restricted. Potential investors are competing for good investment opportunities. The result is that what looks to the lawyer like an abuse of a conflict of interest in a case like this, a taking away of funds that would otherwise go to the stockholder, is not that at all. The stockholder is not going to get those funds because these are monopoly gains, and he is not the monopolist.

The astute, politically well-connected organizer is able to extract this monopoly margin. We then have to use economic theory to tell us the form in which he is going to take his margin. The theory suggests that, often, he will take it by lending to another business he controls.

The same applies to the comingling of investment management and loan business. Schotland argues that while I might go somewhere else with my investment funds, my banker would not like that; and after all, I need my banker. This implies that the bank is a monopoly, not a perfect competitor, in the market for banking services. The fact that it chooses to divide its monopoly return between my investment account and my deposit and loan account, I submit, is a detail. My having to pay this monopoly price is not going to be changed by trying to regulate explicitly what he does with my investment funds. If the banker is constrained in how he handles my investment funds, then my loan rate is going to go up. You cannot understand properly what is happening in these markets by focusing narrowly on the issue of conflict of interest.

That, I think, is the point that I have emphasized.

WILLIAM CARY: In some sense, I have been concerned in this discussion that two people were going off in quite different routes, and I do not feel as if there has been quite an adequate clashing, a confrontation, of views, even though there appears to be a great deal of it.

LAWRENCE WHITE: I think Professor Cary is right that Professors Peltzman and Schotland are passing each other and not really addressing each other. But I think the point at which they are missing each other does not directly concern the question of competition and the benefits or lack of benefits from competition. Instead, the important point is one step prior to the competition issue. The real difference is that they hold opposite paradigms about consumer behavior or, if you like, consumer behavior, investor behavior, and pension holder behavior.

One of the paradigms is the fiduciary paradigm. This is the paradigm of ignorant consumers, ignorant investors, ignorant pension holders, who do not know their own best interests. Not only do they not have the information they are trying to get—the medical information, the investment information, the legal information, the TV repair information— but they do not even know how to assess the information if they somehow get it; they do not know what is good for them; they do not know what is bad for them. They do not learn whether they have good information or bad information. They cannot ask a friend for recommendations as to who is a purveyor of good information and who is a purveyor of bad information, perhaps because the friend does not know or will give them bad advice.

As a consequence, these individuals are totally at the mercy of the purveyor of information. Within this paradigm, it is unclear how, in fact, they choose that purveyor in the first place. Perhaps they throw darts at the phone book, perhaps they do get recommendations from friends, though the recommendations are unreliable. Perhaps they simply choose on the basis of lowest price, regardless of quality, or they choose on the basis of the easy smile or friendly bedside manner. Somehow, they acquire a set of advisers, but they are at the mercy of those advisers.

In this fiduciary world, competition does not work, in the sense of being in the best interests of consumers, because consumers are not choosing properly in the first place. Accordingly, one does not get the nice results that economists normally indicate will be the consequences of competitive markets, and one will get conflict-of-interest situations, because the consumers, investors, and pension holders do not know better. Hence, in this kind of market, we need to rely on professional ethics to limit the self-interests of the seller, or, if we do not trust professional ethics, we try to fall back on legal restrictions, criminal laws, and regulation.

The critical question is: Is this fiduciary paradigm an accurate picture of a significant portion of the world? Are there significant numbers of helpless widows and orphans who simply cannot make good decisions? Or, on the other hand, is the economist's usual paradigm—a world in which consumers are not all that bad at knowing their self-interest—a better view of the world?

This, it seems to me, is where one should start a theory of conflict of interest. One *starts* with a determination of what kind of consumers exist in the world and what is the best way of empirically describing those consumers. One has to think of empirical tests to decide whether consumers are largely choosing in their own best interests or whether they are largely helpless widows and orphans.

Finally, of course, one has to add the important caveat of any economist: Even if one decided that there are significant numbers of widows and orphans who ought to be protected from themselves, is the kind of regulation that, in fact, occurs going to achieve what it sets out to achieve? And what will be its cost to those who are knowledgeable but who are now, because of regulation, being prevented from doing what they would otherwise do?

I think this view of the consumer really lies at the heart of the conflict between Peltzman and Schotland.

FRANKLIN R. EDWARDS: Would anybody like to respond to that?

PELTZMAN: I would only add one thing. There is also a market for information, and there will be an incentive for sellers to inform dumb customers. We have to add that to our story, too.

WHITE: But the fiduciary paradigm says that the incapable customers will not even respond to that market. It says that these helpless widows and orphans simply will never know what their best interests are.

WILLIAM VICKREY: I think what distinguishes bankers from, let us say, doctors, is that bankers are dealing with risky investment decisions, the consequences of which will not become apparent for a long time.

It is a little different from the conflict of interest that arises between, let us say, a legislator and the constituents, where the legislator may have several constituents who pose a tremendous conflict of interest: which people in the constituency to favor.

JOHN HAWKE: It seems to me that we have missed an important point in not looking at the sources of the obligations in conflict. A conflict is a confrontation between an obligation that is legally or morally imposed and either another similar kind of obligation or an individual's self-interest in realizing some profit. I am concerned that we may see conflicts where they do not exist if we do not examine the sources of the obligations.

For example, in one of his first examples, Schotland talks about insider loans at the Madison National Bank. That is a former client of mine, so I happen to know something about it. The question of loans to insiders is also one that the Federal Reserve is terribly interested in right now.

What is wrong with loans to insiders? One thing wrong is that there may tend to be a higher degree of risk when the people in control of credit are making loans to themselves. But assuming that they are making loans within the legal limitations on volume and are not making preferential loans or loans lower than market interest rates, which can be viewed as misappropriation of funds, why is there a conflict of interest? What obligations are in conflict when insiders make loans to themselves?

In the case of Madison National Bank, for example, it just happens that insider loans were the most profitable loans the bank ever made. The bank has never lost a nickel on these loans. I suspect what Schotland is getting at, therefore, is that there ought to be an obligation on management to spread credit around more generally. Or that the conflict is a conflict between directors' desires to make loans to themselves and some implicit obligation or some obligation that, in his view, ought to be imposed by the law, to make loans to a broader spectrum of borrowers.

Is that what we are really talking about in the case of loans to insiders?

SCHOTLAND: First, I cannot, as readily as you, assume that the loans will not be preferential. Our bank failure experience suggests that there is a relatively high incidence of preferential loans. Second, the Federal Reserve for years has been on record as to the need for substantial reenforcement of both Section 22, the limits on insider loans, and Section 23, on loan limits. We have seen that the loan limits are often abused by insider loans, even if the preferential aspect is not there. I think, by definition, you have a higher likelihood of trouble.

Also, I do not think it is just my view of the law that the banker—although I do not care for the label "monopoly"—does have a public license to gather in other people's money and use it to benefit the community. The Madison Bank made no home mortgage loans and made the smallest proportion of consumer loans in the District. It was not doing the job for which I think the statutes say banks get licenses.

Let me make, if I may, one other response, which is also a response to something Peltzman said earlier and to the gentleman's comment about the views of consumers.

I do not think it is a view of consumers' behavior that may be different here: I think it is a view of the market. And I do not understand why people who want competition to work and free market forces to operate do not seize the opportunity and applaud the suggestion to reduce, to the extent we can, nonmarket transactions where preferential pricing is likely to prevail.

If I need my bank for loans, I may suspect that it will take something off my hide over in my trust account. But if the bank is stopped from doing that, it will raise the loan price or the compensating balance price explicitly. That, it seems to me, is exactly the result we want: more explicit market pricing instead of noncompetitive, discriminatory, nonprice terms.

PELTZMAN: I think you are putting the cart before the horse. In a monopoly situation, these combinations of transactions often will mitigate the inefficiency due to the monopoly, so that having separate pricing will be less efficient. I recognize that there is a trade-off here, and it is a trade-off that an economist does not know how to make. The price discrimination that effectively results from all this bundling of the transactions will, as I tried to point out, mitigate economic inefficiency at the cost of inequity. I am saying that we ought to recognize that trade-off. You do not get the explicit pricing without a loss of efficiency, at least in many cases.

VICKREY: What do you have in mind as a case where bundling produces efficiency?

SCHOTLAND: Professor Peltzman cited an example of somebody who is overcharged on a trust account but getting a lower loan rate.

VICKREY: But, prima facie, I think that is a case of inefficiency.

PELTZMAN: Not necessarily; it is a way of selectively cutting loan rates.

VICKREY: Spell that out.

PELTZMAN: What it amounts to, in substance, is that the person who is getting bad (or no) trust service is paying more for a loan than somebody else.

VICKREY: You mean like the greengrocer who makes a big profit on bananas while taking a loss on potatoes?

PELTZMAN: By tying them together?

VICKREY: By bringing you into the store and—

PELTZMAN: A tie-in sale.

VICKREY: Not necessarily a tie-in sale. A loss leader, if you will. In what way is this promoting efficiency? I think you have made an assertion that this can produce efficiency. Now, the prima facie reaction of a person who is accustomed to thinking in terms of performance competition says that deviations from performance competition produce inefficiency, and I think the burden of proof is on you to show where, and how, this is likely to produce inefficiency.

EDWARDS: Professor Peltzman, is your point that in a regulated industry like banking, where regulations fix prices or otherwise constrain behavior so that the competitive price cannot be charged, a tie-in sale may enable the seller to evade regulation and charge the competitive (or monopoly) price?

PELTZMAN: In other words, you correct one error by making another.

EDWARDS: That is one way of putting it.

CARY: Like the fixed rates in the broker-dealer industry, until they were done away with.

I always felt that the reason we did away with fixed commission rates was not the SEC's belief in competition but our desire to eliminate the many abuses prevalent in the industry caused by give-ups and the like resulting from fixed commissions. These practices generated public outcries and, as a consequence, led finally to legislation that did away with them.

EDWARDS: I would like to bring us back to Peltzman's main point, if I may. I think his position is that if a conflict of interest arises under conditions of imperfect competition or regulation, you simply have to look at the cost and benefits of trying to eliminate it. Eliminating the conflict may cause even greater inefficiency and inequity. It is difficult to formulate any general rules and regulations to handle conflict-of-interest situations.

Is that correct?

PELTZMAN: I would put the point a little bit more precisely, that we ought to expect to be faced with the kind of trade-off that I have just discussed. You can frequently improve the efficiency of a monopoly by having price discrimination. The cost of that is inequity. I do not know how to trade equity for efficiency.

All I can do is show that there is that trade-off. I think that this trade-off gets hidden in discussions if you focus on the inequity.

SCHOTLAND: Let us take a concrete example: the stock loan situation. The FDIC did a study of this. There is no question that the group buying control of the bank is getting nonmarket interest rates, 3 percent and 4 percent when the prime is 6 percent, in return for the overlarge corresponding bank balances that will be maintained with the lending bank.

What is the cost of disclosing, at least to the

stockholders of the acquired bank, this fact? I think it is almost silly to say there is a cost there in terms of actually getting the information out. If that is going to inhibit conduct, then we have to decide whether that is conduct which we may want to inhibit.

HARVEY LEVIN: Would Peltzman favor mandatory disclosure in cases like this?

PELTZMAN: One question I would ask is: What good does all this information do? My expectation—again, I do not have the evidence—would be that it would not make a lot of difference to the welfare of the stockholders whether this fact was disclosed or not because banks have to compete for capital. That is my instinct, I might be wrong.

Everything we know in economics about mandatory disclosure in the securities market would be consistent with that judgment. For example, consider the welfare of stockholders before and after the SEC was created and began requiring disclosure of information. I can think immediately of two studies indicating that the SEC has not had much impact on anything in the securities market.

SCHOTLAND: There are studies with other results. This is a very arguable proposition.

PELTZMAN: It is arguable. If you are asking about the more general point whether mandatory disclosure is a good thing or a bad thing, I am not prepared to get into that. It has costs, and it has benefits. We ought to recognize both. It is not one of these free snacks.

WALTER GELLHORN: The fact that mandatory disclosure would not take care of all problems in every instance or be beneficial to all persons who are affected would not seem to me to be an argument against disclosure. Consider Schotland's example of Goldman, Sachs unloading Pennsylvania Railroad paper at the same time that it was busily persuading other people to buy it. I do not know for certain that if Goldman, Sachs's activities had been publicized, it would have prevented everyone from buying paper, but it certainly would have raised questions in some people's minds.

I am not satisfied, however, with all the suggestions that Schotland made for dealing with what seemed to me to be demonstrable evils. Specifically, I am dubious about the advice of encouraging class actions and providing fees for lawyers in order to bring to light some of the improprieties, or, at least, some debatable improprieties.

Class actions with assured fees for lawyers are themselves a social problem, rather than a solution for social problems. I am doubtful that we should rely on them.

On the subject of whether evils exist, I think if you went back to the period before the SEC and thought about the preferred list—the common method of financing when I was a young man going to law school—it was just taken for granted that the new issues of stock went out at an artificial figure and that the insiders went out and sold at the higher figure. That was absolutely commonplace. Regulation has much diminished that evil, it seems to me. In sum, we have accomplished something with regulation, even though some evils still exist.

CARY: Whatever position you take, the Chicago view or the University of Pennsylvania view, it seems to me that disclosure has prevented an enormous number of things from being done that would otherwise be done, and the benefit cannot be quantified.

EDWARDS: I would like to preserve the subject of disclosure for a later session.

PHILLIP CAGAN: I agree with Peltzman's monopoly approach to the problem. Not everything that we are talking about here, however, has to do with monopoly. Goldman, Sachs does not have a monopoly of the commercial paper market, and no banks have a monopoly of the trust business. Some of the cases cited are lags in information. A man leaves a trust to a bank for his family on the basis of its good reputation, but it has slipped a little and no longer obtains the top return on investments, or perhaps it invests for the managers' benefit. They cannot cheat the widow for very much, but in the aggregate, the dishonest or incompetent management may make a lucrative income for themselves or cost all clients together a lot, which could go on for a couple of decades before people stop leaving their trusts to this bank. In the Goldman, Sachs case, somebody was going to lose on Penn Central; it was only a question of who. The firm decided to get out and let somebody else bear the burden.

Consumer misinformation means that a lot of people continue to do business with disreputable characters. I think about those consumers cited earlier and how stupid they were. Yet their behavior differs not a bit from mine! When you lack information, you are stupid, but you may not be able to do much about it, except at inordinate cost.

Obviously, we, the public, make a lot of mistakes, and some people benefit from it. What ought we to do about it? If the information is really so important or useful, what prevents it from being provided now? Why do we have to force or subsidize people to supply this information? If we are not willing to pay the price necessary for its supply now, how can it be so valuable?

I am wondering whether we can really improve this situation by regulation. There is a certain value in being on the spot; somebody is going to benefit from it, and the rest of us are going to get hurt or lose out a little bit. Some people on the spot gain a lot by collecting a little bit from a large number of people. The individual losers will not pay much to avoid such losses.

If there was a big advantage to disclosure, would not suppliers say, "Look, I am going to disclose this. Do business with me." This is widely done. Where it is not, it apparently has no ready market and does not pay. In such cases, how is forcing disclosure going to work? It is incumbent upon proponents of disclosure to show how it will really work to improve each situation. I am skeptical, but I do not prejudge the argument.

With each new regulation on disclosure, however, the sharp operators will discover new ways to take advantage of their special position and information. Disclosure regulations will never keep up with new practices. Will not the need for new disclosure regulations be unending?

SCHOTLAND: I agree. I guess we will constantly be running after problems. I think we have already been running after them for some time.

CAGAN: I find the prospect of an endless stream of new regulations, each closing off some activity or increasing the cost of doing business, alarming.

EDWARDS: It is now time to adjourn. Thank you all very much. I started by saying that one reason we had this session on conflicts of interest is that lawyers, legislators, and policy makers think it is an important subject, while economists do not think it is. I leave it to you to decide whether these views have changed any as a result of our discussion today.

CHAPTER FOUR

# The Economics of Information and the Disclosure Regulation Debate

DISCLOSURE REGULATION IN
FINANCIAL MARKETS: IMPLICATIONS
OF MODERN FINANCE THEORY AND
SIGNALING THEORY

Stephen A. Ross, *Professor of Organization and Management and Economics, Yale University*

## INTRODUCTION

The literature on disclosure regulation is enormous, and it would be folly to attempt to summarize it in any brief space. Equally massive is the breadth of economic issues that come under the heading of disclosure issues. Each such issue has its own wrinkles and requires its own analysis. Despite the differences among them, however, there may be merit in attempting some sort of synthesis. Focusing on the individual aspects of each piece of legislation can often obscure the overall impact and the underlying mode of analysis. This paper is an attempt to formulate an economic framework within which disclosure issues can be examined. A deliberate effort is made to incorporate recent work on the economics of uncertainty. The first task is to identify those elements of disclosure problems that are general and appear to characterize—if not define—the area, and the second is to put these elements together into a cohesive theory.

Disclosure, a fairly new topic to economists, deals with information and its communication within the economic system. Unlike problems involving monopoly and competition, or foreign exchange rates, or farm subsidies, one cannot go back to Ricardo or Mill and quote a pithy phrase. By and large, such informational issues were ignored until fairly recently. Classical economic analysis dealt with situations where people knew the environment within which they were fitted. The consumer knew what goods to purchase, and questions such as whether a product would live up to expectations and what sort of guarantee the manufacturer offered never arose. The producer knew the resulting consequences of decisions—however far ranging—and produced for maximum profit. Investors knew all there was to know about the investments they were to undertake. They did not necessarily know the exact outcome, but no individual knew more than any other. Only nature knew for sure whether there was oil in East Texas, but whatever a well's promoter knew, the investors were also assumed to know.

Of course, the world is not this simple, and people do have different information and hold different opinions about the same economic venture. Furthermore, there is no obvious reason to think that people willingly will share their information with others. To the contrary, much disclosure legislation seems motivated by exactly the opposite view. Individuals who are privy to special information are generally thought to be unwilling to signal that information to the market; it seems a plausible story can always be told to support the notion that it is in their best interests to capitalize on such information before revealing it.

In this paper, some newly developed tools in the economics of information are applied to these issues. The results are not as obvious as the above arguments imply. The first section discusses the irrelevancy of disclosure in the classical economic world, and is followed by a section which describes the neoclassical view hinted at in the discussion about the advantages of possessing inside information. The subsequent section deals with difficulties in establishing competitive markets in information. A section on incentive-signaling analysis develops a new view of the economic forces that can motivate and implement the release of inside information. The next section examines implications for disclosure legislation of traditional and new views, and the last section briefly summarizes conclusions with regard to such legislation. An analytic appendix explicitly models some of the arguments in the text. It can be read independently of the text, but is not as inclusive. Finally, a short annotated bibliography has been included to aid the reader who wishes to look further into the relevant economic literature.

## A WORLD OF PERFECT INFORMATION

To obtain a reference point against which more complex situations involving disclosure and uncertainty may be compared, it is useful to consider a very simple world where none of the problems we will address arise. Suppose that managers, whom we will identify as insiders, and outsiders all possess the same relevant information, so that the value of the firm and its stock will be the same to both parties.

There are at least three ways in which this situation could arise. First, there may simply not be any valuable new information being generated about the firm. Such periods of quietude are not unheard of, and firms in markets that have well-defined and long-standing relationships with the economy are likely candidates. It is important here not to confuse stability with lack of change. Firms in the machine tools sector, for example, find their earnings fluctuating very sharply with movements in the business cycle, but they are stable in the sense in which I am using the term because these fluctuations are highly predictable, given the overall movement in the economy. As a consequence, firm specific information would have little impact upon firm value when it was disclosed, unless it occasioned a break with the past pattern.

Second, all information may already be known by everyone, so that disclosure will have little impact. This point of view is usually identified with the Chicago school of economic thought. The most zealous adherents to this position argue that all information that is pertinent to investors will be leaked to the market through the actions of insiders, whether or not there are disclosure requirements. By the time of any public announcement, the market knows and has already discounted the news. Whether or not this view is correct, for the moment, we should note that it is not a priori correct in a tautological sense; it certainly requires a defense through an elaboration of the mechanism by which such information is transmitted to the financial markets. Several possible transmission mechanisms will, in fact, be examined in subsequent sections.

Third, it is sometimes argued that by simply observing the past performance of a company's stock, the market can predict as well as it could if it possessed inside information. In the first case, there is nothing to disclose; in the second, all information is known by everyone, so that disclosure is redundant; and, in the last, it is now argued that even though there is inside information, it has no impact if it is disclosed. There is no need to dwell long on this argument. While specific pathological examples can be constructed to support it, generally, it is false. At its heart is a misunderstanding of the efficient-markets arguments. Past observations on prices and dividends, as well as the general financial and technical information available on a firm, do provide information about the future; they do not provide *all* the available information but only a portion of it. There is nothing at all "inefficient" about a market where more information is more informative about future possibilities.[1]

---

1. For those familiar with the mathematics of the efficient market theories, let $I_t$ represent all the information available at time $t$ and $S_t$ some subset of $I_t$. While it is true that for a stock with a random value of $P_{t+\tau}$, $\tau$ days in the future, that

$$E\{E\{P_{t+\tau}|I_t\}|S_t\} = E\{P_{t+\tau}|S_t\}$$

if

$$P_t = E\{P_{t+\tau}|I_t\}$$

so that the *current* value will be correctly expected given *only* $S_t$, it is also true that

$$E\{P_{t+\tau}|I_t\} \neq E\{P_{t+\tau}|S_t\}$$

so that more information, $I_t$, is generally superior to less, $S_t$.

## THE EXPLOITATION OF INSIDE INFORMATION AND INSIDER TRADING

In this section, we will begin analyzing the role of inside information by examining the general modes of exploitation available to insiders. The easiest way to approach these arguments is to imagine a single insider who possesses valuable information. Typically, of course, there are many insiders, and their ability to exploit their advantages is limited by the degree of cooperation among them. More specifically, the extent to which each insider monitors the activities of the others, and the extent to which they are unable either to enforce any implicit contracts or monitor any breaches, serves to limit their collusion, so that they may not actually be able to attain much advantage from their information.

Inside information can take a variety of forms. The only requirement we will make is that it not be irrelevant, i.e., given this information, the market would revise its opinions. Within this constraint, though, much is accommodated. Information about a consumer product, if made public, for example, could affect sales and firm returns. A new source of supply, a new invention, an agreed-to line of credit—almost any piece of information—can have value.

From the point of view of stockholders in the firm or, more generally, all claimants to the firm, information can be classified into either good news or bad news according to the simple criterion of whether or not its revelation would increase or decrease the market value of the firm. (There may be conflicts, though, between different claimants, e.g., stockholders and bondholders, but we will ignore these considerations.) In either case, of course, insiders can profit at the expense of outsiders.

The most straightforward method of gain available to insiders is to trade for their own accounts. If the information is good, they will raise the fraction of the shares they hold, say from $S$ to $S'$; if the news is bad, they will cut their holdings down to $S''$ from $S$ (perhaps even taking short positions). This does not exhaust the financial modes of exploitation. Bad news about one firm in an industry (for example, that a new product line is failing) may well be accompanied by good news about other firms. This increases the scope of advantageous personal trading. There are other forms of exploitation on the nonfinancial or consumption side. The executive of a large food company who refuses to let his own children eat the cereal he manufactures may be basing his decision on information outsiders do not possess.

The profitability of these activities is based on some implicit assumptions about the passive behavior of outsiders. Tacitly, it is assumed that insider activities do not communicate or signal information to outsiders, or to the market. Just as the cereal executive might not wish his personal consumption choice to be revealed, so, too, the insider-trader would not wish to communicate his activities. In the

simplest sort of world, any trading by the insider—say, a purchase—
would signal outsiders, who would revise their valuations upward.
When they had revised their selling price to a point where the insider
no longer wished to purchase, they would know that the market price
agreed with the insider's assessment; if it was lower, he would continue to buy.

**181**

*The Economics of
Information and
the Disclosure
Regulation
Debate*

An extreme variant of this is the efficient-markets hypothesis, which
argues that current financial prices in competitive markets will fully
reflect all available information. If insiders acquire information they
then trade on, the new (equilibrium) prices in the securities markets
will reflect this information. By simply observing these prices, then,
outsiders can learn the information possessed by the insiders or, at
least, its implications for value. Thus, everyone would possess the
information and, in the limit, insiders would be unable to profit by
trading on it.

There are, however, several qualifications to this view of instantaneous and perfect signaling of information by price. First, simply
observing, for example, that insiders are selling shares does not serve as
a perfect signal to the market that insiders have revised their anticipations downward on the basis of bad news. There are many other
motives for selling that cloud this simple interpretation. The manager
might be selling for life-cycle reasons, e.g., to pay for his children's
education, to diversify his own portfolio, to buy annuities and bonds
for retirement. Furthermore, any of these activities could actually be
accompanied by an upward revision of the manager's anticipations.
Second, since outsiders will have similar exogenous motives for buying
and selling the firm's shares, there will be a certain amount of leeway
available to the manager to transact without signaling his actions. In
effect, the manager would act as a one-sided trader selling into any
observed excess demand generated by outsiders, thereby limiting his
short-run impact on price. Last, the most obvious way in which the
insider can mask his activities is by conducting them through a third
party. Purchases by "Aunt Tillie" will signal less information than by
the company president. Of course, the demand itself will signal the
outside market, but when it is not identified as coming from an insider,
the impact will be less.

The obvious profit from successful insider trading comes at the
expense of outsiders—the uninformed investors—and forms the core of
the economic analysis of the benefits of disclosure legislation. Requiring disclosure of firm information presumably eliminates these effects,
if timely disclosure can be mandated. Further, disclosure requirements
on insider trading, while it does not eliminate the market's uncertainty
about the insider's true motives and assessment, does communicate
insider trades to the market. Nevertheless, the advantages of insider
information (and, therefore, disclosure regulation) may be overstated in
well-functioning and competitive securities markets.

We have already noted that insider trading, per se, communicates information to the market that tends to mitigate insiders' profits. There is an additional phenomenon at work to cut down the insider's advantage, even if he can trade anonymously. Although outsiders do not possess the same information as insiders, they do know of the existence of insiders. A simple strategy for outsiders to follow, therefore, is to limit the amount of trading they do. By investing for the "long run," outsiders can effectively cut the insiders out of achieving any substantial short-term gains. The market opportunities of the insiders would then be limited to the trading generated by life-cycle considerations and by the exogenous new information received by the outsiders. This strategy would also permit the outsiders to realize the long-run rates of return on which they had based their initial investments—at least insofar as their initial perceptions were valid. By trading for the short run, selling on short-run price rises, and buying on declines, outsiders are trading against the insiders. On average, they will lose. Outsiders may be unknowing, but they are not unsuspecting; and they are not irrational.

In sum, the extent to which insiders can profit from their information depends upon a complex balance of several forces. To some degree, the market outsiders can observe and learn from insider activities. They also have incentives to adopt investment strategies that further diminish insiders' profits. This is not to say, however, that such profit opportunities can be eliminated by wary outsiders. Gathering information about the activities of insiders is costly, as is the adoption of long-run trading strategies that do not fully react to short-run market changes and thereby restrict investor liquidity. These costs leave significant profit opportunities for insiders. Disclosure regulation acts both to increase the quantity of information that is freely communicated and to lower the cost to investors of observing insider transactions. As such, it can promote efficiency, and, as is sometimes argued, enhance equity as between insiders and outsiders.

## MARKETS AND INFORMATION

It has been suggested that rather than trading on inside information, insiders should simply sell their information. In other words, a market could arise in insider information. Such a market would have important advantages; it would transmit information to the public in such a way that investors would pay the marginal value of the information, and information would be supplied up to the point where its marginal value equaled the marginal cost of supplying it. This policy would be socially optimal.

Markets in information, though, are somewhat different from markets in oranges and shoes. There is a public aspect to information that is not present with private goods. To the individual investor, information is of value if that person alone holds it and can exploit it in the fashion of an insider. When the information is publicly held, its private value diminishes, although it may have social value. When an insider sells information, he creates a potential competitor, unless he can bargain with outsiders as a group. It is difficult to see how a competitive market for information could function under such conditions. Most important, there is a moral hazard associated with markets in information. How is the buyer, who by assumption is ignorant, to verify the validity of the information he is buying? This problem is particularly acute in financial markets, where insiders can actually gain by conveying misleading information. If the news is good and the insider can convince the market that prospects are bad, the insider can purchase shares at a lower cost than if outsiders had not been deceived. In addition, individuals who are not insiders also have an incentive to disseminate false information. As long as a person can convince outsiders of possessing superior information, that person will supply it in such a market. The costs of entry in the supply of information are generally quite low. Of course, the market recognizes this and will discount investment advice. The issue of validating genuine inside information, however, remains.

Disclosure legislation can induce individuals to be truthful by exacting penalties for the transmission of false information, but it would be simplistic to think that it is a cure for all moral-hazard problems. The real effect of such legislation is simply to shift the burden of monitoring and verifying from the private sector to the public sector, with no evident gain in economic efficiency. Moreover, such legislation does nothing to eliminate the public aspects of information, which, by limiting its appropriateness to the seller, constricts a private market in information. These considerations all seem to lead inexorably to the view that as a kind of public good, information is a commodity whose allocation is best left to the public sector. However, in the next section, we will argue that strong competitive forces, which up to now we have ignored, will act to force (truthful) information into the open.

## INCENTIVE-SIGNALING ANALYSIS

The situations described above probably strike some readers as having an alien ring. The case of the single insider trading for his own gain is quite different from the situation that prevails in the bulk of modern capitalistic enterprise. Gardiner Means observed long ago that the separation of ownership and control is the central feature of the modern corporation. The above analyses made no such distinction. In fact, the analyses are most appropriate to the situation of the isolated individual investor dealing with financial markets. The role of the insider-manager of a corporation is quite different, and to examine his incentives to disclose information, his relationship with the firm cannot be ignored.

In general, the management of a firm has a long horizon tied to that firm: The economic fortunes of the management depend on those of the corporation. There are many reasons why this should be. The most obvious is that the performance of the company is affected by the actions of the management and serves as a measure of how well the members have performed. Compensation geared to firm performance, therefore, serves as an incentive for managerial performance. Managerial compensation does not have to be tied directly by some specified formula to the earnings or overall performance of the firm. The effect of managerial activities on firm performance will still link the fortunes of the managers with those of the firm: If the firm does poorly, management will be thought to bear some responsibility, and the demand for their services will be less. Conversely, if the firm prospers, management will share some of the credit, and the competitive market will drive their wages up.

There are, however, limits. The compensation of managers is to some extent dictated by the wage level they could receive in competitive jobs. No firm will hire a manager for $1 million a year when the going wage is $100,000. By the same token, stockholders will not permit a $100,000-a-year manager to have the freedom to trade in the firm for his own account and make million-dollar gains. Such activities would be precluded by contract, not because of any moralistic attitudes. Otherwise, such activities would be a form of overcompensating managers for the services they supply. Since the potential gains from such trading described above are generally in excess of managerial compensation schedules, and since the costs of monitoring these activities to limit the managers' total compensations is quite high, the least-cost form of compensation will simply rule out the bulk of insider trading by managers. This is not to say that managers will not still have an incentive to use inside information for their own gain, but rather that stockholders are aware of such incentives and will enter into contracts that penalize such activities.[2]

In the absence of government, the private market would have to erect a structure for monitoring and enforcing these contracts. An important role for the public sector, therefore, is to provide these services. Judicial penalties for fraud and breach of contract are an incentive for management not to violate the no-insider-trading provisions that would be written into their contracts in competitive markets. This is quite different from saying that the public sector mandates disclosure regulation. Rather, in competitive markets for managerial services, managers and stockholders would reach contracts that preclude insider trading, and the role of the law is its usual one of enforcing contracts.

In summary, in a competitive market (with no mandated disclosure), the managers of firms will find their compensation linked directly to the fortunes of the firm on an ongoing basis and will be precluded from profiting directly from inside information. In such a situation, they will

---

2. To the degree that such activities are permitted, they emerge as a competitive component of total managerial compensation. In competitive markets, this component should be small and will be ignored below. Furthermore, from an efficiency viewpoint, there would not necessarily be a need to legislate against it.

have a strong self-interest in disclosing relevant information to the

outside market.

Certainly, management will have an incentive to disclose good information (unless doing so will jeopardize its value to the firm). Such disclosure will raise the value of the firm and, therefore, the manager's compensation. What of bad news? While the same reasoning argues for its suppression, the analysis is not symmetric. If managers are assumed not to disseminate misleading information, then only managers with bad news will say nothing. Outsiders, in turn, will observe some managers spreading good news and others staying quiet, and they will not draw the inference that no news is good news. To the contrary, no news will be regarded as either just that or as bad news. As a consequence, those with no news will suffer by being lumped in with those suppressing bad news. Conversely, those with bad news will gain if outsiders cannot distinguish between firms with nothing to say and firms suppressing bad news. Thus, all managers without bad news will have an incentive to disclose.

But what of the moral-hazard problem of falsely publishing good news reports? What of the related problem faced by those firms that legitimately have nothing to say? We could fall back on the legal mechanism and assert that the dissemination of false information is illegal and, therefore, prohibited. It is not clear, though, precisely how one should define false information under the law (say, to distinguish between a general statement of confidence in future prospects and such a statement based on specific information). Fortunately, there is a more natural mechanism at work to validate information.

Suppose that there were no legal prohibitions whatsoever against disseminating false information. The problem facing the manager with genuine good news is how to signal this information to the market in such a way that it will not be confused with all the misleading and false information being supplied. The manager's problem is similar to that of a producer with a superior product to sell—a better mousetrap. He or she must convince a wary public of the product's virtues. The natural solution to both problems is to offer a guarantee or a warranty.

For concreteness, suppose that a manager knows that his or her company has cleared up some substantial bottlenecks in production by a new cost-reducing innovation and, as a consequence, earnings will be moving up to a new higher level over the next several years. This is complex information, and while its detailed dissemination is possible, outsiders would find it difficult to validate. In other words, while it is true, it is also a prime candidate as a false message. On its face, outsiders with no direct means of checking on the information would tend to discount its validity.

One way in which the manager can signal the validity of this new information is to provide a personal guarantee. Suppose, for example, that the manager announces he will take a 20 percent pay reduction if earnings do not rise as he is predicting. This can serve as a guarantee to outsiders that the information being provided is valid. By explicitly altering and announcing his new compensation schedule, the manager signals the market that he has an incentive to tell the truth. Furthermore, all managers with good news have an incentive to validate their information with such guarantees in order to distinguish themselves from others.

Is the guarantee sufficient? The answer to that question depends upon the incentives that remain for managers who do not have good news to offer similar guarantees, even though they know they cannot fulfill them. In the preceding example, if the announcement were to triple both the company's stock and the manager's salary over the next four years, such a reward might be a sufficient inducement to lie, even if the manager's compensation is reduced later on. But that only means that the guarantee must be raised to eliminate the incentive for others to cheat by false signaling. Once that is done, outsiders will know that there is no longer an incentive to lie and will accept the information as valid (or the validity of the signal).

Of course, the forms that such guarantees can take may not be as direct and as simple as the one in our example. They can be as varied as the complex relationships that the firm has with the outside market. The whole financial structure of the firm, e.g., its debt and equity mix, serves as a means of communication. For example, generally, the failure to pay a dividend is taken as a sign of a reversal in the fortunes of the company and, therefore, results in lower compensation for the managers. A simple announcement of a dividend increase can be used by the firm to signal the market that earnings are rising.[3] This is a strong way of validating management's view that earnings have reached a new higher level; the penalty associated with reneging on dividend payments is high.[4]

What of the managers whose news is bad or, alternatively, have no news at all? Just as the managers with good information have an incentive to signal this to the market to distinguish their firms from others, those with no information also have an incentive to signal. To continue with our example, if the level of dividends has been raised in the past to the maximum level of sustained earnings, then simply retaining it at that level will signal "no news." Presumably, firms anticipating periods with no significant inflows of information will

---

3. Certainly, dividend announcements are anticipated in the open market. Nevertheless, the information anticipating them also is a signal, and the announcement, itself, still may provide a valuable formal validation.

4. How high depends on the exogenous information possessed by outsiders. If the outside market knew that the dividend could not be paid out of earnings, the announcement might not change the assessment of the firm, and the penalty to reneging, at least as it was related to any drop in market values, would not materialize. To put it simply, the signal must square with the outside information; managers cannot signal that a buggy whip company is a General Motors just by announcing that they will lower their pay if they are wrong.

have an incentive to maintain their current levels precisely to signal this and to distinguish themselves from firms receiving adverse news. The "no news" firms are in exactly the analogous situation as the "good news" firms: They must provide a sufficient guarantee to the market to insure, in their case, that they have not received bad news. Firms with bad news are then left with no recourse. They cannot match the guarantees of the "good news" and the "no news" firms; hence, they will be evaluated as having received bad news.[5]

In general, there is a hierarchy of firms from best to worst, based on the relative change in their values that would occur if their inside information were made public. The incentive-signaling mechanism provides a structure that managers use to disclose their information in such a way that outsiders in the market believe it. Those with the best news distinguish their firms from those with the next best, and so on down the line. At the bottom of the hierarchy are those with the worst news, who would like to suppress it, but since it is not in their interest to offer the kinds of guarantees provided by those with better news, the worst news will also be effectively signaled.

We have bypassed many complicated issues (such as timing problems and the force of the different incentive signals), but they do not alter the validity of the incentive-signaling view; they only influence its application to specific circumstances. The following is a summary of the steps in the argument.

1. In earlier sections we have seen that insiders may profit from exploiting their private inside information. Furthermore, the very nature of information makes it unlikely that a private market will arise to trade such news.

2. Under competitive conditions, the difficulty (cost) of assessing and monitoring the returns to the exploitation of inside information will result in managerial compensation schedules that largely prohibit or restrict such activities. In a competitive market for managerial services, these will be the only contracts which will be able to keep managerial compensation at the going market wage. Furthermore, both by direct construction and indirect inferences, the competitive compensation schedule for manager-insiders will link the welfare of the managers and the firm.

3. Given such a compensation schedule, it is in the interest of the managers to disclose (or signal) pertinent information and to provide guarantees concerning its validity in the form of self-imposed penalties in the managerial compensation schedules. The typical form of such signals is to use the financial policies of the firm (e.g., debt policy and dividend announcements) to communicate information.

---

5. For example, if the "bad news" firms tried to maintain their dividend, they would have to finance the shortfall from earnings externally, which, in turn, would signal the bad news to the market.

This incentive-signaling approach (i.e., the use of incentives to signal information) also provides a new format within which to discuss disclosure regulation and the role of information in markets. The complex web of arrangements and interactions between the firm and the market provide a continuing mode for the communication of information about the firm to outsiders in the market. The role of the law in this scenario is to see to it that privately agreed-upon contracts are honored. There is no need for laws legislating that information must be disclosed, since managers have incentives to reveal information. There is a need to enforce the private contracts which stockholders and managers would arguably arrive at; these serve to construct management incentive schedules. In this regard, ethics and honesty can serve along with law. The next section examines the costs and benefits of disclosure legislation, contrasting the incentive-signaling view with the more traditional views.

## EVALUATING DISCLOSURE REQUIREMENTS

Determining the benefits and costs of any particular disclosure legislation hinges on which of the above views of information in economic markets is adopted. The traditional view that insiders will never reveal their information, preferring to exploit it directly (or, that if they did disclose it, outsiders would not believe them) is too simple. On the other hand, the free market argument that management, as the agents of stockholders, will release all information up to the point where the marginal benefit to stockholders just equals the marginal cost is also inadequate. A more complete explanation of the forces in the free market that lead to disclosure is provided by incentive-signaling analysis, which elucidates the competitive incentives for the revelation of inside information.

The two free-market analyses, however, are complementary, and we will lump both theories under the incentive-signaling heading. Presumably, information would not be signaled by managers when the cost of doing so exceeds the benefits. The marginal analysis, in effect, defines the information that will be disclosed, while the incentive-signaling theory explains the mechanism of disclosure.

Which theory is correct—the traditional or the incentive-signaling view? Theories are never right or wrong, and questions like this are naive. The important point is whether the assumptions that underlie the two theories are more or less in accordance with reality. In other words, the question is an empirical one. The incentive-signaling theory is really an extension of the traditional theory, but it arrives at different implications for policy because it makes some assumptions that are different from those implicit in the traditional theory.

The traditional view argues that there are no constraints that prevent the manager from suppressing and exploiting inside information. The incentive-signaling approach argues that the absence of such constraints is incompatible with competitive financial markets and competitive markets in managerial services. If financial markets are competitive, then imperfect competition is implicit in the traditional approach with respect to managerial markets (i.e., barriers to entry into the managerial profession), and vice versa. If managerial services were purchased in a competitive market, the resulting compensation contract would not permit excessive insider trading. (If, however, entry to upper management were controlled by a group or class that bargained for its services, insider trading might well be a feature of the bargains that are struck.)

Consider the debate on disclosure policy that might take place in the absence of the incentive-signaling perspective. The traditionalist would argue that disclosure legislation is warranted because managers simply have no incentive to reveal information in a free market, and because its revelation is of value to outsiders. Such information permits outside investors to improve their decisions in financial markets and, in so doing, to enhance efficiency and improve equity as between insiders and outsiders. The usual free market retort is that if the information is of (net) value, it will be revealed, and if it is not, it will be withheld. Forcing the disclosure of such information, therefore, must inevitably incur costs in excess of the benefits to stockholders. Hence, it is undesirable.

The incentive-signaling theory also argues that relevant information will be disclosed. Further, if information is not disclosed, the theory pinpoints the fault: lack of competition. A likely candidate is an imperfectly competitive market for managers. As we have seen, if managers have some monopoly power, they may be able to strike bargains which permit them to exploit inside information. In such an environment, disclosure legislation can improve the decisions made by outsiders in the market. But it is clear that such legislation does not attack the root of the problem. The bulk of the inefficiency is the result of noncompetitive features in the market for managers. Further, applying a "Coase" type of analysis, we can argue that this market will be unaffected by such legislation. The monopoly power of the managerial class will be unchanged, so that the legislation will only alter the form of the bargains between managers and stockholders; it will not affect their total compensation. The attendant market inefficiency will remain.

Alternatively, financial markets may not be competitive. In this case, ownership of firms may be segmented, and the competitive demand for information may not manifest itself. A firm that withholds information may not suffer in terms of market value. This source of inefficiency is well known. Access to capital markets is substantial, however; so it seems doubtful that lack of competition in capital markets will prevent the disclosure of relevant information. Indeed, the managers of the large financial intermediaries display a continuous demand for such information. The explanation for a failure to disclose relevant information, therefore, would seem to lie primarily with other markets.

Insofar as the failure of other related markets to function efficiently leads to the failure to disclose inside information, there may be benefits to disclosure legislation. These benefits are usually classified as the promotion of efficiency and equity. The efficiency benefits are fairly clear. Presumably, outside investors make better financial decisions with better information, and legislation which promotes the dissemination of information relevant to such decisions has economic value. Just how quantitatively valuable such information is, though, is much harder to evaluate. The holder of a large portfolio of stocks tends to discount much of the specific information firms disclose. (For example, announcement that a firm which has taken on a large contract has incurred a 50-50 chance of a $10 million overrun or underrun may leave the value of the firm unaffected.) Furthermore, the good news and the bad news specific to firms may tend to wash out, leaving investors unaffected. The primary economic impact of such information is indirect—through the influence of financial investment on real investment. The ultimate benefits of the information for stockholders also accrue over a long time, compounding the assessment problem.

The equity benefits of disclosure legislation—as between insiders and outsiders—are more difficult to identify. The case for such benefits seems to rest on the traditional view that outsiders are at the mercy of insiders, and need to be protected from them. In contrast, the incentive-signaling view is that competition forces insiders to disclose their information, and the lack of such disclosure is a consequence of inadequate competition. In particular, if being an insider is such a good deal, then insiders will be in plentiful supply, and none will be able to earn extraordinary returns on inside information. (This is not to say that the unique ability to generate such information—as with a new invention—will not be rewarded.) If this competitive mechanism is not working, the fault must lie with artificial restrictions on the entry of outsiders into the managerial professions. If no such artificial entry barriers exist, there is no equity problem either. All in all, it seems much safer to base the argument for disclosure legislation on efficiency grounds rather than on equity grounds; as we observed above, there is no reason to believe that such legislation will have any influence on total managerial compensation.

## Costs

The costs of disclosure legislation fall into two broad and not wholly separable categories. First, there are the direct costs associated with the economic impact of the legislation on the markets affected. Second, there are the hidden costs of implementing the legislation itself. Let us first focus on the direct effects.

If the legislation results in any additional disclosure, i.e., if it is

effective, firms will incur costs. The costs may be small, as they would be if all that were involved were a simple public announcement or the insertion of some previously withheld information into the annual report. But while such costs of dissemination are generally small, the costs of gathering information can be quite high. This is particularly important when the firm is required to disclose information of a sort that it does not currently use for internal decision making. The requirement that firms disclose the current cost of replacing existing capital equipment is an example of data that may have little or no internal use but are costly to obtain. (The benefits of disclosure are not quite so clear as the costs when the information is not useful internally to the firm.)

The impact of disclosure on the incentives to generate and gather information may be equally important. It is not in the interest of the firm to disclose information when such disclosure would threaten exploitation of it. Trade secrets, the successful testing of a new invention, and the marketing of a new product are examples of inside information that stockholders might want withheld until potential profits could be secured. This desire is not, by itself, sufficient ground to preclude disclosure; if the information results in monopoly abuse, the fact that outside stockholders want it to be withheld is not determining. Nevertheless, disclosure can have the effect of lowering the return to activities that generate information. In the absence of patent protection, for example, the incentives to invent would be severely curtailed. To the extent that such protection does not extend to all forms of innovation, disclosure legislation may have an adverse impact on the supply of such innovations.

Implicit in the above description of the costs of disclosure legislation is the assumption that such legislation is effective. It is in considering the effectiveness of the law that hidden costs must be introduced. Aside from the costs of developing such legislation, once a law has been passed, costs are incurred in three areas: promulgation, monitoring, and enforcement. Promulgation costs are the costs of publishing and announcing the law, as well as the less obvious costs expended by those who must learn and interpret the law. The cost of this learning process is continuous and by no means trivial, but it is largely ignored because of the difficulty in quantifying it. How is one to measure the economic cost to the firm of understanding the requirements of a new law? (The conceptual problem is easy—the practical one, much more difficult.) The growth of the legal and accounting professions in response to the increase in government regulation should not be ignored; this represents a true social cost, to the extent that human resources are diverted to these efforts. I have nothing new to add to the analysis of these costs, but I do have the uncomfortable feeling that they are important, and that omitting them from consideration is unjustified. Recently, in England, Parliament displayed some recognition of these costs when it rejected new legislation that would apply to small businesses on the grounds that the three massive volumes of existing legislation were already a sufficient burden.

Monitoring and enforcement costs are easier to measure, at least in gross terms. If firms are required to disclose information which they would prefer to suppress, the success of this legislation will depend on the effectiveness of the apparatus set up to monitor compliance and the enforcement mechanism used when firms are found to be in violation of the law. These costs range from the bureaucratic costs of investigation to the subtler incremental costs of using the judicial apparatus.

From the incentive-signaling perspective, however, the net costs of these activities may be much less than the gross costs: Such activities may be a substitute for activities that would otherwise be undertaken by the private sector or by other areas of the public sector. The incentive-signaling theory holds that the private sector will supply the monitoring and penalties necessary to assure the disclosure of inside information, either directly or by the use of other procedures supplied by the public sector. From the gross cost of monitoring and enforcing disclosure regulation, then, we must subtract the savings from the elimination of enforcement and monitoring activities by the private sector, and from the diversion of these activities from other segments of the judicial process. Even if disclosure regulation does nothing more than require the disclosure of information that firms currently disclose, it might be beneficial! This will occur if the costs of writing and enforcing private contracts—implicit and explicit—that result in the current disclosure exceed the costs of administering the disclosure regulations. This, in turn, will depend on whether the specialized bureaucratic procedures associated with disclosure regulation are a more or a less costly mechanism for the enforcement of contracts than are conventional alternatives—the law of contracts and fraud. However, if disclosure legislation dictates a special format for disclosure, it is unlikely that it will simply substitute for existing private forms of disclosure. At the extreme, when the legislation actually serves to restrict information, as with new stock offerings or the advertising of new investment projects, it may actually restrict competition and prevent the disclosure of relevant data. These are the costs of the monopoly abuses that such legislation may inadvertently encourage.

In sum, the central message of the incentive-signaling analysis is that the source of a failure by insiders to supply relevant and truthful information to outsiders is the existence of noncompetitive forces in related markets—in particular, the market for managerial services. Given significant barriers to competition, the long-run solution lies in antitrust legislation. Disclosure regulation must be judged as a component of such legislation. It is a short-run remedy for some of the adverse effects of monopoly. Its long-run benefits turn solely on the more delicate issue of whether it is a more efficient means of policing private contracts than are the remedies provided by existing law.

## SUMMARY AND CONCLUSION

This paper has introduced a new structure, the incentive-signaling model, for the analysis of information in financial markets and has examined the implications of this structure for disclosure legislation. While definitive results depend on the empirical magnitudes of the forces involved, the new structure basically supports the view that there are strong market forces tending to lead to adequate disclosure in the absence of disclosure legislation, a view in sharp contrast to the traditional view that disclosure legislation is required because insiders have strong incentives to withhold information. But it does not follow that disclosure legislation is always unnecessary or always inefficient. Such legislation can sometimes provide alternative and, perhaps, cheaper mechanisms for policing arrangements than the private sector would arrive at independently. Finally, if disclosure is inadequate, the incentive-signaling analysis places the blame squarely on the noncompetitive features of the relevant markets. Thus, disclosure regulation can be seen as a substitute for a vigorous antitrust policy.

# APPENDIX A—MODELS OF ALTERNATIVE DISCLOSURES POLICIES

In this appendix, we use a simple but formal model to examine the effects on firm value and on the value of an initial holder's assets from following different disclosure policies.

For simplicity, there are two time periods and two states of nature: $G$ for good news and $B$ for bad news. At time 0, we adopt a disclosure policy; at time 1, the state of nature is revealed, and the disclosure policy is implemented; and at time 2, the firm returns $a$ if the information is good and $b < a$ if it is bad. Diagrammatically, we have the following environment

$$
\begin{array}{c}
\quad\quad 1 \quad\quad\quad\quad 2 \\
0 < \begin{array}{l} G \;\vdash\!\!\!\!\!\!-\!\!\!\!\!\!-\!\!\!\!\!\!\dashv a \\[2mm] B \;\vdash\!\!\!\!\!\!-\!\!\!\!\!\!-\!\!\!\!\!\!\vdash b \end{array} \\
\quad\quad 1 \quad\quad\quad\quad 2
\end{array}
\tag{1}
$$

## 1. MARKET HAS PERFECT INFORMATION, I.E., INFORMATION IS PUBLIC

Let $\pi_a$ be the time 0 value of a claim to a unit of wealth in state $G$ at time 1, and $\pi_b$ the value of a claim in state $B$ at time 1. Furthermore, $\delta\pi_a$ and $\delta\pi_b$ are the current prices for wealth at time 2 in the respective states.[6] In this case

$$
\text{where } V_0 = \delta(\pi_a a + \pi_b b)
\tag{2}
$$

and

$$
V_1 = \begin{array}{l} G \quad\;\; \delta a \\[2mm] B \quad\;\; \delta b \end{array}
\tag{3}
$$

and

$$
V_2 = \begin{array}{l} G \quad\;\; a \\[2mm] B \quad\;\; b \end{array}
\tag{4}
$$

---

**6.** The parameter $\delta$ is the sure rate of discount. If, instead, we permitted $\delta_a \neq \delta_b$, then by observing the public sure rate, the market would be able to distinguish the two states. This would assume away much of interest in the problem of insider trading. To avoid this, we assume equality.

## No insider trading

Again,

$$\text{where } V_0 = \delta(\pi_a a + \pi_b b) \tag{5}$$

but at time 1, the information is not public and

$$V_1 = \gamma_a a + \gamma_b b \tag{6}$$

where $\gamma_a$ and $\gamma_b$ are time 1 contingent prices when the states are unknown.
Since

$$(\pi_a + \pi_b)(\gamma_a a + \gamma_b b) = \pi_a \, \delta a + \pi_b \, \delta b \tag{7}$$

must hold for all $(a,b)$, we have

$$\gamma_a = \left(\frac{\pi_a}{\pi_a + \pi_b}\right)\delta \tag{8}$$

and

$$\gamma_b = \left(\frac{\pi_b}{\pi_a + \pi_b}\right)\delta \tag{9}$$

## Insider Trading Permitted

We retain the assumption that insider trading conveys no information to the market, but, as was discussed in the text, this is not an unambiguous specification of the information that the market possesses. We will deal with this problem below. For the moment, we assume, in addition, that individuals in the market are not even aware that there are inside traders.

At time 1, then, the value of the firm will be simply

$$V_1 = \gamma_a a + \gamma_b b \tag{10}$$

and at time 0

$$V_0 = \delta(\pi_a a + \pi_b b) \tag{11}$$

This is, of course, the same as in the case of no insider trading: From the perspective of the outsiders, there is no difference. However, the actual amount received by outsiders will differ from what they perceive because of the actions of the insiders. At time 1, if the news is $G$, insiders buy the firm; if it is $B$, they will short it. In a perfect market, the only limit on such activities is the total value of the firm. (Even this is not a limit in a sequential model, but we will take it as such here. In theory, for example, the short interest could exceed the total outstanding stock.)

Let $S_0$ denote the percentage of the firm acquired by insiders at time 0, and $S_1$ the percentage acquired at time 1. Since the insiders can adjust $S_1$ to the news, we will let $S_{1a}$ and $S_{1b}$ denote their alternative purchases to emphasize their dependence on the news received. The change in the current value of insider holdings—as perceived by the insiders using market prices—is given by

$$\Delta V = -S_0 V_0 - \pi_a S_{1a}(\gamma_a a + \gamma_b b) + \pi_a(S_0 + S_{1a})\delta a$$
$$-\pi_b S_{1b}(\gamma_a a + \gamma_b b) + \pi_b(S_0 + S_{1b})\delta b \tag{12}$$

To maximize $\Delta V$, the insiders will purchase all the remainder of the firm if the news is good, i.e.,

$$S_{1a} = (1 - S_0) \tag{13}$$

and if it is bad, they will sell their holdings and short the firm, hence

$$S_{1b} = -1 \tag{14}$$

From the formula for $\Delta V$, we have

$$\Delta V > \{\pi_a(\gamma_a a + \gamma_b b) + \pi_b \delta b - V_0\}S_0 \tag{15}$$

and since the coefficient of $S_0$ is negative, the insider will set $S_0$ at 0 initially, barring a short sale. Of course, there is a limit to how far insiders can reduce their initial holdings and remain as insiders, and this is presumably the point at which $S_0$ will be set.

Since the insiders have no impact on firm values, it is in their interest to exploit their information rather than reveal it. In addition, they gain nothing from their original holdings, and as a consequence, insiders would minimize them, buying in only at time 1 with the receipt of good news. Furthermore, since the outsiders will, on average, lose, the insiders can even take advantage of this by short selling the firm at time 0.

Finally, we have assumed that insider trading conveys no information to the market and, therefore, leaves market values unaltered. This is based on an implicit assumption that the firm has sufficient close substitutes traded in the market to leave market prices unchanged. If this is not the case, then insider trading may alter market prices. In such a situation, insiders might adopt a monopsonistic (monopolistic) strategy when they purchase (sell) the firm's outstanding financial instruments. We will ignore this somewhat obvious complication below.

## 3. NO DISCLOSURE RULES AND INSIDER TRADING WITH INFORMATION TRANSMISSION

This is a complicated case, because of the variety of ways and degrees by which information can be transmitted to the market. To make it somewhat more manageable, we will not distinguish within the outsider group and will assume that all outsiders receive their information

simultaneously, i.e., any information is public information.

There is, however, a further difficulty. What precisely is it that communicates the information? Is it the demand or supply of the insider or, perhaps, the resulting market price? If the latter, then what determines the public demand or supply? For example, in our simple world, if there are no exogenous influences on buying or selling, any trading or any price different from $V_1 = \gamma_a a + \gamma_b b$ would instantly communicate the insider's information. We could examine a model with exogenous and probabilistic trading motives that blurred the outsiders' perceptions, but the resulting complications would take us beyond the scope of this paper. Suppose, then, that any insider activity whatsoever communicates the news to the market. In this situation, the insider is locked into a return identical to the market's. Even though he receives the news earlier, any attempt to exploit it results in instant communication.

Presumably, reality lies somewhere between the two extremes described here and in the previous section. It would appear, then, that there is no competitive rationale for insiders to disclose their information. At the worst, they do as well as the outsiders; but at the best, as in the section on "A World of Perfect Information," they make an extra return over and above the market return. As (5) below shows, such a judgment is premature.

## 4. NO DISCLOSURE RULES, BUT INSIDERS KNOWN TO EXIST

In general, the stockholders in a world of perfect information receive less from their holdings than they anticipated. They thought they would receive $V_0 = \pi_a \delta_a a + \pi_b \delta_b b$, but, if they trade at time 1, they actually receive in current value terms

$$\pi_a(\gamma_a a + \gamma_b b) + \pi_b \delta_b b \tag{16}$$

since the insiders purchase the holdings of outsiders if the news is good. If outsiders recognize this, then even though trading per se conveyed no information, the behavior of the insider would be altered. In fact, his initial holdings $S_0$ would now be irrelevant.

One way to insulate themselves is for outsiders simply not to trade. By adopting a policy of "investing for the long run," they will actually hold an investment of value

$$\pi_a \delta_a a + \pi_b \delta_b b \tag{17}$$

This strategy is always available to them and would be a lower limit on the current value of the firm. Further, since this is the value of the firm's returns, it will also be the actual market value of the firm. Such a strategy modifies our previous analysis. The insiders' information is now of no value to them because outsiders do not trade in the intermediate period.

This is a difficulty with the perfect markets arguments, as we have formulated them: There always exists a strategy that makes value independent of the information flow. To determine the actual policy in such a situation, then, requires a complex balancing of several forces that are beyond the scope of the simple theory of this paper. Random personal influences will generate some supply and demand for the firm at time 1 by outsiders, and, presumably, there will be some limited degree of permissible trading activity for insiders. Furthermore, to the extent to which the policy of holding for the long run is not certain, the current market value of the firm will be lessened. The insider who currently, at time 0, has a holding can raise its value with a policy of full disclosure. In addition, to the extent that random influences force insiders to trade even in adverse situations, e.g., selling at time 1 for a consumption purchase even if the news is bad, they will be forced to fully disclose in order to induce outsiders to change their "no trade" policy.

Last, trading by itself conveys market information, and this will limit profits from insider trading. At the extreme, there is no trading by insiders that is not instantly informative and, once again, they will be unable to profit from their special information. (Unless a favorite aunt can be used to "launder" the purchases.)

Let us return to the original issue: Is there some competitive mechanism that forces information outside? For this purpose, we will consider a somewhat more familiar (and less corrupting) setting than the one above.[7]

## 5. THE INCENTIVE-SIGNALING APPROACH IN A CORPORATE ENVIRONMENT

This section formalizes the role of the insider-manager and shows why voluntary disclosure may arise. To capture the ongoing nature of the manager's involvement with a firm, we specify a compensation schedule for the manager of the firm as follows:

$$M = \theta_1 V_1 + \theta_2 V_2 + \omega \qquad (18)$$

where $\theta_1$ and $\theta_2$ are the proportions of the respective market values of the firm that make up the manager's variable compensation schedule. The term $\omega$ is the fixed-wage term. By assumption, changes in the firm's performance leave it unaltered. For simplicity, too, we telescope our problem and look only from time 1 on. We assume, then, that at time 1 the manager-insider is in possession of the news—good or bad—and

---

7. One final point—it should be clear from the above analysis that insiders can increase their gains if they can succeed in conveying misleading information. If, for example, the news is good, then by conveying bad news to the market, the firm value will drop to $\delta_b b$ at time 1 (if the bad news is believed). Purchasing at this price, the insider's profits will be higher than if he buys at $\gamma_a a + \gamma_b b$ from a market that has received no information.

that the market does not currently know what the news is. As before, the current value of the firm is given by

$$V_1 = \gamma_a a + \gamma_b b \qquad (19)$$

Suppose that the news is good. The manager knows that if he reveals the information, his firm's current value will rise to

$$V_1' = (\gamma_a + \gamma_b)a = \delta_a \qquad (20)$$

since at time 1, the firm will return $a$. It is, therefore, in the manager's interests, as given by the above incentive schedule $M$ to disclose this information to the market. By doing so, the manager uniformly increases the market's assessment of his firm and, hence, his own compensation. Conversely, it seems clear that if the news is bad, the same logic implies that the manager will suppress the news.

The story, however, is more complicated. If no information is disclosed, the market will assess the news as bad; after all, any manager with good news is known to have an incentive to reveal it. The only way in which bad news will be suppressed, then, is if all managers are uniformly optimistic. From the compensation schedule, it is easy to see that even managers whose news is bad may behave as though the news is good. As a consequence, the system of disclosure would seem to break down: Any information volunteered by the firms would be discounted.

This pessimism is unwarranted. The problem facing the managers with good news is how to disclose *and* validate it. Conversely, the managers with bad news will try to mask the truth by mimicking the behavior of the managers with the good news. Knowing this, the managers with good news will wish to modify their incentive schedules, perhaps by adopting a penalty of size $L$ at time 2, if their firm fails to attain a return of $a$. In other words, they may modify $M$ to take the form

$$M = \omega + \theta_0 V_0 + \theta_1 \begin{cases} a \text{ if the return is } a \\ -L \text{ if the return is less than } a. \end{cases} \qquad (21)$$

By adopting and announcing such an incentive schedule to the market, managers with good news can validate their information to the market. In other words, such an incentive structure is a valid signal to the market that this manager has actually received good news.

Consider the position of the manager in possession of bad news. The only way for him to convince the market that he, too, possesses good news is for him to adopt a similar incentive schedule. His compensation would then be given by, at best,

$$\omega + \theta_0 a - \theta_1 L \qquad (22)$$

which is less than

$$\omega + \theta_0 b + \theta_1 b \tag{23}$$

if the penalty $L$ adopted by those with good news exceeds

$$\frac{\theta_0}{\theta_1}(a - b) - b \tag{24}$$

Thus, the manager with bad news cannot mimic the manager with good news. As a consequence, good news will be signaled while bad news will be disclosed by default, as it were.

Going back a step to time 0, however, a new possibility is opened up. Suppose at time 0, when all managers are as ignorant as the outsiders, a manager adopts a no-disclosure policy. Now, since at time 0 he tied his hands, the market will not reassess his firm as having received bad news at time 1 when he did not signal. At time 1, then, his firm will still be valued at

$$V_1 = \gamma_a a + \gamma_b b \tag{25}$$

The difficulties with this argument are manifold. A policy of no-disclosure seems untenable. To begin with, market outsiders might believe that the only motive for adopting such a disclosure rule would be that the manager actually knew (or believed) that the news would be bad and was seeking somehow to mask it. If there was any possibility of this being so at time 0, then such a belief would foil this kind of disclosure policy, since $V_0$ would fall on its announcement.

Second, and perhaps more important, a policy of no-disclosure creates strong incentives for its own alteration over time. It is difficult to specify the mechanism that would force management to adhere to it. For example, in a firm whose returns drifted ever upward on continuing good news, the managers would face an ever-widening gap between their present compensation and what they would receive if they disclosed the good news. The incentive to issue valid signals would become overwhelming.

In sum, managers have both the incentive and the means to disclose their information.

# BIBLIOGRAPHY

The seminal article on the use of information is Hirshleifer's. Much of the subsequent work can be viewed as an extension of this original piece. Kihlstrom and Mirman, Grossman, and Grossman and Stiglitz deal with the arguments concerning the extent to which the price system conveys insider information to outsiders. Marshall and Ng generalize Hirshleifer's original results. Jaffe and Rubinstein extend these arguments in many directions, and, in particular, they support the traditional view that the heterogeneity of information is a major source of inefficiency and that disclosure regulation, by sharing information, can promote efficiency. Samuelson's paper is a classic on the relationship between timing and information in speculative markets. Fama provides a good review of the efficient-markets hypotheses.

The moral-hazard problem was first discussed by Arrow, but the new view of information taken here began with Akerlof's work and the seminal book by Spence on equilibrium-information-signaling in job markets. The development of a theory of incentive-signaling and the use of guarantees to signal information is in Ross. Some important theoretical issues in related areas have recently been raised by Rothschild and Stiglitz.

No attempt was made in the paper to discuss the relevant empirical literature. Some key papers in this area are by Stigler, Friend and Herman, and Benston, and the interchange between Benston and Friend and Westerfield. The paper by Jaffe is an important new contribution that examines the effects of regulation on insider trading and argues that there is, indeed, no effect. Overall, I do not think that the empirical issue of whether disclosure requirements have enhanced market efficiency is settled. Furthermore, the new theoretical arguments that have been advanced suggest that the crucial empirical issues may involve difficult tests of monopoly power in related markets.

Akerlof, G., "The Market for 'Lemons': Qualitative Uncertainty and the Market Mechanism," 84 Q.J. Econ., No. 3, pp. 488–500 (Aug. 1970).

Arrow, K. J., *Essays in the Theory of Risk Bearing* (Markham Publishing Co., Chicago 1971).

Benston, G. J., "Required Disclosure and the Stock Market: An Evaluation of the Securities Exchange Act of 1934," 63 American Econ. Rev., No. 1, pp. 132–155 (March 1973).

———, "Required Disclosure and the Stock Market: Rejoinder," 65 American Econ. Rev., No. 3, pp. 473–477 (June 1975).

Fama, E., "Efficient Capital Markets: A Review of Theory and Empirical Work," 25 J. Finance, No. 2, pp. 383–417 (May 1970).

**Friend, I.,** and **E. Herman,** "The SEC Through a Glass Darkly," J. Business, Univ. of Chicago (April 1970).

—— and **R. Westerfield,** "Required Disclosure and the Stock Market: Comment," 65 American Econ. Rev., No. 3, pp. 467–472 (June 1975).

**Grossman, S.,** The Existence of Future Markets, Noisy Rational Expectations and Informational Externalities, unpublished manuscript (Univ. of Chicago, 1974).

—— and **J. Stiglitz,** "Information and Competitive Price Systems," 66 American Econ. Rev., No. 2, pp. 246–253 (May 1976).

**Hirshleifer, J.,** "The Private and Social Value of Information and the Reward to Inventive Activity," 61 American Econ. Rev., No. 4, pp. 561–574 (Sept. 1971).

**Jaffe, J. F.,** "The Effect of Regulation Changes on Insider Trading," 5 Bell J. Econ., No. 1, pp. 93–121 (Spring 1974).

—— and **M. Rubinstein,** *The Value of Information in Impersonal and Personal Markets,* Rodney L. White Center for Financial Research Working Paper No. 16–75 (Univ. of Pa. 1975).

**Kihlstrom, R.,** and **L. Mirman,** "Information and Market Equilibrium," 6 Bell J. Econ., No. 1, pp. 357–376 (Spring 1975).

**Marshall, J.,** "Private Incentives and Public Information," 64 American Econ. Rev., No. 3, pp. 373–390 (June 1974).

**Means, G. C.,** "Industrial Prices and Their Relative Inflexibility," S. Doc. 13, 74th Cong., 1st Sess. (1935).

**Ng, D.,** "Information Accuracy and Social Welfare Under Homogeneous Beliefs," 2 J. Financial Econ., No. 1, pp. 53–70 (March 1975).

**Ross, S. A.,** "The Determination of Financial Structure: The Incentive-Signalling Approach," 8 Bell J. Econ., No. 1, pp. 23–40 (Spring 1977).

**Rothschild, M.,** and **J. Stiglitz,** "Equilibrium in Competitive Insurance Markets: The Economics of Imperfect Information," 90 Q.J. Econ., No. 4, pp. 629–649 (Nov. 1976).

**Samuelson, P.,** "Intertemporal Price Equilibrium: A Prologue to the Theory of Speculation," 79 *Weltwirtschaftliches Archiv,* No. 2, pp. 181–219 (1957).

**Spence, A. M.,** *Market Signalling: Information Transfer in Hiring and Related Processes* (Harvard Univ. Press, Cambridge, Mass., 1974).

**Stigler, G. J.,** "Public Regulation of the Securities Markets," 37 J. Business, Univ. of Chicago, No. 2, pp. 117–142 (April 1964).

# COMMENTARY

Homer Kripke, *Chester Rohrlich Professor of Law, Finance, and Taxation, New York University*

We lawyers have regulated and controlled financial disclosure for more than 40 years, and some of us think that the measure of our success is not clear. I am delighted that the economists in the last 20 years or so have begun to focus their attention on the topic with their remarkably different way of viewing things.

It is, of course, natural that a new economic tool like the signaling concept, which has been developed with acclaim in other fields,[1] should be brought over to the field of financial markets and financial disclosure. It would be gratifying if the transfer were successful, but up to the present time, I do not believe that it has been.

Before proceeding to his incentives-signaling system, Professor Ross prepares a contrast by speaking of what he calls the neoclassical view of the use of nonpublic information by insiders.

His academic orientation leaves me with the feeling that this part of the article is a period piece that ought to be played in the costumes of the eighteenth century. He says that if an insider were observed buying and selling in the market for a company's securities, the insider would be signaling some information. That is true. But the customer is no longer as visible in securities markets as he was under the buttonwood tree where the New York Stock Exchange started. Principals no longer trade in those markets. Professor Ross recognizes that the insider can use a broker for his trading, and, with a concealed source of the trading, the signal of insider trading will be lost. But, he says, "The demand itself will signal the outside market. . . ." I do not understand thi What does the demand signal other than that it is a demand from some

---

1. Spence, *Market Signalling: Information Transfer in Hiring and Related Screening Processes* (Harvard Univ. Press, Cambridge, 1974). For a bibliography on the subject, see McCall, Book Review, 14 J. Econ. Literature, No. 2, pp. 467–468 (reviewing Spence's treatise).

anonymous source? It can come from astute or stupid people, from insiders or outsiders.

What are we to make of Professor Ross's assertion that requiring disclosure of firm information eliminates the opportunity for profitable insider trading if the disclosure is timely? Perhaps that was true in the eighteenth century. But, in the twentieth century (even before the Securities Acts), the telephone and telegraph permit instant execution of insiders' orders as soon as they have inside information, long before company disclosure can impact the markets. How can the dissemination of firm information possibly be compelled on a schedule timely enough to preclude an insider's placing and executing an order before the information comes out?

We also read that a disclosure requirement imposed on the insider trading itself communicates information on insider trading to the market. What good does that do if the insider has already taken advantage of the inside information and has made his trade at an advantageous price before the market impounds the information? We read that insider trading, per se, communicates information to the market that tends to mitigate the insider's profit. I do not understand. Once the insider buys before his information is reflected in the market, he has his advantage. Professor Ross seems to assume that the insider can profit only if he succeeds in keeping his knowledge secret through both the purchase and the sale. This is not so. Obviously, it is not accurate when the insider already owns the securities and when he sells on the basis of insider information, for his cycle is then completed before the market price goes down. It is equally not true when he purchases on the basis of inside information. Once he buys at a price which does not yet reflect the advantageous information, it makes no difference whether the information is then promptly revealed to the public or whether his own purchase signals it and the stock thereafter promptly rises. Either way, he desires this to happen, for he already has his position at a price below the price which impounds the information, and he has an advantage in determining when to sell. He has an advantage even if he has to wait six months, as he does under Section 16(b) of the Securities Exchange Act.[2]

For that reason, I can make nothing out of Professor Ross's suggestions that outsiders can frustrate the insiders' strategy by refusing to trade for the short run and trade only for the long run. The advantage of

---

**2.** For this reason, Section 16(b) of the Securities Exchange Act, which economists sometimes treat as *in pari materia* with Rule 10(b)(5) as to inside information, is really based on an untenable theory. Liability under Section 16(b) is touched off only if the purchase and sale are both made within a six-month period, but, as discussed in the text, the insider has all the advantage necessary if he can trade on the inside information in one direction, and he can then wait out the six-month period and still have the advantage of his information. In contrast, Rule 10(b)(5) (while it has other problems) is correctly based on the concept that if the insider can trade as to only one-half of his cycle on the basis of inside information, he has an advantage over others.

**205**

*The Economics of
Information and
the Disclosure
Regulation
Debate*

insider information can come from trading with insider information on only one point of the cycle, and the question whether the runs are long or short is irrelevant.

Another statement that shows an academic perception is the purportedly factual assertion that stockholders *will* provide contracts that penalize insider trading by managers. Elsewhere in the paper, it is said that if stockholders do not so contract, this is the fault of the imperfect market for managerial services. What period of the world's history does this assume? In 1932, before today's growth of the giant corporation, Berle and Means first pointed out that the managers run the company, and that the stockholders do not.[3] Although I wrote an unfavorable review[4] of the book by Henry Manne on insider trading,[5] his argument that profits from insider trading are looked on as an appropriate means by which corporations reward insiders comes closer to reality than the state of the world that Professor Ross assumes.

Professor Ross makes express reference to the fact that the correctness of what he describes as the neoclassical view of information or his information-signaling view can only be tested empirically, but he announces no program for doing so, nor does he describe a model by which it could be done.

In what kind of real world could Professor Ross's theories be tested: by curing imperfections in the managers' market, which presently precludes competitive forces from pricing managers' services appropriately, thus excluding extraordinary profits from inside information? That would require pulverizing the present giant corporation, so that stockholders really could take control of it in town meetings without the proxy machinery that currently makes corporate democracy a slogan, not a reality.[6] If the corporation were atomized sufficiently, managerial talents might cease to be too specialized to permit ready transfer among industries, and a competitive market in undifferentiated managerial talents might be broader than is possible in the present world of technology. It still would be necessary to outlaw the fringe benefit devices designed to tie the executive to the corporation and preclude the development of this competitive market in managerial talent. In short, we would have to have a tremendous upheaval in the present state of the world to test a contention that the faults of a theory are due to imperfections of a market.

At this point, a remark in Professor McCall's review of the seminal work on signaling becomes relevant:

---

3. Berle and Means, *The Modern Corporation and Private Property* (C.C.H. 1932).

4. Kripke, Book Review, 42 N.Y.U.L. Rev. 212 (1967).

5. Manne, *Insider Trading and the Stock Market* (Free Press, New York 1966).

6. On April 27, 1977, the SEC announced a program for reconsideration of the proxy rules to make another try at increasing corporate democracy. Wall Street Journal, April 28, 1977, p. 17, col. 2.

Too much of modern economic theory resides in a realm remote from economic reality. . . . [A] science is healthy only if its theoretical constructs eventually illuminate empirical phenomena and subsequent theories are enriched by this empirical contact. . . .

A theory that refrains from empirical testing should abstain from policy. . . . Certainly economic theorists recognize that empirical testing is a necessary prelude to policy. Nevertheless, there is a tendency to go directly from theory to policy.[7]

So much for the impression of unreality that I get from this paper. As a noneconomist, I must confess that I get nothing from the comparison of the "neoclassic view" and the incentive-signaling view; so let us proceed to the incentive-signaling view.

In this paper, Professor Ross uses dividend action or nonaction by a board of directors as signaling the insiders' view of their company's prospects, i.e., that it can maintain the indicated dividend rate. This is, of course, obvious enough. We do not need elaborate economic or mathematical theory for the simple proposition that dividend action may convey some information, and the terminology of signaling was commonplace long before the theory. But the signal may be a true or a false picture of management's real view. The heart of Professor Ross's incentive-signaling concept, however, so far as I can comprehend it, is that if the signaler puts his money where his mouth is, so to speak, by guaranteeing the signal, then the signal is not likely to be faked, and will be treated by the market as reliable. Further, the signaler will be rewarded by the company for improving the market for its stock. He suggests, as an example of a "guarantee," that the signaler could offer to take a 20 percent salary reduction if the signal turned out to be false. This is an academic, unrealistic proposal; and he does not supply us in this paper with a realistic one or with a detailed explanation of the theory. He does make a brief reference to the company's "debt and equity mix," which leads us to his earlier *Bell Journal* paper,[8] where he did give a more complete explanation of the theory and an example of the kind of guarantee he has in mind.

In the *Bell Journal* paper, Professor Ross suggests that insiders could signal their confidence in the company's future by creating debt and thus levering the company, giving a guarantee in that, if they are wrong in their optimism, the company will go bankrupt and they will lose their jobs. Thus, they are guaranteeing their optimism by risking their personal careers. It is certainly true that people who incur debt and lead their company into bankruptcy may lose their jobs. General Sutowo, who ran Pertamina, the Indonesian oil monopoly, certainly signaled his confidence in the company by levering it heavily. It turned out that he

---

7. McCall, N. 1 *supra* at 466.

8. Ross, "The Determination of Financial Structure: The Incentive-Signalling Approach," 8 Bell J. Econ., No. 1, p. 23 (Spring 1977).

levered it to death, and he did lose his job,[9] but that does not seem to me to prove the reliability of his signals. Similarly, in the cases of Commonwealth United Corporation, Ling-Temco-Vought, and some other conglomerators of 10 years ago, the insiders incurred vast debt and signaled their confidence in the future, but the penalties paid by the false signalers do not seem to have made the signals reliable.

Or, take Abraham Beame, former mayor of New York City. When he was Comptroller of the City of New York, he was "the man who knew the buck," and he signaled that New York City was sound by having it carry unlimited loads of debt. In line with Professor Ross's thinking, was he rewarded for that by being elected Mayor? The signal was false! He lost his job at the next election, but any satisfaction that the holders of New York City debt got from this enforcement of the "guarantee" was noneconomic. The concept of validation of signaling by penalty seems to me to go nowhere.

In the *Bell Journal* paper, Professor Ross also uses this illustration to reconcile the Miller-Modigliani assertion that capital structure is irrelevant to the value of a firm with the public perception that the firm gains value by appropriate amounts of leverage. He finds the reconciliation in the guarantee. Even if there were any meaning to Professor Ross's theory that the reliability of the signal comes from the guarantee, it is hard to see how this incentive-signaling revelation could reconcile the two views. There must have been debt in the levered companies Miller and Modigliani studied empirically and theoretically, and the validation of the signaling by the possibility of penalty must, therefore, always have been present, even though not yet named and made the cornerstone of an economic theory. And yet, Miller and Modigliani did not find evidence that debt mattered.

Coming back to the signaling by dividends declaration discussed in the present paper, a management almost invariably subjects itself to the possibility of penalty if the signal is false. Management has stock, stock options, phantom stock. Since the share price will fall when the dividend falls, management will pay for the false signal. I have somehow missed what the idea of other penalties adds.

Moreover, I submit that the world is too complex for signaling to have any assured meaning to the market. I read an attempt by one of my distinguished colleagues, a professor of law at a leading law school, to analyze dividend signals and to propose a system of compulsory disclosure by management of its reasons for the action taken (or perhaps not taken), and I persuaded him to abandon his paper. If a management wants to say what it is doing or why, it can resort to the annual report, a press release, or a luncheon speech before the New York Financial Analysts' Society. Those who want to find the information content of dividend signaling need the technology of psychology or game theory, not Professor Ross's exposition.

---

9. New York Times, April 9, 1977, p. 25, col. 1.

As possibly helpful for the future of Columbia's promising Center for Law and Economic Studies, I will conclude with a quotation from my colleague Professor Oskar Morgenstern, the distinguished economist and mathematician:

> [T]he question of the limits of mathematics in economics must be approached cautiously. The limitations arose mostly because a faulty economic model was set up and analyzed mathematically.
>
> . . . . .
>
> [T]he primary task is to discover the true nature of the underlying economic phenomenon and to concentrate efforts in that direction, instead of stopping short and branching out into the mathematical treatment of an ill-defined and vaguely described situation.[10]

---

10. Morgenstern, "Limits to the Use of Mathematics in Economics," *Mathematics and the Social Sciences* 12, 29 (1963).

# DISCUSSION

FRANKLIN R. EDWARDS: Thank you, gentlemen. Perhaps our speaker would like to respond to these remarks before I take questions from the audience.

ROSS: I would like to comment on the apparent counterexamples to the incentive-signaling arguments. Homer Kripke argued that there were large firms—Pertamina and Commonwealth United, for example—that had taken on too much debt, falsely signaling their ability to service it, and had gone bankrupt because of it. Such examples, it is argued, demonstrate the inadequacy of the signaling model.

But there is another way to look at these examples. In the imperfect world we inhabit, the dramatic incident where the insider profits at the expense of the outsider serves an economic function: It warns all outsiders that there are insiders who are ready to take profits at their expense, and it teaches outsiders to protect themselves by writing and monitoring contracts that penalize insiders for doing so.

The alternative world is an economic system where the law or the government insures all securities market transactions. But that would be disastrous; it would shift the burden of monitoring to the government, and investors, always insured, would ignore such risks. Nevertheless, laws do seem to get written more in response to dramatic abuses than to a reasoned consideration. The consequence is often bad law and mismanaged economies.

The individual in the marketplace is ideally placed and is highly motivated to obtain the information that it is to his benefit to know, and to remove this motivation by government guarantee is likely to be both inefficient and ineffective. Competitive markets are a useful tool: they are a way of allocating resources, and they can serve that function very well. Unless it can be demonstrated that there are significant distortions that prevent securities markets from functioning, it is naive to think that passing laws and regulating markets will have beneficial effects.

EDWARDS: Thank you, Steve. I would now like to open the discussion to the audience.

WILLIAM VICKREY: About dividends as a signal, there was a chap several years ago who used dividends very successfully as a signal. His name was Ponzi.

It seems to me that if dividends are going to be an effective signal, there must be some sort of underlying pressure to maintain a dividend level, once reached. If so, I think we have introduced a degree of rigidity into financial operations that is not altogether desirable. It may require companies to maintain extra reserves for the purpose of underpinning the dividend level that has been set. I am not sure that that is a good allocation of capital funds.

ROSS: I disagree with that view. The rigidity that is introduced by having fixed dividends is an irrelevant rigidity. It is costless to the economic system to use such finance signals. There are no productive inefficiencies introduced by having rigidity in a firm's financial structure. That does not mean it is not costly to the manager. But the cost to the manager is a transfer from the manager to others, and not a social cost.

HARVEY GOLDSCHMID: It seems to me that disclosure legislation is an efficient way, and an elegant way, to signal. If you have an SEC that monitors firms, then you can do what Homer Kripke suggests, which is to announce it. The penalty for fraudulent managers seems to me much clearer than with your alternatives.

Dividends are a more complicated signaling device.

ROSS: I am in full agreement with you, and I made a similar point in the paper. I am not advocating market signaling as an alternative to disclosure legislation. Rather, I am suggesting that it is an alternative that would arise in the absence of disclosure legislation. I do not know how costly disclosure legislation is versus raising dividends. That is the key economic question to which, I believe, we do not know the answer.

GOLDSCHMID: Under market signaling, when would bad news come out? If you were president of Penn Central in 1968, with a three-year job horizon and a salary that is sure, why would you announce bad news?

ROSS: You have to recognize that we are talking about two distinct scenarios. One scenario has disclosure legislation in it, in which case the signaling content of the financial structure is altered. Penn Central occurred in a world with disclosure regulation. I agree, incidentally, that disclosure regulations have a signaling function; the law provides specific penalties for lying.

The other scenario is where there is no such legislation, and people use their financial structure to signal and implicitly and explicitly contract to provide information to outsiders. The private sector is a marvelous device for creating its own contracts. When you introduce disclosure legislation, you write these contracts into the public sector. The justification is that it is relatively costless, but this is an empirical issue, to be determined by measurement as well as debate.

EDWARDS: One of the differences between Professor Ross and both Professors Goldschmid and Kripke is that Ross's analysis implies that in a free market, there will exist managerial compensation schemes that will properly penalize or reward managers for their signals.

I interpret Professors Goldschmid and Kripke's remarks as basically saying that that proposition is unrealistic—that such contracts will never happen. It that correct?

GOLDSCHMID: Or that such contracts are not efficient.

EDWARDS: You are saying that market signaling is too costly, or that disclosure regulation is less costly. The relative efficiency of disclosure regulation, however, is not obvious to me.

Professor Kripke said that stockholders could not possibly monitor insider trading. To do it, they would need to have a family tree for every company. But he seems quite willing to say that regulators will be able to monitor the same trading.

KRIPKE: I have no doubt that the SEC's efforts to prevent insider trading may be effective in, say, only 3 percent of the actual cases. The others are concealed. The SEC has difficulty, I am sure, in monitoring insider trading. None of us knows how successful they are. Although I argue that Section 16-B ought to be repealed because all the cases under it involve hardship cases, where somebody made a mistake, the fact is that nobody knows whether it is working well or not, because nobody knows whether it is inhibiting other cases or whether they are simply being concealed.

Now that I understand more fully Professor Ross's argument, that there will be a penalty associated with disclosure of false information, I see that it assumes that we will stop running a welfare state and that we bring back the era of Gilbert and Sullivan's *Mikado*, with Koko and his big snickersnee. Anybody who does not make good cannot excuse this on the ground that we had a depression, or that he did not expect the devaluation of the dollar, or some other excuse, such that he does not suffer any consequences. We need Koko to make this system work.

WILLIAM CARY: I would like to ask Professor Ross how another aspect of disclosure fits into his analytical structure, that is, the prophylactic aspect of disclosure, namely, the old cliche that if you will not do something, you will have to disclose it to *The New York Times.*

ROSS: I would like to comment on several issues. First, I think that there are great incentives not to reveal bad information. But the very fact that you do not say anything is, itself, an indication that you have bad information. If you are silent, you will be lumped in with a pool of two groups—those who have nothing to say, and those who have bad things to say. But people who have nothing to say will have an incentive to inform the market that they are not the ones who have bad news, rather, that their news is neither good nor bad.

In general, there is a hierarchy. In the competitive markets, people with something to sell have an incentive to put their best foot forward. Similarly, people with the best information have an incentive to disclose and guarantee the validity of that information. Further, if you have the top product in the market, you will offer a superior guarantee, and that guarantee will serve as a signal informing the market that your product is of high quality. The sellers with the next best product will be unable to match the top guarantee. Nevertheless, they will do as well as they can to differentiate their product from those which are inferior, and so on down the hierarchy. I see no reason why this sort of signaling will not also arise in securities markets. It would not work perfectly all the time, of course. Occasionally, somebody would breach a contract and get away with something, and this would serve to keep people sensitive to the kinds of guarantees that managers provide.

Second, the issue I am raising is not whether

we should or should not have disclosure rules. Something like disclosure "legislation" and the need for it will arise in any kind of economic system. The issue is whether it is best to rely on the law of contracts and the ordinary judicial rules which apply to private contracts, or, whether we should write additional laws like disclosure legislation. It is really an issue of which is the most effective and least costly system.

EDWARDS: Would a test of your theory be to look at the kinds of managerial compensation contracts or schemes that existed prior to disclosure regulation in the United States?

ROSS: It is very difficult to use historical data to look at past compensation schedules. For one thing, the schedules are not explicit. No one writes down what the manager may suffer if the firm goes bankrupt. It would be possible to test the theory with current data if the law were removed, with the understanding that it would never be put in again.

RONALD GREENBERG: I think the idea of having private contracts obligating managers to disclose information and penalizing them if they are wrong is appealing. But I think the comments pertaining to its practicality are right on target. Could you really get managers to enter into contracts like that?

Another element of impracticality, which I think was brought out by Professor Kripke, is the timing question. He had a question, and I do too, about whether this incentive-signaling system will get all information out simultaneously. I really have trouble with that, because someone has to have the inside information, and that person is going to trade a few seconds before signaling the information.

The laws we now have, such as the *Texas Gulf* case and its progeny, say that you do not have an obligation to disclose information. *Texas Gulf* says that if you are an insider and you have information but you do not trade on it, you do not have to disclose it. If you want to trade on that information to your advantage, you must disclose it. Would insider trading still not be a problem under a market signaling system?

ROSS: I use contracts here in a very abstract way, which may be a source of misunderstanding. Take the case of insider trading, where the manager trades on his information. The current law says that you cannot trade on your information until you have revealed the information, and if you do not reveal it, you have to abstain from trading. That seems to me to be precisely the kind of explicit contract that would arise in a free and competitive securities market. I do not see any reason why we need legislation to bring that about. It seems to me that if we were to remove that part of the current disclosure legislation, all the managers of large corporations would be compelled to sign agreements to the effect that they will not trade on their inside information. If I were a stockholder, I would certainly vote for such a policy.

However, that does not answer the question of whether or not the legislation is useful. It still may be more costly to write such individual contracts. It also may be more inefficient to monitor breaches of those contracts and to enforce them. Certainly, managers as a whole have an incentive to keep them from being enforced. In the long run, then, it might be more efficient to have "standard" contracts that are enforced by explicit legislation rather than to appeal to private enforcement through the general law of contracts. I am merely laying out the battleground on which this kind of legislation ought to be debated. It ought not to be debated on quasi-religious grounds about the power and sanctity of law and regulation.

EDWARDS: I think Ross's point, if I can put it in somewhat different words, is that arguments for disclosure legislation assume that there is no market mechanism by which information will be disclosed, and that managers always have an incentive to take advantage of stockholders.

What Ross is trying to do is move us away from that assumption by specifying the market mechanism that would operate in the absence of regulation, so that we can explicitly examine this mechanism to determine why it is not sufficient. Only after understanding why it fails can we determine the proper disclosure policy to pursue.

GOLDSCHMID: Do we not have some evidence from both the pre-thirties and from other countries that the market does fail?

ROSS: The empirical evidence is ambiguous. Stigler looked at periods before and after the law to see whether or not there was a difference in the performance of new issues one year after they were issued. He was unable to find any significant difference. George Benston did a similar study with similar results. There are, of course, problems with these analyses; all sorts of things are changing simultaneously. I think, at this stage, we have to rely more on logical argument than on empiricism. Logical argument, at least, identifies what kinds of data we need. The data will, we hope, help in the future.

CHAPTER FIVE

# Legal and Economic Perspectives on Consumer Protection in Credit Markets

## CONSUMER PROTECTION IN CREDIT MARKETS: AN ANALYSIS OF REGULATORY REFORM

Robert P. Shay, *Professor of Banking and Finance, Columbia University*

This paper is a first attempt to apply the economic analysis of property rights to the regulatory reform movement affecting consumer credit markets. The first part of the paper develops the analytical framework used and applies it to one limitation of a creditor's remedy to recover debt: the prohibition of wage assignments. The second part reviews and appraises the legal process used by the Bureau of Consumer Protection at the Federal Trade Commission to justify government intervention, and the last part discusses my conclusions.

### AN ECONOMIC FRAMEWORK FOR EVALUATING THE IMPACT OF LIMITATIONS ON THE PROPERTY RIGHTS INVOLVED IN CREDIT AGREEMENTS

#### Property Rights and Economic Theory

The literature pertaining to the economic theory of property rights is an appropriate and useful starting point in a study of the impact of consumer protection regulation on credit markets.[1] This body of thought extends the traditional or classical economic theory of production and exchange to provide

1. That individuals will seek to maximize their own utilities within the limits of the organizations of which they are a part.

---

1. For a summary of this literature, see Furubotn and Pejovich, "Property Rights and Economic Theory," 10 J. Econ. Literature, No. 4, pp. 1137–1162 (Dec. 1972).

The author's work on this subject has been facilitated by a grant from the National Science Foundation under Contract No. C-76-18548 with Abt Associates Inc., of Cambridge, Massachusetts.

2. More than one pattern of property rights can exist and profit (or wealth) maximization of the firm may not always result.
3. That transactions costs may be greater than zero.[2]

The first of these theoretical extensions permits consideration of institutional arrangements which allow individual managers an opportunity to discriminate among credit applicants on bases which may not (or may) be in the interests of owners. (The Federal Equal Credit Opportunity Act of 1975, amended in 1976, exemplifies government intervention to counteract such presumed behavior.) The second extension provides some leeway for firms to behave in suboptimal fashion when penalty-reward systems within the firm militate against optimal performance. The third extension allows for the fact that the transactions costs may be sufficiently high that the adoption of a policy which would maximize output (and wealth) by the firm would result in less than optimal performance because of the costs of defining, exchanging, policing, or enforcing property rights.[3] It is the third aspect, the high transactions costs, that is relevant to consumer credit trade practice regulation. Government intervention to correct malallocation of resources may result in an external effect, or externality, which commonly arises when there is a response of a firm's output, or a person's utility, to the activity of others.[4] Examples of interventions affecting property rights in credit agreements in consumer credit markets are governmental prohibitions or limitations on wage assignments, garnishment, and other creditors' collection remedies. The utility functions of consumer credit applicants will be affected by such changes in property rights, as will the output (or composition of output) of creditors.

If such interventions were to correct creditor behavior, which diverges markedly from standards implicit in competitive markets, government regulation may bring greater equity and efficiency to consumer credit markets. Further, if transactions costs are sufficiently high so that optimal property adjustments are not made privately, governments may intervene with good results.

---

2. *Id.* at 1137.

3. *Id.* at 1143.

4. See Mishan, "The Postwar Literature on Externalities: An Interpretative Essay," 9 J. Econ. Literature, No. 1, p. 2 (March 1971). Mishan goes on to note:

> [G]eneral agreement on the sort of mathematical notation required to indicate the presence of an external effect. Thus, $F^1(x_1^1, x_2^1, \ldots, x_m^1; x_n^2)$ will represent an external effect generated by entity 2 on entity 1. $F^1$ can stand for the utility level of person 1, in which case the $x$s are the amounts of some goods, $x_1, x_2 \ldots, x_m$, utilized by him, $x_n^2$ being the amount of some good $x_n$ (where $x_n$ could, of course, be $x_1, x_2, \ldots,$ or $x_m$) that is utilized by person 2, or produced by an industry 2. Again, $F^1$ can stand for the output of a firm or an industry, in which case the $x^1$s are the amounts of its inputs, while $x_n^2$ is the amount of the input or output of some other firm or industry.

Furubotn and Pejovich, in their review of the property rights literature, note that the concept of property rights does not define merely the
relation between men and things but, "the sanctioned behavioral relations among men that arise from the existence of things and pertain to
their use."[5] Contractual arrangements involved in trade and production
"exist not so much to accomplish the exchange of goods and services
but to permit the exchange of 'bundles' of property rights."[6] Consumer
credit contracts, when made under conditional sales agreements,
involve property rights in the goods financed and deal with conditions
affecting use of the goods during the life of the credit agreement. In loan
contracts, where property is pledged as collateral, similar conditions
affecting the use of the property are set in the agreements. Remedies
available to creditors to collect and recover debts are part of the property
rights of the creditors, while the limitation of creditors' remedies are
property rights of debtors in credit agreements. Other aspects of credit
agreements involving disclosure, rates of charge and other credit terms,
sales of credit-related insurance, late charges, and other matters all
represent types of property rights which are distributed among creditors and debtors in credit contracts.

The basic problem in consumer credit markets is that actual negotiation between creditors and debtors is generally focused upon rates of
charge, credit terms, and sales of credit-related insurance, and not on
the remedies/rights of creditors and borrowers. Disclosure requirements are currently mandated by federal law, as are stipulations affecting credit reporting, credit billing practices, and, as noted above,
antidiscrimination in credit granting. Some creditors' remedies are
limited by federal law, others by state law, and others are enacted or
proposed by the Federal Trade Commission. Still other remedies
remain under the precedent of common law, which traditionally has
decided how property rights are defined in credit agreements. Because
the range of property rights involved in credit agreements is so broad,
the credit contract itself refers specifically to only some of the property
rights involved in credit transactions. In the event of nonperformance
by the debtor, a whole range of legal remedies not specified in the
contract is available to creditors under certain conditions specified by
law (i.e., the right to garnishee wages). It is important to note that it is
not customary to bargain noncontractual items, nor is it customary to
bargain over many of the provisions of "standard" credit contracts
offered to the credit applicant. Yet, there is opportunity to negotiate
items contained in the credit contract which both parties must sign,
and, therefore, a market process does occur which gives the borrower
an opportunity to acquire or sign away property rights. As for the rights
and remedies available to both parties but not specified in credit

**219**

*Legal and
Economic
Perspectives on
Consumer
Protection in
Credit Markets*

---

5. Furubotn and Pejovich, N. 1 *supra* at 1139.

6. *Id.;* and Mishan, No. 4 *supra*.

agreements, it is unlikely that special private arrangements specifying such provisions would be negotiated in consumer credit transactions. Therefore, it is difficult to see how private adjustment of property rights would be feasible in such instances.

## Property Rights and Resource Allocation

A readjustment of property rights resulting from government intervention in consumer credit transactions can affect the allocation of scarce resources in the following ways: a change in the price or readjustment of the terms under which credit is granted, rationing (extension) of credit dependent upon the change in implied cost, and the imposition (removal) of other fees and charges to compensate for the change in the value of property rights in the transaction.

Take, for example, a state's decision to prohibit the taking of wage assignments as a condition for the granting of a loan. The credit applicant, with no assets other than future earning power to pledge as collateral for a loan, may be deprived of the right to borrow money, and the creditor may be deprived of an inexpensive and effective means of recovering the debt in the event of default. The two parties are not given the opportunity to negotiate a second-best alternative (without a wage assignment), which may result in either (1) the lender rejecting the applicant and other similar applicants in favor of expanding loans to better-qualified borrowers at lower rates of charge, or (2) approving loans at higher rates of charge and/or other more restrictive credit terms to the applicant and similar applicants. In both instances, scarce resources will be allocated differently, and third parties may lose or benefit as this process occurs.

## The Demsetz Proposal for Determining When and How to Intervene

Harold Demsetz has provided a useful theoretical framework for analysis of government intervention to realign property rights.[7] Demsetz's framework is general in nature and can be applied to any one or the totality of the property rights involved in consumer credit transactions. Working within the property rights approach, Demsetz accepts the proposition that there may be instances when it is desirable for the government to intervene because the transactions costs of defining, exchanging, policing, or enforcing property rights prevent the market from establishing prices consistent with the social value of the rights that are exchanged. In such circumstances, it may be possible to simulate some of the conditions which would facilitate private adjustments of property rights in a competitive economy with zero transactions costs. Following Coase,[8] a principle of compensation could be utilized

---

7. Demsetz, "Some Aspects of Property Rights," 9 J. Law & Econ. 61–70 (Oct. 1966).

8. Coase, "The Problem of Social Cost," 3 J. Law & Econ. 7 (Oct. 1960).

whereby the insured parties, knowing their own costs as a result of damages under existing property rights, would bargain with the injured parties over compensation to indemnify themselves from further injury. In this instance, if the injuring parties reject the offer, the benefits of the existing property right must exceed the damages, and the absence of externalities ensures that the property right is optimal with regard to social welfare. On the other hand, if the injuring parties find the offers in excess of the benefits, the adjustment of property rights will occur privately.

Demsetz posits conditions where the government would weigh such considerations when contemplating intervention to change property rights:

> The costs and benefits of a prospective change in property rights cannot be treated as a given datum. The marginal costs and benefit curves associated with a prospective realignment of resources are not known by the government. Each affected individual knows his benefit or cost, and in the absence of high exchange cost, this information is transmitted to others in the form of market negotiations. The primary problem of government is the estimation problem. The compensation principle by its assumption that costs and benefits are known begs the most difficult question posed by a prospective change.[9]

Demsetz uses the following marginal benefit–marginal cost schedule (Figure 5-1) to suggest how government might appraise its intervention whenever exchange or policing costs are so high as to prevent useful private adjustments from being made:[10]

Assuming the zero point on both axes to be complete freedom for negotiating parties to include or deny any creditors' remedy or buyers' right in the credit agreement and that all points from zero to $q_2$ represent progressive curtailment of the freedom to contract for such remedies and rights, one can apply Demsetz's framework to the borrowers affected. Then, the marginal benefits, $mb_2$, to those parties who gain from the freedom to contract privately for benefits and rights decline

9. Demsetz, N. 7 *supra* at 68.

10. *Ibid.*

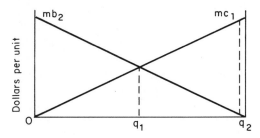

FIGURE 5-1 Marginal benefit–marginal cost schedule.

when such contractual rights are limited, while the marginal costs, $mc_1$, of the parties injured by the freedom to contract for rights and remedies rise as they pay increasing amounts of compensation to curtail creditors' collection remedies and increase their rights. The $q_1$ level of curtailment is obviously optimal.

The basic problems confronted by government are: first, to identify those persons who are injured by unfettered freedom to contract for creditors' remedies and buyers' rights, and to ascertain the economic worth of their injuries and how they would decline (and marginal costs rise) as remedies were curtailed and rights expanded; second, to identify the parties whose benefits are reduced as their property rights in creditors' remedies and limitations on buyers' rights are curtailed, and to ascertain the economic worth of their benefits and how these would decline as the freedom to contract for creditors' remedies and buyers' rights were curtailed; and, finally, by comparing the two, to proclaim the realignment of the property rights and provide for persons forgoing injury to compensate the beneficiaries for their forgone benefits at point $q_1$ in the diagram above.

## APPLICATION OF THE ANALYTICAL FRAMEWORK TO THE PROPOSED FTC LIMITATION OF WAGE ASSIGNMENTS

### Wage Assignments

> A wage assignment is an agreement between debtor and creditor that permits the creditor to receive a portion of the debtor's future wages in the event of the debtor's default on the credit contract. It is usually drafted in the form of an instruction to an employer to pay the creditor (as assignee) a percentage of the debtor's wages at the creditor's demand. The debtor releases the employer from all liability arising out of the latter's compliance with the instrument and waives any requirement that the creditor establish or even allege a default on the part of the debtor.[11]

Wage assignments are to be distinguished from wage garnishments because the former are private contractual arrangements involving debtors, creditors, and employers while the latter are noncontractual and are actuated by court orders after judgment. For legal and analytical purposes, garnishment of wages is a noncontractual attachment of wages by state intervention, whereas wage assignments are negotiated features of credit contracts. In 1974, the FTC staff reported that 20 states had enacted a blanket prohibition of wage assignments on consumer credit transactions, while others restricted their use to specified types of transactions; 11 states permitted assignments only in small loan trans-

---

11. Federal Trade Commission (FTC), Memorandum to Commission from the Division of Special Projects, Bureau of Consumer Protection, That the Commission Propose a Trade Regulation Rule Defining Certain Creditor Remedies as Unfair Trade Practices, p. 203 (April 19, 1974).

actions; 16 states placed no restrictions on the type of transaction, and the remaining states had miscellaneous restrictions.[12] Despite legal challenges, courts have typically upheld the constitutionality of wage assignments, and their future legal status depends upon prospective action by the states or the federal Congress, or adoption by the Federal Trade Commission of the "Proposed Trade Credit Rule Concerning Credit Practices."[13]

## Identifying Injured and Benefited Parties

The types of injury that are usually cited from the use of wage assignments are: discharge by employers, waiver of rights of notice with consequent inability to anticipate the reduction of take-home pay, harassment from threats to invoke the remedy, the placing of a tool in the hands of the unscrupulous to use on the least fortunate, and the impetus given to bankruptcy through credit overextension.

There is need to consider whether credit applicants consider these possible injuries at the time of the application for credit, whether they are capable of making an informed judgment of the benefits versus possible costs of obtaining credit under such conditions, and whether government intervention through prohibition or limitation of the pledge of future wages will lessen the injury. A National Commission on Consumer Finance (NCCF) staff study noted that the frequency with which wage assignments were included in credit contracts was relatively low for all types of credit at commercial banks, finance companies, and retailers, except for personal loans from finance companies (13 percent), suggesting that their use was limited to the segment of the borrowing public where the default risk was relatively high.[14] Credit union loans also often include wage assignments, but they were not included in the NCCF staff study.

In recommending the prohibition of wage assignments by defining them as unfair trade practices, the FTC Bureau of Consumer Protection said:

> This proposal is based upon the contention that wage assignments are unduly injurious to consumers, are unconscionable according to judicially accepted standards of unconscionability, and are contrary to most indicia

---

12. *Id.* at 204–205.

13. FTC "Credit Practices," 16 C.F.R. Pt. 444 (April 11, 1975). Section a3 declares it to be an unfair trade practice "to take or receive from a consumer an obligation which constitutes or contains an assignment of wages;" or (alternate subparagraph) "constitutes or contains an assignment of wages unless the amount of the obligation is three hundred dollars (300.00) or less and no other security interest is taken with respect to the obligation."

14. Greer, "Creditors' Remedies and Contractual Provisions: An Economic and Legal Analysis of Consumer Credit Collection," 5 *Technical Studies* 64–69 Nat'l Comm'n on Consumer Finance Rep. (1972).

of public policy, including state and federal statutes and fundamental constitutional precepts.[15]

To identify the potentially injuring and injured parties, we begin by noting that there must be a wage assignment in the negotiated credit agreement for there to be potential injury of the type noted above. From the applicant's viewpoint, a probability judgment of default must be made in order to evaluate the prospect of employer notification, penalties, and possible harassment involved with default, and these must be weighed against the benefits from the purpose for which credit is being granted. In some instances, this will be the purchase of a good or a service or for the refinancing of existing debts. Such purchases may be emergency needs or frivolity; the refinancing of debt may also forestall bankruptcy or lead more directly to it.

Since wage assignment provisions are not uniformly included in credit contracts, it would appear that any such inclusion would be subject to some consideration by the creditor. Let me suggest that, as noted earlier, the consideration is motivated by the lower expense of collection when a wage assignment is obtained from higher-risk applicants.

Thus, the relevant population to consider in assessing the potential injury from wage assignments is that portion of credit applicants that creditors would require extra compensation to accept in the absence of a wage assignment. Of this group, some proportion of those granted credit will experience default, but neither the creditor nor the debtor can anticipate in advance exactly which of those applicants accepted will default. In this situation, private bargaining would suffice to reach agreement because the creditor could offer the debtor—or the debtor could insist on obtaining—an alternative price for credit without (or with) the wage assignment. But whenever there is a loan rate ceiling above which the creditor cannot charge, there may not be a higher price to forgo wage assignments (and other remedies needed by the creditor to qualify the debtor for credit). Or, alternatively, through ignorance, fear, or inequality of bargaining power, the applicant may not be in a position to bargain forthrightly for credit, and he may not know that he has alternatives to a wage assignment.

Where ignorance of alternatives or transactions costs is appreciable, it is the creditor's decision to allocate resources differently that identifies the parties that benefit or are hurt when government intervention changes property rights. To identify third parties, one has to find out whether creditors will charge higher rates to marginal applicants (rate ceilings permitting) and lower rates to lower-risk sources to encourage more borrowing, or will utilize fewer resources in credit transactions.[16]

---

15. FTC, Memorandum, N. 11 *supra* at 214.

16. For a formal consideration of this process, see Greer, "Rate Ceilings, Market Structure, and the Supply of Finance Company Personal Loans," J. Finance 1363–1382 (Dec. 1974).

To find out whether creditors' adjustments are inconsistent with economic and social welfare, one must begin by weighing whether those denied credit because they cannot pledge future wages are better or worse off. This group includes those who would not have defaulted as well as those who would have defaulted, since defaulters cannot be identified in advance. Those that would not have experienced injury through invocation of wage assignments and who would have been denied credit without wage assignments are hurt by their prohibition.[17] Those who would have defaulted and did not obtain credit would have been spared some injury but would have been deprived of the benefits that the use of credit would have brought in the period before default. The creditor, depending upon his decision regarding the increased collection costs without wage assignments, presumably would undergo lower returns implicit in any second-best alternative.[18] The beneficiaries would be primarily the third parties who would gain from increased credit (at possibly lower cost) or who would obtain better bargains in noncredit sectors.

## Estimating Marginal Benefits and Marginal Costs of Intervention

Obtaining estimates of the value of wage assignments from the affected parties after they are identified poses additional problems, since each individual's estimate is likely to differ because of different utility functions. Such a problem may be alleviated by using sampling techniques, but there are further problems. To what extent can a person estimate the value of an experience never realized? Do individuals possess sufficient information to form a reasonably valid estimate of the economic worth of creditors' remedies and buyers' rights, including wage assignments? Could the prices of remedies be unbundled from the price of credit and be quoted separately? Demsetz shies away from proposed governmental activity to obtain such information:

> If the government should merely question those who alleged that they will be harmed by the activity, it will be in their interest to exaggerate the harmful effects so that they can increase the probability that the activity will be prohibited. Those who allege that they will be harmed if the activity is prohibited have an incentive to exaggerate the benefits they will derive from the activity. Assessing these benefits and costs by simple-minded questionnaires or by relying on the publicity of complaints will lead to the decision being based on inaccurate information, although this is a fair

---

17. Unless it is presumed that all marginal credit risks are better off without credit despite their needs.

18. Under competitive conditions, the statement holds in any circumstance. Under monopolistic or oligopolistic conditions, the observation needs to be modified whenever the firm is not maximizing profits.

description of the way in which the political calculus sometimes operates. However, it is conceptually possible for the government to acquire information of greater accuracy.[19]

Demsetz then introduces the principal of compensation to provide his solution for government intervention:

> Let the government attempt to buy the permission of those who feel that they will be harmed by allowing the activity and also let the government attempt to buy permission to restrict the activity from those who feel that they will benefit from the activity. That action should be taken for which permission can be purchased at lower cost. By assuming the role of middleman, the government through the payment of compensation can increase the accuracy of the information upon which it acts.[20]

It is not apparent how Demsetz would have the government serve as middleman, nor does he extend his analysis beyond pointing out that it is not easy to see why the government could play the middleman role more cheaply than private middlemen.

With regard to wage assignments, in particular, and creditors' remedies and buyers' rights, in general, the transactions costs of publicizing and conducting auctions to determine the ''prices'' of remedies would be high, indeed, since the identity of those who would benefit from any alternative allocation of resources is presently unknown. Nor is it easy to forecast who would be injured by wage assignments on credit contracts ex ante, since the applicants required by creditors to have wage assignments to qualify for credit would include some beneficiaries (who would not default) and some injured parties (who did).

The process of allocating compensation would be difficult, as the funds provided by those who have forgone injury would have to be allocated among creditors, if they are forced to accept second-best alternatives, and among other parties who receive fewer benefits because of creditors' decisions to allocate credit differently. If the creditors' total output of credit remained the same, before and after the change in property rights (wage assignments, in this instance), the beneficiaries of the change could compensate those injured, and the creditor would be the link between the two groups. But if the creditors' output of credit changed as a result of the adjustment of property rights, even the creditor could not identify all the beneficiaries (if less credit were granted than before) or those injured (if the resources used to provide credit came from other sectors of the economy).

The use of the principle of compensation to improve decisions to change property rights has considerable merit, but its implementation presents challenges which require further investigation.

---

**19.** Demsetz, N. 7 *supra* at 69.

**20.** *Ibid.*

## Summary

The application of a theoretical framework derived from the property rights literature to the issues involved in consumer credit protection regulation provides the following insights:

1. The adversary relationships involved in consumer credit protection issues are not basically between the debtor, on the one hand, and the creditor, on the other. Rather, they are between two groups of consumers in our society—those who are harmed if there is freedom to contract for property rights involved in credit transactions, and those who will be harmed if the freedom to contract for those rights is curtailed or prohibited. The creditor may be aligned with either of the two groups as an injured party, but the creditor's share of the total damage will be relatively small.

2. The credit grantor is basically an intermediary between the suppliers of capital, the savers, and the borrowers who seek to utilize credit. Only a modest portion of the funds supplied are from the owners of credit-granting firms. But it is the creditors' adjustment to governmental interventions affecting property rights of credit applicants which determines the parties benefited or injured when property rights are changed.

3. There is, therefore, a need to weigh the marginal benefits versus marginal costs among individuals affected by government intervention to change property rights involved in credit transactions at the time the intervention is contemplated. There is a case to be made for such intervention when the transactions costs are so high that private adjustments of property rights will not be made. Such opportunities may arise when innovations in credit granting techniques or technology change the market values of property rights and when information about such changes in value is not readily recognized or communicated to the marketplace. Yet, if action is taken solely on the claims or allegations of potential injury without consideration of the claims of potential beneficiaries and unknowing third parties, resources will be allocated in a manner which would not maximize economic or social welfare.

## THE LEGAL PROCESS

### The Movement to Borrower Protection

During the last decade, a broad-based attack by consumers and their advocates upon the freedom of borrowers to contract with creditors for the various remedies and rights has joined the long-standing attempt to limit rates of charge on consumer credit agreements. The joining of the attack on creditors' remedies with the attack on interest rate ceilings in the courts, the state legislatures, and the Congress of the United States has merely shifted the grounds on which "predatory" creditors could be prevented from taking advantage of unsophisticated borrowers. The effect on creditors of the deprivation of a remedy that lowers collection costs and decreases bad debts differs little from a lowering of the legal rate ceiling that forces a lowering of revenues. Profits decline when remedies are curtailed with given rate ceilings, since creditors are not able to pass on the increase in costs. Often, the more costly customers (less credit-worthy) will be denied credit.

The interdependence of legal rate ceilings and the limitation of creditors' remedies (or expansion of borrowers' rights) was well-recognized by the NCCF in 1972:

> Underlying the Commission's belief that competition is the best regulator of the consumer credit marketplace is its belief that a competitive system cannot be "half free." If there is to be competition, then it follows that such competition should also be the governor of *rates* as well as other aspects of credit granting (amount, type, and so forth). It would be inconsistent to turn to the industry and attempt to regulate and eliminate practices which affect operating costs but at the same time limit the rate by fiat so that it cannot seek its own level. And yet this is precisely what legislators have done. For example, the effective elimination of some creditors' legal collection devices increases bad debts and collection expenses. When such elimination is not accompanied by a rate structure which recognizes and allows for those increased costs to be covered, less credit is available than would be at equilibrium conditions. The Commission recommends a consistent approach. If there is to be free access, open competition, and elimination of harmful or inappropriate practices, then *inhibiting* rate ceilings should be reviewed and revised to allow competitive forces to operate.[21]

The recent movement for regulation of trade practices has centered on considerations of unconscionability, due process, and unfairness. Changing legal standards are emerging in the courts, and it is likely that a brief review of some of these changing standards will help us appraise whether the interest of all beneficiaries and injured parties are being weighed in the resolution of these issues.

Court decisions regarding unconscionability or due process have been taken to state legislatures and have been used to justify the enactment of statutes which now differ widely among the states. Such decisions also have encouraged the drafting of the Uniform Consumer Credit Code (UCCC) by the National Commissioners of Uniform State Laws and the Model Consumer Credit Act (MCCA) by the Boston College Law Center. Further, both before and subsequent to enactment of the UCCC and MCCA, consumer advocates have pressed due process arguments in the court to invalidate features of state laws which legislate creditors' remedies contrary to their perceived interests. Finally, at the federal level, attempts have been made to further consolidate gains

---

21. National Comm'n on Consumer Finance, *Consumer Credit in the United States: Report of the National Commission on Consumer Finance* 4 (Washington, D.C., Dec. 1972).

by enacting national prohibitions or limitations on remedies in the Consumer Credit Protection Act[22] or through promulgation of trade regulation or trade practice regulation rules by the Federal Trade Commission.

It is important to recognize the sequential aspect involved in the movement to curtail creditors' remedies and expand borrowers' rights in the process of recovering debts after default. During the last decade, actions under common law provided the ammunition for legislative campaigns to enact statutes limiting creditors' remedies or expanding the rights of borrowers. Further ammunition was provided from various newly enacted statutes that could be incorporated in model uniform statutes for legislative enactment. When some states had enacted a number of the provisions of the uniform statutes and recommendations of the National Commission on Consumer Finance, the drive for national uniformity proceeded at the federal level, as impatience with the progress of uniformity at the state level grew. The last step in this sequence involves application of the standard of unfair practices to creditors' remedies and buyers' rights by the Federal Trade Commission. Such action, if taken, would have the effect of making irrelevant many court decisions, including those of the Supreme Court, the actions of many state legislatures, features of the UCCC and MCCA, and some incipient federal legislation.

In the next section, we evaluate three aspects of this wave of credit reform, to see how well they satisfy the tests posed in our theoretical framework for evaluating proposed changes in property rights. They involve, as noted above, unconscionability, due process, and unfair credit practices. I shall focus my attention on the FTC proposed credit practices regulations.[23]

## The FTC Credit Practices Rule

To apply the "unfairness" standard to credit transactions that did not prohibit or require the 11 provisions of the Credit Practices Rule (see Appendix A), the FTC Bureau of Consumer Protection cited three tests from the Commission's unfairness criteria in the Cigarette Rule Statement.[24] These were:

> 1. Whether the practice . . . offends public policy . . . whether, in other words, it is within at least the penumbra of some common-law, statutory, or other established concept of unfairness.

---

**22.** 15 U.S.C.A. §§ 1601–1681 (1970).

**23.** FTC, "Credit Practices," N. 13 *supra*.

**24.** Statement of Basis and Purpose of Trade Regulation Rule 408, Unfair or Deceptive Advertising and Labeling of Cigarettes in Relation to the Health Hazards of Smoking, 29 Fed. Reg. 8350 (1964).

2. Whether it is immoral, unethical, oppressive, or unscrupulous.

3. Whether it causes substantial injury to consumers (or competitors or other businessmen).[25]

The Bureau staff asserted its belief that each of the three criteria, by itself, could support a finding of unfairness, and the Bureau opposed any view that all three were required, citing the *S & H* case, in which the stamp company argued that a showing of consumer injury alone would not constitute unfairness.[26] Yet, the Bureau placed "no independent reliance" upon the second criterion due to its subjectivity and the Bureau's "doubt whether the Commission would be prepared to ban a practice on the basis of a subjective feeling that it is immoral, unscrupulous, reprehensible, or the like."[27]

The FTC Bureau of Consumer Protection utilized a balancing process, under which, first, consumer injury was weighed "against the legitimate interests of industry respondents or the commercial justification for the challenged practice,"[28] and second, an "offensive to public policy" standard was weighed against "the business interest served by a business practice."[29]

The Bureau clarifies how the dual standard was applied in the formulation of the proposed Credit Practices Rule:

> When the foregoing discussion of the public policy/business reasons balance is combined with the similar treatment of the consumer harm/business reasons balance, the complexity of the inquiry becomes manifest. It is not simply a question of public policy *or* consumer injury weighed against business reasons (although in particular cases such a one-dimensional approach may be called for and may well point to a conclusion of unfairness). Typically *both* consumer injury *and* public policy hostility to a given practice call that practice into question. Both indicia of unfairness—the first and third Cigarette tests—will then be summed together and loaded onto the same balance tray. Since the countervailing commercial justification fits into the opposite tray, there are several possible permutations which could eventuate in a finding of unfairness. For example, where the commercial interest is meager or the consumer harm substantial, the Commission need not pause for long over the sketchiness of the public policies which the practice offends.[30]

It is evident that the balancing-of-interests tests of unfairness

---

**25.** FTC, Memorandum, N. 11 *supra* at 49.

**26.** *Id.*, citing FTC v. Sperry & Hutchinson Co., 403 U.S. 233 at 244–245 (1972).

**27.** N. 25 *supra* at 50, in a footnote, the Bureau qualified this statement, with reference to business transactions.

**28.** *Id.* at 51.

**29.** *Id.* at 52.

**30.** *Id.* at 54.

involve the interests of consumers risking potential harm if they are

unable to meet scheduled contractual commitments to creditors versus the interests of the businesses (creditors) which serve them. The Bureau of Consumer Protection chose to cite the number of consumers delinquent 30 days or more, in debt to finance companies, totaling 2,045,000 accounts at the end of 1972, to indicate that the number of consumers potentially subject to creditor remedies was substantial.[31] The Bureau quoted a recent study of the National Council for Consumer Affairs (NCCA) estimating that out of delinquent debts of approximately $2.4 billion on nearly 4.4 million late-paying or nonpaying accounts (including debts owed to finance companies, banks, retailers, and all other consumer-credit grantors), "resort to contractual remedies was estimated to account for recovery of $240 million on 350,000 delinquent accounts annually."[32] But the Bureau indicated doubts as to the accuracy of the NCCA estimates. However, it was unable to measure the area of potential consumer injury more precisely.

Since the balancing process devoted itself to weighing consumer *actual* rather than *potential* injury, the FTC process apparently did not balance the interests of those receiving credit who did not default against the injury done by application of the proposed unfair practice to those who obtained credit and did default. Or, alternatively, if the FTC staff assumed that future removal of actual harm represented benefit to all potential defaulters subject to the unfair credit practice, the granting of credit to those who did repay was assumed to have no economic worth.

PUBLIC POLICY STANDARD

The Bureau cited the following sources for the third Cigarette Rule test:[33]

1. Federal and state constitutional doctrine.

2. State and federal statutory law.

3. Decisional law.

4. The doctrine of unconscionability.

From the Constitution, the Bureau sought to translate established guarantees into "practical reality for disadvantaged consumers."[34] In particular, this would apply to the notion that it is *unfair* to compel a debtor to agree to waive his right to be heard in court before a remedy

---

**31.** *Id.* at 10.

**32.** *Id.* at 11.

**33.** *Id.* at 55–62.

**34.** *Id.* at 55.

could be invoked, i.e., in the case of wage assignments and cognovit notes.[35] In proposing that wage assignments and cognovit notes become unfair credit practices, the FTC would prohibit provisions of credit contracts which the Supreme Court has not declared unconstitutional but to which it has not given blanket approval.[36]

On the basis of state and federal statutory law, the Bureau regards regulation or prohibition by some but not all states as indicative of a practice deemed contrary to the public good and worthy of consideration as an unfair credit practice. For example:

> Of course for reasons of state-federal relations and efficient resource allocation, staff does not propose that the Commission move simply to enforce state laws through its unfairness jurisdiction. But where a substantial number of state legislatures have acted to abolish, regulate, or restrict a practice, the Commission is justified in regarding widespread state concern as the expression of a public policy congenial to across-the-board unfairness relief. . . . [37]

Thus, if a number of states or the federal legislature calls attention to an abusive practice by restricting it or prohibiting it, it becomes a candidate for application to the FTC balancing process to extend it further and make it uniform among all states.

The third source for the public policy standard, decisional law, involves contract provisions which judges have routinely refused to enforce in private disputes. For example:

> Moreover, by gradual accretion, judicial ingenuity has evolved a host of common law and equity principles which may fruitfully be viewed as the embodiment of public policy. Some examples are the doctrines or concepts of unjust enrichment, unclean hands, fiduciary responsibility, penalty clauses, and mitigation of damages. Each of these, and many others, are available to serve. Moreover, certain broad policies are embedded in various bodies of the law, more general than rules or doctrines, but not so vague as to be useless. For instance, the policies of compensation and risk allocation underpin much of tort law. These policies might form the basis for a Commission determination that allocating all risks and burdens to the consumer, and none to the commercial party, is unfair.[38]

For the fourth and final source of the public policy standard, the

---

**35.** *Id.*

**36.** State and federal district courts have rejected challenges to the constitutionality of wage assignments. See Bond v. Dentzer, 494 F.2d 302 (2d Cir. 1974), *cert. denied* 95 S. Ct. 65 (1974); and Beneficial Finance Corp. v. Bond, 372 N.Y.S.2d 374, 83 Misc. 2d 9 (Sup. Ct. 1975). On cognovit notes, see D. H. Overmyer Co. v. Frick Co., 405 U.S. 174, 176–177, 92 S. Ct. 775, 777 (1972).

**37.** FTC, Memorandum, N. 11 *supra* at 56.

**38.** *Id.* at 57, 58.

doctrine of unconscionability, the courts have departed from traditional common-law defenses (where unconscionability was applied to limit the freedom of contract on such grounds as duress, fraud, or incompetence) to apply the doctrine to remove, on substantive grounds, the terms of private agreements that have been formed by unexceptionable means.[39] (The doctrine is split into two parts by Professor Leff, who distinguished procedural from substantive unconscionability along the lines noted above.)[40]

The doctrine is recognized in the Uniform Commercial Code in Section 2-302 and, therefore, is in the statutes of most states. Although the term *unconscionability* is not defined in the U.C.C., the Official Comment to Section 2-302 uses the phrases "the prevention of oppression and unfair surprise . . . and not of disturbance of allocation of risk because of superior bargaining power."

With respect to use of the doctrine of unconscionability by the Commission in determining unfair credit practices, the Bureau staff notes:

> Judicial experience with unconscionability analysis, although still in its formative stages, may hold great lessons for the Commission. The concerns of the courts applying §2-302 closely parallel the Commission's enforcement responsibilities—"oppression and unfair surprise" almost echoes "unfairness and deception." Furthermore, the methodology developed by courts, characterized by a substantive-procedural sliding scale and by a weighing of injury and public policy versus business rationale could be borrowed for unfairness analysis, with some modifications. Also, several hallmarks of substantive unconscionability, developed by courts and commentators, suggest analytically solid grounds for Commission prohibition of practices injurious to consumers. Finally, the decisions on unconscionability thus far amount to a virtual taxonomy of practices and provisions which would be equally suspect in unfairness terms.[41]

SOURCES OF CONSUMER INJURY (OR BENEFITS FROM PROPOSED RULE)

In citing the benefits of the proposed rule, the Bureau indicated three broad categories where removal of unfair credit practices could be found: monetary loss, damage to physical and emotional health, and the production of outrage, frustration, and social unrest.[42] Monetary loss was said to include:

- Evaporated equity in articles that creditors retake from the consumer through repossession.

---

39. Epstein, "Unconscionability: A Critical Reappraisal," 18 J. Law & Econ. 294-295 (1975).

40. Leff, "Unconscionability and the Code—The Emperor's New Clause," 115 U. Pa. L. Rev. 485 (1967).

41. FTC, Memorandum N. 11 *supra* at 61–62, Ns. 75 through 77 omitted.

42. *Id.* at 64.

- Unassertable defenses against payments for defective merchandise, leaving consumers no choice but to pay and then at best to recover through an affirmative lawsuit.

- Straight cash obligations tacked onto the adhesive credit contract. Prominent among these are minimum attorneys' fees and late charges that frequently bear no relation to the costs of legal action or the actual costs of delay when a late payment is received.

- Impairment of earning power. . . . Creditors make it their policy to contact the defaulting debtor's employer and attempt to enlist his help in putting pressure on the debtor to pay (or use wage assignments).[43]

Damage to physical and emotional health was linked to the presence of debt problems accentuated by default and creditors' attempt to collect by using "certain commonly employed remedies:"[44]

- Loss of household goods and goods beyond those at issue in the immediate transaction.

- Threats to job and wages.

- Use of *in terrorem* devices.

Reference was made to a study of debtors who had defaulted to confirm the link between default and physical and emotional health.[45]

The final type of consumer injury, the sense of outrage, frustration, and unrest, was admitted by the Bureau to be "the most difficult to quantify but is no less real for that reason."[46] Examples included "practices that produce an unconditional obligation to pay without the opportunity for a hearing or the right to present defenses, such as wage assignments and confessions of judgment, and in practices that present consumers with the loss or the prospect of loss of far more than they reasonably supposed they were risking in the transaction, such as cross-collateral, blanket security agreements and after-acquired property clauses."[47]

BUSINESS PRACTICES STANDARD (OR COSTS OF PROPOSED RULE)

The Bureau staff cited the arguments noted earlier in conjunction with the discussion of wage assignments as being relevant, suggesting that curtailment of remedies would bring a cost squeeze to the credit industry, forcing it to curtail the credit supply to high-risk customers and to

---

**43.** *Id.* at 66–68.

**44.** *Id.* at 71–74.

**45.** Caplovitz, *Debtors in Default* (Bureau of Social Research, Columbia Univ. 1970–1971).

**46.** FTC, Memorandum, N. 11 *supra* at 76.

**47.** *Id.* at 76, 77.

try to increase credit to lower-risk borrowers.[48] High-risk borrowers would have to turn to creditors who operate with even more repressive tactics within the law, or who operate illegally. Further, the Bureau cited the findings of the National Commission on Consumer Finance, which concluded in a number of instances that abolishing confining remedies would probably tend to force rates up or availability down to a significant extent.[49]

Surprisingly, the Bureau did *not* rebut the business practice argument. Instead, it met the argument in the following way:

> This antireform scenario is plausible enough, and might well have merit if what was proposed was to make legitimate debts either uncollectible or collectible only at prohibitive cost. The rule submitted, however, will do nothing of the sort.
>
> The proposed rule leaves partially or wholly intact a wide range of remedies that will enable the creditor to collect his debts without difficulty and with little or no additional cost. Where additional costs are imposed, the proscribed practice has been found to cause particularly severe and uncontrovertible injury. In a rough sense, the rule attempts to construct a hypothetical negotiated contract between the creditor and a consumer borrower, forcing the creditor to relinquish only those remedies that he might bargain away if faced with the necessity to bargain while still leaving his basic interests protected. If a practice or a remedy appears to be vital to the economic health of the industry, or if consumer injury is debatable, then the practice has been left alone.[50]

It is both interesting and significant that the Bureau limited its proposed rule to those remedies which in its judgment would not impair the health of the credit industry. It suggests that none of the proposed limitations in Appendix A are essential to maintaining the aggregate supply of consumer credit in the marketplace: By prohibiting or limiting certain remedies, the Commission's proposed rule would leave sufficient remaining remedies to accomplish the task of collection and recovery of debts.

The remedies left intact include:

1. *The security interest*   Restricted only to prevent the creditor and lender from "overprotecting his legitimate interest."

2. *Personal liability*   The personal liability of the debtor remains the same, except as protected from increases attributable to payment of attorneys' fees or the sale of encumbered property at less than fair market retail value.

---

48. *Id.* at 78, 79.

49. *Id.* at 80.

50. *Id.* at 80, 81.

3. *Wage garnishment*   The creditor remains able to garnish wages as provided by law, but not to utilize wage assignments in credit contracts.

4. *Self-help repossession*   Remains intact under the proposed rule.

5. *Definition of default*   Leaves definition to the credit contract itself.

6. *Acceleration clauses*   The creditor remains able to declare the entire obligation due and owing upon default of any single installment.

7. *Rebate of unearned finance charges*   Unaffected by the proposed rule.[51]

There is, however, some doubt that the proposed rule will not affect the vital health of segments of the credit industry. The finance industry, the traditional lenders of last resort to high-risk consumers, is particularly exposed to restrictions on security interests and wage assignments in the proposed rule. The Bureau staff also acknowledges that the changes proposed in the Credit Practices Rule may not have the negligible effect implied. Indeed, the Bureau itself drew a second line of defense by stating:

> Despite the foregoing, the possibility that there may be some increase in the price or drop in the supply of consumer credit cannot be ruled out. Cost-free reforms are too much to expect, however diligent an effort is made to insure that costs will be minimized. Even accepting that there may be some price and supply effect as a result of the rule, and that the most likely effect will be the denial of credit to certain high-risk borrowers, the overall effect should be nothing like the catastrophe that has sometimes been suggested.[52]

To explain its prediction of a modest impact, the Bureau staff forecast that the number of high-risk borrowers affected and the amount of their borrowing would be small compared to the total amount of consumer credit users and the total amount of credit outstanding.[53] The staff also noted that increased discrimination by credit grantors to turn away customers whose risk of default is unacceptably high may even benefit these consumers.[54]

## Comparison of FTC Balancing Process with That Implied by the Economic Framework

The property rights–economic theory framework suggests that the adversary relationship between debtors as a group and creditors as a group should not be the basic measure of the benefits versus the cost of

---

51. *Id.* at 81–83, with minor revisions to item 2 to make it consistent with the rule actually proposed.

52. *Id.* at 89.

53. *Id.*

54. *Id.* at 91.

government intervention (see above p. 227). Instead, this framework

recommends that the consumers hurt by the proposed rule should be given an opportunity to estimate the economic worth of the rule change, and then this value should be compared to the estimated worth of the rule change to those consumers protected from injury by the proposed rule. The FTC Bureau's standard weighed only the potential injury removed without considering the urgency of need for credit, which would lower the desire (and estimated worth) for the rule change among those adversely affected. And among those customers who did not default and were not injured by the practices, it is unlikely that their estimate of the rule's worth would be high if its enactment lessened their chances of obtaining credit at current rates of charge.

The problem becomes more apparent when it is recognized that the FTC Bureau's measurement of the breadth of consumer injury was taken solely from a study that dealt only with debtors in default (1,300 defaulters in four large cities), which could not be related to a relevant sample of borrowers whose contracts contained the remedies currently being proposed as unfair credit practices. Defaulters are only a fraction of the relevant borrowing population. Further, the study of the National Commission on Consumer Finance found differences in the amount and price of credit of various types according to the presence or absence or restriction of garnishment, attorneys' fees, waiver of buyer defense, holder in due course, and, among smaller amounts of credit, wage assignments.[55] Further, that study was designed to test the impact of remedies on the *total* amount of credit and its *average* price, and not on the amount and price of credit to borrowers typically requiring the remedies in the proposed rule, where the effects are presumably stronger.

The vagueness of the standard enunciated by the FTC Bureau of Consumer Protection contrasts sharply with its purported attempt to portray the rule as one which simulates how the creditor might bargain away remedies if he were dealing with private interests under competitive conditions.[56] Other than mentioning the questionnaire circulated by the NCCF to creditors, there was little or no indication of how such bargains might have been made.

The public policy standard, as applied by the Bureau to the Credit Practices Rule, does not fit easily into the economic balancing process. It appears more effective as a screening mechanism to select credit practices for possible inclusion within a rule. With consumer injury as a feature already included in the balancing process, the public policy test appears redundant. Since courts and legislatures have already weighed the pros and cons, should their outcomes be quantified and applied to reach a reasoned result? If so, the public policy standard would appear

---

55. Greer, N. 14 *supra* at Ch. 4, p. 153.

56. FTC, Memorandum, N. 11 *supra* at 80.

to be more of a subterfuge to extend the Commission's influence beyond the reaches of decisional law and state legislation which it preempts, than a complement to the consumer injury standard.

## CONCLUSIONS

While this paper has confined itself largely to an abstract analysis of consumer credit protection reform, it may have expressed doubts about the content of the FTC rule, itself. Without going into detail about each of the 10 proposed unfair credit practices, it may be sufficient to note that decisions reached through the application of imperfect information and questionable legal and economic processes may well be accompanied by undesirable results.

It may be appropriate to conclude with a suggested process for evaluating the 10 proposed unfair credit practices. At the risk of over-simplification, I suggest the following approach, using sampling techniques among credit applicants:

1. Identify all the remedies used by creditors to recover debts.

2. Ascertain the number and the amount of credit agreements containing each remedy utilized by creditors to recover debts.

3. Ascertain the proportion of that number and amount of credit agreements containing each remedy which result in credit problems eventually becoming defaults.

4. Ascertain the amount the creditors would be willing to accept to forgo use of the remedy in all the relevant credit agreements.

5. Ascertain the amount the applicants would be willing to pay the creditors to remove each remedy from the credit contract.

6. If the aggregate amount bid by applicants to remove the remedy were greater than the amount required by creditors, change the legal rate ceiling to permit creditors to pass on the increased cost and prohibit use of the remedy, while if the aggregate of the amounts bid by applicants to remove the remedy were less than the amount required by the creditors, retain the status quo.[57]

I suspect that my legal and regulatory colleagues are going to view these proposals with some skepticism, and rightfully so. There are tremendous problems in obtaining this kind of information: all sorts of response bias. But it can be done, and it is necessary if we are to enact useful reforms.

---

**57.** It may also be useful to compare the average price bid among the respondents who have previously experienced default with the average price bid on each remedy by respondents who have not. If this difference is statistically significant, after adjusting for other relevant considerations, we may want to weigh the experience of previous defaulters more heavily in the decision process.

# APPENDIX A—PROPOSED UNFAIR CREDIT PRACTICES RULE

§444.2 Unfair credit practices

In connection with the extension of credit to consumers in or affecting commerce, as commerce is defined in the Federal Trade Commission Act, it is an unfair act or practice within the meaning of Section 5 of that Act for a lender or retail installment seller directly or indirectly:

(a) To take or receive from a consumer an obligation which:

(1) Constitutes or contains a cognovit, confession of judgment, warrant of attorney, power of attorney or other waiver of the right to notice and the opportunity to be heard in the event of suit or process thereon;

(2) Constitutes or contains a waiver or limitation of exemption from attachment, execution or other process on real or personal property held, owned by or due to the consumer;

(3) Constitutes or contains an assignment of wages;

[Alternate subparagraph(3):

(3) Constitutes or contains an assignment of wages unless the amount of the obligation is three hundred dollars ($300.00) or less and no other security interest is taken with respect to the obligation;]

(4) Constitutes or contains a security interest other than a Purchase Money security interest, EXCEPT, where the proceeds of a personal loan are NOT to be PRIMARILY applied to the purchase of consumer goods, the lender may take a security interest in OTHER THAN household goods;

(5) Encumbers goods purchased on different dates from a retail installment seller on a deferred payment basis, unless the contract provides that payments made by the consumer will be credited in full to the earliest purchase to release the goods from encumbrance in the order acquired;

(6) Fails to enumerate and specifically identify each individual item of property encumbered by it;

(7) Fails to provide that if the creditor retakes encum-

bered property from the consumer, the fair market retail value of the property so taken will be credited toward the balance due under the obligation;

(8) Constitutes or contains a provision requiring the payment of attorney's fees or any other costs incident to the collection of the obligation;

[Alternate subparagraph (8):

(8) Constitutes or contains a provision which:

(i) With respect to a consumer loan in which the finance charge calculated according to the actuarial method is more than 18 percent per year, provides for payment by the consumer of attorney's fees:

(A) if the loan is not pursuant to open-end credit and the amount financed is $1,000 or less; or

(B) if the loan is pursuant to open-end credit and the balance of the account at the time of default is $1,000 or less;

(ii) With respect to any other consumer credit transaction, provides for payment by the consumer of attorney's fees unless (A) such fees do not exceed fifteen percent of the unpaid debt at the time of default and (B) such fees become due only after actual referral of the obligation to an attorney who is not a salaried employee of the creditor;]

(9) Provides for charges for late or extended payments which exceed the amount derived from application of the annual percentage rate governing the transaction to the payment or payments late or extended; or

(10) Fails to provide that the creditor shall not, in the course of collecting a debt, communicate or threaten to communicate with the consumer's employer or any agent of the employer or any other person not liable for the debt other than the spouse or attorney of the consumer, except as permitted by order of a court.

(b) To obligate a co-signer other than the spouse of the consumer on any obligation unless:

(1) The co-signer is furnished with a separate statement, at least three days prior to his becoming obligated, which shall contain in ten point bold face type the following information with such limitations as necessary to conform to applicable State law and no other:

(2) Three days or more after receiving the NOTICE TO CO-SIGNER, the co-signer signs a document evidencing the obligation which discloses the full amount he may be asked to repay;

(3) The co-signer is furnished with a completed copy of every document that he is asked to sign or that is furnished to the consumer; and

(4) Any document evidencing the obligation contains the following notice:

No co-signer or surety of this obligation shall be liable thereunder except after the lender or retail installment seller has employed due diligence in attempting to collect the obligation from the principal debtor.

No co-signer or surety of this obligation shall be liable thereunder for more than the total of payments for which the principal debtor is liable at the time that the co-signer becomes obligated.

No co-signer or surety of this obligation shall be liable thereunder unless promptly notified in writing of any default by the principal debtor.

_____
(Date)

BY SIGNING THIS CONTRACT YOU ARE AGREEING TO PAY (*Amount of Contract*) TO (*Name of Lender*), IF (*Name of Principal Debtor*) DOES NOT.

IF FOR ANY REASON (*Name of Principal Debtor*) DOES NOT PAY THIS (*Amount of Contract*) OR ANY PART OF IT WHEN IT IS DUE, YOU MAY BE REQUIRED TO PAY THE AMOUNT WHICH HAS NOT BEEN PAID OR ANY PART OF IT. HOWEVER, BEFORE YOU CAN BE HELD LIABLE FOR THE DEBT, (*Name of Lender*) MUST FIRST DILIGENTLY ATTEMPT TO COLLECT THE DEBT FROM (*Name of Principal Debtor*).

YOU MAY BE SUED ON THIS CONTRACT IF (*Name of Principal Debtor*) DOES NOT PAY AS AGREED FOR ANY REASON. IF (*Name of Lender*) WINS A SUIT AGAINST YOU IN COURT, IT MAY TAKE A PART OF YOUR WAGES EACH WEEK UNTIL THE DEBT IS PAID IN FULL; IT MAY TAKE YOUR SAVINGS OR REAL OR PERSONAL PROPERTY WHICH YOU OWN TO PAY THIS DEBT; AND IT MAY USE OTHER LAWFUL MEANS TO COLLECT THIS DEBT FROM YOU.

YOU MAY BE SUED EVEN IF (*Name of Principal Debtor*) IS NOT SUED IF HE HAS NOT PAID AS AGREED, BUT YOU MAY SUE HIM TO COLLECT ANY MONEY YOU HAVE PAID ON HIS BEHALF.

THIS NOTICE IS *NOT* THE CONTRACT YOU WILL BE ASKED TO SIGN. YOU MUST BE GIVEN A COPY OF THAT CONTRACT AND OF THIS NOTICE.

_____
(Signature of Co-signer)

# COMMENTARY

Leonard Lapidus, *Superintendent, New York State Banking Department*

It has been some time since I read in welfare economics, but there are several aspects of Robert Shay's approach which trouble me (and trouble him as well, I believe). I have some question about whether the economics of externalities is properly applied in examining regulations in consumer credit markets. Externalities—let us say diseconomies—are typically thought to arise in one firm as the incidental effect of the activity of another firm or firms. From a public policy point of view, we are concerned usually about diseconomies of production which incidentally injure innocent citizens. The typical suggested remedies are for government to step in and make sure that private costs reflect all social costs, thereby reducing the uneconomic excess production. The effect of this reduction in output and increase in price is to recast the returns to the factors of production and, normally, to increase the welfare of customers.

In the case of consumer credit regulations, Shay seems to treat debtor and consumer rights—so-called property rights—as externalities. But, clearly, they do not arise incidentally to the production process, and their use by one firm is not a function of the productive activity of other firms.

In fact, property rights are of two sorts. They are either *institutions*—ingrained habitual ways of conducting business, which in the short run are nonnegotiable, or they are *terms* of the contract, which are more or less negotiable. To the extent that property rights are nonnegotiable between private parties, only society or government may effect such changes; so it is reasonable to ask what are the welfare effects of society's effecting changes in them. If they are negotiable, then a prior question must be, what is wrong with the market? Do the particular contract terms not appropriately reflect market forces? That kind of

243

approach leads to a fairly straightforward discussion of the competitiveness of the market rather than to a question of externalities.

What Shay has done, it appears to me, is to attempt to use some of the techniques developed in the externalities literature to measure the effects of changing the property rights of debtors and creditors. I have no real problem with that because the techniques, such as Demsetz's principle of compensation, should be as useful in appraising the marginal costs and marginal benefits attendant on a change in the property rights of debtors and creditors as it is appraising such costs and benefits arising out of externalities. I would assume, however, that if a negotiable contract term arrived at in a competitive market were subject to Demsetz's compensation test, marginal costs and marginal benefits would be equal for the existence of the term and unequal for its nonexistence. The point is that, as Shay has employed it, compensation is a technique for making interpersonal comparisons and not a technique for coping with externalities.

Unfortunately, as Shay realizes, the measurement techniques are not operational even in the static case. And when one contemplates a dynamic world in which equilibrium prices, outputs, and the identity of injuring and injured parties shift, the impracticality of measurement is even more obvious.

But there is a benefit to Shay's approach: Even though measurement is not feasible, the approach requires explicit consideration of *all* parties affected by changes in regulation. To take into consideration *all* parties seems like a self-evident proposition, but it is often—no, frequently—honored in the breach.

I have been close to the political process as it operates in the area of financial regulation, and it is my observation that the parties whose injury or benefit is given greatest weight—leaving aside the whole issue of well-financed interest groups—are those who are articulate and whose injury or benefit is palpable. Unvoiced injury, unseen benefit, and the impact of law and regulation on third parties are given little weight.

This myopia is even true of so-called consumer advocates. The positions taken by advocates of consumer rights derive from their perception of what they believe to be the perception of consumers as to the consumers' self-interest. Consumers are perceived not to understand simple economic reasoning, but rather to believe that

1. Adverse bargains reflect the venality of creditors.

2. Such venality is correctable by legislative imperative.

3. The effects of legislative imperative are direct, specifically effective, and have no spillover effects.

This leads advocates (who often understand more than they appear to) to advocate positions which consumers would applaud, not necessarily positions which would be socially beneficial.

A perfect illustration of this is the usury law that exists in New York State, which sets a ceiling of 8½ percent on mortgage loans to individuals. When market rates are much higher, this unrealistic ceiling inevitably results in funds flowing to those uses not impacted by the usury ceiling. Our studies indicate that in tight money periods, financial institutions in New York State divert increasingly large amounts of their funds available for loans and investments into corporate bonds, FHA or VA mortgages, and out-of-state mortgage loans, all of which are not affected by the ceiling, or that they significantly tighten up on their nonprice terms—resulting in more stringent down-payment requirements and shorter maturities.

As a result, there is an inadequate flow of funds into the local housing market, especially for less affluent potential borrowers, with adverse effects on income and employment in the building industry of New York State.

Moreover, an unrealistically low usury ceiling tends to ignore the fact that keeping interest rates charged to potential home owners at such a low level reduces the earnings of thrift institutions, thereby reducing their ability to pay higher interest rates to savers.

It is only by tracing the effects of the impact of ceilings that one is able to make a proper judgment on their welfare effects. Many legislators and consumer advocates, however, take their positions on the basis of injury to that consumer who would be able to get a cheap mortgage and would, under the proposal, have to pay more for a mortgage.

Aside from the dubious assumption that a typical borrower will be able to obtain mortgage credit at the usury ceiling when prevailing rates are higher, the welfare effect is implicitly taken to be limited to the higher costs inflicted on the successful borrower by the interest rate. Borrowers excluded from the market, borrowers who must pay higher down payments and accept shorter maturities, and labor and capital in the building industry left unemployed as a result of the unavailability of mortgage funds are ignored, or their injury is given little weight.

The position of many consumer groups in favor of Regulation Q illustrates the tendency to decide welfare issues by discounting remote and diffused effects. Regulation Q ceilings decrease the welfare of many "small" savers in favor of increasing the welfare of many fewer borrowers (and of depository institutions). While savers who do not have open market options would seem to be a class of people with natural appeal as being unfairly disadvantaged, nevertheless, borrowers appear to receive the greater degree of sympathy, presumably because individual savers lose only modest amounts of earnings and are relatively inarticulate.

Shay's broad position, that welfare analysis must look broadly to all parties affected by changes in regulations, would be helpful in assessing the Federal Trade Commission (FTC) proposals on consumer credit practices. Indeed, the third criterion in the FTC's general grounds for a finding of "unfairness," "whether it [the practice] causes substantial injury to consumers (or competitors or other businessmen)," provides a sufficient mandate for the FTC to make a full assessment of welfare impacts on all parties. However, the operational tests appear to fall into the error of ignoring unvoiced injury, unseen benefits, and impacts on third parties, and in that respect, the FTC would benefit from a close reading of Shay's criticisms.

# COMMENTARY

Kellis E. Parker, *Professor of Law, Columbia University*

## INTRODUCTION

Professor Shay has presented a nutshell summary of developments in consumer protection and, along the way, has sketched many of the points made in economic assessments of legal problems. As a lawyer whose knowledge of economics would fill a nutshell, I appreciate Shay's lucid discussion of economic concepts. My comments on Professor Shay's paper include a restatement of his objectives, a recapitulation of the main themes in his paper, an assessment of his efforts in attaining his objectives, and an interpretation and criticism of his analysis.

## FROM PROPERTY RIGHTS TO TRANSACTION COSTS

Shay's objectives are to develop a theoretical framework based on an economic theory of property rights and to use this framework to evaluate proposals to prohibit creditor's remedies, particularly wage assignments.[1] Shay states that the economic theory of property rights is based on three theoretical extensions of the traditional or classical economic theory of production and exchange. The first is "that individuals will seek to maximize their own utilities within the limits of the organizations of which they are a part."[2] Law plays both a definitional role (it

---

1. Shay relied on Furubotn and Pejovich, "Property Rights and Economic Theory: A Survey of Recent Literature," 10 J. Econ. Literature, No. 4, 1137–1162 (Dec. 1972); Demsetz, "Some Aspects of Property Rights," 9 J. Law & Econ. 61–70 (Oct. 1966).

2. Shay, p. 1.

defines the scope of permissible utility maximizing activity) and a cautionary role (it aids in defining what activity is utility maximizing).[3] Shay provides an excellent example of the constraints imposed by law on utility maximizing by individuals in credit firms: federal restrictions against refusals to lend or different lending practices based on the race or sex of debtors. Thus, this first principle of classical economic theory boils down to this: An individual will use all means (lawful and unlawful) to maximize utility unless the risks of engaging in unlawful activity are too great.[4]

Shay devoted little attention to the second rule of economic theory that "more than one pattern of property rights can exist and profit (or wealth) maximization of the firm may not always result."[5] But his one-sentence description was loaded with intrigue: "The second extension provides some leeway for firms to behave in suboptimal fashion when penalty-reward systems within the firm militate against optimal performance."[6] Could the second rule also justify the assumption of greater risks because events outside the firm prove the social desirability of suboptimal performance?[7] Suppose the firm has deliberately engaged in unconscionable conduct in the pursuit of utility maximization for an ascertainable period to the disadvantage of a definable class of borrowers, for example, poor people. Should that firm be required to benefit

---

3. Do individuals really know which choices are utility maximizing? Utility, an elusive concept embracing happiness, pleasure, or satisfaction, may be enhanced by maximizing wealth. Furubotn and Pejovich saw the developing property rights literature as an attempt to introduce content into the utility function. Thus, utility is maximized by increasing one's store of property rights. If one defines property rights broadly enough, one can easily lose the specificity sought by adopting the property rights approach. Furubotn and Pejovich defined property rights as "the sanctioned behavioral relations among men that arise from the existence of things and pertain to their use." Furubotn and Pejovich, N. 1 *supra* at 1139. They add that "a theory of property rights cannot be truly complete without a theory of the state." *Id.* at 1140. But, Shay apparently uses a broader definition of property rights: "[t]he remedies available to creditors to collect and recover debts are part of the property rights of the creditors while the limitation of creditors' remedies are property rights of debtors in credit agreements." What are the "things" to which these remedies appertain? The only "thing" is the credit agreement. The consequences of concluding that the so-called credit contract is a "thing" may be significant, since one generally associates contract with a bargaining process in which property rights are exchanged. If the credit document is a "thing," it should be considered one of the goods the debtor receives along with the loan and regulated by the law of products liability. See Leff, "Contract as Thing," 19 Am. U.L. Rev. 131 (1970).

4. The absence of enforcement or the fact of ineffective enforcement may greatly minimize the risks associated with unlawful activities.

5. Shay, p. 1.

6. *Id.*, p. 2.

7. Furubotn and Pejovich saw this as descriptive of the conflict between the utility maximizing decisions of a firm's managers that would not maximize the wealth of the firm's owners (shareholders). N. 1 *supra* at 1147.

borrowers previously disadvantaged for a like period even if reparations would be suboptimal?

The third principle of classical economic theory is that "transactions costs may be greater than zero."[8] "What-is-the-cost-of-what," an expression made famous by Guido Calabresi,[9] is a mystery which Shay fails to solve. The subsequent discussion about externalities would be sharpened by a definition of "what-is-the-cost-of-what."

Illustrations of high transaction costs which generate externalities are plainly and convincingly paraded through the literature. One reads of the beneficial effect *A's* fruit trees receive from *B's* straying bees, the advantage *C's* straying bees receive from *D's* apple blossoms, the damage inflicted by *E's* cattle on *F's* crops, noise from air conditioners, the benefits nonshopping parkers receive from parking in a free lot at a supermarket, etc. Although Shay failed to give an example of how externalities arise in consumer credit transactions, his warning that government regulation could trigger high transaction costs and externalities should be heeded.

## FREEDOM OF CONTRACT

Shay's paper discusses two critical stages of credit transactions: the agreement stage and the default stage. In so doing, he assumes that remedies available at default are either produced by the bargain made during the agreement stage or, in the case of statutory remedies, are affected by such a bargain. The model is attractively simple: *A* borrows money from *B* Finance Company and in exchange gives *B* Finance Company (1) a promise to repay a certain amount in installments and (2) a right to use specified coercive remedies if *A* misses a payment. The bargained-for remedies, therefore, become a part of the creditor's store of property rights just as surely as the bargained-for loan becomes a part of the borrower's supply of property rights. All is fair, Shay tells us, since the high-risk borrower willingly pays a high price for the loan, namely, harsh coercive remedies. Thus, government prohibition of coercive remedies is inefficient if it drives the costs of participating in the agreement stage so high that whole classes of borrowers are deprived of their only bargaining asset, the ability to be subjected to coercive remedies upon default. In this imaginary world of freedom of

---

8. Shay, p. 218.

9. Calabresi, *The Costs of Accidents: A Legal and Economic Analysis* 198 (Yale, New Haven, 1970). An appraisal of the operating and nonoperating costs of the finance industry is presented in Chapman and Shay, *The Consumer Finance Industry: Its Costs and Regulation* (Columbia, New York, 1967). This account does not cover costs imposed on all factors flowing from default. An account of some of those costs is presented in Note, "Resort to the Legal Process in Collecting Debts from High Risk Credit Buyers in Los Angeles—Alternative Methods for Allocating Costs," 14 U.C.L.A.L. Rev. 879 (1967).

contract, government intervention is most pernicious to borrowers who will not default despite their high-risk status.

Shay's world of freedom of contract threatened by government intervention is based on the assumption that consumer credit documents are contracts. But consumer credit documents are standard forms, neither read nor understood by the consumer and drafted by the creditor in ways that discourage reading and understanding. Without the informed consent of the consumer, standard forms are not "contracts."[10]

A contractarian analysis would have value if one were willing to extend one's conception of contracts beyond bargained-for exchange. Such an extension has occurred in cases in which there is no exchange: e.g., *A*, induced by his uncle's promise to pay him $2,000 if he refrains from drinking alcohol for six years, is entitled to the amount promised upon abstaining for the required period. Contract remedies have also been invoked where there is no bargain, e.g., the enforcement of *A's* promise to pay *B* $2,000 for saving his life. Richard Posner, bothered by the absence of exchange, asserts that "[a] better approach would be to treat the breach of a promise likely to induce reliance as a form of negligence actionable under tort law."[11] I have reached a similar conclusion with regard to consumer credit transactions: accident analysis, generally associated with torts, is far more consistent with the realities of credit default than contract.[12]

Default on credit obligations is largely accidental, that is, not intentional. Interruption in income resulting from loss of employment, illness, and divorce accounts for a substantial proportion of debtor defaults.[13] These accidents will not be deterred by the most coercive remedies. Ironically, punishment, a remedial goal not pursued in contract breaches, is courted by creditors when debtors default. Guido Calabresi, in his seminal work on accident costs, stated that the principal goals of any system of accident law are "[f]irst, it must be just or fair; second, it must reduce the costs of accidents."[14]

---

10. Slawson, "Standard Form Contracts and Democratic Control of Lawmaking Power," 84 Harv. L. Rev. 544 (1971). Debtors and creditors do not bargain over the interest to be charged, the service charge, and the remedies to be available to the creditor upon default. The presence of bargaining is the key to Shay's contractarian approach, since what he calls property rights are exchanged after a bargain is struck between the debtor and creditor. One would think that the absence of bargaining in the real world of debtor-creditor transactions would greatly undermine the value of Shay's approach.

11. Posner, *Economic Analysis of Law* 45 (Little, Brown, & Co., Boston 1972).

12. See Wallace, "The Logic of Consumer Credit Reform," 82 Yale L.J. 461, N. 3 (1973).

13. Caplovitz, *Consumers in Trouble: A Study of Debtors in Default* 53–90 (Free Press, New York 1974); Jacob, *Debtors in Court: The Consumption of Government Service* 52 (Rand McNally, Chicago 1969).

14. N. 9 *supra* at 24.

## TOWARD A SINGLE-REMEDY CREDIT SYSTEM

Consider a credit system with only one remedy for default. What standards should govern the selection of that remedy? Shay's preference is for the "best" remedy which is "negotiated" by the parties.[15] Shay asserts that wage assignment is the best remedy for the "credit applicant with no assets other than future earning power to pledge as collateral for a loan;"[16] that government prohibition of wage assignments would compel the two parties "to negotiate a second-best alternative (without a wage assignment)."[17] Shay forecasts that the applicant would either be denied a loan or would have to pay a higher price for it, causing "scarce resources" to be "allocated differently" and "third parties" to "lose or benefit as this process occurs."[18]

One may conclude that the "best" remedy, and thus the only remedy available in this single-remedy system, is the "negotiated" remedy. *A fortiori,* any remedy which the parties agree upon is the best remedy, since that is the price the debtor is willing to pay for default and part of the property rights the creditor is willing to receive in exchange for the loan. A negotiated remedy system would be inefficient, however, given the fact that the costs associated with negotiating an appropriate remedy with each debtor would be prohibitive.[19]

Wage assignments allow creditors to externalize costs by passing them on to others. Job loss and the cost of organizing alternative credit and payment plans are imposed on employers and employees. The creditor has almost unencumbered access to a substantial portion (in some states all) of the debtor's wages. Yet the debtor has no opportunity to raise defenses in advance of this deprivation of property rights.[20]

Given these externalizing effects of wage assignments, one wonders why Shay did not compare them and the externalizing effects he predicts if wage assignments are abolished. Even then, his predictions would retain credibility only if wage assignments were the only available remedy in the credit system. Whether one operates under a single-

---

15. Shay, p. 220.

16. *Id.*

17. *Id.*

18. *Id.*

19. Such costs could be avoided by having the creditor decide upon the appropriate remedies in advance. Accordingly, mass-produced standard form agreements specify the remedies available to creditors upon default. Neither the creditor, the debtor, nor "third parties" would have their wealth maximized by Shay's negotiated remedy system.

20. For a report and comparison of state laws on wage assignments, see Note, "Wage Assignments—§ 444.2(a)(3) of the FTC's Proposed Rule on Credit Practices," 8 Conn. L. Rev. 491–493 (1976). Shay ignores the conflict between the property right the debtor has in his wages and the asserted property interest in the same wages claimed by the creditor. One could not imagine a more suitable occasion for having an arbiter determine whose property right should prevail.

remedy credit system or not, the remedies dispensed should be both fair and cost minimizing.

## THE DEMSETZ THEORY

Harold Demsetz, Coase, and others have added immensely to the excitement of academic discussions of problems and issues familiar to lawyers. The Demsetz theorem is based on numerous assumptions, including the consideration that the particular activity scrutinized harmfully affects some persons while benefiting others. One could ask whether any activity could do otherwise, given a world in which each individual selfishly pursues a maximization of individual, as opposed to societal, utilities. In cases in which collective maximization is also personally maximizing, one could expect other groups to feel that the collective good inures to their detriment. One could imagine the Demsetz theorem being used to support demands for compensation by segregationists who claim injury from integration policies. Perhaps the compensation principle works only when dealing with pure property rights but not at all when dealing with civil rights.

The harmful activity under scrutiny has presumably damaged a definable class of persons for a definable period (a day, a year, 50 years). Is it fair compensation to move to a position where the current benefits and costs are equivalent? Or, in other words, suppose a long period of underintervention by government has produced benefits and savings to some and losses to others. Should government compensate by legislating an equally long period of overintervention? Similar questions are now being raised in employment, education, and housing as the validity of affirmative action, busing, preferential admissions, and benign housing goals are under attack. Credit transactions have not been spared such questions. Housing consumers who claim that their neighborhoods have been excluded from home purchase and improvement mortgages ("redlining") assert that lending institutions should now be forced to invest in those neighborhoods ("greenlining").

Shay attempts to apply the Demsetz model by separating two sets of debtors: those who are benefited by wage assignments and those who are harmed by wage assignments. He does not cite empirical data to support his conclusion that some consumers are benefited and some are not. Indeed, at one point in his analysis, Shay argues that both groups would be injured by government prohibition of wage assignments.

> Those that would have experienced injury through invocation of wage assignments and who would have been denied credit without wage assignments are hurt by their prohibition. Those who would have defaulted and did not obtain credit would have been spared some injury but would have been deprived of the benefits that the use of credit would have brought in the period before default.[21]

---

21. Shay, p. 225 (footnote omitted).

The converse may also be true. All high-risk debtors may be harmed by use of wage assignments and would therefore benefit from abolition. We, therefore, have harm-benefit to debtors from the use of wage assignments and harm-benefit to debtors from the abolition of wage assignments. Instead of considering debtors to be in an adversarial relationship, one could merely recognize that there are varying degrees of harm-benefit and that each debtor will have a unique set of harm-benefit points. (How fast we move from the debtor-creditor adversarial relationship to a debtor-debtor adversarial relationship.) One would have to define harm (loss of civil rights, property rights, opportunities, wealth, satisfactions, pleasures) and benefits (removal of restrictions on civil rights, property rights, opportunities, wealth, satisfactions, pleasures, and net gains therein). Thus, Shay's "adversarial" relationship between debtors is merely descriptive of one aspect of a super-complex of benefits and burdens which variously affect all players, debtors as well as creditors, in the consumer credit game.

## CONCLUSIONS

Shay's analysis would have been more compelling if he had focused on a remedy which has fewer problems of gaining social acceptability. In my opinion, statutes which allow wage assignments are unconstitutional. In *Sniadach* v. *Family Finance Corporation*,[22] the Supreme Court invalidated a Wisconsin statute which allowed prejudgment wage garnishment without prior notice or a hearing. Wage assignments are generally made without notice or a hearing. In *Sniadach*, the Supreme Court noted the extreme hardship wage garnishments inflicted on the debtor, stating that this remedy may "drive a wage-earning family to the wall."[23] Wage assignments have the same insidious power.[24]

Shay's analysis was focused on the efficacy of remedies when, in my opinion, it would have profited from a similar focus on default. Accordingly, the goals of remedies would have been (1) to reduce the costs of defaults by minimizing the activities which cause them; (2) to reduce the economic injury and emotional distress associated with default by spreading the costs; and (3) to reduce the costs of operating the machinery necessary for accomplishing (1) and (2). Attempts to pursue one goal to the exclusion of the other two could be counterproductive. For example, to accomplish (2), a government insurance program could protect creditors against loss from default. Such a program could increase the costs of (1), however, by encouraging creditors to extend credit to anyone regardless of risks. This has occurred with FHA mort-

---

22. 395 U.S. 337 (1969): Compare Fuentes v. Shevin, 407 U.S. 67 (1972); Mitchell v. W.T. Grant Co., 416 U.S. 600 (1974).

23. 395 U.S. at 341–342.

24. See Local Loan Co. v. Hunt, 292 U.S. 235, 245 (1934).

gages. A systems approach to minimize (1), (2), and (3) is therefore needed.[25]

If Shay had employed this kind of analysis, he would have enabled his readers to perceive the difference between statutory prohibition of wage assignments and administrative action to outlaw wage assignments. Administrative prohibition in the face of state approval would increase (3) while having only an appreciable effect on (2). But statutory and regulatory prohibition would satisfy (1) by removing another challenge to one's income and by reducing an opportunity for an overextended person without assets to get credit, it would achieve (2) by reducing the economic and emotional distress accompanying the loss of wages and, sometimes, employment, and it would facilitate (3) by reducing the costs of administrative regulation, since the incidence of default would be lowered.

The value of Shay's analysis resides in its subtle but recurring message: Credit reform efforts must be guided by a concern for the differential impact of reform measures on sets and subsets of debtors and not solely by a desire to deprive creditors of coercive remedies. This is indeed a noble goal. Shay's analysis provides us with a "first attempt" to recognize these competing and conflicting interests and encourages reformers to engage in a searching analysis in advance of change.

---

**25.** I am indebted to Calabresi, N. 9 *supra*, for the seeds of this analysis.

# COMMENTARY

Robert Pitofsky, *Professor of Law, Georgetown University*

There are two principal themes in Shay's paper. The first involves support and elaboration of the argument that the effect of legislation eliminating or modifying current consumer collection practices is not necessarily best viewed as a conflict between the interests of creditors and debtors; rather, a decision to eliminate a particular collection practice, at least at times, may represent a conflict between the interests of one class of debtors and another. That portion of the paper, I believe, is an important and useful insight into the policy argument that often arises in deciding whether to eliminate a particular collection practice.

A second theme of the paper involves an analysis of the possibility of payments of "indemnities" by debtors profiting from the existence of a particular debt collection practice to debtors who are disadvantaged by the availability of that practice—as a substitute for state intervention leading to the elimination of the collection technique. This portion of the paper is an interesting theoretical exercise; as I will argue at a later point, however, I do not see how, as a practical matter, any such indemnity system could be implemented.

In a final section of the paper, Shay expresses some doubts as to whether the Federal Trade Commission, in its pending rule-making proceeding involving credit collection practices, has broadened its focus sufficiently to take into account various relevant considerations— specifically, whether elimination of a debt collection practice will diminish unduly borrowing opportunities for a substantial class of potential debtors. I agree that the focus of any sensible rule making should be broad enough to encompass the question of adverse effects on the credit market, but I am inclined to believe that the Commission has not closed the door on consideration of such factors.

For reasons well described in Shay's paper, elimination of a credit collection practice may have the sole or principal effect of making credit unavailable to a marginal group of borrowers who represent high credit risks and cannot offer conventional types of collateral. Lenders may be willing to make loans to individuals in such groups only if they can be assured in advance of a prompt, reliable, and inexpensive collection procedure upon default.

Accepting all that, I would still like to suggest a few caveats to that assertion, which do not appear in the paper or are referred to only tangentially.

First, it should be recognized that the elimination of a particular creditor's remedy will not *necessarily* diminish credit opportunities for any class of debtors, nor *necessarily* raise the cost of credit to all. There may be so many alternative and similar collection practices in the background that elimination of one technique will be insignificant. Also, the particular collection practice eliminated may be inefficient and counterproductive. I think that may be the situation with respect to wage assignments—the example Shay chose to examine in his paper. There is evidence that many employers follow a policy of firing an employee as soon as a wage assignment notice for that employee is presented. The wage resources available for repayment of a debt, therefore, are eliminated as soon as the wage assignment is imple- mented. Similarly, employees may quit jobs rather than work to a significant extent for a creditor who, they believe, is not entitled to the amount in dispute.

Second, even if a class of potential debtors is denied credit that would have been available if a collection practice were allowed, it does not follow that the elimination of that collection practice is, on balance, an unsound policy judgment. There may be so many adverse conse- quences to certain types of collection activities that they are unjustified as a policy matter, regardless of efficiencies in operation. Shay recog- nizes these points and mentions that wage assignments have been regarded as possibly onerous, because they tend to harass debtors and because they may often predictably lead to discontinuance of employ- ment of the debtor. I would add that there are, at least, two other adverse aspects of wage assignments that are important. Wage assign- ments tend to generate enormous economic pressure on debtors to settle what may be meritless claims by the creditor. Though convinced that the creditor's demand is unjustified, debtors subject to wage assignments may feel that they are not in a position to bargain, resist, or negotiate about the claim. Also, wage assignments necessarily involve a transfer of property without judicial supervision in circum- stances in which there is little doubt as to who has the principal claim to the property. In this respect, wage assignments are not like disputes over repossession. There, a debtor may have paid no more than one payment out of 20 on property bought on credit, so that one can question whether the debtor's possession of the subject of the credit sale entitles the debtor to judicial supervision over transfer on "my property." With wage assignments, however, there is no dispute about to whom the wages belong; the only dispute involves the entitlement of the creditor to those wages.

Third, it is important to note that even if it were true that elimination of a debt collection practice would deny to a class of debtors access to credit (or that the cost of credit to all would rise slightly), it does not follow that those consequences represent a bad thing. Elimination of certain kinds of "efficient" collection practices may make creditors screen their debtor applicants more carefully. The result may be a lower default ratio for the creditor and denial of credit to debtors who probably should not have borrowed in the first place. Thus, an improved screening process may be a desirable development for all concerned.

Turning now to the aspect of the discussion involving the notion of indemnity payments by debtors profiting from the existence of a particular debt collection practice, I note at the outset that I find it very difficult to hold in my mind exactly who are the injured parties and who are the injuring parties. I suppose the injured parties are persons who would have been able to obtain access to credit even if wage assignments were illegal; once they default, they suffer wage assignment collection practices which adversely affect their employment status or some other interest unrelated to their debt obligation. Even assuming, as Shay proposes, that it would be more sensible to pay indemnities to such injured parties than do away with the collection practice, I do not see how one could determine in advance of actual default who the parties would be who would default and who would not. I have always assumed that many debtors default for reasons that were unpredictable at the time of borrowing—illness, unusual personal crises (e.g., divorce, death in the family), loss of job, etc. Even more seriously, I do not see how one could evaluate in advance of default what the nature of any economic injury would be. It is well-established that some employers have an absolute policy of firing people as soon as a wage assignment notice is presented; other employers may adopt that policy on a random basis. Loss of employment is a different kind of injury than might be suffered by a defaulting debtor not employed by companies having such policy. Consider also the problem of a debtor who has a claim that could be vindicated if there were judicial supervision over the creditor's collection practice as opposed to a debtor who does not. Loss of the benefits of that successful claim is one of the injuries resulting from the presence of a wage assignment collection practice, and yet, that kind of injury is almost impossible to evaluate in advance of default.

In sum, I believe the notion of "indemnity" is an interesting angle on debt collection problems and, perhaps, illuminates in a theoretical way some aspects of debtor-creditor rights. I do not see how, as a practical matter, it could be implemented.

Finally, let me say a few words about the Federal Trade Commission's proposed rule-making proceeding relating to creditors' remedies, and about Shay's concern that the scope of that proposed rule making is unduly narrow. I am not going to try to analyze or justify the Commission's substantive proposal, which in effect would eliminate or substantially modify 11 major collection practices.

As I indicated earlier, I believe Shay is right in urging that the Commission take into account the effect of any elimination of collection practices on the access of borrowers to credit and the cost of that credit. Nevertheless, I see no indication in the Commission's statement of goals for the proposed rule making that it will not take that kind of consideration into account. The proposed rule making is regarded by the Commission as authorized by the *S & H* case, and, as Shay indicates, the mandate to the Commission in that decision is so broad that it could incorporate a broad range of considerations.

Also, the Commission's rule-making activities are, at this point, only in the "proposed rule" stage. It has frequently occurred that proposed rules are stated in somewhat vague and less than complete terms, and that policy questions and considerations surface in the course of actual hearings. According to attorneys on the Commission staff, one reason why the proposed rule has been so slow in developing is that investigation and analysis projects, relating to the very issues Shay has raised, have been farmed out to independent economic organizations. Specifically, outside experts have been asked to respond to the question whether the total effect on debtor opportunities to obtain credit would be adversely affected, and to what degree, by a modification of the collection practices listed in the proposed rule. Whether they will properly take these considerations into account remains to be seen.

# DISCUSSION

ELI NOAM: I have a problem with Shay's diagram. One side represents gain, and the other side loss. It seems to me that, with respect to the wage garnishment and wage assignment issues, one's loss is not necessarily a gain for someone else. One's loss of job security is not necessarily a gain for the creditor. It is only a way by which he tries to ensure the repayment of the debt.

SHAY: My point was that the creditor is not the other side of the gain. There are two groups of individuals that are affected by the imposition of wage assignments: the group that will be hurt when the wage assignment gets invoked and the group that would be hurt if the wage assignment were not allowed.

NOAM: But, even there, one group's gain is not necessarily the other group's loss.

SHAY: In my example, the group of borrowers that could not get credit except with the use of wage assignments is hurt if the possibility of putting a wage assignment in the contract is removed and the borrowers do not get credit.

And within this group, there are some who do not repay and against whom the wage assignments are invoked. Among this group, a few may get fired or get hurt in other ways. My two groups are both borrowers, and not the creditor and the debtor, which is implicit in your question.

FRANKLIN R. EDWARDS: I think Noam is raising another point. And that is: If there are benefits to borrowers from restrictions on wage garnishment, is there necessarily a loss to someone else? Must there be a loser for every winner, dollar for dollar?

I think the answer to the question is no.

A usual diagram for the analysis of consumer protection laws is the following. $GN$ and $S_1$ are the demand and supply schedules, respectively, for consumer credit, prior to the enactment of laws that restrict wage garnishment.

Assume, to begin with, that there is no legal rate ceiling, and that restrictions on wage garnishment benefit at least some borrowers, such that the demand schedule shifts from $GN$ to $AM$. In other words, there is a "net" borrower (or consumer) gain: consumer surplus rises from $BFG$ and $CDA$. If, on the other hand, such restrictions also increase lender

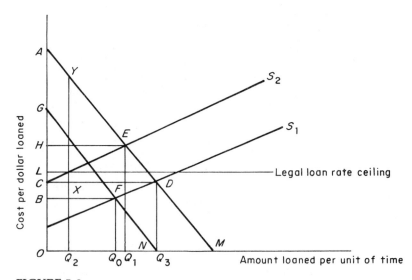

**FIGURE 5-2**

costs, the supply schedule will shift from $S_1$ to $S_2$, and the new consumer surplus will equal only *HEA*, rather than *CDA*. It is, in this case, an empirical question: Will *HEA* be larger or smaller than *BFG*? Or, will consumers, on net, be benefited? In this analytical framework, as opposed to Shay's, there can be a gain without a concomitant loss, or a loss without a concomitant gain, or both a gain and a loss, where borrowers are net gainers or losers.

Shay's analysis focuses largely on disaggregating the demand schedule, or distinguishing one group of borrowers from another. Or, in the case where there is no increase in creditors' costs (or no shift in $S_1$), he is attempting to assess whether there is, on balance, a leftward or rightward shift in *GN*.

Finally, the diagram also shows what will happen if there is an effective loan rate ceiling, such as *OL*. In this case, simultaneous upward shifts in both the cost curve and the demand curve may result in many consumers not being able to borrow at all, or in loan volume of $OQ_2$ rather than $OQ_1$, which greatly diminishes the benefit. With rate ceilings, low-income borrowers are likely to be losers while high-income borrowers are likely to be gainers. In the absence of a rate ceiling, however, it is not clear why low-income borrowers should fare any worse than other borrowers.

HARVEY J. GOLDSCHMID: But are there not also cases of credit contracts where a certain remedy is really an inefficient device? The problem with this analytical view, as well as with the Demsetz framework, is that it assumes rationality on all sides.

We know full well that is not true; that sometimes inefficient remedies are used by creditors.

SHAY: Some creditors say they rarely use the devices of repossessing chattel mortgages. Yet there are creditors who truly believe that the incentive to pay debts is greater when that clause is in the contract.

The reason, quite obviously, is that they feel it has an *in terrorem* effect on a borrower. He will pay off, knowing that the clause is in the contract. There is some logic to that argument, I believe.

On the other hand, creditors may be misjudging borrowers entirely. But for people who do not use consumer credit and who are not subject to the discipline of having this kind of thing in the credit contracts they sign, to say that the creditors are wrong or inefficient makes me wonder from where they derive that insight.

GOLDSCHMID: It may be an empirical question. But, my point is that there certainly are situations where government intervenes to get rid of the irrational, as well as the unfair, with no loss at all.

SHAY: No apparent loss, perhaps.

JOHN HAWKE: It seems to me that one of the purposes of a provision against wage assignments is to protect certain kinds of borrowers against themselves because of the social costs that may be involved if they borrow improvidently. They may be fired from their jobs. They may experience personal bankruptcy. They may increase the burden on the welfare rolls.

How does that social interest, that broader public interest, get taken into account?

SHAY: First, how can you tell in advance who are improvident borrowers? Second, the creditor is really not interested in such borrowers either. Indeed, he uses credit scoring systems and other devices to screen those people out in advance. Third, in attempting to deny credit to improvident borrowers, you will inevitably make mistakes and also deny credit to good borrowers, which may result in a substantial social cost. Finally, the Federal Wage Garnishment Act prevents employers from firing employees because their wages were garnished in court. It does not now cover wage assignments, but, if I were an employer and fired somebody because of a wage assignment, I might wonder about whether a court would uphold that firing. It is not clear how much hurt is going to occur as a result of wage assignments being invoked, relative to the damage done to all applicants needing the wage assignment clause to qualify for credit.

PITOFSKY: Let me just say a word on that point.

I agree with your analysis. It is quite proper. But there is an additional complication. There is a certain amount of literature that supports the view that many creditors take almost no pains whatsoever to screen out debtors for reliability to pay back. Indeed, they are very aggressive in inducing debtors who really should not be borrowing to take monies. Now, one consequence, especially given the fact that there is a rate ceiling which prevents creditors from raising the price of credit across the board to everybody, is that elimination of some of these collection practices is going to lead to a more careful screening process.

That is not necessarily a bad thing. There are many debtors who, if they were screened properly, would not get access to credit, and the creditor would be better off for it, and that class of debtor would also be better off, and, of course, all other debtors who are good credit risks would be better off.

SHAY: Aside from his "heroic" conclusions, Pitofsky's argument bothers me because it assumes that the bulk of creditors do not select borrowers in a rational way.

Creditors in the finance industry turned to empirically-derived, point-scoring systems long before banks did. This is a statistical method of appraising the probability of default in advance for various groups of borrowers, much like the way in which insurance risks are figured. Experience shows that a certain class of borrowers has a high probability of default, just as under-25 drivers are poor insurance risks. This is by no means an irrational way of screening borrowers. Indeed, it is probably the most rational way to do it.

For the smaller suppliers, the situation you described may well be true. There are judgmental measures, and old traditions still hanging on. Only recently have the larger banks gotten rid of those, and they may not have entirely gotten rid of them.

LAPIDUS: To get back to the framework, or diagram, in Shay's paper, I think that is purely an expository device. It is merely meant to show that there are people who are injured. What you want to do is take a look at all the parties who might be injured and all who might be aided. There may be conflict between different classes of borrowers and not only between creditors and debtors. I think that is really the contribution of Shay's paper. Wage garnishment is only used for those people judged to be high risks. In the absence of wage assignment clauses, those people would not be able to get credit, or they would be able to get credit only at a higher price.

In his analytical diagram, Edwards took that group and did the analysis of the consumer surplus for it only. But you have to take all the parties into account. Further, you have to assume that if this group, in fact, can get credit at higher prices without the wage assignment, this group can be charged a different price from other borrowers. In the real world that is not the case: Most debtors will have to pay the higher price. These people have to be factored into the equation as well to determine whether in fact you should eliminate wage assignments.

In sum, it seems to me that when you have a proposal that says to eliminate a certain practice, that is a very heavy burden to carry. What you really want is to identify what is bad about this practice, then propose that we eliminate only those things that are bad.

For example, if it really is unconscionable that somebody should be fired because of a wage assignment, then make it illegal to fire a man who is subject to a wage assignment. I would much rather approach it that way, since wage assignment clauses may help to provide credit to people who otherwise would not get it.

PARKER: Why not use a different approach? Why not insure the creditor against loss? Then you would not have to worry about prohibiting wage assignment clauses.

LAPIDUS: Who pays for the insurance?

PARKER: The same people who are already paying for the benefits received by the high-risk, low-income people. It would just spread it over more people.

LAPIDUS: That means they will pay a higher price for credit.

PARKER: They may pay less than under the scenario you just proposed.

ANN BARTEL: I would like to pursue the suggestion that Parker has made, that one might be able to protect the interests of some of the parties by having a form of government insurance for credit taken out by low-income, high-risk people. It would be a form of wealth redistribution from high-income people to low-income people, since this insurance would certainly be funded out of tax revenues. If that is one of our social goals, then we might want to use this form of insurance even though it may be inefficient.

LAPIDUS: Let me respond to that. A money order company is like a very simple bank. In New York, money order companies are licensees of The State Banking Commission and are not insured under any particular government insurance arrangement. One of them failed recently, with a $5 million liability involving 100,000 people, most of them in New York

City. It was very obvious what we had to do, without very much consideration of the welfare effects, distributive justice, or anything else. We had to make good on those money orders. So, we quickly got up a bill to fund through an insurance arrangement a retroactive liability, which raised all kinds of constitutional questions.

The cost of this insurance will be built into the existing cost structure and will be paid for by people buying money orders and travelers' checks in the future. All this was done with very little consideration of the niceties we are considering today, but it was the *right* thing to do.

HARLAN BLAKE: This is not a comment, just a request for information.

To what degree is the Holder In Due Course Rule comparable in terms of analysis and what, if anything, do we know about the impact of that rule on the functioning of these markets?

SHAY: The Federal Reserve has been charged and is expected to come up with some kind of empirical evaluation of the impact of the Holder In Due Course Rule, but they are having a hard time doing it.

As far as this issue is concerned, it is not one of the 11 items that the FTC has proposed. It is one that is now in effect.

The impact of the removal of the defenses of third-party holders of consumer credit contracts was to make the creditor more careful about the dealer from whom a credit contract was purchased, and to make sure the creditor policed the practices of the dealer better than the consumer could.

The expected adjustment to the Rule would have been to find more purchased contracts specifying recourse to the dealer that were previously nonrecourse in the event of the borrower's default. However, I have not seen or heard of any studies indicating that this has happened.

But as for the reaction that has come from the credit industry; it has adjusted. I think the banks are lending more directly to consumers and buying less paper. The statistics suggest this quite clearly.

Of course, that trend was going on before the rule was passed, and we do not know how much of that trend to attribute to the rule. This is where we stand today.

EDWARDS: Before concluding, I would like to bait the lawyers a little because of what I heard earlier. As economists and lawyers, we can agree that there are both costs and benefits to the regulations we are discussing, and that we would like to know more about them. But, there is one thing on which, I think, we do not agree, and that was represented by comments made by both Pitofsky and Goldschmid. Pitofsky said that prohibiting wage garnishment might improve screening techniques and make the creditors more aware of the risk they are taking; and Goldschmid echoed the same argument when he said that government intervenes to get rid of the irrational.

GOLDSCHMID: I said *sometimes*.

EDWARDS: The economists' response to that—and I think Shay said it—is that creditors already screen in the most cost-efficient way. If they do not screen very much, it is because it is efficient not to screen. It is efficient to take losses rather than use a lot of labor to collect information with which to screen. The frightening thing about "irrationality" arguments is that they can lead to unlimited consumer protection legislation and regulation in all areas, legislation that really has no other basis than the paternalistic claim that people cannot take care of themselves.

PITOFSKY: I think that Shay said that finance companies are screening. He did not say they are screening at an optimal level now.

GOLDSCHMID: It seems perfectly possible to use Shay's analysis rationally, empirically, and wisely, and still conclude that it is wrong.

Also, information problems may well lead you to government regulation at times, in order to protect consumers where information failures are apparent, or errors in risk evaluations are apparent.

LAPIDUS: The error that economists make is to assume that the market works perfectly. In fact, the market does not work perfectly. There are also preconceptions that people have, which we do not question. For example, I think there were preconceptions about women and blacks. But when social pressure was applied and changes were made, those preconceptions were found wanting.

I think that is the kind of thing that lawyers question but economists do not.

## CHAPTER SIX

# Implications of an Electronic Funds Transfer System

## IMPLICATIONS OF THE NEW PAYMENTS TECHNOLOGY FOR MONETARY POLICY

Almarin Phillips *Professor of Economics, Law and Public Policy, University of Pennsylvania*
*Member, National Commission on Electronic Funds Transfer*

In the mid-1930s, John Maynard Keynes expressed the view that

> [T]he ideas of economists and political philosophers, both when they are right and when they are wrong, are more powerful than is commonly understood. Indeed, the world is ruled by little else. Practical men, who believe themselves to be quite exempt from any intellectual influences, are usually the slaves of some defunct economist. Madmen in authority, who hear voices in the air, are distilling their frenzy from some academic scribbler of a few years back. [1]

There is an opposite side to this. Practical men, madmen in authority, and especially academic scribblers often show an amazing ability to resist change. With an historic regularity which is somewhat frightening, a minority of academicians—or, more generally, "voices in the wilderness"—discern a complex of current events which appear to them to portend inevitable changes in the institutional, organizational, political, and social worlds. Which of these "voices" is correct, of course, is not clear as they are set forth. It often is not clear decades later. It is not an exaggeration to say though that, correct or incorrect, they are largely ignored at the time of their expression. Existing paradigms—not just paradigms of science but also paradigms governing the behavior of the extant controlling elements of private and public institutions—exert inertial forces. Until one or another of the voices is shown post hoc to have relevance, they have little influence on a gradual process of intellectual and social change.

---

1. Keynes, *The General Theory of Employment, Interest and Money* 383 (Harcourt, Brace and World, New York 1936).

Consider the history of the deposit financial institutions of the United States. The need for a central bank to assure uniformity, liquidity, and control of the money supply was recognized by some at the time of the founding of the nation. The First and Second Banks of the United States were compromise efforts in the direction of a central bank, but both were aborted. "Free banking"—or "wild cat banking"—emerged, with a nonuniform currency, no provision for the issuance of small denomination coins until 1853, and periodic financial crises. The structure of commercial banking up to the Civil War was obviously affected by the legislative and technological framework within which the systems operated.[2]

The Civil War was the crisis which caused the first fundamental change. Political power shifted from Southern agrarian interests to Northern manufacturing and commercial interests. The Currency Act of 1863 and the National Bank Acts of 1864 and 1865 provided for the federal chartering of national banks, the establishment of reserve requirements against notes and deposits (which favored the sale of government bonds) of these banks, the issuance of National Bank Notes, a prohibition on real estate loans by national banks, a prohibition on branching by national banks (effected by interpretation of the law by the Comptroller of the Currency), and a prohibitive 10 percent tax on state bank notes.

The structure and performance of the system changed rapidly. By 1880, there were about 2,000 national banks, 900 of which were banks which had converted from state to federal charters. Only 650 or so state-chartered banks remained.[3] A saving grace for the latter was the gradual introduction of deposit banking, with special, three-party sight drafts—checks—replacing note issue, despite initial consumer resistance. State banks were also encouraged by generally preferable deposit reserve requirements, easier examination procedures, greater loan powers and, in some states, the ability to branch. By 1900, there were 5,007 state banks and 7,420 national banks, reflecting growing chartering rivalry between the states and the Comptroller of the Currency. By 1920, the numbers had grown to 20,635 and 9,656, respectively. Interestingly, many savings and loan associations—then, usually called "real estate and loan" companies—developed during this period because of the inability or the reluctance of commercial banks to engage in the residential mortgage loan business. Here, we see strong adaptive responses by states and by private financial institutions to the federal

---

**2.** An interesting aspect of this is that mutual savings banks emerged during this period to attract the deposits of small savers. The savings banks were formed in states which were then the population centers of the country and have since spread very little geographically.

**3.** There were, also, perhaps as many as 2,500 "private," unincorporated banks.

legal framework established in the 1860s and to the spread of the new
technology reflected in demand deposit banking. Bank failures and
periodic financial panics remained in the system.

The atmosphere in which the Federal Reserve System was created
was partially the result of these failures and panics. In 1893, 228 state
banks and 69 national banks suspended payments on their deposit
liabilities. In 1907–1908, 141 state banks and 31 national banks failed.
The general milieu was favorable to change, however. The Federal
Reserve System was created during a period when the central government intruded on children's and women's working laws, food and drug
purity, the electoral process for senators, and monopoly and other
corporate abuses. It was the Progressive Era. Again, the law was
changed in response to inadequacies shown to have been characteristic
of the old legislative and regulatory framework, with not a great deal of
attention to the voices who had advocated a central bank in the decades
past.

It has been argued that the elasticity in the currency supply provided
by the Federal Reserve System not only corrected for the inelasticity of
the previous system, but created too much elasticity. The adoption of
the "real bills doctrine" in the act permitted increases in money in good
times and contraction during bad times. This probably accentuated the
amplitude of the business cycle. The Federal Reserve "invented" open
market operations in the 1920s to offset the impact of gold inflows.
Nonetheless, bank failures remained a problem, with 738 suspensions
in 1924, 924 in 1926, and 636 in 1927. When the Great Depression
occurred—abetted by bank failures and Federal Reserve policies to
restrain gold outflows—the failures rose to 1,292, 2,213, 1,416, and
3,891 in 1930, 1931, 1932, and 1933, respectively. Here, bank structure
was changing because of the general economic environment.

During the period 1900 through the 1920s an early trend toward
branching also changed bank structure. The 12,427 banks in existence
in 1900 had only 119 branches. By 1915, 27,390 banks had 785 branches.
In 1920, 30,291 banks operated 1,281 branches, and in 1925, 28,442
banks had 2,525 branches. The early growth of branching was partially
due to technological change—better communication and transportation
services, in particular. By the mid-1920s, however, branching grew
because of the rising number of bank failures. Where permitted by state
law, "sound" state banks often acquired failing banks. Here, structure
changed primarily because of market conditions. The McFadden Act of
1927 extended branching privileges to national banks to reduce the
temptation of these banks to convert their charters, as well as to allow
mergers to soften the effects of failure. The McFadden Act is an illustration of legislative response to the changes occurring in structure and
performance.

Changes in the law during the 1930s were also in response to changes
in bank structure and performance: the Glass-Steagall Act of 1932, the
Emergency Banking Act, the Thomas Amendment, and the Banking Act

of 1933. Supervisory powers of the Comptroller were increased, the Federal Deposit Insurance Corporation was created,[4] national banks were allowed to branch on a full par with state banks, interest on demand deposits was prohibited, controls (Regulation Q) were established for time and savings deposits, and the underwriting, sale, and distribution of securities by banks were prohibited. The Banking Act of 1935 enlarged the supervisory powers of the FDIC (with the effect of largely controlling the chartering of state banks), the Federal Reserve was reorganized, a *de jure* status was given to the Federal Open Market Committee, and Regulation Q was extended to all insured banks. Fifteen states also expanded branching privileges around this time. While some attention may have been paid to the voices of the past, it was largely crisis-borne, ad hoc, problem-oriented legislation which emerged.

During the early years of the Depression, mutual savings banks encountered few failures. The only federal legislation affecting them was their inclusion for FDIC coverage. Failures of savings and loan associations reduced their number from 12,804 in 1928 to 10,744 in 1935. The failures and evidence of at least questionable and, perhaps, fraudulent practices by the associations gave rise to the Federal Home Loan Bank Act of 1932, the Home Owners Loan Act of 1933, and the National Housing Act of 1934. This combination of acts provided for membership in a Federal Home Loan Bank System, with emergency loan powers, the chartering of federal mutual savings and loan associations and the creation of the Federal Savings and Loan Insurance Corporation. The thrift institutions, however, were seldom in direct competition with commercial banks on either the asset or the liability sides of their operations. Markets were segmented into noncompeting groups.

The laws of the 1930s are still those governing the basic aspects of the deposit financial institutions. Of course, there have been many changes in the structure of markets and in the conduct and performance of deposit financial institutions, as well as in legislation and regulation. In the 1950s, after the commercial banks had disposed of great amounts of government obligations acquired during World War II, they turned to the retail market. The services rendered to households were broadened, *de novo* branching and branching by merger increased, and rates paid on savings and time deposits rose absolutely and relative to the rates paid by thrift institutions. Competition for funds began to appear between the thrifts and the commercial banks. By 1966, that competition was strong enough to cause disintermediation, and ceiling rates were imposed on the thrift accounts. Because of the limited services available from the thrifts, a differential was set between the maximums which thrifts and commercial banks could pay. Regulation, in this case,

---

4. Many voices had been advocating this for a decade. Included in these expressions were positions taken by advocates of unit banking states who saw deposit insurance as a means of reducing the pressure for branching powers.

responded to the market realities, with an effort to soften the growing interindustry competition.

Especially in states which prohibited or limited branching, the bank holding company resumed its role as a substitute for branching. In 1956, the Bank Holding Company Act was passed, and in 1970, an important amendment, which included one-bank holding companies within the purview of Federal Reserve controls. By the time of the amendment, nearly 60 percent of all commercial bank deposits were held by holding company banks, with the number of one-bank holding companies having increased from 550 in 1965 to 1,352 in 1970. Structure changed, due to private market decisions, with legislative and regulatory reform following the fact. The holding company "horse" was out by the time the amendment "closed the barn door."

A similar story can be told of the bank merger movement. A total of 1,467 commercial banks ceased independent operations between 1952 and 1960 through mergers, absorptions, and consolidations. The Bank Merger Act was passed in 1960 and amended in 1966 in the wake of the famous *Philadelphia National Bank* case. Under the new standards, the nature of mergers changed, but the number did not decline.

In the 1966 "money crunch," substantial disintermediation occurred between banks and the thrifts. While the extension of deposit rate ceilings to the latter was designed to cure this problem, it planted the seeds for other private responses. One of these was the introduction of C.D.s; another was the expansion of the commercial paper market; another was the Eurodollar market. Increased use also was made of nonbank subsidiaries of bank holding companies for raising funds in markets not subject to deposit rate ceilings. These again illustrate private responses to regulatory constraints.

The disintermediation in the 1969–1970 crunch was different from that of 1966: All the deposit financial institutions were at a disadvantage in buying funds relative to other segments of the money and capital markets. Commercial and finance company paper outstanding rose from $20.5 billion in 1968 to $40.0 billion in 1970. Regulation Q was relaxed for large negotiable C.D.s, but the deposit institutions, nonetheless, lost deposits as businesses and individuals turned to commercial paper and other instruments bearing higher rates. (The Penn Central debacle illustrates the risks of substituting uninsured liabilities for insured bank accounts.) Many types of businesses were ready to sell their own notes to bank and thrift depositors as the gulf between regulated deposit and market rates widened. Consequently, the deposit institutions lacked loan funds. (The 1974–1976 period of high rates caused somewhat less obvious disintermediation because of further relaxation of Regulation Q, with fixed maturity, non-negotiable C.D.s bearing premium rates.)

Through all this, voices for reform could be heard. The Commission on Money and Credit, the Heller Committee, and the Hunt Commission advocated major changes in law and regulation. They were followed by the proposed Financial Institutions Act, (FIA) the Financial Institutions and the National Economy Study, (FINE) and the Financial Reform Act (FRA). There are no outward signs that many of these proposals will be adopted. While technological and market conditions have changed greatly since the 1930s, the voices of reform largely are unheeded because of the inertial and homeostatic forces of private and public organizations.[5]

But there are even greater problems. The proposals embodied in CMC, Heller, Hunt, FIA, FINE, and FRA are old. They were old when they were written and they are older now. They envisage regulatory reform in the context of the ancient ages of the 1950s and 1960s. A few voices, however, are now suggesting that events in the next several years will require even more drastic reform, and still fewer see the prospect of an orderly transition as a distinct probability.

## THE NEW PAYMENTS TECHNOLOGY AND MONETARY POLICY: UNHEEDED ASPECTS OF REFORM

Until very recently, proposals for reform of the financial structure and its regulation have centered on the prohibition of interest on demand deposits, Regulation Q, the asset and liability powers of the thrifts, chartering and branching, reserve requirements, taxation, trust department powers, changes in the organizational framework of regulatory agencies, and housing and mortgage markets. While terms such as *Automatic Teller Machine* (ATM), *Consumer Banking Convenience Terminal* (CBCT), *Regional Switching Unit* (RSU), *Point of Sale* (POS), *Automated Clearing House* (ACH) and *debit card* are now generally familiar, little attention has been given to the impact of electronic funds transfers on the role and the operation of the central bank. Money is still ordinarily defined as $M_1$ or $M_2$, with some other aggregates occasionally mentioned.[6] Quantitative monetary controls seem to be treated as though EFT will not affect them. Arguments persist that mandatory membership, or at least the holding of reserve balances in the Federal Reserve System, is required of all institutions offering third-party payments services, ostensibly to make the quantitative controls more effective.[7] The Chairman of the Board of Governors, the Secretary of the

---

5. The Senate Subcommittee on Financial Institutions, under the leadership of Senator Thomas McIntyre, has worked diligently on reform for several years but, thus far, has been unable to get both houses to agree on omnibus legislation.

6. The staff of the Board of Governors of the Federal Reserve System is reported to be studying the most appropriate definition of money. As of this writing, the results are not public.

7. On this question, see Brunner, "Monetary Growth and Monetary Policy," 27 Banca Nazionale del Lavoro Quarterly Review, No. 111, pp. 271–293 (Dec. 1974); Kopecky, "Nonmember Banks and Empirical Measures of the Variability of Reserves and Money: A Theoretical Appraisal," J. Finance (forthcoming); D. R. Starleaf, "Nonmember Banks and Monetary Control," 30 J. Finance No. 4, pp. 955–975 (Sept. 1975); Kopecky, Nonmember Bank Reserve Assets and Monetary Control (unpublished).

Treasury and others have suggested the payment of interest on reserve balances. Senate bills S. 1664/S. 1669 would provide for interest on reserve balances as well as for nationwide NOW accounts. But the underlying purpose of the reserve proposals is to prevent the further erosion of Federal Reserve membership. Aside from the alleged effects of broad membership on the efficacy of monetary policy, the payment of interest on reserve balances is not regarded as a monetary policy tool.

Central banking in an EFT environment will be different from that of the 1920s, 1930s, 1940s, 1950s, 1960s, and 1970s. Reform of central bank operations will become a critical necessity. This reform is not a substitute for other reforms; it is an addition to the list which should be considered.

There have been voices, but clearly wilderness voices, about basic monetary reforms. In 1960, with a short, terse, and logical argument, James Tobin concluded that the Federal Reserve should pay interest on reserve balances held by member banks.[8] There was no EFT envisioned at that time, and Tobin pushed only to the point that the variable discount rate should be paid on balances in excess of the required membership reserves.

Tobin urged repeal of both the prohibition against interest payments on demand deposits and the ceilings on interest payments on time and savings deposits. This part may seem like an old story, since CMC, Heller, Hunt, FIA, FINE and FRA—not with totally similar conclusions—all addressed these same questions. Tobin's position was a precursor of the primary regulatory problems associated with EFT: The effectiveness and efficiency of monetary policy would be much greater if something approaching his 1960 reform proposals were in place in 1980. Still, given past history, it is difficult to be sanguine about immediate changes.

## THE NEW PAYMENTS TECHNOLOGY AND ALTERNATIVES IN THE HOLDINGS OF TRANSACTIONS BALANCES

It is necessary to consider what an EFT system, with everything "hooked together" is likely to look like in the 1980s. Many variations are possible, with differences in costs and revenues attaching to the alternatives, but Figures 6-1, 6-2, and 6-3 provide an idea of the links and nodes.

Figure 6-1 shows a single commercial bank in the EFT system, with its electronic connections to several classes of customers, including

---

8. James Tobin, "Towards Improving the Efficiency of the Monetary Mechanism," 42 Rev. Econ. & Statistics, No. 3, Pt. 1, pp. 276–279 (Aug. 1960). I am indebted to Carole C. Phillips, who called this paper to my attention, and to James Tobin, with whom I have had a discussion of the relevance of his arguments to the issues of 1980, in an EFT setting, and the immediate need for regulatory reform. Sessions with George Mitchell, former vice chairman of the Board of Governors, and his staff; Willis J. Winn, president of the Federal Reserve Bank of Cleveland; and members of the National Commission on Electronic Funds Transfer have been helpful.

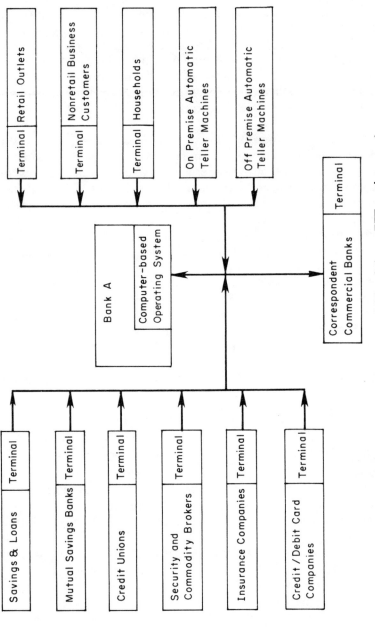

**FIGURE 6-1** A single commercial bank in an EFT environment.

nonbank financial institutions.[9] The bank portrayed, Bank *A,* is rela- **277**
tively large—say, at least $100,000,000 in deposits—but it need not be a
huge multi-billion dollar bank to use the new technologies that are
emerging.

Bank *A* has a computer-based operating system (COS). The system
consists of hardware and software serving internal bank needs and
having input and output devices to handle electronic communications
fund transfers with its customers. Many of these customers have terminals directly linked to the COS of Bank *A.* Thus, some retail outlets will
have terminals for their customers' deposits into the bank, withdrawals
from the bank, check guarantee or check verification, and bank debit
and credit-card transactions where either the bank or a card company is
the host institution. Orders to switch deposits from one type to another
can be handled.[10] These are today's POSs, CBCTs, and RSUs. The retail
outlets may also have terminal hardware and software for payroll
accounting, use of preauthorized loans, inventory control, and general
accounting services performed on the COS.

Nonretail business customers have terminals for similar accounting
purposes, including payroll accounting and employee benefit packages.
Household terminals—perhaps just a telephone with or without non-
verbal alpha-numeric capabilities—allow them to order bill payments,
to use preauthorized lines of credit, and, with a bit more sophistication,
to make deposits from claims on others in the system. The bank's own
ATMs, both on premise and off premise, connect with the COS.

Listed on the opposite side of Figure 6-1, are S&Ls, MSBs, CUs,
brokers, insurance companies, and the debit/credit card companies
whose services are rendered through or by Bank *A.* Finally, in the
bottom portion, the correspondent banks of Bank *A* are shown. All
these have terminals with appropriately designed hardware and software for connections with Bank *A*'s COS.

This arrangement provides many options. All the terminals on the
right-hand side of Figure 6-1 permit customers—business and retail—
to make nearly timeless and low-cost transfers from interest-bearing
accounts to noninterest-bearing accounts, and vice versa. Payors will
need to keep nearly a zero balance in a form like the present demand
deposit. Payees can, by standing order or by discretionary orders, move
funds receipts out of noninterest-bearing accounts and into interest-
bearing accounts.

The terminals on the left-hand side of the figure increase options
further. The deposits of thrift institutions can be debited or credited by
electronic order from any of Bank *A*'s customers. Securities, including

---

9. It is not necessary that this be a commercial bank. A thrift with expanded powers could be
the focal organization. It seems probable, however, that commercial banks will play the
largest switching role for reasons of efficiency as well as of operating powers.

10. Figures 6-2 and 6-3 show the connections among banks which permit customers of banks
other than Bank *A* to use the various terminals.

the debt and equity and holdings of mutual funds, can be bought and sold. Brokers' balances on margin accounts can be used, subject to margin requirements, like checks, with interest at prevailing brokers' rates. These assets will become more liquid and more cash-like. Loan values of reserve life insurance policies also will become more liquid. To the extent that the debit/credit card terminals and the retail outlet terminals are on-line with the COS, the float on noninterest-bearing credit cards will tend to be reduced.

The correspondent banks shown at the bottom of Figure 6-1 can provide essentially the same services to their customers as does Bank *A* for its customers. Each can be connected with the same customer classes as is Bank *A*, but the smaller banks have the option of utilizing smaller computer operating systems. They can purchase computing services from Bank *A* in either a batch or on-line mode when that is the more efficient means of payment. And, of course, their customers can engage in any debit or credit transaction with any of the customers of any business or household in the entire system of which Bank *A* is the central mode.

The part of the EFT system shown in Figure 6-1 is a small subsystem in the totality of the EFTS. In fact, there is little possibility that it would be an economically feasible part if it were independent of a larger system.[11] Figure 6-2 shows the next level of interconnections. Bank *B* and Bank *C* have the same sort of customer connections shown for Bank *A* in Figure 6-1. Each is connected with ACH 1, for interbank clearings. S&L A is represented as having a direct connection with the ACH but (referring to Figure 6-1) could access the ACH through any of the banks belonging to the ACH. The corresponding banks could also access the ACH directly, rather than through a larger bank, if that appeared to be the more economical way to operate.[12]

At the bottom of Figure 6-2, a subnetwork for thrifts appears. They clear among themselves by use of a Mutual Institution Network Transfer System—MINTS—with the latter accessing the ACH. A similar subnetwork could be established for credit unions.

With the interconnections of Figures 6-1 and 6-2 combined, funds transfers of intrainstitutional (e.g., within one bank), interinstitution of the same class (e.g., among commercial banks) and interinstitutional of different classes (e.g., between commercial banks and S&Ls) can be

---

11. One reason for the adverse operating results of some of the present efforts is that the systems are not widely interconnected. They are akin to a telephone system which connects with only a few subscribers. Each telephone has little value until many subscribers are connected through a hierarchy of exchanges.

12. A good guess—but only a guess—is that a hierarchical system of clearing will emerge, rather than every institution being connected directly to a central clearing facility. Judged on the basis of other communication networks as well as on clearing operations of nationwide branching systems of European banks, a hierarchy of exchanges is probably less costly to operate.

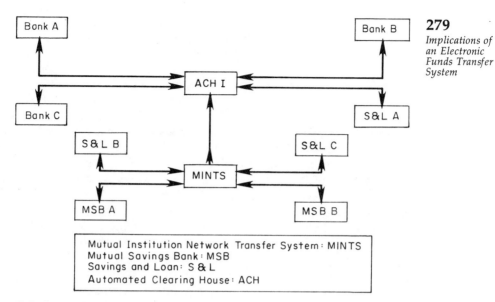

**FIGURE 6-2  Local and regional clearing in an EFT environment.**

effected on a regional and local basis. Many kinds of debit and credit transactions can be handled. And when the figures are combined, systems of debit/credit cards, with one or more of the deposit institutions acting as the host organization, are possible.

The nation as a whole is depicted in Figure 6-3, where a Super ACH clears among the local and regional ACHs.[13] One can now access accounts of businesses and financial institutions for debits or credits with little reference to specific geographic location. An additional level of clearing could be put on top of even the Super ACH to provide international clearing.[14]

With no view of the future and scant regard for today, it is customary

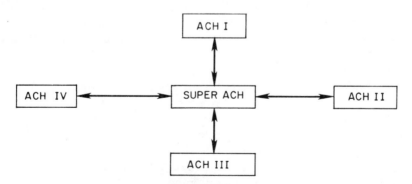

**FIGURE 6-3  National clearing in an EFT environment.**

13. Is the Super ACH the Federal Reserve System?

14. The SWIFT organization is moving in this direction.

to think of transactions balances as being currency plus the demand deposits of banks plus, perhaps, some other aggregates of deposit institution liabilities. It is common to think that the Federal Reserve System, through its open market operations, reserve requirements, and discount rate policies, can control some aggregate of liquid transactions balances in the economy. It is customary to think that this makes some historically defined concept of money—$M_1$, $M_2$, $M_3$, etc.—useful in the control of GNP and inflation, since we all know that GNP = $MV = PT$, with tautologically defined variables.

Money is not so easily defined with an EFT system such as that represented in Figures 6-1, 6-2, and 6-3. Many assets, as viewed by their holders, look more liquid. As noted, intrainstitutional balances and interinstitutional balances are interchangeable with low time and money costs. Whether or not laws are positively permissive, one can use the interest-bearing accounts of banks and thrift institutions for transactions purposes. Moreover, the liabilities of nondeposit institutions, including trust departments of banks, accounts in a mutual fund or with a broker, stock certificates, accumulated reserves in an insurance policy, short- or long-term negotiable municipal, state, or federal obligations, commercial paper, obligations of foreign banks or governments, may be seen by their holders as being nearly equivalent to currency, or to "money in the bank."

## POLICY IMPLICATIONS OF EFTS

From a public policy point of view, there are many worries about the impact of these technological and operational changes. If sleeping peacefully is of concern, one could slumber saying that the only implication is that $V$—some definition of $V$—will rise. Control of $M$—some definition of $M$—will still allow the central bank to keep things in order. The truth is that in an EFT environment with the present regulatory setting, the velocity of $M_1$ or even $M_2$ can rise to close to infinity. The prohibition of interest on demand deposits causes many businesses and households to shift to interest-bearing assets. To the extent that Regulation Q keeps rates on savings and passbook accounts below other market rates, customers will also shift more from them to the liabilities of nondeposit institutions, which bear the higher rates. The greater the difference between the permitted deposit rates and market rates, the greater will be the incentive to shift. What happens to $MV$? As the central bank attempts to control some definition of $M$, with below-market rates of interest, the adaptive market response is to adjust by switching to other types of assets carrying market rates. The velocity of the conventionally defined $M$ thus rises.

On ancillary issues, if businesses and consumers see many more of their assets as liquid, what kind of public policy can be used to avoid aggregative problems reminiscent of the 1920s and 1930s. If one person wants to sell a piece of commercial paper, or a share in a mutual fund, or to take the cash value of an insurance policy, no problems arise. What, however, if the actions become systemic? The answer is clear. There will be an "old-fashioned" liquidity crisis, because of uninsured liabilities being conceived of—correctly from the individual view and incorrectly from the collective view—as money.

Another ancillary issue which frequently appears is found in the argument that everything can be controlled. If markets, as presently controlled and regulated, cause banks to leave the Fed and encourage people to use the liabilities of nondepository institutions for transactions balances, a suggested recourse is to mandate Federal Reserve membership for all institutions in the third-party payment system and to extend the scope of regulation to all. The breadth of the options afforded by EFT makes this option quite impractical.

It cannot be stressed too much that no action may put the payments system on a road to crisis. With Regulation Q, with present reserve requirements, with present regulations on investments, with the present and differential restrictions on branching by brick and mortar versus by terminals, with proclivities to expand control and to insure, the prognosis is one of an eventual and possibly acute crisis, and one in which the traditional deposit institutions, including the Federal Reserve, will lose their roles. It is already going on within them, and between them and the nondeposit institutions.

## THE NEW PAYMENTS TECHNOLOGY: A NEW REGULATORY SCENARIO

Look at a different scenario, a scenario which a few have suggested but which has been resisted by the inertial forces. Suppose that there were no prohibition of interest payments on demand deposits.[15] With interest, businesses and consumers would be more willing to hold transactions balances in the depository institutions that comprise the present system of effectuating the bulk of all payments. In the EFT environment, noninterest-bearing bank demand deposits appear as a distinctly inferior way to hold balances. Data on the quantity and the velocity of $M_1$, particularly in money market cities, shows this clearly today.

If market-determined rates of interest were paid on demand deposits, increases in the velocity of $M_1$ would be slowed. Keeping funds in these deposits would become part of the portfolio management decisions by households and businesses. Control of the $M_1 V_1$ multiple would remain as a useful policy instrument. The new payments technology would be less likely to make monetary policy ineffective.

If market-determined rates of interest were paid on demand deposits, the disintermediation between thrift institutions and commercial banks would be alleviated. Perhaps of greater importance, the tendency

---

15. Or that nationwide NOW accounts were permitted.

for businesses and consumers to shift transactions balances to the uninsured liabilities of nondeposit institutions would be lessened.

The salient point about EFT is that, without the freedom to pay interest on demand deposits, the new technology will tend eventually to make $M_1$ disappear. $V_1$ will rise precipitously. If Regulation Q is set below market rates, savings accounts at deposit institutions will also tend to disappear, although surely less rapidly. Banks will become transactors of payments—with service charges, if they are to exist—and businesses and consumers will look to other assets with market-determined interest rates as their transactions balances.[16]

If interest were paid on demand deposits, the distinction between the historic classification of demand and savings accounts would disappear. The differential reserve requirements on savings and demand deposits would have to be eliminated. If, in an EFT setting, banks and the other deposit financial institutions are to be not just the transactors of payments but, also, the holders of substantial assets and of (insured) liabilities, which the public regards as transactions balances, market rates must be paid on their deposit liabilities.

What of Regulation Q and the allied regulations affecting the thrifts? The argument is clear. If a deposit financial institution must pay market rates to buy money, it follows that to avoid the tendency for customers to use the uninsured liabilities of other institutions as transactions balances, Regulation Q must be phased out. Actually, it has already been partially phased out, even though the enabling statute of the Banking Act of 1933 has not been changed. As severe disintermediation among the deposit institutions and between them and nondeposit institutions has occurred, Regulation Q rates have been relaxed. With EFT, however, the potential for shifting balances is not restricted to negotiable instruments of $100,000 and over. It can easily be accomplished on a balance of $100. The balance can be shifted to a liability of a nondeposit institution. There will remain transactions costs with EFT, but as volume rises, they will be small and offer opportunities to keep assets in the nonregulated sectors.

The recommendations of CMC, Heller, and Hunt are pertinent here. A deposit financial institution cannot buy money at market rates unless it can match these with the rates it charges for selling money with various maturities and risks. The old voices are clear, but the reactions of both the affected institutions and their regulators reflect the inertia. "Keep things as they were years ago" and "Maybe it will go away" seem to be the dominant voices. Few seem to recognize that the technology and market conditions of today and tomorrow make yesterday's modes of operation and regulation ineffective.

---

16. This is not hyperbole. Cash managers of firms with significant liquid asset balances have been managing portfolios to avoid $M_1$ balances for two decades. The experiences with Eurodollars and commercial paper are in point, but one should not neglect NOW accounts and the New England phenomena.

The central bank will also be affected by EFT. The Federal Reserve is properly concerned with the efficacy of its monetary policy tools. The System is intended to influence aggregate spending and regards its quantitative controls as the primary means of doing it. It is clear, however, that standing alone, the old quantitative controls will not work well in an EFT environment. Balances kept at the Fed by deposit institutions are equivalent to having the income from some part of the institution's assets taxed at a 100 percent rate. Noninterest-bearing reserve requirements are a positive inducement to leave the System. And if Federal Reserve membership or reserve requirements for all the present deposit institutions in the third-party payments system were mandated, the result in an EFT environment would be that other institutions—institutions without the 100 percent tax—would tend to substitute their liabilities for those of the present deposit institutions.

There is a way to solve this problem which would retain or improve the effectiveness of quantitative controls. It would both reduce the proclivity of banks to leave the system and provide incentives for nonmembers, including the thrifts, to keep reserve balances with the Fed. This proposal is to pay interest on the balances that deposit financial institutions keep with the Federal Reserve. Unlike the early Tobin proposal, which advocated interest on only excess reserves with a rate equal to the discount rate, the suggestion here is that interest be paid on all balances, with discretionary control over the rate based on policy objectives. Indeed, the rate paid on balances could replace the discount rate as a signaling device to indicate the attitude of the Fed with respect to monetary conditions.

The proposals rest on the fundamental proposition that—ignoring changes in currency in circulation, the Treasury balance, float, and international factors—the total amount of reserves in the System depends solely on Federal Reserve credit outstanding. For example, if Bank A elects to hold more reserves, it is required to reduce its loans and investments. The sale of any of its assets is matched by payments made through some other bank(s) in the system and, via clearing, what Bank A gains in reserves is lost by some other bank(s). There is no net change in total reserves so long as the central bank is neutral.

If the Fed feels that monetary conditions require a tightening of credit, the rate on reserve balances could be raised. The portfolio decisions of individual banks would lean toward holding larger reserve balances. As they attempted to reduce loans and investments, however, market interest rates would tend to rise, paralleling the rate on reserve balances. Total reserves would not rise if the amount of Federal Reserve credit remained unchanged. The loosening of credit would have opposite effects. As is true in all markets, the change in desired reserve holdings may be quite small and still have the appropriate effects. Price changes are influenced at the margin, even if only a small part of the total market is involved.

The new policy would require a coordination with the discount rate and with operating policies at the discount window. If the discount rate were significantly lower than the rate paid on reserve balances, an incentive would exist for institutions to borrow at the window and apply the proceeds towards increased reserves. The same incentive exists now with respect to other loans and investments. The extension of Federal Reserve credit through the window would have to be restricted by discount rate policy and by the implementation of "availability" criteria.

If payments on reserve balances were adopted, mandatory minimums for reserves could be established, but need not be, for third-party payments institutions that elect to hold deposits in the central bank. If there were no strictly defined minimums, balances at the Fed would take on a role similar to "secondary" reserves. They could be drawn down as the condition of individual banks required, but their levels would be subject to safety and soundness tests in the bank examination procedure.

In an EFT environment, it is unreasonable to think that all third-party deposit institutions will voluntarily elect to join the System, even with the inducement of interest payments on reserves. State-chartered institutions might well elect to hold balances with other banks, receiving interest on those balances and accompanying services from those banks. Among those services would be the clearing of accounts through the appropriate ACH and other clearing systems, including the Federal Reserve. It is conceivable that certain larger banks—banks like Bank *A* in Figure 6-1—would retain membership and provide clearing services for nonmembers. Such an arrangement would still subject the nonmembers to state reserve requirements. Moreover, increases or decreases in the rate paid on reserves of the members would be reflected in the rates paid on interbank balances.

Open market operations would work effectively with this arrangement. Most of the initial impact of purchases and sales (of runoffs at maturity) of securities would be on the member banks, but it would be transmitted to nonmembers as fast as it is today. Open market operations might be even more efficient than they now are if more institutions voluntarily elect to hold balances with the Fed.

Another interesting aspect is that policy objectives relating to quantitative goals could be coordinated with those relating to interest rate goals. For any given level of reserves, interest rates could be increased or decreased by variations in the rate paid on reserve balances. For any given rate paid on reserves, the quantity of reserves could be varied by open market operations. The sagacious combination of the two policy tools would permit a larger money supply without the effect of lowering interest rates. Interest rates could be lowered without a larger money supply. Policy trade-offs between the two goals would be possible.

What are the objections? First, some will maintain that paying interest on reserve balances would provide a "windfall gain" to deposit financial institutions, especially present member banks. This is a valid objection only if it is accompanied by the assumption that there exists a good deal of monopoly power in banking markets. If there is, instead, substantial competition, the "windfall gains" will be eroded through the market process. EFT will increase—not decrease—the degree of competition. Still, a "phasing-in" of the new policy might be necessary to prevent short-term windfalls.

A second objection is that the contribution of Federal Reserve earnings to the Treasury would be reduced. This is true. Its importance lies in the answer to the question of who should pay this "tax." At present, bank customers pay it indirectly. With the proposal given here, the tax would fall on general taxpayers.

The final objection may not be expressed, but it could be the most important. Some simply resist change; the status quo is preferable to novel policy. This feeling may be prevalent enough among legislators, regulators, and the banking community to shelve serious consideration of alternatives.

## CONCLUSIONS

The idea that an EFT is coming is not science fiction. As of early 1977, there were 27 ACHs in operation, and five more were being put in place. Most ACH transactions are done in batch mode and involve government social security and veterans' benefits, but the ACHs can be put into a mixed on-line and batch mode as the system develops.

As of the same date, there were at least 184 operating and 149 planned subsystems encompassing parts of what are pictured in Figures 6-1 and 6-2. These 333 subsystems, planned and operating, are just those which can be card-accessed by deposit institution customers. These systems had 1,392 ATMs and 8,283 POS terminals, including check authorization and guarantee terminals, many of which can be upgraded for more complete POS services. There were 2,282 banks, 55 mutual savings banks, 498 savings and loan associations, and 25 credit units involved in the 333 systems. Of these systems, 131 were shared by two or more institutions.[17]

Twenty-seven states have passed EFT laws. A fairly reliable indicator that policy problems exist is the attention being given by the financial institutions, their associations, their regulators, and the legislatures of both state and federal levels. The activities related to EFT must have some precipitating cause. EFT is coming as a market response to new technology.

While the change may be inevitable, it will not be costless to all. Some financial institutions will not try to adapt to the new world, and they will be lost as independent organizations. Some will try to adapt but will elect the wrong time, the wrong hardware or software, or the

---

**17.** These data were compiled by Peat, Marwick, Mitchell & Co. for the National Commission on Electronic Funds Transfer.

wrong marketing strategy, or will be subject to external factors which will cause their failure. Some will succeed. This pattern is common when a major change in technology occurs in an industry. Attempts at protective measures will exacerbate, not alleviate, longer-term adjustment problems. As Alfred Marshall wrote in 1897:

> When one person is willing to sell a thing at a price which another is willing to pay for it, the two manage to come together in spite of prohibitions of King or Parliament or of the officials of a Trust or Trade-Union.[18]

Madmen sometimes are in authority. Economists are frequently defunct as they cling to old thoughts and institutions. The world is, over the centuries, powerfully influenced by thought, but only with a time lag and often with the catalyst of a crisis. Still, it is time for change and time for men of affairs and academic scribblers to look to the future. EFT is going to have pervasive effects on all.

---

18. Marshall, "The Old Generation of Economists and the New," 11 Q. J. Econ., No. 2, pp. 115–135 (Jan. 1897).

# EFT AND BANK SHARING:
# SOME COMPETITIVE QUESTIONS

Elinor H. Solomon, *Senior Economist, Economic Policy Office, Antitrust Division, Department of Justice*

EFT has the potential to expand markets, both geographic and product, and to increase competition and the numbers of competitors in all these broadened markets. With the type of EFT configuration sketched out by Al Phillips, it is possible to have many sellers competing for financial business, and not just in local markets, or even in state markets, but potentially in regional and even national markets. At least theoretically, the future of competition looks good.

On the other hand, how do we get to this ideal world, and what types of hurdles and problems do we face in getting there? One particular and fairly immediate question which troubles us is the matter of bank sharing of EFT facilities.[1]

Suppose that banks representing, say, 80 percent, or 95 percent, or potentially 100 percent, of a state's deposits get together and offer EFT point-of-sale services on a shared basis. Their argument for doing this is that such services constitute a natural monopoly situation. That is, because of large absolute capital requirements, financial risks, and/or scale efficiencies, an efficient package of EFT services can be provided only by a single system. Sellers have to band together and offer these services jointly. This is the classic joint-venture rationale.[2]

---

These remarks are strictly personal and do not necessarily reflect the Department of Justice's views. I am indebted to the comments of Gerald Childs, Thomas Greaney, David Lapides, and Bruce White of the Antitrust Division.

1. See Baker, "Banking Competition in the Age of the Computer: The Economic Revolution in Banking," 90 Banking L.J. 193–212 (1973); Baker, "Competition, Monopoly and Electronic Banking," *Conference on Electronic Funds Transfer* 47–64 (Fed. Reserve Bank of Boston, Oct. 7, 1974).

2. Mead, "The Competitive Significance of Joint Ventures," 12 Antitrust Bull., No. 3, pp. 821–822 (Fall 1967).

One must examine the possible anticompetitive effects of such a joint venture.[3] For example, parental guidance normally is required in a joint venture such as is contemplated here, so that the venture may provide a focal point for discussion of other issues of mutual interest. When a group of banks gets together, say, to offer customer services at retail, this arrangement may well involve not only switching (or clearing) services but also rules and guidelines for the whole customer network.[4] Thus, sharing raises the following issues, among others.

## EFFECTS ON DIRECT AND POTENTIAL COMPETITION

Is there going to be any effect on direct competition in collateral banking activities not governed by the joint venture? Is there going to be any lessening of competition for correspondent banking business, either deposits or the services package, as a result of these joint ventures? Are there going to be any problems at retail, either for merchant, cardholder account, or some normal, conventional bank-lending activities?

Also, will potential competition be affected? Can any one member of the joint venture (or any less comprehensive combination of members) now offer the services separately? Even if this is not now possible, given present scale economies, what about the near-term future? There is expectation of rapid change in technology. Telecommunications costs are going to come down rapidly, particularly if satellites get into the business of transferring data from one processing point to another.[5] Data processing costs will decline. So, if we accept the natural-monopoly approach, and we agree to the joint venture, are we in given

---

3. These issues are discussed also by Bernstein, "Joint Ventures in the Light of Recent Antitrust Developments: Anticompetitive Joint Ventures," 10 Antitrust Bull. Nos. 1–2, pp. 25–29 (Jan.–April 1965).

4. Rules for assessment of the efficiencies versus competitive trade-off are offered by Baxter, Cootner, and Scott, *Retail Banking in the Electronic Age: The Law and Economics of Electronic Funds Transfer* (Allan Held Osmun and Co., Montclair, N.J., 1977). Their analysis classifies joint ventures first according to the extent to which they will achieve scale economies and, therefore, reduce average costs per transaction. Their proxy for scale economies (represented by the elasticity of average-cost curves) is then set against a classification based on market share—the proxy for numbers of possible future competing joint ventures.

   They would find certain joint ventures to be presumptively anticompetitive, where market concentration was high and the scale economies low; they argue that no violation should be found where large-scale economies are realized through the venture, at low levels of market concentration. In their analysis, it is not quite clear how markets would be defined, either product or geographic, or how individual market differences in a legal and institutional framework could be satisfactorily dealt with.

5. Diebold Research Program, reprinted in 22 Datamation, No. 6 (Oct. 1976).

markets locking ourselves into a solution which may not be efficient or optimal five or ten years from now?[6]

Let us look at an illustration. Take the point-of-sale terminal, which is the input point for the customer network. I drop my card into that terminal at the supermarket, and I have funds switched from my account at my Washington bank to the merchant's account by means of this configuration, which has been set up by a group of banks offering the services together.

I could just look at the switch as I would at any type of clearinghouse. But, should our analysis of competition stop with the switch, i.e., the central clearing computer?[7] What about the delivery function? Do we want banks in the telecommunications industry, and in the delivery business directly?

There is also the processing function and, further on downstream, the sale of the retail banking services. But if we look at the successive producing, wholesaling, and retailing tiers—starting not only with the switch and the clearing function, with which we are all familiar, but looking also at the delivery function, correspondent banking functions, and, ultimately, the sale of services at retail—we are looking at possible anticompetitive effects not only in banking but also in other industries.

It also becomes more difficult to define geographic and product markets in which to analyze these effects. Is the "product" the switch? In that case, we are talking about the clearing market which would be analogous to any normal clearinghouse. Should we, rather, look at the whole EFT configuration, starting with the switch and continuing downstream through sale of the ultimate product to the consumer at retail? It may be that some intermediate product market is often more appropriate, depending upon the individual EFT system and its unique characteristics.

## COMPETITION AND ALTERNATIVE EFTS CONFIGURATIONS

Ideally, we hope that the competitive process will generate an optimal market structure. What might that most efficient, as well as competitive, ideal look like? There is no one answer. EFT systems configura-

---

6. Baxter, Cootner, and Scott, N. 4 *supra*, Ch. 6, pp. 101–120; Flannery and Jaffee, *The Economic Implications of an Electronic Monetary Transfer System* (Lexington Books, D. C. Heath and Co., Lexington, Ma., 1973). These economists show that an efficient configuration of processing units and telecommunications lines may dictate larger numbers of competing units within regional nets of electronic funds transfer systems rather than a series of small local statewide monopolies each containing only one system.

7. A switch is nothing more than a computer programmed to perform the communication function of routing messages to their proper destination. In addition, the computer usually performs data processing functions, such as settlement and providing an audit trail for transactions. See U.S. Nat'l Comm'n on Electronic Funds Transfers (NCEFT), Interim Report, *EFT and the Public Interest* (Washington, D.C., Feb. 1977).

tions will ultimately depend not only on technology and market forces but, also, on the ultimate "mix" of competition and regulation in EFT systems, at the various banking and telecommunications levels.[8] A variety of models of "regulated competition" can be envisioned, starting with the pure, competitive model and working up to a public utility type of solution.[9]

## POS Switch in Front of the Banks

In Figure 6-4, one possible configuration displayed places the switch in a central (or hublike) position before, or in front of, the banks which deploy the terminals.[10] The original Atlanta Payments Project envisaged this arrangement, which is the most common configuration.[11] In theory, with this configuration, new systems can access the merchant terminals directly without going through the bank. The customer $A$ places his card in merchant terminals $T_1$ . . . n which are merchant-owned or leased but interconnected into the system. The customer uses a secret code which activates the terminal. Funds are transferred through the switch directly from customer $A$'s account in bank $A$ to the merchant's account in bank $B$.

The conventional bank clearing system may be bypassed altogether as long as (1) the funds transfer is both on-line and local and (2) the funds transfer involves members of the POS system, either primary or associate, i.e., either those owning the facilities and making the initial investment directly or those buying into the system at a later date.

---

8. Flannery and Jaffee, N. 6 *supra* at 64–67. Long and Fenner, *An Electronic Network for Interbank Payment Communications: A Design Study* 12 (Bank Administration Institute, Park Ridge, Ill., 1969). In delineating the optimal (i.e., the least-cost) computer network configuration, the number and location of switching centers is important in estimating network operating costs now and in the future.

   Thus, the authors show that if there are too few message switching centers or if they are not placed so as to minimize circuit costs between the centers and the banks, then communications costs will be unnecessarily high. On the other hand, if there are too many centers, the costs for circuits between banks and the centers would be lower, but the switching center costs themselves would be higher than necessary.

   In either case, the configuration will change as the technology in both the telecommunications and data processing industries is altered.

9. Policy choices in a number of industries, adjusting the mix of competition and regulation, are discussed by Shenefield, "Regulation and Deregulation—Where Do We Stand?" 45 Antitrust L.J., No. 2, pp. 244–289 (Aug. 1976).

10. For all configurations, the entire system is assembled by using services sold by different industries; the entire system consists of a composite of terminals, switch and depository institution-processing centers using equipment obtained from computer equipment manufacturers and tariffed-communication lines provided by regulated communications common carriers.

11. See Atlanta Payments Project, *A Technical Marketing Organizational and Cost Evaluation of a Point-of-Sale Terminal System*, Phase IV, pp. 34, 40–143 (Atlanta, Ga., 1973). A diagram of the system is shown in its 1 *Executive Summary* 4.

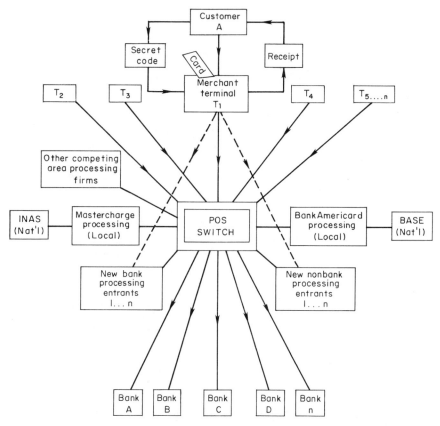

**FIGURE 6-4   Point-of-sale system use and clearing—switch in front of the bank. Note: New systems can access merchant terminals directly; banks not in control.**

Observe that in this configuration, it is not necessary that all system users be members of the joint venture directly. Nonmembers may buy EFT services from correspondents with whom balances are held. If the POS transaction is local and if the merchant's bank $B'$ (or customer's bank $A'$) is not a direct member of the system but, rather, a member's respondent bank, then the transfer will occur on the correspondent's books. The correspondent will hold balances for the user respondent. Correspondent $A$ will debit the account of the respondent bank $A'$ and credit the account of bank $B$. Bank $B$ then turns the balance over to its respondent bank $B'$ for credit to the selling merchant.

Competition exists at many levels and includes several industries. As is shown in Figure 6-4, this system of customer retail electronic banking is, in fact, made up of numbers of different components:

First is the switch (POS), a central processing unit computer, which performs the clearing function, analogous to that performed by the bank clearinghouse in a paper-based system. Clearing through the switch may be either instantaneous, i.e., on-line; or it may be off-line, in which case the Federal Reserve is more likely to get involved along with the switch. Each mode of clearing involves its own particular technical problems.[12]

Second, as an important component of the system, we have the communications lines (solid and dashed in Figure 6-4) analogous in the paper-based system to deliveries of paper checks by airplane, mail, or special courier. Use of these communications lines, to be provided by American Telephone & Telegraph and other specialized common carriers or telecommunications firms, will normally be paid for by the banks and other EFT participating sellers.

Third is the correspondent function, whereby EFT services manufactured and delivered to correspondents ($A,B, \ldots$ n) as wholesalers are, in turn, delivered to respondent banks ($A',B' \ldots n$) with whom they deal, later to be resold to the merchant or cardholder at retail.

Fourth, the bank seller at retail is involved in this system, buying and merchandising EFT services to retail customers either directly or through the intermediary of a correspondent.

Fifth, these retail customers will comprise both merchants and cardholders, the former receiving deposit-related banking services (including regular bank loans) along with authorization, electronic data processing (EDP), and other EFT benefits. Cardholders receive the range of debit and credit card services, including again, overdraft, loan, and funds transfer services.

Sixth, and finally, an important element in the system comprises the computer terminals (T) at retail, which may be either (1) bank-owned or (2) system-owned. In a viable system, terminals owned by one bank within the system will presumably access all others within the joint venture.

Optimally, all members can plug into this system and directly communicate with one another via the switch. Credit unions, financial institutions, life insurance companies, and other users of EFT, such as large merchants capable of offering their own system, will also plug into the centrally located POS switch directly and be able to effect money transfers from buyer to merchant seller at the retail store.

Banks can either become system members or stay out; if the latter course is elected, correspondent member banks ($A,B \ldots n$) may compete to supply EFT services to nonmember banks by providing the best "package" including both service and price.

Ideally, a monolithic EFT system can be avoided. Banks will "buy" both the data processing facilities and the telecommunications lines

---

12. The issues, pro and con, are discussed by Wolkowitz, "The Case for the Federal Reserve System Actively Participating in Electronic Funds Transfer," Banking & Financial Econ., Financial Studies Section (Bd. of Governors of the Fed. Reserve System, March 1977). See also Eisenmenger, Weiss, and Munnell, "The Economics of a National Electronic Funds Transfer System," Conference on Electronic Funds Transfer, 97–110 (Fed. Reserve Bank of Boston, Oct. 7, 1974).

and pay a market-determined price or, where warranted, a regulated price; and banks will sell to a variety of buyers outside the system, who also will pay a market-determined price from a competing number of banks within the local market. Many different types of bank, and nonbank, systems will coexist at retail. Since banks are competing with nonbanks, a minimal bundling of services against deposits may develop. In the ideal EFT world, buyers will know what prices they are paying for each type of EFT service. Merchants may also choose to own or rent terminals independently of banks, thereby retaining control of terminals.[13]

## POS Switch Behind the Bank

This type of world may not develop. For technological or other reasons, a different approach may evolve. Let us turn to Figure 6-5, which shows the POS switch positioned behind the bank. Here, new systems cannot

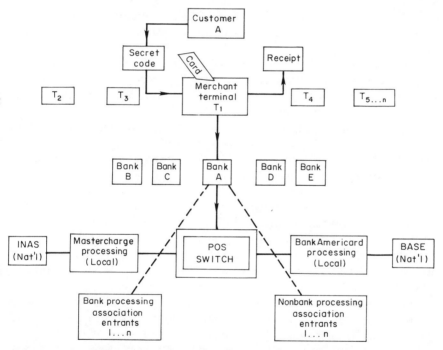

**FIGURE 6-5 Point-of-sale system use and clearing—switch behind the bank. Note: New systems cannot access merchant terminals directly.**

---

**13.** See American Banker, April 6, 1977, p. 1, for remarks of Dale Browning, senior vice president of the Colorado National Bank of Denver, at the American Bankers Ass'n Southern Regional Bank Card Management Workshop. He observed that permissive, not mandatory, sharing of terminals among all financial institutions is the most cost effective; such a system permits charging customers who initiate these transactions, as well as retailers.

access the merchant terminals directly. Nor can they interface directly with the terminals via the POS switch already in place. A merchant (or bank) must now find a bank, and not just a switch, with which to connect. Banks are in greater control.

Any new bank (or nonbank) processing association entrant will have to go through the bank computer systems, operate as processor for a bank member, or purchase banks themselves. Clearly, entry will be more difficult.

The initial steps are the same as in the preceding configuration. The customer presents his card with a picture, signature, account number, and magnetizable strip on the card upon which a random security number can be electronically written. The customer's card is inserted into the merchant's terminal device, which is connected to the sponsoring bank's computer, and the amount of the sale is entered.

This configuration with the POS switch behind the bank may save the establishing-processing bank's money. "On us" transactions can be handled in-house without going through the switch. However, it also may "lock" more clearing balances into the establishing banks. Thus, it raises the specter of greater deposits concentration than under the first (freer) system.

Respondent bank EFT options may be cut further if there is pressure (either informal or compulsory) to get all banks (eligible to join the system) into the system. If they all (large and small) are under the "umbrella" of common ownership, this may remove the possibility of respondents bargaining independently with the city correspondent for EFT services. The presence of explicit system "pricing" rules, either at the wholesale (correspondent) or retail (merchant/cardholder) level, will, of course, heighten this danger and can amount, under some circumstances, to price-fixing.

Observe, also, that in the first case (switch in front of the bank), virtually every merchant terminal ($T_1 \ldots n$) was, in effect, a potential mini-branch of a bank. Further, in that case, a national banking market was possible, in theory, with competition among both banks and nonbanks (e.g., national credit card systems and finance company offices) for consumer loans of varying risk categories.

The second case (switch behind the bank) is more restrictive and could tend to restrict, perhaps artificially, the geographic boundaries of markets for demand deposits and other services.

In addition, entry by processing firms or others attempting to capture components of the business may be impeded. The new entrant has to buy a bank or offer processing services through a bank. The systems offered may tend to be homogenized with less gradations in price and quality. Banks, or at least the state banking regulator, may have the power to exclude certain types of entrants, e.g., those offering a "cheap and dirty" system. Existing correspondent relationships also may tend to be cemented. (Further, the configuration may present more monetary policy problems, such as the possible pyramiding of reserves at a few key correspondent banks.)

It is possible to have a hybrid configuration, where some terminals communicate directly with depository institutions and other terminals with the switch. Most likely, the system that develops will contain such a mixture. The particular hybrid "mix" will depend on circumstances, the markets served, and new technology developments.

## Interregional and National EFT Links

Regional interchange between these local systems is shown in Figure 6-6. The Fed may elect to provide this EFT interface through the Fed Wire in Culpepper, Virginia (although it has no such plans). Interface may also occur through private clearing systems, including credit card clearing systems already in place (NBI's BASE, Bank Wire), or leading banks with the financial resources to develop a system nationwide (e.g., Citibank). Nonbank processing companies are also potentially capable of interregional clearing.

Whatever the case, a competitive struggle may ensue for control of the national switching and clearing business. Although it has recently relaxed processing restraints, NBI's BASE must want to retain the national delivery, as well as processing, business for VISA and, also, for the debit point-of-sale funds transfers it expects to generate in the future from its debit card. Interbank uses its own regional processing centers. Some local point-of-sale systems envisage that credit card processing and authorization functions (including those now offered by Interbank and NBI) are going to be plugged into the local system in order to provide a sufficient volume of transactions to warrant efficient use.[14]

The greatest scale economies in EFT systems will probably be at the level of the switch or central processing unit itself, and it is to be expected that fewer regional than local switching centers will be able to operate. Private regional clearing centers may take on some regional clearing functions now provided by the Federal Reserve, both through their regional check-processing clearing centers (RCPCs) and Fed Wire facilities.

In other words, some switches run either by banks or nonbanks may be expected to perform correspondent and settlement functions for the whole country. They will therefore also hold the necessary clearing reserves and make the short-term loans to respondents that are normally provided by discount operations of a central bank. There may be separate (and disparate) clearing rules established by private banks and credit card systems, and other nonbanks, with respect to clearing

---

14. The Arthur D. Little study throughout makes similar assumptions. See Arthur D. Little, Inc., 1 *The Consequences for Electronic Funds Transfer—A Technology Assessment of Movement Towards a Less Cashless Society*, 158–160 (Nat'l Science Foundation, Jan. 30, 1975). See also Atlanta Payments Project, N. 11 *supra.*

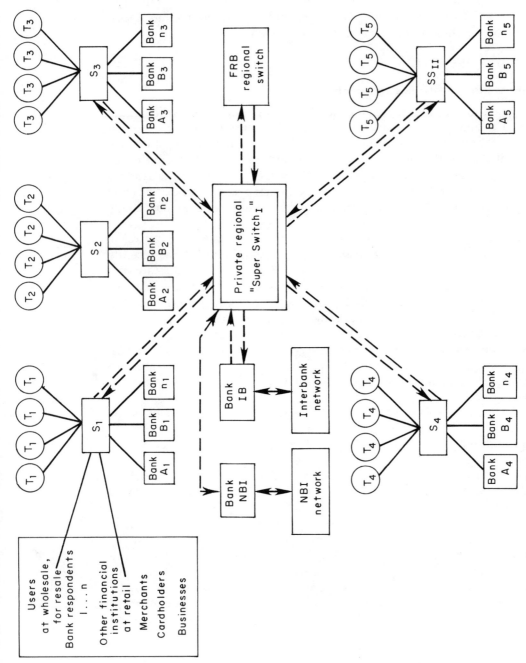

**FIGURE 6-6** Regional clearing of point-of-sale customer networks.

charges. The effects of these rules on entry and competition require **297**

*Implications of an Electronic Funds Transfer System*

study.[15]

## BANK OWNERSHIP OF THE ENTIRE CUSTOMER NETWORK

What are the advantages and disadvantages of having the whole system owned by banks? There are efficiencies in vertical integration by banks or groups of banks. Banks have operated the payment mechanism. They are subject to Fed regulations.

But there are also the usual competitive disadvantages to vertical integration.[16] Also, if in fact we need bank ownership of the whole vertically integrated system, do they have to be banks within the state and, in some cases, with controlling shares of local markets?

Ideally, the markets for EFT services should be regional, or even national, but a number of states have enacted mandatory sharing legislation. In effect, they mandate that when one bank offers EFT services, it is required to let all other banks in the state into the system, and no one else. These sharing statutes may lock us into state or smaller-than-state EFT bank markets, when a more optimal solution would place larger numbers of both bank and nonbank competitors in broader markets. The EFT Commission has suggested that federal antitrust laws should preempt a mandatory state sharing statute on a case-by-case basis.[17]

---

**15.** EFT technology may lead also to a highly concentrated market for bank reserves in the hands of those few banks or firms which operated the regional or national "super-switches." Settlements could be effected for large numbers of institutions without Federal Reserve involvement. If this should happen, there is at least a possibility that monetary policy could become an exercise in implicit bargaining between the central bank and powerful quasi-central banks, including credit card companies and others who were engaged in the interregional clearing operations. See paper of Edward J. Stephens (Federal Reserve Bank, Cleveland) prepared for the Monetary Policy Program of the National Commission on Electronic Funds Transfers; see also the NCEFT, Interim Report, N. 7 *supra* at 95–96.

**16.** The evils of "mixed banking" have been rehashed on numerous occasions in banking history and especially prior to passage of the Glass-Steagall Act of 1935. The history is cited in Board of Governors of the Fed. Reserve System, *Banking Studies* (Waverly Press, Baltimore 1941); Robertson, *The Comptroller and Bank Supervision: A Historical Appraisal* 117–138, 222–228 (Office of the Comptroller of the Currency, Washington, D.C., 1968).

**17.** Sharing questions are discussed by the NCEFT in its Interim Report, N. 7 *supra* at xvii (in summary) and at 49–64 (in text).

In Chapter IV, the Commission endorses procompetitive sharing. It notes (p. 50) that procompetitive sharing will enable sharing where agreed to by the parties and consistent with the antitrust laws. However, sharing, if challenged, would be permitted, required, or prohibited on a case-by-case basis depending upon the effect such sharing would have upon competition in the market involved.

The Commission also recommends (p. 50) federal legislation that would affirm the applicability of the federal antitrust laws to sharing arrangements involving POS or ATM systems and that expressly would nullify the effect of any mandatory sharing legislation.

The NCEFT is analyzing data derived from twenty case studies and has prepared

The pricing of EFT services provided by a number of suppliers is especially difficult. For example, how is system clearing to be priced: on a par basis, with specific charges levied per item (or electronic impulse) cleared; or on a non-par percentage basis? The local POS systems generally price on a per-item basis, while the credit card systems use both methods, with the non-par charge covering, in part, the "free float" period extended by the card-issuing bank to the cardholder.[18]

In addition, suppose the government acts as clearer of last resort, just as, in the present check clearing system, the Federal Reserve acts as a clearer of last resort. In this case, should the Fed (as it does now) provide the base-level clearing services to keep prices down and assure the availability of EFT facilities on an even basis? This may hurt small telecommunications and processing firms, which may want to enter this system at various levels but cannot afford to compete with the Fed.[19]

Last, if artificial interest rate restraints are eliminated and the market is free to determine interest rates on demand deposits (including inter-

---

Internal Working Documents (Nos. 25 and 27), which summarize and discuss the basic or benchmark cost studies. They also provide a conceptual and methodological framework for cost/benefit analysis.

David Walker and the Federal Deposit Insurance Corp. are also updating earlier cost data. See Walker, "An Analysis of EFTS Activity, Levels, Costs, and Structure in the United States," *Conference on Bank Structure and Competition* 1–20 (Fed. Reserve Bank of Chicago Research Dep't, Chicago 1976).

At present, few banks are charging for retail EFTS services, and explicit prices paid by customers for EFT services appear less than for non-EFT services at the present time. See Eisenbeis, *The Competitive Implications Associated with the Use of Electronic Terminals* (internal paper prepared for the NCEFT, Regulators Committee 1977).

18. See Hock, "EFTS or EVE, the Economics of a National Electronic Funds Transfer System," Conference on Electronic Funds Transfer, 65–84 (Fed. Reserve Bank of Boston, Oct. 7, 1974). Mr. Hock discusses the non-par clearing system of National BankAmericard (now VISA). The non-par clearing fee, of 1.95 percent of the face value of the draft, is paid by the selling merchant's bank (assuming it is a principal member) to the cardholder's bank, since the draft is sold at a discount of that amount. The cardholder's bank, in turn, collects from the buyer, after a time lag, at par.

The card-issuing banks with the biggest cardholder base relative to merchant accounts may expect an inflow on the interchange or non-par clearing fee, conceivably raising barriers to new entry in those markets.

For historical experience, see "Federal Reserve Operations in Payment Mechanisms: A Summary," 62 Fed. Reserve Bull., No. 6, p. 481 (June 1976); and George M. Vest, "The Par Collection System of the Federal Reserve Banks," 26 Fed. Reserve Bull., No. 2, pp. 89–92 (Feb. 1940). See also Harding, *The Formative Period of the Federal Reserve System* (Houghton Mifflin Co., Boston and New York 1925).

The curious result of the earlier experience was that the big city correspondent banks generally absorbed the exchange (non-par) charge in order to compete for deposits, while it was the smaller country banks that retained this charge for a long time, despite the Fed's best efforts to stamp it out.

19. See Wolkowitz, N. 12 *supra* at 19–22.

bank),[20] not only might this make monetary policy more effective, in addition, it would very likely result in the "unbundling" of bank services and the pricing of all services individually.[21] As a result, nonbank firms may be able to enter at various levels and compete with banks in providing EFT services, including data processing and maybe even local switching. Depositors will also be able to "shop" for the best price for their deposit inputs, eliminating the archaic barter practices common in banking.[22]

In conclusion, the competitive issues raised by EFTS require careful study, so that the best regulatory reforms can be achieved. The academic community, it is hoped, will continue to provide major input into resolving many of these questions.

**20.** See the staff study of the Board of Governors of the Federal Reserve System, *The Impact of the Payment of Interest on Demand Deposits,* prepared for William Proxmire, chairman, Senate Comm. on Banking, Housing and Urban Affairs, Jan. 31, 1977. The ABA leadership actively supports the new interest-paying consumer checking account. Hutnyan, American Banker, May 16, 1977, p. 1, cols. 1–2.

**21.** These joint competitive and monetary policy issues are described in NCEFT, Interim Report, N. 7, *supra* at Ch. 6, prepared for the Monetary Policy Program of the Commission, whose co-chairman was Almarin Phillips. A bibliography of the consultants' papers is shown in the NCEFT Report, N. 7 *supra* at 81, n. 2.

**22.** Phillips, "Competitive Policy for Depository Financial Institutions," *Studies in the Regulation of Economic Activity: Promoting Competition in Regulated Markets,* 329–366. (Phillips, Ed., Brookings Institution, Washington 1975). See also Phillips, "Competition, Confusion and Commercial Banking," 19 J. Finance, No. 1, pp. 32–45 (March 1964).

Comments by Aspenwall, Mote, and Eisenbeis, "Restructuring the Bank Regulatory Agencies," Conference on Bank Structure and Competition, N. 17 *supra* at 149–163.

# PRIVACY ASPECTS IN EFT SYSTEMS

Alan F. Westin, *Professor of Public Law and Government, Department of Political Science, Columbia University.*

$M$uch has already been written about the potential of individual and associational privacy that would be presented by a comprehensive EFT system. Often, public debate on this matter has seen the fanciful speculations of "total system" EFT enthusiasts met by equally fanciful (though horrified) reactions from civil libertarians.[1]

For example, the enthusiasts project a national or regional EFT system in which almost all of an individual's income sources and recurring obligations would be deposited and automatically paid out of one central account held in a financial utility; a nationwide terminal system would allow immediate debits and credits to the individual's central account from locations across the country; and secure techniques for personal-identity verification would protect against fraud or misuse. This is presented as technologically feasible, increasingly necessary for our transaction-laden financial and consumer-purchase systems, and as a socially desirable innovation.

In reply, civil libertarians have condemned such EFT conceptions as an Orwellian horror delight. An EFT system of this kind would aggregate far more personal information than is being collected by any single financial, retailing, or credit-reporting institution or any existing multiorganizational network. The automated data base of individual accounts would allow managers of the system—and anyone else allowed to use it or able to penetrate it unlawfully—to accomplish unprecedented feats of surveillance: to locate individuals at a given moment, track their movements over time, develop profiles of their spending and saving habits, monitor whether their use of government

---

1. See the discussion of "checkless, cashless society" proposals and reactions in Westin, *Privacy and Freedom* pp. 163–168, 298–326 (Atheneum, New York 1967).

or private funds met various regulatory or program requirements, identify their money-based political, religious, civic, or sexual affairs, and impose various controls over access to funds that could have enormous regulatory consequences for various economic and social groups in the population. Projecting these capabilities of a "total system" EFT onto recent disclosures of the FBI's covert examination of bank records of antiwar and black-protest groups in the late 1960s, the use of White House power over government files by Nixon and his lieutenants during their war on alleged subversives and "political enemies," and similar revelations about breaches of confidentiality from the Watergate-CIA-FBI probes of the past five years, civil libertarians have warned that proposals for developing such a "checkless, cashless society" are extraordinarily dangerous.

The way civil libertarians first reacted in the middle and late 1960s, was, I submit, understandable and proper. Faced by the new technological power of computer and communications systems; the publication of "total system" EFT descriptions and proposals by experts from the business, computer, and government communities, usually without any serious discussion of privacy implications; and the seemingly irresistible momentum of the technological imperative ("if it can be done, it will be done") in the heady 1960s, civil libertarians were providing the necessary "negative" side of the social forecasting debate—asking how a socio-technological development of this magnitude might be misused. I wrote just such an analysis for *Playboy* Magazine in 1968, discussing where then-current proposals for a "cashless, checkless society" and a National Data Center might lead us unless we first strengthened our basic privacy laws.[2]

The trouble with the debate of the 1960s and early 1970s is that it was over a straw man. No "total system" EFT plan had any possibility of being installed then, nor within the 1970s, nor would I see it emerging in the 1980s. Furthermore, even if we got a comprehensive EFT by the year 2000, it would probably bear little relationship to the kind of one-financial-utility, all-accounts-automated, totally preauthorized-payments, "cashless" model that characterized much of the writings in the 1960s. One of the most important findings of the National Academy of Sciences' Project on Computer Data Banks[3] was that there are enormous organizational, legal, competitive, social, and cost-effective constraints on the adoption of "technologically possible" computer and communications systems. The "pure" technological solution is rarely the one that meets those constraints, and, thus, computer-system innovations in the organizational world almost always take longer and are adapted more fully to social policy objectives. At the same time, our society has

---

2. Westin, "The Snooping Machine," Playboy 130–132, 152–157 (May 1968).

3. The report of this project is in Westin and Baker, *Databanks in A Free Society* (Quadrangle Books, New York 1972).

learned that our social *policies* as to individual rights and organizational duties in personal data must be made unmistakably clear and brought up-to-date *before* major new data systems are allowed to be installed.

Overall, then, the past decade of debate over "EFT and privacy" has had one quite useful consequence: It has started society toward a reconceptualization of the right to privacy that individuals should have in various bodies of sensitive financial data that will increasingly be contained in large-scale computerized data bases, and it has sensitized systems developers and organizational leaders working in the EFT field to the need for careful advance planning to respond to those policy considerations. The serious and costly difficulties faced by participants in the Universal Products Code for supermarkets demonstrates vividly the results of a failure to anticipate the consumer's insistence that eye-readable prices be retained on every item at the shelf location, and that a satisfactory system for consumer review at the checkout station also be retained.

It is clear that we *are* already moving from our traditional financial transaction system (say, of the 1950s) toward various less-check and less-cash arrangements. The growing use of bank cards and travel and entertainment cards, the automatic deposit of Social Security checks, and similar specific events are part of this pattern, as are a variety of local pilot projects experimenting with automated deposit or terminal input systems. There is also considerable agreement in the financial and governmental sectors that these moves will increase in the next few decades, some would say inexorably, as a result of high transactional volumes and costs, presumed business and governmental opportunities through new electronic technology, and satisfaction of assumed consumer desires.

Recognizing that we are moving, without any central plan, in the direction of less-check, less-cash arrangements, my discussion concentrates on the key issues of *transition*. How should American society approach change from our existing financial payments system to various, more automated systems? Is there a set of ground rules and a monitoring process that will serve us well with specific automated payment projects in the next decade and will also help us to be better prepared to make social value decisions about the more comprehensive EFT systems that may, at the end of another decade, be ready for serious consideration?

To develop those transitional rules and procedures, we need, first, to assess the current definitions of and safeguards for individual and group privacy in financial transactions. Unfortunately, recent decisions by the United States Supreme Court have adopted a cramped interpretation of the individual depositor's right of privacy in bank records. In *California Bankers Association v. Schultz*,[4] the Court rejected a challenge

---

4. California Bankers Ass'n v. Schultz, 416 U.S. 21 (1974).

to the elaborate record-keeping requirements and inspection powers created by the federal Bank Secrecy Act; the Court held that neither privacy rights nor due process rights were violated by such provisions. In *United States v. Miller,*[5] the Supreme Court wrote an even more disappointing decision, holding that an individual does not have a sufficiently direct constitutional interest in the information maintained in his or her account to be a necessary party to any dissemination of that information beyond the depository institution; more specifically, said the Court, it is the institution that has the property right and the legal standing to contest third-party claims to access to a depositor's account, not the depositor.

When these restrictive decisions of the Supreme Court are laid alongside the absence of a generally prevailing voluntary code for protecting depositor or account-holder privacy among banks, credit card companies, and other financial institutions, the conclusion I reach is that state and/or federal legislation defining such individual depositor rights must be enacted if there is to be a foundation of proper legal protections on which to begin building EFT systems. Or, to put it another way, unless statutes clearly spell out the rights, remedies, and monitoring procedures that govern the handling of sensitive personal information in financial accounts, it will be next to impossible to build properly designed and safeguarded EDP systems.

Beyond this critical first step lies the formulation of a new conception of the individual's right to control the profile of his/her financial transactions in new, multiorganizational data systems. Today, many commentators, especially those from the financial community, treat this new situation as only an extension of what various financial and commercial organizations now know about their customers; following this view, they suggest that all we need to do is to extend current policies, including current confidentiality policies by financial institutions, credit card firms, retail establishments, and commercial reporting agencies.

I submit that this is a fundamentally wrong and unwise approach. When information is merged from a variety of present sources (different kinds of banks, stores, employers, and other income sources, Social Security, card companies, etc.) *not* to make one-time decisions for specific purposes (such as credit, insurance, or employment decisions from commercial reports) but to create and maintain a permanent financial transaction data base and network for an EFT system, then a new *trustee relationship* has been, or should be, held to have been created between the system managers and the individual account holder.

Under this conception, the data rich profile of an individual residing in the EFT data base would be a valuable legal property belonging *only*

---

5. United States v. Miller, 425 U.S. 435 (1976).

to the individual account holder and *not* to "the system." The system managers should be allowed to make use of the information solely for the express purposes of the funds transfer process and its necessary monitoring for security, audit, and other protective purposes. However, any commercial or other gainful use of an individual's transactional history represents the taking of a valuable property right for which both compensation and consent are required.

There may be some who see advocacy of such a property right in personal information as a retrogression in American law, harkening back to the days of liberty-of-contract and substantive due process in the consitutional jurisprudence of 1890–1937. While I am not forgoing for an instant the defense of privacy rights that rests on personal liberty grounds (e.g., First and Fourth Amendment bases) or on positive legislation such as the Federal Privacy Act of 1974 and its counterpart in nine states, I am convinced that a propertied-privacy approach is also vital if we are to develop a coherent protection of the privacy rights of individuals as consumers in an increasingly data-rich commercial civilization.[6]

Today, American law is steadily writing into statutes or regulatory rules that personal information given to organizations (both governmental and private) for an express purpose, reflecting an information bargain between individual and organization, cannot be used for additional purposes not within the original agreement unless the later consent of the individual is obtained or it is mandated by law (and within the limits of the original transaction). This is true with medical records, educational records, credit-insurance-and-employment reporting by commercial agencies, and many other areas. When we, therefore, contemplate the kind of master file that a broad EFT plan would create, even far short of the year 2000-type systems, I submit we should treat this as a new and concretely valuable collection of sensitive, personal data. It ought not to be thought in any way to become the property of the EFT system, subject to be sold by the system to business advertisers, political candidates, religious groups, civic causes, magazines, or Fruit-of-the-Month clubs without the say-so of the financial account holder.

What would follow from this approach is that every account holder would have to be offered options by the EFT system as to *any* additional uses made of his/her data. A check-off system could be created, whenever an individual opened the account, offering various options. One is that data should *never* be provided to anyone. Another is that data could be provided for all uses checked off on a list, and at so much compensation directly to the individual for such use. Still another option might be a blanket permission for marketing and solicitation uses, at a particularly high rate of payment for giving such permission.

---

6. See *Privacy and Freedom*, N. 1 *supra* at 330–364.

The beauty of computer systems is that such a privacy-respecting check-off system installed at the outset and revised periodically, would be eminently feasible as a technological matter. The privacy of those who want no additional commercial, charitable, or other uses made of their data could be respected, while a specific payment per use could be automatically credited to the individual's account whenever each authorized use was made.

One can anticipate cries of outrage from some members of the direct mail industry, who have been buying and selling our personal profiles for decades without our getting a cent for it. But the age of clean air and water as economic "free goods" is over, and so ought to be the age of free commercial use of our personal profiles. In a market economy, any scarce commodity that buyers want becomes an object of value, sold on contract terms. The sooner American consumers wake up to the fact that amassed personal facts about them are becoming the necessary currency of marketing in our economy, the sooner we will have a new and more humanistic exchange theory of value for the electronic age.

So far, I have been addressing the disposition of account holder data for private, commercial purposes other than management of the EFT system itself. Equally, if not more, important will be the issues of what access government authorities would have to the system, in a range of entries starting from minimum regulatory agency oversight to insure the integrity of the system and its security, all the way, at the other extreme, to a general right to access the system for criminal investigations, legislative inquiries, civil process, regulatory program enforcement, or internal security programs.

Logically, one can hypothesize three basic answers to this question: (1) no access whatever for any governmental purpose; (2) access for whatever purposes would today allow entry to individual financial records, and under present safeguards; and (3) an intermediate policy of specifically limited entries under express conditions and procedures.

Option 1, I think, is unrealistic and probably unwise. Unlike the immunity our society bestows by law or by practice on a handful of informational resources (psychiatric-incident registers, priest-penitent confidences, etc.), I cannot believe that financial accounts in an EFT-type data base ought to have such wholesale immunity.

Option 2 is equally unpersuasive, given my already expressed position that our current law of financial privacy is dangerously outdated and weak.

This leaves option 3, whose evaluation obviously depends on an elaboration of what "specifically limited entries and express conditions and procedures" would mean. For me, this would mean the following kinds of rules:

(1) Any law enforcement inquiry that involved inspection of EFT records directly related to First-Amendment-protected activity—religion, press, speech, and assembly, and especially, records of private associations—would be presumptively improper. A special judicial

warrant system would pass on proof of probable cause and probe whether there was another investigative technique that might be used instead with less harmful impact on personal rights (as the Omnibus Crime Control Act of 1968 does with regard to wiretapping and electronic eavesdropping). No general searches of the EFT data base for possible "hits" on lists of "suspected persons" should be allowed, on the theory that these would be equivalent to the general warrants forbidden by the Fourth Amendment in the precomputer era.

(2) Before any automated payment from a government social-benefit program was included in an EFT system, the legislature ought to require that a privacy-impact statement be drawn up and presented by the executive agency involved (state or federal) indicating any techniques of enforcement using the rest of the EFT system that were proposed (collation of payments with other program payments, seeking location information on delinquent program participants, etc.). This ought to be subject to public-notice proceeding at which various private groups could appear and testify on the issue of whether those enforcement techniques were too violative of the overall confidentiality pledges of the EFT system. If a national EFT system were authorized by Congress at some point in the future, there should be language of a declaratory character mandating the protection of privacy and confidentiality interests of the individual and rights of individual access to all information contained in his/her file and to an audit record of all uses made of it. This language would become the standard that courts could use in reviewing the fidelity of later additions to the EFT system and uses of its data, with judicial power to entertain class action as well as individual law suits and to hold both legislative and administrative actions to the declared policy of the EFT system.

(3) While we do not know what shape a future EFT-type system would take, it is not too soon to start thinking about the kinds of institutional arrangements our society might require to be appended to local or regional pilot programs that are being developed, or to early national experiments. I think a searching public-notice proceeding before a national or state regulatory commission ought to be required before an EFT-type system is initiated, with the commission specifically charged to consider safeguards for individual rights in its decision about the acceptability of the proposal. In addition, if a national EFT-type system were attempted, a board of overseers with private as well as public members should be created to monitor continuously the rules and operation of the system, including, specifically, its individual rights practices, and to report to Congress annually on the way such practices were being observed, the need for additional protections, etc.

To sum up, I have assumed that the next several decades will see the gradual development of various forms of less-cash, less-check payments mechanisms, but not the "total system" plan of the comprehensive, automatic, one-big-utility variety. At what stage partial payments systems on a local or regional basis, or national payments programs for

specific income purposes (like Social Security checks) will be deliberately merged into a single national payments system, I cannot predict,
but I doubt whether this will come within the next 10 to 15 years.

Therefore, I see the transition toward a privacy-respecting system of
EFT arrangement as requiring the following:

1. Congress should deal with the serious problems of privacy in bank and
credit card records that need redress, *before* we go any further to more
comprehensive financial transaction systems.

2. Pilot programs of automated financial transactions should formulate
clear rules of individual rights and protective procedures of the type
discussed earlier, as applied to the specific contexts of those
experiments.

3. Congress should create the oversight commission of private and public
members, the public-notice proceedings, the declaratory standards, and
the protective procedures mentioned earlier at the point, if we reach it,
at which a national EFT-type system is created.

If we pass through the next decade or two under such controlled
experiment conditions, American society will then be in a good position to assess any plans that may be offered for a comprehensive
national EFT system, and to judge whether such a plan would be a
privacy respecting boon to American enterprise or a dangerously
Orwellian step.

# DISCUSSION

FRANKLIN R. EDWARDS: We have heard three speakers on three different aspects of EFT systems.

Dr. Phillips tells us that if we do not bring EFT under present regulations, the Federal Reserve will not be able to control total spending in the economy and we will be subject to great cyclical swings in economic activity. People will also begin using nondeposit liabilities for transaction purposes, which are uninsured and not covered by the usual solvency regulations, so that you have the makings of an old-fashioned bank panic.

Professor Westin says that we should not bring this system on line without proper safeguards to protect the privacy of individuals, and he suggests a transitional plan to evaluate our ability to protect individuals.

Dr. Solomon says that although EFT should, in principle, expand markets and interbank competition, the exact opposite may occur unless EFT development is carefully thought out, by both regulatory and antitrust officials.

WILLIAM VICKREY: I think this system is not going to come about very quickly. It has certain similarities to the kind of system that I have been trying to promote for 20 or 25 years, for charging people according to the precise use they make of city streets. This scheme would have all kinds of favorable effects on the efficiency with which these facilities are used and

would be a source of revenue to the proper authorities. Instead of being a burden on the taxpayer, it would actually confer a benefit on the average taxpayer. This system involves sophisticated electronic equipment of the same sort. I have learned that it is not easy to get a sophisticated electronic scheme accepted by the general public. We already have a great outcry against the coding of packages, of prices, and so on. Some of this is misunderstanding of just how it is going to work and what it is going to do, but there are all sorts of people who say that they do not want this kind of system. They want the results, but none of the fancy, mysterious electronic stuff.

PHILLIPS: It is perfectly clear that when the paper check system came into use in the last decade of the nineteenth century, it did not totally replace cash. EFTs will also not fully replace either cash or checks, but it is an alternative payments mode that will clearly change the degree to which cash and checks are used in the payment system.

JOHN HAWKE: The Justice Department's position on mandatory sharing apparently is that it is a bad thing. On the other hand, the Department has been advancing the idea that for certain essential facilities, there ought to be required sharing—or that the antitrust laws compel sharing.

Do you see any inconsistency in this position? Where do you draw the line between good sharing and bad sharing?

SOLOMON: The National Commission's (on Electronic Funds Transfer) interim report lists four different types of sharing. The Commission endorses so-called pro-competitive sharing where agreed to by the parties and consistent with the antitrust laws. Sharing must be looked at on a case-by-case basis. Whether it is good or bad depends upon the effect that it has upon competition in the market involved.

In the case of an essentially "natural monopoly," where the competitive solution is impossible because of scale efficiencies, the Department might advance the idea of required sharing, with full-user access. On the other hand, if it is possible to have competing systems, either now or within some reasonable time frame, the Department might very well oppose sharing because of its adverse effects on potential or direct competition. I do not see any inconsistency. It all depends upon the particular circumstances.

HAWKE: I have trouble determining how you will conclude that a natural monopoly exists. In a paper-based clearinghouse situation, for example, the Justice Department probably would take the position that those are natural monopolies, although promoting the idea of competition among ordinary clearinghouses.

PHILLIPS: The issue is really more complicated. You can have a shared system where the sharing is at the terminal; or you can have a shared system, even if the terminal is a proprietary terminal of one or a few financial institutions. If switching—sharing—is done through the computer system of the host banks, it, in fact, opens up the system to others. One bank can own the terminal and still have sharing. Card numbers, presumably, will tell the operating system to which bank to go. You use a card at one terminal. It may go directly to Bank *A*. Bank *A* does the switching through the hierarchy of switching that goes on through the system. It is a shared system, but here the sharing and access to it by a variety of financial institutions comes from the switching gear, not because the particular terminal is a shared terminal. Sharing can be at any level in the hierarchy of switching in the system. In addition, the lines used are telecommunications lines: satellite or microwave relay arrangements, regular telephone lines, etc. This makes it look very much like AT&T will be tremendously involved in EFT. AT&T is currently very interested in various sorts of terminals. They have had a history of attempting to control telephone terminal devices and will probably offer EFT terminals, too.

IBM is also moving into the area. If the computer is an IBM computer or of another manufacturer, the manufacturer will have an interest in software compatibility and in terminal facilities. IBM is, of course, moving in this direction, but it has a very small share.

BERNARD SHULL: In this movement toward EFTs, do you visualize any very substantial, or radical, institutional changes?

PHILLIPS: Yes, I do. And one of the reasons I think the reports of the CMC and Heller and Hunt and FIA and FINE and FRA are more relevant today is that they would allow freedom for existing financial institutions to adapt to the new system.

There is bound to be a shaking out. The electronics technology is emerging very fast. And even if you had the most sagacious managers of financial institutions that you could find—an assumption I would like to make—when the technology is changing so rapidly, decisions as to the when, where, and how of utilization of that technology and the associated marketing can result in an awful lot of managerial errors. Take the Glendale experience, for example. Sears, Roebuck went to a terminal system on Singer machines. What did Singer do? Went out of business! Somebody goes to a GE system, and GE goes out of business! These are the kinds of unforeseeable problems that crop up. You just do not know where, when, and how to hook into the system. So, even if all of the 14,500 bank presidents are very wise men, they are bound to make mistakes in an environment of rapid technological change and increased competition.

I would not regard it as a terrible social disaster if the number of banks went gradually from 14,500 to half that number, but the Independent Bankers Association would not like it very much (any more than the brokers would). The new technology is going to replace the older ones, and some banks will not make the transition successfully.

SANFORD ROSE: I do not see why you say that the velocity of money under EFTS will pose a great problem for monetary control. Even if there is a rising trend in velocity, or a greater variability around that trend, I do not see why there is a control problem. There might be some sort of a cosmetic problem—they may have to reverse themselves more frequently—

but I do not think that would be a very serious problem.

PHILLIPS: The problem is similar to what occurred back in the twenties with respect to checks. Then, the argument was about what to do about checks. Are they part of $M$? Fisher said that we ought to look at the equation $MV$ plus $M_1V_1$, divided by $T$, where we have $M$ and $V$ for currency and $M_1V_1$ for checking accounts. If this were not done, of course, checks would have the effect of increasing the velocity of $M$.

What I am saying is that in the EFT environment, the potential for $V$ to change, and to change radically, is much greater. Of course, you can say, "I will not look at $M_1$ any more. I know its velocity has been going up. I will look at $M_1$ plus $M_2$, and maybe plus $M_3$, or something like that." While $V_1$ has been relatively unstable, $V_2$ has been stable, so far. But is it going to remain stable?

Suppose I can go from a savings account to a demand deposit by telephone within my own institution; and go from a thrift institution to my transaction balance in the bank virtually timelessly and costlessly; and go from the liabilities of other institutions to my transaction balance. All this may get us up to $M_{27}$, at which point I begin to worry about the pure monetarists saying, "Well, all we have to do is expand our definition of money and everything will be O.K." I think we will have real velocity problems as EFT emerges. It is useful to talk about controlling $M_1$ if $V_1$ is fairly constant because this will control total expenditures in the system, but if velocity can go all over the place, it is no longer a very useful framework.

PHILLIP CAGAN: I agree. Anything that allows people to cluster their spending more easily creates a policy problem. Aggregate spending in the economy becomes too high or too low at various times. There are lots of reasons why you get such variability in spending, which we observe as part of the business cycle. Governments have attempted to control the amount of this clustering on the grounds that such control would benefit everyone.

The gold standard was one answer to the problem, and we have created a lot of problems for ourselves by abandoning it. Presently, we are creating even more problems by going further away from gold. The EFTS is merely a new development of this trend. The process started long ago.

We initially controlled demand deposits in banks in order to provide some control over the amount of spending, but in recent years, that control has been eroded. There was a time when if you had a savings account in a commercial bank, you could not transfer funds from that account without going to the bank in person with your passbook. The idea was that no assets other than checking accounts and currency should be used as a medium of exchange. We wanted a monetary quantity that we could control. This is now being eroded by such things as phone transfers and NOW accounts. You can make a request over the telephone and have your funds that same afternoon. We are creating all kinds of substitutes for demand deposits. The EFTS simply takes another step. Even if we do not have EFTS, we are still developing problems.

The money supply $M_1$ today is about $300 billion, and we are transacting GNP of $1.5 trillion. Suppose it gets to the point where we have only $50 billion of $M_1$, and perhaps $1 billion of $M_2$, and GNP transactions of $1.5 trillion. You then have a very high velocity of money, and the possibility of clustering expenditures at points in time becomes greater.

ROSE: Yes, but the Fed gets continuous reports on the state of the economy. Presumably, it can still adjust the monetary base to compensate for such changes in velocity.

CAGAN: Yes, the Federal Reserve will continue to have its traditional controls. But EFTS will make it a lot easier for the economy to disregard, to a considerable extent, the intended effects of the controls on spending.

What do we do about this trend? The old answer was: "Do not allow money substitutes. Keep institutions from offering anything that looks like a checking account." We also said: "If you are going to offer anything that looks like a checking account, you must be a member of the Federal

Reserve and you will have to observe reserve requirements." There was never an inalienable right to offer checkable deposits, or money. The original purpose of the government intervention in this area was to control the quantity of money.

Professor Phillips suggests that we can avoid the problem by making checking accounts more attractive, and thereby stabilizing their quantity. I do not believe that will be enough. The interest rate offered on them will probably not be adaptable enough. If you see people spending too much, presumably you induce them to stop spending and hold checking accounts by suddenly increasing the interest rate on checking accounts. How do you operate and obtain the results fast enough?

VICKREY: But if you increase the rate on checking accounts, you will increase other interest rates, and you will slow down investments.

CAGAN: Yes, you will affect interest rates, but not directly, only if you can produce a change in the quantity of money. Under the present system, you change the quantity of money, and that affects people's spending. Under Professor Phillips' proposal, you change the interest rate on checking accounts, and that, supposedly, will induce people to change the amount of such accounts they want to hold, and, finally, spend. It is more roundabout and, very likely, much slower.

EDWARDS: Professor Phillips is saying that we already have these problems and that, when we go on to EFTS, they will become worse. Professor Cagan's point, as I understand it, is that we should not go in that direction at all. We should go back and prevent the creation of substitutes for demand deposits.

CAGAN: We cannot turn the clock back, and we cannot stop EFTS, nor should we give up such greater efficiency of transactions. But there is reason to worry that the monetary system will not be anchored to anything, and the implications for the price level are not clear. We need to find a way to allow improvements like EFTS and, at the same time, maintain control over the quantity of the medium of exchange by sharply limiting the growth of assets that are close substitutes for whatever assets we call and control as money.

## CHAPTER SEVEN

# Credit Allocation Schemes: Truths and Fictions

## CREDIT ALLOCATION AND HOUSING

Stanley Diller, *Bond Portfolio Strategist, Goldman, Sachs & Co.*

In current usage, the term *credit allocation* covers the many programs through which government tries to influence the allocation of resources by channeling credit toward desired uses. Government does not try to control credit, as such, but rather, to change the way money is spent or—which comes to the same thing—the way real resources are allocated. In housing, for example, government tries to keep credit cheap in order to boost housing demand and construction. Most housing programs focus on the amount of credit offered to would-be home buyers; the price of credit is left to market forces. In some cases, government agencies use the funds obtained through open-market borrowing to buy mortgages or lend to those that do; in others, thrift institutions are given various tax incentives to favor mortgage investments. Government policies to channel public deposits into thrift institutions are also part of the housing program.

These programs run counter to a key proposition in credit theory, namely, that credit is fungible. It is not possible—in theory or in practice—to isolate segments of the credit market for the purpose of changing the balance of supply and demand forces in these segments. Increased government borrowing raises rates in the government sector and attracts funds from other sectors of the market, causing the rates in these sectors to go up as well. Buying mortgages with the proceeds from government borrowing lowers mortgage rates and deters other mortgage investors. The net effect is a standoff that changes the cast of characters in each market without affecting the amount and the cost of credit. Evidence to this effect is given in the next section.

The author wishes to acknowledge the support provided by Citibank and to thank the following for their help: Paul Derosa, Thomas Barneby, Mary Mongibelli, John Winder, and Robert McGill.

The argument is less definitive when the credit programs include subsidies. Lowering the cost of a given type of credit—e.g., mortgage credit or municipal credit—should increase the use of this type of credit. But keep in mind that the purpose of credit programs is to change final spending; credit is merely a tool. Lowering the cost of mortgage credit can increase mortgage lending without affecting housing construction. A home mortgage is merely a loan collateralized by a house. The house can be old or new. If the mortgage rate is subsidized, homeowners can refinance their homes; buyers can make a smaller down payment to take advantage of the cheap credit. In other words, subsidizing mortgage credit need not lead to more housing: instead, it could lead to more loans against existing houses. We cannot say for sure that there would be no additional construction from subsidized mortgage credit; we *can* say that the value of the additional construction would be far less than the amount of new mortgage money resulting from the subsidy. A subsidy directly on the purchase price would lead to more housing per subsidy dollar and fewer arbitrary windfalls than a credit subsidy.

These arguments follow from the fact that credit is fungible. Credit fungibility permits investors to look beyond the superficial differences among securities in pursuit of the basic goals of high yields and low risk. Further, because all loans ultimately lead to cash, borrowers can transform an apparently designated loan into a source of general funds. In other words, the borrower pools the cash obtained from all sources. By definition, cash is fungible.

The same can be said of funds supplied to financial institutions. Thrift deposits do not lead directly to mortgages. If additional evidence for this point were needed, surely it stands out in the failure of housing starts to respond to the sharp increase in thrift deposits in 1976. Instead, the deposits were used to acquire government securities and to pay off government advances to the thrifts. The point is that the thrifts have enough control over their spending to separate effectively the variability of deposits from that of mortgage lending.

The above examples of the fungibility of credit speak to the ineffectiveness of credit allocation programs. Our analysis suggests that because of credit fungibility, the desirable effects of these programs are, at best, not worth the cost or at worst, nonexistent. When their side effects are also taken into consideration, these programs look even worse: Credit allocation is inherently regressive. Most of the programs work through financial intermediaries, on whom less wealthy households and businesses rely more than their wealthier counterparts. Wealth gives people more financial alternatives. If intermediaries are discouraged from making certain kinds of loans or from giving customers a full return on their investments, they will lose the business of their wealthy customers. But less fortunate customers have nowhere else to go. Small savers cannot beat the controlled deposit rate, no matter how high other rates may be. As a result, less wealthy households and businesses disproportionately bear the brunt of these programs.

Curiously, this point is lost on some observers, who in other matters show a healthy regard for the smaller players in the economic game. It is left to the Federal Reserve Board to deplore the regressivity of these programs. The Board's former chairman, Arthur Burns, has testified to this effect many times.

While the fungibility of credit and the regressive distributive effects of credit allocation programs are fundamental to the general question of credit allocation, a third topic closely identified with the issue is housing. Housing is the real reason behind much of the demand for credit allocation and serves as a case study of the misunderstandings that have led to the demand for credit allocation. Our aim in dealing with this topic is to separate the matter of housing from the matter of credit. Any housing problem that exists is unrelated to credit. The controlling question in housing is the *demand for houses,* not the *supply of credit.* Cheap credit, at best, is an anodyne for the fortunate people who already own or can afford to own a house; for the others, it is a bane. In any case, to improve the mortgage market, it makes more sense to encourage its integration with the capital market than to magnify its separation.

## FUNGIBILITY OF CREDIT

### Credit Markets

Programs to allocate credit come in conflict with the relentless pursuit of maximum portfolio returns by all types of investors. Government may wish to support some group by buying or causing others to buy certain securities. Other things being equal, the increased demand for the securities would raise their price and lower their yield. Rather than accept a lower yield, private investors will switch into securities whose demand has not been inflated artificially. If these investors took as many dollars out of the market as government put in, they would neutralize the allocation program. As for the increased demand in the market into which the private investors fled, that, too, should be neutralized by the increased supply of government securities used to finance the program.

The counterattack by investors illustrates the fungibility of credit. Investors are wedded not to any security but to a desired yield to which they cling long after they have abandoned the security. Substitution by insurance companies of agency securities for mortgages illustrates the point. In this event, the program comes full circle, an exchange of paper that leaves intact the underlying credit flows. At other times, the exchange is less direct but no less telling.

One common allocation method channels public funds into institutions on whom pressure is brought to make investments in which the government is interested. These programs cannot evade the fungibility of credit. First, the government is hard pressed to control the institutions' access to funds. As shown below, the public is willing to shift into higher yielding assets when deposit rates fall behind. No amount of huckstering on behalf of these institutions and their purported aims can stifle the public's pursuit of a fair return on its savings. Second, credit is fungible even within the institutions. No matter how cheaply the funds are obtained, they merely contribute to the pool of funds the institutions are pledged to deploy on behalf of their depositors. Third, the funds are fungible to the final borrower, as well. He, too, tries to minimize borrowing costs and maximize investment yield. For these reasons, the government's grip on credit flows is largely verbal, lacking as it does control over the incentives that govern behavior. Two factors underlie the subversive impact of the fungibility of credit on credit allocation programs.

First, the government cannot preempt a sufficient share of any credit market to forestall neutralizing actions by the remaining part of the market. The contest between the two sides is evident in government's traditional interest in modifying the term structure. At times, it tries to raise the short rate in relation to the long rate, ostensibly to discourage foreign outflow of short-term capital while encouraging domestic investment. At other times, it tries to keep the short rate relatively low to dissuade thrift deposits from seeking a higher return. These efforts are doomed by the relatively modest share of United States Treasury debt to total debt (about 15 percent). The attempt to raise the short-term rate relative to the long-term would encourage private issuers of short-term securities to lengthen their debt in order to avoid the higher short-term borrowing costs. Private long-term borrowers would increase the size of their offering at the now lower long-term rate, investing the excess cash receipts in short-term securities at the higher rate. Of course, investors also would react along the lines already noted. In combination, these actions would overwhelm the government's program.

Second, investors are more willing to vary their holdings in pursuit of higher yields than generally is thought. Their failure to completely equalize yields on different securities, by changing their portfolio, is misunderstood. The persistence of yield differentials and the strong preference by some types of investors for certain securities are consistent with yield maximizing behavior. Investors respond not to nominal yields but to *effective* yields, that is, the yields to them after taxes and operating costs and after allowance for the (risk) characteristics of different securities. The interplay among these factors gives rise to nominal yield differentials that equalize yields at the margin. In other words, at this point, no investor can improve his bottom line by switching his portfolio.[1]

---

1. In this context, risk is a form of negative yield. A more risky security must have a higher nominal yield in order to equalize its effective yield.

Not all investors will shift into higher yielding securities when relative rates change, because not all of them are at the margin. For example, a rise in the commercial paper rate relative to the rate on savings deposits entices some investors to switch before others. The ones moving first have the lowest transactions costs—generally, those with large portfolios—and the least taste for the convenience of a savings account. Similarly, a rise in the corporate bond rate will not entice insurance companies to forgo their comparative advantage in private placements until the public rate rises enough to offset the premium available to them. In other words, differences between effective and nominal rates vary with the conditions of investors. These differences lead to thresholds of investors' reactions to changes in yields. Investors near the margin of indifference between securities react to small changes in rates; their threshold, the magnitude of change required for them to move, is small. Investors with a greater stake in existing holdings have a large threshold. But virtually all investors have *some* threshold; there are some offers they cannot refuse.

The sizes of these thresholds determine the success of government attempts to divert credit flows. They determine what changes in yields the market will tolerate before offsetting flows occur. Larger thresholds imply more segmented markets within which yields are more susceptible to government influence. In contrast, smaller thresholds keep relative yields within narrower limits. The thresholds are analogous to thermostats and related controls, which set the bounds within which an equilibrium state is permitted to move.

Suppose, for example, government tried to force down utility bond yields with a buying program. As yields fell, some investors would substitute industrials for utilities, taking advantage of the higher prices on utilities. The first to move would be the investors with the lowest threshold, the least preference for utilities. If government bought through this first line of defense and opened greater yield spreads, it would entice investors with greater thresholds, that is, those less disposed to alter their portfolios. The first group of investors could be professionals trading for eighths and quarters. As they exhausted their supply of securities—and their capacity for short selling—their offering prices would rise, thereby opening up greater yield differentials. Other investors would comb their attics for securities to sell. There is no way the government could sustain the utility rate below rates on comparable securities.

## Consumer Flexibility

Traditionally, households have chosen the convenience and liquidity of savings accounts over marketable securities. Their use of thrift deposits merely reflects their preference for convenience and liquidity in light of yield differentials with alternate savings vehicles. During most of the postwar period before 1966, the average rate paid by savings and loan associations exceeded the commercial paper rate (see Figure 7-1). When the differential rose, for the first time during 1966 and then later during successive credit crises, the cost of convenience and liquidity grew. Households with enough funds to acquire short-term securities switched from savings accounts. Figure 7-2 depicts the inverse relationship between changes in annual increases in holdings by the household sectors of thrift deposits and of short-term government agency securities. Before 1965, this relationship barely is noticeable because the flows barely changed. In other words, the holdings of both agencies and savings accounts grew at relatively constant rates between 1953 and 1965. After that, as interest rates began to rise, holdings of the two types of assets fluctuated. The changes in the flows were about equal in size and opposite direction, suggesting a high degree of substitutability between the savings forms.[2]

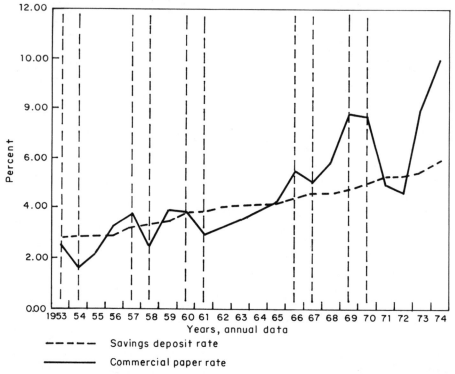

— — — — Savings deposit rate

————— Commercial paper rate

FIGURE 7-1  Interest rates on commercial paper and savings deposits. Note: The interest on commercial paper is an annual average of monthly data of the 90-day dealer placed commercial paper rate. (SOURCES: *Commercial paper rate: Board of Governors of the Federal Reserve System*, Federal Reserve Bulletin, *vol. 62, no. 1, Jan. 1976. Savings deposit rate: United States League of Savings Associations,* Savings and Loan Association Fact Book, *Average Annual Yield on Savings Accounts in Savings Associations.*)

---

2. Changes in flows are shown in the chart in order to avoid the effects of strong trends in both series. Only accounts that are large enough to cover the minimum denominations available on market securities can chase after higher yields. The smaller accounts have no alternative but to continue their trend. This trend dominates the data.

Policy loans obtained by customers of life insurance companies are another form of savings withdrawal. The interest rates on these loans are fixed by law at the time the policies are written. When market rates rise above these fixed rates, many policyholders elect to borrow in order to invest at the higher market rate or to substitute for higher cost loans from the usual sources. The flow of policy loan disintermediation is described in Figure 7-3. The evidence strongly supports the proposition that investors are willing to rearrange their portfolios in favor of higher yielding assets. When administered rates are set too low, credit will flow out of these areas.

Another example of the responsiveness of private investors to market conditions is given by the relationship between the fraction of short-term assets held by households in the form of savings deposits and the differential between average rates paid on thrift deposits and the commercial paper rate. (Due to the unavailability of thrift deposit rates on a quarterly basis, the rate paid by commercial banks on savings accounts was used. The substitution does not affect the substance of the results.) This relationship is shown in the accompanying regression, which relates changes in the ratio of savings deposits to total short-term assets

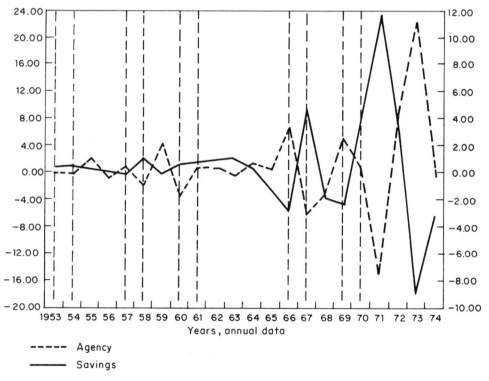

-- -- -- Agency

———— Savings

**FIGURE 7-2  Annual changes in household ownership of thrift deposits and short-term government securities, in billions of dollars.** (SOURCE: *Board of Governors of the Federal Reserve System,* Flow of Funds Accounts, 1946-1975: First Differences of Flows, U.S. Government Agency Securities and Deposits at Thrift Institutions Held by Households, *pp. 10-12.*)

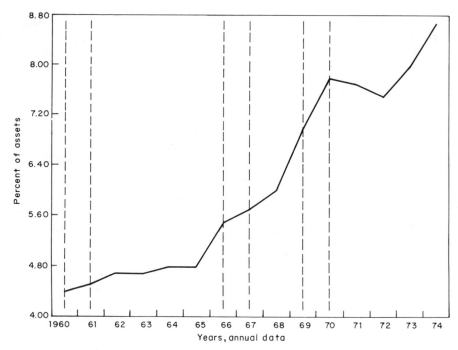

**FIGURE 7-3    Policy loans.** (SOURCE: *Institute of Life Insurance,* Life Insurance Fact Book, *p. 79.*)

to rate differentials just noted. In addition, since the flows of funds into savings accounts have a strong seasonal component, seasonal dummy variables are added.[3]

$$\frac{\text{Savings accounts}}{\text{Short-term assets}} = \underset{(-5.32)}{-.67} + \underset{(3.94)}{.34}(R_t - R_{cp}) + \underset{(9.17)}{1.63D_1} + \underset{(8.63)}{1.54D_2} + \underset{(2.80)}{.50D_3} \text{(1)}$$

$$R^2\text{adj.} = .74$$
$$\text{Durbin-Watson} = 2.24$$
$$(t - \text{values in parenthesis})$$

where $\dfrac{\text{Savings accounts}}{\text{short-term assets}}$ = ratio of savings accounts held by house-hold sector to total short-term assets held by household sector.

---

**3.** *Dependent Variable:* Board of Governors of the Fed. Reserve System, *Flow of Funds Accounts 3rd Quarter 1975, Household Sector* [hereinafter cited as *Quarterly Flow of Funds*]. *Independent Variable:* Thrift Rate—*Federal Reserve Survey of Total Time and Savings Deposits*—average of most common rate paid on savings and consumer-type time deposits. Data prior to 1967 is based on Federal Reserve Bank of Chicago, *Survey of Total Time and Savings Deposits.* Commercial Paper Rate—Fed. Reserve Bull., Table A26, "Money Market Rates."

$R_t - R_{cp}$ = interest rate on commercial bank savings deposits minus commercial paper rate.

$D_1, D_2, D_3$ = seasonal dummy variables for first, second, and third quarters, respectively.

The predicted value of the savings ratio in, say, the third quarter is equal to $(-.67 + .50) + .34$ times (interest differential); and for the fourth quarter, it is $-.67 + .34$ times (interest differential).

The regression, run with quarterly data from 1953 to mid-1975, indicates that for each percentage point increase in the thrift rate relative to the commercial paper rate, the short-term assets held in the form of savings accounts increase by .34 percentage points relative to total short-term assets.

## Institutional Flexibility

Financial institutions also display more flexibility in their investment choices than generally is thought. The innate characteristics of certain institutions, legal constraints, and conventional yield spreads among securities inspire portfolio choices that become identified with the type of institution. These choices are not rigid. They are products of the facts facing the institution at a given time. As the facts change, the portfolio decisions adapt.

An instance of a large change in an institutional portfolio is given by the decline in life insurance company holdings of 1 to 4 family residential mortgages relative to total assets. Figure 7-4 compares the interest rates on new home mortgages with the Aa utility rate. Until 1965, the mortgage rate maintained a premium over the utility rate, often in excess of a percentage point. Beginning in 1965, the gap between the two rates closed and by 1968 disappeared altogether, after which the two series more or less overlap. Figure 7-5 shows insurance companies' holdings of 1 to 4 family residential mortgages as a percentage of their total assets. The life companies started to lighten their holdings of these mortgages in the early 1960s, but did so much more rapidly beginning in 1966, when the gap between the mortgage rate and the utility rate narrowed. After that point, holdings of 1 to 4 family residential mortgages declined rapidly. From an average in the 1950s of about 20 percent of their portfolio, the percentage fell to less than 9 percent by 1974.

## Commercial Banks' Access to Funds

Commercial banks' access to funds is affected by Federal Reserve controls on interest rates and reserves. These controls influence the banks' ability to compete for funds. During recent high interest rate periods, beginning with the one in 1966, banks had difficulty holding deposits at controlled interest rates in the face of higher market rates. Between the fourth quarter of 1968 and the first of 1970, the volume of certificates of deposit (CDs) was reduced by more than half. As described below, banks sought to replace these funds from uncontrolled sources. Such activities and the Federal Reserve's responses illustrate the fungibility of credit.

The banks had been increasing their use of the Eurodollar market to raise funds for credit demands and to offset runoffs of CDs since 1966. By 1969, borrowings had risen to $15 billion. To counter this evasion of interest rate ceilings, the Fed imposed, effective September 1969, a 10 percent marginal reserve requirement on net liabilities to foreign branches that exceeded the daily average outstanding amounts in the four weeks ended May 28. As the cost of Eurodollars rose, the banks turned to the domestic money markets to raise nondeposit funds. A few large banks had issued unsecured short-term notes in 1966, but the Fed quickly amended Regulations D and Q so that the paper was treated as a deposit and therefore subject to reserve requirements and rate ceilings. But bank-holding-company paper was not covered by such regulation. Bank holding companies and other bank affiliates began borrowing in the commercial paper market during 1969. They, in turn, used the funds to purchase loans and investments from the affiliated banks.

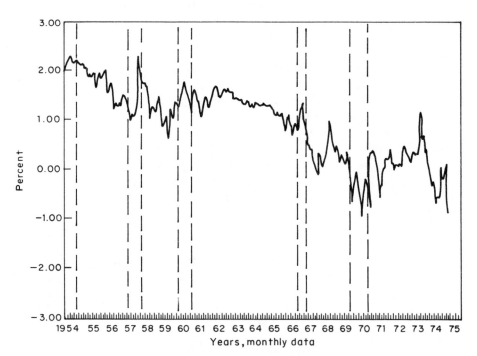

**FIGURE 7-4  Interest rate differential between new home mortgages and Aa utilities.** (SOURCES: *FHA-HUD Conventional New Home Mortgage Rate,* Federal Reserve Bulletin, *Table A43, "Term and Yields on New Home Mortgages"; Aa Utility Rate: Citibank Corp.*)

Bank-related commercial paper outstanding grew from a $1.2 billion level in June 1969 (first available numbers) to $7.8 billion in just a year.

Again, the Fed reacted to the circumvention. On August 17, 1970, it announced that, effective October 1, all funds raised in this way by member banks from affiliates were subject to reserve requirements, thereby reducing the attractiveness of this source of funds. Banks also tried to use loan repurchase agreements (RPs) with their nonbank corporate customers in 1969. These, too, were not subject to reserve requirements or interest rate ceilings. The Fed again stepped in, and, effective August 28, 1969, amended Regulations D and Q to provide that RPs entered into with anyone other than a bank and on any asset except United States government and/or United States agency securities would be classified as deposits subject to regulation. On May 16, 1973, the Fed suspended rate ceilings on all maturities of large CDs and imposed marginal reserve requirements on issues of CDs of more than $10 million. However, small deposits still were subject to regulation. As a result, banks lost deposits once more in the 1973–1974 period as interest rates reached postwar highs. Those commercial banks with the most alternatives were able to cope the best.

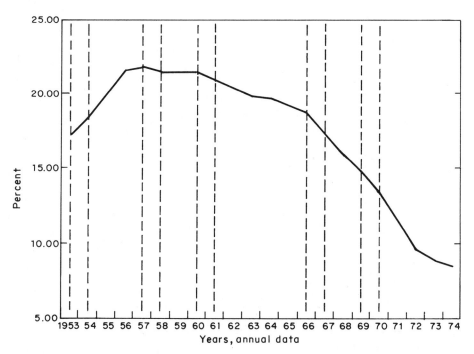

**FIGURE 7-5  Insurance companies' ratio of holdings of 1 to 4 family residential mortgages to total assets. (**SOURCES: *Board of Governors of the Federal Reserve System,* Flow of Funds Accounts, 1946–1975: *Home Mortgages Held by Life Insurance Companies, pp. 146–148; Total Assets of Life Insurance Companies, pp. 125–127.*)

The goal of credit allocation is not to control credit itself but final spending. This goal, also, is thwarted by fungibility. Borrowers who wish to acquire different forms of capital equipment do not care where they obtain their funds. Within reasonable bounds of convenience, they are concerned mainly with borrowing at the lowest cost. Hence, the expansion of a given credit form need not signify anything about a corresponding growth of real assets. If mortgages, for example, were to become a very low-cost form of borrowing, households and even businesses would do all they could to meet their financing needs for any purpose by expanding their mortgage debt. The effect of this strategy would be to raise the ratio of mortgage debt to the housing stock. In fact, mortgages already are a relatively low-cost source of funds. Not surprisingly, there is substantial evidence to indicate that mortgages are used as an all-purpose credit form.

The variation in the loan-to-value ratio is shown in Figure 7-6. Between 1952 and 1965, the ratio of the mortgage debt outstanding to the value of the housing stock rose continuously from less than 25 percent to almost 45 percent. After that, it declined somewhat through the first quarter of 1971 and gently rose to the present. A similar picture

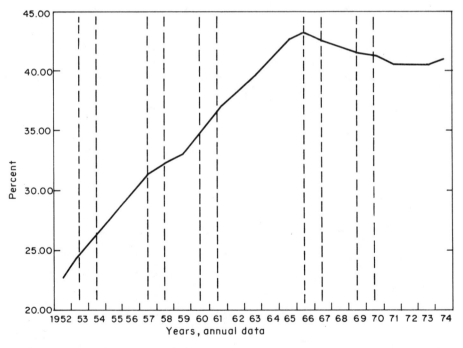

**FIGURE 7-6  Ratio of mortgage debt to housing stock.** (sources: *Mortgage Debt Outstanding: Board of Governors of the Federal Reserve System,* Flow of Funds Accounts, 1946–75, pp. 146–148; *Value of Housing Stock: John C. Musgrave,* "New Estimates of Residential Capital in the United States, 1925–1973," Survey of Current Business, *vol. 54, no. 10, Oct. 1974, pp. 32–38.*)

is given in Figure 7-7, which plots the ratio of changes in net mortgage

debt outstanding to outlays on new 1 to 4 family residential housing, including land costs. The ratio doubled from about .4 to about .8 between 1952 and 1964, declined to about .6 in 1970, and rose from there to well over 1.[4]

Figure 7-8 plots the difference between the consumer installment credit rate and the new home mortgage rate. The mortgage rate declined relative to the consumer loan rate through 1965, the period of steep rise in the mortgage loan-to-value ratio. After that, the mortgage rate rose relative to the consumer rate, a period in which the loan-to-value ratio was fairly flat.[5]

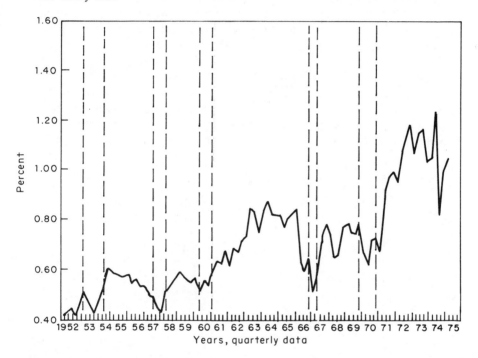

**FIGURE 7-7   Ratio of mortgage debt to aggregate outlays (including cost of land but excluding home improvement expenditures) on residential investment.** (SOURCES: *Mortgage Debt Outstanding: Board of Governors of the Federal Reserve System,* Flow of Funds Accounts, 1946–1975, *pp. 146–148; Outlays on New 1 to 4 Family Housing: Bernard Gelb,* Mortgage Debt for Non-Real Estate Purposes, *The Conference Board, New York, 1972, p. 78.*)

---

4. Mortgage Debt Outstanding: Board of Governors of the Fed. Reserve System, *Flow of Funds Accounts, 1946–1975,* pp. 146–148. Value of Housing Stock: Musgrave, "New Estimates of Residential Capital in the United States, 1925–1973," 54, Survey of Current Business, No. 10, pp. 32–38 (Oct. 1974); Outlays on New 1- to 4-Family Housing: Gelb, *Mortgage Debt for Non-Real Estate Purposes,* 78 (Conference Board, New York 1972). (Follow-up data obtained by telephone.)

5. Interest Rate on Consumer Installment Debt: Estimated series obtained from Citibank. New Home Mortgage Rate: FHA-HUD Conventional New Home Mortgage Rate, Fed. Reserve Bull., Table A43, "Term and Yields on New Home Mortgages."

The general impression one gets from Figures 7-6 and 7-7 is of a rising use of mortgage funds. The discussion that follows attempts to put this phenomenon in perspective. Three influences act on the aggregate loan-to-value ratio: (1) the size of the down payment; (2) the refinancing of mortgages; and (3) the turnover of houses. Since mortgages provide one of the least expensive forms of household debt, the mortgagor has a clear incentive to minimize his down payment in the event he needs borrowed funds for other purposes, like the purchase of securities.

A major deterrent to greater use of mortgage borrowing for general purposes is the large, front-ended administrative cost connected with refinancing a mortgage. Since the procedure involves terminating the outstanding mortgage and creating a new one, the costs are comparable with those encountered in the closing on the purchase of a house, one of the more expensive paper rituals. Unless the loan involves a substantial sum over a long period, the front-end fees likely are prohibitive, even in comparison with the higher interest rates payable on installment loans. There is little question that a decline in these largely gratuitous costs would stimulate mortgage refinancing for much broader purposes.

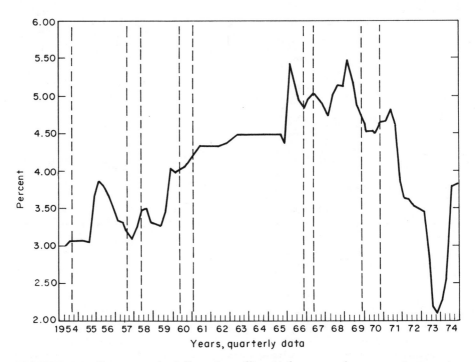

**FIGURE 7-8  Consumer installment credit rate less new home mortgage rate.**
(SOURCES: *Interest Rate on Consumer Installment Debt: estimated series obtained from Citibank Corp. New Home Mortgage Rate: FHA-HUD Conventional New Home Mortgage Rate,* Federal Reserve Bulletin, *Table A43, "Term and Yields on New Home Mortgages."*)

The major reason for the increased loan-to-value ratio on residential housing is the turnover of existing houses. As a result of the appreciation of houses, as well as the amortization of outstanding mortgages, the size of the buyer's mortgage very likely exceeds the outstanding balance on the seller's. Even if the seller applies his proceeds to the purchase of a new house, the size of his down payment likely is less than the difference between the amounts of the buyer's new mortgage and the one he retires. Often, the seller will purchase another existing house and apply the net proceeds (after mortgage retirement) of the earlier sale to improvement of his newly purchased house. Even allowing for that, sellers, on balance, come away with cash from their housing transactions. Surely, that is the case when an estate disposes of a house and distributes the proceeds to the government and the heirs. Often, a family whose head is nearing or in retirement will exchange its existing house, on which the outstanding mortgage may be quite small, for a smaller house or even a rental unit. The buyer of the family's house will obtain a mortgage that reflects its current market value. The balance on the existing mortgage likely will be smaller because its original size reflected the value of the house before its subsequent appreciation and because it has been reduced by amortization.

## HOUSING

### Introduction

Housing is the major focus of credit allocation programs currently in force—and underlies many of the ones proposed as well. Its importance stems from the assumed influence of credit on housing and of housing on the overall economy. In no other sector of the economy is credit given such a central role. The argument in this section is that credit is not the source of any housing problem. Increasing the volume of credit at market rates will not boost construction activity because sufficient credit already is available, and always has been, for those willing to pay the market rate. As noted previously, forcibly shifting funds from one market to another does not work. It is unfair—and futile—to channel the funds of small savers at low interest rates to thrift institutions in the hope that the funds *somehow* would increase the supply and lower the cost of mortgage money. Far from increasing construction, this policy merely deprives small savers of a fair return and managers of thrift institutions of the incentive to develop market-tested products. The recriminations that follow the withdrawal of thrift deposits when market interest rates increase also introduce an irrelevant issue to the debate on monetary policy that obfuscates the important questions. The same amount of credit would be absorbed by the housing industry regardless of interest rate ceilings on deposits and of the federal agency programs that largely offset the ill effects of these ceilings.

People borrow in order to buy something; they do not buy something because they have borrowed. (They buy skis because they want to ski; they do not ski *because* they have skis.) For this reason, the demand for credit is called a derived demand; it is derived from the underlying demand for the product to be acquired with the borrowed funds. When this demand is present, availability of funds is no problem: If some borrowers were deprived temporarily, they would bid up the rate slightly to attract funds. Why should lenders care whether their loans are used to buy houses or anything else?

The main thesis of this section is that the volume of mortgage credit in use is determined by the demand for houses—not the other way around. To increase the demand for mortgage credit for housing use, it is necessary to increase the demand for houses. People do not buy houses simply because they are able to obtain a mortgage. This point would be deemed trivial in any area besides housing. Why not for housing? Because in housing, a theory is acceptable only if it does not discuss the price of the house. Yet, it is to the increase in prices to which one must turn for an explanation of the secular slowdown in home building activity.

## Secular Demand for Housing

It is important to distinguish between the demand for housing *services* and the demand for housing *stock*. The first is a question of consumption, comparing the gain in satisfaction from an additional dollar's worth of housing service with that from, say, automotive service. In this connection, it makes no difference whether the house is bought or rented, or whether it is a single-family or a multiple-family house. Rather, the question is one of how much to spend on living quarters instead of on something else. In contrast, the desired stock of housing involves investment rather than consumption. Here, the relevant comparison is with other sources of income (i.e., other assets), not with other objects of consumption—for example, whether to buy a house yielding a certain rental income (either payments from tenants or the imputed income of an owner-occupied dwelling) or to buy a bond or other capital asset. This question concerns not how much to spend on housing services but, rather, how to invest one's money.

There is no underlying demand for housing stock as such, but only for housing services. In this respect, housing is like a machine. A company does not need machines, per se, but only the services provided by them. It can obtain these services through buying the machines, leasing them at various terms, or even buying output from others who have them. The decision *whether* to obtain the services of machines depends upon factors different from those governing the decision of *how* to obtain these services.

The demand for housing services largely depends upon three considerations—income, price, and demographic factors. The trends in these variables account for most of the secular demand for housing services. The consensus among researchers is that the demand for housing services increases in proportion to increases in household income and decreases in proportion to increases in price.[6] Leaving aside demographic factors, which do not bear on this study, the demand for housing services involves the interplay of income and price effects: the first generally causing upward pressure and the second, downward pressure on demand.

While the consumer is concerned with the choice between housing services and other forms of consumption, the investor wishes to obtain the best return on his investment. A prospective home owner must deal with both decisions: how much of his income to devote to housing service, and whether to obtain this service from an owned or a rented house. Clearly, the second is an investment decision, since the person in question has the alternative of buying a security with the funds he otherwise would apply to the house, and applying the income from the security to the rental on a house.

In the normal course of events, growing population and growing per capita income put pressure on the existing housing stock. As vacancy rates decline, the competition for the remaining space drives up rents, including imputed rents on owner-occupied dwellings. The rising actual and imputed rental prices drive up the rate of return on the housing stock in place. As returns on the existing stock rise relative to the returns available on other assets, investors try to purchase existing houses in order to obtain the higher return. As investors bid for the higher-yielding asset, in this case the houses, they cause the price to rise. As a result, yields on houses fall, until they coincide with those of other assets with comparable risk.

But the prices on the existing housing stock cannot rise indefinitely. Except during brief transition periods, no one would pay more for an existing house than the cost of constructing a new one. Therefore, as the prices of existing stock overtake construction costs, they trigger new construction. Building programs take time. During the building period, the prices of existing assets could rise above construction costs. Those who pay these prices take losses when new buildings come on stream and drive down rents. There is a lot of money to be lost from this kind of miscalculation.[7]

---

6. Another way to state these points is as follows: The elasticity of demand with respect to income and price, respectively, is equal to one and minus one. See Muth, "The Demand for Non-Farm Housing," (Harberger, Ed., *The Demand for Durable Goods*, Univ. of Chicago Press, Chicago 1960).

7. Insufficient attention is given to the role of construction costs in setting the ceiling on the prices of existing houses. Artificial floors on construction costs raise the ceiling on the prices of existing stock. The reverse also is true: technological improvements in construction procedures, or other sources of lower costs, lower the price ceiling on existing stock. (Of course, other factors determine whether the existing stock sells at the ceiling.) One reason for the relatively poor market performance of prefabricated and modular housing, in spite of their sometime cost advantages, is their seemingly greater potential for cost-saving improvements in the comparison with on-site construction. The potentially lower building costs reduce the prospect for capital gain for owners of existing prefabs. The smaller potential gain reduces the expected rate of return on these houses and thereby discourages demand. The relationship between construction costs and the value of

The volume of residential construction activity after World War II reflects the combined influence of trends in household income and the price of housing services. In the five to eight years following the war, the sharp increase in household formation, together with the depletion of the housing stock during the war years, gave rise to a substantial boom in residential construction. Since that time, residential construction has accounted for a declining share of gross national product, except for the sharp housing boom during the early seventies. Figure 7-9 gives the ratio of fixed investment in residential structures to GNP in constant dollars.[8]

One thesis of this section is that the almost continuous decline in the share of GNP devoted to residential construction is due mainly to increasing costs of residential construction, not to a lack of credit or to declining consumer interest in housing.

EFFECT OF INCOME AND PRICE ELASTICITY

The following simulation illustrates this point. Assume that over a given period, the percentage change in the real housing stock depended upon the percentage change in real income and the percentage change in the relative costs of residential construction. That is

$$\Delta H_{real} = \Delta Y_{real} * E_y + \Delta P_{cstn} * E_p \qquad (2)$$

where $\Delta H_{real}$ = percentage change in real stock of housing
$\Delta Y_{real}$ = percentage change in real income
$E_y$ = income elasticity of demand for housing
$\Delta P_{cstn}$ = percentage change in relative cost of construction
$E_p$ = price elasticity of demand for housing

The simulation involves inserting the actual data for the changes in the real housing stock, real income, and relative prices. Then, the income elasticity is set to unity and the equation solved for the implicit value of the price elasticity; alternatively, the price elasticity is set to

---

existing stock makes for a community of interest between homeowners and the construction industry that likely helps explain the public's tolerance for restraints of trade in the construction industry. The more construction costs rise, the greater the potential capital gains on the existing stock.

8. The housing stock data are for the net value of private nonfarm, 1- to 4-family residential capital in billions of 1958 dollars; they are obtained and interpolated to produce a quarterly series, from Musgrave, N. 4 *supra*. The real income series used follows Milton Friedman's conception of permanent income as refined by Michael Darby in "The Allocation of Transitory Income Among Consumers' Assets," 62 American Econ. Rev., No. 5, pp. 928–941, Data Appendix (December 1972); all of which is based on real disposable income, taken from U.S. Dep't of Commerce, *Survey of Current Business, National Income Accounts of the United States*, Table 2.1. The relative cost of construction is the ratio of the price deflator for nonfarm residential structures and total GNP, *ibid*. at Table 8.1.

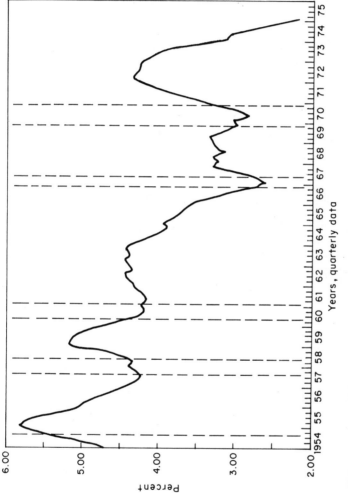

**FIGURE 7-9  Real residential, nonfarm expenditures as a percentage of real GNP.** (SOURCE: *U.S. Dept. of Commerce*, Survey of Current Business, National Income Accounts of the United States, Table 1.2.)

unity and the equation solved for the implicit value of the income elasticity. The objective is to discover whether the estimates of the implicit elasticities approximate unity, since that is the consensus value of both elasticities. If they do, the equation gives a simple and plausible explanation for the current status of housing. The results are as follows:

| | assume $E_y = 1$ | assume $E_p = 1$ |
|---|---|---|
| | implicit $E_p$ | implicit $E_y$ |
| 1947–1973 | −.68 | 1.05 |
| 1954–1973 | −1.18 | 0.97 |

The results are consistent with the proposition that the growth in the housing stock has not kept up with the growth in real income *because* the *relative* price of construction has been rising. As a result of rising construction costs, residential construction has accounted for a declining fraction of GNP.[9]

RISING CONSTRUCTION COSTS

Figure 7-10 shows the changes in the relative price of construction (i.e., the ratio of the price deflator for residential construction to the GNP deflator). Until the early sixties, the relative price of residential construction gradually declined, albeit modestly and from a high level.

---

9. Similar results obtain from regression analysis of the same data. Results for the following two regressions are given:

$$H = b_1 + b_2\,Y + b_3\,P + b_4\,r + u \qquad (3)$$

$$\frac{H}{Pop} = b_1 + b_2\frac{Y}{Pop} + b_3\,P + b_4\,r + y \qquad (4)$$

where $H$ = real housing stock
$\quad Y$ = real permanent income
$\quad P$ = relative price of construction
$\quad r$ = Baa interest rate
$\quad Pop$ = number of households

| regression | estimated | elasticities |
|---|---|---|
| | Y | P |
| (1) | 1.07 | −1.17 |
| (2) | .97 | −.95 |

| | $b_1$ | | $b_2$ | | $b_3$ | | $b_4$ | | | Durbin- |
|---|---|---|---|---|---|---|---|---|---|---|
| *Regression* | *coef* | *t* | *coef* | *t* | *coef* | *t* | *coef* | *t* | $R^2$ | *Watson* |
| 1 | 508.54 | 9.63 | 1.03 | 25.83 | −455.68 | −8.15 | −11.24 | −5.37 | .98 | .10 |
| 2 | 7.75 | 9.10 | .95 | 12.52 | − 6.59 | −6.81 | − .13 | −3.64 | .88 | .11 |

The Baa rate is from Moodys Investors Services. Data pertaining to the number of households are from the U. S. Bureau of the Census, *Current Population Reports,* Series P-20. Other sources are reported in *Flow of Funds Accounts,* Musgrave, and Gelb, N. 4 *supra.*

During this period, the decline in relative expenditures on residential

construction (Figure 7-9) also was modest. After that point, relative
prices started to rise and the relative position of construction declined.
(The housing boom of the early 1970s is considered below.)

The major factor behind rising construction costs has been labor
costs. Residential construction is highly labor intensive. In 1974, compensation of labor accounted for 77 percent of the value added (i.e.,
sales less purchased materials), compared with 57 percent for the nonfarm private economy as a whole.[10] While materials costs, particularly
lumber—which accounts for almost 40 percent of all materials and
equipment used in single-family houses, contributed to the recent rise
in construction prices, they were not the major factor for the whole
period in question.[11]

Figures 7-11(a), 7-11(b), and 7-11(c) describe the movement of labor
costs. In Figure 7-11(a), output per workhour, after having risen sharply
through the fifties, stopped growing for the remainder of the period.
With rising compensation rates (shown in Figure 7-11(b)), flat produc-

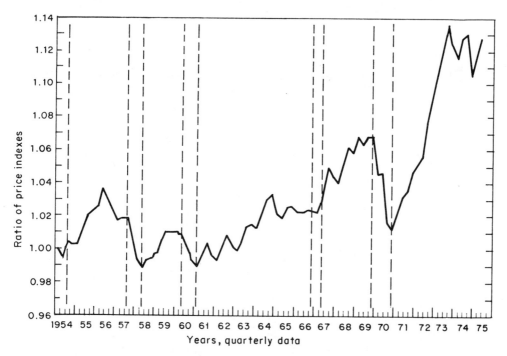

**FIGURE 7-10    Ratio of price index for nonfarm residential construction to price index
of GNP (1954=1.00).** (SOURCE: *U.S. Dept. of Commerce,* Survey of Current Business,
National Income Accounts of the United States, *Table 8.1.*)

10. *National Income Accounts,* N. 8 *supra* at Table 1.22.

11. One study of construction costs was especially useful: Ball, "Labor and Material Requirements for Construction of Private Single-Family Houses," Bureau of Labor Statistics, Bull.
1755, originally published in the Monthly Labor Rev. (Sept. 1971).

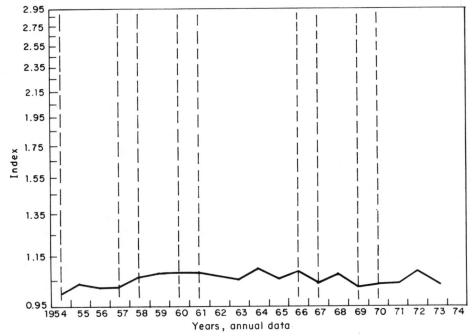

**FIGURE 7-11 (a) Index of output per workhour in contract construction
(1954=1.00). (**SOURCE: *U.S. Dept. of Labor, Bureau of Labor Statistics, unpublished
series.*)

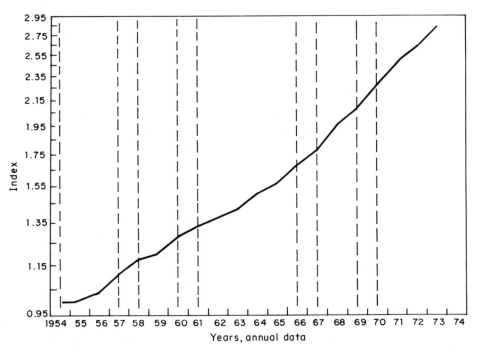

**FIGURE 7-11 (b) Index of compensation per workhour in contract construction
(1954=1.00). (**SOURCE: *U.S. Dept. of Labor, Bureau of Labor Statistics, unpublished
series.*)

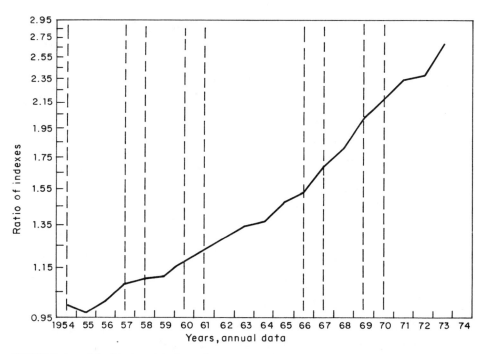

FIGURE 7-11 (c)   **Ratio of index of compensation per workhour to index of output per workhour (1954=1.00).** (source: *U.S. Dept. of Labor, Bureau of Labor Statistics, unpublished series.*)

tivity meant rising unit-labor costs, or higher labor costs per unit of output (shown in Figure 7-11(c)).

Reasons for the rising unit-labor costs are not hard to find. Technology is not available to make on-site construction a significantly more capital-intensive process. What capital substitutions *are* made arise from the use of purchased materials. As a result of increased capital intensity, technological improvements, and improved quality of labor throughout the economy, wage rates tend to rise. Industries experiencing less productivity growth are forced to pay wage rates that are pushed upward by rising productivity elsewhere in the economy. As a result, their unit-labor costs rise.

Another factor responsible for rising labor costs is the restrictive behavior of construction unions, which limit the number of eligible workers through nepotism and other discriminatory practices.[12]

---

**12.** The adverse impact of restricting entry into construction unions and trade groups (not to mention other employment syndicates like teamsters, municipal employees, and, in some respects, professional groups) is not limited to higher prices of housing. With members holding largely semiskilled and unskilled jobs, these groups constitute a growing fraction of the declining number of nonskilled jobs or, at least, jobs that do not require formal education. These jobs should be open to blacks and other low income groups who, with this opportunity, soon would become middle income groups. There is little question that the solution to our urban problems lies in opening up such jobs. Conversely, the cost of restricted entry must include a substantial part of the very large costs of our urban

The rising costs of construction ultimately affect the costs of owner-occupied housing services, as shown in Figure 7-12. Clearly, the rising relative costs of housing services discourage this form of consumption.[13]

## Cyclical Demand for Housing

The cyclical variation of construction activity has been a major political concern at most times and in most places. Yet, current discussion of the cycle is dominated by the relatively recent phenomenon of so-called disintermediation, and, more generally, the effect of monetary policy on the construction industry. Never mind that bank interest ceilings did not even exist before the thirties, while the construction cycle did; or that other countries finance mortgages differently without noticeably dampening the construction cycle. Still, one might infer from popular discussion that the whole problem would disappear if interest ceilings were abrogated (desirable though that may be on other grounds). What,

---

problem and the political malaise it engenders. But the adverse impact is not limited to the people denied entry into the employment groups. In many cases, members of the groups are enticed by the artificially high wages to work below their mental capacity and are discouraged from acquiring the education preparatory to more rewarding work. Moreover, society has to forgo the services these underemployed workers would have performed had they worked up to their capacity. Finally, the workers lock themselves into a good, but not great, situation with little to bequeath save co-option into the same situation.

13. The sharp decline in the relative price index for rentals (Figure 7-12) is both striking and informative. Part of the disparity between the relative price index for home ownership and for rentals is illusory. The homeowners' index includes interest charges, which, as noted above, the homeowner can recover. The rental index is not affected by the high nominal interest rate because competition among landlords excludes this recoverable cost from the rental price. The relative decline in the rental index likely is due to the increase in multiple-unit building activity at a time of relatively weak demand for urban residences where most apartments are located. During the late sixties and early seventies, the syndication of tax-sheltered real estate investments became popular. Investors who had relied upon tax-exempt bonds for tax-sheltered income suddenly were drawn into the depreciation game with the consequent overbuilding of multiple-unit dwellings. Coming on top of the falling demand for urban residences, this overbuilding brought about the sharp decline in relative rents.

The impact of taxes on the merits of ownership versus rental is a matter of some confusion. The simplistic idea that the tax-deductibility of mortgage interest payments favors ownership clearly ignores the similar advantage enjoyed by owners of multiple-unit dwellings. Competition among landlords would force this advantage into the rents. The more sophisticated, and accurate, view is that the advantage of ownership lies in the nontaxability of income in kind—like owner-occupied housing service. But, owners of multiple-unit dwellings have the right to depreciate their houses, often at accelerated rates. Moreover, since such owners are likely to be, on average, in a higher tax bracket than the average homeowner, the depreciation is worth more to them than the tax exemption is to the average homeowner. Again, competition should force these tax advantages into the rents. The upshot is that it is far from obvious what the net effect is of taxes on the relative merits of home ownership versus rental.

then, caused the construction cycles before interest ceilings? Before the Federal Reserve System? In other countries?

The thesis of this section is that the construction cycle is brought about by changes in the vigor with which prospective homeowners compete with other investors for the limited resources available—not just credit, but all resources.

During a business expansion, businessmen try to anticipate the increased demand for goods by laying claim to machines. The increased demand for machines stimulates the competition for credit and raises the real interest rate. In contrast, the demand for housing services does not rise as much. People do not change their housing style in response to what may prove to be temporary changes in income. When the interest rate rises above the service yield on houses, the value of the housing stock must decline, and with it the demand for credit with which to add to the stock. A stable demand for housing service leads to an unstable demand for housing stock because the real interest rate, used to discount the stream of housing services, varies with the unstable demand for machines.

The willingness of prospective home buyers to withdraw from the market temporarily is explained by the relatively low cost of postponing purchase. Forgoing one or two years' services of a house involves a

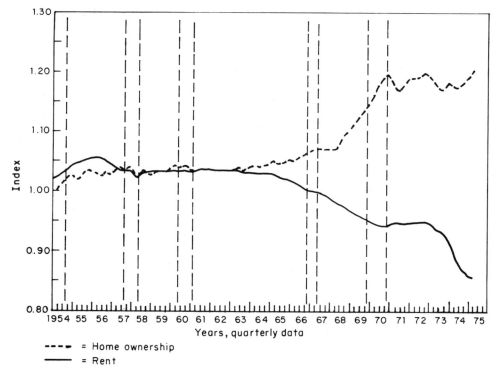

FIGURE 7-12 **Consumer price indexes of home ownership and rent (1954=1.00).** (SOURCE: Monthly Labor Review, *Nov. 1, 1975, Table 23.*)

minor loss over its long life. Moreover, this postponement enables the would-be home buyer to obtain the relatively high rates of return on the paper issued by business investors in machines. It is far less advisable to postpone the purchase of machines and forgo the advantage of immediacy. A profitable opportunity either is seized or lost to the competition. Lacking such desideratum, the would-be home buyer says, "Let them have the money."

In addition to competing for funds with which to acquire the machines, would-be buyers must compete for the machines as well. They compete in the speed with which they place their orders for the equipment. The longer they wait, the more likely the price of the goods will rise as capacity limits are reached, and the greater is the chance that they will be shut out entirely. Perceptions of cyclical advance tend toward uniformity among executives who are wired to the same media. Paying more for credit is less painful than losing one's place in the queue for machines.

In these circumstances, the national interest is served from postponement of residential construction. By encouraging such postponement, the rise in the real interest rate enables businessmen to obtain the credit with which to speed up their purchases of scarce machines and, thereby, to supply the products for which demand is less postponable. By altering the sequence of purchases, the variation in real interest rates allows a greater consumption of goods and services stretched over the whole cycle.

## Test of the Cyclical Housing Model

A direct test of the discursive housing model just described requires estimates of the expected rate of return on the housing stock and the real rate of interest. When the former exceeds the latter, construction of new homes should rise—the more so, one might expect, the greater the difference in the two rates. It is easy to devise a statistical model that uses this idea to predict expenditures on new homes. However, the data present a problem. There is no way to observe directly either the real rate of interest or the expected return on capital. Instead, it is necessary to devise an indirect method that tests the theory without calling for the unavailable data or making do with farfetched proxies that replace the theory as the focus of attention.

The housing model given above (the Model) hypothesized a competition for funds between the housing and business sectors leading to a single interest rate, with which each sector compares its expected rate of return before deciding whether to invest. The statistical model used to test the housing model (the Test) substitutes correlative data for the rates of return and interest in order to simulate the investment decision: Instead of pitting expected yields in the housing and business sectors against the real interest rate, as in the Model, the Test pits the market values against the replacement costs of the stocks of the respective sectors. The two comparisons come to the same thing. The advantage of

the latter comparison lies in the availability of data.

The ratios of market value to replacement costs of the stocks of corporate assets and owner-occupied housing, respectively, are given by:

$$Q_M = \frac{\text{market value of corporate assets}}{\text{replacement cost of same}} \tag{5}$$

$$Q_H = \frac{\text{market value of 1- to 4-family residential housing stock}}{\text{replacement cost of same}} \tag{6}$$

The numerator of $Q_M$ estimates the market value of outstanding stocks and bonds of nonfinancial corporations,[14] while the denominator is the current dollar value of assets held by nonfinancial corporations.[15] The numerator of $Q_H$ is estimated by dividing the sum of net rent and interest payments for owner-occupied homes by the Baa rate, and the denominator is an estimate of the current value of the residential capital stock.[16]

In theory, the demand for increased stock of housing depends only on $Q_H$. As long as the value of existing stock exceeds replacement cost, it pays to increase the stock.[17] Why, then, introduce $Q_M$? The problem is that the estimate of $Q_H$ is inadequate. The numerator, an estimate of the market value of the housing stock, does not reflect enough of the cyclical movement in housing values. This estimate is based on the well-known formula for valuing perpetuities—present value equals annual income divided by the appropriate interest rate.[18] National Income Accounts' estimates of net rental income and interest on owner-

---

14. The market value of stock is estimated by dividing total dividend payments by the Standard and Poor's (S&P) 500 stock dividend-price ratio; the market value of bonds is estimated by dividing total net interest payments (National Income Accounts) by the S&P Baa bond rate. This method is described by Tobin in "A General Equilibrium Approach to Monetary Theory," 1 J. Money, Credit & Banking, No. 1, pp. 15–29 (Feb. 1969). Updates were obtained from an unpublished distribution by John Ciccolo.

15. *Flow of Funds Accounts, 1946–1975,* N. 4 *supra* at 105.

16. Net rent and interest are given on an annual basis in the National Income Accounts. For the present purpose, they were interpolated into quarterly data. The 1- to 4-family residential housing stock valued at replacement cost, were obtained from Musgrave, N. 4 *supra* at Table 2. Note that the numerator refers to owner-occupied housing and the denominator to 1- to 4-family housing. This discrepancy, which has little effect on the *variation* of $Q_H$, is unavoidable.

17. Strictly, the comparison is made at the margin, that is, the value of the next unit of stock relative to the cost of the next unit. The model given here is a rough macro-model that abstracts from the rising cost and diminishing productivity of capital, as more is acquired, and from differences in the types of capital—factors that necessitate evaluations at the margin. These refinements add little to the result obtained from considering average values and costs in a disequilibrium context; closing the disequilibrium gap swamps the refinements.

18. For example, the present value of $1 in perpetuity at 5 percent interest is $20 (1/.05).

occupied housing gives a plausible estimate of service income. But the Baa bond rate is not a good measure of the opportunity cost of investment funds, the appropriate denominator for this purpose: It neither rises enough during business expansions nor falls enough during contractions. The inadequacy of the Baa rate for this purpose is itself a testable proposition, since the direction of its errors can be anticipated and offset by a theoretically justified variable. That variable is $Q_M$. During cyclical expansions, the rising $Q_M$ implies upward pressure on the real interest rate. The rise in $Q_M$ could compensate for the insufficient decline in $Q_H$ resulting from the insufficient rise in the Baa rate. This mechanism implies that housing expenditures are negatively related to $Q_M$ and, of course, positively related to $Q_H$. In effect, the $Q$s are both components of a single variable, which, if measured correctly, would give the ratio of the value to the replacement cost of the existing stock of housing.

To test these ideas, the $Q$s were introduced in a regression to explain housing expenditures. The dependent variable in this regression is defined as follows: the nominal expenditures on nonfarm, 1- to 4-family homes divided by the current dollar value of the previous quarters' housing stock.[19]

The $Q$s were lagged because market signals should precede expenditures. The lags shown below (two quarters for $Q_H$ and four quarters for $Q_M$) gave the best result. The results of fitting the model to the quarterly data from 1954 through 1973 are:

$$\frac{\text{Housing expenditure } (t)}{\text{Housing stock } (t-1)} = 6.57 + 3.38 \ Q_H(t-2) - 3.50 \ Q_M(t-4) \quad (7)$$
$$\phantom{xxxxxxxxxxxxxxxxxxxxxxxxxx} (10.87) \phantom{xxxxxxxx} (-16.67)$$

$R^2$ (adj) = .88

The results are striking for such a simple model (seemingly free of spurious relationships between the dependent variable and its own shadow—for example, housing starts with mortgages or with their own lagged value). The coefficients of $Q_H$ and $Q_M$ are statistically significant ($t$-values given below the coefficients) and sufficiently close in magnitude to suggest that the difference between the $Q$s would fit the data almost as well—that is to say, one variable $Q_H - Q_M$, could do virtually the whole job. This result adds to the credibility of the interpretation of $Q_M$ as an adjustment to $Q_H$.

Further evidence of the soundness of the model is given from the improvement in the regression that results from a theoretical refinement. The formula for the present value of a perpetuity—income divided by interest rate—assumes a constant income, like the coupon on a bond. Expected inflation, which imparts a trend to the expected service income of housing, is no problem as long as the same expected

---

19. Expenditure figures were obtained from *Quarterly Flow of Funds*, N. 3 *supra*. The housing stock data were obtained from Musgrave, N. 4 *supra* at Table 7-2.

rate of inflation is included in the interest rate.[20] But if the expected

price of housing services rises at a faster rate than the expected rate of inflation, it will result in an expected capital gain on the housing stock that effectively will reduce the interest rate used to discount the service value stream. This effect should be incorporated into $Q_H$.[21]

Theoretically, it is possible to redefine $Q_H$ in order to incorporate the expected capital gains or losses, represented as the difference between the expected change in the price of housing services and the expected rate of inflation. But, the correction requires knowledge of this differential. Clearly, the ratio $s_o/r\text{-}g$, the numerator of $Q_H$, is very sensitive to errors in estimating $g$. In particular, if the estimate of $g$ exceeded the Baa rate in any quarter, the ratio would explode.

To evade this problem while retaining some of the advantages of an improved equation, it is enough to enter $g$ as a separate variable in the regression. (It is entered with two lags to align it with $Q_H$.) The variable entered for this purpose is a four-term moving average of the price index of home construction, which, as noted above, influences the prices of existing houses. The regression results follow:

$$\frac{\text{Housing expenditure } (t)}{\text{Housing stock } (t-1)} = 6.10 + 4.08 Q_H(t-2)$$
$$(13.65)$$
$$- 3.87 Q_M(t-4) + .11 g(t-2) \quad (8)$$
$$(-19.96) \qquad\qquad (5.28)$$

$$R^2 = .91$$

---

20. Let $s_o$ = current service value
$p$ = expected rate of inflation
$r$ = real interest rate
$t$ = units of time

The present value of the perpetual stream of service income from the housing stock, assuming no expected inflation, is given by:

$$PV = s_o \int_0^\infty e^{rt}\, dt = \frac{s_o}{r}$$

Assuming the expected rate of inflation imparts a growth rate to the nominal service value equal to the percentage point increase in the interest rate (in other words, neutral inflation), the $PV$ is unaffected:

$$PV = \int_0^\infty e^{(p-(r+p))t}\, dt = \frac{s_o}{r}$$

Where $r + p$ = the nominal interest rate. In other words, neutral inflation washes out. But, if the service value on housing grows by $g$ percentage points faster than the rate of inflation, the present value of the stream becomes

$$PV = s_o \int_0^\infty e^{(g-r)t}\, dt = \frac{s_o}{r-g}$$

21. $Q_M$ already includes this effect, since its numerator is taken from the actual market value of corporate assets, a number that discounts any expected capital gains or losses.

Introducing the price variable clearly improves the overall fit of the regression, thereby adding to the creditability of the theoretical underpinnings of the model. That the introduction of $g$ affects the coefficient of $Q_H$ more than the coefficient of $Q_M$ also adds to the plausibility of the explanation given for this variable.

Figure 7-13 plots the predicted expenditures on residential construction against actual expenditures.[22] The regression does a fairly good job of following the cycles in housing expenditures; in particular, it caught the boom in 1971.

The test demonstrates the feasibility of devising a theoretically sound, noncredit model of housing that does not depend on autoregressions or other legerdemain.

## Role of Credit in Housing

In light of the analysis just given, it is hard to explain the widespread view that housing problems are credit problems. In virtually no other area is credit assumed to play such an important role, or are market

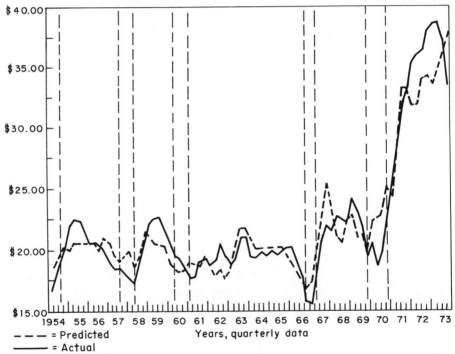

FIGURE 7-13 **Housing expenditures, predicted and actual (in millions of dollars).**
(SOURCE: *Actual expenditure data from Board of Governors of the Federal Reserve System,* Flow of Funds Accounts, 3rd Quarter 1975; *Predicted expenditures from regression derived by author.*)

---

22. Both series are obtained by multiplying both the actual and predicted series by the housing stock, the denominator of the dependent variable.

failures assumed to be so pervasive. Few people understand the overall system—especially the incentives of the thrifts and the role of the government agencies. The image of the thrifts battling giants on behalf of the little man's right to a home is pervasive and irresistible. The fact is, forcing savings into thrift institutions at below-market rates does not cause them to make loans they do not want to make, or to accept less than the best yields available. The thrifts have responsibility to maximize the yield on their portfolios, subject to their legal constraints. They have no mandate to subsidize mortgage rates.[23] Forcing low-cost money into thrifts does not keep down mortgage rates; it merely increases the thrifts' profits.

There is little basis for the popular view tying housing starts to thrift deposit flows. Only about three-quarters of the value of savings deposits at thrift institutions are used to finance residential mortgages, and of that, only about one-third of residential mortgages made by thrifts apply to new homes. In other words, only about one-quarter of the value of thrift deposits are used to finance new home mortgages—far less than one would infer from the public's concern for deposit flows.[24] Surely the tenuous relationship between deposits and new homes gives little support to a policy of depriving depositors of a fair return for the purpose of increasing new home construction.

Perhaps one reason the role of thrift deposits is exaggerated is the

---

23. Historically, the thrust of credit policies toward housing has been to divert, not to subsidize, credit. Except for some special, and ephemeral, programs, mortgagors are expected to pay the market rate, including the premiums for insured loans. The next section argues that forcing money through thrift institutions at below-market rates does *not* reduce mortgage rates. It merely taxes small savers for the benefit of the managers and stockholders, if any, of the thrifts. Even the explicit subsidy programs have questionable purpose. As with most subsidy programs, the groups who lobby for and ultimately write the law are not the consumers, each of whom obtains, at best, a small gift, but rather sellers who see additional money with each new transaction. For example, in 1975, Congress enacted a cash subsidy, ostensibly to new home buyers, which in fact accrued entirely to builders. Since it was limited to houses already in existence and, thus, in fixed supply, it could change only the price, not the quantity, of new houses for sale. A provision of the law giving the subsidy prohibited the sale price from exceeding any previously advertised price. It did not take much imagination to beat the provision. There is no obvious answer to the question why it was the taxpayers' obligation to bail out builders who had incorrectly assessed demand. There *is* an obvious answer to the question why this bailout was sold to the public as a populist device to support the poor home buyer against the machinations of a callous financial establishment. I am indebted to Paul Derosa for this point.

24. From *Flow of Funds Accounts*, N. 4 *supra*; United States League of Savings Ass'ns, *Savings and Loan Association Fact Book* (1974); and Federal Deposit Insurance Corp., Assets and Liabilities—Commercial & Mutual Savings Banks (Washington, D.C., 1974); the percentage of home mortgages to liabilities was 65 percent in 1974. U.S. Dep't of Housing and Urban Development, *The Supply of Mortgage Credit, 1970–1972*, and succeeding monthly issues: 33 percent of all 1- to 4-family loan originations were for new homes. The figures for loan purchases are not available. Purchases account for only 22 percent of the net increase in holding of home mortgages. The 33 percent is applied to these holdings.

prominent role of government agencies in supporting them. When market interest rates rise above Federal Reserve ceilings, those depositors with enough funds to cover the threshold costs of open market investments (see next section) withdraw their funds and seek higher yields. But, the government does not leave the thrifts without money to lend. In effect, there is a two-tier system: The agencies sell securities at market yields to the larger (more fortunate) savers and re-lend the proceeds to the thrifts. The result is that the depositors without alternatives get the lower yield, while those with a big enough investment to buy marketable securities get the higher rate. The agencies serve effectively as an extension of the thrifts, attracting the marginal savings without killing the low-rate market for the thrifts.

It is clear the present system of financing long-term mortgages with liquid liabilities is an anachronism. Unstable interest rates expose the thrift institutions to the risk of adverse spreads between short-term borrowing rates and long-term lending rates. Imposing interest rate ceilings simply translates unstable spreads into unstable deposit flows. The system is ineffective and inequitable. It would be unfair even if it produced lower mortgage rates. There is little basis for the argument that since depositors and mortgagors are members of the same economic group at different stages of the lift cycle, they can offset their losses on savings with lower borrowing costs.[25] Depositors and mortgagors need not be the same people. Urban dwellers are less likely to want mortgages than are suburban or rural dwellers. Surely depositors from purportedly "redlined" districts are not made whole with low-cost loans.

## REGRESSIVITY OF CREDIT ALLOCATION

### Introduction

The value of any policy can be judged only in light of its total impact: of the change in the state of the world it brings about. Some of these changes simply are unavoidable, a form of pollution. Like most economic controls, credit programs work through large groups in order to economize on enforcement costs. The large groups in credit programs are the financial institutions. Financial institutions serve as converters, assemblers, and packagers of credit, largely supplied by households who abjure a voice in its final use. Generally, they can pass along increased costs to their customers, either with higher prices or reduced quality of service. Since the less wealthy households and smaller busi-

---

**25.** The idea that American society is made up of economic classes within which a gain to one member compensates a loss to another contradicts the major premise of democratic government that the basic unit of measurement is the individual.

nesses rely relatively more on institutions for their financial needs, they bear a disproportionate brunt of a rise in the costs of these institutions. They are also less able to replace these services when costs increase.

Forcing institutions to discriminate *in favor* of these groups cannot offset the factors just noted. Distorting their portfolios raises the effective costs of the institutions. The overall supply of institutional credit must decline. If lower-cost credit is diverted forcibly to some borrowers, the cost to other borrowers will have to rise in order to preserve the institutions' yield on its own capital. The larger borrowers, with alternate sources of credit, will go elsewhere, leaving the smaller borrowers to absorb the higher costs. The failure of institutions to offset forced reductions in price with higher prices on other business will lower their profits and reduce their access to capital and their ability to extend credit. As already noted, a decline in institutional credit is relatively more damaging to smaller borrowers.

At best, credit allocation schemes make some groups better off, while others are left holding the bag. These programs are inherently regressive because the people caught holding the bag are those without alternatives.

The purpose of this section is to supply evidence and analysis in support of these points:

1. Diversion of credit from business borrowers toward mortgages or other uses discriminates against smaller businesses, who rely more upon bank credit than do larger businesses.

2. Less wealthy households and small businesses not only rely more upon financial institutions but also are less able to avoid higher financial costs or to offset reduced availability of services.

3. Prohibition against payment of interest on demand deposits works against small businesses, who tend to maintain larger demand balances.

4. Ceilings on savings deposit rates work against less wealthy households, who maintain a larger share of their wealth in this form.

5. Limitations on installment credit work against poorer households, who rely more upon this form of credit.

## Business Finance

There are three reasons for the dependence of smaller companies on bank credit (in declining order of importance): (1) they are less able to raise public credit; (2) a greater fraction of their liabilities are short-term; and (3) they are less able to finance themselves.[26]

Credit standing rather than size per se is the important factor in

---

26. See Appendix A for evidence to support these propositions.

raising public credit. However, the two are related closely. In part, they are related because size provides some measure of a company's ability to survive brief reversals. In addition, larger companies generally are better known to the public and therefore less suspect. Still, size alone is not enough: Other factors come into play; more so for debt than for equity securities; much more so for short-term than for long-term securities; still more so, for all types of securities during periods of high interest rates. Credit standing is more important in raising public than private credit. The risk differential is greater in the public market. Private lenders—including banks, insurance companies, pension funds, and others—are set up to evaluate and monitor credit standing. Their costs of information and servicing are lower than those of public investors, who may have only a passing interest in the borrower. Moreover, private negotiation facilitates use of special terms and conditions that improve the quality of the loan. These special conditions are less feasible in public markets, where standardization of indentures is necessary to the maintenance of liquid-after-markets. However, to provide nonstandardized terms at acceptable risk, banks—and other institutions—must incur far greater overhead costs than the broker-dealers through whom open market securities pass.[27]

Borrowers with sufficient public standing have no reason to defray these expenses when their access to public credit makes these costs superfluous.[28] The effect of rising borrowing costs to banks on their marginal money is to raise the borrowing costs for less-than-prime borrowers, who are forced either to pay a greater quality differential on the open market or a higher bank rate.

---

27. Some observers falsely attribute the higher costs of bank credit for low-risk borrowers to the need for banks to maintain reserves against deposits. Except in extreme cases, the *average* cost of funds to the bank *is* lower than that of open-market borrowers. Lower-cost money depends upon the bank's ability to offer payments and savings services that attract deposits at below-market rates. Required reserves, in effect, constitute a tax on the right to obtain these deposits at rates held down by government ceilings. It is true that an individual bank cannot control the volume of these deposits and that, as a result, it has to pay market rates for required funds in excess of its rate-controlled deposits. If the bank is willing to borrow for very short terms and bear the risk of changing interest rates, it can buy federal funds and make repurchase agreements which provide additional funds without adding to required reserves. Otherwise, it must issue certificates of deposit, commercial paper, or other sources of funds that increase required reserves. It is at this point that bank borrowing costs rise above market rates as banks are forced to tie up cash as reserves against additional borrowings.

28. The sources of long-term credit are subject to similar conditions as those just described for short-term credit, except that their quality requirements are less stringent than those in short-term markets. Companies with acknowledged credit standing can issue long-term debt in the public market. But, as in the short-term market, the quality differential, that is, the interest premium which the market requires to offset its perception of higher risk, grows more rapidly in the public than in the private market. Imposing restrictions on private (largely institutional) lenders would affect the availability of credit more to smaller and financially weaker companies than it would to larger and financially stronger companies.

A company's demand for bank credit is not an all-or-nothing proposition. There is a small group of very large and well-regarded corporations with little or no reason to call on a bank for credit. Below this group, there exists a continuum of companies whose short-term credit needs are satisfied in varying degrees by banks. At one end of the spectrum are companies that seldom, and maybe never, borrow from banks; at the other end are those who rely entirely on nonpublic sources of credit, such as bank credit. Between these limits are companies whose external short-term credit is met in varying proportions by the public market, banks, and other intermediaries. The proportions vary among companies, mostly in accordance with their public access, and with changes in the availability of public funds.

Implicit in this ordering of borrowers is the schedule of borrowing costs they face. In choosing its source of credit, the borrower compares its risk differential in the public market with the sum of the risk differential and intermediary costs involved in a bank loan. Companies with the best public position, facing no risk differential from either source, have little reason to incur intermediary costs. Barring other considerations, they avoid bank debt. Less favored companies may find that the public risk differential they face increases with the extent of their public borrowings. These companies will favor the public source as long as the resulting differential survives the comparison just noted. When the public costs overtake the bank costs, the borrower switches to the bank.

The continuous relationship between the public borrower and its commercial paper dealer, analogous in many respects to a bank relationship, facilitates the borrower's transfer between the public and bank sources. The relationship enables the borrower to accommodate his public borrowings to his need for funds and to availability. Changes in the public's perception of risk will influence the relative advantages of public and bank credit. In periods of heightened uncertainty, public differentials increase, forcing borrowers to reduce the public share of their debt, in many cases to zero. During these periods, the public, in effect, prefers to interposition banks between the lenders and the ultimate borrowers, in order to take advantage of both the banks' superior credit facilities and, implicitly, banks' access to a lender of last resort.

Similarly, borrowers will exploit their ability to shift between sources of credit in response to changes in the effective public-bank differential arising from inertia in the bank rate.[29] If the rate were held

---

**29.** The major differences between the effective and the stated rates are the following: (1) most arrangements for bank loans require the borrower to maintain average balances with the lending bank (compensating balances) equal to some fraction (frequently 10 percent) of the outstanding loan. In this case, the effective rate is 10 percent more than the stated rate; (2) most issuers of commercial paper maintain lines of credit with banks to cover them in the event the availability of public credit diminishes as well as to increase

down for political or other reasons, the point at which the costs of public borrowing overtake bank borrowing would occur at a lower rate of public borrowing.

To effect this transferability between markets, borrowers must maintain lines of credit or commitments with banks. These lines contribute to the quality of a borrower's outstanding paper, not by guaranteeing bail-out money in the event the borrower goes sour but, rather, by facilitating its adaptation to changing market conditions.

## Household Finances

The composition of assets and liabilities in a household's portfolio reflects its owner's opportunities. No one *prefers* to pay more interest on a loan than others pay or to receive a lower yield on savings than others receive on theirs. Differences in household financial behavior are explained much better by differences in opportunities than by differences in desires.

The most important reason for differences in portfolio composition is the size of the portfolio or, its correlative, wealth. Small portfolios cannot generate orders of sufficient size to make the purchase of marketable securities worthwhile. Costs per dollar invested are too high. As a result, households with relatively low net worth tend to maintain larger deposit balances relative to their wealth. This group is hurt more when Regulation Q ceilings on savings deposits become effective: Wealthier groups can withdraw their funds and purchase marketable securities; the less wealthy households cannot.

The following analysis provides some evidence for the proposition that less wealthy households rely more upon financial institutions than do wealthier households.

Data on the composition of household portfolios were obtained from two independent household surveys. The first, the Survey of Financial Characteristics of Consumers, was conducted by the Census Bureau for the Board of Governors of the Federal Reserve System. The survey covers the balance sheets as of December 31, 1962, of 2,557 *households*. The second was conducted by the Survey Research Center, Institute for Social Research, the University of Michigan. It covers the balance sheets and other information pertaining to 2,576 *families* interviewed during

---

public confidence in the company's ability to repay the debt (so-called backup lines). To obtain these lines, a company is required to maintain balances with the bank on which no interest is paid. Alternatively, the company may obtain a commitment from the bank for which it pays a fee as well as maintains balances. The commitment is a more binding obligation of the bank than a line, and the charges, accordingly, are higher. The cost of these lines and commitments, without which, in many cases, a company cannot issue commercial paper, contribute to the effective costs of borrowing in the commercial paper market.

1970.[30] Various tabulations of the surveys are given in their published versions. Additional tabulations were obtained from the Board and the Center.[31]

**351**

*Credit Allocation Schemes: Truths and Fictions*

Figures 7-14 and 7-15 show the shares of wealth held in certain forms by households with different levels of income. The data were taken from the Board and the Center, respectively. The points marked off along the horizontal axes represent the mean values of the income groups provided by the tabulations of the two surveys. Clearly, access to the raw data would permit more continuous curves with clearer points of inflection. But, at the moment, these data are available, and they do have a message.

The share of wealth held in the form of savings deposits declines with rising income. The key factor in this decline is the declining cost (and, therefore, the rising net yield) of alternate investment media,[32] whose share of wealth rises with increasing household income.

Short-term marketable securities make good substitutes for savings deposits. But these securities generally trade in relatively large denominations. The additional yield available on a relatively small investment may not offset the cost and inconvenience of buying and selling the securities. As a result, open market securities do not provide practical alternatives to small depositors. But the inconvenience is the same for investments of any size—it is a fixed cost—and unit transactions costs tend to decline as the size of the order increases; and total interest returns rise proportionally with the size of the investment. Eventually, the yield differential on marketable securities overtakes the added costs when the size of the investment reaches a certain threshold. At that point, the switch is made. This threshold size declines as the yield differential between marketable securities and savings deposits increases. As the threshold declines, the switch into marketable securities becomes practical for a greater number of depositors.

In Figures 7-14 and 7-15, the share of wealth held as checking deposits is the same at all levels of income. This finding runs counter to the widely held opinion that the relative need for cash (i.e., currency plus checking—or demand deposits) declines with increasing wealth, an idea that mainly rests on the view that the need for cash rises more

---

**30.** Projector and Weiss, *Survey of Financial Characteristics of Consumers* (Bd. of Governors of the Fed. Reserve System, Washington, D.C., Aug. 1966); Katona, Mandell, and Schmiedeskamp, *1970 Survey of Consumer Finances* (Survey Research Center, Institute for Social Research, University of Mich., Ann Arbor 1971).

**31.** The author is indebted to Sven Thoresen of the Board of Governors of the Federal Reserve System and Evelyn Hansmire of the Survey Research Center, Institute for Social Research, The University of Michigan, for their help in working with the respective surveys.

**32.** As defined in the charts, savings deposits consist of deposits held at commercial banks (including certificates of deposit) and thrift institutions. Investments consist of marketable securities, own business, and real estate other than primary owner-occupied homes.

slowly than the volume of payments.[33] Often, an analogy is drawn between required cash on hand and business inventories, which tend to rise more slowly than business sales. Money, like inventories, is held in store to offset temporary imbalances between inflow and outflow. The gap between inflow and outflow rises more slowly than either flow. Less money is required relative to the money flow to offset the imbalance. Money also is held as a source of liquidity—or flexibility. The demand for liquidity actually may rise with wealth. Liquidity, likely, is a luxury good—that is, one for which the demand rises more rapidly than income. Liquidity also is an adjunct to investment and is therefore more valuable to wealthier people.

One implication of this finding is that the failure to pay interest on demand deposits does *not* have a regressive impact on income distribution. Higher income (as well as wealthier) households keep at least as much money on hand, relative to income or wealth, as poorer households. All groups forgo proportionately the same yield. The difference

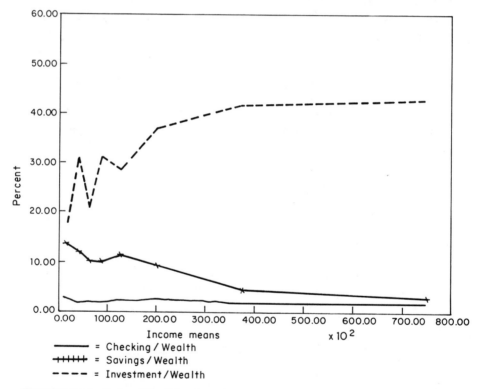

**FIGURE 7-14  Federal Reserve data. (**SOURCE: *Dorothy S. Projector and Gertrude S. Weiss,* Survey of Financial Characteristics of Consumers, *Board of Governors of the Federal Reserve System, Washington, D.C., August 1966.*)

---

**33.** Changes in the aggregate demand for money through time are influenced by other factors besides increasing wealth. These other factors are not involved in the current discussion.

in the costs of substitutes as wealth increases is the major reason for the difference in the impact of wealth on savings—and demand deposits. For savings deposits, rising wealth lowers the cost of substitutes; for demand deposits, it does not.

Figures 7-16 and 7-17 give the share of installment-to-total debt as household income increases. Both surveys clearly show the declining importance of installment debt as household income increases. Actually, the data understate the relatively greater importance of installment credit on low-income households. Wealthier households can sell assets to obtain funds for consumer purchases; if necessary, they can forgo credit altogether. While both rich and poor need to cushion imbalances between the inflow and outflow of cash, wealthier families have the option of self-financing, as well as a choice of credit.

The availability of installment credit does not elicit as much concern as that of most other forms of credit. The desirability of bridging imbalances in cash flow is acknowledged with less fervor when installment loans are involved than when mortgages, business loans, or government loans are involved. In part, the relatively high costs of

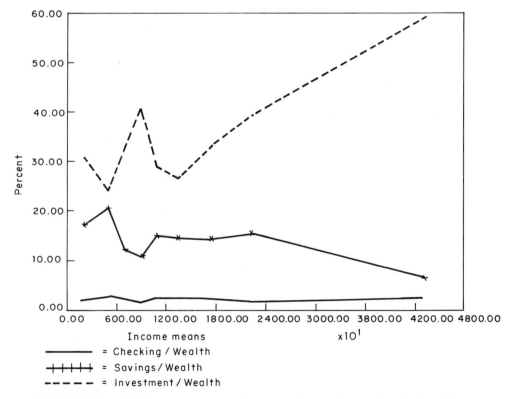

**FIGURE 7-15  Michigan survey data. (**SOURCE: *George Katona, Lewis Mandell and Jay Schmiedeskamp, 1970 Survey of Consumer Finances, Survey Research Center, Institute for Social Research, The University of Michigan, Ann Arbor, 1971.*)

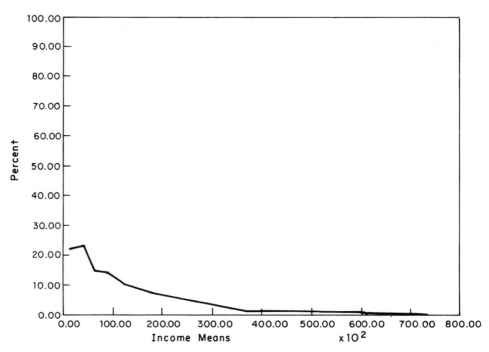

**FIGURE 7-16** **Installment debt/total debt: Federal Reserve Data.**(SOURCE: *Dorothy S. Projector and Gertrude S. Weiss,* Survey of Financial Characteristics of Consumers, *Board of Governors of the Federal Reserve System, Washington, D.C., August 1966.*)

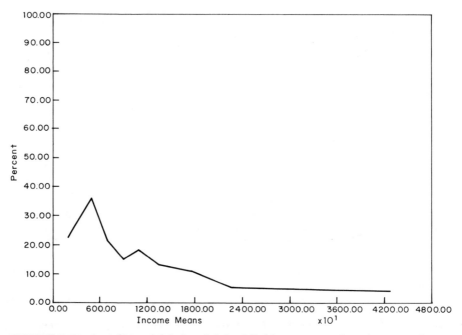

**FIGURE 7-17** **Installment debt/total debt: Michigan survey data.** (SOURCE: *George Katona, Lewis Mandell, and Jay Schmiedeskamp,* 1970 Survey of Consumer Finances, *Survey Research Center, Institute for Social Research, The University of Michigan, Ann Arbor, 1971.*)

these loans, reflecting the high administrative costs per dollar loan value, taint their image. In part, people who determine social mores do not need installment credit. Most of all, consumer purchases do not embody the tangible ethic of a house, the social stability that is associated popularly with a very durable asset. It frequently is overlooked that stability—especially when it is enforced by a mortgage—can thwart movement and flexibility, essential factors in a modern economy.

# APPENDIX A—EVIDENCE OF THE RELATIONSHIP OF COMPANY SIZE TO SOURCE OF CREDIT

The key factors in the relative use of bank loans and commercial paper are the interest rate spread on the two types of debt and a given company's sensitivity to the spread. Sensitivity depends upon a company's access to the commercial paper market. Access requires a good credit standing because the market specializes in high-quality securities that for many investors—mainly nonfinancial corporations—provide alternatives to cash. For them, default risk must be minimized. Credit standing is related—but not limited—to a company's size, measured by sales, assets, or net worth. Other factors contribute to credit standing, like liquidity of assets and stability of earnings. Some of these factors are related to industries or other groupings. Suitable proxies for these relationships play a role in the statistical work that follows.

The following regressions[34] fit differences in company debt to certain characteristics of the companies. The data for each observation were taken from a Standard and Poors' report on a given company. There are as many observations as there are companies. The dependent variable is the following ratio for the $i$th company:

$$\frac{\text{commercial paper outstanding}}{\text{commercial paper plus bank loans}}$$

---

34. Only limited data are available on breakdowns of short-term debt into bank loans and commercial paper classified by the size and industry of the borrower. Standard and Poor's quarterly rating reports on issuers of commercial paper have certain limitations. First, company data, as distinct from group data, are difficult to work with because of the large number of extraneous factors they introduce. Second, the data available at a given time provide balance sheet information—including breakdowns of outstanding debt—that span a short period during which there is relatively little variation in the interest rate spreads. (The solution to this problem is to collect data over a longer period.) The data used in this section cover a period of only three months. As a result, the interest rate effect is barely noticeable. Third, the data are limited to companies that are in the commercial paper market. Therefore, the sample is biased toward the larger, more credit-worthy companies. The effect of this bias is to obscure most of the major point of the section, namely, that access to public credit declines (therefore, that reliance on banks increases) as company size declines. As noted, a threshold size exists for corporate access to the commercial paper market. For any practical interest rate spread, companies below this threshold size cannot borrow in the commercial paper market. These companies are excluded from the sample. For those beyond the threshold size, access improves with credit standing and, therefore, with size. In this gray area, more factors than size are at work. These factors elude the model described, which is intended only to demonstrate the role of size. These two points—the sample bias and the failure to specify other factors for companies that have passed the threshold size—account for the relatively low explanatory power of the regressions. *Note:* Due to their special features, finance companies were excluded from the sample. A few other special cases were excluded in advance as a result of unusual features.

This variable was chosen because it measures the *relative shares* of the two types of short-term debt, the matter to be explained. The independent variables are:

1. *Company size:* The logarithm of total assets was used to measure size. (The difference between assets and sales in this context is considered below.) The logarithmic form was used because the cumulative effect of size appears to increase at a decreasing rate.

2. *Industry proclivity for bank loans:* The proxy used is the ratio of bank loans to total liabilities for the industry to which the given company belongs.[35] This variable is added because certain industries rely more than others upon bank loans. Some reasons for these differences are considered below.

3. *Interest rate spread:* This variable is measured by the difference between the Citibank prime rate and the 90-day commercial paper rate (prime minus paper). No attempt was made to adjust for effective rates because, in a short period, the nominal and effective rates move together.

The results follow:

| Regression number | Independent variables | Regression coefficient | t-value | $R^2$ adj |
|---|---|---|---|---|
| 1 | Constant | .277 | — | .065 |
|   | log assets | .059 | 4.71 | |
| 2 | Constant | .329 | — | .130 |
|   | log assets | .070 | 5.70 | |
|   | industry loan/ | | | |
|   | liability ratio | −1.699 | 4.83 | |
| 3 | Constant | .286 | — | .138 |
|   | log assets | .067 | 5.51 | |
|   | industry loan/ | | | |
|   | liability ratio | −1.630 | 4.62 | |
|   | bank-paper rate | .038 | 1.73 | |

The reported results are consistent with the following conclusions:

1. Even for companies past the access threshold, size has a positive influence on the relative use of commercial paper. Allowance for industry proclivity uncovers a greater size effect.

2. The tendency for some industries to rely more upon bank loans is supported by the significance of the proclivity variable (regressions 2 and 3). That the industry variable (bank loans to total debt) is related to the relative use of commercial paper by particular companies indicates a common element among the companies within an industry that justifies

---

35. For this purpose, the industry is defined by a two-digit SEC code as given by the Census Bureau.

use of the word "proclivity." A better specification of the proclivity variable should improve the results all around.

3. The interest rate spread does not have a significant effect on the proportion of bank loans and commercial paper. Given the limitations of the data noted earlier, this result is far from definitive.

The *composition* of short-term liabilities is only one factor in the importance of bank loans to small businesses. Another is the tendency of smaller companies to keep a larger share of their liabilities short-term. As mainly short-term lenders, banks are more important to smaller companies on this account alone. The two points—more bank credit relative to short-term liabilities and more short-term liabilities relative to total—work in the same direction.

The decline in the ratio of short-term to total liabilities as company size increases is shown in Figure 7-18 for major sectors of the economy. The ratios of short-term to total liabilities for each size class, measured along the vertical axes, were divided by the same ratio for the total sector.[36] This normalization technique narrows the range of data among sectors without altering the indicated relationships within sectors. The measure of size, along the horizontal axes, is the logarithm of assets. The logarithm is used because the cumulative effect of company size on the use of short-term liabilities increases at a decreasing rate. The numbers along the horizontal axes actually are the logarithms of the *means* of the size intervals given in the statistical source. Intervals below $1 million in assets were excluded.[37] A regression line was computed and drawn through the points to give a better sense both of the direction and the uniformity of the relationship. These charts provide clear evidence of the inverse relationship between corporate size and the relative use of short-term liabilities.

Two mutually consistent hypotheses are offered here to explain, in part, the pattern just described. The first is that larger companies are better able to finance themselves and, therefore, have less need to incur short-term liabilities. The second is that larger companies are involved in fewer market transactions relative to their total revenues. Other things being equal, larger companies tend to add more value to their product—i.e., to buy less from other companies—than do smaller companies. Fewer transactions lead to less short-term debt. These points are considered in turn.

There are two ways to meet temporary needs for cash: (1) incur short-term liabilities as the need arises; or (2) maintain a portfolio of liquid assets for sale when cash is needed. Holding cash itself for this purpose

36. The data were taken from Internal Revenue Service, *Statistics of Income, 1970.*

37. These data were excluded because (1) the financial conditions of very small companies are related intimately to those of the major stockholders—therefore, the group does not define a meaningful class; and (2) the size intervals within this class are too similar to enable meaningful dispersion.

is uneconomical in view of opportunity costs. The assets must provide a

yield. But it is not practical to manage a liquid asset portfolio that is too
small to cover administrative costs.

The second strategy is more appealing to larger companies. In many
cases, their incentive is enhanced by better access to long-term debt,
which helps them maintain their liquid asset portfolios. Clearly, each

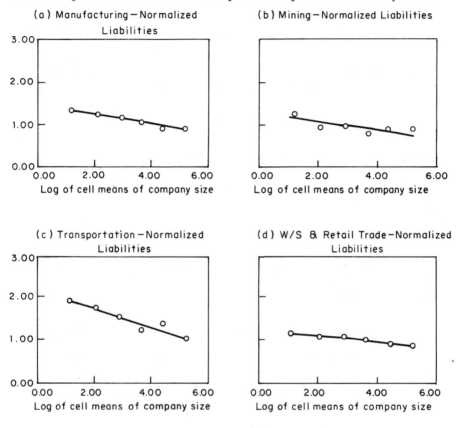

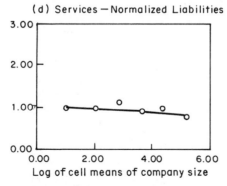

**FIGURE 7-18  Ratio of short-term to total liabilities in relation to size of
company.** (SOURCE: *From* Statistics of Income, 1970, *Internal Revenue Service.*)

company must decide whether the negative interest spread it incurs (relative to its own long-term liabilities and to its opportunities for higher-yielding real assets), in addition to turnover costs, is preferable, on average, to the costs of going into and out of short-term debt. The more volatile a company's cash needs are, the higher the turnover costs in the second method. Greater stability in their cash flows also favors larger companies for self-financing.

The advantage larger companies have enjoyed in short-term financing mainly has been due to the costs of portfolio management. Advances in computer technology in recent years have nullified much of the *real* advantage of size. However, the regulatory environment has not kept pace with technology. Allowing payment of competitive interest on demand deposits or, even better, encouraging an overdraft system, *in effect* would enable banks to manage liquid portfolios on behalf of their smaller corporate depositors, providing them with the benefits of scale formerly available only to larger corporations. The costs of the current ban on interest payment on demand deposits likely are borne by smaller companies more than by any other identifiable group.

By internalizing more of their production, larger companies effectively substitute administrative decision for market transactions. One division is *told* to obtain a part from another division, instead of soliciting bids from vendors. Whether the buying division pays "transfer" dollars, a form of scrip, or incurs an accounting liability, its transactions do not affect the balance sheet of the parent company. By making fewer outside purchases, larger companies have less occasion to incur short-term debt. Their more internalized production, in part, is due to the greater capital intensity of larger companies within a given industry. Smaller companies do not produce in sufficient volume to make economical use of some types of equipment available to larger competitors. They often purchase the output of vendors, who spread the costs of the equipment among many small customers. Smaller companies also tend to face less stable demand than larger companies in the same industry and, therefore, are reluctant to suffer fixed charges during periods of insufficient demand. Instead, they buy what they need to service revealed demand, leaving the vendor to worry about idle capacity. (The vendor has less to worry about because his customers face partly offsetting risks and because he charges for whatever risks remain.) While there are no rules on this point, the companies who own the equipment—integrated producers and vendors—finance long-term, and those who purchase the parts finance short-term.

Size is not the only source of variation in corporate financial policies. As noted above, certain correlatives of size, rather than size itself, affect these policies. For companies of a given size, capital intensity, vendor purchases, and stability of revenues vary across industries. Capital-intensive utilities, even small ones, are more inclined to borrow long than, say, retailers of the same size.[38] Air frame manufacturers are more involved with banks than most other companies of comparable size because they rely upon vendor purchases and have relatively unstable revenues. As a result, they act more like smaller companies in other industries that are more vertically integrated (i.e., purchase less from outside vendors) and more stable. It is important to allow for these industry effects when trying to relate company size to the structure of balance sheets.

The data obtained from Standard and Poors' commercial paper ratings provide some evidence on the relationship between company size and the use of bank loans. The regression below relates the ratio of a company's outstanding bank loans to its total assets to: (1) the ratio of outstanding bank loans to total liabilities of the industry to which the company belongs; and (2) the logarithm of the company's total assets. The variable to be explained is the amount of bank loans outstanding relative to the size of the company—measured, in this case, by value of assets. The industry loan-to-total-liability ratio is based upon a two-digit industry classification.[39]

The logarithm of assets for the given company serves the same role as in the statistical work described above. The regression follows:

$$\text{Dependent variable:} \frac{\text{Bank loans outstanding}}{\text{Total assets}}$$

| Regression number | Independent variable | Regression coefficient | t-value | $R^{2*}$ |
|---|---|---|---|---|
| 1 | Constant | 6.77 | 5.37 | .082 |
|   | log assets | −1.04 | 5.06 | |
| 2 | Constant | 6.66 | 5.42 | .125 |
|   | log assets | −1.31 | −6.16 | |
|   | industry loans / total liabilities | 21.79 | 3.81 | |

*274 degrees of freedom

Asset size has a significantly negative effect on the relative importance of bank loans to a company. Its measured effect is increased both

---

**38.** Capital intensity does not imply heavy equipment. A stable inventory of soft goods can be the basis for a capital intensive business. Inventories, typically, are financed short-term, not because they turn over, but because the value held at a given time is unstable and because the changes in their market value tend to vary with short-term interest rates.

**39.** As given by the Census Bureau. Data on bank loans by industry are taken from Federal Trade Commission, *Quarterly Financial Report For Manufacturing Corporations*. The data are averages over the quarters of 1970. Data for this variable are used to estimate the proclivity for bank loans of the industry to which the company in question belongs. The measure provides a very rough proxy for the factors described above. A finer industry breakdown should work better.

in magnitude and statistical significance when the industry effect is introduced.

The industry loan-to-liability ratio should reflect the financial incentives of the industry along lines described above. It is difficult to find good proxies for these incentives. In the regression that follows, the ratio of total assets to total sales for the given industry is used as a proxy for the degree of vertical integration. (The basis for this estimate is given above.) The other independent variable in the regression that follows is the ratio of inventory-to-sales.[40]

$$\text{Dependent variable: } \frac{\text{Bank loans outstanding}}{\text{Total liabilities}}$$

| Independent variables | Regression coefficients | t-values | $R^{2*}$ |
|---|---|---|---|
| Constant | 9.83 | 4.61 | .268 |
| $\dfrac{\text{Assets}}{\text{Sales}}$ | −.04 | −3.49 | |
| $\dfrac{\text{Inventory}}{\text{Sales}}$ | .37 | 2.65 | |

*32 degrees of freedom

The relative importance of bank loans to an industry is related inversely to the ratio of assets to sales and directly to the ratio of inventory to sales.

An indirect way to relate bank loans to company size involves short-term liabilities. Other things being equal, the more dependent a company is on short-term liabilities, the more dependent it likely will be on bank loans. In fact, the case is even stronger: When short-term liabilities are important, bank loans likely account for a larger fraction of short-term liabilities. Some evidence of the second point was given earlier. Here, some evidence of the influence of company size on the importance of short-term liabilities is given. The data used are taken from *Statistics of Income*.[41] The size classifications used are the same as those described in connection with Figure 7-18. Reported results are limited to those obtained with data on manufacturing industries. The proxy used to represent an industry's proclivity for short-term liabilities, namely the asset-to-sales ratio, does not work well for nonmanufacturing industries, at least at the two-digit level.

The dependent variable in the regressions that follow is the ratio of short-term liabilities to total liabilities for companies in a given size

---

**40.** *Id.*

**41.** See IRS, N. 36 *supra* at 32–64.

class and a given industry. For this purpose, the value of total assets is

the measure of size. The lowest size class used in a given industry is the one containing all firms with total assets valued between $1 million and $5 million. The open-ended class—more than $250 million—was omitted because the class mean was not available.

Independent variables are (1) the logarithm of assets, in this case, the class means of the asset-size classes ($1 million to $5 million, $5 million to $10 million, etc.) and (2) the ratio of total assets to sales of the companies in the respective size classes. Reasons for specifying these variables were given above.

For the companies in a given size-class in a given industry, the dependent variable in the following regressions is the ratio:

$$\frac{\text{Short-term liabilities}}{\text{Total liabilities}}$$

| Independent variable | Regression coefficient | t-value | $R^{2*}$ |
|---|---|---|---|
| | (unweighted) | | |
| Constant | 82.78 | 36.85 | .585 |
| log assets | −2.87 | −5.06 | |
| assets/sales | −.25 | −6.84 | |

*123 degrees of freedom

The size and industry effects—respectively, the log of assets and the assets to sales ratio—have roughly comparable influences on the ratio of short-term to total liabilities. This point is reflected in the roughly equal t-values of the coefficients on the two variables. The negative coefficients on the two variables are consistent with the previous discussion.

As noted earlier, large companies incur relatively less short-term liability, partly because they use more self-financing. Varying their holdings of liquid assets (i.e., cash and marketable securities) substitutes for short-term borrowing. This method is practical only if the company can hold down its cash position, which ties up capital in nonyielding assets. The task of minimizing the share of liquid assets held as cash is easier (1) the more predictable the company's cash transactions are and (2) the greater the efficiency with which its holdings of marketable securities can be varied. Since there are economies of scale in trading short-term securities, the second point favors larger companies.

These two factors, stability and scale, were noted earlier for their positive influence on vertical integration. They play a similar role here: Financing is part of production; it can be made or bought, like any other input. The choice of financing method, therefore, is just another make-or-buy decision.

The following regression illustrates the influence of stability and size on the share of liquid assets held in the form of cash.[42] The dependent variable is the ratio

$$\frac{cash}{cash + government\ securities}$$

held by companies of a given size in a given industry. The independent variables are the same ones reported in the previous regression.

| Independent variable | Regression coefficient (unweighted) | t-value | $R^{2*}$ |
|---|---|---|---|
| constant | 1.05 | | .145 |
| log assets | −.006 | −0.54 | |
| assets/sales | −.191 | −3.33 | |

*99 degrees of freedom

Other things constant, the fraction of liquid assets held as cash declines with the size and vertical integration of the corporation. If one interprets all liquid asset holdings as a form of self-financing (or vertical integration), then one can conclude that the unit cost of self-financing declines with the share held in cash, as the size and integration of the company increases. Finally, as the cost of self-financing declines, so does the need for short-term loans, including bank loans.[43]

The empirical studies described in this section lead to the following conclusions: (1) Smaller companies are less prone than larger companies to substitute lower cost commercial paper for bank loans. (2) The ratio of short-term to total liabilities increases with decreasing company size. (3) For companies of a given size, the greater the ratio of assets to sales, the smaller the ratio of short-term to total liabilities. This relationship helps explain differences among industries and by company size within industries. (4) The greater reliance of smaller companies on bank loans, therefore, stems from (a) their greater reliance on short-term liabilities and (b) the greater importance of bank loans in their short-term liabilities. (5) The effects of company size accumulate at a decreasing rate. For this reason, the logarithm of size is a more significant variable than size itself.

42. The data were taken from *Internal Revenue Service Source Book, 1970,* for manufacturing companies only. The data exactly parallel those used in the regression on liabilities reported above.

43. Actually, self-financing replaces bank loans more than it replaces open-market borrowing. Like the latter, self-financing ultimately is a means to avoid intermediation costs. The choice between self-financing and open-market loans (i.e., asset or liability management) turns more on the company's desired leverage—that is, whether to use its or the public's capital—than on operating costs.

# CREDIT ALLOCATION AND CONSUMER EXPENDITURES: THE CASE OF INSTALLMENT CREDIT CONTROLS

Michael J. Hamburger, *Adviser, Federal Reserve Bank of New York*

Burton Zwick, *Associate Director, Economic and Investment Research, Prudential Insurance Company of America*

One of the factors that distinguishes central bank policy in the United States from that in most other countries is the tendency to rely on techniques that influence the total volume of money and credit and not their distribution among different sectors of the economy. During the last several years, however, the public debate over credit allocation has intensified. In June 1974, Chairman Reuss of the House Committee on Banking, Currency and Housing introduced a bill "to amend the Federal Reserve Act to permit the Federal Reserve Board to allocate credit to national priority needs." In May 1975, the House Banking Committee passed a bill that would require a sample of federally insured banks to provide figures on the dollar volume of loans to specific categories of lenders. Support for the use of selective credit policies to alter the allocation of real resources has also come from Andrew Brimmer, a former member of the Board of Governors of the Federal Reserve System, who advocates the use of differential asset reserve requirements for commercial banks in order to encourage the movement of funds into particular sectors of the economy.[1]

In addition to their use as instruments to alter resource allocation, selective credit policies have been proposed as an aid to the conduct of general monetary and stabilization policy. Henry Kaufman, one of Wall

While responsibility for this paper is ours alone, we are indebted to Marcelle Arak, Fred Levin, Thomas Mayer, Laurence Meyer, James O'Brien, and Charles Sivesind for valuable comments. Marie Cavanaugh provided valuable research assistance. The material in the paper does not necessarily reflect the views of the Federal Reserve Bank of New York. (Reprinted with permission from the *Journal of Finance*, vol. 32, Dec. 1977, where this article appeared under the title "Installment Credit Controls, Consumer Expenditures and the Allocation of Real Resources.")

1. Andrew Brimmer, The Banking Structure and Money Management, address before the San Francisco Bond Club, April 1970; Brimmer, *Central Banking and Credit Allocation* (Graduate School of Bus., Univ. of Texas, Austin 1975).

Street's most widely quoted analysts and interpreters of financial market developments, has argued that interest rate ceilings, limits on housing and consumer finance, and other forms of credit controls can help the Federal Reserve "to keep credit expansion reasonable."[2] Moreover, while expressing strong opposition to any formal system of credit allocation by commercial banks, the Board of Governors of the Federal Reserve System in its conduct of general monetary policy on several occasions has taken an active role in counseling banks on their loan strategies. For example, in September 1974, the Board released a statement by the Federal Advisory Council (FAC) on bank lending policies designed both to encourage banks to lend for certain specified purposes and—of equal importance—to discourage lending for other purposes. The Board mailed the FAC statement to all member banks in the system, indicating that it could be "helpful to banks in formulating their lending policies" in the current period of credit restraint.[3]

A minimum requirement for selective credit policies to accomplish either of the above objectives is for these policies to affect the composition of real expenditures.[4] The purpose of this paper is to consider whether—apart from the social and administrative costs of regulatory programs and apart from the problems of permitting political decisions to preempt the decisions of the market—selective credit policies do in fact affect the composition of real expenditures, particularly consumer durable expenditures. We focus on consumer durable expenditures because of the imposition of minimum down payment and maximum maturity requirements on installment credit from 1948, fourth quarter, through 1949, second quarter, and from 1950, fourth quarter, through 1952, first quarter. This control program represents one of the few direct and open attempts to impose credit controls in this country during the post-World War II period, and the presumed effectiveness of installment credit controls during these periods has served as an important basis of support for many of the recent proposals for selective credit policies.[5]

---

2. Henry Kaufman, Forces of Change in the American Credit Markets, address before the Financial Times conference on New York as a World Financial Center, June 11, 1974.

3. Board of Governors of the Fed. Reserve System, "FAC Statement on Bank Lending Policies," 60 Fed. Reserve Bull., No. 9, pp. 679–680 (Sept. 1974).

4. Even if real expenditures are affected, problems in timing or general coordination with other policies may limit the effectiveness of selective credit policies for stabilization. The use of selective credit controls to affect conditions in financial markets without reference to real resource allocation, as in the case of margin requirements in the stock market, will not be considered or evaluated in this paper.

5. Residential construction is another sector of the economy where selective credit policies have been employed to influence the level of expenditures. Here, the United States Government has tried in a number of different ways to subsidize mortgage credit for the purpose of stimulating housing expenditures. For an analysis of the efficacy of these policies, see Meltzer, "Credit Availability and Economic Decisions: Some Evidence from the Mortgage and Housing Markets," 29 J. Finance, No. 3, pp. 763–777 (June 1974); Jaffee,

The first section of the paper presents evidence to test the effects of

the installment credit controls of the 1948–1952 period on the level of consumer durable expenditures. The evidence is based on the parameter estimates of a fully specified model of the demand for consumer durable goods. In the next section, this evidence is compared with that of previous investigations. We also attempt to determine the expenditure effects of installment credit controls and other selective credit policies in today's economy by analyzing the recent loan behavior of banks in the Second Federal Reserve district. The last section is a summary and conclusion.

## THE EFFECTS OF INSTALLMENT CREDIT CONTROLS ON CONSUMER DURABLE EXPENDITURES

This section presents evidence on the effects of the 1948–1952 installment credit controls obtained from the estimation of the parameters of a stock adjustment model of the demand for automobiles and for other durable goods. A brief outline of the model, whose parameters were originally estimated with quarterly data from 1953 to 1964,[6] is presented in the first part of this section. The results of the tests for the effects of installment credit controls follow.[7]

In the model, the desired real stock of consumer durable goods $(\bar{A})$ is expressed as a linear function of $Y$, aggregate income valued in constant prices, $r$, a vector of yields on financial assets and liabilities, and $P$, the

---

"Housing Finance and Mortgage Market Policy," *Government Credit Allocation* 93–122 (1975); William E. Gibson, "Protecting Homebuilding from Restrictive Credit Conditions," *Brookings Papers on Economic Activity* 647–700 (Brookings Institution, Washington, D.C., 1973); and Penner and Silber, "The Interaction Between Federal Credit Programs and the Impact on Allocation of Credit," 63 American Econ. Rev., No. 5, pp. 838–852 (Dec. 1975). For general surveys of the issues relating to the use of selective credit policies, see Silber, "Selective Credit Policies: A Survey," 26 Banca Nazionale del Lavoro Q. Rev. No. 107 (Dec. 1973); and Mayer, "Financial Guidelines and Credit Controls," 4 J. Money, Credit & Banking, No. 2, pp. 360–374 (May 1972).

6. See Michael Hamburger, "Interest Rates and the Demand for Consumer Durable Goods," 57 American Econ. Rev., No. 5, pp. 1131–1153 (Dec. 1967).

7. In an examination of several durable goods expenditure models, Juster and Wachtel report that the Hamburger model performs as well or better than the alternatives considered. Juster and Wachtel, "Anticipatory and Objective Models of Durable Goods Demand," 1 Explorations in Economic Research, No. 2, pp. 340–392 (Fall 1974). We had initially hoped also to use a durable goods expenditures model developed by Evans and Kisselgoff. Evans, *Macroeconomic Activity: Theory, Forecasting, and Control* 151–183 (Harper and Row, New York 1969); Evans and Kisselgoff, "Demand for Consumer Installment Credit and Its Effect on Consumption," *The Brookings Model: Some Further Results* 41–83 (Duesenberry et al., Eds., Rand McNally & Co., Chicago 1969). Unfortunately, their work involves the use of some proxies for credit terms and controls which we were unable to reconstruct or to obtain from Evans. Since their work makes an attempt to evaluate the effects of the 1948–1952 credit controls, our results are compared to those originally reported by Evans and Kisselgoff in text accompanying N. 23.

price of durable goods relative to the price of all other goods and services purchased by consumers. That is,

$$\bar{A} = a + bY + cr + fP \tag{1}$$

where the parameters $b$, $c$, and $f$ denote the long-run effects of the independent variables on the desired stock. Except for the inclusion of $r$, this formulation of the demand function for consumer durable goods is similar to those that have been used elsewhere.[8]

Using the standard stock adjustment relation,

$$\Delta A_t = \theta(\bar{A}_t - A_{t-1}) \qquad 0 \leqslant \theta \leqslant 1 \tag{2}$$

where $\theta$ is the reaction coefficient and $A$ is the actual stock of durable goods, and using a transformation suggested by Nerlove,[9] the following equation for $X$, the *flow* of consumer durable expenditures, is obtained:

$$X_t = a' + b'[Y_t - (1 - d)Y_{t-1}] + c'[r_t - (1 - d)r_{t-1}] \\ + f'[P_t - (1 - d)P_{t-1}] + (1 - \theta)X_{t-1} + v_t \tag{3}$$

where $d$ represents the percentage of depreciation of the asset per time period.[10] Introduction of lagged values of the independent variables in eq. (1), i.e.

$$\bar{A} = a + bY_{t-n_1} + cr_{t-n_2} + fP_{t-n_3} \tag{4}$$

allows for differences in the speed with which expenditures on consumer durables begin to respond to alternative stimuli. Use of $t^*$ as a shorthand device for $(t - n_1)$, $(t - n_2)$ and $(t - n_3)$ yields the following alternative form for eq. (3):[11]

$$X_t = a' + b'[Y_{t^*} - (1 - d)Y_{t^*} - 1] + c'[r_{t^*} - (1 - d)r_{t^*} - 1] \\ + f'[P_{t^*} - (1 - d)P_{t^*} - 1] + (1 - \theta)X_{t-1} + v_t \tag{5}$$

---

8. See, e.g., Gregory C. Chow, "Statistical Demand Functions for Automobiles and Their Use in Forecasting," *The Demand for Durable Goods* 149–178 (Harberger, Ed., Univ. of Chicago Press, Chicago 1960); Fromm and Klein, "The Complete Model, A First Approximation," *The Brookings Quarterly Econometric Model of the United States* 681–738 (Duesenberry, Fromm, Klein, and Kuh, Eds., Rand McNally & Co., Chicago 1965); Stone and Rowe, "The Market Demand for Durable Goods," 25 Econometrica, No. 3, pp. 423–443 (July 1957).

9. Nerlove, *Distributed Lags and Demand Analysis for Agricultural and Other Commodities* (Washington, D.C., 1958).

10.
$$z' = \frac{z\theta}{1 - g} \text{ for } z = a,b,c,f$$

where $g$ is the coefficient of $X_t$ in the following equation for $D$, depreciation: $D_t = gX_t + dA_{t-1}$

11. The values of $t^*$ will generally not be the same for all of the explanatory variables. For nonzero values of $n_1$, $n_2$, and $n_3$, eqs. (4) and (5) imply that the adjustment of expenditures to changes in the explanatory variables is negligible for some time period, then rises abruptly to its maximum, and declines geometrically thereafter. Of course, actual expen-

The quantity of real money balances may affect the demand for consumer durables either as a measure of the ability of consumers to make large purchases or down payments[12] or as a proxy for total consumer wealth.[13] If the stock of real money balances is added to the explanatory variables of eq. (5), the following equation is obtained:[14]

$$X_t = a' + b'[Y_{t^*} - (1 - d) Y_{t^*-1}] + c'[r_{t^*} - (1 - d)r_{t^*-1}]$$
$$+ f'[P_{t^*} - (1 - d)P_{t^*-1}] + h'[M_{t^*} - (1 - d)M_{t^*-1}] \qquad (6)$$
$$+ (1 - \theta)X_{t-1} + v_t$$

Using eq. (6), two tests were carried out to determine the effects of the 1948–1952 controls on installment credit on the level of consumer durable expenditures. The first involved the use of the 1953–1964 parameter estimates of eq. (6), as presented by Hamburger.[15] Values of automobile and of other durable goods expenditures for the 1948–1952 period, as implied by 1953–1964 parameter estimates, were compared with the actual values of expenditures during this earlier period. The errors in the prediction of the two expenditure components are presented in Figure 7-19 (the equations are included in Appendix A). The

---

ditures, even if lagged, would probably not start off at their peak response but are more likely to build up gradually to the peak and then taper off. Hence, the adjustment pattern used here may be overly restrictive. However, given our interest in assessing the effects of installment credit and related variables on the demand for consumer durable goods, this pattern seems to provide a reasonable first approximation. It should be noted that at the time the model was originally estimated, many of the current distributed-lag computer algorithms were not widely available.

12. See Klein, "Major Consumer Expenditures and Ownership of Durable Goods," 17 Oxford University, Institute of Statistics, Bull., No. 4, pp. 387–414 (Nov. 1955).

13. See Klein, "A Postwar Quarterly Model: Description and Application," in National Bureau of Economic Research, Conference on Research in Income and Wealth, 28 *Models of Income Determination* (Studies in Income and Wealth) 11–36 (Princeton Univ. Press, Princeton 1964).

14. The stock of real money balances can be introduced into equation 6 either as a determinant of the flow of automobile expenditures or as a determinant of the desired stock of automobiles. The use of $M_t$ as a determinant of the flow rather than the desired stock has no effect on the form of the regression equations estimated below or on the meaning of the short-run adjustment coefficient of $M$. What is affected, of course, is the interpretation of the parameter of $M$ as a long-run coefficient. For further elaboration on this point, see Hamburger, N. 6 *supra*.

15. *Ibid.* The values of $d$ estimated by Hamburger using quarterly data are .08 for automobiles and .15 for other durable goods. The .08 estimate of the quarterly depreciation rate on automobiles corresponds to an annual rate of depreciation of .28, which is quite similar to the rates assumed or implied by the works of Chow, N. 8 *supra*; Charles S. Friedman, "The Stock of Automobiles in the United States," 45 *Survey of Current Business*, No. 10, pp. 21–28 (Oct. 1965); and Evans, *Macroeconomic Activity*, N. 7 *supra*. The estimated annual rate of depreciation for other consumer durables is almost .50, which seems unusually high. Except for the interest rate, the lags of the explanatory variables are three-quarters or less. For the interest rate, a lag of five-quarters provides the highest coefficient of determination in the automobiles equation, and a lag of six-quarters provides the closest fit in the equation for other consumer durables.

line across each section of the chart is drawn at the level of the average algebraic value of the errors. The average absolute values of the errors, for both automobiles and other consumer durables, are fairly large, indicating some difficulties in using the 1953–1964 parameter estimates to explain the 1948–1952 period. However, for both types of expenditures, the average absolute values of the errors are no greater for the quarters involving controls on installment credit than for other quarters, indicating that controls by themselves do not impair the explanatory power of the equations. This is one bit of evidence suggesting that the controls had little effect on consumer expenditures.

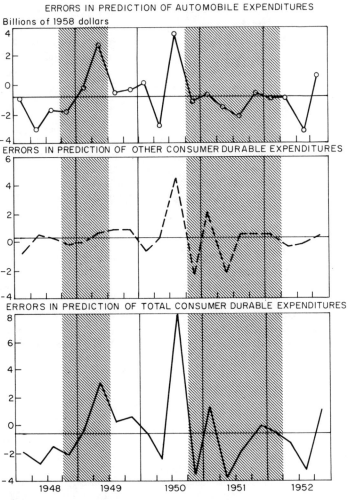

FIGURE 7-19 Errors in expenditure predictions. Note: Shaded areas represent periods when Regulation *W* controlling consumer credit was in effect. Horizontal lines are drawn at full sample means.

Of greater importance for the present analysis are the average *algebraic* values of the errors, since they would reveal any tendency of the model to overestimate expenditures during control quarters. For automobile expenditures, the average algebraic value of the errors for the quarters involving installment credit restrictions is essentially identical to the average error for other quarters. For other durable goods expenditures, the average value of the errors for the control quarters is slightly less than for the noncontrol quarters. During the control quarters, the average annual level of other durable goods expenditures relative to the predicted levels is $560 million (or 3 percent) less than during the noncontrol quarters. For total durable goods, the corresponding decrease during the control periods is about 1½ percent. Thus, the results suggest that while expenditures on consumer durable goods other than automobiles were affected in the anticipated direction by the imposition of the 1948–1952 controls on installment credit, the effect was quantitatively trivial.

Because of the relatively large errors in the out-of-sample predictions of eq. (6), the equation was reestimated for the 1948–1952 period to allow for adjustments in the lags on the independent variables. With this single modification, the standard errors of the equations, for both automobiles and other consumer durables, were reduced by about one-third. A dummy variable was then introduced, 1 for quarters involving controls on installment credit and 0 for the other quarters of the 1948–1952 period, and eq. (6) was reestimated. In the automobile equation, the coefficient of the dummy variable for credit controls is $-.06$ with a $t$-statistic of $-.08$, and the coefficients of the other variables are virtually unaffected by its introduction (equation included in Appendix A). In the other durable goods equation, the coefficient of the dummy variable for credit controls is $-.43$, its $t$-statistic is $-.69$, and there is some tendency for its introduction to reduce the significance of some of the other coefficients (equations included in Appendix A). These results, like those obtained with the 1953–1964 parameter estimates, suggest that the installment credit controls of the 1948–1952 period had no significant effect on the level of consumer durable expenditures.[16]

---

16. Both sets of results presented in this section are subject to a number of potential sources of bias. To begin with, we assume that whatever other effects credit controls may have, they do not alter the coefficients of the independent variables in the expenditure equations. To test the importance of this restriction, the equations were reestimated, allowing for differences in all the parameters during the control and noncontrol quarters. The results support our procedures: taken together, the differences in the slope coefficients (in both equations) are not significant, even at the 10 percent confidence level. Moreover, allowing for these differences does not alter the finding that the intercept dummy variable is both quantitatively and statistically trivial, e.g., the absolute value of its $t$-statistic never exceeds 0.5.

Second, the present model does not make explicit allowance for all the factors that affected durable goods expenditures during the 1948–1952 period. However, for the exclusion of any variable to bias the estimate of the effects of credit controls, the impact of the omitted variable on expenditures must be different during the control and noncontrol

**PREVIOUS STUDIES OF THE EFFECTS OF SELECTIVE CREDIT POLICIES**

The literature on selective credit policies includes numerous investigations of their effects on financial markets and on the balance sheets of particular financial institutions. These are not our concern. Instead, we review two studies and cite several others which deal specifically with the effects of selective credit policies on the allocation of real expenditures and resources. These studies are not presented as an exhaustive list of the material in this area; rather, our purpose is to provide an indication of the type of evidence that has been used to support the efficacy of consumer credit controls.

As part of the study on consumer installment credit commissioned by the Federal Reserve Board, Don Humphrey studied the relation between fluctuations in income and fluctuations in durable expenditures and installment credit.[17] In his analysis, he focused extensively on the early postwar period that includes the installment control periods analyzed above. To avoid misinterpretation of Humphrey's conclusions, we reproduce an extensive passage from the summary that appears at the beginning of his paper.

> Before the Second World War, fluctuations in disposable personal income usually produced corresponding movements in consumer expenditures

---

quarters. In particular, for the omission of a variable to lead to the understatement of the effects of controls, the omitted variable must cause expenditures to increase in quarters when credit is restricted relative to other quarters. Otherwise, the variable's omission would not cause the effects of controls to be understated, and could, indeed, overstate them. For example, supply constraints associated with the Korean War may have affected expenditures. Since controls on supplies and materials were completely absent until late 1951, our impression is that their effects on expenditures were small. In any case, their application during the war is positively, rather than inversely, related to the imposition of credit controls, and omission of this variable would tend to overstate the estimated effect of credit controls. Scare buying in anticipation of controls undoubtedly increased expenditures during the third quarter of 1950. Since this factor involves a shift of expenditures from the next several quarters (when controls were imposed) to this noncontrol quarter, its omission, like that of the Korean War supply constraints, causes the effects of credit controls to be overstated. Any pent-up demand from World War II that persisted into the 1948–1952 period presumably affected the control and noncontrol quarters similarly. Hence, its omission exerts no upward or downward bias on our estimate of the effects of credit controls.

Finally, it may be appropriate to consider alternative specifications of the credit controls intercept dummy variable. One possibility is to assume that credit controls have an initial impact on expenditures which declines over time as suppliers and demanders of credit find ways to circumvent the controls. We did not test this hypothesis explicitly because of the imprecision in its specification. However, an evaluation of the patterns of the residuals in Figure 7-19 suggests that this alternative formulation is unlikely to perform any better than the one tested.

17. Humphrey, "Installment Credit and Business Cycles," *Consumer Installment Credit*, Pt. II, pp. 3–55 (Bd. of Governors of the Federal Reserve System, Washington, D.C., 1957).

and installment credit. As a result credit expansion and contraction intensified the fluctuations in expenditures. In the postwar decade, however, consumer durable goods expenditures do not generally parallel income cycles before 1953. . . .

Since income and installment credit move in opposite directions more often than in the same direction, the influence of credit on disposable personal income is generally stabilizing for the more important cycles before 1953.

On the other hand, our findings show that installment credit fluctuates in the same direction as consumer durable goods expenditures during three-fourths of the postwar decade and undoubtedly intensifies the cyclical swings in durable goods expenditures.[18]

Since an increase in the supply or availability of credit, given the general determinants of demand, may increase the demand for durable goods, a positive correlation between installment credit flows and durable goods expenditures may reflect the effect of credit flows on expenditures. On the other hand, since an increase in the demand for durable goods, given the overall supply of credit in the economy, may increase the amount of installment credit supplied by lenders, a positive correlation between installment credit flows and durable goods expenditures may reflect the effect of expenditures on the supply of credit. From our point of view, what is interesting about Humphrey's statements, particularly since they seem to reflect a general view among many of the supporters of credit controls, is that, *without introducing any additional evidence,* he assumes that closer synchronization of the movements of installment credit to the movements of durable goods expenditures than to the movements of income reflects the effects of credit on expenditures rather than vice versa.

Another passage from Humphrey's summary is also of interest:

Net credit change fell sharply when regulation of installment credit was reimposed in September 1948, and again in September 1950. In each instance, moreover, the ratio of net credit change to income remained well below precontrol levels until restrictions were relaxed in the final quarter of controls. *A regression of installment credit extended against durable goods expenditures shows that less credit was extended per billion dollars of expenditures during periods of credit regulation than the average relationship for the decade.*[19]

What is striking about these comments, again because they seem to represent a typical orientation among many who have supported controls, is the impression that, as controls are introduced, the decrease in installment credit relative to expenditures represents evidence about

---

18. *Id.* at 4.

19. *Id.* at 5 (emphasis added).

the effectiveness of controls. As far as we can tell, this interpretation is based on the premise that control of credit, apart from the control of expenditures, is itself a useful goal of credit controls; or that the decrease in the use of credit per dollar of expenditures necessarily implies a reduction in the absolute level of expenditures. As controls are introduced, at no time is the decrease in the ratio of credit to expenditures interpreted as an indication that, while controls do effectively reduce the volume of credit, purchasers manage to maintain their level of expenditures by reducing savings or obtaining alternative forms of credit.[20]

To summarize, Humphrey reports evidence of (1) a closer synchronization of movements of installment credit to the movements of durable expenditures than to the movements of income, and (2) a decrease in the use of credit per dollar of expenditures as controls are introduced. Then, on the basis of these findings, he concludes that (1) the volume of credit affects expenditures and (2) credit controls, by reducing the use of credit, reduce the level of expenditures. This evidence and these conclusions appear to be major foundations on which belief in the effectiveness of the installment controls of the 1948–1952 period is based. However, the evidence he presents is subject to the alternative interpretation that (1) expenditures affect the volume of credit; and (2) credit controls cause people to reduce savings or obtain alternative forms of credit in order to maintain expenditures. Support for both components of the latter view is provided by the simple correlation between the changes in installment credit outstanding and consumer durable expenditures during the 1948–1974 period. Over the entire period, the $R^2$ between these variables is .55, but it drops to essentially zero (.025) during the 1948–1952 interval. This implies that although consumers customarily use installment credit to finance a substantial portion of their purchases of durable goods, they had little difficulty finding substitute sources of finance when the availability of this credit source was restricted during the late forties and early fifties.[21] We conclude that Humphrey's analysis provides no support for the efficacy of credit controls on expenditures.[22]

---

20. For example, Lewis Bassie, the discussant of Humphrey's paper, argues that "[i]n several postwar situations, changes in [credit] terms played a distinct part in determining the course of credit changes and, *presumably*, the purchases that might have been based on credit" (emphasis added), and cites evidence of a change in the credit/expenditure ratio as an indication that expenditures were affected by a change in the supply of credit. Bassie, "Comment," *id.* at 56–69.

21. It also may be worth noting that the 1948–1952 evidence described by Humphrey is inconsistent with the notion that expenditures were not affected by the 1948–1952 controls *because* the restrictions imposed on maturity and down payments were not sufficiently binding to affect the demand for consumer credit. As Humphrey reports, the volume of credit was affected by the imposition of controls (or at least the ratio of credit to expenditures); only expenditures were not affected.

22. As indicated earlier, the present survey is not intended to be exhaustive. In this connection, it may be noted that another recent review cites a different set of references from

An alternative type of evidence is presented by Evans and Kissel-goff.[23] Proceeding along the lines of the previous section, these authors formulate and estimate demand equations for automobiles and "other durable" goods and test for the effects of credit terms and credit controls within these relationships. In the automobile equation, but not in the other durables equation, Evans, using quarterly data from 1948 to 1964, reports a statistically significant effect of a "credit control" dummy variable, that takes the value of −1 for quarters of the 1948–1952 control periods, 0 for all other quarters from 1948 through 1954, and 1 for all quarters thereafter. An even stronger coefficient is reported for a "credit-term" variable—an index of the average monthly payment on installment loans for new cars. This variable is a function of the price of new cars, the maturity of the loan contract, the finance charge rate, and the percent of down payment.

The usefulness of the credit-terms variable as an indicator of the effects of credit controls is subject to considerable question because of the endogeneity problem. As in the case of credit flows, credit terms, as measured by down payment and length of contract, are endogenously determined through the simultaneous interaction of the supply and demand for expenditures and credit. A positive relation between durable expenditures and ease of credit terms (e.g., a lengthening of the contract) reflects the effect of credit terms on the demand for durable goods, or, alternatively, some degree of complementarity in the demands for durable goods and installment credit. In the latter case, one assumes that consumers exert some control over the credit contracts they enter into. However, in the Evans and Evans and Kisselgoff analyses (and in an earlier study by Suits[24]), the terms of these contracts

---

those included here. P. Smith, "A Review of the Theoretical and Administrative History of Consumer Credit Controls," in I. Kaminow and J. O'Brien, Eds., *Studies in Selective Credit Policies,* Federal Reserve Bank of Philadelphia, 1975. Smith's discussion seems to imply that consumer credit controls have an important impact on specific types of consumer expenditures. However, our reading of his source material suggests a different interpretation. While there appears to be a clear indication that controls influence the quantity of credit extended, we find little, or no, evidence of an effect on expenditures. The McCracken, et al. analysis (Paul W. McCracken, James C. Mao and Cedric Fricke, *Consumer Installment Credit and Public Policy,* Bureau of Business Research, Graduate School of Business Administration, University of Michigan, Ann Arbor, 1965, pp. 143–155) does not contain a single reference to the expenditure statistics. Moreover, the conclusion of the Dyckman contribution to the McCracken study (Thomas R. Dyckman, "Installment Credit in the 1955 Auto Sales Year: A Case Study," in McCracken, et al., *Id.,* pp. 181–240) seems more compatible with our view than with Smith's. Dyckman argues: "The rise in consumer automobile installment debt and the easing credit terms [in 1955] were responding to the increase in demand for new automobiles and to easy general credit conditions. Credit functioned as a permissive and not as a causal factor." *Id.,* p. 240.

**23.** Evans, N. 7 *supra*; Evans and Kisselgoff, N. 7 *supra.*

**24.** Suits, "The Demand for New Automobiles in the United States, 1929–1956," 40 Rev. of Econ. & Statistics, No. 3, pp. 273–280 (Aug. 1958).

are assumed to be entirely determined on the supply side of the credit market.[25]

The evidence relating to Evans' dummy control is not sensitive to the endogeneity problem that affects the credit terms variable and is opposite to the evidence presented in the previous section. Hence, it is important to consider the relative validity of the two analyses. Several factors favor acceptance of the earlier results and the conclusions derived from them. First, questions may be raised as to whether Evans' dummy variable measures what it is intended to. As noted above, the variable equals −1 for the control quarters, 0 for all other quarters from 1948 to 1954, *and* takes the value of +1 for all quarters after 1955. It is not clear what factors are picked up by the positive values of the control variable during the last part of the sample period and what they contribute to its significance. Moreover, neither study finds any significant impact of a credit controls dummy variable on the demand for durable goods other than automobiles. Finally, the evidence of the first section is based not only on estimation within the 1948–1952 period but also on a comparison of actual and predicted values derived from estimation outside the period.[26] While Evans' results cannot be completely discounted, each of these factors suggests that his findings, at least by themselves, are not sufficient to reverse the conclusions reached above.[27]

Because of changes in the economy since the 1948–1952 period, our evidence does not necessarily imply that credit controls would be ineffective today or in the future. To consider the potential effects of controls in today's economy, it is useful to consider the behavior of borrowers and lenders implied by current economic theory and recent

---

25. Moreover, the Evans and Kisselgoff credit-terms variable is, at least to some extent, misspecified. As a measure of the stringency of credit terms, one would expect the variable to be positively related to the size of the down payment and inversely related to the length of the installment contract. However, as constructed by Evans and Evans and Kisselgoff, the average monthly payment falls as the contract is lengthened (as desired), but also falls as the down payment is increased (opposite to what is desired).

26. Moreover, even within the period in which the Evans automobile equation is estimated, 1948–1964, its statistical fit is not as close as the equation reported in the first section. Of particular interest is the inclusion of a statistically significant interest rate in our specification. Evans' formulation does not include the interest rate, and this omission may help to explain the significance of his credit controls variable. Ideally, we would have reestimated Evans' regression with an interest rate, or at least determined how the interest rate behaved in the periods for which he used dummies, but, as mentioned in N. 7 *supra*, we were unable to reconstruct his data or to obtain them from him.

27. In a study of several types of expenditures, Cohen reports a positive relation between expenditures and credit flows for some sectors though not for others. Cohen, "Integrating the Real and Financial via the Linkage of Financial Flow," 23 J. Finance, No. 1, pp. 1–27 (March 1968). As mentioned above, a positive relation between credit and expenditures may reflect the effects of expenditures on credit rather than the effects of credit on expenditures. We believe that problems regarding the interpretation of Cohen's results, as well as the mixed nature of the results, limit their impact on our conclusions about the effects of selective credit policies.

empirical evidence. Theory suggests that borrowers choose overall portfolios of assets and liabilities. They do not select particular assets according to the availability of particular liabilities. This focus on overall portfolios implies that a decrease in the availability of a particular form of credit will encourage the creation of new forms of credit and new uses of existing forms of credit to finance the existing demand for assets.

The general innovative capability of the United States financial industry is well documented.[28] Two forms of evidence about recent loan behavior of banks in the Second Federal Reserve District provide a specific illustration of how lenders may respond to the pressure for new forms of credit in the consumer area. First, there are survey data which indicate that rates of automobile loans, from 1972 to 1975, have been approximately the same as the rates on unsecured personal loans. The second form of evidence, gathered by actual attempts to obtain automobile and unsecured personal loans from several banks in the Second Federal Reserve District, reveals that, for most borrowers, the rates on these loans are identical. When confronted with the initially surprising result that secured and unsecured loans carry the same rate, several loan officers of these banks indicated that automobile collateral (and presumably other collateral in the form of consumer durable goods) has no value, implying that the costs of repossessing and reselling such goods is greater than or equal to their market value. Others indicated that, in a few marginal cases, the use of an automobile as collateral would enable a borrower to qualify for a loan that would be denied on an unsecured basis.

These results do not imply that personal and installment loans are identical assets for commercial banks. However, they suggest that, in order to reduce the loss in volume and in earning assets from restrictions on automobile or other installment credit, banks would be likely to extend unsecured personal loans in place of many of the installment loans whose extensions were subject to control. This response would reduce the expenditure effects of any installment credit controls. Thus, the capacity to alter real resource allocation through selective credit policies is unlikely to be greater today (and may well be less) than it was during the 1948–1952 period.[29]

## SUMMARY AND CONCLUSION

With particular reference to durable goods expenditures, this paper reconsiders the question of the efficacy of selective credit controls in altering the allocation of real expenditures and resources. Several types

---

28. See, e.g., William L. Silber, Ed., *Financial Innovation* (Lexington Books, D.C. Heath & Co., Lexington, Mass., 1975).

29. To the extent that the bank lending practice described here existed in the 1948–1952 period, the present analysis provides an explanation of the results for that period rather than indicating any difference in the efficacy of controls.

of evidence are examined. First, we consider the explanatory power of a stock adjustment model of the demand for consumer durable goods. Although the model makes no allowance for credit controls, there is no tendency for it to overestimate expenditures when controls are operative. Moreover, the imposition of controls does not impair the model's explanatory power. The implication is clear: Credit controls do not affect expenditures.

Second, we review the evidence that has been presented previously to support the efficacy of selective credit policies in limiting expenditures. It is unpersuasive. Indeed, in many early studies, it seemed sufficient to demonstrate that the imposition of controls reduced the flow of credit. This assumes, of course, that there is a close and stable relationship between the volume of expenditures and the amount of credit extended. However, as indicated above, it is precisely when controls are introduced that this relationship breaks down. We interpret this entire set of evidence as indicating that, when controls on the extension of installment credit were imposed in the past, consumers, in an attempt to maintain durable goods expenditures, either reduced their stocks of savings or obtained alternative forms of credit.

To determine the likely effect of credit controls and other selective credit policies in today's economy, we examined the portfolio behavior of individuals, firms, and financial institutions, in conjunction with evidence about the loan behavior of banks in the Second Federal Reserve District. This analysis suggested that, in today's economy, the capacity of credit controls or other selective credit policies to alter the allocation of real resources is no greater, and may well be less, than in the past. While no single piece of evidence in the paper may be sufficient to indicate that selective credit policies exert no effect on the composition of real expenditures, the cumulative effect seems sufficient to shift the burden of proof from those who think selective credit policies exert no effect on the composition of real expenditures to those who think that they do.

# APPENDIX A—PARAMETER ESTIMATES OF EQUATIONS OF AUTOMOBILE AND DURABLE GOODS EXPENDITURES 1953–1964 AND 1948–1952*

| | Automobile expenditures | | Other durable goods expenditures† | | |
|---|---|---|---|---|---|
| | 1953 –1964 | 1948 –1952 | 1953 –1964 | 1948 –1952 | 1948–1952 |
| Intercept | 1.29 | .74 | 3.31 | 6.88 | 6.11 |
| | (.83) | (.22) | (1.60) | (1.02) | (.88) |
| Y | .205 | .165 | .096 | .206 | .207 |
| | (.058) | (.067) | (.018) | (.054) | (.054) |
| | [1] | [2] | [0] | [2] | [2] |
| r | −2.83 | −8.24 | −.804 | −6.17 | −5.88 |
| | (1.08) | (3.99) | (.363) | (3.04) | (3.14) |
| | [5] | [2] | [6] | [4] | [4] |
| r_sv | | | −2.20 | 6.30 | 7.14 |
| | | | (.90) | (8.53) | (8.79) |
| | | | [0] | [0] | [0] |
| P | −.169 | −.177 | −.332 | −.385 | −.269 |
| | (.109) | (.178) | (.101) | (.324) | (.370) |
| | [0] | [1] | [0] | [0] | [0] |
| M | .183 | .256 | .113 | .300 | .218 |
| | (.113) | (.175) | (.036) | (.127) | (.172) |
| | [3] | [2] | [3] | [3] | [3] |
| D | | −.059 | | | −.430 |
| | | (.709) | | | (.623) |
| $X_{t-1}$ | .582 | .663 | .780 | .100 | .142 |
| | (.075) | (.131) | (.042) | (.192) | (.205) |
| $R^2_{adj}$ | .913 | .775 | .995 | .612 | .596 |
| DW | 1.21 | 2.63 | 2.54 | 1.89 | 2.01 |

*Standard errors are in parentheses below the regression coefficients. The numbers in square brackets denote the lags associated with the dependent variables. All variables are defined and transformed as described here in pages 372 to 377 and in Michael Hamburger, "Interest Rates and the Demand for Consumer Durable Goods," *American Economic Review*, vol. 57, no. 5, Dec. 1967, pp. 1131–1153.

†For the 1948–1952 period, two equations for "Other durable goods expenditures" are shown in order to indicate the slight effect of the dummy variables. Only one equation for automobile expenditures is shown for this period, because there the effect of the dummy variable was trivial.

# COMMENTARY

Lester C. Thurow, *Professor of Economics and Management, Massachusetts Institute of Technology*

The paper "Credit Allocation and Housing," by Stanley Diller, essentially springs from a vision of perfectly competitive capital markets. Each saver sends his savings into the capital markets and is paid a competitive (equal) rate of interest by the financial intermediaries. Financial intermediaries, in turn, allocate the savings to those lenders who are willing to pay the highest rate of interest. With the exception of allowing for differences in risk and the costs of making loans (economies of scale in handling large borrowers), all borrowers pay at the same rate of interest. Differences between lending rates and borrowing rates reflect the financial intermediaries' costs (including a necessary profit) of making loans. The level of the competitive interest rate insures that the demand for savings equals the supply of savings. In such a world, no one cares to whom he lends or from whom he borrows. The same conditions are available everywhere. In such a world, social priorities are quite properly left in the government budget.

The question then becomes one of whether the real world is close enough to a perfectly functioning world that we can afford to operate on the premise that the real world functions perfectly. Alternatively, we could ask what changes would be necessary to bring the real world close enough to a perfectly functioning world to make the assumption valid.

By assuming that financial markets meet the tests of perfect competition, Diller misses the main point of credit allocation. If credit markets are not now neutral with respect to their lending policies (i.e., only looking at risks of repayment in making loans), government policies may be necessary to establish neutrality. Once neutrality is established, we can argue whether the government should go beyond neutrality and establish preferential lending sectors. I am not in favor of preference, but I am in favor of neutrality. As I shall argue, credit markets are not now neutral.

While a host of deviations between such a model and the real world could be noted, there are three major facts of life that are not in accordance with the ideal world. First, not all savings are allocated in the capital markets. In the ideal world, they should be. Second, private credit rationing is a pervasive fact of the real world. In the ideal world, it does not and cannot exist. Third, customer relationships are thought to be important. In the ideal world, the whole concept of a regular and valued customer does not exist. To some extent, these are not three independent deviations. The latter two spring principally from the first.

Corporate retained earnings are the major source of unallocated savings within the capital markets. They enjoy special tax and legal advantages. They are subject to neither the allocation procedures of the capital marketplace nor to the allocation desires of their owners (the individual shareholders). From the point of view of Diller's paper, all earnings (including depreciation charges) should be paid out as dividends and then brought back into the firm in the form of borrowings or equity issues. Corporate taxation should be abolished, but all dividends and depreciation allowances above the initial investment would be taxed as personal income in an integration of the corporate and personal income tax. As a result, corporations would be forced to compete for all their capital needs. Unless this is done, corporations have two major advantages in the country's capital markets. First, they have tied savings for which they do not have to compete. Second, their tied savings (cash flow) can be used as collateral to obtain extra funds in the capital markets. This is especially potent given Regulation Q. Conversely, the supply of savings for which others must compete is smaller than it should be.

Our actual financial markets are marked by credit rationing and by preferences for large regular corporate customers over small, irregular, noncorporate customers. Why? The answer lies in imperfect knowledge and in the tied savings of the corporate sector. Profit-maximizing financial intermediaries obviously want to cultivate the business of corporations with large flows of tied savings (cash flows). In our real world of oligopoly relationships, such a connection is the best method for maximizing long-run profits. Yet, from the point of view of economic efficiency, such long-run profit maximization will result in too few funds being allocated to the infrequent noncorporate borrower.

Logically, all the assumptions that lead to Diller's conclusions lead to the abolition of retained cash flow. Simple economic efficiency considerations demand it; yet Diller does not recommend it.

The absence of such a recommendation coupled with a recommendation to abolish Regulation Q leads to a paper that can best be described as self-serving. It is against special provisions for noncorporate sectors of the economy, but it does not favor the removal of those regulations and provisions which constitute special provisions for corporate America. Given a large imperfection in favor of corporate borrowers, there are *only* two options. Create equal preferences within the financial markets for noncorporate borrowers or stop the preferences for corporate borrowers. I am willing to stop the special preferences for corporate borrowers, but I suspect that, realistically, we must focus on equal preferences for noncorporate borrowers. Without such preferences, credit rationing will allocate too many funds to the corporate sector. This is not a question of equity but of efficiency.

## AN EXAMINATION OF SPECIAL CASES

Before examining the possible countervailing preferences that could be created for small, irregular, noncorporate borrowers, it is necessary to examine the special cases that are advanced for special financial regulations for special sectors. The areas usually cited include housing, state and local governments, agriculture, exports, and small businesses. In addition to its absolute merits, however, each case needs to be examined with an eye to alternative solutions. Are special financial regulations or institutions the best way to solve the problem?

### State and Local Governments

The basic problem of state and local government finance is not a problem of borrowing power but of taxing power. The relevant question is not, "How do we borrow more?" but, "How do we raise more tax revenue?" Revenue sharing and more use of the personal income tax completely dominate special borrowing provisions as a method of solving the financial problems of state and local governments. States are large institutions that can compete in the credit markets, and they can easily establish financial intermediaries to obtain borrowing economies of scale for small local governments in their jurisdictions. If the taxation problem were solved, the borrowing problem would not exist. Unless the tax problem is solved, there is no way to solve the borrowing problem.

The current tax exemption on state and local government bonds constitutes an inefficient subsidy, but legally, it cannot be eliminated by the federal government. The federal government can only bribe state and local governments to issue taxable bonds by offering them a larger direct subsidy than the financial markets now indirectly allocate them. Other than this change, I can think of no reasons why special provisions should be made for state and local governments, once neutrality has been established.

### Exports

The current system of export credit subsidies is another place where Diller was not looking. He is against special provisions that might constitute aid to noncorporate America, but he does not recommend the removal of export credit guarantees. Maybe a case could have been made for these special provisions in the days of fixed exchange rates, but in a system of flexible exchange rates, there is no case to be made for them. Whatever sudsidy is given in the export credit system (by the United States or other countries) is simply offset in induced changes in the exchange rate with no net gain to the United States.

## Agriculture and Small Business

Agriculture and small business would benefit from any general program to ensure equitable treatment for the small, irregular, noncorporate borrower, but the case for special provisions over and beyond this must rest on the argument that small, independent entrepreneurs contribute something to the country over and beyond their economic output. This may be true, but I would agree with Diller that the noneconomic benefits which different sectors produce should be rewarded in government budgets, not in regulations of the financial system. There simply is no method of regulation that yields everyone a gain equal to his noneconomic benefits. In addition, the whole society, not just savers, should be forced to compensate for such noneconomic benefits.

## Housing

If housing generates positive or negative externalities, private money markets will provide too little or too much housing, since all the benefits or costs of housing are not considered in each individual investment decision. Housing is probably subject to two types of externalities. First, a whole set of sociological externalities may flow from housing. These are popularly thought to include crime, alienation, and other factors. As a result, when social benefits are included, too little is invested in housing. Second, housing is subject to financial externalities because the value of your house depends upon how well your neighbors maintain their houses. Knowing this, each individual in the neighborhood has an incentive to undermaintain his own home, since doing so will have little effect on its value as long as all the other homes in the neighborhood are well maintained. Conversely, it does little good to maintain your own home if others are not maintaining theirs. The result of individual economic rationality, however, is collective irrationality. Too little is invested in housing maintenance, and housing (and commercial property) deteriorates much faster than economic rationality would warrant. Special incentives may be necessary to offset private inefficiency.

Social costs and benefits also are created by the seasonality of construction in northern climates. Each person wishes to build his home in the good weather period when construction costs are lowest; each person legitimately ignores the social costs of idle resources during periods of bad weather. Some of these costs are absorbed by the factors of production in the industry, but many are absorbed by society through unemployment compensation, inflation, and restrictive work rules. Rational social policies may call for much more bad weather construction than will ever occur as a result of individual decision making.

As a result, even in a world of perfect markets, some government program would be necessary to stop such collective irrationality from taking place. Individual housing decisions will lead to too little being invested in housing. Some form of incentive is needed to inject the sociological benefits of housing into the private economic calculus and to prevent the social costs of seasonality and neighborhood deterioration.

In addition, when a society decides upon its optimum distribution of private money incomes through its tax policies, society is de facto deciding on its optimum distribution of marketable economic goods. There may be goods, however, that society wishes to distribute in a different manner. Such goods are "merit wants," and the usual preference is to distribute them more equally than the general basket of goods and services. There is no method for doing this through the private market mechanism, however, since there can be only one distribution of money income. Consequently, these goods are furnished through government policies, even though they do not meet the classical tests of pure public goods. The most common such merit wants are education, housing, and health care. Society seems to have indicated that it wants these particular goods to be more equally distributed than other marketable economic goods. If you like, we are more communistic with respect to some goods than others.

Thus, the question arises as to how housing can be more equally distributed than the distribution of money income. Private market mechanisms will never bring about such a distribution without government interference of some sort.

As a result, a strong case can be made that private market mechanisms will not lead to an optimum (from an efficiency or equity viewpoint) investment in housing or to an optimum distribution of this investment across the population, even if the current preferences for corporate borrowers are eliminated. While a case can be made for more housing investments than would occur in a perfectly competitive private market, this does not mean that special credit provisions—above and beyond those needed to establish neutrality—could be created to solve the problem. If such a situation exists, budgetary provisions are clearly preferable.

Diller misses the point when he demonstrates that there is a natural cycle in the relative size of residential lending and business lending as monetary policies tighten. Of course there is. Residential buyers drop out because they cannot afford to pay the competitive rates. The question is not whether society should allow it to occur. Is it good social policy to collapse the housing sector of the economy during a period of tight money? What happens to the long-run supply characteristics of the industry if we periodically force it out of business?

## THE EXISTENCE OF CREDIT CRUNCHES

If the Diller view of the world is correct, credit crunches where the private markets allocate credit on something other than the price of credit (i.e., the interest rate) cannot exist. Yet, we all know that they do exist. In the fall of 1974, it was common to call a mortgage lending institution and be told that the mortgage rate was 10 percent, but that the institution was not making any loans. No attempt was made to determine the riskiness of the borrower or the maximum interest rate that he or she was prepared to pay. The institution simply was not making mortgage loans, regardless of the credit worthiness of the borrower.

I would simply ask Dr. Diller why he thinks credit crunches exist. Given that they do exist, neutrality should call for some changes to eliminate them. Any time a market is allocating credit based on something (old and valued customers, etc.) other than price, it is being inefficient. How would he remove this inefficiency? The answer is simple. To remove credit crunches and private credit allocation, you would have to eliminate both Regulation Q and retained corporate earnings. Efficiency calls for it. Why not recommend it?

The question is not answered by demonstrating that housing demand would probably fall faster in perfectly competitive capital markets than nonhousing demand—we all believe that. The questions revolve around reductions in housing demand imposed by private credit rationing that are greater than those that would occur in a perfectly competitive capital market. Regressions without credit crunch variables for periods of nonprice rationing prove nothing, since they simply bury the effects of nonprice rationing into estimations of price elasticities that are too high.

## INTERNAL INCONSISTENCIES

In addition to assuming, rather than proving, the existence of neutrality (with the exception of an appropriate risk premium for each borrower, everyone pays the same interest rate and can borrow whatever he or she wants), the Diller paper is marred by internal inconsistencies. He wants to work both possible arguments, even when they conflict with each other.

If fungibility of credit means that credit allocation policies cannot work, it also means that credit allocation policies cannot hurt anything.

Either they are effective and could distort credit allocation in possibly perverse ways, or they are ineffective and could not possibly distort credit in perverse ways. If Diller believes his statement that "government cannot preempt a sufficient share of any credit market to forestall neutralizing actions by the remaining part of the market," I would suggest we all go home and not waste time and money persuading Congress to adopt possible credit policies. Whatever it does, it cannot do any harm.

On the contrary, I think that it can do harm, because it can be effective. Using credit allocation schemes, the Swedes, for example, have been able to increase residential lending and building while at the same time reducing business lending and investment.[1] If policies can make a difference, as I believe they can, we have a duty to avoid bad policies and adopt good ones.

I find his disdain for the impact of interest rates inconsistent, since he himself in his regressions finds that interest rates have a very large impact on real housing demand.

He also ignores the cash flow problem faced by any family. A house may be a great investment, but if you cannot meet the monthly carrying charges, you cannot make this great investment. Diller is correct to point out that factors other than credit costs have raised the monthly carrying charge, but credit costs are a substantial part of the problem. Because of the cash flow problem, you cannot simply dismiss high gross interest rates on the grounds that the rate of appreciation has been high enough to generate low net interest costs. The individual pays the gross cost today, and only at some far distant date (at death?), reduces it to its ultimate net cost.

He talks about the restrictions in housing caused by unions, but does not seem to realize that the vast proportion of housing built in the United States is built by nonunion labor. Union-built single family homes are almost nonexistent. As a result, entry restrictions in unions are hardly going to impact the cost of housing. Conversely, eliminating them is also not going to impact the cost of housing. All the discussion of the relative price of construction also ignores a large literature demonstrating that the price deflators in the GNP accounts exaggerate the amount of inflation that has occurred, since the GNP accounts systematically underestimate the amount of productivity that has taken place in the construction industry.

## CONCLUSIONS

I agree with all Diller's conclusions. Existing rules and regulations should be removed, and no system of credit allocation that simply

---

1. House Comm. on Banking & Currency, Staff Rep., *Foreign Experience With Monetary Policies to Promote Economic and Social Priority Programs*, 92nd Cong., 2d Sess. 27 (May 1972).

focuses on banking institutions alone should be instituted. I would note, however, that it is the banking institutions themselves, and not some perverse coalition of the poor, that keeps Regulation Q in existence. I would only add to this list the provision that we should require the payout of all corporate cash flow, abolish the corporate income tax, and then sit back to enjoy the benefits of an enlarged, effective, neutral capital market.

In the end, the problem comes down to one of establishing neutrality among potential borrowers. If we are ready to eliminate the special provisions that exist for corporate borrowers—principally, Regulation Q and tax incentives for retained earnings—neutrality could be established without having to move in the direction of credit allocation. If, however, we are unable to eliminate the special provisions that exist, there is a second-best argument for moving to some sort of asset-reserve requirement. Under a system of asset-reserve requirements, the government places a 100 percent reserve requirement on some fraction of each and every financial institution's assets, unless this fraction is invested in the desired sectors. For example, if national goals called for investing 25 percent of national savings in housing and other preferred sectors, each financial institution would have a 100 percent reserve requirement on that fraction of its assets. As long as it invested 25 percent of its assets in housing, however, it would not have to leave any reserves with the government. If it had invested only 20 percent of its assets in housing, 5 percent of its assets would have to be held with the government as required reserves. If it invested nothing, 25 percent of its assets would be held as reserves. Thus, *all* financial institutions are essentially given the option of making interest paying loans in the housing field or making an interest-free loan to the government. Different asset-reserve requirements are essentially different tax rates.

The asset-reserve requirement has several advantages over the present system for aiding housing. First, it works. It can insure that housing gets whatever fraction of total funds policymakers think housing should get. Credit crunches have no effect on its effectiveness. Funds cannot flow away from housing, since there are no financial institutions that can avoid housing investment. Every financial institution is required to be a housing institution to some degree. (This does not mean, however, that every financial institution must operate in the housing field at the retail level. Specialized housing institutions could issue bonds for those institutions with no expertise in housing and no desire to get into this business.) Second, it is a simple, straightforward regulation that does not require the cumbersome and complex set of regulations necessary to maintain the present system. Third, it does not discriminate between the small saver and the big saver. Each can receive the same interest returns. Fourth, institutions are not locked out of other areas. If a savings and loan society has a good industrial lending opportunity, it can make such a loan. Fifth, the government does not have to raise the taxes necessary to finance the fiscal alternative, and it does not need to build a bureaucracy large enough to manage a large, direct involvement in the housing field.

To the extent that asset-reserve requirements are used to correct the two capital market imperfections on which I have been focusing, they are regulations called for by simple, economic efficiency. No equity considerations emerge. To the extent that asset-reserve requirements are used to stimulate social rather than private benefits, there is an equity issue. It is fair to force savers to invest part of their funds for social, as opposed to private, goals. Once again, this comes back to the previous second-best question as to whether an asset-reserve requirement is a better or a worse tax than other taxes that might be used to obtain the same goal.

The answer to this question is obviously a matter of value judgment that I have not been elected to make. Relative equity, however, is often easier to determine. Let me venture the hypothesis that a system of general asset-reserve requirements that shifted the same quantity of funds into these sectors as the present system of regulations would be more equitable than the present system of rules and regulations. Horizontal inequities among savers would certainly be eliminated. Given the progressivity of savings rates, such a regulatory tax on savings would certainly be a progressive tax.

Finally, it must be noted that asset-reserve requirements (formal or informal) are used in many developed countries. Based on two studies conducted by myself and some colleagues at M.I.T. for the United States House Banking and Currency Committee, they seem to be the only effective regulatory mechanism for moving funds into priority areas.[2] This does not eliminate the need to choose between the fiscal and regulatory approach, however, since the fiscal approach can also work. Nor would adoption of the asset-reserve requirement allow the elimination of all budgetary expenditures for the same areas. Asset-reserve requirements can move funds into particular areas, but they really cannot be used to move funds to particular individuals. If the goal is low-income housing, as opposed to just housing, for example, expenditure programs and asset-reserve requirements would need to be coordinated. Without programs to move the necessary funds into the desired areas, however, distributional policies simply cannot work.

But let me emphasize once again that asset-reserve requirements are not the first-best solution. At best, they are only second-best. The first-best solution is to establish a capital market where all the country's savings are allocated neutrally across potential borrowers. With the

---

2. For the discussion of how various foreign countries attempt to aid sectors of social priority, see House Comm. on Banking & Currency, Staff Rep., *Activities by Various Central Banks to Promote Economic and Social Welfare Programs*, 91st Cong., 2d Sess. (Dec. 1970); and House Comm. on Banking & Currency, *Foreign Experiences with Monetary Policies to Promote Economic and Social Priority Programs*, 92nd Cong., 2d Sess. (May 1972).

exceptions of different risk premiums that reflect the probability of repayment and different charges for administrative costs, everyone pays the same interest rate and has equal access to credit. We do not have that at the moment—credit crunches prove its nonexistence—but there is no reason why we cannot have it if we are willing to practice rather than preach the virtues of free competitive markets.

# COMMENTARY

Dwight M. Jaffee, *Professor of Economics, Princeton University*

When I first read Stanley Diller's paper I was a bit upset, because I agreed with it so much, and as a commentator, that is not a pleasant situation. Indeed, to be a critic, I was going to have to play the role of devil's advocate. When I later learned that Lester Thurow was also commenting and that he takes the devil's position with such enthusiasm, I was much relieved. Thurow's paper has changed little since he presented it a number of years ago at a Federal Reserve Bank of Boston conference. Ed Kane and Eli Shapiro were the discussants at that conference, and in my view, they did a first-rate job of illustrating the flaws of Thurow's analysis.[1]

Thurow's paper is sufficiently important that I will briefly summarize the critique by Kane and Shapiro. Their main point was that corporate retained earnings and the provision of financial services to corporations by banks are not basically related. There is little ground for arguing that the banking system or the financial markets take funds away from priority sectors, such as housing markets or state and local governments, because corporations do a large amount of saving through retained earnings. In fact, if corporations were forced to distribute these earnings and were required to issue equity to carry out new investments, there would be hardly any difference in the way banks would operate. It does not matter to a bank whether a firm's deposit account has been developed through retained earnings or from equity issues. Thurow makes the comment that Diller was self-serving on this score. To the contrary, in my view, Diller would have been self-

---

1. See Thurow, "Proposals for Rechanneling Funds to Meet Social Priorities," *Policies for a More Competitive Financial System* 179–204 (Fed. Reserve Bank of Boston, Conference Series No. 8, Boston, 1972).

serving *only* if he had suggested that corporations *should* distribute their savings and then come to certain brokerage firms with additional underwriting business to obtain new equity funds.

The second point is that the real reason for a tie-in relationship between the corporations and the banks is the prohibition against interest payments on demand deposits. Banks which want to obtain demand deposit balances have no normal market mechanism with which to compete for these funds. Consequently, they do use nonmarket, nonprice means to induce corporations to maintain demand deposit balances. This is the real source of the problem. If we allow interest payments on demand deposits, then AT&T's dollars will be no better than mine, and there will be no reason for the bank to give special services to them.

The prohibition against interest on demand deposits is a fine example of the sort of problem one gets into with selective credit controls. Somewhere deep in the past, the Depression in this case, somebody for some reason legislated a prohibition against the payment of interest on demand deposits. Years later, we need additional regulations, such as selective credit controls, to offset the negative effects of this prohibition. It would seem a more rational course simply to eliminate the original bad legislation.

A third point concerns the issue of housing. Thurow argues that all housing is worthy of social priorities, and that anything that promotes housing is good. This is just not the case. Many can agree that low-income housing is worthy of some social priority. But, mortgage subsidy programs do little, if anything, to aid low-income housing. Mortgage subsidy programs are regressive in their mortgage market effects, they are regressive in their savings deposit effects, and they have very modest effects on housing in general. The effects they have do not benefit low-income people. Mortgage subsidies are just the wrong way to go.

It is very hard to get this point across to Congress, in part because the housing lobby is so strong. I, personally, have come to the view that if the housing people want mortgages so badly, then give them all the mortgages they want; but do it in the least costly way. Because credit is so fungible (as are mortgage funds), the least-cost method is for Ginny Mae, or some other government agency, to buy the required amount. This is a solution many European countries have used. Purchasing the mortgages directly is much better than using selective controls—asset-reserve requirements, and the like.

Thurow says that asset-reserve requirements work, are simple, and do not discriminate. My response is that they will not work, they are incredibly complex, and they will clearly discriminate. He points to Sweden as an example. I spent a year in Sweden studying its policies for managing housing and mortgage markets. My conclusion is just the opposite of his.

The first point is that Sweden has achieved a stable growth in housing. Factually, then, I agree with Thurow and disagree with Diller. The reason for the stability in Swedish housing, however, is not the magic of regulated markets, but the large excess demand for housing that existed from World War II until 1971. People were doubling up all over the country, and the government would not allocate the necessary real resources to housing. They used a permit system: They allocated five permits one year, six the next, and seven the next, which resulted in a very nice time trend. The Swedish "success" has little to do with mortgage markets and financial markets. They used a real resource constraint to achieve a stable growth in housing. More or less, this is also true of most European countries. They plan and allocate real resources, and the result is stability in those markets.

But stability is not itself a virtue. If you talk to many Swedish economists, the sector of their economy that they are least happy with, indeed that they are embarrassed about, is housing. During this period of excess demand, they were building skyscrapers out in the Tundra, 50 miles from Stockholm, and people were queueing to get into these units because of the shortage. Around 1971, supply and demand crossed, and there was a sudden excess supply. Only then was it discovered that they had built the wrong kind of housing. Sweden is wealthy, and, not surprisingly, there is a high income elasticity in their housing demand. Families did not want to live on the fifteenth floor, in a one-room apartment, out in the middle of nowhere. Suddenly, they found that all this smooth growth of housing produced the wrong kind of housing.

Their solution was perhaps even more interesting than the problem. The political solution was not to say, "Well, we made a mistake and we should build new housing." Rather, the solution was to say, "We must subsidize the rent on the existing units so it is low enough that people will actually want to live in those units." Sweden uses a system of short-term mortgages, and rent in this system is basically a markup over the mortgage rate. So, the way to subsidize rent in Sweden is to lower mortgage rates.

How did they get the mortgage rate lower? They simply told the banks to purchase the low-coupon securities. If the banks showed any reluctance, they were reminded of certain pending legislation—pending for 30 years—to nationalize the banking system. In view of this, the only question for the banks was how to allocate the bonds among themselves.

There is a moral in all this: Selective controls can work—you can make them work. But, the controls cannot be subtle. Asset-reserve requirements are too subtle a device. In Sweden, the direct approach works, but only because it has certain characteristics: It is a small country, there are five banks, and the people have a philosophical bent toward socialist principles. When we have tried it here, we have discovered that the costs are too great. The whole scenario of Regulation Q, and its ramifications, bears this out. We will not pursue selective credit policies all the way, and there is no sense in going half way.

Returning to Diller's paper for a minute, there are a couple of points I would have stressed differently, although from his oral presentation, I can see that we are really in very close agreement.

The first is that one has to distinguish between the effects one can achieve in the financial markets and the effects one can achieve in real resources. Selective credit policies can influence financial markets and can make money flows go hither and yonder. The problem is that real resources, not financial flows, are the real objective, and there the going gets much tougher.

The second point concerns the question of money crunches and credit rationing. Here, I lean more toward Thurow. I think credit crunches do occur. They are cyclical phenomena that last, typically, for two or three quarters, and when they do occur, they create a problem—one that we well might want to do something about. The solution is basically simple: Direct the government agencies into these markets and have them buy up mortgages during the brief period in which the private market for some reason has become disorganized. There is another side to that coin. When you get into a boom period such as we had in 1971, 1972, and 1973, those same government agencies should be out selling mortgages; they do not always do that.

One last point we might want to discuss further. If you have an economy that you are trying to cool down, some sector must reduce its call on real resources. For reasons that have already been mentioned, housing turns out to be a likely candidate. The problem is that housing production is relatively labor intensive in the United States. It is labor intensive all over the world, but more so in the United States. One reason for this could be the big cycles in housing: To minimize its losses, the construction industry consists of small units. The last thing construction companies are about to do is invest in heavily capital-intensive techniques. There is a cause and effect circle here. It might be that if we stabilized housing more, we might encourage more capital-intensive construction techniques, which would have long-term benefits in terms of lower housing prices.

# COMMENTARY

George Cooper, *Professor of Law, Columbia University*

I have a dual advantage over everyone else in this discussion. I know less about economics in general, as the only lawyer amongst a group of economists, and I know less about the subject at hand, not being an expert on credit markets. Nonetheless, Frank Edwards has asked that I try to join the issue from the viewpoint of an objective observer.

Unfortunately, I do not see that there is any issue to be joined. Everyone seems to say that pursuing governmental policies to allocate credit either is going to be ineffective, or if effective, will be a relatively inefficient technique compared to other more direct means of accomplishing the ultimate goals.

The only argument even advanced for using credit allocation strategies is Professor Thurow's position that the ability of corporations to retain earnings, coupled with the tax inducement for them to do so, gives them an unfair source of credit that needs to be neutralized somehow. Well, President Carter pledged himself to integrate the corporate and individual income taxes, and most proposals to do this would tend to encourage, if not necessitate, the regular payout of corporate profits, thus negating Professor Thurow's argument. This tax integration appears a very likely tax reform of the next several years. The Republican administration also urged it. Thus, to the extent that Professor Thurow's argument is valid, future tax reform is likely to undercut it. Moreover, I share the doubts of other speakers as to the basic validity of the argument. The problem of tax-induced retained earnings has a myriad of implications, and it needs to be dealt with directly. Credit allocation techniques would merely offset some of the supposed undesirable effects of these retained earnings while generating a whole new set of undesired, as well as desired, dislocations. The inherent inefficiency of pursuing an indirect strategy, such as credit allocation, to cope with the perceived excess power of corporations seems obvious.

But notwithstanding the fact that no real case has been made for it, let us assume that one wants to continue to pursue the argument, and ask why is it that using governmental policies to allocate credit is going to be unsuccessful. This lack of success is not, I believe, because the total fungibility of credit markets will prevent credit allocation from having any effect at all, as Dr. Diller suggests. Unless I have misunderstood Dr. Diller's analysis, he misperceives the effects of fungibility. Take one simple example he gives of the government trying to increase the allocation of credit to utilities by intervening in the market and buying utility bonds. Dr. Diller says that when the government does this, it drives prices up, causing yields to fall and private investors to begin moving away, meaning that the government has merely displaced private investors. That analysis is accurate if the utilities sit there and simply watch what is happening and do not do anything about it. It seems more likely, however, that when the prices begin to go up on the bonds, the utilities will begin to take an interest in projects which they had previously forgone because of the cost of borrowing. The utilities will then issue more bonds to take advantage of the increased demand until a new equilibrium is reached. To this extent, we will wind up with more credit in the utility area. Dr. Diller may be partially right in that we cannot expect a dollar-for-dollar increase in credit for utilities simply because of the new money that the government put there, but there will undoubtedly be some increase.

Moreover, even if Dr. Diller were correct in his fungibility analysis, there surely are some governmental credit intervention techniques which *can* be effective in reallocating credit. Certainly, government subsidy techniques can do that. I do not think, for example, that even Dr. Diller would deny that the tax exemption of municipal bonds has increased the amount of credit going to states and municipalities as distinguished from the private sector.

The problem, therefore, is not the lack of ability to have any effect with credit allocation techniques, but rather, the likely inefficiency of those techniques in achieving ultimate goals.

We need to look at each particular technique and ask two simple and obvious questions about it: First, is it going to be at all effective in changing credit flows in the way intended? Some techniques are almost totally ineffective, at least in achieving the purposes for which they are undertaken. For example, Dr. Diller's criticism of Regulation Q on the ground that it is wholly misguided is very powerful.

Second, to the extent that a technique is at least somewhat effective in altering the distribution of credit, we need to explore more precisely what its effects are likely to be in terms of the allocation of real resources and contrast that to available alternatives. Let us, for example, look at

Professor Thurow's asset-reserve proposal, with its emphasis on stimulating housing. If Professor Jaffee is right, it will probably be somewhat effective, especially if you extend it to enough financial institutions. But what will those effects be? Here, we move into speculative terrain as we try to sort out the implications of this indirect approach for coping with problems in the housing market.

Dr. Diller suggests that to the extent that banks are forced to devote more loans to housing, the money that the banks are lending is going to be diverted from somewhere else, and he suggests that it is going to come from small business. That may be right, although I would generalize more and say that loan funds would be reallocated away from the most marginal aspect of the banking business, the lowest profit end of it. To the extent that small business has few credit alternatives, it may well be that the profitability of small-business loans is not so low as to make them first in the queue for termination. However, let us assume that it will be small business that will lose out. I am not sure it much matters; whoever is squeezed out will presumably shift to another activity. The small businesses which are squeezed out of credit markets will presumably move over and enter the housing area, or be replaced by other small businesses who participate because of the new demand in housing and the new credit available in that area. The end result is not that any group in particular is knifed in the process. Rather, borrowers in general who were formerly doing one thing will be induced to do something else, and that, after all, is the purpose of reallocating credit: to get more people out of other things and into housing.

On the distribution question, it seems to me that there is no reason, on the face of it, to assume that this reallocation will have an invidious distributional effect among classes of producers. Only if housing producers are inherently less worthy than other producers would this be a problem, and I know of no reason to suspect any such inherent tendency. One also has to ask how effective the policy would be in accomplishing any redistributional goal. What would the distributional effects be among consumers? Here, I have my doubts. I subscribe to the view that most of this shift of funds to housing will go into middle-income or upper-income housing. The effect of the shift of credit will be to marginally lower the cost of housing. Low-income housing is more than marginally unprofitable, it is off-the-wall unprofitable, and nobody is going to be induced into it by marginally lowering the cost. Thus, we could expect to get more middle-income and upper-income housing, which is not bad, but it is also a relatively low-priority governmental goal.

What all this points up is that a simple subsidy for desired classes of housing would be a cleaner and more efficient program. The effects of credit allocation are so complex and speculative, and the means of bringing it about so difficult, that we should prefer more direct and simpler strategies. In other words, what everybody here has suggested is probably true. If you want to use governmental policies to bring about changes in demand, the more effective way to do it is to directly attack the demand with specific subsidies rather than to try an indirect massage of the credit markets. Credit regulation makes sense when credit qua credit is the problem, not when we expect to influence something else, like real spending, with credit.

# DISCUSSION

FRANKLIN R. EDWARDS:  Does anyone wish to address a question to one of the speakers?

HARVEY LEVIN:  Who benefits from the selective controls you are talking about? Many of you said that they do not have any impact at all, and one of you said that they do have some effects but not the ones that are intended. Could any of the panelists comment on the distributional effects of these controls? Perhaps Lester Thurow?

THUROW:  If you look at any of these rules and regulations, there are some obvious beneficiaries. If nothing else, there is an income effect. The government is essentially putting credit into the system, and the total supply of credit is larger. Even if you think that every market is completely fungible, when the total supply increases, something happens in each component, and somebody wins and somebody loses.

For example, suppose that the government put money into the credit markets, that housing had a very elastic demand, and that everything else had an inelastic demand. Then, it would not make much difference where the government put the money; it would have an impact on housing. Given that the money goes into housing, how much of it really lowers the price to the purchaser, how much raises the income of people building houses, etc.? To argue that it does not have any impact just does not make any sense. Even if you want to go so far as to argue that there are no substitution effects, which I would not want to argue, you have to say that there are at least some income effects.

LEVIN: On which groups in specific?

THUROW: Who defends Regulation Q? The banks! Who defends Davis Bacon? The labor unions!

RONALD GREENBERG: I do not understand why retained earnings are thought to be responsible for lack of neutrality in the credit market.

THUROW: I am talking about retained cash flow. It is in the bank after you have paid off your suppliers, your laborers, and the government. You can decide to pay it out to the shareholders—no question about that. The question is whether it ought to go to the owner or to the manager. If it went to the owner and not the corporate manager, would it be spent in exactly the same way? If you look at the real rates of return on capital investment, as calculated by the FTC or anybody else, you will see enormous differences. I would suggest that if you had been a shareholder of United States Steel and had gotten all their retained earnings, you would not have put it back into United States Steel the way managers actually did. The capital market exists, to some extent, to capitalize this disequilibrium in the real capital market out of existence. The argument, however, is that managers are not a pass-through device.

BERNARD SHULL: Professor Thurow, is the assumption underlying your position on retained cash flow that instead of funds being bid for in competitive financial markets, they are obtained in imperfectly competitive credit markets?

THUROW: No, you obtain funds in product markets which may or may not be perfectly competitive, but then they are not allocated in a competitive capital market. If you look at the rate of return on capital investment, making adjustments for risk, you will not find everybody earning the same rate of return as you would in the perfectly competitive capital markets that we all envision. This indicates that managers must make different decisions than a perfectly competitive capital market would. For example, if you look at drugs, you find that the drug industry has had the highest rate of return every year in the postwar period, twice the average. How can that happen for a 25-year period if everyone is making optimal real capital investments? It is not "risk" if they have the highest rate of return every year. If ex-ante risk never shows up as ex-post risk, it is not risk.

PAUL DEROSA: My question is to both Professor Thurow and Professor Jaffee. They seem to agree that during periods of monetary stringency, the mortgage markets break down. I think they are in agreement that the cause of this is that deposits are redirected away from thrift institutions and into the open market.

But the government has established a set of institutions to ameliorate that negative aspect of Regulation Q. They have developed the Federal Home Loan Bank System, Fanny Mae, and Ginny Mae. These institutions were developed, in effect, to soothe the problem of disintermediation. In light of these additional institutions, how can one now justify being concerned about credit crunches?

THUROW: If they could actually offset the disintermediation, you would not have the problem we have. But they simply cannot swing enough money around to offset what the private sector is doing.

JAFFEE: I thought that most of what you said was right. These institutions, Fanny Mae and the Federal Home Loan Bank Board, have been around a long time. They are not recent innovations directed at this problem. Also, I think that the problem has been around a long time. One aspect of the problem is that the mortgage rate moves sluggishly up or down, and this has been a feature of the mortgage market going back to the beginning of the century. You can find reports in the 1900s discussing why the mortgage rate is so sluggish in clearing the market.

The thrust of your point is that these institutions, the Bank Board and Fanny Mae, should be able to clear the market. I think that is right, and it is a question of how quickly they react and how much they are willing to throw into the balance. There is also an offsetting effect. The Bank Board has to get the permission of the Treasury before it can finance these advance loans to the S & Ls, and the two times that the Treasury has said "no" to them were during the 1966 and 1970 credit crunches.

PHILLIP CAGAN: The argument that monetary policy often works to discriminate among different sectors of the economy because it works through financial markets is a common one. In times of monetary restraint, those sectors of the economy that are heavily dependent on borrowing must cut back and bear most of the burden of restraining aggregate demand. The issue, however, is whether or not this is desirable.

I would like to address this question to Professor Jaffee, since I remember that he said we might want to do something about the housing sector because we do not want to see people cut back or forced into bankruptcy when we have a period of severe monetary restraint. During periods of monetary restraint, somebody has to cut back. Why not the sector that is most sensitive to the interest rate? If it happens to turn out to be the housing sector, what is wrong with that?

I remember when I was on the Council of Economic Advisors in 1970, and one of these financial crunches was going on. One of the things that really came in loud and clear to Washington was that the home building industry was very unhappy with monetary restraints. They were going out of business, and they said that if we wanted to see a home building industry in this country, we had better do something about it. We were all shaking in our boots, but we were too late to do anything about it, so the crunch ran its course, and the housing industry went through the wringer. Yet, a year later, there was the housing industry again. I am wondering if it is as bad as they say it is, and whether or not this is a pretty good industry to cut back. When they cut back, labor flows out, and when times get better, it comes back again. It does not seem so inefficient or socially costly.

The question is: What are the criteria in deciding who does get cut back in times of restraint?

JAFFEE: Fundamentally, I agree with what you are saying. Housing is an asset where the demand is shiftable, and what difference does it really make over the lifetime of a person when he buys his house?

CAGAN: I was not thinking of the buyer, I was thinking of the industry, or the suppliers.

JAFFEE: I certainly do not know what the truth is about this. It is a perplexing problem because there is a possibility that it is circular. If you run the economy in such a way that housing fluctuates widely, you get a housing industry which is arranged such that it can live through these things, and does. Is that optimal?

Indeed, I was just talking to somebody in New Jersey about the 1974–1975 difficulties. He was saying that it was remarkable how much of the industry is still here in 1976. Maybe it is not remarkable. The production technique used in housing is labor intensive and is very easy to turn on and off. Entrepreneurs, somehow, get through those years: They hire less labor, and they do not have specialized capital that is sitting unused during such periods.

WILLIAM VICKREY: The unemployment insurance system bears part of the cost, as well.

JAFFEE: Indeed, that is involved, too.

JOHN PERKINS: Perhaps another social cost is that, with housing subject to wide fluctuations, home builders do not develop innovative approaches to building homes that are more efficient but not as adaptable as are present techniques.

JAFFEE: I think that is right. But the issue still remains: Who is to cut back and how should this be determined? And why should it not be the housing sector?

WILLIAM K. JONES: I am not advocating the subsidization of middle-income housing, but I seem to have missed something in the analyses of Professors Jaffee and Cooper. Suppose we build 10 percent more middle-income housing, and these houses are filled by middle-income people. Presumably, these people came from some place. They did not just arrive from the tundra of the north or come up out of the ocean. Presumably, they are moving out of other housing in order to get into the newly constructed middle-income housing. One would assume that they are moving out of the upper level of the existing housing just below that being constructed. Why, then, does the construction of middle-income housing not help everybody in housing below the people who move in? Why do you not have everybody moving up a notch to take advantage of houses or premises that the person below has vacated? Is there something that I am not comprehending?

JAFFEE: That is called the filter-down theory.

JONES: I think of it as the moving-up phenomenon.

JAFFEE: You are an optimist. First of all, it is not true that somebody has to be leaving a house. A major effect of the subsidy programs is to cause people that were doubling up in existing units, young married people living with their parents, etc., to move out and form two separate households and live in two separate units. In that case, you are not freeing any housing units.

JONES: But, if they are in a position to buy middle-income houses, they would also be in a position to bid away existing housing from someone who is less well off in economic terms. It is really the same phenomenon.

THUROW: Trickle-down works to some degree, but we also have other government economic policies. In the post-war period, the large subsidies have gone to middle-income housing through instruments like tax deductibility of mortgage interest payments and local taxes. We also have had other government policies, like interstate highways, which were tearing down low-income housing. We did not, in fact, augment the stock of low-income housing. We were subtracting low-income housing as fast as we were adding it.

JAFFEE: I think the answer to your question is that the filter-down approach is not very efficient. If you create a new unit which is just slightly above the low-income housing you are hoping to free, that would not be too inefficient. But if you subsidize palaces, then you give somebody a palace in order to free some of these low-income units, and that is very inefficient.

VICKREY: The question is, also, whether in building the palace, you build it on a vacant lot, or instead, demolish a lot of low-income housing to build it.

EDWARDS: Our time is up. On behalf of the Center and myself, I want to thank all the participants for a most interesting and stimulating session.

## CHAPTER EIGHT

# Multinational Banking: Theory and Regulation

## REGULATORY ISSUES AND THE THEORY OF MULTINATIONAL BANKING

James W. Dean, *Associate Professor of Economics, Simon Fraser University*

Herbert G. Grubel, *Professor of Economics, Simon Fraser University*

Banks in most countries of the world traditionally have carried on *international* banking activities through their dealings in foreign exchange and the financing of foreign trade. In this paper, we are not concerned with these kinds of banking activities. Our focus is on the analysis of *multinational* banking, which involves the operation of branches, agencies, offices, or subsidiaries of one country's banks in other countries.

Multinational banking has developed dramatically since the end of World War II and has led to a situation where the banks of most major countries have branches, agencies, offices, or subsidiaries in all other major countries. A matrix relating the nationality of parent banks by the country or area in which they have multinational banking activities in 1968–1969 showed about 70 percent of all cells filled with a total of 2,744 entries.[1] Since then, growth in multinational banking has been very rapid. For example, in 1965, 13 United States banks had 211 foreign branches whose assets represented 2.6 percent of total United States domestic banking assets; by 1974, 129 United States banks had 737 branches abroad with assets equal to 17.7 percent of total United States banking assets.[2]

---

We acknowledge the useful comments on an earlier draft made by participants at seminars at the Columbia University Law School Center for Law and Economic Studies, Simon Fraser University, the University of Washington, and Yale University, especially H. Bloch, P. Callier, F. Edwards, D. Gordon, J. Tobin, and R. Vernon.

1. Lees, Int'l Banking & Finance 15 (John Wiley and Sons, New York 1974).

2. Aliber, "International Banking: Growth and Regulation," 10 Colum. J. World Bus., No. 4, p. 10 (Winter 1975); Brimmer and Dahl, "Growth of American International Banking: Implications for Public Policy," 30 J. Finance, No. 2, p. 345 (May 1975).

Foreign banks with branches in the United States rose from 19 in 1965 to 39 in 1974, and the number of their branches went from 36 to 57 during the same time period. Similar growth took place in the number of agencies of foreign banks, from 35 to 75, primarily in states where laws prohibited the opening of branches. The assets of these foreign branches and agencies rose from 1.4 percent to 5.4 percent of the total United States bank assets.[3]

This growth of multinational banking has led to demands for the control, regulation, and supervision of foreign banks in the United States. Legislation has been proposed which "will inevitably have repercussions in other countries and may be used as a precedent for new legislation elsewhere."[4] The proposed United States legislation has been analyzed in great detail by a number of authors.[5] We will not consider the regulatory issues surrounding multinational banking from the point of view of United States conditions and proposed legislation. Instead, we will discuss multinational banking more broadly and focus on issues which have to be addressed by legislators in all countries with multinational banks.

The key ingredient of our analysis is the presentation of an outline of a theory of multinational banking,[6] with an emphasis on explaining the factors motivating its development. We distinguish four groups of factors consisting of (1) benefits associated with lending and borrowing, (2) real banking economies affecting interest rate spreads, (3) government policies affecting real costs, and (4) government policies affecting lenders or borrowers. We argue that to the extent that multinational banking is based on the exploitation of national bank regulations which discriminate in favor of foreign banks, it is inefficient, and that

3. *Id.*

4. Hutton, "The Regulation of Foreign Banks—A European Viewpoint," 10 Colum. J. World Bus. No. 4, p. 109 (Winter 1975).

5. Aliber and Brimmer, N. 2 *supra*; Edwards, "Regulation of Foreign Banking in the United States: International Reciprocity and Federal-States Conflicts," 13 Colum. J. of Transnat'l L., No. 2 (1974); Edwards and Zwick, "Foreign Banks in the United States: Activities and Regulatory Issues," 10 Colum. J. World Bus., No. 1 (Spring 1975); Ganoe, "Controlling the Foreign Banks in the U.S.," Euromoney (June 1975); R. A. Johnston, "Proposals for Federal Control of Foreign Banks," Fed. Reserve Bank of San Francisco Econ. Rev. (Spring 1976); Perkins, "The Regulation of Foreign Banking in the United States," 10 Colum. J. World Bus., No. 4 (Winter 1975); Welsh, "The Case for Federal Regulation of Foreign Bank Operations in the United States," 10 Colum. J. World Bus., (Winter 1975).

6. There is relatively little literature dealing directly with the theory of multinational banking. See Aliber, "Towards a Theory of International Banking," Fed. Reserve Bank of San Francisco Econ. Rev. (Spring 1976); Lees, *Foreign Banking and Investment in the United States: Issues and Alternatives* (Macmillan, London 1976); Lees, N. 1 *supra*. The vast literature dealing with Eurocurrency markets is only indirectly relevant to an understanding of multinational banking. This literature is reviewed and synthesized creatively in Little, *Euro-Dollars: The Money Market Gypsies* (Harper and Row, New York 1975); some valuable new insights are presented in Hewson, *Liquidity Creation and Distribution in the Eurocurrency Markets* (D. C. Heath and Co., Lexington, Mass., 1975).

such discrimination should be eliminated by legislation applying all regulations equally to domestic and foreign banks, even though this will reduce multinational banking and will likely lead to increased governmental control and reduced competition. We then deal with the risk of externalities from multinational banking, arguing that some form of deposit insurance is desirable socially, and that its existence would obviate the need for a lender of last resort. Arguments for the control of multinational banks on the grounds that they interfere with national monetary sovereignty, and that they cause inflation, are shown to be fallacious. They are based on mistaken views about the existence of a Phillips-curve trade-off and about Eurocurrency multipliers.

## MOTIVES FOR MULTINATIONAL BANKING

The motives for multinational banking can best be explained by first showing that the existence of a United States bank in Paris (or of a German bank in London, etc.) involves a puzzle. The puzzle is why any owner of funds prefers to deposit them in the form of dollars with the United States bank in Paris rather than with a United States bank in New York, or in the form of francs or dollars in a French bank in Paris. An analogous puzzle arises from the motives which lead to the borrowing of dollar funds from a United States bank in Paris rather than from a United States bank in New York, or of francs or dollars from a French bank in Paris. What are the sources of advantage of the United States bank in the foreign country? Its foreign competitors have a clear advantage in the knowledge of local conditions, in traditional ties with the economy, and in connections with the government. Also, the loans and deposits of its competitors are extremely close substitutes in any use and with respect to such properties as negotiability and default risk. Similarly, why do customers prefer to deal with the United States bank in Paris rather than with its head office in New York?[7]

The broad explanation is simply that the United States banks' effective rates on borrowing and lending simultaneously are more favorable than those of its competitors abroad and of its head office in New York.

---

7. The example presented in the text covers only the case of dollars lent and borrowed through the intermediation of banks located abroad, which are known as Eurodollars. In the real world, there are other Eurocurrencies, and analogous problems arise in explaining why they are lent and borrowed through banks located abroad. To keep our exposition simple, we formulate the analysis in terms of Eurodollars alone. We have chosen to develop the analysis in terms of Paris because both German and British conditions are subject to special conditions, which distract from their use as prototypes of host countries for multinational banks. As we shall see later, Germany is the only country in which Eurocurrency deposits are subject to minimum reserve requirements, while U.K. banks operate under an unusual system which dichotomizes the severity and scope of controls in domestic and foreign business; furthermore, they draw on a very large stock of international banking experience accumulated during the period of Britain's global economic dominance before World War II.

This explanation can be represented graphically in Figure 8-1, which shows that a United States bank can function in Paris only if it offers the public effective lending and borrowing rates on dollars (Eurodollars) which are above and below, respectively, those on similar services provided by United States banks in New York or a French bank in Paris.

This "explanation" is not an explanation; it is a description of a truism. A genuine explanation of multinational banking requires an analysis of the causes of this divergence between the effective lending and borrowing rates without which multinational banking would not exist. We now turn to such an analysis, grouping causes under four basic headings and numerous subheadings in each main group. This arrangement of the sources of comparative advantage of multinational banks does not imply that each operates independently. Often, one is operative only in conjunction with others; often, they occur together. However, we believe that the following taxonomy is useful for an understanding of regulatory issues of multinational banking, even though, as a theoretical exercise, it cannot cover all the complex real-world cases.

## Benefits Associated with Specific Lenders and Borrowers

In this section, we consider cases where the *nominal* lending and borrowing rates on different currencies offered by different banks can be identical, while the *effective* rates may still be more favorable for certain customers because of reasons specific to them.

TRANSACTIONS COST SAVINGS

Consider the subsidiary manufacturing company of a United States parent in France, which regularly imports and exports goods payable in dollars. Because payments and receipts rarely are synchronized perfectly, the company often has short-term investable funds or needs to borrow in the money market. Such a firm saves foreign exchange

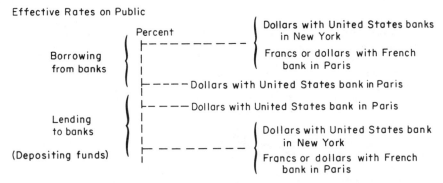

FIGURE 8-1  Necessary conditions for existence of multinational banks.

transactions costs and reduces the risk of exchange losses by dealing in dollars rather than francs. These savings lower its effective cost of borrowing and raise its effective return on lending in dollars, so that dealing in dollars is more advantageous than dealing in francs, even if the posited lending and borrowing rates in francs are equal to, or more favorable than, those on dollars.

The preceding analysis explains why a company resident in France will deal in dollars rather than francs. There remains the question of why it deals with a United States-owned rather than a French-owned bank. We return to this question in detail below. Here, we assert simply that the company tends to turn to the United States bank because of long-established commercial ties between the company's and the bank's United States parents, or because the French bank is subject to regulations which raise its costs relative to those of the United States bank.

Savings on transactions costs are greatest with the use of dollars, since dollars serve as a key currency in world trade and finance. Some other currencies, however, may also give rise to this type of multinational banking business.

### FORWARD EXCHANGE BENEFITS

At a given difference in short-term lending rates on francs and dollars, the relationship between spot and forward rates can make it profitable for someone with a stock of investable francs and a future requirement for franc balances to lend dollars. For such a lender, the effective return on dollars is above that on francs, and the lender would deal in that market. Similar circumstances can induce borrowers in need of francs to enter the dollar market. Either customer relations or government relations can direct these lenders and borrowers to the United States bank rather than to a French bank.

The forward exchange rate tends to adjust to equalize effective yields on franc and dollar money market instruments with equal default and liquidity characteristics. However, for the forward rate to adjust, some transactions must take place. Inframarginal investors can benefit from these profit opportunities. During speculative periods, the resultant arbitrage operations can often be quite large.[8]

### NONECONOMIC REASONS—ANONYMITY

The lenders and borrowers in Eurodollar markets, in principle, are unknown to United States authorities and are not subject to United States jurisdiction. These characteristics of Eurodollar deposits and loans have been of great importance to the Soviet Union, which, during

---

8. For a portfolio approach to forward exchange market analysis, see Grubel, *Forward Exchange, Speculation and International Capital Flows* (Stanford Univ. Press, Stanford, Cal., 1966).

the 1950s, had temporary dollar balances from gold sales which they intended to use for the payment of grain shipments from the United States. Cold War ideology and tensions made it preferable to hold these dollars with a British bank in London rather than with a United States bank in New York. Similar advantages of anonymity and absence of United States jurisdiction presently appeal to the owners of dollar balances in Arab countries and to the governments of developing countries, which borrow Eurodollars to finance development projects and payments imbalances. These factors (influencing the effective lending and borrowing rates on dollars) are enhanced by the key currency role of the dollar and, specifically, by the advantages of liquidity and exchange stability it confers.

In our analytical framework, the advantages of anonymity and escape from United States jurisdiction are considered to have a value which can be expressed as a dollar equivalent annual yield. As such, multinational banking (Eurodollar) lending and borrowing rates are more favorable inframarginally than those on francs in Paris or dollars in New York, even if nominal rates are the same.[9]

### LIQUIDITY AND SAFETY

Multinational banks, typically, are the largest banks of the industrial countries. Consequently, deposits or other debt instruments issued by their branches to attract funds are considered by lenders to have low risks of default (which is a form of nonpecuniary yield). Thus, even if nominal interest rates on the obligations of these banks were the same as those on local banks, many depositors would consider the effective yield on the multinational bank obligations to be higher.

Debt instruments issued by multinational banks are also relatively liquid because of the reputation of the issuers and because they are denominated in key currencies, for which there exist broad and deep markets. This liquidity feature raises the nonpecuniary yield of the debt instruments issued by multinational banks, and it explains why a lender would prefer to deal with the French branch of a United States bank in dollars rather than with a French bank in francs.[10]

### CREDIT RATIONING

Consider a potential borrower in France who cannot obtain credit at any cost because of credit rationing by the French banking system.

---

9. Readers of an earlier draft of this paper with practical experience in multinational banking commented that anonymity is not an important motive for lenders and borrowers. However, as the well-known episode of Russian loans indicates, there is at least the potential for this motive to be important.

10. Although it is practically inconceivable that governments would let these banks fail, it still seems reasonable to assume that, *ceteris paribus*, potential customers will evaluate risk differences among private banks.

Such a firm will turn to the Eurodollar market and borrow from a multinational bank, even at rates above those quoted in the market for franc borrowers in Paris. The firm will borrow from a multinational bank in Paris rather than in New York because the former bank has better access to credit information about French borrowers. (We examine this type of multinational banking activity further on pages 417 to 418.)

## Real Banking Economies Affecting Spread

In this section, we discuss the real economies enjoyed by multinational banks which can result in narrower spreads between the nominal lending and borrowing rates noted in Figure 8-1. The comparative advantage accruing to multinational banks from these economies is probably the most important explanation of their success and will significantly influence their future growth. These economies also differ fundamentally from the advantages discussed elsewhere in this paper in that they would give rise to multinational banks, even in the absence of government regulations, even if customers were perfectly homogeneous, and even if risk considerations alone determined the portfolio composition of banks. In the real world, of course, the narrower spreads and motives attributable to individual customers operate simultaneously and cannot be separated through observation.[11]

SCALE AND INFORMATION ECONOMIES

It is well known that multinational banks follow or accompany their major customers who have established production and trading facilities abroad. The most plausible explanation for this behavior is that they are afraid their customers will turn to foreign or other United States banks for their business abroad, leading to the potential loss of business not only with the foreign branch but also with the domestic parent.

This concern makes sense only in the context of imperfect competition, where there are important information costs. The theory of imperfect competition among firms is a broad subject and can explain with some degree of success why oligopolistic banks tend to compete through advertising, tie-in services, and the provision of convenient banking locations, since these save customers real resources. The marginal cost of such bank branches is low, as they draw on the advertising, managerial and accounting, and product development system of the headquarters, thereby exploiting important economies of scale in the use of these resources. Seen from this point of view, multinational banking is simply an extension of domestic forms of nonprice competition.

---

11. For an application of portfolio choice under uncertainty to the theory of banking, see O'Bannon, Bond, and Shearer, *Money and Banking: Theory, Policy and Institutions* (Harper and Row, New York 1975).

However, such economies of scale in international branch banking, taken by themselves, do not give rise to a competitive advantage (in dealing with a particular United States manufacturing subsidiary in Paris) over local French banks or other United States-owned rivals. Presumably, all such competitors enjoy the same kinds of economies of branch banking. The source of the comparative advantage which accrues only to the United States bank in Paris arises from the historical working relationship between the parent of the bank and the manufacturing firm in the United States. The advantages accrue in the form of highly specific and continuously current information about the condition of the manufacturing firm's sales, finances, and personnel. While such information can be acquired in the market by other banks at some cost, it accrues to the firm's main bank in the natural course of doing business, and at practically zero cost.

Two authors have concluded that the low marginal cost of using existing information constitutes the most important explanation of direct foreign investment in manufacturing.[12] While there is a subtle difference in the types of knowledge relevant for the explanation of multinational banking and direct manufacturing investment, the similarities are great enough to suggest that, in an important sense, the theory of multinational banking developed there is part of the general theory of direct foreign investment. It follows that multinational banking, like direct foreign investment, increases global allocative efficiency through the wider use of existing knowledge. Thus, any regulation of multinational banking should be evaluated in the light of its effect on this source of global welfare gains.

Multinational banks enjoy additional cost savings of a special type that is not available to multinational manufacturing firms. These economies arise in connection with the international flow of short-term capital in response to interest rate differentials caused by divergent monetary policies. We will discuss this phenomenon below in greater detail. The point important here is that funds flow between ultimate lenders and borrowers in two countries through a chain of banks (often of considerable length) and through what is known as the interbank market. This market is most developed in London and is similar to the United States Federal Funds Market. In each link of the chain, the banks are well known to one another, so that the marginal cost of credit investigations is near zero, since the perceived risk of default is very small. The spread between lending and borrowing rates can, therefore, be very narrow. This type of linkage can lead to a deposit by a small, internationally unknown French lender going to a Japanese borrower of similar characteristics, with a minimum of private and social investment in information gathering about credit worthiness.

---

12. See Richard E. Caves, "International Corporations: The Industrial Economics of Foreign Investment," 38 Economica, No. 149, pp. 1–27 (Feb. 1971); Kindleberger, *American Business Abroad* (Yale Univ. Press, New Haven 1969).

Prudent investment principles, which in many countries are reinforced by regulation, prevent individual banks from lending large sums to any one borrower. These limitations are overcome by the formation of banking consortia among multinational banks. These consortia have made loans of unprecedented size in recent years to governments and quasi-governmental institutions, such as utilities. Such loans can be made at low cost because of the relatively simple credit investigation and administration required and because of the low risk for each individual bank.[13] On the other hand, experience in dealing with borrowers from developing countries has not been extensive, and fears are now being voiced about the ability and political will of some of these borrowers to meet their obligations.

The multinational banks participating in international loan consortia, typically, are those who have moved abroad to accompany their manufacturing customers. These banks have tended to stay out of the normal retail business of commercial banks in local markets and, besides serving the manufacturing firms, have acted more like brokers than bankers in bringing together large lenders and borrowers. One result is that these banks enjoy low costs of portfolio management.[14] Another is that they are able to minimize exchange and liquidity risks through the close matching of maturities and currency denominations in their asset and loan portfolios.[15]

The economies arising from the participation in loan consortia and from the characteristics of the business and portfolio composition of many multinational banks permit them to operate profitably on narrower margins than can their domestic competitors. These economies are an alternative or supplementary explanation (to those advanced above) for the phenomenon described in Figure 8-1. Further, their presence implies the existence of welfare gains, whose reduction must be considered as a cost to any regulation which reduced the scope of multinational banking.

REDUCED NONPRICE COMPETITION

It is well known that most national banking systems in Western countries are characterized by oligopolistic market structures, and that

---

13. It has been shown that in recent years losses from defaults have been smaller for international than national loan portfolios of U.S. banks. Ruckdeschel, "Risk in Foreign and Domestic Lending Activities of U.S. Banks," 10 Colum. J. World Bus., No. 4 (Winter 1975).

14. See Little, N. 6 *supra* at 30–31.

15. See Hewson, N. 6 *supra*. However, it has been suggested that this matching of maturities in balance sheets may hide the fact that many short-term loans are, in fact, long-term, since they are rolled over almost automatically. Although such loans may be subject to cancellation, it is doubtful that they are as liquid as genuine short-term loans.

banks engage in many forms of nonprice competition. Such rivalry raises costs and results in inflated spreads between lending and borrowing rates. Multinational banks, typically, are not part of the local oligopoly structure and are not committed to nonprice competition. Furthermore, the multinational banks, which concentrate on serving the subsidiaries of manufacturing firms abroad and which engage in wholesale and consortia banking, do not need to compete through oligopolistic product differentiation because of the nature of their business competition. As a result, these banks have lower marginal and average costs than their domestic competitors, and they offer narrower spreads between their lending and borrowing rates.

In the longer run, these advantages of multinational banks may be eroded as domestic bank oligopolies are weakened, and as competition through marginal cost pricing is established. Such a trend is now discernible in many countries. Domestic banks must increasingly compete with multinationals directly, in loan consortia and in other large-scale operations. As competition among domestic and foreign banks increases, however, the latter will continue to prosper through the exploitation of the other comparative advantages discussed above.

### RETAIL BANKING AND PRODUCT DIFFERENTIATION

The retail banking systems of most countries are characterized by imperfect competition and by efforts on the part of banks to differentiate their products in minor ways with the aid of advertising. According to the theories of direct foreign investment, it is the low marginal cost of using abroad the differentiated products and advertising developed for the domestic market which motivates manufacturers to open foreign facilities.[16] These motives also are operative in multinational banking, where appealing packages of consumer services and advertising developed for home use have found a place in the foreign market. An outstanding example of multinational banking based on these principles is the opening of "money boutiques" by Citibank in London during the 1960s. (These permitted a segment of the British population which had previously been neglected by British banks to obtain bank loans.) Other examples are the Japanese and British retail banks in California, which appeal to ethnic minorities; and the United States and Canadian banks in the Caribbean and other Central American countries.[17]

The intrusion of multinational banks into domestic bank oligopolies frequently stimulates competition, particularly through the develop-

---

16. The dynamics of this process, which includes the aging and obsolescence of products, has led to Vernon's product-cycle explanation of foreign trade. Vernon, "International Investment and International Trade in the Product Cycle," 80 Q.J. Econ., No. 2 (May 1966).

17. For a history of Canadian banking in this vein, see Baum, *The Banks of Canada in the Commonwealth Caribbean* (Praeger, New York 1974).

ment of new services. Often, the original comparative advantage of the foreign banks is so eroded that they withdraw. For example, the money boutiques in London were ultimately closed; and with the help of government policies, domestically owned banks are slowly replacing United States and Canadian retail banks in Latin America. Such developments are consistent with the theory of direct foreign investment, which stresses that in industries in which technology and products are relatively stable, as they are in banking, the primary source of comparative advantage of multinationals is absent.[18] For this reason, multinational retail banking probably will become an increasingly less important part of multinational banking in the future.

## Government Policies Affecting Real Costs

### MINIMUM RESERVE REQUIREMENTS AND DEPOSIT INSURANCE

In all Western countries, banks are required to maintain minimum reserve deposits with their central banks, ostensibly as a liquidity backing for their demand deposits and as a means of enhancing monetary control. These minimum reserves, however, do not provide an effective liquidity buffer, since only a small fraction of them can be used to meet unforeseen net deposit withdrawals. Consequently, banks have either to maintain additional liquidity to protect themselves against the consequences of unforeseen large deposit withdrawals or to rely on use of the lender-of-last-resort facilities at a premium cost. Therefore, the required minimum deposits maintained at the central bank, which typically earn no interest, are a tax on domestic banking, and this cost is passed on to consumers through an increased spread between lending and borrowing rates.

Discriminatory treatment also exists in connection with the payment of premiums on compulsory deposit insurance: Deposits in domestic currencies are, and those denominated in foreign currencies are not, subject to this charge. While the amounts involved are small, especially in relation to the tax through minimum deposit requirements, the premiums do affect the difference in the spread between lending and borrowing rates in domestic and foreign currency banking.

We have already mentioned the absence of minimum reserve requirements on foreign currency denominated liabilities as one of the most important sources of comparative advantage of multinational

---

**18.** See Caves and Kindleberger, N. 2 *supra*. However, in a world of dynamic changes, such as the development of electronic transfer technology and systems, the success of multinational retail banking depends on the speed and ease with which these innovations are available to domestic banks as compared with multinationals. Since the computer-based banking innovations are marketed primarily by multinational computer firms, it is unlikely that they will be a major dynamic source of comparative advantage for multinational retail banking in the future.

banks. In terms of the analytical framework of Figure 8-1, this absence of minimum reserve requirements can explain on price-theoretic grounds a substantial portion of the difference in the spread between lending and borrowing rates on national and multinational banking activities. Germany's policy to require such minimum reserves on foreign currency deposits has resulted in the exodus of Eurodollar business and multinational banking from that country. In recent years, the volume of multinational banking in Germany has been far below what one would expect on the basis of German trade and productive capacity.[19] However, since such business has not ceased entirely in Germany, this situation is both evidence of the importance of the discriminatory minimum reserve requirements and of the fact that other motives discussed in this paper encourage the operation of multinational banks.

REGULATION OF DOMESTIC BANKING

Multinational banks in the United States can have branches in different states and can engage in merchant banking activities; domestic banks cannot.[20] British banks are subject to administratively expensive foreign exchange controls on their business originating with British subjects; and all European banks are subject to many kinds of regulations on their domestic banking activities. On the other hand, in Europe, *international* banking business is relatively free from regulation. It has proved to be technically feasible as well as economically possible for British and other European banks to achieve effective separation between their domestic and international banking operations. Multinational banks, of course, also benefit from the discriminatory treatment of domestic and foreign business.

To the extent that branching and merchant banking in the United States (and the absence of controls on international banking in Europe) result in real cost savings, the multinational banks in these countries (and the foreign banking divisions of European banks) can operate on narrower spreads between lending and borrowing rates than can banks engaged solely in domestic operations. Under these conditions, therefore, national banking regulations discriminating between domestic and foreign business constitute a motive for multinational banking.

However, not all national banking regulations favor multinational banking. During the 1960s, United States balance of payments policies,

---

**19.** In the *Bank for International Settlements Annual Report* for 1976 (p. 78), it is shown that, in December 1975, the external liabilities of German banks in foreign currency were only $10.6 million; for other countries, they were as follows: Belgium-Luxembourg, $39 million; France, $39 million; and United Kingdom, $118 million.

**20.** The literature on U.S. legislative proposals deals with this issue in some detail (See N. 5 *supra.*)

in the form of the Interest Equalization Tax and the Voluntary Credit Restraint programs, served to tax or restrict dealings of United States wealthholders with multinational banks abroad, as well as borrowing by foreigners from United States banks. Furthermore, many countries treat interest income from bank deposits owned by foreigners as investment income and, therefore, apply a withholding tax on such earnings, normally of 15 percent. Domestic depositors are not subject to such withholding taxes, although they have to report earnings from bank deposits as regular income. These United States balance of payments policies have ended, and the quantitative importance of the withholding taxes on foreigners is not very great, so that at present, legislation discriminating against multinational banking is not a serious matter. However, there still exists in many countries discriminatory legislation of this sort. Also, balance of payments crises or domestic problems may at any time induce such legislation.

## Government Policies Affecting Lenders or Borrowers

### MONETARY POLICIES

Historically, international short-term capital flows always have interfered with the ability of countries to manage aggregate demand through monetary policy. Multinational banks have become a most efficient conduit for such short-term capital flows and have further reduced governments' ability to conduct independent stabilization policies.

The method by which multinational banks are efficient conduits of international capital flows has already been discussed. It rests on the exploitation of economies of information. For example, consider small, rural bank $A$ in the United States, which is in portfolio equilibrium when (as a result of expansionary monetary policy) it receives an additional demand deposit. This deposit creates an incentive to make a loan. Often such a loan will go to the U.S. Federal Funds Market, but, *ceteris paribus,* this market will be in disequilibrium as a result of the hypothesized infusion of funds. As a result, United States bank $B$ with foreign branches may find it profitable to lend the money in the European interbank market, where it may be re-lent several times among banks in different countries before it ends up as a loan to an ultimate German borrower. This process takes place with a minimum of delay and costs, since each link of the lending chain is known to its immediate business partner through regular dealings. The ultimate effect is a transfer of funds from an unknown, small lender in a country with easy credit conditions to a similarly small and unknown borrower in a country with tight credit conditions (just as in the United States, the federal funds market arbitrages excess demand and supply throughout the United States).

Typically, loans through the multinational banking network are carried on in dollars or other key currencies. Thus, the German borrower who needs deutsche marks to finance his activities sells his dollar proceeds in the foreign exchange market, normally covering his repayment obligations in dollars through a forward exchange purchase. Under fixed exchange rates, the dollars sold by the borrower are bought by the German central bank, which pays for them with deutsche marks, creating an increase in the high-powered money base of the German banking system. This action interferes with the German central bank's efforts to pursue a restrictive monetary policy. In the United States, on the other hand, the outflow of the funds keeps up interest rates and reduces the quantity of loans to potential domestic borrowers, thereby frustrating the United States policy goal of easier credit (which we assumed to be the initial source of the disequilibrium).

International capital flows of this sort, going through multinational banks, have been important sources of disturbance during the period of fixed parity exchange rates. Since exchange rates have become more flexible in recent years, the problem is less serious, though worries about the loss of reserves and control over the money supply have been replaced by concerns over the excessive fluctuations of exchange rates brought about by these capital flows.

However, it is clear that the advantages in operating costs enjoyed by multinational banks (discussed in the two preceding sections) permit them to operate as low-cost conduits of international short-term capital flows, and that this has made the interest elasticity of capital flows greater than it has ever been, with concomitant implications for national monetary sovereignty and exchange rate instability. We return to these implications below in our discussion of potential multinational banking legislation.

## U.S. INTEREST CEILINGS

For historic reasons, U.S. financial markets have been encumbered by legislation limiting the maximum interest rates that can be paid or charged on certain types of liabilities and assets. During the inflationary period of the late 1960s and early 1970s, nominal market interest rates on these assets in the U.S. market would have exceeded the legislated ceilings. Multinational banks in foreign countries were not subject to these interest ceilings and, therefore, were able to offer U.S. lenders more attractive rates. Consequently, funds moved abroad, and potential U.S. borrowers who were rationed out of credit at the legislated rates in the United States obtained loans abroad.

The circumvention of U.S. interest ceilings provided a strong stimulus for U.S. banks to open foreign branches, since it allowed them to continue to serve their traditional U.S. customers. In fact, negotiations with borrowers and lenders go on as usual in the United States. Once a bank deposit is negotiated at the high interest rate, it is simply transferred to the foreign branch of the U.S. bank in the name of the bank's customer. Alternatively, the U.S. borrower is credited with the amount of his loan in the branch abroad, which he typically asks to have transferred to the U.S. parent with which he normally does his banking business. In effect, the foreign branches of U.S. banks engaging in these activities tend to serve as nothing more than a legally acceptable device for the avoidance of U.S. interest rate ceilings.

In recent years, inflationary pressures have eased, and maximum interest ceilings have been raised or abandoned. As a result, this motive for multinational banking has disappeared. At one point, some analysts argued that U.S. multinational banking would cease once interest ceilings became ineffective. This prediction has not materialized, and the continued prosperity of U.S. multinational banking is evidence of the importance of the other motives analyzed above.

## Summary and Conclusions

The analysis presented in this part of the paper suggests that there are four classes of motives for multinational banking. The first two are associated, respectively, with banks' customers and with banks themselves. They are based on real economies and make multinational banking appear as an institutional innovation that increases the global efficiency of resource allocation. These real economies include the lower operating costs due to transactions cost savings, economies of scale in operation and risk diversification, the use of knowledge at zero marginal cost, and the savings from not participating in oligopolistic forms of nonprice competition. Some of these economies accrue through product improvements which benefit consumers, such as the increased liquidity and safety of financial instruments, the anonymity of financial dealings, and the ability to circumvent domestic credit rationing.

The third set of motives arises from the government policies which affect the real cost of operations and provide discriminatory advantages to multinational over foreign operations: minimum reserve requirements, compulsory deposit insurance, limitations on types of bank-related activities, etc. The fourth set of motives affects lenders and borrowers and arises from the international short-term capital flows induced by differential aggregate demand management policies and by U.S. interest rate ceilings.

This analysis of motives for multinational banking has important implications and provides a useful framework with which to examine the merits of regulating multinational banks.

## REGULATORY ISSUES

In the following analysis, we assume that existing national regulations of domestic banking are socially optimal and inviolate. Under this assumption, it is obvious that multinational banks must be subjected to the same controls as national banks, given that society wishes to curtail or eliminate the perceived negative externalities associated with banking generally. This assumption also permits us to avoid discussion of issues raised by the possibility that some domestic banking regulations are inefficient, to the point that efficiency is increased by exempting multinational banking from such regulations. While this approach may be subject to the criticism that it fails to deal with some of the most interesting public policy issues, it can be defended on the ground that, in spite of many economists' arguments that some domestic regulations are inefficient, politicians seldom change them (possibly because the public's perception or evaluation of externalities is different from that of economists).

We shall assume also that national demand management, exchange rate policies, and controls are here to stay, even though they may have to be modified to deal with the consequences of multinational banking activities. We thus rule out the argument that there would be no grounds for the control of multinational banks if only governments gave up attempts at demand management, simply let their money supplies grow at steady rates, and removed all exchange controls and let their exchange rates float freely.

In sum, we assume that demands for the regulation of multinational banks are justifiably based on arguments that, first, multinational banks prevent the elimination of some types of externalities, and, second, that multinational banking gives rise to new types of negative externalities.

## Failure to Eliminate Negative Externalities

One set of problems arises because some domestic bank regulations do not apply to multinational banks. For example, in the United States, domestic banks are barred from nationwide branch banking and from certain types of investment banking, while multinational banks are not. This discriminatory treatment should be eliminated because the operation of foreign banks in this manner interferes with the attainment of the social goals the legislation was designed to achieve: to inhibit the development of powerful nationwide banks and of concentrated financial institutions. It therefore seems appropriate to put foreign-owned banks in the position where it is illegal for them to branch nationally and to engage in financial market activities other than banking.

MINIMUM RESERVE REQUIREMENTS

For multinational banking in countries other than Germany and the United States, the most important type of discrimination arises from the absence of minimum reserve requirements on foreign currency deposits. This fact has contributed fundamentally to the rapid growth of the Eurodollar business, since the latter is not subject to the tax implicit in reserve requirements. This discrimination between domestic and multinational banking has resulted in the loss of some control by national authorities over the quantity and type of lending undertaken in the Eurodollar market.

We do not now go into the arguments and evidence concerning the Eurodollar market's ability to create liquidity. There already exists a very large literature concerned with Eurodollars.[21] Suffice it to say that the evidence increasingly suggests that the Eurodollar market has not resulted in the creation of large quantities of new liquidity. On the basis of this evidence, we conclude that the inflationary impact of the Eurodollar markets probably does not justify the imposition of minimum reserve requirements on foreign currency deposits.

However, the absence of such minimum reserve requirements has still created an inefficiency: It has led to the expansion of financial intermediation in an area greater than would have occurred in the presence of neutral requirements on all bank deposits. This overexpansion in the Eurodollar market has received a great deal of attention, especially in the case of loans to developing countries' governments and to public enterprise. Such overexpansion is inefficient on price-theoretic grounds because it leads to the purchase of relative quantities of services which do not reflect true social scarcities.

The preceding argument presents a strong case for imposing minimum reserve requirements on foreign currency deposits, and we endorse such a policy.[22]

DEPOSIT INSURANCE

The absence of mandatory deposit insurance on foreign currency deposits in all countries favors multinational banking and the growth of the Eurodollar business. Deposit insurance has been instituted to reduce the externalities arising from runs on banks and liquidity crises, which have historically accompanied the failure of certain banks. As in the case of the effect of multinational banking on the magnitude and composition of the global credit market, there is no reliable evidence on

---

21. That literature is summarized and synthesized in Little and Hewson, N. 6 *supra.*

22. Arguments have been made in the literature that minimum reserve requirements are not required to assure monetary control. See Johnson, *Reserve Requirements and Monetary Control,* Discussion Paper No. 66 (Econ. Council of Canada, 1976). If this is the case, then the interest-free minimum reserve requirements on domestic-currency deposits also represent an inefficiency, since they, too, are not necessary to assure control over the money supply. Therefore, the absence of minimum reserve requirements on foreign-currency deposits increases efficiency and should not be eliminated. This subject cannot be discussed satisfactorily here, although we note that whether or not reserve requirements *enhance* (as opposed to *enable*) monetary control is an open question. We believe that Johnson's argument strengthens Tobin's case for paying interest on excess reserve deposits. See Tobin, "Towards Improving the Efficiency of the Monetary Mechanism," 42 Rev. of Econ. & Statistics, No. 3 (Aug. 1960). This would reduce the taxation implicit in reserve requirements and would enhance their attractiveness for control over the money supply.

the magnitude of the externalities, actual and potential, arising out of the absence of required insurance on foreign currency deposits.

However, it seems to us that the cost of including foreign currency deposits in national compulsory insurance schemes, or of creating a global insurance agency for these types of deposits, is relatively low in comparison with the potential benefits. There are important problems of moral hazard associated with deposit insurance, and none of the methods available for dealing with that phenomenon is perfect. However, there exist methods of classifying risk categories, charging differential insurance premiums and selecting levels of coinsurance which assure that depositors are protected and portfolio management principles are not distorted excessively.[23]

In principle, insurance for foreign currency deposits can be incorporated into existing national schemes by the amendment of national legislation. On the other hand, the lack of uniformity among national insurance programs and the absence of such programs in some countries suggest that a global effort may be desirable. Under the sponsorship and supervision of the International Monetary Fund (IMF), the Bank for International Settlements (BIS), or the World Bank, such an insurance agency could operate in a self-financing manner through the levy of appropriate premiums. Flexibility in the setting of premiums and in borrowing in capital markets against future premium income (in the case of large losses) would permit such an institution to operate successfully, even in the absence of current and reliable information on risk.

LENDER OF LAST RESORT

It is well known, from both banking theory and the analysis of historic events, that liquidity crises can be prevented by the existence of adequate deposit insurance. This insurance, in principle, does not need to be backed by any central banks. If accumulated insurance reserves turn out to be inadequate for covering large losses, the insurance agency can always borrow in the capital market on the strength of future insurance premiums. The recent involvement of the Federal Reserve System in United States bank failures was caused by the existence of large aggregate deposit liabilities in individual accounts exceeding the $40,000 insured limit—not because the United States deposit insurance agency was unable to meet its obligations.

In the past, liquidity crises usually resulted from fears of bank failure due to bankruptcy of one bank, which led to massive deposit withdrawals throughout the system. With the institution of deposit insurance, such withdrawals have ceased to be a problem, and the discount window of the lender of last resort has been used, instead, to avoid the

---

23. See Edwards and Scott, "Regulating the Solvency of Depository Institutions: A Perspective for Deregulation," in this volume.

effect of stringent monetary policy. We conclude that there exists no strong need for the creation of a lender of last resort for multinational banks.

This view is reinforced by the fact that the Eurocurrency markets are very efficient and flexible. First, the banks themselves are well protected by their policies of matching maturities of assets and liabilities, which is possible to a large extent by the imaginative use of roll-over loans and flexible interest rates. Second, even large deposit withdrawals can readily be offset by the attraction of new deposits drawn from national money supplies of all Western countries through necessary interest rate adjustments. Finally, it should be remembered that large deposits cannot be, and are not, withdrawn in cash; at worst, they are shifted between different banks or even different countries, so that they never leave the global capital market, which the multinational banks have integrated so effectively, and can always be borrowed back.

## NEED FOR COLLECTIVE ACTION

Attempts to eliminate the externalities caused by multinational banks through the imposition of minimum reserve requirements on foreign currency deposits and the inclusion of such deposits in compulsory insurance schemes gives rise to the need for collective action by all countries. Without such action, multinational banking activities will simply move to countries without such legislation. The problem is very similar to that caused by the existence of income (and other) tax havens. If international agreement cannot be reached, it may be necessary for major countries to pass national legislation to eliminate directly the advantages accruing to their nationals from taking refuge in foreign shelters. United States personal and corporate income tax legislation is replete with precedents for such regulations.

## THE COSTS OF CAPTURING EXTERNALITIES

Policy changes designed to control or eliminate the externalities from multinational banking will come, unfortunately, at a cost. With minimum reserve requirements, deposit insurance, and disclosure regulations will come increased government intervention. Like domestic banks, multinational banks will be required to conform to certain standards of portfolio composition, ratios of equity to loans, and other safety rules.

Such interference with the freedom of banks to operate may result in multinational banks becoming less competitive and innovative. If the past is any guide to the future, increased government regulations will lead to the creation and maintenance of oligopolies among multinational banks, and between them and domestic banks (typically, with tacit agreement by government). These costs will have to be weighed carefully before any policies are enacted.

In sum, we believe that neutrality in the treatment of multinational and domestic banks is a desirable policy objective, even though it will lead to a reduction in the level of multinational banking and may carry a risk of reduced competition. The proposed United States legislation for the control of multinational banking basically is designed to achieve such neutrality. German banking legislation is in the same spirit. We suggest that other countries should follow the precedents set by these two countries. It is in the interest of an efficient global banking system for government regulation to eliminate the negative externalities that sometimes arise from the free operation of markets.

## The Generation of New Externalities

Control over the activities of multinational banks has been advocated because the resulting increased capital flows allegedly have reduced national monetary sovereignty, and because the Eurocurrency markets have arguably led to an uncontrolled expansion of international liquidity.

### NATIONAL MONETARY SOVEREIGNTY

During the 1960s and early 1970s, most Western countries were engaged in efforts to reduce unemployment through expansionary monetary and fiscal policies, attempting to trade greater employment for some increased inflation along their Phillips curves. In some countries, attempts to increase money supplies as part of these policies led to short-term capital outflows, to reserve losses, and to exchange rate devaluation, as other countries failed to pursue these policies to the same degree. During these times, many economists and policymakers argued that, under the regime of fixed parity exchange rates, countries had lost their monetary sovereignty because international short-term capital flows prevented them from achieving the money supply increases and low interest rates deemed necessary for the attainment of target unemployment rates.

The loss of monetary sovereignty is, of course, a matter of degree, and the development of multinational banking and the Eurocurrency markets was considered to have added to the severity of this control problem. During the last decade, there have been many recommendations to curb the activities of multinational banks in order to increase national monetary sovereignty. However, most countries which have had experience with controls over international short-term capital flows have found them to be ineffective in anything but the shortest run. Money is simply too fungible a commodity to be prevented from flowing across borders by controls which are consistent with the maintenance of market economies. Many economists have argued that the solution lies in the adoption of floating exchange rates, which we have had since the international monetary upheavals of 1971.

Experience with floating exchange rates has shown that monetary sovereignty (defined as having control over the money supply) is more attainable with than without exchange rate flexibility. However, having control of the money supply does not necessarily imply the attainment of the goal of lower employment. The reason for this problem is now accepted almost universally: There is no trade-off between unemployment and inflation over any time span relevant to economic policymaking. We accept this view, of the absence of a Phillips curve trade-off, and conclude that the most important historical motive for the control of multinational banks and Eurocurrency markets—that they are obstacles to the attainment of monetary sovereignty and low unemployment—has disappeared.

There remains the problem that multinational banking may affect the ability of monetary policy to combat national business cycles. We believe that this problem does not justify the institution of controls over multinational banks for two reasons. First, in today's world, international economic interdependencies in forms other than money market integration are so great that business cycles tend to be worldwide, and international short-term capital flows aid rather than hinder global recovery efforts. Second, floating exchange rates permit countries increased freedom to pursue domestic stabilization policies. Capital flows complicate, but do not make impossible, the task of stabilization.

Generally, the argument against the regulation of multinational banks to control international capital flows is that such control can be achieved only at the cost of heavy interference with free markets and allocative efficiency. The more the operations of these banks are curbed, the more the world suffers from the loss of savings in financial intermediation and the availability of new market instruments. The dubious advantages of monetary sovereignty and control over business cycles are more than outweighed by these losses in allocative efficiency.

INFLATION

We turn, finally, to the discussion of arguments for direct control over multinational banks and Eurocurrency markets, based on the view that these institutions have increased the world money supply (through the operation of large expansion multipliers) and therefore are responsible for the worldwide inflation of recent years. In the preceding section, we pointed out that there now exist increasing theoretical understanding and empirical evidence that leakages from Eurodollar markets are so great that Eurodollar multipliers are, in fact, quite small, and that net liquidity creation through maturity transformation by multinational banks has been very small.[24] In recent years, worldwide inflation has

---

24. See Little, N. 6 *supra* at Ch. 5; and Hewson, N. 6 *supra*.

been the result of past efforts by major countries to exploit the Phillips curve trade-off. Aggregate increases in the world's national money supplies, unmatched by increases in real output, are quite capable of explaining the inflation without any reference to Eurocurrency deposits[25]—which, at any rate, are counted almost completely in national money supply statistics.[26] For these reasons, it appears to us to be counter to the interest of global price stabilization efforts to regulate the activities of multinational banks and Eurocurrency markets through direct controls, though we endorse the imposition of minimum reserve requirements on foreign currency deposits for the efficiency reasons discussed above.

## SUMMARY AND CONCLUSIONS

Our review of the motives for multinational banking suggests that its recent growth has been caused by two sources of comparative advantage: natural economies brought to the fore by technological innovations, and implicit tax advantages arising from discriminatory reserve requirements and other legislation, which, in most countries, favors multinational banks.

We have presented arguments in favor of legislation which would eliminate the distortions created by this favorable treatment of multinational banks, and which would permit countries to continue to capture the externalities which prompted the domestic legislation. United States legislation proposed for the regulation of multinational banks roughly follows this principle by advocating prohibitions on multinational banks' national branching and merchant banking activities. In other countries, the primary implication of this principle is the institution of minimum reserve requirements and compulsory deposit insurance on foreign currency deposits where compulsory insurance exists for domestic deposits. This legislation would probably curtail the growth of multinational banking, but the existence of natural comparative advantages would assure its continued existence and permit the world to enjoy the benefits of increased efficiency in world capital markets.

The institution of compulsory deposit insurance for multinational banks is recommended on the grounds that it is relatively cheap and simple and would reduce the risk of financial crises which might sweep the world economy. In the presence of deposit insurance, the need for a lender of last resort is much diminished. Indeed, we feel it is not necessary. Also, the very global integration of capital markets achieved by multinational banks removes the need for a lender of last resort.

---

25. See Heller, *International Reserves and World Wide Inflation*, IMF Staff Papers (March 1976).

26. For a discussion of this very technical subject by an expert from the BIS, see Mayer, "The BIS Concept of the Net Size of the Euro-Currency Market and Its Relation to the World Money Supply," Euromoney (May 1976).

The case for the regulation of multinational banking on the ground that it interferes with national monetary sovereignty is rejected on the ground that the employment-generating benefits from national monetary sovereignty are illusionary, due to the absence of any policy-relevant, Phillips-curve trade-off. Also, there is no justification for restricting multinational banks on the ground that they cause inflation. These banks reallocate but do not create liquidity, at least to a significant degree.

The proposed guideline for the regulation of multinational banks will assure their continued existence. However, there is some danger that the industry will become less competitive and less efficient—government regulation normally has these effects. While this is an important point to consider when designing specific legislation, it is not by itself a sufficiently strong argument to invalidate the legislative changes proposed in this paper.

# COMMENTARY

Henry S. Bloch, *Executive Vice President, E. M. Warburg, Pincus & Co., Inc.;*
*Adjunct Professor of Law and International Relations, Columbia University*

The first question raised by Grubel and Dean is why banks engage in multinational operations. In my opinion, one cannot really argue that the same economic, legal, and political reasoning applies to all banks in all countries at all times. Banks in different countries have different motives for engaging in multinational banking. United States banks have located preferentially in the markets of United States multinational corporations. They also, like other banks, need overseas loci to operate in the Eurodollar markets. No doubt, they have responded to United States tax law (the Interest Equalization Tax, which is no longer in effect); capital transfer laws (no longer in effect); and to other regulatory devices. It is also true that over a number of years, United States banks had an advantage over European banks because of the interest rate differential. Multinational banking follows both corporations and trade.

Much of the success of multinational banking depends on a foreign bank's ability to infiltrate the domestic market, provide services, and adapt itself to the practices of the marketplace. Price competitiveness is obviously a *conditio* sine qua non. There are modern banks with a long-established international practice. An early example is the British, who have banking facilities in their former colonies, and, in many cases, continue to operate successfully in newly independent countries. The same can be said of the French and the Dutch, as well. Canadian multinational banking has a place of its own, partly due to the concentration of business in a few very large banks, and partly due to the Canadians' understanding of Commonwealth practices. Japanese and German banks are liquid institutions endowed with great size, and they have stronger ties to their own multinational corporations than do United States banks to theirs.

The second issue raised is whether big banks can challenge a country's monetary sovereignty. This is certainly true for small nations
which have no banking system of their own. A number of smaller
countries had to develop banking systems of their own so as not to be at
the mercy of swings in money supply dictated by foreign banks' cash
transfer practices. Almost any country must have some control over its
money supply. Even small countries have proved themselves able to
hold their own against big banks, but they have had to use regulatory
measures. Unfortunately, such measures have sometimes also been
self-defeating. However, I generally agree with the position presented
here by Grubel and Dean.

It is of interest that the French Left put nationalization of banks at the
top of its program but specifically declared that it would have refrained
from nationalizing foreign banks. Let us look at the numbers: of the
total footings of French banks, between 1,300 and 1,400 billion francs in
1977, a figure which includes government-owned banks, private banks,
the so-called *banques mutuelles et coopératives,* and foreign banks, only
between 80 and 90 billion francs are the footings of foreign banks.
Obviously, even the Left sees no danger to sovereignty from a foreign
bank influence, and even left extremists see the advantages of foreign
banking.

The third issue is whether foreign banks in the United States enjoy a
great competitive advantage over domestic banks. Instead of reviewing
the papers submitted, let us quote Governor Mitchell's statement before
Congress on the principal regulatory advantages for foreign banks
operating through branch and agency forms of organization:

(1) branches and agencies are not legally subject to any of the reserve
requirements or other regulations effecting monetary policy that are
placed on the operations of their primary competitors—large national
and State member banks in our major financial markets;

(2) branches and agencies are not subject to any federal restrictions on
multi-State banking and thus can be established in any State that
permits entry, even if a foreign bank has a State or federally-chartered
subsidiary bank in another State (44 foreign banks have commercial
banking operations in more than one State, Table 17 of Appendix);

(3) a foreign bank maintaining only branches and agencies is not subject to
the prohibitions of the Glass-Steagall Act, and thus can maintain those
banking operations and at the same time have an interest in a securities
firm in the U.S. (20 foreign banks with commercial banking operations
in the U.S. have interests in U.S. broker-dealers, Table 18 in
Appendix);

(4) a foreign bank maintaining only branches and agencies is not subject to
the Bank Holding Company Act of 1956, as amended, and thus can
engage directly or indirectly in the United States in any type of nonbanking activities and can invest in any United States commercial firm,

so long as it has the power to do so under the laws of its home country; and

(5) branches and agencies are not subject to any federal bank examination, regulation, or supervision of the type carried out by the Comptroller of the Currency, the Board, or the FDIC.[1]

It is also true that the proposed regulation will not put foreign and domestic banks on the same footing.

The objective, in a large country where free competition is the desirable working hypothesis, should be equality of treatment. Once a foreign bank is granted entry, there should be neither advantages nor disadvantages as against domestic banks. In order to accomplish this, foreign banks will have to be federally, not state, controlled.

Each country also has to accept a certain responsibility for the banks operating within its borders, and each home country has to respect the sovereignty of the host country in which its banks operate.

A fourth issue, of major concern lately to all those who study the banking system, is the soundness of multinational banks. Basically, the soundness of a system is determined by its operators, not by its regulators. There has been constant improvement in the internal reporting systems, the internal guidelines, the systems of supervision and training, and the internal controls of banks. To me, the fact is inescapable that this improvement in self-controls in some banks has made greater progress towards solvency than improvements in supervisory procedures. However, I would also recommend that we develop a uniform reporting system as soon as possible. The Comptroller of the Currency is now seeking to develop a comprehensive country exposure report in cooperation with the Federal Reserve System and the FDIC. Much work has to be done to refine it and to develop a comparable system of information.

One of the solutions recommended by Grubel and Dean is compulsory deposit insurance for international banks. As a general ground rule, this has great theoretical appeal. Empirically, however, deposit insurance can apply only to limited amounts because of limitations upon the ability of the insuring organization to make good in case of failure. And Eurodollar operations are undertaken only on a large scale.

Unquestionably, the multinational banks must be encouraged to be wary of their overseas deposit structures. Huge depositors, Middle Eastern and others, have been known to move capital very quickly, thus making for a fragile deposit structure. A fragile deposit structure is just as dangerous as a fragile loan portfolio. By and large, the Eurodollar customer and the wholesale banking customer deal in large sums which far exceed the maximum that any insurance system could allow without

---

1. Statement by George W. Mitchell, Vice Chairman, Board of Governors, Federal Reserve System, Before the Subcomm. on Financial Institutions of the Senate Comm. on Banking, Housing and Urban Affairs, 94th Cong., 1st Sess. 6–7 (Jan. 28, 1976).

endangering its own health. As a bank's Eurodollar depositor and

Eurodollar borrower are often identical, or if not, have a confluence of interest, it is rather useful for the depositors to know that they do have a responsibility vis-à-vis the banks—a remark particularly relevant to certain petrodollar depositors.

A lender of last resort is the ultimate guarantor of the integrity of the banks in its jurisdiction. In my opinion, the home country has the first responsibility for its own multinational banks when it comes to the question of last-resort lending.[2] It is impossible to split the foreign and domestic operations of a single bank.

It does not follow, however, that the host country should exempt from its regulations banks operating within its borders. Coordination of regulations among different countries would be desirable, as would be disclosure practices. As different countries require different types of reporting, it might also be useful to develop a uniform model into which all information can be translated by use of a code. Such a model might be accepted by several countries.

It is also desirable for informal consultations between central banks and their examiners to be extended. There is need for continued and systematic consultations among all domestic banking authorities dealing with international banking, and with all foreign authorities dealing with American banking. The consultation mechanism of central banks is now informal and quite secretive.

Having made a strong case for the role of the central banks, I am still concerned with other very specific issues of bank regulation. State-owned banks in a number of countries have been able to make major export loans in the national interest. Foreign insurance and guarantee programs allow foreign banks in a number of countries to extend export credits to less developed countries without incurring risk to the latter. U.S. banks are subject to very strict U.S. regulation, which results in classifying certain less developed countries' risks as substandard, and the banks do not have the support of insurance and credit mechanisms necessary to allow export financing to such countries. The U.S. regulatory program is now so risk averse that it possibly has begun to inhibit U.S. exports to less developed countries. The automatic classification of countries into noncreditworthy categories makes it difficult to grant credit in those countries, whatever the purpose or whatever the conditions. To quote Governor Wallich of the Federal Reserve System:

> The regulatory authorities will have to develop techniques that will allow bank examiners to comment on risks taken in foreign lending without doing irreparable damage to the credit standing of particular countries.[3]

---

2. This is also stated by Governor Mitchell. Cf. *id.*

3. See Henry C. Wallich, "How Much Private Bank Lending Is Enough," address given at a Symposium on Developing Countries' Debt, sponsored by the Export-Import Bank, Washington, D. C., April 21, 1977.

In summary, although my general position is that informal approaches are more effective than formal international cooperation in bank supervision, there will be instances where bilateral understandings for the exchange of information will become necessary. A multilateral agreement, even within the framework of the Common Market, will probably not be concluded for decades to come. Meanwhile, the self-control mechanisms of banks must continue to improve, and national regulations must become more sensitized to international requirements. The central banks will probably remain the best international channels of information, and they must continue to share their international contacts and experience with other national regulatory authorities.

# COMMENTARY

Raymond Vernon, *Herbert F. Johnson Professor of International Business Management, Harvard University Graduate School of Business Administration*

Dean and Grubel aspire, in short compass, to describe the forces that have led to the growth of multinational banking, to assess the macroeconomic implications of that growth, and to prescribe a set of policies that would produce results more to the taste of the authors. The purpose of the paper is so ambitious that it is hard for the authors to avoid, at times, appearing somewhat shallow in their analysis and dogmatic in their prescriptions.

Perhaps the authors could avoid this impression in a book-length exposition of the subject. But not altogether, I fear. Part of the seeming dogmatism and shallowness arises out of the heavy commitment of the authors to a neoclassical view of how the world actually operates, as well as a heavy preference for "allocative efficiency" in the classical sense as a key objective for economic policy. Let me comment briefly on each of these emphases.

## HOW MULTINATIONAL BANKING OPERATES

The authors point out—rightly, no doubt—that the extraordinary improvement in international communication and travel had something to do with the growth of multinational banking. That development, I think they would agree, was a necessary but not a sufficient condition for some banks to branch out across international borders and for others to form international consortia. The sufficient condition, however, was the multinational spread of the large customers of these banks, the so-called multinational enterprises. This was a phenomenon of consummate importance and far more significant in helping the enterprise get a foothold abroad than the trivial tactics, such as advertising, on which their analysis dwells. It is no coincidence, therefore, that the banks which were most prone to multinationalize were also those most prominent in serving multinational manufacturers and extractive enterprises.

The propensity of banks to follow their customers abroad was due partly to the fact that they had an inside track in securing the business of the foreign subsidiaries of such customers, and partly to a fear of the consequences if they failed to follow their customers abroad. As the banks' strategists saw it, if they failed to corral the subsidiary's business abroad, rival banks would have an entry wedge into the multinational network of their customers, and that entry could lead eventually to a rivalry for the business of other members of the same network, including the business of the parent, itself. Accordingly, banks followed their customers abroad, partly in anticipation of fresh profits and partly to reduce the risk of competition for the earnings that were coming from the rest of the customer's multinational network. In an extension of the same kind of strategy and in a reflection of the same sort of worry, some banks followed the leaders into new locations, even if their own customers had not yet established themselves in these areas, hoping not to be left too far behind in the competitive race.

It has been typical of the experience of multinational banks that, whatever their original motivation may have been in establishing overseas branches and subsidiaries, those branches and subsidiaries have been drawn gradually into the domestic economy of the countries in which they have settled. That stage has been manifested partly by a growth in deposits in the national currency and Eurocurrencies, and by a growth of loans to non-Americans. In some cases, the multinational banks have accelerated the process by a familiar device: They have exported from their home-base some facility or service which had not yet been adopted in the host economy, and they have used their quasi-technological edge to establish a foothold in that economy. Services of the type described in the discussion paper, such as Citibank's "money boutiques," illustrate this tactic. In other cases, computer services have been offered to handle the back office work of commercial customers; new money market instruments have been introduced; and so on. As a rule, in a world in which communication is increasingly efficient, these initial leads have been relatively short-lived—a few years or a decade, at most. But, they often have been critical in the first penetration of customer markets. Besides, multinational banks could sometimes renew their wasting technological advantages by introducing added innovations, as long as innovations were being produced somewhere in their network.

Now, a word on future developments. Projections unavoidably are statements of faith; but some projections are more plausible than others. And the authors' expectations that the multinational banking phase will shake down into a period of quiescent oligopoly run counter to my own. The number of multinational banks seems likely to increase, not to decline. The Soviet Union, for instance, is already in the business;

the Middle East countries are not far behind; and one sees early stirrings out of Brazil, Mexico, and even India. In other sectors of business, such as oil, copper, aluminum, automobiles, and heavy chemicals, the steady increase in the number of multinational enterprises vying with each other in national markets has been weakening national oligopolies, not the other way around.[1] And, I see no reason why multinational banking should be an exception in this regard.

## THE DIRECTION OF PUBLIC POLICIES

The authors' discussion of government policies toward multinational banking strikes me, on the whole, as reasonable enough: a combination of measures to equalize the regulatory impact on all the competitors in the market, whether national or foreign; and a preference for avoiding additional regulatory restraints wherever they can. But they seem to me to overlook some important problems and to dismiss others a bit too readily.

One of these is the problem created by the sloshing around of short-term funds and the short-term fluctuations in exchange rates that these movements help create. They suggest that central banks need not worry quite so much about the adequacy of their reserves, now that flexible rates seem here to stay. Yet, central bank intervention proceeds at a very heavy rate and large foreign exchange borrowings from the International Monetary Fund are still in the picture. The authors' assumptions, therefore, do not seem to fit very well with the world as we know it. We all have learned that fixed exchange rates were a source of repeated crisis and trauma for the major monetary areas. And we are now learning that flexible exchange rates can be a source of persistent, sometimes acute, headache. Insofar as multinational banks can be said to facilitate the flow of short-term funds, therefore, they are part of a problem that cannot be dismissed easily.

In addition, the authors seem to me to be oversimplifying the key issues of public policy by concentrating mainly on the Phillips curve, the trade-off between inflation and unemployment. As far as most professional economists are concerned, that is certainly a central issue. But politicians, government administrators, and the public at large have other worries, as well. For instance, they worry about the fact that multinational banking facilities make it somewhat easier for United States customers to avail themselves of offshore tax havens—a perfectly legal use of such facilities, but one that continues to be troublesome to many. Some also worry about the possibility that multinational banking appears to increase the dominance in the U.S. economy of those U.S. banks that are already the country's leaders. And, some are concerned about the fact that in periods of credit stringency, the multina-

---

1. For the evidence on this score, see Vernon, *Storm over the Multinationals: The Real Issues* 80–87 (Harvard Univ. Press, Cambridge 1977).

tional banks can garner funds from their London branches that may well have originated in the United States. When, for instance, Midwest banks lend dollars to these London branches and those branches lend the dollars to their New York parents, the supply of funds to state and municipal borrowers in the United States tends to decline, while the funds to industrial borrowers are increased. Relative changes in the terms of borrowings, such as these, are of the essence in national policy and national politics, and they cannot be addressed by concentrating on macroeconomic magnitudes and the Phillips curve.

The essence of my comments, therefore, is this: The theory of multinational banking on which the authors rely, while adequate as far as it goes, suffers from an air of unreality. And the regulatory issues with which the authors deal, while of considerable significance, leave many problems untouched, problems that could, in the end, determine the way in which the public regulatory mechanism addresses—and indeed ought to address—the issue of regulating multinational banking.

# DISCUSSION

FRANKLIN R. EDWARDS: Today's session is a little bit out of the mainstream of what we have been discussing up to now. We have been focusing on domestic regulatory issues. Today, we are going to focus on the regulatory problems which arise because financial institutions are transnational, or multinational, or international.

YOSHI TSURUMI: I question whether economic efficiency should be the supreme criterion for evaluating banking regulations, or the regulation of multinational banks. What I have failed to see in the primary paper and in the authors' presentations is how neutrality is established in the United States between domestic and foreign banks. I also fail to see how the establishment of neutrality is going to curb the growth of monopoly by multinational banks in the United States.

DEAN: I do not think that there is any danger of the growth of monopoly by international banks in the United States. That is not an issue. It is just that the United States banking lobby at present—and I think rightly so—is concerned that, in some respects, multinational banks are treated favorably. That is why I did not quite agree with Professor Bloch's remarks that international banks are not favorably treated under United States regulation.

It is my understanding that there are now three bills before the United States Congress, actively pushed by the domestic banking lobby, that would impose equal regulations on the foreign banking community.

Why is the United States banking lobby so concerned if, in fact, foreign banks have no advantages under the present banking system?

BLOCH: You have a very good point. However, I did not quite say that United States and foreign banks are treated equally. I said there is a gray area; the issue is not so clearcut. You also often find that lobbies attempt to impose additional restrictions on foreign institutions, even when they do not enjoy any advantages.

DEAN: The major thrust behind the banking lobby comes from the small domestic banks, which do not have multinational banking options open to them.

BLOCH: That is right.

EDWARDS: As I understand your paper, you have two major points. One is that neutrality should be a goal of regulation; and the second concerns what you call the externalities associated with the soundness of the international financial system.

Neutrality is a very debatable issue. We could sit here for hours, at least, and debate the pros and cons of who is treated better, and not come to any conclusion.

Further, I do not think that we can look at the activities of political lobbyists as indications of unfair treatment. They might want to put multinational banks in a worse position, regardless of the position they are in already.

I would like to shift our attention to the solvency issue, or to the soundness issue, and talk about your proposal for instituting deposit insurance in place of a lender of last resort. As I understand your paper, you are against a lender of last resort because of the political difficulties of coordinating an international lender of last resort, and you feel that deposit insurance would be an easier and more foolproof device for assuring soundness.

My problem with this proposal is that, if you look deeply at how most current deposit insurance systems work, you quickly discover that when you have a uniform premium system, you need a host of other solvency regulations to support the system. Even if you have variable premiums, the "moral hazard" problem may still be very tricky.

Consequently, it is not clear to me that you could successfully impose deposit insurance on a worldwide basis without first getting international cooperation on all kinds of solvency regulations.

It seems to me that having a lender of last resort is no more politically infeasible than is deposit insurance.

GRUBEL: The problem with the lender-of-last-resort facility in the United States and in most Western countries is that it has been abused and has become a way in which commercial banks are able to circumvent the attempt of central banks to make monetary policy. They use the rediscount facilities, not so much in order to keep from becoming insolvent but in order to avoid monetary tightness. That is the way in which it has degenerated. What prompted my argument is that with deposit insurance, we no longer need a lender of last resort.

In the same way, I am afraid that if the International Monetary Fund were made the lender of last resort, it would eventually grow into a system whereby the banks would get further liquidity above that which is available in other countries. I do not think that is desirable.

I know that there are certain difficulties associated with deposit insurance, but because of these considerations, I have made the judgment that we should put more emphasis on trying to develop a sound system of insurance.

GERALD M. MAYER, JR.: I remember the days of June 1974, when a number of banks in New York participated in an operation called Dawn Patrol. At seven o'clock in the morning, we would survey all the payments being made by international banks to determine whether we should recall these payments in the clearinghouse. All this was a result of the Herstadt Bank affair, and the Herstadt failure was the result of two things: One, there was no deposit insurance in Germany, and, two, there was ultimately a failure by the BundesBank to act as the lender of last resort. It almost created monetary havoc, and the BundesBank, I think, has tacitly, and now legally, acknowledged that it probably did not handle the situation in the most sophisticated manner.

I do not think you could ever replace the stability rendered by an effective lender of last resort with a deposit insurance system. They are complementary. A lender of last resort is never sure—you never know if the central bank is going to step in, nor should you; but the fact that such a move is available to a banking system is, I think, absolutely essential to the proper functioning of the system.

I cite what was done with the Franklin National Bank, what was done with the Hamilton Bank here, and what has been done with a number of other banks that have failed in this country. Had it been left only to deposit insurance, I do not think it would have worked.

CANTWELL MUCKENFUSS: I am from the FDIC. Deposit insurance is a misnomer. If you believe that all that is insured are deposits of $40,000, you would simply look to the resources available in the insurance fund as the source of confidence. In point of fact, a deposit insurance system is far more complex. If you look at the Franklin failure or the Hamilton failure, a more accurate

name for what was done would be the "federally assisted purchasing and assumption corporation." Without going into the technicali-
ties of those cases, what was used instead of
insurance was a panoply of tools for dealing
with disruptive bank failures.

ROBERT MUNDELL:     When you start to insure the deposits of banks
in, say, Iran and Mexico, where revolutions
may occur, you also have to ask whether it is
private or public money that is going to provide the implicit resources. If it is public
money, whose public money is it? And, is it
going to be public money with all the same
rights attached?

MICHAEL ADLER:     Professor Grubel, given those relationships
among interest rates described in your paper,
why do large United States firms ever borrow
domestically, rather than from the foreign currency market?

GRUBEL:     Since I know how well-informed you are,
would you please provide the answer?

ADLER:     I do not know the reason.

GRUBEL:     Well, I suppose the first question is to ask how
big a phenomenon it is. Does General Motors
of Germany deposit a lot of money with whatever their main bank is in New York rather
than with the branch of an American bank in
Europe? That is really what you are implying.
Before I spend much time thinking about it, I
would like to know whether, in fact, they do
this and to what extent they do it.

To change the subject, I am puzzled by Ray
Vernon's statement that he has a different paradigm, and that transaction costs are not so
important.

Could someone among the practitioners here
please explain what words you use in order to
describe the motives for First National City
going to Frankfurt when some big multinational customer also goes to Frankfurt? What is
it in the terminology of the theory of multinational enterprises that explains why they find

it necessary to go to Frankfurt? You say they are worried that if they do not go, they will lose business. But why?

VERNON: Let us distinguish two kinds of transaction costs. One is the cost associated with borrowing from a distant lender or lending to a distant borrower. From a narrow technical point of view, I assume this is minimal to the point of being zero nowadays.

The other is a process by which a potential borrower decides from what institution to borrow. It involves another kind of transaction and another kind of transaction cost, because he will want to have a perception of the subsequent choices that will derive from the borrowing relationship he is establishing. Or, stated differently, he may regard the whole chain of future transactions as being related and not independent of one another. The bank has to ask whether it wants to make such an investment in this customer—in effect, a lumpy investment. The marginal cost of subsequent transactions between the bank and the local subisidiary will be very low because it will know the subsidiary and the subsidiary will know the bank.

This kind of decision is the quintessence of a lot of multinational business—deciding whether or not to make such a lumpy investment.

It is this second kind of transaction cost that you have to keep your eye on, not the first.

GRUBEL: But what is it that the American bank has and can offer more cheaply to the American subsidiary abroad that a Frankfurt bank cannot give the American subsidiary?

VERNON: You are breaking the problem down in a way that is wise to avoid. There are two streams of transactions. One is the independent borrowing and lending between a subsidiary and a local bank. The other is a stream of interrelated transactions involving headquarters and other subsidiaries.

Before the fact, the bank manager cannot know what the mix is going to be, nor can central headquarters. So, the question is: Can the bank position itself in an optimal way for both kinds of transactions?

GRUBEL: I still do not see why First National City has to, or would want to, follow its customer to Frankfurt. Why cannot a Frankfurt bank provide services more cheaply, since it knows the local conditions, knows the government, and has all the comparative advantages on a natural basis?

MAYER: Let me take a shot at this. I think there is an implication of neatness in our discussion which just does not exist in the real market. The world is a sloppy place, and we have to organize ourselves purposely to function in a sloppy world.

EDWARDS: Economists see order in disorder.

MAYER: Precisely. But, bankers do not see this order. We see a marketplace made up of many marketplaces. Many things happen at different times and without being anticipated.

GRUBEL: I do not believe for a moment that you cannot give me a good reason why First National City went to Frankfurt. Were you going to lose that company if you did not go?

MAYER: I think that when we perceive opportunities in a market, we go to that market. The market opportunity may exist because our customers are there. In other cases, it exists because we think our customers should be there.

GRUBEL: But what have you got that gives you a comparative advantage?

EDWARDS: Professor Bloch?

BLOCH: The question before us is how the international banking network has arisen as a consequence of multinational corporate activities and what the interrelationship is between such international corporate activities and international banking.

American international banking is relatively new. Overseas banking is only partially due to international corporate activities. American banks also have engaged in overseas activities because of legislative provisions, many of which are no longer in effect: the Interest Equalization Tax, capital transfer limitations, guidelines governing overseas lending. These limitations affected not only banks but also the corporations. Also, both corporations and banks are pushed towards overseas financial vehicles by United States tax legislation.

However, once American corporations required complex overseas financial activities, and once it became clear that these activities required strong banking support, the powerful American banks were natural candidates to furnish the supporting services. Their ability to mobilize capital abroad because of the strong backing of their home base played a major role in American overseas development. Further, their excellent communications network made it possible for them to render services in exchange transactions, trading, and other financial activities, services which are very lucrative.

The method of doing business by American corporations also differs considerably from that of European corporations. American bankers know this method and therefore have a major advantage in serving their compatriots.

The expanding export business of U.S. companies also required intensive financing, especially since the U.S. government does not give its own exports the same kind of financial backing as do a number of competitor nations. Multinational corporations are in an advantageous position if a U.S. bank is responsible for the payment of foreign trade debts.

The reverse is also true: The great expansion of Japanese and German banking in the United States, which took place during recent years, directly followed the expansion of investments in the U.S. by firms from those countries. Again, differences in the method of doing business is probably of critical importance.

It is not, however, easy to pinpoint specific instances of multinational corporations actually triggering the establishment of a United States banking activity. But let me give you one example: When General Motors started its huge European plant near Antwerp, the Chase Manhattan Bank established a banking activity in that city, together with a Belgian bank. That this relationship between Chase and General Motors is symbiotic should be obvious. It is usually much more effective to serve a corporation on a global basis, with credits and debits distributed throughout the international banking network, thus maximizing the utilization of funds and optimizing foreign exchange management.

EDWARDS:     If I may intervene for a moment, I think that this discussion is partially substantive and partially semantic. It depends upon what we call transaction costs, or upon what we call real economies. I think we all agree, if I may render an assessment here, that there are some real economies to multinational banking, and that these are often referred to by different names. Although it would be useful to know more about them, let us assume for purposes of argument that they exist and move on to another issue.

We have also agreed that neutrality in the regulatory treatment of multinational banks is a good idea, and that we want soundness, whether through an effective lender of last resort or through a sound deposit-insurance system.

Let me turn briefly to what Professor Vernon said in his remarks about large banks. He said that, even though there are real economies associated with multinational banks, if these banks got to be very large and powerful, they still might not be a good thing. Would you stop multinational banking from developing for this reason? Is this concern an overriding public policy issue? And, what remedies do you have in mind?

VERNON: I have not turned my mind to the question of public policy with respect to international banking. I thought I should use my comparative advantage to discuss how international banking came to be. I thought I was being terribly brave even to discuss some public policy considerations. I raised the issue of monopoly because I think it is important to United States policy. It is a social and political problem, as well as an economic problem. Empirically, however, I suggest that probably multinational banking on the whole may be having the opposite effect in most banking markets: It may be increasing competition. My point was a narrow one. It was only that you dare not stop with the allocative efficiency question to express the United States menu of political tastes.

COHEN: Isn't one of the reasons U.S. banks go abroad so they can provide large U.S. corporations with funds, no matter what domestic monetary policy is? Smaller U.S. banks are not able to do this.

GRUBEL: Why can't the American manufacturing subsidiary go directly to Paris? Why do large corporations need U.S. banks to have overseas branches to circumvent monetary policy?

EDWARDS: We are getting close to the end of the hour.

GRUBEL: May I just say something about economic efficiency as an objective. When George Schultz left the Treasury, he said that allocative efficiency is like a compass we have to use to know where we are going. When we turn to questions of policy, it is very much like sailing a ship: One has to tack the way the wind goes, but we still must keep on looking at the compass. If we give up the compass, we are dead. We will not know where to go at all. We will be tacking back and forth wildly.

MUNDELL: To end with a kind of nasty comment: Given the number of unanswered questions that Pro-

fessors Grubel and Dean and others have
admitted exist, such ignorance itself seems
like a strong argument for not regulating anything. Under these circumstances, the chances
are great that any kind of regulation will be
wrong.

EDWARDS: That seems a fitting summary on which to end.

## CHAPTER NINE

# A Survey of Studies on Banking Competition and Performance

## MARKET STRUCTURE, COMPETITION, AND PERFORMANCE IN FINANCIAL INDUSTRIES: A SURVEY OF BANKING STUDIES

Arnold A. Heggestad, *Chairman and Professor, Department of Finance, Insurance and Real Estate, University of Florida*

The United States commercial banking industry has a unique and paradoxical structure. While there are more than 14,000 commercial banks, regulation and the character of most banking services greatly constrict banking markets, so that there are only a small number of alternatives available to most consumers. Local customers face a banking structure that is more monopolistic than competitive.

The industry is also intensely regulated. Federal and state regulators prescribe who may offer financial services, which services they may offer, where they may offer them, and how they must conduct their business.

Several efforts have been launched in recent years to reform the regulatory structure. There has been pressure to expand the power of nonbank financial intermediaries, to allow interstate branching, to allow bank expansion into nonbank activities, and to drop many of the regulations designed to protect the banking industry from "excessive" competition. Many of these reforms would directly and indirectly alter the structure of local banking markets, largely by changing the number of banking alternatives available to consumers. To evaluate the structural impact of these reforms, therefore, it is necessary to know how market structure affects the performance of banks.

Since the path-breaking studies by Schweiger and McGee[1] and

The author wishes to thank F. R. Edwards, J. J. Mingo, and S. A. Rhoades for their extensive comments. They are not, of course, responsible for errors. Financial support from the National Science Foundation (Contract Number NSF-C76-18548) and the Center for Public Policy Research at the University of Florida is gratefully acknowledged.

1. Schweiger and McGee, "Chicago Banking," 34 J. Bus., No. 3, pp. 203–366 (July 1961).

Edwards,[2] there have been many studies of the structure-performance relationship in banking, with findings that are often superficially quite different. This paper surveys and analyzes these studies. Three basic issues are addressed. First, does market structure matter, or is the banking industry so highly regulated that market structure is simply not a relevant factor in determining market performance? Second, which aspects of market structure are most important, and, therefore, which types of regulatory reform will have the greatest impact? Finally, what aspects of bank performance are most sensitive to differences in market structure?

The first section of the study discusses the theoretical relationship between structure and performance and its applicability to commercial banking. The next section describes the existing market structure in commercial banking. In the following section, some general issues encountered when evaluating the empirical literature are discussed. Empirical studies then are described and analyzed in the two succeeding sections. Finally, the last section contains conclusions and suggestions for future research.

## ECONOMIC THEORY AND THE STRUCTURE-CONDUCT-PERFORMANCE MODEL

The structure-conduct-performance model is a general statement on the determinants of market performance. Simply stated, the conduct or rivalry in a market is determined by market structure conditions, especially the number and size distribution of firms and the condition of entry. This rivalry leads to unique levels of prices, advertising, profits, and other aspects of market performance. Through the link of conduct, the performance of firms in a market is tied to the structure of the market.

Traditional economic theory has extensively developed the analysis of firm and market behavior under conditions of perfect competition and monopoly. In these polar cases, rational profit maximizing behavior leads to predictable prices and other aspects of performance. Under conditions of perfect competition, the consumer welfare is maximized, while firm welfare is maximized under monopoly.

Most markets do not fall neatly into either the perfect competition or the monopoly category. Chamberlin and Robinson initiated formal study of markets falling between these polar extremes.[3] As the structure of markets becomes increasingly monopolistic, a critical question is

---

2. Edwards, "Concentration in Banking and Its Effects on Business Loan Rates," 46 Rev. of Econ. & Statistics, No. 3, pp. 294–300 (Aug. 1964).

3. Chamberlin, *The Theory of Monopolistic Competition* (Harvard Univ. Press, Cambridge 1933); Robinson, *The Economics of Imperfect Competition* (Macmillan, London 1933).

whether performance will become more like that found in monopoly markets, or will, instead, remain reasonably competitive. Chamberlin's approach,[4] which still seems the most reasonable, was to assume that firms will wish to achieve jointly the same price-output configuration as would a monopolistic firm, since by doing so, they will maximize their joint profits. The critical question, therefore, becomes under what conditions firms will be able to coordinate their activities to achieve this result. Even though it is in all their interests to set the monopoly price, each firm may believe it can do better by cutting its price relative to the group. Stigler[5] has delineated the conditions that lead to such price-cutting behavior—conditions largely based on the probability of other firms detecting price-cutting and retaliating. The most important of these conditions is the number and size distribution of firms. The greater the number of firms, the greater the difficulty in detecting and preventing price-cutting. In addition, the difficulty of detection is affected by the number of buyers, market growth, consumer loyalty, and product differentiation. Stigler's model predicts that prices will be higher (and performance worse) in markets with fewer firms, and in markets with lower growth rates, many customers, little customer turnover, and substantial product differentiation.

Potential, as well as actual entry, also restricts the ability of firms to maintain their monopoly positions. An expectation of high profits will entice new firms to enter the market. Existing firms have two options: They may set an entry-forestalling price[6] that makes it unprofitable for new firms to enter, or they may continue to charge the higher (monopoly) price. In the latter case, new entry will occur, and the increased number of firms will eventually drive prices and profits down. In both cases, barriers to entry influence the equilibrium price and performance.

Thus, economic theory ties market structure to firm performance, especially price performance. This relationship has also been subjected to numerous statistical tests in nonfinancial sectors, and in most cases, the theoretical relationship has been shown to hold empirically.[7] If it were not to hold in banking, therefore, it might be because of institutional characteristics specific to banking markets. The extensive regulation in banking may conceivably dictate conduct independent of market structure.

---

4. See Chamberlin, *id.*

5. Stigler, "A Theory of Oligopoly," 72 J. Political Econ., No. 1, pp. 44–61 (Feb. 1964).

6. See Bain, *Barriers to New Competition* (Harvard Univ. Press, Cambridge 1956).

7. For an excellent survey of this literature, see Weiss, "The Concentration-Profits Relationship and Antitrust," *Industrial Concentration: The New Learning* 184–233 (Goldschmid, Mann, and Weston, Eds., Little, Brown & Co., Boston 1974).

## Regulatory Environment

The commercial banking industry is subject to a wide range of regulations.[8] At least three major goals of regulations can be identified, all of which are interdependent and possibly conflicting.[9] The first, and certainly most important, is to maintain bank soundness. Confidence in the strength of individual banks and in the soundness of the banking system is believed to be critical to the economy. The second goal is to achieve an efficient intermediation process, the *raison d'être* of financial industries.[10] The final goal is to provide desired levels of specific bank products or services. Two such products are demand deposits and credit to the housing sector.

To achieve these goals, regulations are imposed on both bank managers and bank markets. Direct regulations on management behavior include the setting of investment criteria, prohibitions of interest on demand deposits, rate ceilings on savings deposits, usury laws, and capital requirements. Other regulations set specific standards of performance. These include the Equal Credit Opportunity Act and the Truth in Lending Act. Since these regulations impact directly on the firm and its ability to adapt to market forces, they may well change the impact of a given market structure. In particular, for a given degree of monopoly, they make it easier to achieve a cartel-like stability in banking markets.

The remaining regulations operate directly on market structure. The most important are the chartering laws. Permission from the Comptroller of the Currency or the state banking commission is necessary to obtain a charter. Historically, it has been difficult to obtain a charter. Peltzman[11] estimates that the chartering laws reduced new entry by about 50 percent between 1937 and 1962. Edwards and Edwards[12] demonstrate that this estimate is excessive, but that the true restriction still exceeds 40 percent. A similar but less restrictive procedure is required to enter markets with new branches. Of course, in those states that limit or forbid branching, this form of restriction is absolute. Regulators also establish policies applicable to mergers.

The United States has a dual banking system with regulation divided

8. These regulations are surveyed in Golembe and Hengren, *Federal Regulation of Banking* (American Institute of Banking 1975).

9. For a thorough discussion, see Jacobs, "The Framework of Commercial Banking Regulation: An Appraisal," 1 Nat'l Banking Rev., No. 3, pp. 343–357 (March 1964); and Edwards and Scott, "Regulating the Solvency of Depository Institutions: A Perspective for Deregulation," in this volume.

10. See Benston and Smith, "A Transactions Cost Approach to the Theory of Financial Intermediation," 31 J. Finance, No. 2 pp. 215–231 (May 1976).

11. Peltzman, "Entry in Commercial Banking," 8 J. Law & Econ., 11–50 (Oct. 1965).

12. Edwards and Edwards, "Measuring the Effectiveness of Regulation: The Case of Bank Entry Regulation," 17 J. Law & Econ., No. 2, pp. 445–460 (Oct. 1974).

between state and several federal authorities.[13] State regulations are not uniform; some states are considerably more severe than others.[14] Similarly, there are differences between the federal agencies. As a result, the extent and the severity of regulation vary significantly among markets. For example, branching laws, chartering conditions, holding company restrictions, and powers of thrift institutions differ between markets. Thus, variation in the degree of regulation is, itself, an element of market structure.

## CONCENTRATION LEVELS

Banks offer many products to different types of consumers. Depending on the size of transaction, the geographic market for the bank product will differ considerably.[15] Household demand for safety deposit boxes will be limited to a very small area, such as a neighborhood. Conversely, the demand for large commercial loans will cover the entire nation. The bulk of commercial banking operations, however, including most households and small businesses, is limited to a fairly small geographic area. Banking markets have been approximated in most studies of bank performance and in most court cases by the Standard Metropolitan Statistical Area (SMSA), or by the rural county, or by some combination of counties.[16] This may not be entirely appropriate. As Talley notes, "the bank regulatory agencies, the Department of Justice, and the courts frequently employ SMSAs and counties as approximations for banking markets, partly because deposit data on an office basis are readily available for these geographic areas."[17]

Most banking markets, defined as SMSAs and counties, are highly concentrated. One measure of concentration is the Herfindahl Index, and its corresponding "numbers-equivalent." A market with a num-

---

13. For an elaboration on the regulatory organization, see Scott, "The Dual Banking System: A Model of Competition in Regulation," in this volume.

14. For a tabulation of differences, see *A Profile of State Chartered Banking* (Conference of State Bank Supervisors, Washington, D.C., 1975).

15. Several studies have analyzed the size of banking markets for different products. See, e.g., Lozowick, Steiner, and Miller, "Law and Quantitative Multivariate Analysis: An Encounter," 66 Mich. L. Rev., No. 8, pp. 1641–1678 (June 1968); Eisenbeis, "Local Banking Markets for Business Loans," 2 J. Bank Research, No. 2, pp. 30–39 (Summer 1971); Gelder and Budzeika, "Banking Market Determination: The Case of Central Nassau County," 52 Fed. Reserve Bank of New York Monthly Rev., No. 11, pp. 258–266 (Nov. 1970); Stolz, "Local Banking Markets, Structure, and Conduct in Rural Areas," *Bank Structure and Competition* 134–149 (Fed. Reserve Bank of Chicago, 1972).

16. This has been the judicial standard since United States v. Philadelphia Nat'l Bank, 374 U.S. 321 (1963). In recent litigation, however, this simple approximation has been challenged. See United States v. Connecticut Nat'l Bank, 418 U.S. 656 (1974).

17. Talley, "Recent Trends in Local Banking Market Structures," *Staff Economic Studies*, No. 89, p. 5 (Bd. of Governors of the Fed. Reserve System, May 1977).

bers-equivalent of, say, $N$ will arguably be as competitive as a market with $N$ firms of equal size.[18] The distribution of numbers-equivalent banks in the United States banking markets in 1973 based on total deposits is presented in Table 9-1. Two facts are evident. First, although there is a wide range in concentration, the average market is highly concentrated. Only 10 percent of the SMSAs have a numbers-equivalent of more than 9.3 equal size banks. The average SMSA market has a numbers-equivalent of only 4.5 banks, i.e., it is no more competitive than if it had 4.5 banks of equal size. Second, rural counties are considerably more concentrated. Only 20 percent of the rural counties have markets with a numbers-equivalent that exceeds 3.9. The average rural county has less than 2.2 banks of equal size. Thus, banking at the local level is highly concentrated with few alternatives open to local customers.

**TABLE 9-1. Cumulative Distribution of Numbers-Equivalent Banks in United States Banking Markets**

| *Percent of markets with numbers-equivalent greater than the indicated level* | *Numbers-equivalent banks in SMSAs* | *Numbers-equivalent banks in rural markets, or non-SMSA counties* |
|---|---|---|
| 10 | 9.3 | 5.0 |
| 20 | 7.0 | 3.9 |
| 30 | 6.1 | 3.4 |
| 40 | 5.3 | 2.9 |
| 50 | 4.7 | 2.6 |
| 60 | 4.3 | 2.2 |
| 70 | 3.8 | 1.9 |
| 80 | 3.4 | 1.7 |
| 90 | 2.9 | 1.0 |
| 100 | 1.7 | 1.0 |
| Mean | 4.5 | 2.2 |
| Median | 4.7 | 2.6 |

*Source:* Heggestad and Mingo, "The Competitive Condition of U.S. Banking Markets and the Impact of Structural Reform," 32 J. Finance, No. 3, pp. 649–661 (June 1977).

---

**18.** The Herfindahl Index is

$$H = \sum_{i=1}^{N} S_i^2$$

where $S_i$ is the share of the market held by firm $i$ and where there are $N$ firms in the market. The reciprocal of the Herfindahl Index is the "numbers equivalent," which is the number of equal size firms that would give a Herfindahl Index of a given value. See Adelman, "Comment on the 'H' Concentration Measure as a Numbers-Equivalent," 51 Rev. of Econ. & Statistics, No. 1, pp. 99–101 (Feb. 1969).

**The Condition of Entry**

**455**

*A Survey of
Studies on
Banking
Competition and
Performance*

The condition of entry varies systematically across markets. In banking, entry takes place by branching, by holding company expansion, or by the formation of new banks. Entry barriers can be natural economic constraints that impose a cost disadvantage on new entrants, or they can be legal constraints. Most banking studies allege that the legal constraints are the most significant.[19]

Chartering limitations are important in preventing new firms from entering markets. Obtaining a charter requires approval by either the state banking commissioner or by the Comptroller of the Currency, and to the extent that state commissioners are more lax or more stringent than the Comptroller, legal entry barriers may differ across markets.

Permission to open branches or to form holding company affiliates is also required. The various laws on branching and holding company affiliation have caused a patchwork design in entry barriers. Donald Baker recently summarized the situation:

> Fifteen states prohibit branch banking altogether while 16 others limit branch banking to local markets. Still others provide "home office" protection to existing banks, and a few even protect branch offices the same way. Finally, 11 states prohibit multiple bank holding companies by statute, and 5 others restrict them in lesser ways. As a result of these various limitations, only 12 states remain with statewide *de novo* branching and freedom of holding company entry.[20]

Other legal restrictions on entry are more subtle. Alhadeff[21] shows that the legal lending limit of 10 percent of capital to any one borrower may force new banks to raise significant capital before obtaining a charter. Otherwise, they would have little flexibility in competing for business loans. Of course, this regulation would not be a barrier for branches or holding company affiliates, since these are backed by the capital structure of their entire organization.

Perhaps the most important economic barrier is the need to attain minimal efficient size. Although minimal efficient size may not be large in banking,[22] it may still be sufficient to restrict entry into small markets. This barrier would again be smaller for large banks entering from other markets via branching or holding company affiliation.

Existing firms in a market may also have a product differentiation advantage. Depositors tend to stay with their existing banks, so that

---

19. One notable exception is Alhadeff, "Barriers to Bank Entry," 40 Southern Econ. J., No. 4, pp. 589–603 (April 1974).

20. Baker, "Chartering, Branching, and the Concentration Problem," *Policies for a More Competitive Financial System* 25–26 (Fed. Reserve Bank of Boston, 1972).

21. Alhadeff, N. 19 *supra.*

22. See George J. Benston, "The Optimal Banking Structure: Theory and Evidence," 3 J. Bank Research, No. 4, pp. 220–237 (Winter 1973).

new banks must pay more competitive rates, charge lower loan rates, or advertise more to succeed. Existing banks frequently maintain their advantage by advertising extensively and by establishing widespread branching networks to usurp convenient sites from new entrants.

In summary, the condition of entry may vary significantly across banking markets. Both legal and economic restrictions play a role in foreclosing entry in some markets; in other markets, entry is easier, but never free. Thus, a well-specified model of structure and performance in banking must incorporate variations in entry barriers.

## STRUCTURE-PERFORMANCE STUDIES IN BANKING

There have been more than 40 studies of the impact of market structure on performance in banking. These studies are summarized in Table 9-2. Most have attempted to isolate the concentration dimension of market structure and determine its impact on prices and profits. A few have considered other aspects of performance. In almost every case, the data have been cross-sectional observations, drawn from many sets of markets and covering many time periods. In general, the studies find that concentration is an important determinant of performance, but that the impact of the other structural variables on performance is less predictable.

Before discussing the results of these studies, we consider some general theoretical and empirical problems that arise when interpreting and evaluating them. These include the theoretical and econometric specifications of the models, the definition of key variables, and some measurement problems. No study surmounts all these problems, but some succeed more nearly than others.

### Specification Problems

The structure-performance studies in banking suffer a weakness common to all structure-performance studies: There is no rigorous theoretical model that relates concentration to equilibrium price levels, or to any other dimension of performance.[23] The models used in industrial organization studies are, of necessity, ad hoc adaptations of theoretical models (such as those of Stigler or Saving). While this has proved reasonably satisfactory for other industries, banking may be different. Banking markets are highly concentrated, and regulation is pervasive. Banks are also multiproduct firms, operating with different degrees of

---

**23.** Development of such a model would require specification of the complex behavior patterns within markets. Stigler has developed a model which implies a weak relationship between the Herfindahl Index and price, based on a theory of cooperation among firms. Stigler, N. 5 *supra*. Saving has developed a model which ties the concentration ratio to the price-cost margin (Lerner Index), but his assumptions, including perfect collusion and a structure dominated by one firm, are so stringent as to be virtually devoid of empirical significance in banking. Saving, "Concentration Ratios and the Degree of Monopoly," 11 Int'l Econ. Rev., No. 1, pp. 139–146 (Feb. 1970).

**TABLE 9-2  Structure-Performance Studies in Commercial Banking**

| Study | Performance measures | Concentration measure | Other market structure measures | Control variables | Sample | Period | Effect of concentration | Effect of other market structure variables | Comments |
|---|---|---|---|---|---|---|---|---|---|
| Schweiger and McGee (1961) | Automobile loan rates; installment loan rates | Number of banks | Branching vs. unit banking | | 11 large cities | 1960 | Higher rates with fewer banks | | No econometric tests |
| Edwards (1964) | Business loan rates (Federal Reserve Survey) | 3 bank concentration of total deposits by SMSA | Branching variables; size of SMSA | Demand and cost variables | 49 SMSAs | 1955; 1957 | Significant in 1955, not in 1957; effect small | No effect of branching | |
| Edwards (1965) | Average loan rates; average savings rates; profitability; portfolio selection | 2 bank concentration ratio of total deposits by SMSA | Branching variables | Demand and cost variables | 36 SMSAs; 1400 banks | 1962 | Significant for average rates but not profitability | Branching leads to higher average loan rates and more risky portfolios | Average price subject to measurement error |
| Jacobs (1965) | Number of banks; number of bank offices; changes in numbers of banks | | Branching variables | Population and income | 49 states | 1946–1963 | | (1) Branching has no effect on the number of offices (2) Greater increases in banking offices in branching states | Ignores the effects of market power which may bias tests |
| Flechsig (1965) | Business loan rates (Federal Reserve Survey) | 3 bank concentration ratio of total deposits by SMSA | | Demand and cost variables; regional variables | 49 SMSAs for 1955; 19 SMSAs for 1960 | 1955; 1960 | No effect | | Concentration effect found by Edwards removed by arbitrary regional variables |

**TABLE 9-2  Structure-Performance Studies in Commercial Banking  (Continued)**

| Study | Performance measures | Concentration measure | Other market structure measures | Control variables | Sample | Period | Effect of concentration | Effect of other market structure variables | Comments |
|---|---|---|---|---|---|---|---|---|---|
| Kaufman (1966) | Average loan rates; average savings rate; profitability; portfolio selection | 3 bank concentration ratio of total deposits in rural counties; number of banks | Distance to financial center; S&L assets relative to bank assets | Demand variables | Bank averages in 99 counties | 1959; 1960 | Significant, especially on profitability | Little effect | Average prices subject to measurement error |
| Phillips (1967) | Short term business loan rates (Federal Reserve Survey) | 3 bank concentration ratio of total deposits in SMSAs | | Loan size; bank size; demand variables; regional variables | 11 SMSAs | 1960; 1962 1964; 1966 | Concentration significant, but its effect is small | | Careful attempt to approximate actual effective rates |
| Meyer (1967) | Business loan rates (Federal Reserve Survey) | 3 bank concentration ratio of total deposits in SMSAs | | Demand and cost variables | SMSA average rate | 1955; 1957 | Concentration significant, but its effect is small | | |
| Peltzman (1968) | Market value of bank stock relative to book value | | State branching laws; entry rates | Bank size; regional variables | 256 banks | 1962 | | Branching laws have no effect; entry rates reduce value | Ignores market related variables that would affect firm value |
| Taylor (1968) | Average loan rates; portfolio selection | Number of banks (SMSA) | | Loan mix; SMSA mix; bank size | 1315 banks | 1962 | No effect | | Average price subject to measurement error |

| | | | | | | | |
|---|---|---|---|---|---|---|---|
| Bell and Murphy (1969) | Estimated demand deposit service charges | Alternative measures of 3 bank concentration based on different sizes of deposits and numbers of accounts | Estimated marginal cost | 14 banking market areas | 1966 | Positive and significant for all measures | Average service charge subject to measurement error |
| Lanzillotti and Saving (1969) | Number of bank offices | State branching laws | Demand variables | States | 1947–1960 | More offices in unit states but branching states faster to adjust to changes in demand | Ignores market related variables that could affect the optimal number of offices |
| Weiss (1969) | Offering of no service charge on checking accounts | Number of banks; 3 bank concentration of demand deposits; Herfindahl Index of demand deposits by SMSA | | 25 SMSAs | 1968 | Higher concentration related to the absence of free checking | Statistical tests subject to substantial errors |
| Aspinwall (1970) | Mortgage rates | 3 firm concentration ratio based on total deposits of mortgage lending firms; number of institutions offering mortgages | Demand and loan characteristic variables | 31 SMSAs | 1965 | Significant, but the effect is small | |

459

## TABLE 9-2 Structure-Performance Studies in Commercial Banking (Continued)

| Study | Performance measures | Concentration measure | Other market structure measures | Control variables | Sample | Period | Effect of concentration | Effect of other market structure variables | Comments |
|---|---|---|---|---|---|---|---|---|---|
| Emery (1971) | Profitability as measured by deviations from the capital market line | 5 bank concentration ratio based on total state deposits | Branching laws | | 980 banks | 1967–1968 | No effect | Higher profits in statewide branching compared to limited branching compared to unit branching | Very interesting approach but state concentration inappropriate measure of market power |
| Fraser and Rose (1971) | Average loan rates; average deposit rates; profitability; portfolio selection | 1 bank concentration ratio based on total deposits in small cities; number of banks | Presence of S&L | Demand and cost variables | 193 banks in 78 small towns and cities | 1966;1967 | Small effect in 1967; no effect in 1966 | No effect, except on deposit mix | Average prices subject to measurement error |
| Jacobs (1971) | Business loan rates (ABA survey) | 3 bank concentration ratio of total deposits by SMSA | Branching variables | Demand, costs, and customer relationship variables | 8500 loans at 160 banks | 1966 | Concentration significant, but the size of the effect is small | Rates highest in unit banking areas and lowest in statewide branching areas | |
| Klein and Murphy (1971) | Savings rates; demand deposit service charge | Alternative concentration ratios based on dollar volume and numbers of accounts | | Demand and cost variables | 164 SMSAs | 1968 | No effect on savings rates, but service charge increases with concentration | | Approximation of average rates may be subject to measurement error |
| Vernon (1971) | Profitability | 3 bank concentration ratio of total deposits by SMSA | Branching variables | Leverage, size region, and owner vs. manager controlled | 85 of 200 largest banks | 1961–1966 | Profits fall significantly with concentration | High profits in branching states | Counter-theoretical results |

| Study | Performance/dependent variables | Market structure measure | Control variables | Sample | Period | Results | Comments |
|---|---|---|---|---|---|---|---|
| Bryan (1972) | Profitability | Number of competitors and bank perception of strength of competition in the SMSA | Cost and market demand variables | 1,000 banks | 1963–1967 | None | Multicollinearity present with three competition variables in the same equation |
| Fraser and Rose (1972) | Average loan rates; average deposit rates; average service charges; profitability; portfolio selection | Number of banks in the rural town; distance to financial center and presence of S&L | Demand variables | 154 banks in 1, 2, or 3 bank towns | 1965; 1966 | Virtually no effect; Little effect | Average prices subject to measurement error |
| Fraser and Rose (1972) | Average loan rates; average deposit rates; portfolio selection | Structural change due to new entry | Controls by paired banks | 24 new banks in 23 towns | 1960–1966 | Entry significantly improves portfolio selection but not rates | Average prices subject to measurement errors |
| Stuhr (1972) | Mortgage interest rate; time deposit rate | Various market share measures approximating interinstitutional competition |  | 25 New York banks | 1967 | S&Ls strongly compete with banks; there is some interinstitutional competition for loans | Does not control for concentration |
| Ware (1972) | Average loan rates; average savings rates; average service charges; profitability; portfolio selection | 4 bank concentration ratio of total deposits in rural counties | Demand variables | 57 rural counties—bank averages of performance | 1969; 1970 | Never significant; Seldom significant | Average price subject to measurement error |

**TABLE 9-2  Structure-Performance Studies in Commercial Banking  (Continued)**

| Study | Performance measures | Concentration measure | Other market structure measures | Control variables | Sample | Period | Effect of concentration | Effect of other market structure variables | Comments |
|---|---|---|---|---|---|---|---|---|---|
| Edwards (1973) | Advertising intensity | 3 bank concentration ratio of total deposits by SMSAs | | Demand and cost variables | 36 of the largest United States banks in 23 SMSAs | 1965 | No effect | Little effect | Evidence that simple profit maximization may not be the objective of some banks |
| Edwards and Heggestad (1973) | Uncertainty avoidance (variance of profits divided by average profits) | 3 bank concentration ratio based on total deposits in SMSAs | Branching variables | Demand, cost, and diversification variables | 66 of 100 largest banks | 1954–1966 | Increased uncertainty avoidance with high concentration | Little effect | |
| Fraser, Phillips and Rose (1974) | Index of performance including many balance sheet items | 1 bank concentration ratio of total deposits or number of banks by rural county | Presence of S&Ls | Demand and cost variables | 1,206 Texas banks | 1969; 1970 | Virtually no effect | Little effect | Canonical correlation test but based on data that are subject to measurement error |
| Yeats (1974) | Average loan rates; average savings rates; profitability; portfolio selection | Herfindahl Index on total county deposits, the change in the Herfindahl Index, and market share stability | | Demand and cost variables | Tennessee and Louisiana counties | 1970 | Small effect of concentration but important effect for changes in concentration | | Average price data subject to measurement error; study considers critical concentration ratio |
| Alhadeff and Alhadeff (1975) | Bank concentration of total deposits in counties, states and nationally | | Structural change due to entry | | Sample of counties | 1948–1966 | | New entry significantly reduces national & local (small county) concentration | Difficult to abstract from other factors |

| Study | Performance measures | Market structure measure | Controls | Sample | Year | Finding | Finding | Comments |
|---|---|---|---|---|---|---|---|---|
| Beighley and McCall (1975) | Lerner Index; average loan rates | 3 bank concentration ratio based on installment loans by SMSA | Loan characteristics | 184 banks in 7 SMSAs | 1968 | Concentration has important effect | No effect | Only 7 different observations on concentration |
| Fraser and Alvis (1975) | Average loan rates; average savings rates; portfolio selection | High vs. low concentration markets based on deposits | Demographic, demand, and cost variables | 309 banks in unit banking states | 1972 | Little or no effect | | Average price data subject to measurement error; alternative statistical tests used |
| Jessup and Stolz (1975) | Number of banks in rural markets | Unit vs. branching | | 90 rural counties | 1970 | | No difference between unit and branching states | No controls for concentration |
| Heggestad and Mingo (1976) | Installment loan rates; deposit service charges; savings rates; measures of nonprice competition | Herfindahl Index of total SMSA deposits | Demand and cost variables | 236 banks in 52 SMSAs | 1973 | Effect significant for 8 of 11 performance variables; the effect is large when aggregated | No effect | Survey data of actual rates charged to households; effect may be nonlinear |
| Heggestad and Rhoades (1976) | Market share stability | 3 bank concentration ratio based on total deposits by SMSA | Branching, holding company activity, merger activity, average bank size | 228 SMSAs | 1966–1972 | Greater stability with high concentration | No effect | Stability is a measure of the presence of rivalry in the market |
| McCall and Peterson (1976) | Average loan rates; average savings rates; average service charges; profitability; portfolio selection | Market share | Structural change due to entry | Controls by paired bank approach | 42 banks in towns with less than 3 banks | 1966–1969 | | Entry significantly improves portfolio selection and reduces prices | Average price data subject to measurement error |

**TABLE 9-2  Structure-Performance Studies in Commercial Banking  (Continued)**

| Study | Performance measures | Concentration measure | Other market structure measures | Control variables | Sample | Period | Effect of concentration | Effect of other market structure variables | Comments |
|---|---|---|---|---|---|---|---|---|---|
| Mingo (1976) | Average loan rates; portfolio selection; leverage; profitability | Herfindahl Index based on total deposits by SMSA | Acquisition by a holding company | Demand and cost variables | 384 banks | 1966 | No effect on earnings but impacts on leverage and portfolio selection | Strong interaction effect between holding company affiliation and concentration | Average price data subject to measurement error |
| Rose (1976) | United States Senators' vote on the Helm's Amendment to the Financial Institutions Act of 1975 | 5 bank concentration ratio of total deposits at state level | | Bank size, bank assets relative to personal income | 90 Senatorial votes | 1975 | No effect | | New approach, but state concentration may not be the appropriate measure of concentration for this purpose |
| Rose and Fraser (1976) | Average loan rates; average savings rates; average service charges; portfolio selection | Several alternative measures of concentration at the county level | Presence of S&Ls | Demand and cost variables | 704 banks in 90 Texas counties | | Concentration important, but the measured effect depends on the index | Little effect | Average price data subject to measurement error |
| Stolz (1976) | Interest rate on household and farm loans; savings rates; demand deposit service charges; non-price competition variables | Herfindahl Index on total deposits in service area banking markets | Market share, holding company presence, thrift presence, Production Credit Association presence | Demand and cost variables | 333 banking offices in 75 rural counties | 1975 | Concentration affects most nonprice variables, only one of the price variables (farm loan rates) | Production Credit Association reduce farm loan rates; market share often has the opposite effect of the concentration ratios | Market definition innovative but not comparable with other studies; good survey data |

| Study | Dependent variable | Structure variable | Other variables | Control variables | Sample | Period | Result | Result | Comments |
|---|---|---|---|---|---|---|---|---|---|
| White (1976) | Number of bank offices | Herfindahl Index on total deposits in SMSAs | Number of thrift associations | Demand and cost variables | 40 large SMSAs | 1970 | Less offices with high concentration | More offices where thrifts are present | Evidence against simple profit maximization as objective; investigates critical level of concentration |
| Edwards (1977) | Expense preference (labor expense) | Separation of monopoly and competitive markets | Branching variables | Demand and cost variables | 44 SMSAs | 1962; 1964; 1966 | Evidence of expense preference by monopoly banks; nonlinear effect of concentration | Little effect | |
| Heggestad (1977) | Profitability; risk; adjusted profits | 3 bank concentration ratio of total deposits by SMSAs | | Demand and cost variables | 238 banks in SMSAs | 1960–1970 | Significant but small, stronger for risk adjusted profits | | Evidence against simple profit maximization as objective |
| Heggestad and Mingo (1977) | Demand deposit service charge; new car loan rates | Herfindahl Index of total deposits in SMSAs | Presence of mutual savings bank offering demand deposit (NOW accounts) | Demand and cost variables | 236 banks in 52 SMSAs | 1973 | Significant but nonlinear. | Service charges dramatically lower when thrift allowed to compete | Evidence that most SMSAs are effectively monopolized |
| Heggestad and Rhoades (in press) | Market share stability | 3 bank concentration ratio of total deposits by SMSAs | Multimarket links, branching | Market growth | 187 SMSAs | 1960–1972 | Significant reduction in rivalry | Links reduced rivalry, also less rivalry in unit banking states | Test of the impact of extra-market structure. |

*Source:* See Bibliography.

monopoly power in a variety of specific product and geographic markets.

Many of the banking studies make no attempt to develop a conceptual model. As a result, they often omit important variables and are subject to interpretation problems. Also, little thought is usually given to the appropriate functional form of the estimating equations. Improvement in theoretical modeling is an obvious first priority of future research.

## Estimation Problems

In general, a model of the structure-performance relationship in banking (or any other industry) would make the equilibrium price for any product a function of:

1. The level and elasticity of market and firm demand.

2. The firm's cost function.

3. The prices and quantities of related financial products, and their interaction with the firm's demand and cost functions.

4. The objective functions of firms in the market.

5. The interaction among firms in the market.

Taking all of these factors into consideration, each firm would simultaneously, or iteratively, reach the equilibrium price.[24] Market structure enters this model by its effect on the interaction among firms.[25]

The estimating equations are generally of the form

$$P = f(D, C, M, S, X) \tag{1}$$

where $D$ = a set of variables to reflect market demand conditions
$C$ = a set of variables to reflect differences in costs across firms and markets
$M$ = the degree of monopoly in the market as measured by the concentration ratio
$S$ = other market structure variables, such as proxies for barriers to entry
$X$ = a set of control variables related to a specific product's characteristics.

---

**24.** For a simple example of this determination, see Edwards and Heggestad, "Uncertainty, Market Structure, and Performance: The Galbraith-Caves Hypothesis and Managerial Motives in Banking," 87 Q. J. Econ., No. 3, pp. 455–473 (Aug. 1973).

**25.** Some studies to be discussed later also argue that market structure may affect firms' objective functions. See Edwards and Heggestad, N. 24 *supra*; Edwards, "Managerial Objectives in Regulated Industries: Expense-Preference Behavior in Banking," 85 J. Political Econ., No. 1, pp. 147–162 (Feb. 1977).

P is generally the price of a specific product, although it may represent other dimensions of performance as well. The unit of observation in the studies is either the firm or the market. Multivariate statistical techniques, such as multiple regression, are almost always used to estimate the parameters of the equation.

Eq. (1) is essentially a reduced-form equation. As such, the estimated coefficients are combinations of the structural coefficients in the unspecified and, generally, unspecifiable, demand functions, cost functions, objective functions and reaction functions. Great care, therefore, must be taken in interpreting the values and signs of these reduced-form coefficients, since the structural coefficients that comprise them may have conflicting effects. For example, permissive branching in a market may lower entry barriers which, *ceteris paribus*, should lower prices, but it may also increase bank costs which should raise prices. The two effects may even cancel each other out and show a nonsignificant coefficient in the reduced form eq. (1). This result, obviously, should not be interpreted as meaning that branching affects neither bank costs nor competition.

Several econometric problems are pervasive throughout the studies. First, the imprecise theoretical models often lead to omitted variables in eq. (1), which can result in a bias in the estimate of the effect of monopoly power. Suppose the true model is:

$$P = \beta_1 + \beta_2 M + \beta_3 S \tag{2}$$

where $\beta_1$, $\beta_2$, and $\beta_3$ are constant parameters, but that the model that is actually estimated is

$$P = \hat{\beta}_1 + \hat{\beta}_2 M \tag{3}$$

If the degree of monopoly, $M$, and entry barriers, $S$, the omitted variable, are correlated across markets, the estimate of $\hat{\beta}_2$ will be biased upward. Specifically, it can be shown that

$$E(\hat{\beta}_2) = \beta_2 + \beta_3 \alpha_2 \tag{4}$$

where $E$ is the expectations operator and $\alpha_2$ is determined by the regression[26]

$$M = \alpha_1 + \alpha_2 S \tag{5}$$

If $S$ represents the degree of difficulty of new entry, $\beta_3$ should be positive; i.e., prices will be higher where entry barriers are higher. If concentration is also high in those markets, or where entry barriers are high, $\alpha_2$ will also be positive. Thus, from eq. (4) it can be seen that $\hat{\beta}_2$ will overstate the effect of monopoly power, since it will include both the positive effect of monopoly on price ($\beta_2$), and the positive effects of entry barriers and monopoly ($\beta_3 \alpha_2$). If this were the only omitted variable, the direction of the bias would be clear. However, the omis-

---

26. See Kmenta, *Elements of Econometrics* (Macmillan, New York 1971).

sion of other important variables often compounds this misspecification problem.

A second econometric problem arises from the difficulty of properly measuring monopoly. Any such measure is, at best, an approximation of the true degree of monopoly, or

$$M^* = M + U_i \tag{6}$$

where $U_i$ is a (hopefully) random term which represents the measurement error. In this situation, at a minimum, the estimated coefficient of the effect of monopoly on performance is inconsistent. Maddala shows that this type of measurement error could lead, and in fact is likely to lead, to a downward bias in the estimation of (or an understatement in) the effect of monopoly power.[27] Thus, there are at least two econometric difficulties in the estimation of the effect of monopoly, and they are, as specified in our example, likely to conflict. Variations in the degree to which these problems are present may be one explanation for the conflicting results of some studies.[28]

A third econometric difficulty lies in specifying the functional form of the estimating equation. Because of the lack of a clear theoretical model, most studies adopt a linear functional form that assumes a given change in monopoly will have the same absolute effect on performance, no matter what the level of concentration before the change. Two recent studies have demonstrated that, at least for some products, the concentration-price relationship is nonlinear.[29] Linear equations, therefore, may be a misspecification and result in biased estimates.

Finally, the coefficient of determination ($R^2$) measures the percentage of variation in the dependent variable (or price) explained relative to the variable's total variation. Typically, this value is low in these studies: the average $R^2$ is approximately .15. This may be the result of three factors.[30] First, there may be omitted variables that are important in explaining the variation in prices or performance across markets. Second, the functional form of the models may be misspecified—a

---

27. See Maddala, *Econometrics* (Macmillan, New York 1977). The amount of the downward bias is related to the degree of measurement error. This may explain why the estimates of the Herfindahl Index-price relationship are generally stronger than the concentration ratio-price relationship. The Herfindahl Index is a superior measure of monopoly power.

28. There are so many econometric problems that it is difficult to determine the net effect. An additional downward bias will occur if there is measurement error in the dependent variable, and the error is correlated with the error in measuring monopoly. Maddala, *id.* at 302–303. This is quite likely in the studies that estimate effective loan rates by average returns from loans based on balance sheet data, which may explain why most of these studies fail to find a structure-performance relationship.

29. Heggestad and Mingo, "The Competitive Condition of U.S. Banking Markets and the Impact of Structural Reform," 32 J. Finance, No. 3, pp. 649–661 (June 1977); Heggestad and Mingo, "Prices, Nonprices and Concentration in Commercial Banking," 8 J. Money, Credit & Banking, No. 1, pp. 107–117 (Feb. 1976).

30. For elaboration, see Kmenta, N. 26 *supra.*

linear model may be inappropriate. Finally, the effect of the independent variables may be weak compared to other random factors. This latter condition is often the case with cross-sectional data.[31] Thus, while the low $R^2$'s of most structure-performance studies may indicate omitted variables or misspecification, they are most likely to reflect the random nature of cross-sectional data.

## Measurement of Monopoly Power

There are three major aspects of measuring monopoly in banking markets: choosing the appropriate general index of monopoly power, choosing the appropriate economic variable with which to measure differences in bank size, and accounting for differences in institutional competition (or for competition between banks and nonbank financial institutions).

The variable used should, if possible, be related to the specific product under study, although a variable based on total bank deposits may be appropriate when studying general bank performance. For example, measurement of monopoly in the consumer loan market should ideally be based on the distribution of consumer loans among banks. With few exceptions,[32] however, studies use measures based on deposit data. Although this seems like a serious error, the use of deposits, as a proxy variable, to measure monopoly may not lead to serious error for two reasons. First, the various measures of monopoly in banking, using different data, are likely to be highly correlated. For example, the size of a bank's total deposits is often, not unexpectedly, highly correlated with the distribution of its consumer or business loans. Thus, estimates of the effect of monopoly power will be, at least, asymptotically unbiased and efficient.[33] Second, all measures are only approximations of monopoly, in any case. Although a large bank may have no consumer loans, it still may be a viable force in the consumer loan market, since it could readily offer these loans. Thus, a measure based upon a common data base, such as deposits, may better represent this potential competitive force.

Few of the studies incorporate interinstitutional competition in their monopoly measures. Among banking markets, there are substantial differences in the strength of specialized competing institutions. Credit unions, for example, compete with banks more in some markets than in others. A study that looks only at the concentration of bank deposits, and ignores credit union deposits, may overstate the degree of monop-

---

31. A typical $R^2$ on a household demand function using survey data is .20. See Kmenta, N. 26 *supra* at 234.

32. E.g., Beighley and McCall, "Market Power and Structure and Commercial Bank Installment Lending," 7 J. Money, Credit & Banking, No. 4, pp. 449–467 (Nov. 1975).

33. This, of course, is not true if the use of deposits as a proxy variable adds additional measurement error.

oly. The severity of the error, of course, will depend on the competitive strength of credit unions in the particular market.[34]

The final issue is the appropriate general index of monopoly power. Most studies use the number of banks in the market, or a concentration ratio which measures the share of the largest $N$ firms in the market. Recent studies have also used the Herfindahl Index and its corresponding numbers-equivalent. Using only the number of banks ignores differences in relative sizes among banks. Also, while concentration ratios reflect some differences in size among banks, they do not capture all elements of dispersion; they, also, do not reflect the number of competing firms. The Herfindahl Index is responsive to both the size dispersion of firms and the number of firms, and is therefore a superior measure. However, all these measures are actually so highly correlated that the choice of index is not of critical importance for testing structure-performance hypotheses.[35]

## Measurement of Entry Barriers

Theory suggests that entry barriers are an important dimension of both structure and performance. Few studies adequately control for differences in entry conditions across markets. The most important entry barrier is the legal requirements associated with obtaining a new charter, which none of the studies attempt to measure because of the lack of an adequate index. For example, a measure of this might be the regulatory rejection rates in the particular market, but even this is flawed because applications for charters will be partially a function of the probability of success in obtaining a charter. Past rejection rates may also not be good predictors of present regulatory attitudes toward entry.

State laws regarding branching and holding company formulation also represent entry barriers. Even in legally unrestricted branching states, permission to open branches must be obtained. Studies have accounted for these differences by the use of binary variables which reflect differences in state law, but these ignore regulatory differences within states or within regions with comparable laws.

The nonregulatory barrier to entry, relative-minimal-efficient-size-of firm, is usually handled by simply including a variable for the size of the market, since in banking, it is reasonable to assume the minimum

---

34. Specialized institutions, generally, only offer partial substitutes to commercial bank products. Thus, to include their deposits equally with banks may understate the degree of monopoly. A method to account for this would be to adjust the weight of nonbank-product values by the degree of substitutability between their products and bank products.

35. See Rose and Fraser, "The Relationships Between Stability and Change in Market Structure: An Analysis of Bank Prices," 24 J. Industrial Econ., No. 4, pp. 251–266 (June 1976).

efficient size of firm is the same in all markets.[36] Product differentiation, often achieved through advertising and by a proliferation of branches,[37] might be captured by the past advertising expenses of existing firms and by a measure of banking convenience, such as the population density relative to banking office density.[38] Few studies attempt to control for product differentiation.

## CONCENTRATION AND PERFORMANCE: THE EVIDENCE

This section surveys findings of studies that examine the impact of concentration on performance. These studies are summarized in Table 9-2. They examine many aspects of performance: loan rates, rates on deposits, service charges, and profits. In addition, recent studies analyze nonprice competition and the motives of bank managers.

### Impact of Concentration on Loan Rates

The effect of concentration on loan rates has received substantial attention. Loans are an important bank output, and they are usually not regulated.

The studies employ cross-sectional data and, generally, estimate an equation such as

$$R = f(M, LC, S, D, C) \tag{7}$$

where $R$ = either the rate on specific loans or the average return on some set of loans

$M$ = generally the three bank concentration ratio using total deposits

$LC$ = a vector of variables of loan characteristics, such as the type, size, and maturity of the loan

$D$ = a set of demand variables, such as measures of market economic activity and market growth

$C$ = a variable (usually bank size) to reflect differences in banks' cost functions due to economies of scale

Overall, the results of these studies have not been consistent. How-

---

36. Market size is an important variable determining the entry rate in Texas. See Rose, "The Attractiveness of Banking Markets for *De Novo* Entry: The Evidence from Texas," 7 J. Bank Research, No. 4, pp. 284–293 (Winter 1977).

37. See White, "Price Regulation and Quality Rivalry in a Profit-Maximizing Model: The Case of Branch Banking," 8 J. Money, Credit & Banking, No. 1, pp. 97–106 (Feb. 1976).

38. The fact that these variables are often not significant when entered in reduced form equation (see e.g., Edwards, "Advertising and Competition in Banking," 18 Antitrust Bull., No. 1, pp. 23–32 (Spring 1973)) for advertising does not necessarily mean that they do not affect entry barriers. Rather, they may structurally affect several market dimensions, e.g., entry and costs, and cancel each other out in the reduced form equation.

ever, closer examination reveals a distinct pattern: The studies that evaluate the impact of concentration on *average* loan rates find little or no relationship; the studies that analyze the effect of concentration on *actual* rates on *specific* kinds of loans find concentration to be important. Thus, differences in results may well be tied to data differences rather than to underlying economic inconsistencies.

Business loan rates, in particular, have consistently been statistically linked to concentration, although the impact of concentration on these rates is not large. Increases in concentration clearly increase loan rates, but not by a large amount. Edwards[39] uses a Federal Reserve Survey of loan rates in 49 metropolitan areas and finds that concentration is important in 1955, a slack year, but that this effect disappears in 1957, a period of tight money. His results for 1955 have been substantiated by later studies, especially by Phillips[40] and Jacobs.[41] In an extensive survey of 8,500 loans, Jacobs finds a strong statistical relationship between concentration and business loan rates, after adjusting for the important bank-borrower relationship, which is ignored in other studies due to data limitations. It is interesting to note that all three studies find the magnitude of the concentration coefficient to be virtually the same—a 10 percentage point increase in the concentration ratio increases loan rates approximately 6 basis points.[42]

Household or consumer loan rates should be the most sensitive to differences in market structure, since these customers are largely constrained to local markets. In a univariate econometric study, Schweiger and McGee[43] find standardized automobile loan rates and installment loan rates to be higher in markets with fewer banks. They did not evaluate these differences for statistical significance, however. Similarly, Beighley and McCall[44] find a strong relationship between the percentage markup over marginal cost on consumer loans and the Gini coefficient of firm size dispersion.[45] (Their study offers a promising new technique, although it is limited to only seven SMSAs.)

Heggestad and Mingo[46] examine the rates on standardized automo-

---

39. Edwards, N. 2 *supra*.

40. Phillips, "Evidence on Concentration in Banking Markets and Interest Rates," 53 Fed. Reserve Bull., No. 6, pp. 916–926 (June 1967).

41. Jacobs, *Business Loan Costs and Bank Market Structure: An Empirical Estimate of Their Relations*, Occasional Paper 115, National Bureau of Economic Research (distributed by Columbia Univ. Press, New York 1971).

42. See Edwards, "Review of Business Loan Costs and Bank Market Structure," 27 J. Finance (Sept. 1972).

43. Schweiger and McGee, N. 1 *supra*.

44. Beighley and McCall, N. 32 *supra*.

45. The Gini coefficient measures the inequality in firm sizes within a market. The greater the inequality, the greater the monopoly power present in the market.

46. Heggestad and Mingo (1976), N. 29 *supra*.

**473**

*A Survey of
Studies on
Banking
Competition and
Performance*

bile loans charged by 332 banks. They find a strong effect for concentration, especially in unconcentrated markets: a merger between two banks with 15 percent and 5 percent market shares, respectively, would, on average, increase loan rates by 41 basis points. However, after a certain critical level of concentration is reduced (Herfindahl Index of .14), rates would not increase with further increases in concentration. Household rates appear to be more sensitive to changes in concentration than business loan rates, as economic theory might suggest. For business loan rates, Edwards[47] estimates the *ceteris paribus* effect of going from the least concentrated market to the most concentrated market in his sample to be 36 basis points. A similar change for household rates in the Heggestad-Mingo study would be 79 basis points.[48]

Stolz[49] replicates the Heggestad-Mingo survey in rural markets, but he does not find a relationship between concentration and new car loan rates. Stolz does not use the traditional market approximations: SMSAs and rural counties. Rather, he develops market areas based on "areas of convenience." These definitions of banking markets differ substantially from the market definitions used in other studies; so his results are not comparable.

The bulk of the studies which examine loan rates estimate them by using the average loan revenue from a bank's loan portfolio, taken from the bank's financial report. This rate is obtained by dividing the total interest and fees on loans received by the bank during the year by the bank's total loans outstanding at the end of the calendar year. This rate has both advantages and disadvantages. Its major disadvantage is the likelihood of measurement error. Interest rates vary, depending on the type of loan, its maturity, and its risk characteristics. Even if two banks charge identical prices on comparable loans, if they have different loan mixes, their average rates will be different. The bank that holds more consumer loans or more risky business loans will, for example, appear to charge higher rates. Further, some recent studies have found the proportion of these types of loans in banks' portfolios to be correlated with concentration.[50] Consequently, this measurement error will bias statistical estimates of the concentration-loan rate relationship.

The advantage of the measure is its availability. Hypotheses can be tested for a wide range of banks over many different time periods. One group of studies has analyzed large samples across many markets. Edwards[51] finds average rates increase with concentration. His results

---

**47.** Edwards, No. 2 *supra.*

**48.** These are not exactly comparable, however, because of differences in the average rate.

**49.** Stolz, N. 15 *supra.*

**50.** See, e.g., Mingo, "Managerial Motives, Market Structures, and the Performance of Holding Company Banks," 14 Econ. Inquiry, No. 3, pp. 411–424 (Sept. 1976).

**51.** Edwards, "The Banking Competition Controversy," 3 Nat'l Banking Rev., No. 1, pp. 1–34 (Sept. 1965).

have apparently not held up; Taylor[52] finds that virtually all variation in average rates is explained by portfolio composition. However, Taylor's statistical technique does not allow for the simultaneous impact of both concentration and portfolio composition on loan rates, and it is, therefore, a biased test.

To avoid the problems associated with variations in regulations across states, several studies restrict their sample to markets within a single state. In most cases, they define the market to be the rural county or the small town, as opposed to the SMSA, which is used frequently in national studies. Studies have been made of Texas by Fraser and Rose,[53] Louisiana and Tennessee by Yeats,[54] Iowa by Kaufman,[55] and Ohio by Ware.[56] The results show no pattern.

Fraser and Rose[57] find that in Texas, the share of the largest firm (the one bank concentration ratio) had no influence on loan rates in 1966 and only a small influence in 1967. Then, using 1965 and 1966 data for small towns in the Eleventh Federal Reserve District (primarily Texas), they find[58] that the number of banks has no influence on average rates in small towns. Finally, their last study[59] covers 704 unit banks in 90 Texas counties in 1970. In this study, they use alternative measures of monopoly. Again, the number of banks is not correlated with the average returns from loans, but a better measure of monopoly, the Herfindahl Index, is. Thus, with Texas data, for some years and for some measures of monopoly, market structure affects rates; while for other years and for other measures, it does not. This pattern of inconsistency continues with other states. With Iowa data, structure matters; with data from Louisiana, Tennessee, and Ohio, it does not. These differences probably reflect the measurement-error problem associated with differences in loan portfolio mixes, among states and at different time periods.[60]

In summary, although the results of the numerous concentration-

---

52. Taylor, "Average Interest Charges, the Loan Mix, and Measures of Competition: Sixth Federal Reserve District Experience," 23 J. Finance, No. 5, pp. 793–804 (Dec. 1968).

53. Fraser and Rose, "More on Banking Structure and Performance: The Evidence from Texas," 6 J. Financial & Quantitative Analysis, No. 1, pp. 601–611 (Jan. 1971); Fraser and Rose, "Banking Structure and Performance in Isolated Markets: The Implications for Public Policy," 17 Antitrust Bull., No. 3, pp. 927–947 (Fall 1972); Rose and Fraser, N. 35 *supra*.

54. Yeats, "Further Evidence on the Structure-Performance Relation in Banking," 26 J. Econ. & Bus., No. 2, pp. 95–100 (Winter 1974).

55. Kaufman, "Bank Market Structure and Performance: The Evidence from Iowa," 32 Southern Econ. J., No. 4, pp. 429–439 (April 1966).

56. Ware, "Banking Structure and Performance: Some Evidence from Ohio," Fed. Reserve Bank of Cleveland Econ. Rev. 3–14 (March 1972).

57. Fraser and Rose (1971), N. 53 *supra*.

58. Fraser and Rose (1972), N. 53 *supra*.

59. Rose and Fraser, N. 35 *supra*.

60. See N. 28 *supra*.

loan rate studies differ, there is a pattern. Studies that use survey data of actual rates, or estimates of actual rates for particular types of loans, generally find that concentration is important. This holds for business loan rates, consumer rates, and mortgage rates.[61] The results of studies using average loan rates, on the other hand, are quite inconsistent. Some find concentration to be important; others do not. Given the complexities involved in controlling for differing loan portfolios, the use of average loan revenue to estimate actual interest rates is so imprecise that little confidence can be placed in the results of these studies.[62]

## Concentration and Deposit Competition

Deposits are the primary input into a bank's production of loans. A profit-maximizing bank will seek additional deposits as long as the cost of obtaining the last dollar of deposits is less than the revenue from lending that dollar. Deposit markets are heavily regulated, however: Payment of interest on demand deposits is prohibited, and Regulation Q limits the interest rate that banks can pay on savings deposits.

Market structure may still influence competition for deposits, but in a limited way. First, there may be variations in the rate paid on savings deposits, at least up to the legal maximum. Second, banks can vary their service charges on demand deposits up to the point of offering free checking services. Third, as Hodgman[63] has demonstrated, competition for deposits may take the form of lower rates on loans to depositors. Finally, the bank may use nonprice forms of competition to lure depositors. Theoretically, an analysis of the impact of concentration on service charges and savings rates must consider the substitutability between nonprice competition and price competition that is encouraged by rate regulation. The next two subsections analyze price competition for deposits, followed by a section which analyzes nonprice rivalry.

DEMAND DEPOSIT SERVICE CHARGES

There are three ways to estimate or measure demand deposit service charges, and all present at least some difficulties in interpretation. The

---

61. Aspinwall, "Market Structure and Commercial Bank Mortgage Interest Rates," 36 Southern Econ. J., No. 4, pp. 376–384 (April 1960). The pattern does not hold with Flechsig, who uses arbitrary regional variables that cancel out the concentration effect, nor with Stolz. Flechsig, "The Effect of Concentration on Bank Loan Rates," 20 J. Finance, No. 2, pp. 298–311 (May 1965); Stolz, N. 15 *supra*.

62. In an earlier analysis of structure performance studies, Benston also concludes that the studies using average revenue from loans are simply not meaningful. Benston, N. 22 *supra*. He also, however, strongly criticizes the survey data which Edwards uses in his early study. Edwards, N. 2 *supra*.

63. Hodgman, *Commercial Bank Loan and Investment Policy* (Univ. of Ill., Bureau of Bus. & Econ. Research, Champaign, Ill., 1963).

first, and most accurate, is to conduct a survey of actual charges on representative checking accounts.[64] This determines the price of a specified level of service. As Osborne[65] points out, however, banks usually have a schedule of prices, and such a surveyed price may not reflect the actual prices that most consumers pay. An alternative is to estimate service charges from the Federal Reserve Functional Cost Analysis program data. The virtue of these data is that it permits average service charges to be estimated after holding constant differences in account activity and average account size. The final, and totally unsatisfactory, method is simply to divide a bank's total service charge revenue by its year-end demand deposits. This measure is dependent on average account size and transaction activity, which are not held constant. A bank could have a low average service charge but still have a very high service charge on small accounts if a large volume of its deposits are large commercial deposits. Similarly, a bank with very active accounts could have low charges per transaction but still have high average charges per dollar of demand deposits.

The results of these studies are not consistent. Heggestad and Mingo,[66] using survey data, find that service charges increase with concentration, but in a nonlinear fashion. After a critical level of concentration is reached (Herfindahl Index of .099), service charges no longer increase with concentration. At concentration levels below .099, service charges do increase with concentration. These results do not hold up in rural markets: Stolz[67] finds service charges are not influenced by concentration using his "area of convenience" approximations to banking markets.

Bell and Murphy[68] use functional cost analysis data to estimate service charges and find that, for 14 New England markets in 1965, "adjusted" service charges vary directly with the level of concentration. Using similar data for 1969, Klein and Murphy[69] affirm this effect (for 164 SMSAs). Bell and Murphy's New England study is further supported by Weiss,[70] who finds that average concentration is higher in a

---

64. For example, Heggestad and Mingo asked: "What is the least amount that the bank would charge a customer for a regular or special demand deposit account in which 20 checks are written and 2 deposits are made during the month? Assume his average balance is $200 and the account never falls below $100." Heggestad and Mingo (1976), N. 29 *supra*.

65. Osborne, "Survey of Empirical Findings on the Cost of Checking Accounts," *Review* 7–15 (Fed. Reserve Bank of Dallas, May 1977).

66. Heggestad and Mingo (1976, 1977), N. 29 *supra*.

67. Stolz, N. 15 *supra*.

68. Bell and Murphy, "Impact of Market Structure on the Price of a Commercial Bank Service," 51 Rev. of Econ. & Statistics, No. 2, pp. 210–213 (May 1969).

69. Klein and Murphy, "The Pricing of Bank Deposits: A Theoretical and Empirical Analysis," 6 J. Financial & Quantitative Analysis, No. 2, pp. 747–761 (March 1971).

70. Weiss, "Commercial Bank Price Competition: The Case of 'Free' Checking Accounts," New England Econ. Rev. 3–22 (Fed. Reserve Bank of Boston, Sept.–Oct. 1969).

sample of New England markets that do not offer free checking than it is in markets that do offer this service.

Studies using "average service charges," not surprisingly, produce conflicting and inconsistent results. Fraser and Rose[71] find no relationship between either the number of banks or the one-bank concentration ratio (in Texas and in small southwestern towns) and this measure of service charge. In a later sample, however, the same authors[72] find these structural variables to be related to service charges. These conflicting results no doubt reflect the poor quality of their service charge variable.

In summary, once again the evidence is mixed. In general, the weight of the evidence is that concentration does influence price competition for demand deposits. The studies that do not find this effect are either based on a noncomparable market definition (Stolz) or use poor measures of service charges.

INTEREST ON TIME AND SAVINGS DEPOSITS

In most periods, Regulation Q sets ceiling rates on savings deposits that are far below the rates that banks would be willing to pay in a free market. It is not surprising, therefore, that few studies find that the degree of concentration affects the level of savings rates actually paid. Studies that do find such an effect are Heggestad and Mingo,[73] Edwards,[74] and Kaufman.[75] Others, such as Stolz,[76] Ware,[77] and Klein and Murphy,[78] find no effect.

## Concentration and Nonprice Competition

The severe regulatory restrictions on the ability of banks to compete by varying the price they pay for deposits forces them to adopt nonprice strategies to obtain deposits: increases in the number of their offices, extending their banking hours, advertising intensively, etc. This kind of behavior is usually not optimal. For example, Scherer[79] demonstrates that firms in an oligopolistic market (as commercial banking) are likely to advertise more than is socially optimal. This tendency, combined

---

71. Fraser and Rose (1971, 1972), N. 53 *supra*.

72. Rose and Fraser, N. 35 *supra*.

73. Heggestad and Mingo (1976), N. 29 *supra*.

74. Edwards, N. 51 *supra*.

75. Kaufman, N. 55 *supra*.

76. Stolz, N. 15 *supra*.

77. Ware, N. 56 *supra*.

78. Klein and Murphy, N. 69 *supra*.

79. Scherer, *Industrial Market Structure and Economic Performance* (Rand McNally, Chicago 1970).

with rate regulation, is likely to lead to excessive use of nonprice competition.

The strongest nonprice competition results are obtained in studies by Heggestad and Mingo,[80] Stolz,[81] and White.[82] Both Heggestad and Mingo and Stolz find that in low concentration markets, banking hours are longer and the likelihood is higher that such services will be offered as 24-hour automated-teller service.[83] White finds a similar result with respect to the intensity of branching: He finds that the number of branches rises as the Herfindahl Index falls. *Ceteris paribus,* in low concentration markets where branching is permitted, consumers have better access to banking services.

Only Edwards[84] has analyzed the determinants of advertising in banking. He finds that concentration does not influence the advertising intensity of banks. His sample of very large banks, however, may not be representative of most United States banks. Further study of this issue is needed.

### Concentration and Profitability

Profitability may be looked upon as a summary index of performance. High profits in a market signal a need for more resources; they indicate a need for more competition and more entry into those markets. The concentration-profitability relationship in banking has been found to be quite weak, which is surprising, since many studies find that price and nonprice competition is affected by concentration.

All profit studies, except Peltzman,[85] use year-end income and balance sheet data. While these data may be subject to "window dressing" to satisfy regulators, they are the best available. Rates of return calculated on book value of equity capital and on total assets have been studied.

Neither of these measures is ideal. For example, if banks with monopoly power have higher capital-to-asset ratios, perhaps because they are more conservative or because they have made greater absolute profits over time and have retained these funds, their ratios of profits to capital may be low, even though their net return on assets is high.

---

80. Heggestad and Mingo (1976), N. 29 *supra*.

81. Stolz, N. 15 *supra*.

82. White, "Searching for the Critical Industrial Concentration Ratio: An Application of the 'Switching of Regimes' Technique," *Studies in Nonlinear Estimation* 61–76 (Goldfeld and Quandt, Eds., Ballinger, Cambridge, Mass., 1976).

83. The Stolz results parallel Heggestad and Mingo in nonprice dimensions but not in price dimensions.

84. Edwards, N. 38 *supra*.

85. Peltzman, "Bank Stock Prices and the Effect of Regulation of the Banking Structure," 41 J. Bus., No. 4, pp. 413–430 (Oct. 1968).

Alternatively, the ratio of profits-to-assets is influenced by portfolio mix, like the average loan rate. A bank may have a low profits-to-assets ratio because it has a portfolio of safe assets. If the bank is highly levered, however, its owners could still be earning a high return on equity, even though the bank's profit-to-asset ratio is low.

In a world of uncertainty, investors are concerned about the riskiness of their investments as well as the level of their profits. Studies comparing profitability across firms cannot ignore this factor. A low level of relatively secure profits may be preferred to a higher level of risky profits. Only the studies by Emery,[86] Edwards and Heggestad,[87] and Heggestad[88] consider this issue.

No study finds a relationship between concentration and the rate of return on equity, except for Fraser and Rose,[89] and then only in one of the two years they study. Others, including Bryan,[90] Ware,[91] and Yeats[92] find no relationship. In fact, Vernon[93] finds that such returns are higher in competitive markets. Thus, the evidence does not indicate higher returns on equity in monopolistic markets.[94]

The effect of concentration on the profits-to-assets ratio is stronger. Heggestad[95] finds that the average return on banks' assets (over the period 1960–1970) increases with concentration. The relationship is stronger when profit levels are adjusted for differences in risk, measured by differences in banks' profit variability. These results confirm earlier studies by Edwards[96] and Kaufman[97] in unit banking states.

In all these studies, the effect of concentration on profits is small. This is not surprising, given the nature of bank regulation. On the one hand, regulators, who are primarily concerned with bank soundness,

---

86. Emery, "Risk, Return and the Morphology of Commercial Banking," 6 J. Financial & Quantitative Analysis, No. 2, pp. 763–776 (March 1971).

87. Edwards and Heggestad, N. 24 *supra*.

88. Heggestad, "Market Structure, Risk and Profitability in Commercial Banking," 32 J. Finance, No. 4, pp. 1207–1216 (Sept. 1977).

89. Fraser and Rose (1971), N. 53 *supra*.

90. Bryan, *The Determinants of Bank Profits*, Research Paper No. 8 (American Bankers Ass'n, Dep't of Research & Planning, Washington, D.C., 1972).

91. Ware, N. 56 *supra*.

92. Yeats, N. 54 *supra*.

93. Vernon, "Separation of Ownership and Control and Profit Rates, the Evidence from Banking: Comment," 6 J. Financial & Quantitative Analysis, No. 1, pp. 615–625 (Jan. 1971).

94. This may reflect the regulators' desire to maintain high capital in banking, and the fact that they can place greater pressure on banks in concentrated markets. Thus, capital levels are higher in monopolistic markets.

95. Heggestad, N. 88 *supra*.

96. Edwards, N. 51 *supra*.

97. Kaufman, N. 55 *supra*.

will not allow low or negative profits for very long; on the other hand, they are unlikely to permit high profits to exist for long, since these may be a sign that regulators are being too protective and should ease entry restrictions in these markets.[98]

## Concentration and Managerial Motives

Several recent studies have questioned the traditional assumption that large multiproduct firms with monopoly power are profit maximizers.[99] Firm preferences may change with monopoly power. If so, the theoretical underpinnings of the structure-performance models are even less secure. Recent empirical evidence also indicates that this may be more than just a possibility.

Edwards and Heggestad,[100] using a sample of large banks, find evidence consistent with the hypothesis that the degree of uncertainty avoidance in banks increases with their monopoly power.[101] As firms gain monopoly power, they may become more risk averse. This implies that changes in monopoly power can lead to changes in the character of a bank's portfolio, which may not show up (or may show up in unpredicted ways) in the traditional measures of performance. For example, monopolistic banks may be less likely to innovate, or less willing to make risky loans, or may reduce their leverage. Heggestad[102] supports these results with his finding that concentration has a greater effect on risk-adjusted profits than on simple average profit rates.

Mingo[103] offers additional evidence to challenge the assumption of profit maximization. In an evaluation of the effect of affiliation of independent banks with holding company banks, he finds the effect to vary with market concentration. In low concentration markets, where market forces are strongest, affiliation has no influence on the "independent" bank's degree of leverage; in concentrated markets, affiliation leads to a significant drop in its capital-to-asset ratio. Thus, conservative risk-avoiding banks may be able to exist in monopoly markets but not in competitive markets. The more profit-oriented holding companies were only able to reduce the capital ratios of the monopolistic banks they acquired.

Edwards[104] provides a different approach to determining the impact

---

98. For a theoretical elaboration of these points, see Edwards and Edwards, N. 12 *supra*.

99. See, e.g., Williamson, "Managerial Discretion and Business Behavior," 53 American Econ. Rev., No. 5, pp. 1032–1057 (Dec. 1963); Galbraith, *The New Industrial State* (Houghton Mifflin, Boston 1967).

100. Edwards and Heggestad, N. 24 *supra*.

101. Their model cannot differentiate between changes in management preference and changes in the investment frontier.

102. Heggestad, N. 88 *supra*.

103. Mingo, N. 50 *supra*.

104. Edwards, N. 25 *supra*.

of monopoly on managerial behavior, an approach which may also

explain why researchers have not found a strong concentration-profit
relationship in banking. He argues that managers in banks with
monopoly power have expense-preference utility functions: As banks
obtain more monopoly power, they tend to hire more staff, pay higher
wages, and become less conscious of costs. His empirical findings are
consistent with this behavior: Banks in highly concentrated markets
use more labor, everything else being equal. These findings suggest
that monopoly may lead to higher costs and greater inefficiency (implying lower profits than would otherwise exist). This aspect of performance will undoubtedly be given greater attention in future research.

## Is There a Critical Level of Concentration?

Many theoretical models of oligopoly argue that firms explicitly or
implicitly collude to reach the cartel (monopoly) solution, and that at
some number of firms or some level of concentration, this collusion will
break down due to the incentive individual firms have to cut prices
secretly. White[105] terms this point the "critical" concentration level.
Increases in concentration above this level, for example, will not
increase prices, since the monopoly price will have been attained
already. This approach directly challenges the assumption of a linear
concentration-performance relationship.

Heggestad and Mingo[106] estimate the critical concentration ratio for
two bank products: consumer loans and demand deposit services. They
find that loan rates increase with the Herfindahl Index until that index
reaches a value of .14 (a numbers-equivalent of 7) and that further
increases do not cause an increase in loan rates. For demand deposit
service charges, the critical Herfindahl Index is .099: for markets with a
Herfindahl Index greater than .099, a further increase in concentration
does not increase service charges.[107] The implication of these results is
far reaching: For these specific products, well over 80 percent of the
United States banking markets are already effectively monopolized,
and this may be true of other bank products as well.

This finding may also explain some of the inconsistent results of
previous studies. Generally, the studies of rural markets find that
structure does not matter. Rural markets, however, are more highly
concentrated than city markets (Table 9-1), so that these studies may be
examining markets that are already effectively monopolized. If their
data samples had included markets with a complete range of concentration levels, their result might have been different.

---

105. White, N. 82 *supra*.

106. Heggestad and Mingo (1977), N. 29 *supra*.

107. The critical level need not be identical for all aspects of performance. For example,
Edwards finds a critical three-bank concentration ratio for expense preference behavior of
.76—a value somewhat higher than the levels for bank prices. Edwards, N. 25 *supra*.

If it is true that many banking markets effectively are monopolized already, this may be a strong justification for undertaking major structural reform in the industry. In these circumstances, minor reforms, such as tougher merger laws, are unlikely to have much impact on performance.

## OTHER DIMENSIONS OF STRUCTURE

There are other dimensions of market structure besides concentration which vary among markets, and their impact on performance also needs to be analyzed. These include the condition of entry, interinstitutional competition, and "extra-market structure," or structural considerations outside the market that influence behavior in the market.

### Entry Barriers

The impact of entry barriers on performance has been evaluated by two alternative approaches. The first is to include explanatory variables representing the condition of entry in models explaining performance. With this type of formulation, the simultaneous impact of entry barriers and concentration, as well as other factors, can be estimated. While this is a desirable approach, data problems often limit its applicability. The alternative approach is to evaluate the impact of *actual* new entry on the performance of existing banks—a before and after comparison.

Attempts to include entry variables in the estimating equations have been limited to distinguishing between the different types of branching and holding company laws. Presumably, states with unrestricted branching laws, or which liberally permit holding company expansion, have lower entry barriers, since they allow entry by existing firms. The problem is that these variables may also reflect differences in banks' costs due to differences in organizational structure and bank size.

Studies using this approach reach conflicting conclusions. Jacobs[108] finds that loan rates to small firms are lowest in statewide branching states and highest in unit banking states; Emery[109] and Vernon[110] find higher profits in statewide branching states; and Peltzman[111] finds branching laws have no effect on bank stock prices. Neither Emery nor Peltzman, however, includes variables to reflect differences in local market power, so little confidence can be placed in their results. In a different context, Lanzillotti and Saving[112] find that, *ceteris paribus*, unit

---

108. Jacobs, N. 41 *supra*.

109. Emery, N. 86 *supra*.

110. Vernon, N. 93 *supra*.

111. Peltzman, N. 85 *supra*.

112. Lanzillotti and Saving, "State Branching Restrictions and the Availability of Branching Services," 1 J. Money, Credit & Banking, No. 4, pp. 778–788 (Nov. 1969).

banking states have more bank offices, while Jessup and Stolz[113] find that branching laws have no effect on the number of rural offices.

The studies of the impact of actual entry are more consistent. McCall and Peterson[114] find that *de novo* unit entry into highly concentrated rural markets increases savings deposit interest rates. On the other hand, *de novo* branching entry has little effect. Their results differ in some specifics but basically substantiate the Fraser-Rose[115] study, which finds that entry significantly improves performance, especially in the portfolio selection of existing firms. Similarly, Peltzman[116] finds that entry rates into states reduce the returns of existing banks, and this result is supported in a dynamic context by findings of Edwards and Edwards.[117]

## Extra-Market Structure

In two recent bank merger cases, the Supreme Court questioned the assertion that domination of a state by a few banks will adversely affect performance.[118] In both cases, the merger in question would not have directly altered the local structure, although it would have increased the level of concentration in the state as well as the degree of interdependence among the largest banks in the state.

Two recent studies analyze the impact of this type of "extra-market" structural change on performance. Rose[119] considers the impact of state concentration ratios on the political process. He tests the hypothesis that domination of a state by a few banks leads to control of the political process. The largest banks, for example, might be able to get laws passed that are favorable to their interests. As a test case, Rose examines the impact of state banking concentration on the votes of 90 senators on a bill that would delay nationwide NOW accounts. The level of concentration appears to have no effect on their votes. His approach is novel and deserves more attention.

Heggestad and Rhoades[120] empirically evaluate the impact on market

---

113. Jessup and Stolz, "Customer Alternatives Among Rural Banks," 6 J. Bank Research, No. 2, pp. 135–139 (Summer 1975).

114. McCall and Peterson, *The Impact of De Novo Commercial Bank Entry*, Working Paper 76-7 (Fed. Deposit Ins. Corp., Div. of Research, 1976).

115. Fraser and Rose (1972), N. 53 *supra*.

116. Peltzman, N. 85 *supra*.

117. Edwards and Edwards, N. 12 *supra*.

118. United States v. Connecticut Nat'l Bank, 418 U.S. 656 (1974); United States v. Marine Bancorp., 418 U.S. 602 (1974).

119. Rose, *Industry Concentration and Political Leverage: An Empirical Test*, unpublished paper (Bd. of Governors of the Fed. Reserve System, Washington, D.C., 1976).

120. Heggestad and Rhoades, "The Influence of Multi-market Links on Local Market Competition," *Review of Economics and Statistics* (forthcoming).

performance of "links" between the dominant banks in markets throughout a state. Edwards[121] and Solomon[122] argue that when firms have contact with each other in many markets, they may develop strong interdependence. For example, they may restrict rivalry in one market out of fear of retaliation in another market where they may be more vulnerable. Heggestad and Rhoades find evidence to support this contention: *ceteris paribus,* there is less competition in a banking market where the dominant banks in that market also meet often in other markets. These findings take on considerable significance in the light of the prospect of nationwide branching via EFT systems.

## Interinstitutional Competition

Most studies of banking performance focus on banking structure and do not take into account competition from other types of financial institutions. Further, the studies that have attempted to do so have used very imprecise measures of interinstitutional competition. There is some evidence to suggest that this factor may be quite important in explaining performance. Heggestad and Mingo[123] find that demand deposit service charges are much cheaper (by $1.52 per month) in markets where thrifts are allowed to offer NOW accounts. Similarly, Stolz[124] finds that farm loan rates are lower in markets with production credit associations; and White[125] finds that the presence of thrifts increases the number of commercial bank offices within SMSAs. This dimension of competition is likely to be an extremely important determinant of performance in the future, since the prospect is for more direct competition among all kinds of financial institutions.

## CONCLUSION

Empirical knowledge about the impact of market structure on bank performance has an important bearing on merger and antitrust policy as well as on the many proposals for regulatory reform. It already has been studied extensively, notwithstanding the severe difficulties in theoretical modeling, in econometric specification and estimation, and in obtaining the required data. Some conclusions can be drawn from these studies.

The weight of the evidence supports the view that market structure is an important determinant of performance in banking. Of the 36 studies

---

121. Edwards, N. 51 *supra.*

122. Solomon, "Bank Merger Policy and Problems: A Linkage Theory of Oligopoly," 2 J. Money, Credit & Banking, No. 3, pp. 323–336 (Aug. 1970).

123. Heggestad and Mingo (1977), N. 29 *supra.*

124. Stolz, N. 15 *supra.*

125. White, N. 37 *supra.*

listed in Table 9-2 that specifically test the impact of either the number of banks or the level of concentration (using either a concentration ratio or the Herfindahl Index) on performance, 23 find that structure matters. Further analysis tips the scales even further: of the 10 studies that use the best price measures (survey data of actual rates), 8 find an important relationship. Many of the studies that do not find a relationship are plagued with data and econometric difficulties. For example, balance sheet derived average loan rates are very poor measures of actual loan rates: 7 of the 13 studies that use this data do not find a relationship. The evidence also is increasing over time. Of the 19 studies completed between 1961 and 1973, 11 find that structure matters. In contrast, of the 17 studies published since 1973, 12 find such a relationship.[126]

Market structure is also economically important. Since the performance of the industry in virtually every product examined is influenced by structure, the aggregate effect of a change in structure may be substantial. Further, recent work, which finds that a critical level of concentration exists, suggests that previous linear specifications of the structure-performance relationship may have underestimated the effect on concentration in moderately concentrated markets.

There are several areas where more research is needed. First, more effort should be expended in modeling behavior in the industry. The simple structure-performance model commonly used is not sufficient to explain behavior. Second, several studies are now casting doubt on the assumption that profit maximization is the sole goal of banks. More work is needed to verify and determine the implications of these results. Nonprofit maximizing behavior may impact on entirely different aspects of performance. Third, further study is needed of the impact of structural variables other than concentration. These include interinstitutional competition, barriers to entry, overall state concentration, and extra-market linkages. Fourth, further theoretical and empirical work needs to be done on the functional form of the concentration-performance relationship. Recent work indicates that the assumption of linearity may not be appropriate. Knowledge of this form is critical to evaluating regulatory reform proposals. Finally, many of these issues require the use of performance data that have, up to now, not been available. Greater effort should be expended by the regulatory agencies to gather and make available data for evaluating these questions.

---

126. Two earlier surveys of this literature are more tentative in their conclusions about the impact of market structure on performance. Guttentag and Herman, "Banking Structure and Performance," The Bull., Nos. 41–43 (New York Univ. Graduate School of Bus. Ad., Institute of Finance, Feb. 1967); Benston, N. 22 *supra*. Both were published, however, before the strong results obtained by the studies published since 1973.

**Adelman, M. A.:** "Comment on the 'H' Concentration Measure as a Numbers-Equivalent," Review of Economics and Statistics, Vol. 51, No. 1 pp. 99–101 (Feb. 1969).

**Alhadeff, David A.:** "Barriers to Bank Entry," *Southern Economic Journal,* Vol. 40, No. 4, pp. 589–603 (April 1974).

—— and **C. P. Alhadeff:** "Bank Entry and Bank Concentration," Antitrust Bulletin, Vol. 20, pp. 471–483 (Fall 1975).

**Aspinwall, Richard C.:** "Market Structure and Commercial Bank Mortgage Interest Rates," Southern Economic Journal, Vol. 36, No. 4, pp. 376–384 (April 1970).

**Bain, J. S.:** *Barriers to New Competition* (Harvard Univ. Press, Cambridge 1956).

**Baker, Donald:** "Chartering, Branching, and the Concentration Problem," *Policies for a More Competitive Financial System* 21–39 (Fed. Reserve Bank of Boston 1972).

**Beighley, H. Prescott,** and **Alan S. McCall:** "Market Power and Structure and Commercial Bank Installment Lending," Journal of Money, Credit and Banking, Vol. 7, No. 4, pp. 449–467 (Nov. 1975).

**Bell, Frederick W.,** and **Neil B. Murphy:** "Impact of Market Structure on the Price of a Commercial Bank Service," Review of Economics and Statistics, Vol. 51, No. 2, pp. 210–213 (May 1969).

**Benston, George J.:** "The Optimal Banking Structure: Theory and Evidence," Journal of Bank Research, Vol. 3, No. 4, pp. 220–237 (Winter 1973).

—— and **Clifford W. Smith, Jr.:** "A Transactions Cost Approach to the Theory of Financial Intermediation," Journal of Finance, Vol. 31, No. 2, pp. 215–231 (May 1976).

**Boczar, Gregory:** "The Evidence on Competition Between Commercial Banks and Finance Companies," Journal of Bank Research, Vol. 6, pp. 150–154 (Summer 1975).

**Bryan, William R.:** *The Determinants of Bank Profits,* Research Paper No. 8, (American Bankers Ass'n, Dep't of Research and Planning, Washington, D.C., 1972).

**Chamberlin, Edward H.:** *The Theory of Monopolistic Competition* (Harvard Univ. Press, Cambridge 1933).

**Conference of State Bank Supervisors,** *A Profile of State Chartered Banking* (Washington, D.C., 1975).

**Edwards, Franklin R.:** "Managerial Objectives in Regulated Industries: Expense-Preference Behavior in Banking," Journal of Political Economy, Vol. 85, No. 1, pp. 147–162 (Feb. 1977).

————: "Advertising and Competition in Banking," Antitrust Bulletin, Vol. 18, No. 1, pp. 23–32 (Spring 1973).

————: "Review of Business Loan Costs and Bank Market Structure," Journal of Finance, Vol. 27 (Sept. 1972).

————: "The Banking Competition Controversy," National Banking Review, Vol. 3, No. 1, pp. 1–34 (Sept. 1965).

————: "Concentration in Banking and Its Effects on Business Loan Rates," Review of Economics and Statistics, Vol. 46, No. 3, pp. 294–300 (Aug. 1964).

———— and **Arnold A. Heggestad:** "Uncertainty, Market Structure, and Performance: The Galbraith-Caves Hypothesis and Managerial Motives in Banking," Quarterly Journal of Economics, Vol. 87, No. 3, pp. 455–473 (Aug. 1973).

———— and **James H. Scott:** "Regulating the Solvency of Depository Institutions: A Perspective for Deregulation," in this volume.

**Edwards, Linda N.,** and **Franklin R. Edwards,** "Measuring the Effectiveness of Regulation: The Case of Bank Entry Regulation," Journal of Law and Economics, Vol. 17, No. 2, pp. 445–460 (Oct. 1974).

**Eisenbeis, Robert A.:** "Local Banking Markets for Business Loans," Journal of Bank Research, Vol. 2, No. 2, pp. 30–39 (Summer 1971).

**Emery, John T.:** "Risk, Return and the Morphology of Commercial Banking," Journal of Financial and Quantitative Analysis, Vol. 6, No. 2, pp. 763–776 (March 1971).

**Flechsig, Theodore G.:** "The Effect of Concentration on Bank Loan Rates," Journal of Finance, Vol. 20, No. 2, pp. 298–311 (May 1965).

**Fraser, Donald R.,** and **Joel B. Alvis:** "The Structure-Performance Relationship in Banking: A Dichotomous Analysis," Review of Business and Economic Research, Vol. 2 pp. 35–57 (Fall 1975).

————, **Wallace J. Phillips, Jr.,** and **Peter S. Rose:** "A Canonical Analysis of Bank Performance," Journal of Financial and Quantitative Analysis, Vol. 9, pp. 287–296 (March 1974).

———— and **Peter S. Rose:** "Banking Structure and Performance in Isolated Markets: The Implications for Public Policy," Antitrust Bulletin, Vol. 17, No. 3, pp. 927–947 (Fall 1972).

———— and ————: "Bank Entry and Bank Performance," Journal of Finance, Vol. 27, pp. 65–78 (March 1972).

———— and ————: "More on Banking Structure and Performance: The Evidence from Texas," Journal of Financial and Quantitative Analysis, Vol. 6, No. 1, pp. 601–611 (Jan. 1971).

**Galbraith, John Kenneth:** *The New Industrial State* (Houghton Mifflin, Boston 1967).

**Gelder, Ralph H.,** and **George Budzeika:** "Banking Market Determination: The Case of Central Nassau County," Federal Reserve Bank of New York Monthly Review, Vol. 52, No. 11, pp. 258–266 (Nov. 1970).

**488**

**Golembe, C. H.,** and **R. E. Hengren,** *Federal Regulation of Banking* (American Institute of Banking 1975).

**Guttentag, Jack M.,** and **Edward S. Herman:** "Banking Structure and Performance," The Bulletin, Nos. 41–43 (New York Univ. Graduate School of Bus. Ad., Institute of Finance, Feb. 1967).

**Heggestad, Arnold A.:** "Market Structure, Risk and Profitability in Commercial Banking," Journal of Finance, Vol. 32, No. 4, pp. 1207–1216 (Sept. 1977).

—— and **John J. Mingo:** "The Competitive Condition of U.S. Banking Markets and the Impact of Structural Reform," Journal of Finance, Vol. 32, No. 3, pp. 649–661 (June 1977).

—— and ——: "Prices, Nonprices and Concentration in Commercial Banking," Journal of Money, Credit and Banking, Vol. 8, No. 1, pp. 107–117 (Feb. 1976).

—— and **Stephen A. Rhoades:** "The Influence of Multi-market Links on Local Market Competition," Review of Economics and Statistics, Vol. 60, No. 4 (Nov. 1978).

—— and ——: "Concentration and Firm Stability in Commercial Banking," Review of Economics and Statistics, Vol. 58, pp. -43–452 (Nov. 1976).

**Hodgman, Donald R.:** *Commercial Bank Loan and Investment Policy* (Univ. of Ill., Bureau of Bus. and Econ. Research, Champaign, Ill., 1963).

**Jacobs, Donald P.:** *Business Loan Costs and Bank Market Structure: An Empirical Estimate of Their Relations,* Occasional Paper 115, Nat'l Bureau of Econ. Research (distributed by Columbia Univ. Press, New York 1971).

——: "The Interaction Effect of Restrictions on Branching and Other Bank Regulations," Journal of Finance, Vol. 20, pp. 332–348 (May 1965).

——: "The Framework of Commercial Banking Regulation: An Appraisal," National Banking Review, Vol. 1, No. 3, pp. 343–357 (March 1964).

**Jessup, Paul F.,** and **Richard W. Stolz:** "Customer Alternatives Among Rural Banks," Journal of Bank Research, Vol. 6, No. 2, pp. 135–139 (Summer 1975).

**Kaufman, George G.:** "Bank Market Structure and Performance: The Evidence from Iowa," Southern Economic Journal, Vol. 32, No. 4, pp. 429–439 (April 1966).

**Klein, M. A.,** and **Neil B. Murphy:** "The Pricing of Bank Deposits: A Theoretical and Empirical Analysis," Journal of Financial and Quantitative Analysis, Vol. 6, No. 2, pp. 747–761 (March 1971).

**Kmenta, Jan:** *Elements of Econometrics* (Macmillan, New York 1971).

**Lanzillotti, R. F.,** and **Thomas R. Saving:** "State Branching Restrictions and the Availability of Branching Services," Journal of Money, Credit and Banking, Vol. 1, No. 4 pp. 778–788 (Nov. 1969).

**Lozowick, Arnold H., Peter O. Steiner,** and **Roger Miller:** "Law and Quantitative Multivariate Analysis: An Encounter," Michigan Law Review, Vol. 66, No. 8, pp. 1641–1678 (June 1968).

**Maddala, G. S.:** *Econometrics* (Macmillan, New York 1977).

**McCall, Allan S.,** and **Manferd O. Peterson:** *The Impact of De Novo Commercial Bank Entry,* Working Paper 76-77 (Fed. Deposit Ins. Corp., Div. of Research, 1976).

**Meyer, Paul A.:** "Price Discrimination, Regional Loan Rates, and the Structure of the Banking Industry," Journal of Finance, Vol. 22, pp. 37–48 (March 1967).

**Mingo, John J.:** "Managerial Motives, Market Structures, and the Performance of Holding Company Banks," Economic Inquiry, Vol. 14, No. 3, pp. 411–424 (Sept. 1976).

**Orr, David,** and **Paul MacAvoy:** "Price Strategies to Promote Cartel Stability," Economica, Vol. 32, pp. 186–197 (May 1965).

**Osborne, D. K.:** "Survey of Empirical Findings on the Cost of Checking Accounts," Review 7–15 (Fed. Reserve Bank of Dallas, May 1977).

**Peltzman, Sam:** "Bank Stock Prices and the Effect of Regulation of the Banking Structure," Journal of Business, Vol. 41, No. 4, pp. 413–430 (Oct. 1968).

———: "Entry in Commercial Banking," Journal of Law and Economics, Vol. 8, pp. 11–50 (Oct. 1965).

**Phillips, Almarin:** "Evidence on Concentration in Banking Markets and Interest Rates," Federal Reserve Bulletin, Vol. 53, No. 6, pp. 916–926 (June 1967).

**Robinson, Joan:** The Economics of Imperfect Competition (Macmillan, London 1933).

**Rose, John T.:** "The Attractiveness of Banking Markets for *De Novo* Entry: The Evidence from Texas," Journal of Bank Research, Vol. 7, No. 4, pp. 284–293 (Winter 1977).

———: *Industry Concentration and Political Leverage: An Empirical Test,* unpublished paper (Bd. of Governors of the Fed. Reserve System, Washington, D.C., 1976).

**Rose, Peter S.,** and **Donald R. Fraser:** "The Relationships Between Stability and Change in Market Structure: An Analysis of Bank Prices," Journal of Industrial Economics, Vol. 24, No. 4, pp. 251–266 (June 1976).

**Saving, Thomas R.:** "Concentration Ratios and the Degree of Monopoly," International Economic Review, Vol. 11, No. 1, pp. 139–146 (Feb. 1970).

**Scherer, Frederic M.:** *Industrial Market Structure and Economic Performance* (Rand McNally, Chicago 1970).

**Schweiger, Irving,** and **John S. McGee:** "Chicago Banking," Journal of Business, Vol. 34, No. 3, pp. 203–366 (July 1961).

**Scott, Kenneth E.:** "The Dual Banking System: A Model of Competition in Regulation," in this volume.

**Solomon, Elinor Harris:** "Bank Merger Policy and Problems: A Linkage Theory of Oligopoly," Journal of Money, Credit and Banking, Vol. 2, No. 3, pp. 323–336 (Aug. 1970).

**Stigler, George J.:** *The Organization of Industry* (R. D. Irwin, Homewood, Ill., 1968).

———: "A Theory of Oligopoly," Journal of Political Economy, Vol. 72, No. 1, pp. 44–61 (Feb. 1964).

**Stolz, Richard W.:** "Local Banking Markets, Structure, and Conduct in Rural Areas," *Bank Structure and Competition* 134–149 (Fed. Reserve Bank of Chicago, 1972).

**Stuhr, D. P.:** "Competition and Commercial Bank Behavior," *Bank Structure and Competition* 184–202 (Fed. Reserve Bank of Chicago, 1972).

**Talley, Samuel H.:** *Recent Trends in Local Banking Market Structures,* Staff Economic Studies, No. 89, p. 5 (Bd. of Governors of the Fed. Reserve System, May 1977).

**Taylor, Charles T.:** "Average Interest Charges, the Loan Mix, and Measures of Competition: Sixth Federal Reserve District Experience," Journal of Finance, Vol. 23, No. 5, pp. 793–804 (Dec. 1968).

United States v. Connecticut National Bank, 418 U.S. 656 (1974).

United States v. Marine Bancorporation, Inc., 418 U.S. 602 (1974).

United States v. Philadelphia National Bank, 374 U.S. 321 (1963).

**Vernon, Jack R.:** "Separation of Ownership and Control and Profit Rates, the Evidence from Banking: Comment," Journal of Financial and Quantitative Analysis, Vol. 6, No. 1, Jan. 1971, pp. 615–625.

**Ware, Robert F.:** "Banking Structure and Performance: Some Evidence from Ohio," Federal Reserve Bank of Cleveland Economic Review 3–14 (March 1972).

**Weiss, Leonard:** "The Concentration-Profits Relationship and Antitrust," *Industrial Concentration: The New Learning* 184–233 (Harvey J. Goldschmid, H. Michael Mann, and J. Fred Weston, Eds., Little, Brown & Co., Boston 1974).

**Weiss, Steven J.:** "Commercial Bank Price Competition: The Case of 'Free' Checking Accounts," New England Economic Review, 3–22 (Fed. Reserve Bank of Boston, Sept.-Oct. 1969).

**White, Lawrence J.:** "Searching for the Critical Industrial Concentration Ratio: An Application of the 'Switching of Regimes' Technique," *Studies in Nonlinear Estimation* 61–76 (S. M. Goldfeld and R. E. Quandt, Eds., Ballinger, Cambridge, Mass., 1976).

———: "Price Regulation and Quality Rivalry in a Profit-Maximizing Model: The Case of Branch Banking," Journal of Money, Credit and Banking, Vol. 8, No. 1, pp. 97–106 (Feb. 1976).

**Williamson, Oliver E.:** "Managerial Discretion and Business Behavior," American Economic Review, Vol. 53, No. 5, pp. 1032–1057 (Dec. 1963).

**Yeats, Alexander J.:** "Further Evidence on the Structure-Performance Relation in Banking," Journal of Economics and Business, Vol. 26, No. 2, pp. 95–100 (Winter 1974).

# *Appendixes*

## APPENDIX 1—BIOGRAPHICAL INFORMATION ON FACULTY SEMINAR SERIES SPEAKERS AND COMMENTATORS

**Bloch, Henry S.,** *Executive Vice President, E. M. Warburg, Pincus & Co., Inc., Adjunct Professor of Law and International Relations, Columbia University*

D.L., 1937, Nancy; Dr. Hon. Causa, 1969, Brussels

Chairman, director, UNITAR Seminar on International Monetary System (1972). Mr. Bloch has an extensive background in the teaching of both law and economics, and many years of service to the United Nations. He has served as financial adviser to governments, companies, and financial institutions in Asia, Latin America, Africa, and Europe. Recent publications include *Financial Integration in Western Europe* (1969); *The Global Partnership, International Agencies and Economic Development* (1968).

**Cooper, George,** *Professor of Law, Columbia University*

LL.B., 1961, Harvard; B.S., 1958, University of Pennsylvania

On the Columbia faculty since 1966; Visiting Professor, Harvard (1974–1975); Associate Covington & Burling, Washington, D.C., (1963–1966). Has been active as a litigator and consultant in civil rights, poverty, fair employment, and tax law. Author of law review articles on tax and fair employment matters. Recent publications include *Fair Employment Litigation* (co-author) (1975).

**Dean, James W.,** *Associate Professor of Economics, Simon Fraser University*

Ph.D., 1973, M.A., 1968, Harvard; B.S., 1962, Carleton

Canadian Council Leave Fellowship spent interviewing international bankers in Europe (1975–1976); Consultant, The Fraser Institute, developed financial data base for British Columbia (summer 1975); Consultant, Mac-

491

Millan Bloedel, Ltd., writing "Two Year Economic Outlook for Major Industrialized Countries" (summer 1974). Recent publications include "A Comment on the 1977 Bank Act Revision," *Canadian Public Policy*, Summer 1976; "Papers on the 1977 Bank Act Revision: A Reply," *Canadian Public Policy*, Winter 1977; "The Neutrality of Foreign Exchange In Flows," (with P. Kennedy), in progress.

**Diller, Stanley,** *Bond Portfolio Strategist, Goldman, Sachs & Co.*

Ph.D., 1966, Columbia; B.A., 1961, Queens College

Employed at Goldman, Sachs since 1976; Citibank (1974–1976); Research Associate, National Bureau of Economic Research (1966–1974); SEC (1968–1970); taught at Graduate School of Business, Columbia University (1966–1968, 1971–1974). Recent publications include: Study on credit allocation for Citibank (1976); chapter on primary capital markets for the SEC's *Institutional Investor Study* (1971); "The Expectations Component of the Term Structure," in *Essays on Interest Rates*, NBER (1971); *Seasonal Variation of Interest Rates*, NBER (1970); "Term Structure of Interest Rates" in *Economic Forecasts and Expectations*, NBER (1969).

**Edwards, Franklin R.,** *Professor of Business, Graduate School of Business, Columbia University*

J.D., 1968, New York University; Ph.D., 1964, M.A., 1960, Harvard; B.A., 1958, Bucknell

Senior Economist for the Comptroller of the Currency (1964–1966); Editor, *The National Banking Review* (1964–1966); Federal Reserve Board (1963–1964). Recent publications include "Measuring the Effectiveness of Regulation: The Case of Bank Entry Regulation," *J. of Law and Econ.* (October 1974); "Managerial Objectives in Regulated Industries: Expense-Preference Behavior in Banking" (forthcoming in *J. of Political Econ*).

**Gellhorn, Walter,** *University Professor Emeritus, Columbia University*

LL.B., 1931, Columbia; A.B., 1927, Amherst (and many honorary degrees)

Member of the Faculty of Law at Columbia (1933–1973); University Professor (1973–1974); University Professor Emeritus at Columbia since 1974. President, A.A.L.S. (1963); Council, American Philosophical Society (1970–1973); Council, Administrative Conference of the United States, since 1967. Recent publications include *When Americans Complain* (1966); *Ombudsmen and Others* (1966); *Cases and Comments on Administrative Law* (with Byse), 6th ed. (1974).

**Grubel, Herbert G.,** *Professor of Economics, Simon Fraser University*

Ph.D., 1961, Yale; B.A., 1958, Rutgers; Abitur, 1954, Germany

Since 1972 at Simon Fraser; Senior Policy Adviser, U.S. Treasury, International Division (1971); Associate Professor, University of Pennsylvania (1966–1969); Assistant Professor, University of Chicago (1963–1966). Associate Editor, *Journal of Finance* (1972–1974). Recent publications include *International Economics* (1976); *Intra-Industry Trade: The Theory and Measurement of International Trade in Differentiated Products* (with P. J. Lloyd) (1975).

**Hamburger, Michael,** *Economist, Federal Reserve Bank of New York*

Ph.D., 1964, M.S., 1962, Carnegie-Mellon University; B.S., 1959, Syracuse

Dr. Hamburger has been at the Federal Reserve since 1966, serving in various capacities. He is the author of several publications, among the most recent of which are "The Expectations, Hypothesis and the Efficiency of the Treasury Bill Market" (with Elliott Platt), *Review of Economics and Statistics* (May 1975); "Inflation, Unemployment and Macroeconomic Policy in Open Economies: An Empirical Analysis" (with Rutbert Reisch), in *Institutions, Policies and Economic Performance*, Karl Brunner and A. H. Meltzer, eds. (1976).

**Heggestad, Arnold A.,** *Chairman and Professor, Department of Finance, Insurance, and Real Estate, University of Florida*

Ph.D., 1973, M.A., 1970, Michigan State University; B.A., 1965, University of Maryland

On the University of Florida faculty since 1974; Economist, Division of Research and Statistics, Federal Reserve Board (1970–1974); Economist, Federal Trade Commission (1965–1967). Recent publications include *Studies in Public Regulation of Financial Services: Costs and Benefits to Consumers—A Bibliography*, in press; "The Effect of Market Structure on Risk and Profitability in the Commercial Banking Industry," *Journal of Finance*, September 1977.

**Horvitz, Paul M.,** *Assistant to the Chairman for Policy, FDIC*

Ph.D., 1958, Massachusetts Institute of Technology; M.B.A., 1956, Boston University; B.A., 1954, University of Chicago

Dr. Horvitz has been at the FDIC since 1967, first as Assistant Director, then Director of Research. Formerly Senior Economist, Office of the Comptroller of the Currency (1963–1966); Assistant Professor of Finance, Boston University (1960–1962); Financial Economist, Federal Reserve Bank of Boston (1957–1960).

**Jaffee, Dwight M.,** *Professor of Economics, Princeton University*

Ph.D., 1968, Massachusetts Institute of Technology; B.A., 1964, Northwestern University; 1960–61, Oberlin College

On the Princeton faculty since 1968; Consultant to the U.S. Treasury, Federal Home Loan Bank Board, Department of Housing and Urban Development; Member, New Jersey Economic Policy Council (1976–). Associate Editor, *Journal of Monetary Economics* (1975–), *Journal of Finance* (1974–). Recent publications include *Credit Rationing and the Commercial Loan Market* (1971); *Economics of a Monetary Economy* (forthcoming).

**Kripke, Homer,** *Chester Rohrlich Professor of Corporation Law, Finance and Tax, New York University*

J.D., 1933, A.B., 1931, University of Michigan

Director, Securities Institute, NYU; General Counsel, Allied Concord Finance Corporation (1964–1966); private practice (1960–1964 and 1933–1938); Assistant General Counsel, C.I.T. Financial Corp. (1944–1960); Assistant Solicitor, SEC (1934–1944). Member, Permanent Editorial Board of Uniform Commercial Code and Executive Committee of National Bankruptcy Conference. Member of SEC's Advisory Committee on Corporate Disclosure; consultant to American Law Institute's Federal Securities Code Project. Professor Kripke has written widely in the field of securities, legal-accounting problems, Uniform Commercial Code, and consumer credit. Publications include *Materials on Consumer Credit* (1970) and *Accounting for Business Lawyers* (with Fiflis) (1971).

**Lapidus, Leonard,** *First Deputy Superintendent, New York State Banking Department*

Ph.D., 1975, M.A., 1960, New York University; B.S., 1951, City College of New York

Before joining the New York State Banking Department in 1975, Dr. Lapidus served with the Federal Reserve Bank for 13 years. Recent publications include "Commercial Banks and Thrift Institutions: The Differing Portfolio Powers," *Banking Law Journal,* May 1975; "Thoughts on Investment Strategy for Thrift Institutions," *Business Economics,* September 1975.

**Niskanen, William,** *Director of Economics, Ford Motor Company*

Ph.D., M.A., University of Chicago; B.A., Harvard

Director of economics for the Ford Motor Company since July 1975. Prior to joining Ford, Dr. Niskanen taught three years in the Graduate School of Public Policy at the University of California, Berkeley; was Assistant Director for Evaluation, Office of Management and Budget (1970–1972); Senior Research Associate, Institute for Defense Analyses, Wash. D.C. (1964–1970); and worked in the Office of Systems Analysis, Defense Department (1962–1964). Recent publications include *Bureaucracy and Representative Government.*

**Parker, Kellis E.,** *Professor of Law, Columbia University*

J.D., 1968, Howard; B.A., 1964, University of North Carolina

Consultant, NAACP Legal Defense Fund (1972–); Executive Committee, National Committee against Discrimination in Housing (1974–). Professor Parker began his teaching career at the University of California at Davis Law School, where he directed a clinical program training students and lawyers as community developers. Joined the Columbia faculty in 1972. Author of *Modern Judicial Remedies* (1975).

**Peltzman, Sam,** *Professor of Business, Graduate School of Business, University of Chicago*

Ph.D., 1965, Chicago; B.B.A., 1960, City College of New York

Member of the Faculty, University of California at Los Angeles (1964–1973); Editor, *Journal of Political Economy* (1974–); Research Associate, National Bureau of Economic Research, (1974–); Senior Staff Economist, Council of Economic Advisers, Executive Office of the President. Recent publications include "The Effects of Auto Safety Regulation," *J. Polit. Econ.* (July/August

1975), and numerous articles on drug industry regulation.

**Phillips, Almarin,** *Professor of Economics and Law, University of Pennsylvania*

Ph.D., 1953, Harvard; M.A., 1949, B.S., 1948, University of Pennsylvania

Dean, School of Public and Urban Policy, University of Pennsylvania (1976–1978); Member, National Commission on Electronic Funds Transfer (1975–); Consultant, Secretary of the Treasury (1973–); Co-Director, President's Commission on Financial Structure and Regulation (1970–1971); Consultant, Board of Governors of the Federal Reserve System (1962–1973). Professor Phillips has served as consultant or adviser to numerous other commissions, research organizations, economics publications, and government agencies. Recent publications include *Promoting Competition in Regulated Markets* (editor and contributor), The Brookings Institution (1975); "Regulatory Reform for the Deposit Financial Institutions: Retrospect and Prospects," *J. of Fin. and Quant. Analysis* (1974).

**Pitofsky, Robert,** *Commissioner, Federal Trade Commission, Professor of Law, Georgetown University Law Center*

LL.B., 1954, Columbia; B.A., 1951, New York University

Director, Bureau of Consumer Protection, FTC (1970–1973); Professor of Law, NYU (1963–1970). Of Counsel, Arnold & Porter; Chairman, Board of Directors, Institute for Public Interest Representation, Georgetown (1973–). Recent publications include *Cases and Materials on Trade Regulation* (with Handler, Blake, and Goldschmid) (1975); "Regulation under Fire: Consumers, the Environment, the Economy and the Impact of Change—A Panel," 8 *Colum. J. L. & Soc. Prob.* 33 (1971).

**Ross, Stephen A.,** *Professor of Economics, Finance and Public Policy, University of Pennsylvania*

Ph.D., 1969, Harvard; B.S., 1965, California Institute of Technology

Member, National Science Foundation Review Panel (1976–1977); Associate Editor, *Journal of Economic Theory* (1975–), *Journal of Financial Economics* (1974–), *Management Science* (1976–). Recent publications include "A Survey of Modern Option Pricing Theory" (with J. C. Cox), *Journal of Finance* (May 1976); "The Determination of Financial Structure: The Incentive-Signalling Approach," *Bell Journal of Economics*, forthcoming.

**Schotland, Roy A.,** *Professor of Law, Georgetown University Law Center*

LL.B., 1960, Harvard; A.B., 1954, Columbia

Professor since 1970. Associate Dean, Georgetown (1970–1972); Chief Counsel, SEC Institutional Investor Study (1969–1970); Visiting Professor, University of Pennsylvania (1968–1969); Associate Professor and Professor, University of Virginia (1964–1970); private practice, New York City (1963–1964); Editorial Assistant, Special Study of Securities Markets, SEC (1962–1963); Law Clerk, Justice Brennan, U.S. Supreme Court (1961–1962). Consultant, House Committee on Interstate and Foreign Commerce (1972), Federal Reserve Board (1974–1975), and House Banking Committee (1975–1976).

**Scott, James H., Jr.,** *Associate Professor of Business, Graduate School of Business, Columbia University*

Ph.D., 1975, M.S., 1970, Carnegie-Mellon University; B.A., 1967, Rice University

Visiting Assistant Professor, Stanford University (1974–1975); Assistant Professor, University of Wisconsin (1972–1975); Research Fellow, Federal Reserve Bank of Cleveland (1971–1972); Instructor, Carnegie-Mellon University (1969–1971). Research Coordinator, Institute for Quantitative Research in Finance; reviewer, *The Bell Journal of Economics*. Recent publications include "Bankruptcy, Secured Debt, and Optimal Capital Structure," and "Ambiguities in the Cross-Section Analysis of Per Share Financial Data: Comment," *J. of Finance* (both forthcoming).

**Scott, Kenneth E.,** *Professor of Law, Stanford Law School*

LL.B., 1956, Stanford University; M.A., 1953, Princeton University; A.B., 1949, College of William and Mary

Before joining the Stanford faculty in 1968, Professor Scott served as General Counsel, Federal Home Loan Bank Board (1963–1968); Chief Deputy Savings and Loan Commissioner, State of California (1961–1963); and practiced law in New York City and Los Angeles (1956–1961). Recent publications include "In Quest of Reason: The Licensing Decisions of the Federal Banking Agencies," 42 *U. Chi. Law Rev.* (1975); "Two Models of the Civil Process" 27 *Stan. Law Rev.* (1975).

**Shay, Robert P.,** *Professor of Banking and Finance, Graduate School of Business, Columbia University*

Ph.D., M.A., B.S., University of Virginia

Director, Consumer Credit Management Program, Arden House; member, Governing Board, Credit Research Center, Purdue University; Consultant Economist, National Commission on Consumer Finance (1970–1972). Professor Shay has just completed a revision of his 1970 book, *Licensed Lending in New York*.

**Shull, Bernard,** *Professor of Economics, Hunter College*

Ph.D., 1957, University of Wisconsin; M.A., 1954, University of Illinois; B.A., 1952, Temple University

Consultant, Federal Reserve Board, Justice Department, and President's Commission on Financial Structure and Regulation. Various positions (1965–1970) with the Board of Governors of the Federal Reserve System, including Chief of the Banking Markets Section and Associate Adviser to the Board of Governors. Economist at the Federal Reserve Bank of Philadelphia (1958–1963); Senior Economist, Office of the Comptroller of the Currency; Associate Editor of the *National Banking Review*.

**Solomon, Elinor H.,** *Senior Financial Economist, Department of Justice*

Ph.D., 1948, Harvard-Radcliffe; M.A., 1945, Radcliffe; A.B., 1944, Mt. Holyoke

Before joining the Justice Department in 1966, Dr. Solomon was a lecturer at American University (1964–1967) and an economic consultant (1960–1969). She was a Financial Economist with the Federal Reserve Board (1949–1957) and was employed by the State Department (1957–1959). A number of her articles have appeared in professional journals.

**Thurow, Lester C.,** *Professor of Economics and Management, Massachusetts Institute of Technology*

Ph.D., 1964, Harvard; M.A., 1962, Oxford University; B.A., 1960, Williams College

Research Associate, Kennedy School of Government, Harvard (1968–); Assistant Professor of Economics, Harvard (1965–1968); Staff Economist for the President's Council of Economic Advisors (1964–1965); Consultant (1965–1968); weekly economic commentator on WGBH-TV, Channel 2, Boston (1969–1975); Associate Editor, *Quarterly Journal of Economics* and *Review of Economics and Statistics.* Consultant to various government agencies and private corporations. Recent publications include *The Economic Problem* (1974); *Generating Inequality: The Distribution Mechanisms of the Economy* (1975).

**Vernon, Raymond,** *Herbert F. Johnson Professor of International Business Management, Harvard University*

Ph.D., 1941, Columbia; B.A., 1933, City College of New York

Director, Harvard's Center for International Affairs (1973–); Director, Harvard's Multinational Enterprise Project (1965–). Professor Vernon has served as a consultant to various UN agencies, to the U.S. government, and to a dozen governments in the less-developed world on issues dealing with international trade and investment. Recent publications include *The Economic Environment of International Business* (1975); *The Oil Crisis* (ed.) (1976).

**Westin, Alan F.,** *Professor of Public Law and Government, Columbia University*

Ph.D., LL.B., Harvard; B.A., University of Florida

Editor in Chief, *The Civil Liberties Review* (1972–); Director, Project on Computer Databanks, National Academy of Sciences (1969–1972); Associate of Harvard University Program on Technology and Society (1967–1973). Currently Consultant, Privacy Protection Study Commission and Office of Technology Assessment, U.S. Congress. Presidential Appointee to National Wiretapping Commission (1973–1976); Consultant, Senate Committee on Government Operations (1974); Consultant, New York State Identification and Intelligence System; Chairman, Privacy Committee, American Civil Liberties Union. Recent publications include *Databanks in a Free Society* (1972); *Privacy and Freedom* (1967); "The Technology of Secrecy," in Norman Dorsen and Stephen Gillers (eds.), *None of Your Business: Government Secrecy in America* (1974).

**Young, William F.,** *James L. Dohr Professor of Law, Columbia University*

LL.B., 1949, B.A., 1947, University of Texas

Visiting Professor at Stanford University (1970), University of California

(1962–1963), and Duke (1952–1953). Member of the Faculty of Law of the University of Texas (1949–1956), except for a year as a graduate fellow at Harvard. Recent publications include: *Cases on Contracts* (with Jones and Farnsworth) and *Cases on Insurance*.

**Zwick, Burton,** *Economist, Federal Reserve Bank of New York*

Ph.D., 1969, Carnegie-Mellon University; M.B.A., 1965, B.A., 1963, Harvard

Associate Professor of Finance, University of Tennessee (1974–1975); Assistant Professor of Finance, UCLA (1968–1974). Professor Zwick is the author of several articles on macroeconomic topics in major economic journals.

# APPENDIX 2—FACULTY SEMINAR SERIES PARTICIPANTS

In addition to this volume's contributing authors, seminar participants included the individuals listed below. Unless otherwise indicated, all are members of the Columbia University Faculties.

**Adler, Michael**
*Professor of Business*

**Anderson, Ronald**
*Assistant Professor of Business*

**Baker, Richard C.**
*Assistant Professor of Business*

**Banks, Robert S.**
*Vice President and General Counsel*
*Xerox Corp.*

**Bartel, Ann**
*Assistant Professor of Business*

**Bassett, Bruce**
*Professor of Business*

**Berger, Curtis J.**
*Professor of Law*

**Blake, Harlan M.**
*Professor of Law*

**Bloch, Ernest**
*Professor of Business*
*New York University*

**Cagan, Phillip**
*Professor of Economics*

**Cary, William L.**
*Professor of Law*

**Chamberlain, Neil**
*Professor of Business*

**Chung, Un Chan**
*Assistant Professor of Business*

**Cohen, Robert**
*Conservation of Human Resources Project*

**Danthine, Jean-Pierre**
*Assistant Professor of Business*

**Derosa, Paul**
*Citibank, N.A.*

**Farnsworth, E. Allan**
*Professor of Law*

**Figueredo, Fernando J.**
*Associate in Comparative Law*

**Ginzberg, Eli**
*A. Barton Hepburn Professor of Economics*

**Golden, Soma**
*Director, Bagehot Fellowship Program*
*School of Journalism*

**Goldschmid, Harvey J.**
*Professor of Law*
*Director, Center for Law and Economic*
*Studies* .

**Greenberg, Ronald**
*Assistant Professor of Business*

**Harriss, C. Lowell**
*Professor of Economics*

**Hawke, John D.**
*General Counsel, Board of Governors*
*Federal Reserve System*

**Hellawell, Robert**
*Acting Dean and Professor of Law*

**Hopkins, Stephen A.**
*Government Relations Unit*
*Citibank, N.A.*

**Johnsen, Thore**
*Assistant Professor of Business*

**Jones, William K.**
*Professor of Law*

**Kelly, Chris**
*Director, Doctoral & Research Services*
*School of Business*

**Kolesar, Peter J.**
*Associate Professor of Business*

**Kuhn, James**
*Professor of Industrial Relations*

**Lerner, Abba**
*Professor of Economics*
*Queens College*

**Levin, Harvey**
*Professor of Business*
*Hofstra University*

**Lindsay, Robert**
*Professor of Business*
*New York University*

**Marcuse, Peter**
*Professor of Urban Planning*

**Marty, Alvin**
*Professor of Economics*
*City College of New York*

**Mayer, Gerald M., Jr.**
*Vice President*
*Citibank, N.A.*

**Meginniss, James R.**
*Associate in Business*

**Mundell, Robert**
*Professor of Economics*

**Muckenfuss, Cantwell**
*Comptroller of the Currency*

**Nadiri, M. Ishag**
*Professor of Economics*
*New York University*

**Noam, Eli**
*Assistant Professor of Business*

**Ordover, Janusz A.**
*Professor of Economics*
*New York University*

**Papademos, Lucas**
*Assistant Professor of Economics*

**Perkins, John**
*Associate in Business*

**Pontecorvo, Giulio**
*Professor of Business*

**Pozen, Robert**
*Professor of Law*
*New York University*

**Reese, Willis L. M.**
*Professor of Law*

**Robock, Stefan**
*Professor of International Business*

**Rose, Sanford**
*Fortune Magazine*

**Rosen, Sumner**
*Associate Professor of Social Work*

**Rudy, John P.**
*Vice President*
*Citibank, N.A.*

**Sametz, Arnold W.**
*Director, Solomon Brothers*
*Center for the Study of Financial Institutions*
*New York University*

**Schrag, Philip G.**
*Professor of Law*

**Simmons, Judson**
*Associate in Law*

**Tsurumi, Yoshihiro**
*Visiting Professor of Business*

**Vickrey, William**
*Professor of Political Economy*

**Vojta, George**
*Executive Vice President*
*Citicorp*

**Weiss, Elliot J.**
*Investor Responsibility Research Center, Inc.*

**Welsh, Gary**
*Assistant General Counsel*
*Federal Reserve System*

**Werner, Walter**
*Professor of Business Law*

**White, Lawrence**
*Professor of Business*
*New York University*

**Widick, Jack B.**
*Senior Lecturer in Business*

**Wilkinson, Maurice**
*Professor of Business*

**Wolf, Charles**
*Professor of Business*

**Yavitz, Boris**
*Dean and Professor of Business*

# Index